BARRON'S

HOW TO PREPARE FOR THE

TOEFL® TEST

TEST OF ENGLISH AS A FOREIGN LANGUAGE

11TH EDITION

Pamela J. Sharpe, Ph.D.
The Ohio State University

BARRON'S

**To my former students
at home and abroad**

© Copyright 2004, 2001, 1999, 1996, 1994, 1989, 1986,
1983, 1979, 1977 by Barron's Educational Series, Inc.

All inquiries should be addressed to:
Barron's Educational Series, Inc.
250 Wireless Boulevard
Hauppauge, New York 11788
http://www.barronseduc.com

Library of Congress Catalog Card No.: 2003070920
International Standard Book No. 0-7641-2315-7 (book only)
International Standard Book No. 0-7641-7576-9 (book with compact disks)
International Standard Book No. 0-7641-7578-5 (book with CD-ROM)
International Standard Book No. 0-7641-7579-3 (cassettes only package)
International Standard Book No. 0-7641-7577-7 (compact disks only package)

Library of Congress Cataloging-in-Publication Data

Sharpe, Pamela J.
    How to prepare for the TOEFL test : test of English as a foreign
language / Pamela J. Sharpe. — 11th ed.
        p.   cm.
    ISBN 0-7641-2315-7 (book only) — ISBN 0-7641-7576-9 (book with
compact disks) — ISBN 0-7641-7578-5 (book with CD-ROM)
    1. English language—Textbooks for foreign speakers. 2. Test of
English as a Foreign Language—Study guides. 3. English language—
Examinations—Study guides. I. Title.

PE1128.S5   2004
428'.0076—dc22   2003070920

PRINTED IN THE UNITED STATES OF AMERICA
9 8 7 6 5 4 3 2 1

CONTENTS

INTRODUCTION

QUESTIONS AND ANSWERS CONCERNING THE TOEFL

REVIEW OF LISTENING

PREVIEW OF SPEAKING

REVIEW OF STRUCTURE

REVIEW OF READING

REVIEW OF WRITING

TOEFL MODEL TESTS

To the Teacher

Rationale for a TOEFL Preparation Course

Although *Barron's How to Prepare for the TOEFL* was originally written as a self-study guide for students who were preparing to take the TOEFL, in the years since its first publication, I have received letters from ESL teachers around the world who are using the book successfully for classroom study. In fact, in recent years, many special courses have been developed within the existing ESL curriculum to accommodate TOEFL preparation.

I believe that these TOEFL preparation courses respond to three trends within the profession. First, there appears to be a greater recognition on the part of many ESL teachers that student goals must be acknowledged and addressed. For the engineer, the business person, the doctor, or the preuniversity student, a satisfactory score on the TOEFL is one of the most immediate goals; for many, without the required score, they cannot continue their professional studies or obtain certification to practice their professions. They may have other language goals as well, such as learning to communicate more effectively or improving their writing, but these goals do not usually exert the same kinds of pressure that the required TOEFL score does.

Second, teachers have recognized and recorded the damaging results of test anxiety. We have all observed students who were so frightened of failure that they have performed on the TOEFL at a level far below that which their performance in class would have indicated. The standardized score just didn't correspond with the score in the gradebook. In addition, teachers have become aware that for some students, the TOEFL represents their first experience in taking a computer-assisted test. The concepts of working within time limits, marking on a screen, and guessing to improve a score are often new and confusing to students, and they forfeit valuable points because they must concentrate on unfamiliar procedures instead of on language questions.

Third, teachers have observed the corresponding changes in student proficiency that have accompanied the evolutionary changes in ESL syllabus design. Since this book was first written, we have moved away from a grammatical syllabus to a communicative syllabus, and at this writing, there seems to be growing interest in a content-based syllabus. Viewed in terms of what has actually happened in classrooms, most of us have emphasized the facilitation of communication and meaning and de-emphasized the teaching of forms. As we did so, we noticed with pride the improvement in student fluency and with dismay the corresponding loss of accuracy. Some of our best, most fluent students received disappointing scores on the test that was so important to them.

Through these observations and experiences, teachers have concluded that (1) students need to work toward their own goals, (2) students need some time to focus on accuracy as well as on fluency, and (3) students need an opportunity to practice taking a standardized test in order to alleviate anxiety and develop test strategies. With the introduction of the Computer-Based TOEFL, the opportunity to gain experience taking a computer-assisted model test has also become important to student confidence and success. In short, more and more teachers have begun to support the inclusion of a TOEFL preparation course in the ESL curriculum.

Organization of a TOEFL Preparation Course

Organizing a TOEFL preparation course requires that teachers make decisions about the way that the course should be structured and the kinds of supplementary materials and activities that should be used.

Structuring

Some teachers have suggested that each review section in this book be used for a separate class; they are team teaching a TOEFL course. Other teachers direct their students to the language laboratory for independent study in listening comprehension three times a week, checking on progress throughout the term; assign reading and vocabulary study for homework; and spend class time on structure and writing. Still other teachers develop individual study plans for each student based on previous TOEFL part scores. Students with high listening and low reading scores concentrate their efforts in reading labs, while students with low listening and high reading scores spend time in listening labs.

Materials and Activities

Listening. Studies in distributive practice have convinced teachers of listening comprehension that a little practice every day for a few months is more valuable than a lot of practice concentrated in a shorter time. In addition, many teachers like to use two kinds of listening practice—intensive and extensive. Intensive practice consists of listening to problems like those in the review of listening in this book.

By so doing, the student progresses from short conversations through longer conversations to mini-talks, gaining experience in listening to simulations of the TOEFL examination. Extensive practice consists of watching a daytime drama on television, listening to a local radio program, or auditing a class. Creative teachers everywhere have developed strategies for checking student progress such as requiring a summary of the plot or a prediction of what will happen the following day on the drama; a one-sentence explanation of the radio program, as well as the name of the speaker, sponsor of the program, and two details; a copy of student notes from the audited class.

Speaking. One of the best ways to support students who are fearful of speaking is to address the issue of confidence. Developing a positive attitude toward the speaking tasks is a key to success on this section of the TOEFL.

Another important strategy is to make 60-second telephone assignments. The TOEFL Academic Speaking Test (TAST), which is a preliminary version of the Speaking Section on the Next Generation TOEFL, is currently administered by telephone. To prepare our students for this new experience, some of us are experimenting with phone-in speaking practice by using telephone answering machines to record our students when they call. In this way, the students can become accustomed to the telephone tasks and we can provide more realistic feedback for them.

Structure. Of course, the focus in a review of structure for the TOEFL will be on form. It is form that is tested on the TOEFL. It is assumed that students have studied grammar prior to re-

viewing for the TOEFL, and that they are relatively fluent. The purpose of a TOEFL review then is to improve accuracy. Because accuracy is directly related to TOEFL scores and because the scores are tied to student goals, this type of review motivates students to pay attention to detail that would not usually be of much interest to them.

Among ESL teachers, the debate rages on about whether students should ever see errors in grammar. But many teachers have recognized the fact that students *do* see errors all the time, not only in the distractors that are used on standardized tests like the TOEFL and teacher-made tests like the multiple-choice midterms in their grammar classes, but also in their own writing. They argue that students must be able to recognize errors, learn to read for them, and correct them.

The student preparing for the TOEFL will be required not only to recognize correct answers but also to eliminate incorrect answers, or distractors, as possibilities. The review of structure in this book supports recognition by alerting students to avoid certain common distractors. Many excellent teachers take this one step further by using student compositions to create personal TOEFL tests. By underlining four words or phrases in selected sentences, one phrase of which contains an incorrect structure, teachers encourage students to reread their writing. It has proven to be a helpful transitional technique for students who need to learn how to edit their own compositions.

Reading. One of the problems in a TOEFL preparation course is that of directing vocabulary study. Generally, teachers feel that encouraging students to collect words and develop their own word lists is the best solution to the problem of helping students who will be faced with the dilemma of responding to words from a possible vocabulary pool of thousands of words that may appear in context in the reading section. In this way, they will increase their vocabularies in an ordered and productive way, thereby benefiting even if none of their new words appears on the test that they take. Activities that support learning vocabulary in context are also helpful. In this edition, a Glossary of Campus Vocabulary supports comprehension of listening as well as of reading items that are, for the most part, campus based.

In order to improve reading, students need extensive practice in reading a variety of material, including newspapers and magazines as well as short excerpts from textbooks. In addition, students need to check their comprehension and time themselves carefully.

It is also necessary for students who are preparing for the Computer-Based TOEFL to practice reading from a computer screen. The skill of scrolling through text is different from the skill of reading a page in a book. To succeed on the TOEFL and after the TOEFL, students must develop new reading strategies for texts on screens. An English encyclopedia on CD-ROM is an inexpensive way to provide students with a huge amount of reading material from all the nonfiction content areas tested on the TOEFL. By reading on screen, students gain not only reading comprehension skills but also computer confidence. Again, it is well to advise students of the advantages of distributed practice. They should be made aware that it is better to read two passages every day for five days than to read ten passages in one lab period.

Writing. There are many excellent ESL textbooks to help students improve their writing. Because TOEFL topics include opinion, persuasion, and argument, some teachers tend to emphasize these types of topics in composition classes.

The extensive list of writing topics published in the *Information Bulletin* for the Computer-Based TOEFL and listed on the TOEFL web site offers teachers an opportunity to use actual TOEFL topics in class. In order to help students organize their thoughts, the topics can be used as conversation starters for class discussion. In this way, students will have thought about the topics and will have formed an opinion before they are presented with the writing task on the TOEFL.

It is also a good idea to time some of the essays that students write in class so that they can become accustomed to completing their work within thirty minutes.

Although teachers need to develop grading systems that make sense for their teaching situations, the scoring guide that is used for the essay on the TOEFL is general enough to be adapted for at least some of the assignments in an ESL composition class. By using the guide, teachers can inform students of their progress as it relates to the scores that they can expect to receive on the essay they will write for the TOEFL.

Staying Current

So many changes have been made in the design and content of the TOEFL over the years that one of the greatest challenges for teachers is to remain current and to help our students prepare for the format that they will see when they take the TOEFL. Now there are three TOEFL formats—the Paper-Based TOEFL, the Computer-Based TOEFL, and the Next Generation TOEFL—each of which requires slightly different preparation. In addition to the explanations and examples of each format that are provided in this book, the official TOEFL web site is a good resource for the most recent changes. Refer often to updates at *www.toefl.org*.

Networking with ESL Teachers

One of the many rewards of writing is the opportunity that it creates to exchange ideas with so many talented colleagues. At conferences, I have met ESL teachers who use or have used one of the previous editions of this book; through my publisher, I have received letters from students and teachers from fifty-two nations. This preface and many of the revisions in this new edition were included because of comments and suggestions from those conversations and letters.

Thank you for your ideas. I hope that by sharing we can help each other and thereby help our students more. Please continue corresponding by mail or by e-mail.

Pamela Sharpe
1406 Camino Real
Yuma, Arizona 85364
sharpe@teflprep.com

Acknowledgments

With affection and deep appreciation I acknowledge my indebtedness to the friends, family, and colleagues who have been part of the TOEFL team for so many years:

The late Dr. Jayne Harder, former Director of the English Language Institute at the University of Florida
for initiating me into the science of linguistics and the art of teaching English as a second language;

Robert and Lillie Sharpe, my parents,
for their enthusiastic encouragement during the preparation of the first manuscript and for their assistance in typing and proofreading previous editions;

The late Dr. Tom Clapp, former Dean of Continuing Education at the University of Toledo
for the maturity and confidence that I gained during our marriage because he believed in me;

Carole Berglie, former Editor at Barron's Educational Series
for her guidance in seeing the first edition of the manuscript through to publication, and to all of the editors at Barron's for their contributions to later editions;

Wendy Sleppin, Project Editor at Barron's Educational Series
for her invaluable insights and wise counsel during every stage of development and publication; acknowledgment does not begin to express my gratitude for her collaboration during our long association;

Debby Becak, Production Manager at Barron's Educational Series
for the suggestions and designs, large and small, that have improved every chapter;

Joan Franklin, President, and John Rockwell, Editor, at Cinema Sound
for casting and directing the talent voices and bringing the script to life;

Michele Sandifer, Copy Editor
for her constructive criticism and helpful corrections throughout the manuscript;

Kathy Telford, Proofreader at Proofreader's Plus
for her skillful review of the pages, her attention to the important details in the writing process, and her positive approach to errors;

Roxanne Nuhaily, Associate Director of the English Language Program at the University of California, San Diego
for field testing the items for the computer adaptive model test;

Dr. Sheri McCarthy-Tucker, Associate Professor at Northern Arizona University
for analyzing and calibrating the items for the adaptive model test;

Karen McNiel, Reading Coordinator at Yuma High School and Dr. Jean Zukowski-Faust, Professor at Northern Arizona University
for reviewing the reading level and collaborating in the revision of selected reading passages in the computer-based model tests;

Dennis Oliver, Professor at Estrella Mountain Community College
for coauthoring the Glossary of Campus Vocabulary in a collaborative project for Test University (*testu.com*);

Faye Chiu, Director at Test University
for managing the transformation from print to CD-ROM on this and previous editions;

John T. Osterman, my husband—a special thank you
for the unconditional love, the daily interest in and support for my writing career; each revision of this book is better than the last, and every new and revised year with John is the best year of my life.

Permissions

Timetable for the TOEFL

THE THREE TOEFL FORMATS

	Paper-Based TOEFL	Computer-Based TOEFL	Next Generation TOEFL
Tutorial	No questions	Variable	Variable
Listening	50 questions	30–50 questions	33–34 questions
Speaking	No questions	No questions	6 questions
Listening/Speaking	No questions	No questions	Included
Structure	40 questions	20–25 questions	No questions
Reading	50 questions	45–55 questions	36–39 questions
Reading/Speaking	No questions	No questions	Included
Writing	1 question	1 question	2 questions
Listening/Writing	No questions	No questions	Included
Reading/Writing	No questions	No questions	Included
TIME	3 hours	4 hours, 30 minutes	4 hours

Note: The actual times will vary in accordance with the time the supervisor completes the preliminary work and begins the actual test. On the Computer-Based TOEFL and the Next Generation TOEFL, the time for the tutorial will vary from one person to another. Exact numbers of questions will also vary slightly from one test to another for statistical purposes. This is a good estimate.

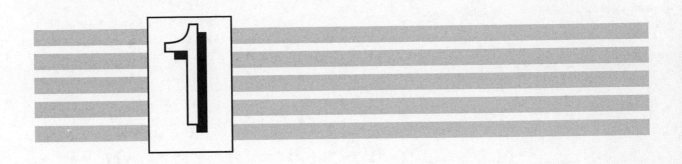

INTRODUCTION

Study Plan for the TOEFL

Many students do not prepare for the TOEFL. They do not even read the *Information Bulletin* that they receive from Educational Testing Service along with their registration forms. You have an advantage. Using this book, you have a study plan.

Barron's TOEFL Series

There are three books in the Barron's TOEFL series to help you prepare for the Test of English as a Foreign Language. Each book has a different purpose.

Barron's Practice Exercises for the TOEFL. A book for learners who need additional practice for the TOEFL. It includes a general preview of the TOEFL examination and almost one thousand exercises. Six separate audio CDs accompany the book to give you practice in listening and speaking. You may have used *Barron's Practice Exercises for the TOEFL* before using this book. Many students use *Barron's Practice Exercises for the TOEFL* as a workbook for the book you are using now.

Barron's How to Prepare for the TOEFL. A book for learners who need review and practice for the TOEFL. It includes questions and answers about the TOEFL examination, a detailed review for each section of the examination, and eight model tests similar to the Computer-Based TOEFL examination. Several sets of additional materials are available to supplement this book, including a separate package of cassette tapes, a separate package of audio compact disks, or the book may be accompanied by compact disks for audio only, or a CD-ROM for use with a computer. A computer-adaptive test like that of the Computer-Based TOEFL is found on the CD-ROM. In addition, Model Test 9 in the book and on the CD-ROM provides an opportunity to practice taking a Next Generation TOEFL test.

Barron's Pass Key to the TOEFL. A pocket-sized edition of *Barron's How to Prepare for the TOEFL.* It is for learners who need review and practice for the TOEFL and want to be able to carry a smaller book with them. It includes questions and answers about the TOEFL examination, basic tips on how to prepare for the TOEFL, and four model tests from *Barron's How to Prepare for the TOEFL.* Two audio CDs accompany the book to give you practice in listening and speaking.

More About This Book

In preparing to take the TOEFL or any other language examination, it is very important to review the language skills for each section of the examination and to have an opportunity to take model tests that are similar to the actual examination. Reviewing will help you recall some of the language skills you have studied in previous classes and other books. Taking model tests will give you the experience of taking a TOEFL before you take the actual examination. If you plan to take the Computer-Based TOEFL or the Next Generation TOEFL, it is especially important for you to practice using the CD-ROM that supplements this book.

Remember, the purpose of the book is to provide you with a detailed review of the language skills for each section of the TOEFL examination and to provide you with opportunities to take model tests similar to the actual TOEFL examination. By studying this book, you should renew and sharpen your skills, increase your speed, and improve your score.

Planning to Take the TOEFL

Most learners who use Barron's *How to Prepare for the TOEFL* take the test immediately *after* they have finished studying this book. More than one million Barron's students have been successful on the TOEFL. You can be successful, too.

Study Plan I—For Intermediate Level Learners

- First, use *Barron's Practice Exercises for the TOEFL*.
- Then use this book, *Barron's How to Prepare for the TOEFL*.

Study Plan II—For High Intermediate Level or Advanced Learners

- Use this book, *Barron's How to Prepare for the TOEFL*.
- Follow the Twelve-Week Calendar.

A Twelve-Week Calendar

Week One

- Read Chapter 1, "Introduction."
- Read Chapter 2, "Questions and Answers Concerning the TOEFL."
- Request a copy of the TOEFL *Information Bulletin* or download it from the TOEFL web site.
- Register for your test date.
- Take Model Test 1 to determine which sections will be most challenging.

Week Two

- Focus on Listening.
- Refer to Chapter 3 and review the listening problems.
- Mark problems that you need to study.

Week Three

If you are taking the Next Generation TOEFL:
- Focus on Speaking.
- Refer to Chapter 4 and preview the speaking problems.
- Mark problems that you need to study.

If you are taking the Computer-Based TOEFL or the Paper-Based TOEFL:
- Use this time to review one of the other sections that you identified as challenging when you took Model Test 1.

Week Four

If you are taking the Computer-Based TOEFL or the Paper-Based TOEFL:
- Focus on Structure.
- Refer to Chapter 5 and review the structure problems.
- Mark problems that you need to study.

If you are taking the Next Generation TOEFL:
- Use this time to review one of the other sections that you identified as challenging when you took Model Test 1.

Week Five

- Focus on Reading.
- Refer to Chapter 6 and review the reading problems.
- Mark problems that you need to study.

Week Six

- Focus on Writing.
- Refer to Chapter 7 and review the writing problems.
- Mark problems that you need to study.

Week Seven

- Take Model Test 2 and write the essay.
- Refer to the Explanatory Answers in Chapter 10.
- Mark items that you need to review.

Week Eight
- Take Model Test 3 and write the essay.
- Refer to the Explanatory Answers in Chapter 10.
- Mark items that you need to review.

Week Nine
- Take Model Tests 4 and 5 and write the essays.
- Refer to the Explanatory Answers in Chapter 10.
- Mark items that you need to review.

Week Ten
- Take Model Tests 6 and 7 and write the essays.
- Refer to the Explanatory Answers in Chapter 10.
- Mark items that you need to review.

Week Eleven
- Review all the problems that you have marked in the review chapters.
- Take Model Test 8 and write the essay.
- Refer to the Explanatory Answers in Chapter 10.
- Mark items that you need to review.

Week Twelve
- Focus on the test format

If you are taking the Paper-Based Model Test:
- Review all the items that you have marked in the model tests.

If you are taking the Computer-Based TOEFL:
- Take the Computer-Adaptive TOEFL if you have the CD-ROM.

If you are taking the Next Generation TOEFL:
- Take Model Test 9 in the book or on the CD-ROM.

Adjusting the Calendar

Ideally, you will have twelve weeks to prepare for the TOEFL. But, if you have a shorter time to prepare, follow the plan in the same order, adjusting the time to meet your needs.

Plan for Preparation

To improve your scores most, follow this plan:

- *First,* if you have taken the TOEFL before, you already know which section or sections are difficult for you. Look at the part scores on your score report. If your lowest score is on Listening, then you should spend more time reviewing Section 1. If your lowest score is on Section 2 or Section 3, then you should spend more time reviewing them.

- *Second,* spend time preparing every day for at least an hour instead of sitting down to review once a week for seven hours. Even though you are studying for the same amount of time, research shows that daily shorter sessions produce better results on the test.

- *Finally,* do not try to memorize questions from this or any other book. The questions on the test that you take will be very similar to the questions in this book, but they will not be exactly the same.

What you should try to do as you use this and your other books is learn how to apply your knowledge. Do not hurry through the practice exercises. While you are checking your answers to the model tests, *think* about the correct answer. Why is it correct? Can you explain the answer to yourself before you check the explanatory answer? Is the question similar to others that you have seen before?

Plan for Additional Preparation

Although this book should provide you with enough review material, some of you will want to do more in order to prepare for the TOEFL. Suggestions for each section follow.

- *To prepare for Listening.* Listen to radio and television newscasts and weather reports, television documentaries, lectures on educational television stations, and free lectures sponsored by clubs and universities. Attend movies in English. Try to make friends with speakers of American English and participate in conversations.

- *To prepare for Speaking.* Talk on the telephone in English with a friend. Ask each other your opinions about conversational topics. Use a timer to become accustomed to answering in 60 seconds.

- *To prepare for Structure.* Use an advanced grammar review book. If you are attending an English course, do not stop attending.

- *To prepare for Reading.* Read articles in English newspapers and magazines, college catalogs and admissions materials, travel brochures, and entries that interest you from American and English encyclopedias. Try to read a variety of topics—American history, culture, social science, and natural science.

- *To prepare for Writing.* Refer to the TOEFL *Information Bulletin* for the Computer-Based TOEFL or visit the TOEFL web site at *www.toefl.org*. Actual essay topics for the TOEFL are listed in the TOEFL *Information Bulletin* and on the web site. For a fee, the test developers will grade one of your practice essays. Click on "Score It Now."

A Good Start

Learn to relax. If you start to panic in the examination room, close your eyes and say "no" in your mind. Tell yourself, "I will not panic. I am prepared." Then take several slow, deep breaths, letting your shoulders drop in a relaxed manner as you exhale.

Concentrate on the questions. Do not talk. Concentrate your attention. Do not look at anything in the test room except the answers that correspond to the question you are working on. Do not think about your situation, the test in general, your score, or your future. If you do, force yourself to return to the question. If you do not understand a problem and you do not have a good answer, do your best. Then stop thinking about it. Be ready for the next problem.

Do not cheat. In spite of opportunity, knowledge that others are doing it, desire to help a friend, or fear that you will not make a good score, *do not cheat*. On the TOEFL, cheating is a very serious matter. If you are discovered, your test will not be scored. Legal action may be taken by Educational Testing Service (ETS).

Advice for Success

Your attitude will influence your success on the TOEFL examination. You must develop patterns of positive thinking. To help in developing a positive attitude, memorize the following sentences and bring them to mind after each study session. Bring them to mind when you begin to have negative thoughts.

I know more today than I did yesterday.
I am preparing.
I will succeed.

Remember, some tension is normal and good. Accept it. Use it constructively. It will motivate you to study. But don't panic or worry. Panic will cause loss of concentration and poor performance. Avoid people who panic and worry. Don't listen to them. They will encourage negative thoughts.

You know more today than you did yesterday.
You are preparing.
You will succeed.

There is more "Advice for Success" at the end of each review chapter. Please read and consider the advice as you continue your study plan.

2

QUESTIONS AND ANSWERS CONCERNING THE TOEFL

The TOEFL is the Test of English as a Foreign Language.

Almost one million students from 180 countries register to take the TOEFL every year at test centers throughout the world. Some of them do not pass the TOEFL because they do not understand enough English. Others do not pass it because they do not understand the examination.

The following questions are commonly asked by students as they prepare for the TOEFL. To help you, they have been answered here.

TOEFL Programs

What is the purpose of the TOEFL?

Since 1963, the TOEFL has been used by scholarship selection committees of governments, universities, and agencies such as Fulbright, the Agency for International Development, AMIDEAST, Latin American Scholarship Programs, and others as a standard measure of the English proficiency of their candidates. Some professional licensing and certification agencies also use TOEFL scores to evaluate English proficiency.

The admissions committees of more than 4,400 colleges and universities in the United States, Canada, and many other countries worldwide require foreign applicants to submit TOEFL scores along with transcripts and recommendations in order to be considered for admission.

Many universities use TOEFL scores to fulfill the foreign language requirement for doctoral candidates whose first language is not English.

Which TOEFL testing programs are available now?

The official TOEFL examination is currently administered at test sites around the world in three different formats: the Paper-Based TOEFL (PBT), the Computer-Based TOEFL (CBT), and the Next Generation TOEFL. The language proficiency skills are tested on every format, but they are tested in different ways.

In addition to the official TOEFL administrations, some schools and agencies administer the institutional TOEFL for their students and employees. The institutional TOEFL is usually the Paper-Based format.

What is the Computer-Based TOEFL program?

The CBT is a computer-adaptive test that is offered as an official standard for language proficiency worldwide. The CBT is also called the Official TOEFL.

The Computer-Based TOEFL has four sections: Listening, Structure, Writing, and Reading. The Writing is equivalent to the Test of Written English (TWE) on the Paper-Based TOEFL. The CBT is an adaptive test, which means that everyone who takes the TOEFL during the same administration may not see and answer the same questions. The computer selects questions for you at your level of proficiency. There are three subscores—Listening, Structure/Writing, and Reading. The total score is based on a scale of 0–300.

What is the Paper-Based TOEFL?

The PBT is a pencil and paper test that is offered for two purposes. One purpose of the PBT is for placement and progress evaluations. Colleges or other institutions use the PBT to test their students. The scores are not valid outside the place where they are administered, but the college or institution accepts the PBT that they administer as an official score. This PBT is also called an Institutional TOEFL.

The other purpose of the PBT is to supplement the official Computer-Based TOEFL in areas where computer-based testing is not possible. The scores are usually valid outside the place where they are administered. This PBT is also called a Supplemental TOEFL.

The Paper-Based TOEFL has three sections: Listening Comprehension, Structure and Written Expression, and Reading. In addition, the TWE is a required essay that provides a writing score. The PBT is a linear test, which means that everyone who takes the TOEFL during the same administration will see and answer the same questions. The total score is based on a scale of 310–677.

What is the Next Generation TOEFL?

The Next Generation TOEFL is a computer-assisted test that will be introduced in September 2005 worldwide. The Next Generation TOEFL has four sections: Listening, Speaking, Reading, and Writing. The Speaking Section was already introduced in 2003 as the TOEFL Academic Speaking Test (TAST) and can be taken and scored without the other sections. On the four-part Next Generation TOEFL, most of the questions are independent, but some of the questions are integrated. For example, you may be asked to listen to a lecture or read a text and then speak about it or write a response. The total score will probably be based on a scale of 0–100.

What is the Institutional TOEFL program?

More than 1,200 schools, colleges, universities, and private agencies administer the Institutional TOEFL. The Institutional TOEFL is the same length, format, and difficulty as the official Paper-Based TOEFL, but the dates and the purposes of the Institutional TOEFL are different from those of the official TOEFL.

The dates for the Institutional TOEFL usually correspond to the beginning of an academic session on a college or university calendar. The Institutional TOEFL is used for admission, placement, eligibility, or employment only at the school or agency that offers the test. If you plan to use your scores for a different college, university, or agency, you should take one of the official TOEFL tests. For more information about the Institutional TOEFL Program, contact the school or agency that administers the test.

How can I order an *Information Bulletin*?

There are three ways to order a TOEFL *Information Bulletin*.

Download	*www.toefl.org*
Phone	1-609-771-7100
Mail	TOEFL Services
	P.O. Box 6151
	Princeton, NJ 08541-6151
	U.S.A.

Many schools and educational advising centers also have copies of the TOEFL *Information Bulletin* in their counseling centers. If you order your TOEFL *Information Bulletin* by mail, it is correct to limit your correspondence to two sentences. For example:

REQUEST FOR THE TOEFL *INFORMATION BULLETIN*

(write your address here)
(write the date here)

TOEFL Order Services
P.O. 6151
Princeton, NJ 08541-6161
U.S.A.

Dear TOEFL Representative:

Please send me a copy of the TOEFL *Information Bulletin.* Thank you for your earliest attention.

Sincerely yours,

(write your name here)

The TOEFL *Information Bulletin* is often available overseas in the U.S. embassies and advising offices of the United States Information Service, binational centers, IIE and AMIDEAST Counseling Centers, Fulbright offices, and ETS Regional Registration Centers as well as from international TOEFL representatives.

May I choose the format of my TOEFL—Computer-Based TOEFL, Paper-Based TOEFL, or Next Generation TOEFL?

When the Computer-Based TOEFL is phased in for the area where you will take your TOEFL, you must take the Computer-Based TOEFL. The TOEFL web site lists the areas where the Supplemental Paper-Based TOEFL has been reintroduced on a temporary basis. When the Next Generation TOEFL appears in 2005, the plan is to phase out the Computer-Based TOEFL and retain a minimum number of Supplemental Paper-Based TOEFL sites.

Which language skills are tested on the Computer-Based TOEFL?

In general, the same language skills are tested in all TOEFL formats. Some differences occur in the number of sections and the types of questions used to test the language skills, however. Charts that outline the differences are included in the Quick Comparisons in the review chapters for each section of the TOEFL. The chart below shows the four sections on the Computer-Based TOEFL.

Section 1   Listening
Section 2   Structure/Writing
Section 3   Reading
On the Computer-Based TOEFL, the essay counts 50 percent of the total score for Section 2.

Which language skills are tested on the Paper-Based TOEFL?

In general, the same language skills are tested in all TOEFL formats. Some differences occur in the number of sections and the types of questions used to test the language skills, however. Charts that outline the differences are included in the Quick Comparisons in the review chapters for each section of the TOEFL. The chart below shows the three sections on the Paper-Based TOEFL.

Section 1   Listening
Section 2   Structure
Section 3   Reading

Does the TOEFL have a Composition Section?

The Computer-Based TOEFL has a Writing Section. On the Writing Section and on the TWE (Test of Written English), you must write a short essay on an assigned topic. The essay should be about 300 words long. The topic is typical of academic writing requirements at colleges and universities in North America. You have 30 minutes to finish writing. Both the Writing Section and the TWE are described in greater detail in the Tutorial for the Writing Section.

The Paper-Based TOEFL does not have a Composition Section. However, you are also required to take the TWE. It is a short essay on an assigned topic. The essay should be 300-350 words long. The topic is usually an opinion question. You have 30 minutes to finish writing. The TWE rating is reported as a separate score from that of the TOEFL.

Does the TOEFL have a Speaking Section?

The Computer-Based TOEFL does not have a Speaking Section. Only the Next Generation TOEFL includes a Speaking Section.

A Speaking Section is planned for the Paper-Based TOEFL, but it has not been included in the test yet. It will probably be administered by telephone.

Are all the TOEFL tests the same length?

The forms for the TOEFL vary in length. Some items are included for research purposes and are not scored. On the Computer-Based TOEFL, items are selected by the computer based on the level of difficulty and the number of correct responses from previous items. Difficult items are worth more points than average or easy items.

All of the forms for the Paper-Based TOEFL are the same length—140 questions. Occasionally, additional questions are included for research purposes, but they are not included in the section scores.

How do the Paper-Based TOEFL and the Institutional TOEFL compare with the Computer-Based TOEFL?

The Paper-Based TOEFL and the Institutional TOEFL are different from the Computer-Based TOEFL for several reasons. First, taking a test with a pencil and paper is different from taking a test with a computer. Second, the test designs are different. The Paper-Based TOEFL and the Institutional TOEFL are linear tests. This means that all the questions appear in a row and everyone receives the same questions. The Computer-Based TOEFL has two sections, Listening and Structure, that are computer-adaptive. This means that only one question appears on the screen at a time, and everyone does not receive the same questions. Everyone begins with a question of average difficulty. If you answer it correctly, you are given a more difficult question. If you answer it incorrectly, you are given an easier question. You receive more points for answering difficult questions correctly than you do for answering average or easy questions correctly.

For a more detailed comparison of the Paper-Based TOEFL with the Computer-Based TOEFL, please refer to the Quick Comparisons in each review chapter of this book.

Is the Computer-Based TOEFL fair?

The Computer-Based TOEFL is fair because the computer is constantly adjusting the selection of items based on your previous responses. It allows you to achieve the maximum number of points that you are capable of based on your English language proficiency. In addition, everyone receives the same test content and the same proportion of question types—multiple-choice and computer-assisted.

What if I have little experience with computers?

The beginning of the official Computer-Based TOEFL has a Tutorial to help you become familiar with the computer before you begin your test. In the Tutorial, you will review how to use a mouse, how to scroll, and how to answer all the question types on the test. The Tutorials on the CD-ROM are similar. If you would like to work through the official Tutorial before the day of your Computer-Based TOEFL, you can download it at no charge from the TOEFL web site at *www.ets.org/cbt/cbtdemo.html*.

Registration

How do I register for the TOEFL?

There are three ways to register for the Computer-Based TOEFL. If you plan to pay by credit card—VISA, MasterCard, or American Express—you may register by phone. Call Candidate Services at 1-800-468-6335 to make an appointment for a test in the United States, or phone your Regional Registration Center to make an appointment for a test in another country. The phone numbers for the regional centers are listed in the TOEFL *Information Bulletin*. If you plan to pay by check, money order, or credit card, you may register by mail. To arrange a test in the United States, Canada, Puerto Rico, or a U.S. territory, return the voucher request form in your TOEFL *Information Bulletin,* along with your registration fee, to TOEFL Services in Princeton, New Jersey. A mailing label is provided in the TOEFL *Information Bulletin.* To arrange a test in all other locations where the Computer-Based TOEFL is offered, return the International Test Scheduling Form to your Regional Registration Center. Mailing labels are provided in the TOEFL *Information Bulletin.* Be sure to sign the form and include your registration fee. You may be asked to choose two days of the week and two months of the year as well as two test centers. If no appointments are available on the dates you have requested, you will be assigned a date close to the request you have made.

The *Information Bulletin* for the Paper-Based TOEFL has a registration form in it. Using the directions in the TOEFL *Information Bulletin,* fill out the form and mail it to the TOEFL Registration Office. Be sure to sign the form and include your registration fee. To register online, visit *www.toefl.org*.

When should I register for the TOEFL?

If you are taking the TOEFL as part of the application process for college or university admission, plan to take the test early enough for your score to be received by the admission office in time to be considered with your application. Usually, a test date at least two months before the admission application deadline allows adequate time for your scores to be considered with your admission application. Test centers often receive more requests than they can accommodate on certain dates. Try to schedule your appointment by phone or mail at least a month before the date you prefer to take the TOEFL, especially in October, November, December, April, and May. You must call at least three days before the appointment date that you are requesting.

What are the fees for the TOEFL?

In the United States, the registration fee for both the Computer-Based TOEFL and the Paper-Based TOEFL is $130 U.S. The fee may be paid by check, credit card, money order, bank draft, or U.S. postal money order. In Canada, the fee is $130 U.S. plus taxes. In other countries, the registration fee is also $130 U.S. However, because of exchange rates, the actual cost may vary from one country to another. For exact fees in local currency and options for payment, refer to the TOEFL *Information Bulletin*.

Which credit cards will be accepted?

Only MasterCard, VISA, and American Express may be used to pay for TOEFL registration fees and services.

May I pay by check or money order?

In order to pay for the Computer-Based TOEFL (CBT) by check or money order, you should complete a voucher request form and mail it to the TOEFL Office with your payment. This form and an envelope for it are bound in the middle of the TOEFL *Information Bulletin* for the Computer-Based TOEFL. You can also find these materials on the TOEFL web site. You will receive a CBT voucher by return mail.

In order to pay for the Paper-Based TOEFL by check or money order, include payment with your registration form. Checks, bank drafts, and money orders must be drawn on a bank in the U.S. Canadian checks will be subject to taxes. Do not send cash or demand drafts.

Which currencies will be accepted?

Payments at the current exchange rate for the U.S. dollar may be made in the following currencies:

Australian dollar, British pound, Canadian dollar, Danish krone, Euro, Hong Kong dollar, Japanese yen, New Zealand dollar, Norwegian kroner, Singapore dollar, Swedish krona, Swiss franc.

Is there a fast way to send mail to the TOEFL Office?

For the fastest delivery, use e-mail on the TOEFL web site. For rush mail delivery, use the express courier delivery address:

TOEFL Services (25-Q-310)
Distribution and Receiving Center
225 Phillips Blvd.
Ewing, NJ 08628-7435
U.S.A.

Will Educational Testing Service (ETS) confirm my registration?

If you register for the Computer-Based TOEFL, you will receive an appointment confirmation number. If you do not receive an appointment confirmation number or if you lose your appointment confirmation number, call 1-800-GOTOEFL (1-800-468-6335) in the United States or call your Regional Registration Center outside the United States. The phone numbers for regional registration centers are listed in the TOEFL *Information Bulletin.*

If you register for the Paper-Based TOEFL, you will receive an admission ticket. Your admission ticket is your confirmation. You must complete the ticket and take it with you to the test center on the day of the test along with your passport. If you have not received your admission ticket two weeks before the test, contact TOEFL Services.

May I change the date or cancel my registration?

In the United States, Canada, Puerto Rico, and U.S. territories, call Candidate Services at 1-800-468-6335. Be sure to call by noon, three business days before the date of your appointment, or you will not receive a partial reimbursement of your registration fee, usually $65. If you want to choose a different date, you may be asked to pay a rescheduling fee of $40. In all other locations, call your Regional Registration Center by noon, five business days before the date of your appointment, or you will not receive a partial reimbursement of your registration fee. If you want to choose a different date, you may be asked to pay a rescheduling fee of $40. You must provide your appointment confirmation number when you call. You will be given a cancellation number.

Test date changes are not permitted for the Paper-Based TOEFL; however, you may receive absentee credit. If you cancel your test, the refund request form and the unused admission ticket must arrive within 60 days of your test date for you to receive $65 cash or a $65 credit toward registration for a different date. Mail the form and the admission ticket to TOEFL Services or fax them to 1-609-771-7500. Allow ten weeks for the refund to arrive.

May I give my appointment to a friend?

Appointments cannot be reassigned or exchanged among friends.

How should I prepare the night before the TOEFL?

Don't go to a party the night before you take your TOEFL examination, but don't try to review everything that you have studied either. By going to a party, you will lose the opportunity to review a few problems that may add valuable points to your TOEFL score. By trying to review everything, though, you will probably get confused, and you may even panic. Instead, select a limited amount of material to review the night before you take the TOEFL. And remember, you are not trying to score 100 percent on the TOEFL examination. No one knows everything. If you answer 75 percent of the questions correctly, you will receive an excellent score.

May I register on the day of the TOEFL?

Registration of candidates on the day of the test is permitted for only the Computer-Based TOEFL, but most of the time there is no space. Candidates who arrive at the center are admitted only if a seat is available.

Registration is not available for the Paper-Based TOEFL on the day of the test administration.

Test Administration

Where are the test centers?

The most recent listing of the test centers for the TOEFL administrations worldwide is found in the current TOEFL *Information Bulletin* or on the TOEFL web site.

May I change my test center assignment?

You may go to another center on the date printed on your admission ticket, but you may or may not find a seat and test materials available.

What kind of room will be used for the TOEFL?

Rooms used for the Computer-Based TOEFL are small. They are like the study areas in a library or in a language laboratory. Usually only six to fifteen students are at individual computer stations. Each student has a headset.

Rooms used for the Paper-Based TOEFL tend to be large, but they vary greatly from one test site to another. The seats are usually school desks. It is a good idea to wear clothing that allows you to adjust to warm or cold room temperatures.

What should I take with me to the examination room?

For the Computer-Based TOEFL, take your appointment confirmation number and your official identification. Also take the institution and department codes for the schools or agencies to which you will report your scores. These codes can be found in the TOEFL *Information Bulletin.* You will not need a watch because the computer screen has a clock face on it. Books, dictionaries, tape recorders, cellular phones, pagers, highlighters, pens, and notes are not permitted in the examination room. Some centers will have lockers for you to store your possessions but it is really better not to take with you anything that you cannot take into the examination room.

For the Paper-Based TOEFL, take your admission ticket, photo identification form, and official photo identification with you. Taking three sharpened pencils and a watch would be helpful, although most examination rooms will have clocks. Books, dictionaries, tape recorders, cellular phones, pagers, highlighters, pens, and notes are not permitted in the examination room. Don't forget the institution and department codes for the schools or agencies to which you will report your scores.

What kind of identification is required?

In the United States, only your valid passport will be accepted for admission to the Computer-Based TOEFL examination. In other countries, your valid passport is still the best identification, but if you do not have a passport, you may refer to the TOEFL *Information Bulletin* for special directions. Your photograph will be taken at the test center and reproduced on all official score reports sent to institutions. Your identification will be checked against the new photograph. In addition, all Computer-Based TOEFL sessions will be videotaped. Be sure to use the same spelling and order of your name on your registration materials or phone registration, the test center log that you will sign when you enter the test area, the forms on the computer screens, and any correspondence that you may have with TOEFL Services, Candidate Services, or other local representatives.

The test center supervisor will not admit you to the Paper-Based TOEFL examination if you do not have official identification. In the United States, only your valid passport will be accepted. The supervisor will not allow you to enter with an expired passport or a photocopy of your passport. In other countries, your valid passport is still the best identification, but if you do not have a passport, you may refer to the TOEFL *Information Bulletin* for special directions. Be sure that your photo identification form and your passport picture look like you do on the day of the examination. If not, you may not be admitted to the examination room. Be sure to use the same spelling and order of your name on your registration materials, admission ticket, answer sheet, and any correspondence that you may have with either TOEFL Services or your Regional Registration Center.

Will I sign a confidentiality statement?

Before you begin the Computer-Based or Paper-Based TOEFL, you may be asked to sign a confidentiality statement. You will agree to keep confidential the content of all test questions. The purpose of this procedure is to protect the security of the test.

Where should I sit?

You will be assigned a seat. You may not select your own seat. It is usually better not to sit with friends anyway. If you do, you may find yourself looking at friends instead of concentrating on your test materials. You may even be accused of cheating if you appear to be communicating in some way.

What if I am late?

Report to the test center 30 minutes before the appointment for your TOEFL. You will need a half hour to check in. If you arrive late, you may not be admitted, and your fee may not be refunded.

How long is the testing session of the TOEFL?

The time for the Computer-Based TOEFL will vary, depending on your familiarity with computers. A computer Tutorial is offered at the beginning of the session for those who need some practice using the computer before taking the Computer-Based TOEFL. In general, the Computer-Based TOEFL takes between four hours and four hours and 30 minutes, including the Tutorial. When you finish, you may leave the room quietly.

The total time for the testing session of the Paper-Based TOEFL is three hours. Since the instructions are not included as part of the timed sections, the actual time that you will spend in the examination room will be about three hours and 30 minutes. When you finish, you must sit quietly until the supervisor dismisses the group.

How much time do I have to complete each of the sections?

Work as rapidly as possible without compromising accuracy. Check the Timetable for the TOEFL on page x for an estimate.

Are breaks scheduled during the TOEFL?

A 10-minute break is scheduled during the Computer-Based TOEFL. It usually occurs between the Structure and the Reading Sections.

No breaks are scheduled for the Paper-Based TOEFL.

Is there a place to eat lunch at the test centers?

Some of the testing centers are conveniently located near restaurants, but many, especially the mobile centers, are not. You may want to take a snack with you to eat before or after your test.

How can I complain about a test administration?

If you feel that the test situation was not fair, you have a right to register a complaint by mail or by fax. Within three days of the date of the test, write a letter to Test Administration Services. Their address appears on page 12. If you prefer to send a fax, the fax number is 1-609-771-7500. Mention the date of your test, the city, and the country. Explain why you feel that the test was not fair.

Examination

What kinds of questions are found on the TOEFL?

The majority of the questions on the Computer-Based TOEFL are multiple-choice. Some other types of questions are also on the Computer-Based TOEFL. These questions have special directions on the screen. You will have many examples of them in the Model Tests in this book.

All the questions on the Paper-Based TOEFL are multiple-choice.

How do I answer the test questions?

When you are presented with a multiple-choice question on the Computer-Based TOEFL, read the four possible answers on the screen, point the arrow, and click beside the answer that you choose. The oval will change from white to black. When you are presented with other types of questions, follow the directions on the screen.

To answer test questions on the Paper-Based TOEFL, read the four possible answers in your test book, and mark the corresponding space on the answer sheet.

How do I mark the answers?

MARKING THE ANSWER SCREEN: COMPUTER-BASED TOEFL

One question is shown on the computer screen. One answer is marked on the screen.

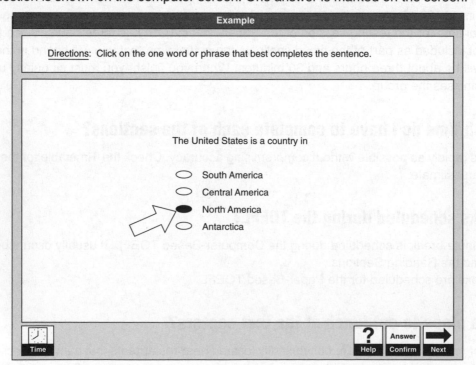

MARKING THE ANSWER SHEET: SUPPLEMENTAL PAPER-BASED TOEFL

One question is shown in the test book. One answer is marked on the answer sheet.

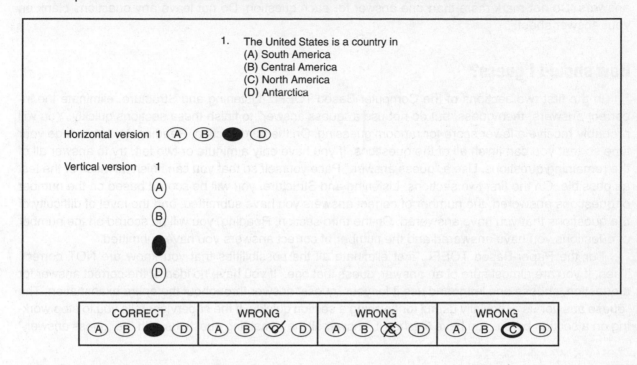

On the Computer-Based TOEFL, you will have an opportunity to practice marking the answers to questions on the computer screen before the examination begins. The Tutorial will include all the different types of questions on the Computer-Based TOEFL.

May I make notes in the test book or on the scratch paper?

There is no test book for the Computer-Based TOEFL. All the questions and the answer options are presented on the computer screen. You may not use the scratch paper for your essay to make notes for any other section of the test.

You are not allowed to make marks in your test book for the Paper-Based TOEFL. You may not underline words or write notes in the margins of the test book. Doing so is considered cheating.

May I change an answer?

On the first two sections of the Computer-Based TOEFL, Listening and Structure, you can change your answer by clicking on the new answer. You can change your answer as many times as you wish until you click on the **Confirm Answer** button. When you click on **Confirm Answer**, you move to the next question, and you cannot go back to a previous question. On the third section of the Computer-Based TOEFL, Reading, you can change your answer as many times as you wish. You may go on to the next question and back to the previous questions. The CD-ROM that supplements this book will provide you with practice in choosing and changing answers on the computer screen.

You may erase an answer on the answer sheet of the Paper-Based TOEFL if you do so carefully and completely. Stray pencil marks may cause inaccurate scoring by the test-scoring machine.

If I am not sure of an answer, should I guess?

Try to answer every question on the Computer-Based TOEFL. Your score will be based not only on the difficulty of the questions but also on the number of questions answered.

If you are not sure of an answer on the Paper-Based TOEFL, you should guess. The number of incorrect answers is not subtracted from your score. Your score is based only on the number of correct answers. Do not mark more than one answer for each question. Do not leave any questions blank on your answer sheet.

How should I guess?

In the first two sections of the Computer-Based TOEFL, Listening and Structure, eliminate the incorrect answers, then guess, but do not use a "guess answer" to finish these sections quickly. You will probably receive a lower score for random guessing. On the third section, Reading, try to manage your time so that you can finish all of the questions. If you have only a minute or two left, try to answer all of the remaining questions. Use a "guess answer." Pace yourself so that you can finish as much of the test as possible. On the first two sections, Listening and Structure, you will be scored based on the number of questions answered, the number of correct answers you have submitted, and the level of difficulty of the questions that you have answered. On the third section, Reading, you will be scored on the number of questions you have answered and the number of correct answers you have submitted.

For the Paper-Based TOEFL, first eliminate all the possibilities that you know are NOT correct. Then, if you are almost sure of an answer, guess that one. If you have no idea of the correct answer for a question, choose one letter and use it for your "guess" answer throughout the entire examination. The "guess answer" is especially useful for finishing a section quickly. If the supervisor tells you to stop working on a section before you have finished it, answer all the remaining questions with the "guess answer."

What should I do if I discover that I have marked my answers incorrectly?

Marking your screen incorrectly on the Computer-Based TOEFL is not possible because the computer program will present only one question on each screen. If you change your mind after you have confirmed a response on the Listening or Structure sections, the computer will not allow you to return to a previous question on these two sections, and you will not be able to change the answer that you have confirmed. As you see, it is very important to be sure of the answer before you click on **Confirm Answer**.

Do not panic if you have marked an answer incorrectly on the Paper-Based TOEFL. Notify the supervisor immediately. If you have marked one answer in the wrong space on the answer sheet, the rest of the answers will be out of sequence. Ask for time at the end of the examination to correct the sequence. The TOEFL test supervisor may or may not allow you to do this. To save time finding the number on the answer sheet that corresponds to the problem you are reading, to avoid mismarking, and to save space on your desk, use your test book as a marker on your answer sheet. As you advance, slide the book down underneath the number of the question that you are marking on the answer sheet.

May I choose the order of the sections on my TOEFL?

You may not choose the order. Listening, Structure, and Reading are tested in that order on both the Computer-Based TOEFL and the Paper-Based TOEFL. The essay is written last. When you have finished with a section, you may not work on any other section of the test.

What if I cannot hear the tape for the Listening Section?

You have your own headset for the Computer-Based TOEFL. Before the Listening Section begins, you will have an opportunity to adjust the volume yourself. Be careful to adjust the volume when you are prompted to do so. If you wait until the test begins, you may not be able to adjust it.

The supervisor for the Paper-Based TOEFL has the responsibility of making sure that everyone is able to hear the tape. If you cannot hear it well, raise your hand and ask the supervisor to adjust the volume.

May I keep my test?

TOEFL Services publishes copies of TOEFL tests and makes them available for purchase. Visit the TOEFL web site for more information. If you try to keep or copy TOEFL tests from your test administration, the TOEFL Office may take legal action.

What can I do if I do not appear to take the test?

There is a $65 refund for the Computer-Based TOEFL if you cancel your test five business days before the date of your appointment.

If you do not appear to take the Paper-Based TOEFL test without canceling your appointment, you cannot request a refund. If you cancel your appointment, then you are entitled to a refund of $65. Write to TOEFL Services to make your request. You must contact them within 60 days of the date of the TOEFL administration that you have missed.

Score Reports

How is my TOEFL scored?

Total Computer-Based TOEFL scores range from 0–300. First, each of the sections of the TOEFL is graded on a scale from 0–30. Then the scores from the sections are added together. Finally, the sum is multiplied by 10 and divided by 3.

For example, the following scores were received on the sections:

Listening	23
Structure and Writing	25
Reading	27
	75

$75 \times 10 = 750 \div 3 = 250$ Total TOEFL Score

Total Paper-Based TOEFL scores range from 310–677. First, each of the three sections of the TOEFL is graded on a scale from 31–68. Then the scores from the three sections are added together. Finally, the sum is multiplied by 10 and divided by 3.

For example, the following scores were received on the three sections:

Listening Comprehension	52
Structure and Written Expression	48
Vocabulary and Reading Comprehension	50
	150

$150 \times 10 = 1,500 \div 3 = 500$ Total TOEFL Score

The Test of Written English (TWE) rating is reported as a separate score on a scale from 1–6.

How are the Structure and Writing scores combined on the Computer-Based TOEFL?

The Structure score counts half of the section score on the Computer-Based TOEFL, and the essay counts half of the score. The rating scale of 1–6 for the essay is converted to a statistical equivalent of the points in the Structure Section.

How do I interpret my score?

There are no passing or failing scores on either the Computer-Based TOEFL or the Paper-Based TOEFL. Each agency or university will evaluate the scores according to its own requirements. Even at the same university, the requirements may vary for different programs of study, levels of study (graduate or undergraduate), and degrees of responsibility (student or teaching assistant).

The following summary of admissions policies are typical of U.S. universities. This assumes, of course, that the applicant's documents other than English proficiency are acceptable.

TYPICAL ADMISSIONS POLICIES OF AMERICAN UNIVERSITIES

Paper-Based TOEFL Score	Policy	Computer-Based TOEFL Score
650 or more	admission assured for graduate students	280 or more
600–649	admission assured for undergraduate students	250–279
550–599	admission probable for graduate students	213–249
500–549	admission probable for undergraduate students	173–212
450–499	individual cases reviewed	133–172
449 or less	referral to English language program probable	132 or less

Refer to the TOEFL *Information Bulletin* or web site for a detailed chart of percentile ranks for total TOEFL scores. This will help you interpret your score relative to the scores of others taking the examination.

How do the scores on the Supplemental Paper-Based TOEFL compare with those on the Computer-Based TOEFL?

A concordance table is a table that shows comparisons. A concordance table for the Paper-Based TOEFL and the Computer-Based TOEFL has been mailed to all institutions that use TOEFL scores for admissions decisions. A copy of the concordance table is printed in the TOEFL *Information Bulletin* and posted on the TOEFL web site. A shorter version of the table follows:

Paper-Based TOEFL	Computer-Based TOEFL
677	300
650	280
600	250
550	213
500	173
450	133
400	97

If I score very poorly on one part of the TOEFL, is it still possible to receive a good total score?

If you feel that you have done very poorly on one part of a section, do not despair. You may receive a low score on one part of a section and still score well on the total examination if your scores on the other parts of that section and the other sections are good.

When can I see my scores?

After you complete your Computer-Based TOEFL, you can view your estimated score on the screen. You will be able to see section scores for both Listening and Reading as well as for the multiple-choice part of the Structure Section. However, the essay, which is included as half of the Structure score, will not have been graded. The estimated score that you will see shows a total score range based on a very poorly written essay or on a very well written essay. For example, your score range might be 150–220.

You are entitled to five copies of your test results, including one personal copy for yourself and four official score reports. Your official scores for all sections will be mailed to you about two to five weeks after you take your Computer-Based TOEFL. However, you will have a very good idea of how you performed on the test after you see the estimate.

For the Paper-Based TOEFL, you are entitled to five copies of your test results, including one personal copy for yourself and four official score reports. You will receive your copy four or five weeks after you take the test.

How can I know my scores sooner?

If your essay is typed instead of handwritten, your scores will be mailed sooner. If you would like to know your score on the same day that the report is mailed, you may use the TOEFL phone service. Using a touch-tone phone, call the TOEFL Office. You will hear prompts to enter your appointment number, your test date, your date of birth, and a credit card number. The fee to hear your scores by phone is $10 plus any long-distance charges that apply.

To call toll-free from the United States or Canada, touch 1-888-TOEFL-44, which is 1-888-863-3544. To call with long-distance charges from all other locations, touch 1-609-771-7267.

What can I do if I want to register a complaint?

For the Computer-Based TOEFL, submit your complaint in writing to:

CBT Administration
Computer-Based Testing Network Group
Educational Testing Service
Mail Stop 16-2
Rosedale Road
Princeton, NJ 08541
U.S.A.

Occasionally, on the Paper-Based TOEFL, the computer will score an answer sheet incorrectly because of the way you have marked it. If you feel your score is much, much lower than you expected, you have a right to register a complaint. To do so, submit your complaint in writing to:

CBT Administration
Paper-Based Testing
Educational Testing Service
Mail Stop 16-2
Rosedale Road
Princeton, NJ 08541
U.S.A.

May I cancel my scores?

After you view your score on the screen, you will be given the option to report or cancel your scores for the Computer-Based TOEFL. If you choose to report your scores, you will then choose four institutions to receive your score report. All of this is arranged by responding to questions on the computer screen.

If you do not want your Paper-Based TOEFL scores to be reported, you have a right to cancel them. To cancel your test scores, you must complete the score cancellation section of your TOEFL answer sheet, or you must write, e-mail, call, or fax TOEFL Services. If a signed request is received at TOEFL Services within seven days of the date of the test, your scores will not be reported.

How will the agencies or universities of my choice be informed of my score?

Two to five weeks after the Computer-Based TOEFL testing, your official score reports will be forwarded directly to the agencies and/or universities that you designated on the information section on the computer screen the day of the examination. Personal copies of score reports are not accepted by institutions without confirmation by TOEFL Services. Scores more than two years old are not considered valid on the Computer-Based TOEFL.

Four or five weeks after the Paper-Based TOEFL testing, your official score reports will be forwarded directly to the agencies and/or universities that you designated on an information section at the top of the TOEFL answer sheet the day of the examination. Personal copies of score reports are not accepted by institutions without confirmation by TOEFL Services. Scores more than two years old are not considered valid on the Paper-Based TOEFL.

How can I send additional reports?

You can use a form in the TOEFL *Information Bulletin* to have official score reports for the Computer-Based TOEFL sent to institutions that were not listed on your computer screen. If you use the form, do not send a letter because correspondence will cause a delay. If you prefer, the TOEFL Office offers a telephone service for additional score reports. To use the service, you will need a touch-tone phone. Call 1-888-TOEFL-44 in the U.S. or 1-609-771-7267 from all other locations. For the Computer-Based TOEFL, you will be asked to provide your appointment confirmation number, a credit card number, your test date, and both the institution and department codes for the schools you wish to add to your score report list. You will use the numbers on your touch-tone phone to enter the numbers for all of the dates and codes. The fee for this service is $12 per call and $12 for each report. Official score reports will be mailed the same day as your telephone request.

You can use a form in the TOEFL *Information Bulletin* to have official score reports for the Paper-Based TOEFL sent to institutions that were not listed on your answer sheet. If you use the form, do not send a letter because correspondence will cause a delay. You may also request official score reports by phone for the Paper-Based TOEFL. To use this service, you must have your admission ticket, a credit card, and a touch-tone phone. Use the same telephone numbers that appear above for the CBT. Call from six in the morning to ten at night, New York time. The fee for this service is a $12 charge to your credit card per call, a $12 charge per score report, plus a charge to your telephone bill for the long-distance call. Official score reports will be mailed three days after your telephone request.

May I take the TOEFL more than one time?

You may not take the Computer-Based TOEFL more than once a month. For example, if you take the Computer-Based TOEFL in July, you must wait until August to take it again.

You may take the Paper-Based TOEFL as many times as you wish in order to score to your satisfaction.

If I have already taken the TOEFL, how will the first score or scores affect my new score?

TOEFL scores are considered valid for two years. If you have taken the TOEFL more than once but your first score report is dated more than two years ago, TOEFL Services will not report your first score. If you have taken the TOEFL more than once in the past two years, TOEFL Services will report the score for the test date you request on your score request form.

Is there a direct correspondence between proficiency in English and a good score on the TOEFL?

There is not always a direct correspondence between proficiency in English and a good score on the TOEFL. Many students who are proficient in English are not proficient in how to approach the examination. That is why it is important to prepare by using this book.

What is the relationship between my score on the Model Tests and my score on the TOEFL?

Calculating an exact TOEFL score from a score that you might receive on a Model Test is not possible. This is so because the actual TOEFL examination has a wider variety of problems.

The Model Tests have been especially designed to help you improve your total TOEFL score by improving your knowledge of the types of problems that most often appear on the TOEFL. These problem types are repeated throughout the Model Tests so that you will have practice in recognizing and answering them.

By improving your ability to recognize and correctly answer those types of problems that most often appear on the TOEFL, you will improve your total TOEFL score.

Can I estimate my TOEFL score after I have prepared?

To estimate your TOEFL score after you complete each of the Model Tests, use the Score Estimates in Chapter 11 of this book. After you complete the Computer Adaptive Test on the CD-ROM that supplements this book, you will see an estimate of your TOEFL score.

Will I succeed on the TOEFL?

You will receive from your study what you give to your study. The information is here. Now, it is up to you to devote the time and effort. Thousands of other students have succeeded by using *Barron's How to Prepare for the TOEFL.* You can be successful, too.

The Next Generation TOEFL

When will the Next Generation TOEFL be administered?

The Next Generation TOEFL will be phased in. There will be three stages:

2003	The Speaking Section will be offered by telephone for practice. To purchase a practice test, visit the official TOEFL web site at *www.toefl.org* on the Internet. Click on the TAST (TOEFL Academic Speaking Test). The cost is $30 U.S.
2004	Several full-length forms of the Next Generation TOEFL will be made available on the Internet at no cost. Visit *www.toefl.org* and follow the directions to take advantage of this opportunity.
2005	The Next Generation TOEFL will replace the Computer-Based TOEFL (CBT) world-wide as the official TOEFL examination. In some remote areas, the Paper-Based TOEFL will be offered. A telephone version of the Speaking Section is planned to supplement the Paper-Based TOEFL.

Which language skills are tested on the Next Generation TOEFL?

In general, the same language skills are tested in all TOEFL formats. Some differences occur in the number of sections and the types of questions used to test the language skills, however. Charts that outline the differences are included in the Quick Comparisons in the review chapters for each section of the TOEFL. The chart below shows the four sections on the Next Generation TOEFL.

Section 1   Listening
Section 2   Speaking
Section 3   Reading
Section 4   Writing

Does the Next Generation TOEFL have a Composition Section?

The Next Generation TOEFL has a Writing Section that includes both independent writing and integrated writing. The independent writing is a response to a question that asks your opinion about a familiar topic. You have 30 minutes to complete the independent writing task. The integrated writing is a response to a question about the content of a short reading passage, a short lecture, or both. You have 20–30 minutes to complete the integrated writing task.

Does the Next Generation TOEFL have a Speaking Section?

The Next Generation TOEFL has a Speaking Section that includes both independent speaking and integrated speaking. The independent speaking is a response to a question that asks for your opinion about a familiar topic. You have 15 seconds to prepare and 45 seconds to respond. The integrated writing is a response to a question about the content of a short reading passage, a short lecture, or both. You have 20–30 seconds to prepare and 60 seconds to respond. You may use notes while you speak.

Are all the Next Generation TOEFL tests the same length?

All of the forms for the Next Generation TOEFL are about the same length. It is not an adaptive test.

How do I register for the Next Generation TOEFL?

The *Information Bulletin* for the Next Generation TOEFL will have a registration form in it. Using the directions in the TOEFL *Information Bulletin*, fill out the form and mail it to the TOEFL Registration Office. Be sure to sign the form and include your registration fee. To register online, visit *www.toefl.org*.

What are the fees for the Next Generation TOEFL?

The fees for the Next Generation TOEFL have not been determined. However, they will be about the same as those for the Computer-Based TOEFL.

Where are the test centers?

The test centers for the Next Generation TOEFL will be announced on the TOEFL web site *www.toefl.org*. Many test centers are being planned at school sites throughout the world.

How long is the testing session of the TOEFL?

The total time for the testing session of the Next Generation TOEFL is about four hours.

How much time do I have to complete each of the sections?

Work as rapidly as possible without compromising accuracy. Refer to page x to see the Timetable for the Next Generation TOEFL.

What kinds of questions are found on the TOEFL?

The majority of the questions on the Next Generation TOEFL are multiple-choice. Some other types of questions are also on the Next Generation TOEFL. These questions will have special directions on the screen. You will have examples of them in Model Test 9.

How do I answer the test questions?

When you are presented with a multiple-choice question on the Next Generation TOEFL, read the four possible answers on the screen, point the arrow, and click beside the answer that you choose. The oval will change from white to black. When you are presented with other types of questions, follow the directions on the screen. This is similar to the way that the test questions on the Computer-Based TOEFL are answered.

May I make notes in the test book or on the scratch paper?

You are allowed to take notes and use them to answer questions on the Next Generation TOEFL. You will be given paper for that purpose when you go into the test room.

May I change an answer?

On the Listening Section of the Next Generation TOEFL, you can change your answer by clicking on the new answer. You can change your answer as many times as you wish until you click on the **Confirm Answer** button. When you click on **Confirm Answer**, you move to the next question, and you cannot go back to a previous question. On the Speaking Section, you will be cued with a beep to begin and end speaking. Everything that you say during the recording time will be submitted. You cannot change an answer. On the Reading Section, you can change your answer by clicking on the new answer. You can change your answer as many times as you wish, and you can go back to previous answers on the same reading passage. When you begin a new reading passage, you may not return to the previous passage to change answers. On the Writing Section, you can revise your essays as much as you wish until the clock indicates that no time is remaining. If you submit your essays before time is up, you cannot return to them. The CD-ROM that supplements this book will provide you with practice in choosing and changing answers on the computer screen.

If I am not sure of an answer, should I guess?

If you are not sure of an answer, you should guess. The number of incorrect answers is not subtracted from your score. Your score is based on only the number of correct answers.

How should I guess?

First, eliminate all of the possibilities that you know are NOT correct. Then, if you are almost sure of an answer, guess that one. If you have no idea of the correct answer for a question, choose one letter and use it for your "guess answer" throughout the entire examination. The "guess answer" is especially useful for finishing a section quickly. If the supervisor tells you to stop working on a section before you have finished it, answer all the remaining questions with the "guess answer."

How is the Next Generation TOEFL scored?

The Next Generation TOEFL will have section scores for each of the four sections. The range for each section score will be 0–25. Then the scores for the four sections will be added together. Although final scoring has not been determined, the total score range for the Next Generation TOEFL will probably be 0–100. Check the TOEFL web site at *www.toefl.org* for the latest information about the scoring scale.

How do I interpret my score?

Admissions policies have not yet been decided by American universities. For the latest information about scoring, visit *www.toefl.org* on the Internet.

How do scores on the Next Generation TOEFL compare with those on the Computer-Based TOEFL?

A concordance table comparing the two tests is not yet available from the test developers. However, the TOEFL formats have been carefully calibrated so that scores on one format equate with scores on another format. If you score well on the Computer-Based TOEFL, for example, you should score well on the Next Generation TOEFL also.

When can I see my scores?

After you complete your Next Generation TOEFL, you can view your estimated score on the screen. You will be able to see section scores for both Listening and Reading, but the Speaking and Writing Sections will require additional time to evaluate. The estimated score that you will see shows a total score range based on a very low score on the Speaking and Writing Sections and a very high score on the Speaking and Writing Sections.

You will be entitled to five copies of your test results, including one personal copy for yourself and four official score reports. You will receive your copy about five weeks after you take the test, but you will have an idea of how you performed on the test after you see the estimate.

How can I know my scores sooner?

You may be able to use the TOEFL phone service to receive your report on the same day that it is mailed. Watch the *www.toefl.org* web site for more information about this option.

May I take the TOEFL more than one time?

You may take the Next Generation TOEFL as many times as you wish in order to score to your satisfaction. There may be a limit to the number of times that you may take the test in a one-month time period. More information about these limits will be published at a later date.

Updates

Visit the TOEFL web site at *www.toefl.org* or my web site at *www.teflprep.com* for the latest information about the TOEFL.

This web site helps students and professionals prepare
for the Test of English as a Foreign Language (TOEFL®). You are invited
to <u>practice</u> with the types of questions that appear on the TOEFL, visit the
TEFL Prep Center <u>Bookstore</u>, and ask Dr. Pamela Sharpe questions about her
books. The TEFL Prep Center web site also has information about
<u>scholarships</u> and <u>news</u> about the TOEFL.

| *Welcome* | *The Practice Page* | *The TEFL Center Bookstore* | *TOEFL News* | *Scholarship Opportunities* | *Dear Dr. Sharpe* |

If you are not seeing images or if the page is loading improperly,
you may want to use these links to download <u>Netscape Navigator</u> or
<u>Internet Explorer</u>, available at no cost.

TOEFL is a registered trademark of Educational Testing Service.
The TEFLPREP Center bears sole responsibility for this web site's content
and is not connected with the Educational Testing Service.

REVIEW OF LISTENING

Overview of the Listening Section

**QUICK COMPARISON—LISTENING
PAPER-BASED TOEFL,
COMPUTER-BASED TOEFL, AND NEXT GENERATION TOEFL**

Paper-Based TOEFL	*Computer-Based TOEFL*	*Next Generation TOEFL*
Three types of questions are presented in three separate parts. Part A has short conversations; Part B has long conversations and class discussions; Part C has mini-talks and lectures.	Three types of questions are presented in three sets. The first set has short conversations; the second set has longer conversations and class discussions; the third set has lectures.	Two types of questions are presented in six sets. The first sets each have a long conversation. The next sets each have one lecture.
The talks and lectures are about 2 minutes long.	The lectures are about 3 minutes long.	The lectures are about 5 minutes long.
Everyone taking the TOEFL answers the same questions.	The computer selects questions based on your level of language proficiency.	Everyone taking the same form of the TOEFL answers the same questions.
There are no pictures or visual cues.	Each short conversation begins with a picture to provide orientation. There are several pictures and visual cues with longer conversations and lectures.	Each conversation and lecture begins with a picture to provide orientation. There are several pictures and visual cues with lectures.
You hear the questions, but they are not written out for you to read.	The questions are written out on the computer screen for you to read while you hear them.	The questions are written out on the computer screen for you to read while you hear them.
Everyone taking the TOEFL proceeds at the same pace. You cannot pause the tape.	You may control the pace by choosing when to begin the next conversation or lecture.	You may control the pace by choosing when to begin the next conversation or lecture.
The section is timed. At the end of the tape, you must have completed the section.	The section is timed. A clock on the screen shows the time remaining for you to complete the section.	The section is timed. A clock on the screen shows the time remaining for you to complete the section.
You may not replay any of the conversations or lectures.	You may not replay any of the conversations or lectures.	You may not replay any of the conversations or lectures.
All of the questions are multiple-choice.	Most of the questions are multiple-choice, but some of the questions have special directions.	Most of the questions are multiple-choice, but some of the questions have special directions.
Every question has only one answer.	Some of the questions have two or more answers.	Some of the questions have two or more answers.

Paper-Based TOEFL	*Computer-Based TOEFL*	*Next Generation TOEFL*
You answer on a paper answer sheet, filling in ovals marked Ⓐ, Ⓑ, Ⓒ, and Ⓓ.	You click on the screen in the oval that corresponds to the answer you have chosen, or you follow the directions on the screen.	You click on the screen in the oval that corresponds to the answer you have chosen, or you follow the directions on the screen.
You can return to previous questions, erase, and change answers on your answer sheet.	You cannot return to previous questions. You can change your answer before you click on **Confirm Answer**. After you click on **Confirm Answer**, you cannot go back.	You cannot return to previous questions. You can change your answer before you click on **OK**. After you click on **OK**, you cannot go back.
You may NOT take notes.	You may NOT take notes.	You may take notes while you listen to the conversations and lectures.

Directions and Examples for Listening Questions

The Listening Section of the TOEFL tests your ability to understand spoken English as it is heard in North America. This section is included in the Paper-Based TOEFL, the Computer-Based TOEFL, and the Next Generation TOEFL. The section is different for each of the three TOEFL formats—the Paper-Based TOEFL, the Computer-Based TOEFL, and the Next Generation TOEFL.

Paper-Based TOEFL (PBT)

The directions for the Paper-Based TOEFL are reprinted with the permission of Educational Testing Service (ETS) from the official *Information Bulletin* for the Supplemental Paper-Based TOEFL.

Section I — Listening Comprehension

In this section of the test, you will have an opportunity to demonstrate your ability to understand conversations and talks in English. There are three parts to this section, with special directions for each part. Answer all the questions on the basis of what is stated or implied by the speakers you hear. Do **not** take notes or write in your test book at any time. Do **not** turn the pages until you are told to do so.

Directions: In Parts A and B, you will hear conversations between two people. After each conversation, you will hear a question about the conversation. The conversations and questions will not be repeated. After you hear a question, you will read the four possible answers in your test book and choose the best answer. Then, on your answer sheet, find the number of the question and fill in the space that corresponds to the letter of the answer you have chosen.

Here is an example.

On the recording, you will hear: **Sample Answer**
                                         ● Ⓑ Ⓒ Ⓓ

  (woman) *I don't like this painting very much.*
    (man) *Neither do I.*
  (narrator) *What does the man mean?*

In your test book, you will read:
    (A) He doesn't like the painting either.
    (B) He doesn't know how to paint.
    (C) He doesn't have any paintings.
    (D) He doesn't know what to do.

You learn from the conversation that neither the man nor the woman likes the painting. The best answer to the question, "What does the man mean?" is (A), "He doesn't like the painting either." Therefore, the correct choice is (A).

Directions: In Part C of this section you will hear several talks. After each talk, you will hear some questions. The talks and questions will not be repeated.

After you hear a question, you will read the four possible answers in your test book and choose the best answer. Then, on your answer sheet, find the number of the question and fill in the space that corresponds to the letter of the answer you have chosen.

Here is an example.
On the recording, you will hear:
  (narrator) *Listen to an instructor talk to his class about a television program.*
    (man) *I'd like to tell you about an interesting TV program that'll be shown this coming Thursday. It'll be on from 9 to 10 pm on Channel 4. It's part of a series called "Mysteries of Human Biology." The subject of the program is the human brain — how it functions and how it can malfunction. Topics that will be covered are dreams, memory, and depression. These topics are illustrated with outstanding computer animation that makes the explanations easy to follow. Make an effort to see this show. Since we've been studying the nervous system in class, I know you'll find it very helpful.*

Sample Question   **Sample Answer**
  You will hear: Ⓐ Ⓑ ● Ⓓ
    (narrator) *What is the main purpose of the program?*

In your test book, you will read:
    (A) To demonstrate the latest use of computer graphics.
    (B) To discuss the possibility of an economic depression.
    (C) To explain the workings of the brain.
    (D) To dramatize a famous mystery story.

The best answer to the question, "What is the main purpose of the program?" is (C), "To explain the workings of the brain." Therefore, the correct choice is (C).

Sample Question   **Sample Answer**
  You will hear: Ⓐ Ⓑ Ⓒ ●
    (narrator) *Why does the speaker recommend watching the program?*

In your test book, you will read:
    (A) It is required of all science majors.
    (B) It will never be shown again.
    (C) It can help viewers improve their memory skills.
    (D) It will help with course work.

The best answer to the question, "Why does the speaker recommend watching the program?" is (D), "It will help with course work." Therefore, the correct choice is (D).

Remember, you are **not** allowed to take notes or write in your test book.

Computer-Based TOEFL (CBT)

The directions for the Computer-Based TOEFL are reprinted with the permission of Educational Testing Service (ETS) from the official *Information Bulletin* for the Computer-Based TOEFL.

The Listening section of the test measures the ability to understand conversations and talks in English. You will use headphones to listen to the conversations and talks. While you are listening, pictures of the speakers or other information will be presented on your computer screen. There are two parts to the Listening section, with special directions for each part.

On the day of the test, the amount of time you will have to answer all the questions will appear on the computer screen. The time you spend listening to the test material will not be counted. The listening material and questions about it will be presented only one time. You will not be allowed to take notes or have any paper at your computer. You will both see and hear the questions before the answer choices appear. You can take as much time as you need to select an answer; however, it will be to your advantage to answer the questions as quickly as possible. You may change your answer as many times as you want before you confirm it. After you have confirmed an answer, you will not be able to return to the question.

Before you begin working on the Listening section, you will have an opportunity to adjust the volume of the sound. You will not be able to change the volume after you have started the test.

QUESTION DIRECTIONS — Part A

In Part A of the Listening section, you will hear short conversations between two people. In some of the conversations, each person speaks only once. In other conversations, one or both of the people speak more than once. Each conversation is followed by one question about it.

Each question in this part has four answer choices. You should click on the best answer to each question. Answer the questions on the basis of what is stated or implied by the speakers.

Here is an example.

On the computer screen, you will see:

On the recording, you will hear:
(woman) Hey, where's your sociology book?
(man) At home. Why carry it around when we're just going to be taking a test?
(woman) Don't you remember? Professor Smith said we could use it during the test.
(man) Oh, no! Well, I've still got an hour, right? I'm so glad I ran into you!

You will then see and hear the question before the answer choices appear:

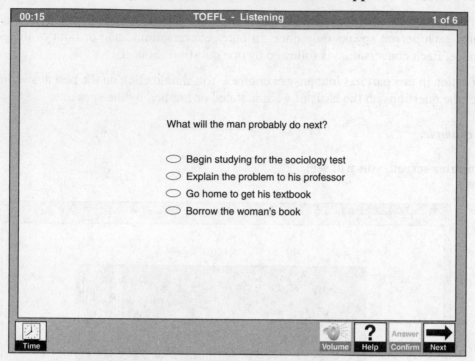

To choose an answer, you will click on an oval. The oval next to that answer will darken. **The correct answer is indicated on the next screen.**

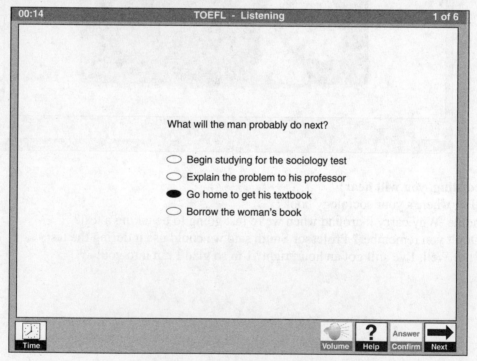

After you click on **Next** and **Confirm Answer**, the next conversation will be presented.

QUESTION DIRECTIONS — Part B

In Part B of the Listening section, you will hear several longer conversations and talks. Each conversation or talk is followed by several questions. The conversations, talks, and questions will not be repeated.

The conversations and talks are about a variety of topics. You do not need special knowledge of the topics to answer the questions correctly. Rather, you should answer each question on the basis of what is stated or implied by the speakers in the conversations or talks.

For most of the questions, you will need to click on the best of four possible answers. Some questions will have special directions. The special directions will appear in a box on the computer screen.

Here is an example of a conversation and some questions:

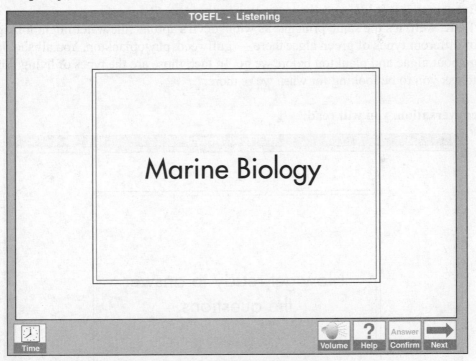

(narrator) Listen to part of a discussion in a marine biology class.

(professor) A few years ago, our local government passed a number of strict environmental laws. As a result, Sunrise Beach looks nothing like it did ten years ago. The water is cleaner, and there's been a tremendous increase in all kinds of marine life — which is why we're going there on Thursday.

(woman) I don't know if I agree that the water quality has improved. I mean, I was out there last weekend, and it looked all brown. It didn't seem too clean to me.

(professor) Actually, the color of the water doesn't always indicate whether it's polluted. The brown color you mentioned might be a result of pollution, or it can mean a kind of brown algae is growing there. It's called "devil's apron," and it actually serves as food for whales.

(man) So when does the water look blue?

(professor) Well, water that's completely unpolluted is actually colorless. But it often looks bluish-green because the sunlight can penetrate deep down and that's the color that's reflected.

(woman) But sometimes it looks really green. What's that about?

(professor) OK, well, it's the same principle as with "devil's apron": the water might look green because of different types of green algae there — gulfweed, phytoplankton. You all should finish reading about algae and plankton before we go. In fact, those are the types of living things I'm going to ask you to be looking for when we're there.

After the conversation, you will read:

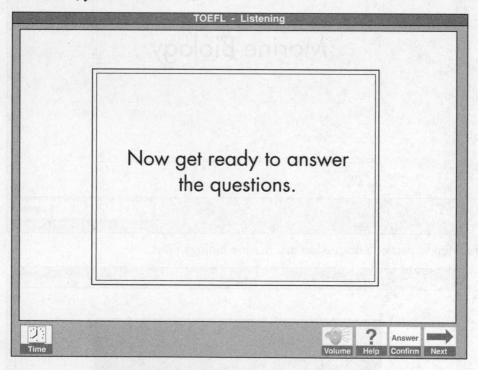

Then, the first question will be presented:

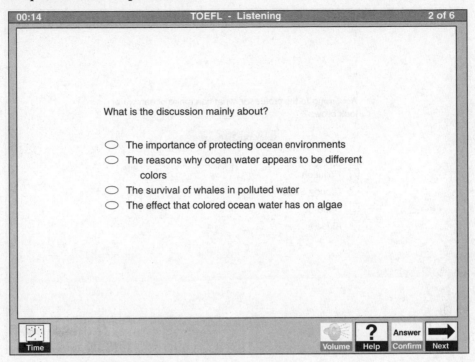

To choose an answer, you will click on an oval. The oval next to that answer will darken. The correct answer is indicated on the screen below.

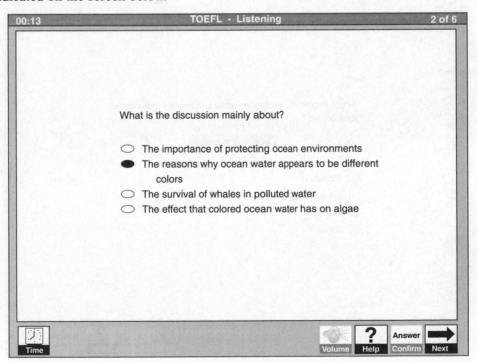

After you click on **Next** and **Confirm Answer, the next question will be presented:**

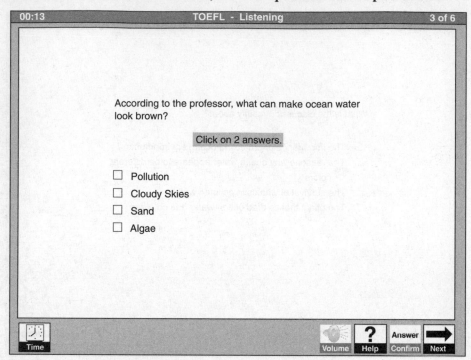

To choose your answers, you will click on the squares. An "X" will appear in each square. The correct answer is indicated on the screen below.

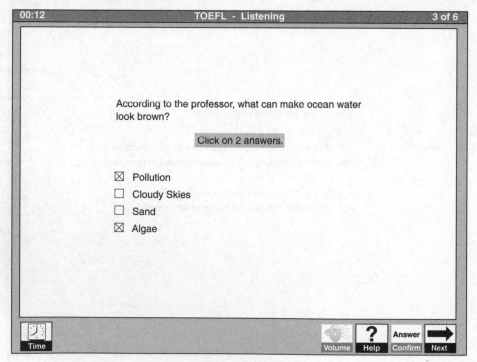

Sometimes the screen changes several times during a conversation or talk, as in the next example.

Here is an example of a talk and some questions:

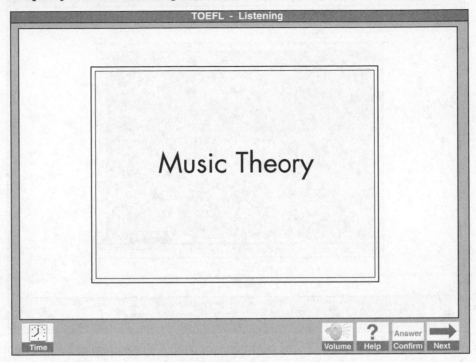

(narrator) Listen to part of a talk in a music theory class.

(professor) I'm sure if I asked you, you'd be able to tell me the common meaning of the word "interval."

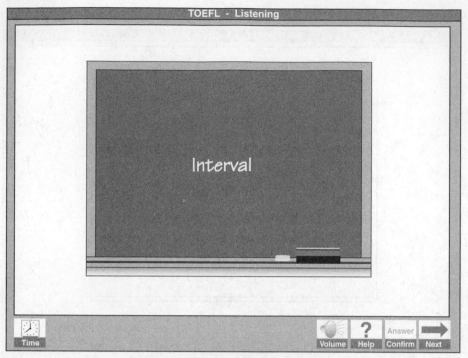

(professor) An interval is the period of time between two events. For example, buses might stop at a certain location every ten minutes—that is, at ten minute intervals. In the typical sense of the word, an interval is a period of time. But in music theory the word has a different meaning. A musical interval is the distance between two notes. So, if two notes are far apart, the musical interval between them is large. If two notes sound close together, the musical interval is small. The smallest musical interval is actually no distance at all between two notes. It's called "the unison," and that's the interval when two notes are exactly the same.

(professor) Today, I'd like to focus on a way of analyzing musical intervals by looking at the precise mathematical relationship that exists between musical notes. To do this, I've made some sounding boxes.

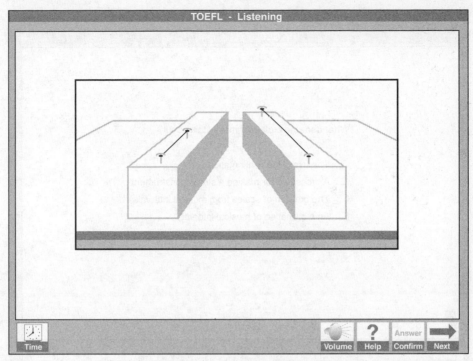

(professor) As you can see, they're just boxes made of wood with strings wrapped around two nails on the top. Now, the only difference between these two sounding boxes is the length of the string. I made the strings two different lengths to show you how this affects the sound. In fact, if you measured the length of the two strings, you'd see that the long string is exactly twice the length of the short string. So, the ratio between the short string and the long string is one to two. That's a pretty basic ratio, mathematically, and it produces one of the most basic intervals in Western music—the octave.

After the talk, you will read:

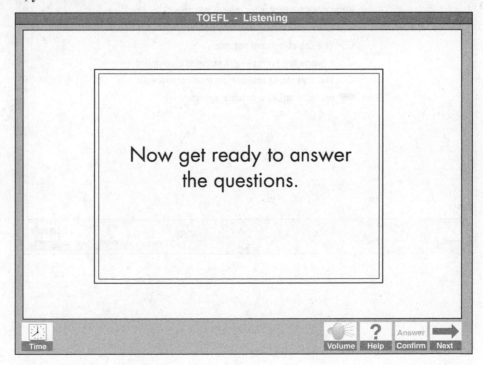

Then, the first question will be presented:

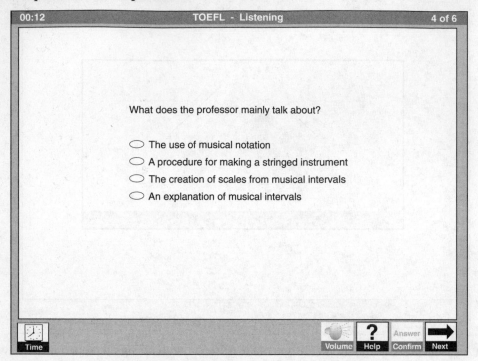

To choose an answer, you will click on an oval. The oval next to that answer will darken. The correct answer is indicated on the screen below.

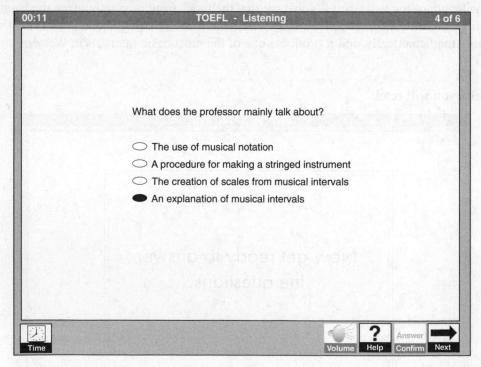

After you click on **Next** and **Confirm Answer**, **the next question will be presented:**

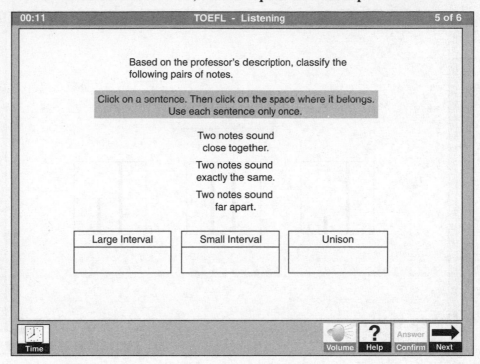

To choose your answers, you will click on a sentence and then click on the space where it belongs. As you do this, each sentence will appear in the square you have selected. The correct answer is indicated on the screen below.

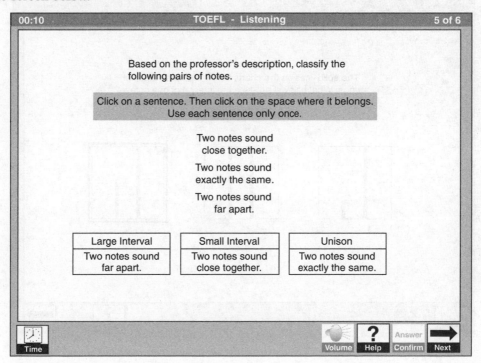

After you click on **Next** and **Confirm Answer**, **the next question will be presented:**

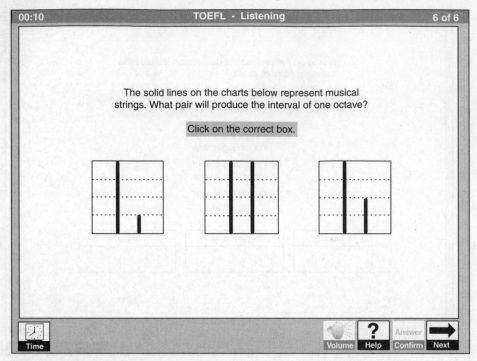

To choose your answer, you will click on the box. As you do this, the box will become highlighted. The correct answer is indicated on the screen below.

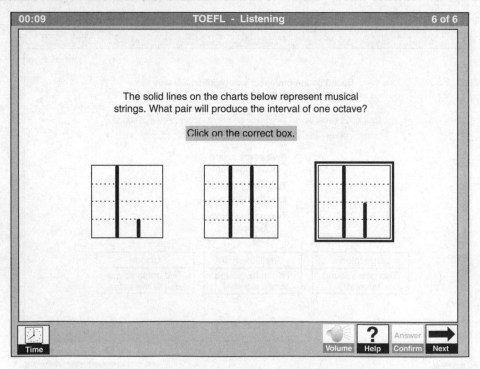

Next Generation TOEFL

There are usually 33 or 34 questions in two parts on the Listening Section of the Next Generation TOEFL. The conversations, talks and lectures are presented only one time. You may take notes. The topics are all academic. The questions are either multiple-choice with four possible answer choices or computer-assisted with special directions on the screen. It takes 25 minutes to complete the questions. The time for the conversations, talks, and lectures is not included in the 25-minute estimate.

There are two types of tasks included in the Listening Section: independent listening tasks and integrated listening tasks.

Independent Listening

Directions: In the independent listening tasks, you will hear long conversations, class discussions, and lectures in an academic setting. They include natural pauses and they are presented at a normal rate for native speakers. You may take notes. After each conversation, discussion, or lecture, you will hear several questions. After every multiple-choice question, choose the best answer choice from four possible answers. After every computer-assisted question, follow the special directions on the screen to complete the answer.

Here is an example of a conversation and some questions:

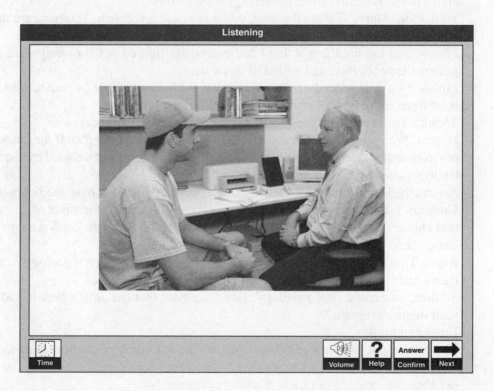

Note: On the Next Generation TOEFL, the **Answer Confirm** button may appear as **OK** with a check (✔) mark.

(narrator) Listen to part of a consultation in a professor's office.

Marty:	Do you have a minute, Dr. Peters? I mean, I know this isn't your office hour, but . . . could I ask you a question?
Dr. Peters:	Sure. Come on in, Marty. What's the problem?
Marty:	Well, I'm not sure. I got this letter, uh, it's a letter about my grant . . . and I don't understand it very well.
Dr. Peters:	Let's see it.
Marty:	. . . It's from the Financial Aid Office. . . . Are they going to cancel my student aid?
Dr. Peters:	I would hope not. Hmmn. Oh, I see. Here's what happened. You're only registered for three hours next semester. See here, there's a check mark in this box...the one that says "credit hours," then there's a number three beside it, so that must mean that you're not signed up for enough credit hours. . . . It looks like you only have one three-hour class next semester.
Marty:	That's true, but . . . but I plan to register for another class, I mean, during open registration. Um . . . I heard about a new environmental science course . . . it's supposed to be really good, and there's a field trip and everything, so uh I'm waiting for it. It hasn't been assigned a sequence number yet. . . but by open registration, well, I'm sure the number will be on the list, you know, the list they have printed out for classes that aren't in the schedule when the schedule comes out.
Dr. Peters:	Well, then, Marty, if that's the case, you don't have a problem. You're aware that the terms of your grant require you to take at least six hours a semester.
Marty:	I know, and I really thought that I had everything figured out, but, well, I've never gotten a letter before, and it kind of threw me.
Dr. Peters:	I think it's a new procedure. Don't worry about it. But uh, just be sure to sign up for at least three more hours before the beginning of the semester.
Marty:	Thanks, Dr. Peters. I'm really glad you were in your office today.
Dr. Peters:	Hmmn. Wait a minute, Marty. Um . . . do you have a back-up plan if the class . . . the environmental science doesn't have enough students...or, if it's closed by the time you try to register for it?
Marty:	Not really. Um . . . maybe I should though . . . since I have to have the hours, I mean.
Dr. Peters:	Umhum. I think you should go into registration with a course in mind to . . . as a second choice. That way, when you get to the head of the line, you know what to do, and . . . and you won't have to make a hasty decision.
Marty:	Right. That's a good idea. Actually, I was thinking about taking a geology course, but then I heard about the environmental science class.
Dr. Peters:	So then, you could find a geology class . . . a class that fits your schedule and works in your degree program?
Marty:	I'm sure I could.
Dr. Peters:	You don't want to take a class that wouldn't count toward graduation. But anyway, there are a lot of geology classes that . . . they are general studies classes, and you can use them for one of your basic science requirements.
Marty:	Right. Okay. Well, thanks. I'll check out the schedule and I'll find something, but . . . well, I hope that environmental science class works out for me.
Dr. Peters:	Me, too. And it should. That class isn't offered every year, so there should be enough interest. I'd get there early though, at open registration.
Marty:	I will. I'm going on the first day, early in the morning.
Dr. Peters:	Good. Well, I hope it all goes well for you.
Marty:	I think it will. Thanks so much . . . for explaining the letter and everything.
Dr. Peters:	No problem. Glad I could help.

After the conversation, you will read:

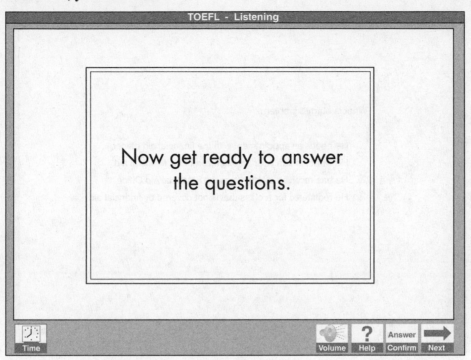

Then, the first question will be presented:

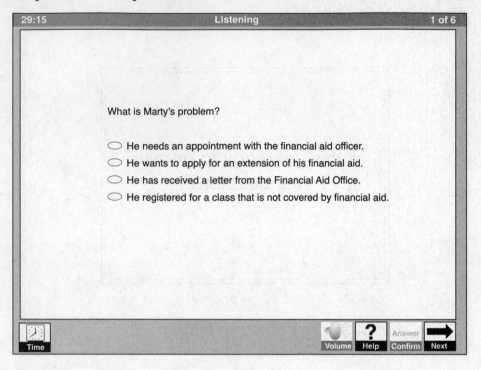

To choose an answer, you will click on an oval. The oval next to that answer will darken. The correct answer is indicated on the screen below.

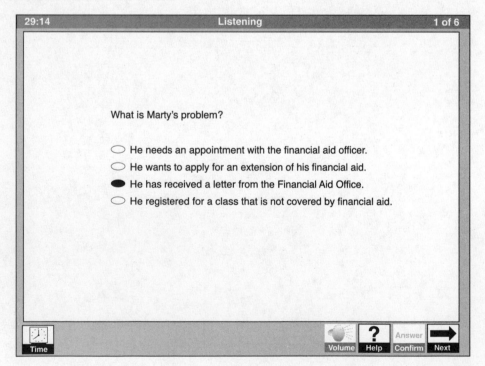

After you click on **Next** and **Confirm Answer, the next question will be presented.**

In this example, you will listen to part of the conversation again. Then you will answer a question.

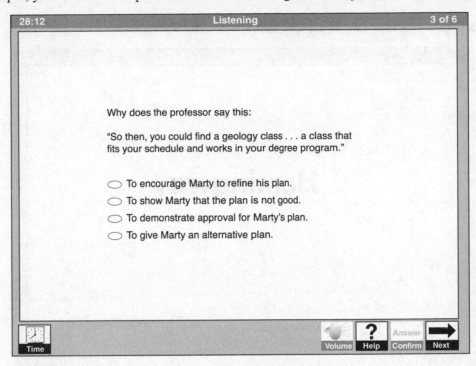

To choose your answers, you will click on an oval. The oval next to the answer will darken. The correct answer is indicated on the screen below.

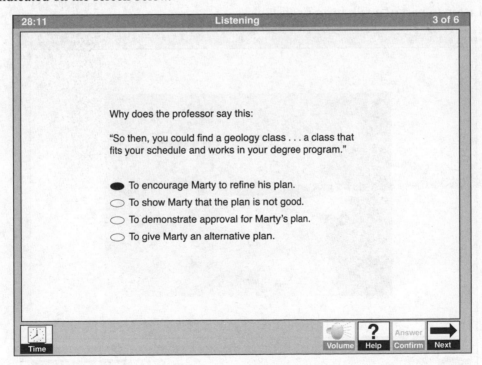

Sometimes the screen changes several times during a conversation or talk, as in the next example.

Here is an example of a talk and some questions:

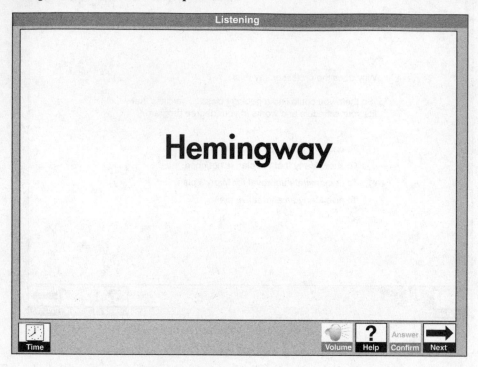

(narrator) Listen to part of a talk in an English class.

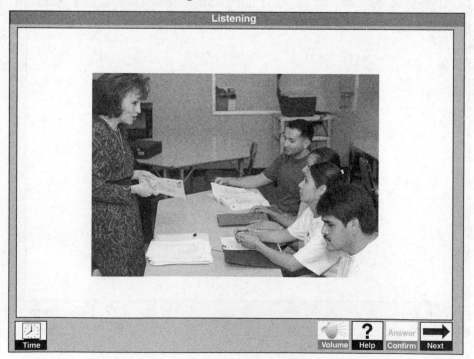

(**professor**) So today we'll talk about Earnest Hemingway. But before we actually read and discuss his works, I'd uh I'd like to look at his life . . . how the writing fits into it. Okay, first, we'll talk about the years he spent as a newspaper reporter because that experience was very influential uh for his writing career as a novelist. Um . . . after he graduated from high school, he chose not to go to college, accepting a job instead for the Kansas City *Star*. Later he would say that he learned how to write fiction in the newsroom, because the style required for the newspaper contained short sentences and active verbs, and uh he learned synthesis and clarity by writing news copy. So Hemingway was quoted as saying, "Those rules were the best rules I ever learned for the business of writing." Later, he worked for other newspapers, and . . . but the *Toronto Daily Star* offered him an overseas correspondent's assignment, and so he really began his writing career as an ambitious young American newspaperman in Paris after the First World War. His early books were published in Europe before they were released in the United States, but his first true novel *The Sun Also Rises* came out in 1926, and established him as a literary force in the United States. It was a fairly autobiographical novel about a World War I veteran who became a news correspondent in Paris after the war.

So I'll mention here that the autobiographical nature of the novel was pretty typical of Hemingway. He always wrote from experience rather than from imagination. Although often he would write from the . . . the um . . . distance that time or another place might provide. Here's what I mean. He was living in Key West at the time that he wrote *Farewell to Arms,* and published it in 1929, but it was a reflective novel in which he recounted his adventures as an ambulance driver in Italy during the First World War. Then in *For Whom the Bell Tolls,* published in 1940, he retold his memories of the Spanish Civil War that took place in the 30s.

Okay. He had a lot of short stories to his credit as well, in anthologies and magazines. But, you'll probably notice that there are eleven years between *Farewell to Arms* and *For Whom the Bell Tolls,* and those were difficult years in a way because the critics and the public expected every work to be a masterpiece, and they just weren't.

Nevertheless, perhaps more than any other twentieth-century American writer, he was responsible for creating a style of literature. The Hemingway style was hard, economical, and powerful. Remember the newspaper training. It lured the reader into using imagination in order to fill in the details.

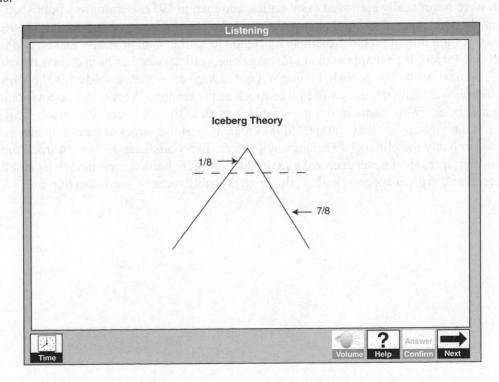

(professor) In fact, Hemingway's theory of writing has been referred to as the iceberg theory. Because he thought it was important to omit the right thing from a story or a story line in a book. And he compared that with the structure of an iceberg where uh only uh I think it's 1/8 of the iceberg that can be seen above the water, whereas the rest, the remaining 7/8 under the surface . . . that's what causes it to move. So, that's where the imagination comes in. The reader has to fill in the details under the surface.

So twelve more years of . . . of experimentation really—short stories and slim novels that sold well but were never really approved of by critics, and then in 1952, Hemingway published *The Old Man and the Sea*. I am guessing that many of you have read it already. For those who haven't, it's a short, compelling tale of an old fisherman's struggle to haul in a giant marlin that he had caught in the Gulf of Mexico. It first appeared in *Life* magazine, selling over 5 million copies almost immediately. The next week, the publisher brought it out in hard cover, and it sold 50,000 copies before they could restock. And the critics liked it as much as the readers. What is the fascination with this rather small book? Well, some critics interpreted it as uh as the . . . allegory of man's struggle against old age; others . . . they interpreted it as man against the forces of nature. In any case, this book was probably the climax of Hemingway's career. Two years later, he was awarded the Nobel Prize for literature. He'd never received a major literary prize before, even though he had achieved commercial and critical success, and . . . the prize probably meant a great deal to him.

After the talk, you will read:

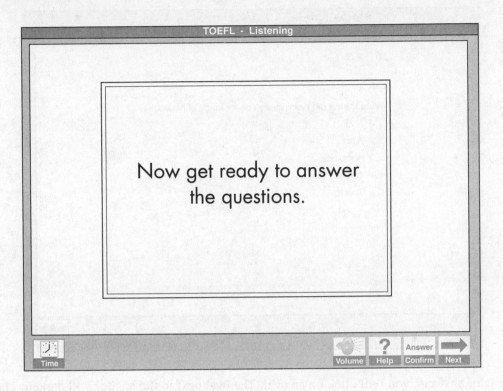

Then, the first question will be presented:

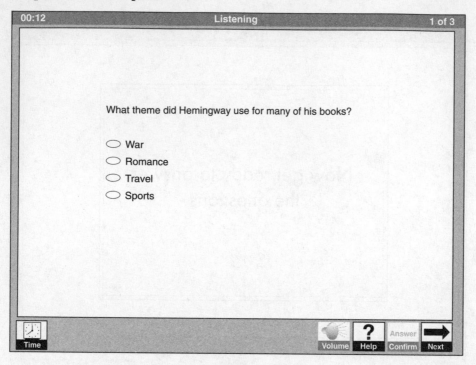

To choose your answers, you will click on an oval. The oval next to the answer will darken. The correct answer is indicated on the screen below.

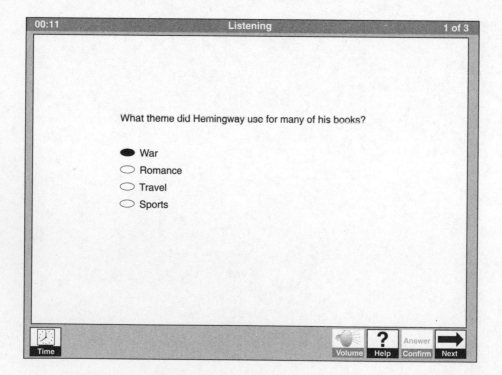

After you click on **Next** and **Confirm Answer**, the next question will be presented.

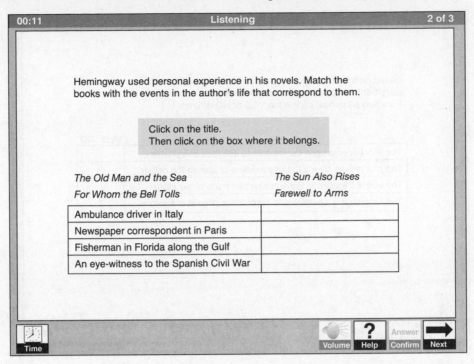

To choose your answers, you will click on a title and then click on the space where it belongs. As you do this, each title will appear in the square you have selected. The correct answer is indicated on the screen below.

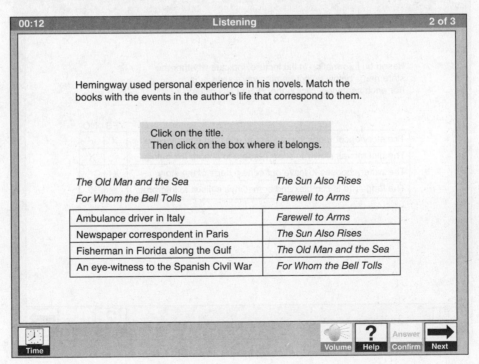

After you click on **Next** and **Confirm Answer**, the next question will be presented:

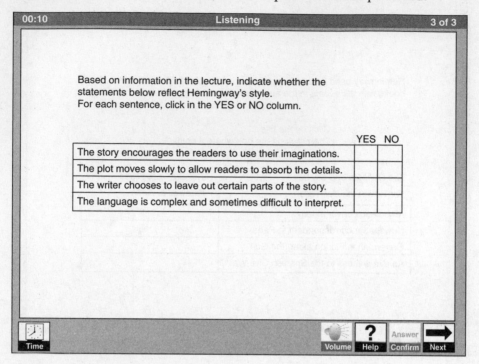

To choose your answer, you will click on the box. As you do this, an X will appear in the box. The correct answer is indicated on the screen below.

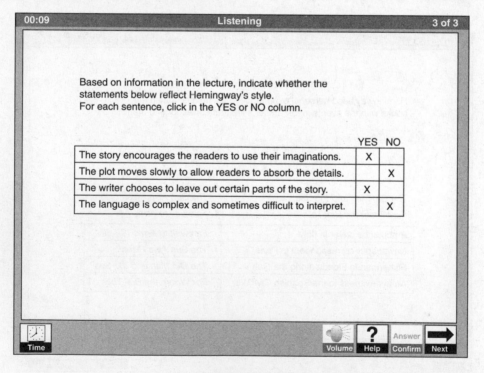

Integrated Listening

Directions: In the integrated listening tasks, you will hear and respond to long conversations, class discussions, and lectures in an academic setting. The language includes natural pauses and is presented at a normal rate for native speakers. You may take notes. After each conversation, discussion, or lecture, you will hear a question that requires you to respond by speaking or writing. Integrated examples are shown in the Directions and Examples for Speaking in Chapter 4 and the Directions and Examples for Writing in Chapter 7.

Review of Problems and Questions for the Listening Section

This Review can be used to prepare for both the Paper-Based TOEFL and the Computer-Based TOEFL. For the most part, the same types of problems are tested on both the Paper-Based TOEFL and the Computer-Based TOEFL; however, questions on Informal Conversations and Tours are found only on the Paper-Based TOEFL and are not addressed in this book.

Most of the questions on both the Paper-Based TOEFL and the Computer-Based TOEFL are multiple-choice. Some of the questions on the Computer-Based TOEFL are computer-assisted. The computer-assisted questions have special directions on the screen.

Although the computer-assisted questions in this book are numbered, and the answer choices are lettered A, B, C, D, the same questions on the CD-ROM that accompanies the book are not numbered and lettered. You need the numbers and letters in the book to refer to the Answer Key, the Explanatory Answers, and the Transcript for the Listening section. On the CD-ROM, you can refer to other chapters by clicking on the screen. The questions on the CD-ROM that is available to supplement this book are like those on the Computer-Based TOEFL.

TYPES OF PROBLEMS IN THE LISTENING SECTION

Problems like those in this Review of Listening frequently appear on Parts A, B, and C of the Listening section of the TOEFL.

Part A   Short Conversations

1 Details

2 Idiomatic Expressions

3 Suggestions

4 Assumptions

5 Predictions

6 Implications

7 Problems

8 Topics

Part B   Longer Conversations

9 Academic Conversations

Part C   Talks and Lectures

10 Class Discussions

11 Academic Talks

12 Lectures

Types of Problems in Short Conversations

1   Details

Details are specific facts stated in a conversation.

In some short conversations, you will hear all of the information that you need to answer the problem correctly. You will NOT need to draw conclusions.

When you hear a conversation between two speakers, you must remember the details that were stated.

EXAMPLE

Man:	Front desk. How may I help you?
Woman:	I'd like to arrange a wake-up call for tomorrow morning at seven o'clock, please.
Narrator:	When does the woman want to get up tomorrow?
Answer:	Seven o'clock in the morning.

2   Idiomatic Expressions

Idiomatic expressions are words and phrases that are characteristic of a particular language with meanings that are usually different from the meanings of each of the words used alone.

In some short conversations, you will hear idiomatic expressions, such as "to kill time," which means to wait.

When you hear a conversation between two speakers, you must listen for the idiomatic expressions. You will be expected to recognize them and restate the idiom or identify the feelings or attitudes of the speaker.

It will help you if you study a list of common idioms as part of your TOEFL preparation.

EXAMPLE

Man:	I'm single. In fact, I've never been married.
Woman:	No kidding!
Narrator:	What does the woman mean?
Answer:	She is surprised by the man's statement.

3   Suggestions

A *suggestion* is a recommendation.

In some short conversations, you will hear words and phrases that make a suggestion, such as "you should," "why don't you," or "why not."

When you hear the words and phrases that introduce a suggestion, you must be able to recognize and remember what the speaker suggested, and who made the suggestion.

EXAMPLE

Woman:	Oh, no. Dr. Thompson's class is closed.
Man:	Already?
Woman:	I know. This is only the first day of registration.
Man:	Well, it's offered every term. Why don't you just take it next semester?

| Narrator: | What does the man suggest that the woman do? |
| Answer: | Wait until next semester to take Dr. Thompson's class. |

4   Assumptions

An *assumption* is a statement accepted as true without proof or demonstration.

In some short conversations, an assumption is proven false, and the speaker or speakers who had made the assumption express surprise.

When you hear a conversation between two speakers, you must be able to recognize remarks that register surprise, and draw conclusions about the assumptions that the speaker may have made.

EXAMPLE

| Woman: | Let's just e-mail our response to Larry instead of calling. |
| Man: | *Larry* has an e-mail address? |

| Narrator: | What had the man assumed about Larry? |
| Answer: | He would not have an e-mail address. |

5   Predictions

A *prediction* is a guess about the future based on evidence from the present.

In some short conversations, you will be asked to make predictions about the future activities of the speakers involved.

When you hear a conversation between two speakers, you must listen for evidence from which you may draw a logical conclusion about their future activities.

EXAMPLE

Man:	Could you please book me on the next flight out to Los Angeles?
Woman:	I'm sorry, sir. Continental doesn't fly into Los Angeles. Why don't you try Northern or Worldwide?

Narrator:	What will the man probably do?
Answer:	He will probably get a ticket for a flight on Northern or Worldwide Airlines.

6   Implications

Implied means suggested, but not stated. In many ways, implied conversations are like prediction conversations.

In some short conversations, you will hear words and phrases or intonations that will suggest how the speakers felt, what kind of work or activity they were involved in, or where the conversation may have taken place.

When you hear a conversation between two speakers, you must listen for information that will help you draw a conclusion about the situation.

EXAMPLE

Woman:	Where's Anita? We were supposed to go to the library to study.
Man:	Well, here is her coat, and her books are over there on the chair.

Narrator:	What does the man imply about Anita?
Answer:	Anita has not left for the library yet.

7   Problems

A *problem* is a situation that requires discussion or solution.

In some short conversations, you will hear the speakers discuss a problem.

When you hear a discussion between two speakers, you must be able to identify what the problem is. This may be more difficult because different aspects of the problem will also be included in the conversation.

EXAMPLE

Woman:	It only takes two hours to get to New York, but you'll have a six-hour layover between flights.
Man:	Maybe you could try routing me through Philadelphia or Boston instead.

| Narrator: | What is the man's problem? |
| Answer: | His flight connections are not very convenient. |

Topics

A *topic* is a main theme in a conversation or in a piece of writing.

In some short conversations, the speakers will discuss a particular topic.

When you hear a conversation, you must be able to identify the main topic from among several secondary themes that support the topic.

EXAMPLE

Man:	Tell me about your trip to New York.
Woman:	It was great! We saw the Statue of Liberty and the Empire State Building and all of the tourist attractions the first day, then we saw the museums the second day and spent the rest of the time shopping and seeing shows.
Narrator:	What are the man and woman talking about?
Answer:	The woman's trip.

Types of Problems in Longer Conversations

Academic Conversations

Academic conversations are conversations between students and professors or other academic personnel on a college or university campus.

In some longer conversations, you will hear an academic conversation between two speakers.

When you hear a conversation, you must be able to summarize the main ideas. You may also be asked to recall important details.

EXAMPLE

Joe:	Hi, Dr. Watkins. Are you busy?
Dr. Watkins:	Oh, hello, Joe. Come in.
Joe:	Thanks. You've probably graded our midterms.
Dr. Watkins:	Just finished them. Frankly, I was surprised that you didn't do better on it.
Joe:	I know. I had two midterms on the same day, and I didn't organize my time very well. I spent too much time studying for the first one, and then I ran out of time to study for yours.
Dr. Watkins:	I see.
Joe:	So I was wondering whether I could do a project for extra credit to bring my grade back up. I'm sure I have a B or even a C after that midterm, but before that I had a solid A.

Dr. Watkins:	Did you have anything in mind for your project?
Joe:	Well, I was thinking that I could develop a reading list, using the main topics from the midterm. And then, if the list looks okay to you, I could write a summary of each of the readings. But, if you don't like that idea, I'd be happy to do any project you would approve.
Dr. Watkins:	Actually, that sounds like a good plan. In fact, I have a reading list that might work for you.
Joe:	Better yet.
Dr. Watkins:	Good. If you do summaries for all of these articles, the extra points should put you back on track for an A.
Joe:	Thanks. Thanks a lot.
Question:	What is Joe's problem?
Answer:	His grade in the course is low because of his midterm.
Question:	Why didn't Joe do better on the midterm?
Answer:	He spent too much time studying for a midterm for another class.
Question:	What does Joe want to do?
Answer:	He wants to complete some additional assignments to earn extra points.
Question:	How does Professor Watkins respond to Joe's proposal?
Answer:	She is helpful.

Types of Problems in Talks and Lectures

10 Class Discussions

Class discussions are conversations that occur in classrooms.

In some talks, you will hear a class discussion between two, three, or more speakers.

When you hear a discussion, you must be able to summarize the important ideas. You will usually NOT be required to remember small details.

It will help you to audit some college classes.

EXAMPLE

Miss Richards:	Good morning. My name is Miss Richards, and I'll be your instructor for Career Education 100. Before we get started, I'd appreciate it if you would introduce yourselves and tell us a little bit about why you decided to take this class. Let's start here....
Bill:	I'm Bill Jensen, and I'm a sophomore this term, but I still haven't decided what to major in. I hope that this class will help me.
Miss Richards:	Good, I hope so, too. Next.
Patty:	I'm Patty Davis, and I'm majoring in foreign languages, but I'm not sure what kind of job I can get after I graduate.
Miss Richards:	Are you a sophomore, too, Patty?
Patty:	No. I'm a senior. I wish I'd taken this class sooner, but I didn't know about it until this term.

Miss Richards: Didn't your advisor tell you about it?

Patty: No. A friend of mine took it last year, and it helped her a lot.

Miss Richards: How did you find out about the course, Bill?

Bill: The same way Patty did. A friend of mine told me about it.

Question: In what class does this discussion take place?

Answer: Career Education.

Question: What are the two students talking about?

Answer: They are introducing themselves.

Question: Why is the woman taking the course?

Answer: To help her find a job after graduation.

Question: How did the students find out about the course?

Answer: From friends who had taken it.

11 Academic Talks

Academic talks are short talks that provide orientation to academic courses and procedures.

In some talks, you will hear academic talks on a variety of college and university topics.

When you hear a talk, you must be able to summarize the main ideas. You must also be able to answer questions about important details. You will usually not be asked to remember minor details.

EXAMPLE

Since we'll be having our midterm exam next week, I thought I'd spend a few minutes talking with you about it. I realize that none of you has ever taken a class with me before, so you really don't know what to expect on one of my exams.

First, let me remind you that I have included a very short description of the midterm on the syllabus that you received at the beginning of the semester. So you should read that. I also recommend that you organize and review your notes from all of our class sessions. I'm not saying that the book is unimportant, but the notes should help you to identify those topics that we covered in greatest detail. Then, you can go back to your book and reread the sections that deal with those topics. I also suggest that you take another look at the articles on reserve in the library. They have information in them that is not in the book, and although we didn't talk much about them in class, I do feel that they are important, so you can expect to see a few questions from the articles on the exam. Oh, yes, I almost forgot. Besides the twenty-five objective questions, there will be five essay questions, and you must choose three.

EXAMPLE

Question: What does the speaker mainly discuss?

Answer: The midterm exam.

Question: When will the students take the exam?
Answer: Next week.

Question: According to the professor, what should the students do to prepare?
Answer: Study their notes, the articles on reserve, and appropriate sections of the book.

Question: What is the format of the exam?
Answer: Twenty-five objective questions and five essay questions.

12   Lectures

Lectures are short talks that provide information about academic subjects. They are like short lectures that might be heard in a college classroom.

In some talks, you will hear academic information in a short lecture.

When you hear a lecture, you must be able to summarize the important ideas. You must also be able to answer questions that begin with the following words: *who, what, when, where, why?*

It will help you to listen to documentary programs on radio and television. Programs on educational broadcasting networks are especially helpful. Listen carefully. Ask yourself questions to test your ability to remember the information.

EXAMPLE

The vast array of fruits presents a challenge for scientists who try to classify them, but they are usually classified into several types according to the origin of their development. Simple fruits are derived from flowers with just one pistil. Here is a diagram of a simple fruit. Some of the most obvious examples include cherries, peaches, and plums, but coconuts are also simple fruits.

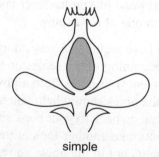

simple

As you can see, the second classification of fruits, aggregate fruits, differs from simple fruits in that each flower has several pistils. Examples of aggregate fruits are blackberries, raspberries, and strawberries. Now, let's look at a diagram of an aggregate fruit.

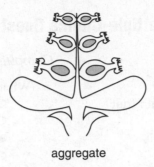

aggregate

The third type, a multiple fruit, develops from a group of flowers that grow in clusters. When the walls of the pistils thicken, then they bond and become incorporated into a single fruit. The classic example of this type is the pineapple, but figs are also classified as multiple fruits. Here is a diagram of a multiple fruit for comparison with the other two types.

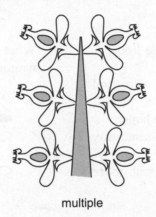

multiple

Selective breeding creates new varieties of fruit, usually larger, juicier, and more appealing than the smaller natural fruits. However, even laboratory fruits seem to adhere to this general typology.

Okay, I'm going to put some specimens into the lab for you to examine. There will be three trays—the first with samples of simple fruits, the second with samples of aggregate fruits, and the third with samples of multiple fruits. Please examine both the flowers and the fruits themselves, and this is important—please look at the three trays in this order—simple fruits, aggregate fruits, and multiple fruits.

TYPES OF QUESTIONS

Multiple-Choice Questions

Paper-Based TOEFL

1. What is the lecture mainly about?
   - Ⓐ Laboratory assignments with fruit
   - Ⓑ Selective breeding of fruit
   - Ⓒ Basic classifications of fruit
   - Ⓓ A definition of fruit

2. Which of the fruits is an example of a multiple fruit?
   - Ⓐ Pineapples
   - Ⓑ Cherries
   - Ⓒ Strawberries
   - Ⓓ Blackberries

3. What distinguishes laboratory fruits from natural fruits?
   - Ⓐ They do not taste as sweet as natural fruits.
   - Ⓑ Laboratory fruits tend to be larger.
   - Ⓒ They are not classified the same way as natural fruits.
   - Ⓓ Laboratory fruits are bred with more pistils.

4. Which of the following fruits will NOT be placed into the first tray in the lab?
   - Ⓐ Coconuts
   - Ⓑ Plums
   - Ⓒ Peaches
   - Ⓓ Raspberries

Computer-Based TOEFL

What is the lecture mainly about?
- ○ Laboratory assignments with fruit
- ○ Selective breeding of fruit
- ● Basic classifications of fruit
- ○ A definition of fruit

Which of the fruits is an example of a multiple fruit?
- ● Pineapples
- ○ Cherries
- ○ Strawberries
- ○ Blackberries

What distinguishes laboratory fruits from natural fruits?
- ○ They do not taste as sweet as natural fruits.
- ● Laboratory fruits tend to be larger.
- ○ They are not classified the same way as natural fruits.
- ○ Laboratory fruits are bred with more pistils.

Which of the following fruits will NOT be placed into the first tray in the lab?
- ○ Coconuts
- ○ Plums
- ○ Peaches
- 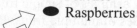 ● Raspberries

Answer Sheet

1. Ⓐ Ⓑ ● Ⓓ
2. ● Ⓑ Ⓒ Ⓓ
3. Ⓐ ● Ⓒ Ⓓ
4. Ⓐ Ⓑ Ⓒ ●

Computer-Assisted Questions

Two-Answer Questions. On some of the computer-assisted questions, you will be asked to select two answers. Both answers must be correct to receive credit for the question.

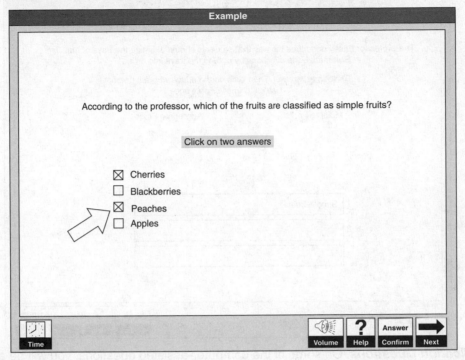

Visual Questions. On some of the computer-assisted questions, you will be asked to select a visual. The visual may be a picture, a drawing, or a diagram.

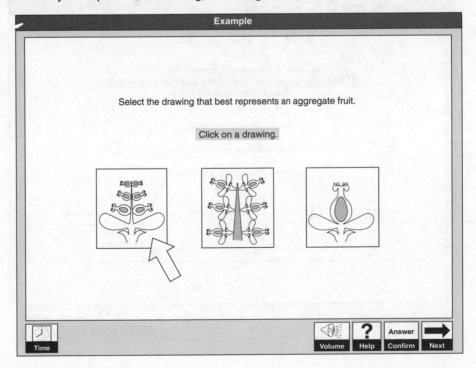

Sequencing Questions. On some of the computer-assisted questions, you will be asked to sequence events in order. The events could be historical events or the steps in a scientific process. All answers must be sequenced correctly to receive credit for the question.

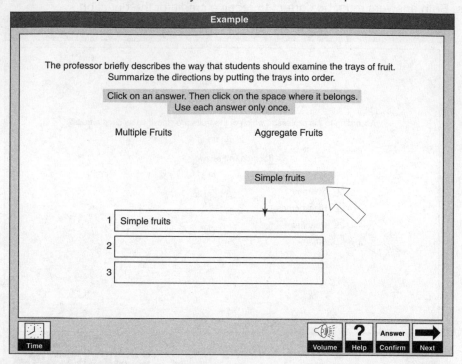

Classification Questions. On some of the computer-assisted questions, you will be asked to classify information by organizing it in categories.

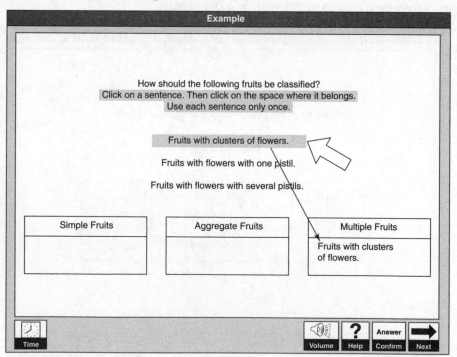

Computer Tutorial for the Listening Section

In order to succeed on the Computer-Based TOEFL, you must understand the computer vocabulary used for the test, and you must be familiar with the icons on the computer screens that you will see on the test. First, review the vocabulary. Then study the computer screens in this Tutorial.

Testing Tools: Vocabulary, Icons, and Keys

General Vocabulary for the Computer-Based TOEFL

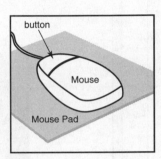

Mouse	A small control with one or two buttons on it.
Mouse Pad	A rectangular pad where you move the *mouse*.
Arrow	A marker that shows you where you are moving on the computer screen. Move the *mouse* on the *mouse pad* to move the **Arrow** on the screen.
Click	To depress the button on the *mouse* is to **Click** the *mouse*. **Click** the *mouse* to make changes on the computer screen.
Icon	A small picture or a word or a phrase in a box. Move the *arrow* to the **Icon** and *click* on the **Icon** to tell the computer what to do.

Icons for the Computer-Based TOEFL

Dismiss Directions	An example of an *icon*. *Click* on **Dismiss Directions** to tell the computer to remove the directions from the screen.
Oval	The *icon* beside the answers for the multiple-choice test questions. Move the *arrow* to the **Oval** and *click* on one of the **Ovals** to choose an answer.
Next	An example of an *icon*. To see the next question on the screen, *click* on **Next** first and then *click* on **Confirm Answer**.
Confirm Answer	An example of an *icon*. *Click* on **Confirm Answer** after you *click* on **Next** to see the next question on the screen. Remember, *click* on **Next**, **Confirm Answer** in that order.
Help	An example of an *icon*. *Click* on the question mark to see a list of the *icons* and directions for the section.
Time	An *icon* of a clock in the bottom left corner of the screen. *Click* on the clock face to hide or show the time you have left to finish the section of the test you are working on. Five minutes before the end of each section of the test, the clock will appear automatically. Remember, the time appears in numbers at the top of the screen, not on the clock face. You cannot use the clock during the recording.

Specific Vocabulary for Section 1

Volume	One additional *icon* at the bottom of the screen in the Listening section. *Click* on **Volume** to go to a screen with an *up arrow* and a *down arrow*. *Click* on the *up arrow* to make the recording louder. *Click* on the *down arrow* to make the recording softer. Remember, you can change the volume while the speaker is giving directions, but not after the directions have concluded.

COMPUTER SCREENS FOR THE COMPUTER-BASED TOEFL

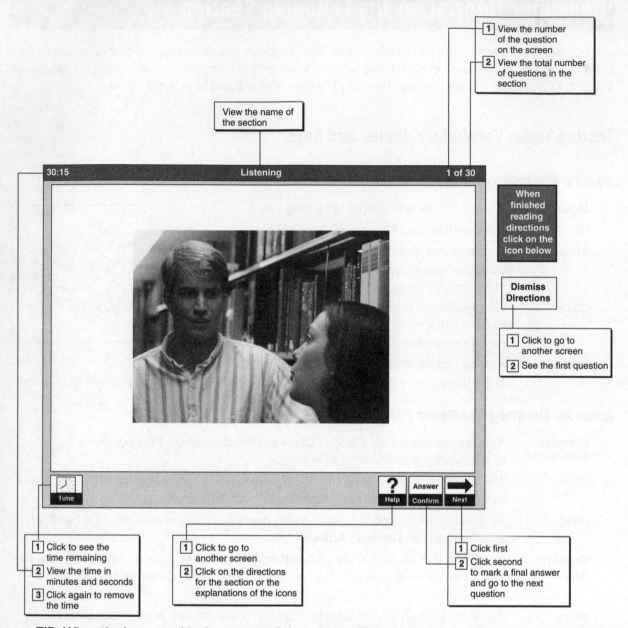

View the name of
the section

1 View the number
of the question
on the screen

2 View the total number
of questions in the
section

30:15   Listening   1 of 30

When
finished
reading
directions
click on the
icon below

**Dismiss
Directions**

1 Click to go to
another screen

2 See the first question

Time

? Help

Answer Confirm

→ Next

1 Click to see the
time remaining

2 View the time in
minutes and seconds

3 Click again to remove
the time

1 Click to go to
another screen

2 Click on the directions
for the section or the
explanations of the icons

1 Click first

2 Click second
to mark a final answer
and go to the next
question

TIP: When the icons are black, you can click on them. When they are gray, they are not functioning. For example, **Confirm Answer** is gray until you click on **Next**. Then **Confirm Answer** is black. Remember the order to click on these two icons.

Computer Screens for Section 1

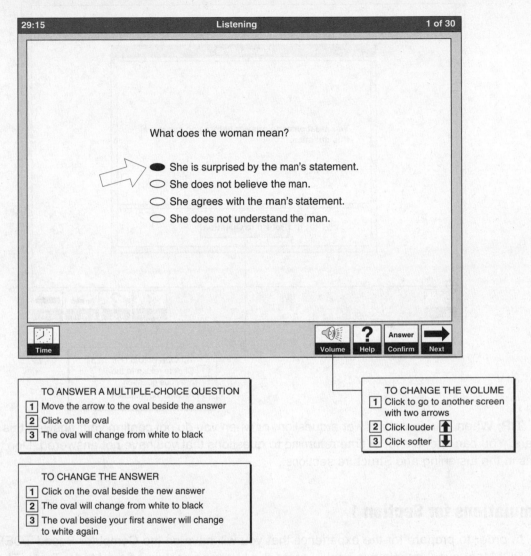

TIP: Most of the questions on the Computer-Based TOEFL are multiple-choice. When you learn to move the arrow to the oval and click on the oval, you will be able to answer most of the questions.

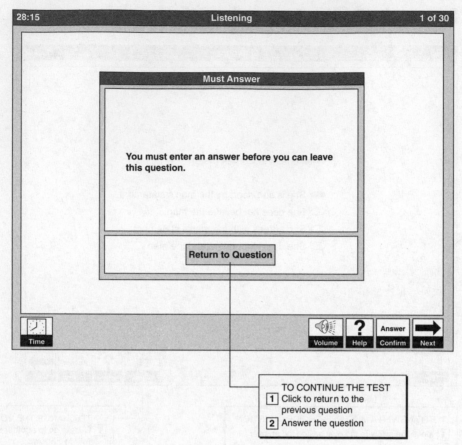

Must Answer

You must enter an answer before you can leave this question.

Return to Question

Time   Volume Help Answer Confirm Next

TO CONTINUE THE TEST
1 Click to return to the previous question
2 Answer the question

TIP: When you do not answer a question, or when you do not confirm your answer, this screen appears. You can spend a lot of time returning to questions that you have not answered. Don't skip questions in the Listening and Structure sections.

Simulations for Section 1

In order to prepare for the experience that you will have on the Computer-Based TOEFL, use the CD-ROM that supplements this book. Locate the Listening section on the Model Tests. The computer will simulate features of the Listening section on the Computer-Based TOEFL. These Model Tests are computer-assisted.

As part of your study plan, be sure to review all of the questions in all of the Model Tests. Use the Explanatory Answers on the CD-ROM or in Chapter 10. Finally, take the Cumulative Model Test on the CD-ROM. This test is computer-adaptive, which means that the computer will select questions for you at your level of language proficiency.

If you do not have a computer, you can simulate some of the features of the Computer-Based TOEFL. In Section 1 of Model Tests 1–8 in Chapter 8, the questions are written out for you to read while you listen to them. This is different from the Paper-Based TOEFL. Instead of the CD-ROM, you may be using either an audio compact disk or a cassette. Pause the tape or compact disk occasionally to give yourself more control of the time for each question. But be careful not to pause too often or you will not be able to complete all of the questions within the total time allowed for the section.

Preview of Listening on the Next Generation TOEFL

The Next Generation TOEFL will include comprehension passages with natural speech at a rate that is normal for native speakers and a style that is appropriate for campus conversations and academic classroom interactions.

Chapter 12 of this book is a Glossary of Campus Vocabulary to help you understand the campus context. The next edition of this book will include a new, revised Listening Chapter to provide you with strategies to comprehend natural speech in academic situations.

Watch for *Barron's How to Prepare for the TOEFL, 12th Edition* to be published when the Next Generation TOEFL is introduced.

Advice for the Listening Section

Be sure to adjust the volume before you begin. Before you begin the Listening section, you will have an opportunity to adjust the volume on your headset. Be sure to do it before you dismiss the directions and begin the test. After the test has begun, you may not adjust the volume.

Do not let the visuals of people distract you from listening to the short conversations. We all respond in different ways to pictures. If you become too involved in looking at the pictures, you may pay less attention to the recording. For the most part, the pictures of people are for orientation to the short conversation. After you look briefly at the picture, give your full concentration to the conversation. If you take the Model Tests on the CD-ROM that may supplement this book, first practice by watching the screen during the short conversation and then by closing your eyes or looking away during the conversation. Find the best way for you to listen to this part of the test.

Focus on the visuals of objects, art, specimens, maps, charts, and drawings in the talks. In general, the pictures of people are for orientation to the talks, whereas the visuals of objects, art, specimens, maps, charts, and drawings support the meaning of the talks. Do not focus on the pictures of people. Do focus on the other visuals that appear during the talks. They could reappear in a question. When you take the Model Tests, practice selective attention. Disregard the pictures of the lecturer and the students, and be alert to the other visuals.

Be sure to read the question while you are hearing it. The questions will be shown on the screen while you are hearing them. If you find that it is to your advantage to close your eyes or look away during the short conversations, be sure to give your full attention to the screen again while the question is being asked. During the questions for longer conversations and talks, watch the screen carefully. By using the Model Tests, you will be able to develop a rhythm for interacting with the screen that is to your advantage.

Advice for Success

This advice from Dr. Charles Swindell is framed on the wall of my office near my computer so that I can see it every day. I am happy to share it with you:

"The longer I live, the more I realize the impact of attitude on life. Attitude to me is more important than facts. It is more important than the past, than education, than money, than circumstances, than failures, than successes, than what other people think or say or do. It is more important than appearance, giftedness, or skill. The remarkable thing is, we have a choice every day regarding the attitude we will embrace for that day. We cannot change our past . . . we cannot change the fact that people may act in a certain way. We cannot change the inevitable. The only thing we can do is play on the one string we have, and that is our attitude. I am convinced that life is 10 percent what happens to me and 90 percent how I react to it. And so it is with you. We are in charge of our attitudes."

Henry Ford said it another way:

"If you think you can or you think you can't, you are probably right."

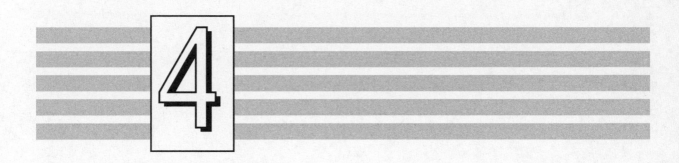

PREVIEW OF SPEAKING

Overview of the Speaking Section

**QUICK COMPARISON—SPEAKING
PAPER-BASED TOEFL,
COMPUTER-BASED TOEFL, AND NEXT GENERATION TOEFL**

Paper-Based TOEFL	Computer-Based TOEFL	Next Generation TOEFL
There is NO speaking section.	There is NO speaking section.	Three types of questions are presented in six sets. The first two sets have a general question; other sets have questions about campus and academic topics. After you see and hear the general questions, you will have 15 seconds to prepare your answers and 45 seconds to record them. After you hear the campus and academic questions, you will have 20–30 seconds to prepare each answer and 60 seconds to record it.

Directions and Examples for Speaking Questions

The Speaking Section of the TOEFL tests your ability to speak in English about a variety of general and academic topics. The Speaking Section is not included in either the Paper-Based TOEFL or the Computer-Based TOEFL. It is included in the Next Generation TOEFL.

Paper-Based TOEFL (PBT)

There is no Speaking Section on the current format of the Paper-Based TOEFL; however, there are plans for a telephone administration of speaking for future tests.

Computer-Based TOEFL (CBT)

There is no Speaking Section on the current format of the Computer-Based TOEFL.

Next Generation TOEFL

There are usually six questions in two parts on the Speaking Section of the Next Generation TOEFL. The questions are presented only one time. You may take notes. The topics are both general and academic. There are two types of tasks included in the Speaking Section: two independent speaking tasks and four integrated speaking tasks.

Independent Speaking

Directions: In the independent speaking tasks, you will hear questions about familiar topics. You can use your personal experience and general knowledge to answer. After each question, you have 15 seconds to prepare your answer, and 45 seconds to record it.

This is an example of an independent speaking question:

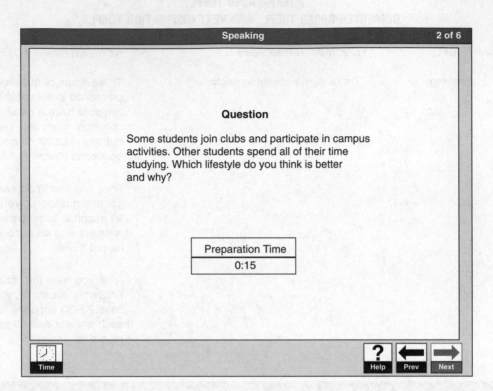

Speaking   2 of 6

Question

Some students join clubs and participate in campus activities. Other students spend all of their time studying. Which lifestyle do you think is better and why?

Preparation Time
0:15

Time   Help   Prev   Next

This is an example of an answer that receives an excellent rating:

"When I go to college, I plan to join at least one club and participate in some of the activities. Being part of a club is a good way to make friends because . . . you have something in common, and . . . and if I can make friends with Americans, I'll probably improve my English. And activities are also a good way to relax. Studying all the time is uh stressful, and breaks are good for your health. Um . . . another reason to participate in activities is to demonstrate that you lead a balanced life. Some of the scholarship committees are looking for additional qualities, like leadership or community service as well as high grades, and when you have extra . . . extra-curricular activities on your application, it can help you get a scholarship or admission to graduate school. So I think students who study all the time . . . they miss out on a lot of opportunities for friendship and maybe even for a scholarship."

Checklist for Independent Speaking

☑ The talk answers the topic question.
☑ The point of view or position is clear.
☑ The talk is direct and well-organized.
☑ The sentences are logically connected to each other.
☑ Details and examples support the main idea.
☑ The speaker expresses complete thoughts.
☑ The meaning is easy for the listener to comprehend.
☑ A wide range of vocabulary is used.
☑ There are only minor errors in grammar and idioms.
☑ The talk is within a range of 100–150 words.

Integrated Speaking

Directions: In the integrated speaking tasks, you will hear a lecture or read a passage about an academic topic, or you may listen to a lecture and read a related passage about an academic topic. You can take notes to prepare your answer. After each lecture or reading passage, you will hear a question that requires you to respond by speaking. You will have 20–30 seconds to prepare your answer, and 60 seconds to record it.

This is an example of a lecture:

(professor) Okay. Let's continue our discussion about the way that psychologists gather information. First, let me remind you that many of us reject the idea that the social sciences can be studied with the same methods that scientists use in the natural or physical sciences. We believe that human behavior is contextualized, that is, that the behavior is intensely personal and subjective, and must always be studied within the natural context of the behavior, not in an artificial, experimental setting. So, that said, let me talk about a couple of methods that we use.

One of the most useful methods is the interview. Unlike surveys that contain set answers from which the subject must select, the interview allows us to ask open-ended questions. This gives subjects the option of explaining why they hold a certain opinion and that can be very useful in understanding what motivates people and what would be likely to change their behaviors. Of course the problem is that it is extremely time consuming as compared with something more quantitative, like say, the survey.

So, one way to interview a larger number of people more efficiently is to bring them together in a focus group. Focus groups are situations in which groups of people are brought together with a researcher to focus on a topic not only to articulate their opinions but also to explain them to each other. The researcher learns by listening to the group and draws conclusions from their interactions. The advantages are obvious—focus groups provide data from a group much more quickly and cost effectively than would be possible if each individual were interviewed separately, and they provide a way for researchers to follow up and clarify responses that may be stated in an ambiguous way.

This is an example of an integrated speaking question:

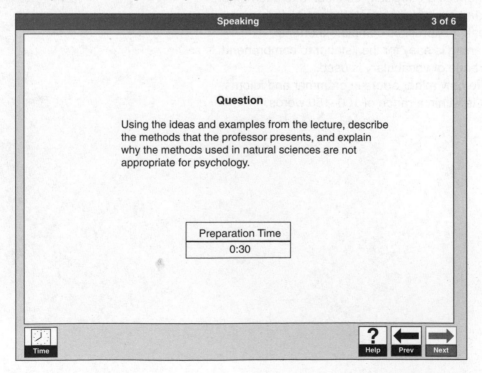

Speaking · 3 of 6

Question

Using the ideas and examples from the lecture, describe the methods that the professor presents, and explain why the methods used in natural sciences are not appropriate for psychology.

Preparation Time
0:30

Time · Help · Prev · Next

Here is an example of an answer that receives an excellent rating:

"The methods used to study natural sciences can't be used to study social sciences because human behavior is best observed in a real context. In spite of . . . in spite of the fact that it is efficient and relatively . . . quick, a survey may be the least useful method since it uh . . . it includes a limited range of answers. On the other hand, interviews have open-ended questions, which uh which allow the subjects to explain the reasons why they answered in a certain way. But it takes a lot of time to interview an adequate sample. Focus groups allow researchers to . . . to gather data from a larger number of people and uh more quickly than individual interviews. In a focus group, the researcher listens to a group and makes conclusions about their opinions uh . . . following up and clarifying comments. The way subjects interact is also interesting to the researcher. So a focus group is probably the best option for gathering data."

Checklist for Integrated Speaking

☑ The talk answers the topic question.
☑ There are only minor inaccuracies in the content.
☑ The talk is direct and well-organized.
☑ The sentences are logically connected to each other.
☑ Details and examples support the main idea.
☑ The speaker expresses complete thoughts.
☑ The meaning is easy for the listener to comprehend.
☑ A wide range of vocabulary is used.
☑ The speaker paraphrases, using his or her own words.
☑ The speaker credits the lecturer with wording when necessary.
☑ There are only minor errors in grammar and idioms.
☑ The talk is within a range of 100–150 words

Preview of Problems and Questions for the Speaking Section

Introduced as the TOEFL Academic Speaking Test (TAST)

This preview can be used to prepare for the Next Generation TOEFL Speaking Section or the TOEFL Academic Speaking Test (TAST). The TAST was introduced in 2003 as a first version of the TOEFL Speaking Section. Although minor modifications will be made in the second version of the TAST when it is included in the Next Generation TOEFL, this preview will be a good way to begin your preparation.

The Next Generation TOEFL Speaking Section, like the TAST, will measure your ability to speak in English about a variety of general and academic topics. There are six questions. The total time is 20 minutes. Although the administration is currently by telephone, the plan is to design a Speaking Section on the Internet.

There is no Speaking Section on the current format of the Paper-Based TOEFL or the Computer-Based TOEFL. However, there are plans for a telephone administration of speaking for future Paper-Based administrations.

TYPES OF QUESTIONS IN THE SPEAKING SECTION

Questions like those in this Preview of Speaking appear on the TOEFL Academic Speaking Test, soon to be reintroduced as the Next Generation TOEFL Speaking Section.

1 Experiences
2 Preferences
3 Reports
4 Examples
5 Problems
6 Summaries

Question 1—Experiences

In this question, you will be asked to speak about a personal experience. This may be a place, a person, a possession, a situation, or an occasion. After you hear the question, you will make a choice from your experience and then explain why you made that choice. You will have 15 seconds to prepare and 45 seconds to speak.

EXAMPLE QUESTION

Where would you like to study in the United States?

Task
• Describe your experience
• Explain the reasons for your choice

Directions

Read Question 1, the Example Notes, and the Example Answer. Use the Checklist to learn how to rate a speaking response for this type of question.

EXAMPLE NOTES

Washington, D.C.
- Family in area—advice, help
- International city—food, stores
- Tours—sites, trains to other cities
- Universities—excellent, accepted at one

SCRIPT FOR EXAMPLE ANSWER

I'd like to study at a university in Washington, D.C. because I have family in the area, and . . . and it would be nice to have them close by so I could visit them on holidays and in case I need advice or help. I've been to Washington several times, and I like it there. It's an international city, and there are restaurants and stores where I can buy food and other things from my country while uh I'm living abroad. And Washington is an exciting place. I've gone on several tours, but I still have many places on my list of sites to see. Also, um . . . there are trains to New York and Florida so I could take advantage of my free time to see other cities in the United States. Um . . . as for the universities, there are several excellent schools in Washington, and . . . and I'd probably be accepted at one of them.

Checklist
✔ The talk answers the topic question.
✔ The point of view or position is clear.
✔ The talk is direct and well-organized.
✔ The sentences are logically connected to each other.
✔ Details and examples support the main idea.
✔ The speaker expresses complete thoughts.
✔ The meaning is easy for the listener to comprehend.
✔ A wide range of vocabulary is used.
✔ There are only minor errors in grammar.
✔ The talk is within a range of 125–150 words.

Question 2—Preferences

In this question, you will be asked to speak about a personal preference. This may be a situation, an activity, or an event. After you hear the question, you will make a choice between two options presented and then explain why you made that choice. You will have 15 seconds to prepare and 45 seconds to speak.

EXAMPLE QUESTION

Some students live in dormitories on campus. Other students live in apartments off campus. Which living situation do you think is better and why?

Task
- Choose between two options
- Explain the reasons for your preference

Directions

Read Question 2 and the Example Answer. Use the Checklist to learn how to rate a speaking response for this type of question.

Example Notes

Dormitories
- More interaction—practice English, study
- Less responsibility—meals, laundry, cleaning
- Better location—library, recreation, classroom buildings

Script for Example Answer

A lot of my friends live off campus, but I think that living in a dormitory is a better situation uh especially for the first year at a new college. Dormitories are structured to provide opportunities for interaction and for making friends. As a foreign student, it would be an advantage to be in a dormitory to practice English with other residents and even to find study groups in the dormitory. And dorm students have . . . uh have less responsibility for meals, laundry, and . . . and cleaning since there are meal plans and services available as part of the fees. Besides, there's only one check to write, so the bookkeeping's minimal. And the dormitory offers an ideal location near the library and um all the recreational facilities and . . . and classroom buildings.

Checklist
✔ The talk answers the topic question.
✔ The point of view or position is clear.
✔ The talk is direct and well-organized.
✔ The sentences are logically connected to each other.
✔ Details and examples support the main idea.
✔ The speaker expresses complete thoughts.
✔ The meaning is easy for the listener to comprehend.
✔ A wide range of vocabulary is used.
✔ There are only minor errors in grammar.
✔ The talk is within a range of 125–150 words.

Question 3—Reports

In this question, you will be asked to listen to a speaker and read a short passage on the same topic. The topic usually involves a campus situation, and the speaker's opinion about it. After you hear the question, you will be asked to report the speaker's opinion and relate it to the reading passage. You will have 30 seconds to prepare and 60 seconds to speak.

Example Question

The man expresses his opinion of the proposal in the announcement. Report his opinion and explain the reasons he gives for having that opinion.

Task
- Summarize a situation and an opinion about it
- Explain the reason or the background
- Connect listening and reading passages

Directions
Read the Announcement in 45 seconds. Then read the Conversation followed by the Example Answer. Use the Checklist to learn how to rate a speaking response for this type of question.

Reading

> Announcement concerning a proposal for a branch campus
> The university is soliciting state and local funding to build a branch campus on the west side of the city where the I-19 expressway crosses the 201 loop. This location should provide convenient educational opportunities for students who live closer to the new campus as well as for those students who may choose to live on the west side once the campus is established. The city plan for the next ten years indicates that there will be major growth near the proposed site, including housing and shopping areas. By building a branch campus, some of the crowding on the main campus may be resolved.

Talk
I understand that a branch campus on the city's west side would be convenient for students who live near the proposed site and might attract more local students, but I oppose the plan because it will redirect funds from the main campus where several classroom buildings need repair. Hanover Hall for one. And uh a lot of the equipment in the chemistry and physics labs should be replaced. In my lab classes, we don't do some of the experiments because uh because we don't have enough equipment. And we need more teachers on the main campus. I'd like to see the branch campus funding allocated for teachers' salaries in order to decrease the student-teacher ratios. Most of the freshman classes are huge, and there's very little interaction with professors. Um . . . a branch campus would be a good addition but not until some of the problems on the main campus have been taken care of.

EXAMPLE NOTES

Plans to open a branch campus
- Convenient for students near
- Might attract more students

But will redirect funds from main campus
- Buildings need repair
- Equipment should be replaced
- More teachers—smaller classes

SCRIPT FOR EXAMPLE ANSWER

The man concedes that the branch campus might be advantageous for students living close to the new location, but he's concerned that the funding for a branch campus will affect funding on main campus for . . . for important capital improvements such as classroom buildings that are in need of repair. Um . . . and equipment in the science labs is getting old, so it needs to be replaced. And he also points out that more teachers are needed for the main campus in order to reduce student-teacher ratios, which . . . which would improve the quality of the teaching and interaction in classes. So the man feels that more attention should be given to the main campus and funding should be allocated to improve the main campus before a branch campus is considered.

Checklist

✔ The talk summarizes the situation and the opinion.
✔ The point of view or position is clear.
✔ The talk is direct and well-organized.
✔ The sentences are logically connected to each other.
✔ Details and examples support the opinion.
✔ The speaker expresses complete thoughts.
✔ The meaning is easy for the listener to comprehend.
✔ A wide range of vocabulary is used.
✔ There are only minor errors in grammar.
✔ The talk is within a range of 125–150 words.

Question 4—Examples

In this question, you will be asked to listen to a speaker and read a short passage on the same topic. The topic usually involves a general concept, and a specific example of it. Sometimes the speaker provides a contradictory point of view. After you hear the question, you will be asked to explain the example and relate it to the concept. You will have 30 seconds to prepare and 60 seconds to speak.

EXAMPLE QUESTION

Explain the Wug experiment and why the results supported the basic theory of child language acquisition.

Task

• Explain how an example supports a concept
• Connect listening and reading passages

Directions

Read the Textbook Passage in 45 seconds. Then read the Lecture followed by the Example Answer. Use the Checklist to learn how to rate a speaking response for this type of question.

Reading

> The telegraphic nature of early sentences in child language is a result of the omission of grammatical words such as the article *the* and auxiliary verbs *is* and *are* as well as word endings such as *-ing*, *-ed*, or *-s*. By the end of the third year, these grammatical forms begin to appear in the speech of most children. It is evident that a great deal of grammatical knowledge is required before these structures can be used correctly, and errors are commonly observed. The correction of grammatical errors is a feature of the speech of preschoolers four and five years old. The study of the errors in child language is interesting because it demonstrates when and how grammar is acquired.

Lecture

English uses a system of about a dozen word endings to express grammatical meaning—the *-ing* for present time, *-s* for possession and plurality, and . . . the *-ed* for the past, to mention only a few. But uh how and when do children learn them? Well, in a classic study by Berko in the 1950s, investigators . . . they elicited a series of forms that required the target endings. For example, a picture was shown of a bird, and . . . and the investigator identified it by saying, "This is a Wug." Then the children were shown two similar birds um to . . . to elicit the sentence, "There are two ——." So . . . if the children completed the sentence by saying, "Wugs," then it was inferred that they had learned the *-s* ending. Okay. Essential to the study was the use of nonsense words like "Wug" since the manipulation of the endings could have been supported by words that the children…had already heard. In any case, charts were developed to demonstrate the uh the gradual nature of grammatical acquisition. And the performance by children from 18 months to four years confirmed the basic theory of child language that the . . . the gradual reduction of grammatical errors . . . these are evidence of language acquisition.

EXAMPLE NOTES

Word endings—grammatical relationships
- *-ed* past
- *-s* plural

Wug experiment—Berko
- nonsense words—not influenced by familiar
- manipulate endings
- data about development

SCRIPT FOR EXAMPLE ANSWER

In English, there are several important word endings that express grammatical relationships, for example, the *-ed* ending that signals that the speaker's talking about the past and the *-s* ending that means "more than one" uh when it's used at the end of a noun. So, when children learn English, they um . . . they make errors in these endings, but they gradually refine their use until they master them. In the Wug experiment, Berko developed nonsense words to get children to use endings . . . so . . . so the researchers could uh follow their development. It was important not to use *real* words because the children might have been influenced by a word they'd heard before. So this experiment provided data about the time it takes and the age when endings are learned. It supported the basic theory of child language that um . . . sorting out grammatical errors is a feature of the speech of . . . of four year olds and a stage in language acquisition.

Checklist
- ✔ The talk relates an example to a concept.
- ✔ There are only minor inaccuracies in the content.
- ✔ The talk is direct and well-organized.
- ✔ The sentences are logically connected to each other.
- ✔ Details and examples support the talk.
- ✔ The speaker expresses complete thoughts.
- ✔ The meaning is easy for the listener to comprehend.
- ✔ A wide range of vocabulary is used.
- ✔ The speaker paraphrases, using his or her own words.
- ✔ The speaker credits the lecturer with wording.
- ✔ There are only minor errors in grammar.
- ✔ The talk is within a range of 125–150 words.

Question 5—Problems

In this question, you will be asked to listen to a conversation and explain a problem and the solutions that are proposed. You will have 20 seconds to prepare and 60 seconds to speak.

EXAMPLE QUESTION

Describe the woman's budgeting problem and the two suggestions that the man makes. What do you think the woman should do and why?

Task

- Describe a problem and several recommendations
- Express an opinion about the better solution
- Propose an alternative solution

Directions

Read Question 5 and the Example Answer. Then read the Conversation. Use the Checklist to learn how to rate a speaking response for this type of question.

Conversation

Woman:	Did your scholarship check come yet?
Man:	Yeah, it came last week. Didn't yours?
Woman:	No. That's the problem. And everything's due at the same time—tuition, my dorm fee, and let's not forget about books. I need about 400 dollars just for books.
Man:	Well, do you have any money left from last semester, in your checking account, I mean?
Woman:	Some, but not nearly enough. The check won't be here until the end of the month, and I won't get paid at work for two more weeks . . . I don't know what I'm going to do.
Man:	How about your credit card? Could you use that?
Woman:	Maybe, but I'm afraid I'll get the credit card bill before I get the scholarship check, then I'll be in worse trouble because of, you know, the interest rate for the credit card on top of everything else.
Man:	I see your point. Still, the check might come before the credit card bill. You might have to gamble, unless . . .
Woman:	I'm listening.
Man:	Well, unless you take out a student loan. A short-term loan. They have them set up at the Student Credit Union. Isn't that where you have your checking account?
Woman:	Umhum.
Man:	So you could take out a short-term loan and pay it off on the day that you get your check. It wouldn't cost that much for interest because it would probably be only a few weeks. That's what I'd do.

EXAMPLE NOTES

Problem—not enough money
- Books
- Tuition
- Dorm

Solutions
- Use credit card
- Take out a student loan

SCRIPT FOR EXAMPLE ANSWER

The woman doesn't have enough money for her expenses. Um . . . she has to pay tuition, and her dorm fee is due at the same time. Besides, she needs to buy books. So the problem is everything has to be paid now, and she won't get her scholarship check until the end of the month, and she won't be paid at work for two weeks. The man suggests that she use her credit card because she won't have to pay it off until the end of the month, but the problem is . . . the . . . the interest would be substantial if the scholarship check is delayed. The other idea—to take out a student loan—that seems better because the loan could be paid off on the day the check arrives instead of a fixed date, and it wouldn't cost much to get a short-term loan at the Student Credit Union. So . . . I support applying for a student loan.

Checklist

✔ The talk summarizes the problem and recommendations.
✔ The speaker's point of view or position is clear.
✔ The talk is direct and well-organized.
✔ The sentences are logically connected to each other.
✔ Details and examples support the opinion.
✔ The speaker expresses complete thoughts.
✔ The meaning is easy for the listener to comprehend.
✔ A wide range of vocabulary is used.
✔ There are only minor errors in grammar.
✔ The talk is within a range of 125–150 words.

Question 6—Summaries

In this question, you will be asked to give a summary of an academic lecture. You will have 20 seconds to prepare and 60 seconds to speak.

EXAMPLE QUESTION

Using examples from the lecture, describe two general types of irrigation systems. Then explain the disadvantages of each type.

Task
• Comprehend part of an academic lecture
• Summarize the main points

Directions
Read Question 6, the Lecture, and the Example Answer. Use the Checklist to learn how to rate a speaking response for this type of question.

Lecture
Two types of irrigation methods that are used worldwide are mentioned in your book. Flood irrigation . . . that has been a method in use since ancient times . . . and we still use it today where water is cheap. Basically, canals connect a water supply like a river or a reservoir to the fields where ditches are constructed with valves uh valves that allow farmers to siphon water from the canal, sending it down through the ditches. So that way the field can be totally flooded, or smaller, narrow ditches along the rows can be filled with water to irrigate the crop. But, this method does have quite a few disadvantages. Like I said, it's contingent upon cheap water because it isn't very efficient, and the flooding isn't easy to control, I mean, the rows closer to the canal usually receive much more water, and of course, if the field isn't flat, then the water won't be evenly distributed. Not to mention the cost of building canals and ditches and maintaining the system. So let's consider the alternative—the sprinkler system. In this method of

irrigation, it's easier to control the water and more efficient since the water is directed only on the plants. But, in hot climates, some of the water can evaporate in the air. Still, the main problem with the sprinklers is the expense for installation and maintenance because there's a very complicated pipe system and that usually involves a lot more repair and even replacement of parts, and of course, we have to factor in the labor costs in feasibility studies for sprinklers.

EXAMPLE NOTES

Flood
- Not efficient
- Difficult to control—flat fields
- Initial expense to build canals, ditches
- Requires maintenance

Sprinkler
- Complicated pipe system
- Expensive to install, maintain—repair, replace
- Labor cost

SCRIPT FOR EXAMPLE ANSWER

Two methods of irrigation were discussed in the lecture. First, flood irrigation. It involves the release of water into canals and drainage ditches that flow into the fields. The disadvantages of the flood method . . . um . . . well, it isn't very efficient since more water is used in flooding than the crops actually...uh, need, and also it isn't easy to control. Another problem is the initial expense for the construction of the canals and the connecting ditches as well as . . . as maintenance. And besides that, if the fields aren't flat, the water doesn't—I mean, it isn't distributed evenly. The second method is sprinkler irrigation which uses less water and provides better control, but there is some evaporation, and the pipe system's complicated and can be expensive to install and maintain, and there's usually a lot more labor cost because the equipment must be repaired and replaced more often than a canal system.

Checklist

✔ The talk summarizes a short lecture.
✔ There are only minor inaccuracies in the content.
✔ The talk is direct and well-organized.
✔ The sentences are logically connected to each other.
✔ Details and examples support the main idea.
✔ The speaker expresses complete thoughts.
✔ The meaning is easy for the listener to comprehend.
✔ A wide range of vocabulary is used.
✔ The speaker paraphrases, using his or her own words.
✔ The speaker credits the lecturer with wording.
✔ There are only minor errors in grammar.
✔ The talk is within a range of 125–150 words.

Computer Tutorial for the Speaking Section

The Speaking Section of the Next Generation TOEFL is being introduced as a telephone test. It is called the TAST (TOEFL Academic Speaking Test). Later, the TAST will be integrated into the Next Generation TOEFL as the Speaking Section, and it will be administered on the Internet. For now, dial the telephone number that you receive when you register. Then, follow the directions that you hear. You will be told when to prepare each answer and when to begin speaking. It is important to speak directly into the telephone. Speak up. If your voice is too soft, the rater will not be able to grade your answers.

Advice for the Speaking Section

Become familiar with the types of questions you will be asked. If you are listening to the kinds of questions that you expect to hear, you will be more prepared to organize your answers. That is why it is so important to study using the review section in this book, and to practice using the model test.

Develop a sense of timing for the short speaking answers. You will be speaking for only 45–60 seconds, and that isn't very long to develop a complete answer. When you are answering the practice questions in this book, set a kitchen timer for 60 seconds and begin speaking. When the bell rings, stop. Did you complete your thought, or did you have more to say? Always use the timer when you are practicing. Soon you will develop a sense of the timing for the questions, and you will know how much you can say in a short answer.

Practice using the telephone to speak. Call a friend to practice some of the speaking questions by phone. Speak directly into the phone. Ask your friend to confirm that you are speaking at a good volume to be heard clearly.

Maintain a positive attitude toward the experience. It is natural to be a little anxious about speaking in a second language, but it is important not to become negative and frightened. Negative thoughts can interfere with your concentration, and you may not hear the questions correctly. Take some deep breaths before each question, and say this in your mind, "I am a good speaker. I am ready to speak." If you begin to have negative thoughts during the test, take another deep breath, and think "confidence" as you breathe in. Focus on listening to the questions. Focus on taking notes.

Choose a quiet place to take your test. Choose a room with a telephone where you can be alone. Close the door. Make a sign for the door asking friends and family not to enter while you are taking your test. Turn off pagers and cell phones. Eliminate other distracting noises. If you are disturbed while you are taking your test, you will not hear the questions, and you will lose valuable preparation time. Gather the materials that you need for the test. Always have an extra pencil in case you need it. Then, clear the desk or table that you will use for taking notes. If you see only the questions and your notes, you will focus more easily.

Advice for Success

Do you talk to yourself? Of course you do. Maybe not aloud, but all of us have mental conversations with ourselves. So the question is *how* do you talk to yourself?

Negative Talk	Positive Talk
I can't study all of this.	I am studying every day.
My English is poor.	My English is improving.
I won't get a good score.	I will do my best.
If I fail, I will be so ashamed.	If I need a higher score, I can try again.

How would you talk to good friends to encourage and support them? Be a good friend to yourself. When negative talk comes to mind, substitute positive talk. Encourage yourself to learn from mistakes.

REVIEW OF STRUCTURE

Overview of the Structure Section

**QUICK COMPARISON—STRUCTURE
PAPER-BASED TOEFL,
COMPUTER-BASED TOEFL, AND NEXT GENERATION TOEFL**

Paper-Based TOEFL	*Computer-Based TOEFL*	*Next Generation TOEFL*
Two types of questions are presented in separate parts. Part A has incomplete sentences, and Part B has sentences with underlined words and phrases.	Two types of questions are presented at random in one continuous section. You may see two incomplete sentences, one sentence with underlined words and phrases, another incomplete sentence, and so forth.	There is NO Structure Section.
All of the questions are multiple-choice.	All of the questions are multiple-choice.	
Everyone taking the TOEFL answers the same questions.	The computer will select questions based on your level of proficiency.	
Every question has only one answer.	Every question has only one answer.	
You have twenty-five minutes to complete the section.	You may control the pace by choosing when to begin the next question, but the section is timed. A clock on the screen shows the time remaining for you to complete the section.	
You answer on a paper Answer Sheet, filling in ovals marked Ⓐ, Ⓑ, Ⓒ, and Ⓓ.	You click on the screen either in the oval or on the underlined word or phrase.	
You can return to previous questions, erase, and change answers on your Answer Sheet.	You cannot return to previous questions. You can change your answer before you click on **Confirm Answer**. After you click on **Confirm Answer**, you will see the next question. You cannot go back.	
The score on the Structure Section is not combined with the score on the essay in the Test of Written English (TWE).	The score on the Structure Section is combined with the score on the essay in the Writing Section.	

Directions and Examples for Structure Questions

The Structure Section of the TOEFL tests your ability to recognize standard written English as it is used in North America. The Structure Section is included in the Paper-Based TOEFL and the Computer-Based TOEFL, but it is not included as a separate section in the Next Generation TOEFL.

Paper-Based TOEFL (PBT)

The directions for the Paper-Based TOEFL are reprinted with the permission of Educational Testing Service (ETS) from the official *Information Bulletin* for the Supplemental Paper-Based TOEFL.

Section 2 —
Structure and Written Expression

This section is designed to measure your ability to recognize language that is appropriate for standard written English. There are two types of questions in this section, with special directions for each type.

Structure

Directions: These questions are incomplete sentences. Beneath each sentence you will see four words or phrases, marked (A), (B), (C), and (D). Choose the **one** word or phrase that best completes the sentence. Then, on your answer sheet, find the number of the question and fill in the space that corresponds to the letter of the answer you have chosen.

Look at the following examples:

Example I   **Sample Answer**

Geysers have often been compared to volcanoes   Ⓐ ● Ⓒ Ⓓ
_ _ _ _ _ they both emit hot liquids from below
the Earth's surface.

(A) due to
(B) because
(C) in spite of
(D) regardless of

The sentence should read, "Geysers have often been compared to volcanoes because they both emit hot liquids from below the Earth's surface." Therefore, you should choose answer (B).

Example II   **Sample Answer**

During the early period of ocean navigation,   Ⓐ Ⓑ Ⓒ ●
_ _ _ _ _ any need for sophisticated instruments
and techniques.

(A) so that hardly
(B) where there hardly was
(C) hardly was
(D) there was hardly

The sentence should read, "During the early period of ocean navigation, there was hardly any need for sophisticated instruments and techniques." Therefore, you should choose answer (D).

Written Expression

Directions: In these questions, each sentence has four underlined words or phrases. The four underlined parts of the sentence are marked (A), (B), (C), and (D). Identify the **one** underlined word or phrase that must be changed in order for the sentence to be correct. Then, on your answer sheet, find the number of the question and fill in the space that corresponds to the letter of the answer you have chosen.

Look at the following examples:

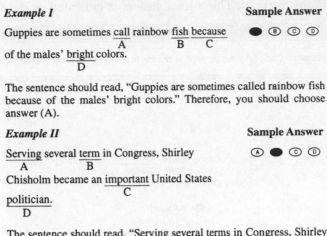

Example I   **Sample Answer**

Guppies are sometimes <u>call</u> rainbow <u>fish</u> <u>because</u>   ● Ⓑ Ⓒ Ⓓ
                       A   B   C
of the males' <u>bright</u> colors.
              D

The sentence should read, "Guppies are sometimes called rainbow fish because of the males' bright colors." Therefore, you should choose answer (A).

Example II   **Sample Answer**

<u>Serving</u> several <u>term</u> in Congress, Shirley   Ⓐ ● Ⓒ Ⓓ
   A   B
Chisholm became an <u>important</u> United States
                       C
<u>politician</u>.
    D

The sentence should read, "Serving several terms in Congress, Shirley Chisholm became an important United States politician." Therefore, you should choose answer (B).

Computer-Based TOEFL

The directions for the Computer-Based TOEFL are reprinted with the permission of Educational Testing Service (ETS) from the official *Information Bulletin* for the Computer-Based TOEFL.

This section measures the ability to recognize language that is appropriate for standard written English. There are two types of questions in this section.

In the first type of question, there are incomplete sentences. Beneath each sentence, there are four words or phrases. You will choose the one word or phrase that best completes the sentence.

Here is an example.

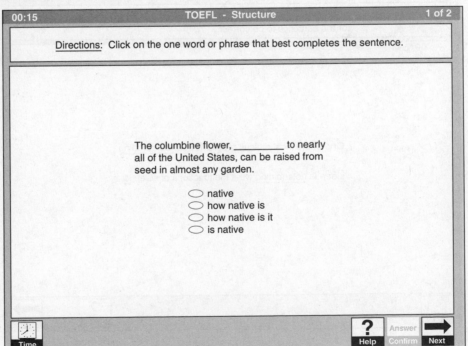

Clicking on a choice darkens the oval. The correct answer is indicated on the screen below.

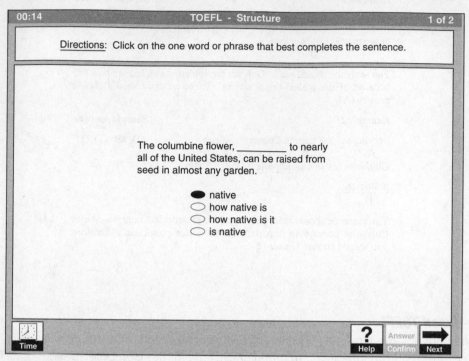

After you click on **Next** and **Confirm Answer**, the next question will be presented.

The second type of question has four underlined words or phrases. You will choose the one underlined word or phrase that must be changed for the sentence to be correct.

Here is an example:

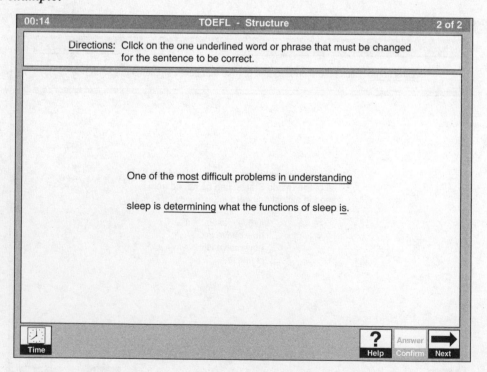

Clicking on an underlined word or phrase will darken it. The correct answer is indicated on the screen below.

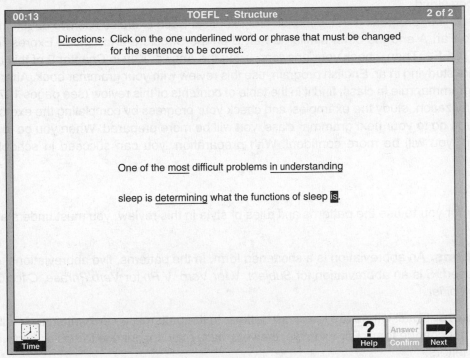

The sentence should read: One of the most difficult problems in understanding sleep is determining what the functions of sleep are. After you click on **Next** and **Confirm Answer**, the next question will be presented.

Next Generation TOEFL

There is no Structure Section in the Next Generation TOEFL. Structure is scored on the rating scale for both the Speaking Section and the Writing Section.

Review of Problems and Questions for the Structure Section

This Review can be used to prepare for both the Paper-Based TOEFL and the Computer-Based TOEFL. For the most part, the same types of problems are tested on both the Paper-Based TOEFL and the Computer-Based TOEFL. All of the questions on both the Paper-Based TOEFL and the Computer-Based TOEFL are multiple-choice. Computer-assisted questions have special directions.

Strategies and Symbols for Review

Strategies

How will this Review of Structure help you?

It won't teach you every rule of English grammar, but it will provide you with a review of the problems in structure and written expression that are most commonly tested on the TOEFL.

Use this review to study and to check your progress. Follow three easy steps for each problem.

1. *Review the generalization.* First, read the explanation and study the word order in the chart. Then, close your eyes, and try to see the chart in your mind.

2. *Study the examples.* Focus on the examples. First, read them silently, noting the difference between the correct and incorrect sentences. Then, read the underlined parts of the correct sentences aloud.

3. *Check your progress.* First, complete the exercise. Each exercise has two questions—one similar to Part A and the other similar to Part B on the Structure and Written Expression section of the TOEFL. Then, check your answers, using the Answer Key in Chapter 9 of this book.

If you are studying in an English program, use this review with your grammar book. After your teacher presents a grammar rule in class, find it in the table of contents of this review (see pages 107–109). Refer to the generalization, study the examples, and check your progress by completing the exercise.

When you go to your next grammar class, you will be more prepared. When you go to your TOEFL examination, you will be more confident. With preparation, you can succeed in school and on the TOEFL.

Symbols

In order for you to use the patterns and rules of style in this review, you must understand five kinds of symbols.

Abbreviations. An abbreviation is a shortened form. In the patterns, five abbreviations, or shortened forms, are used: *S* is an abbreviation for *Subject, V* for *Verb, V Ph* for *Verb Phrase, C* for *Complement,* and *M* for *Modifier.*

Small Letters. Small letters are lowercase letters. In the patterns, a verb written in small (lowercase) letters may not change form. For example, the verb *have* may not change to *has* or *had* when it is written in small letters.

Capital Letters. Capital letters are uppercase letters. In the patterns, a verb written in capital (uppercase) letters may change form. For example, the verb *HAVE* may remain as *have,* or may change to *has* or *had,* depending upon agreement with the subject and choice of tense.

Parentheses. Parentheses are curved lines used as punctuation marks. The following punctuation marks are parentheses: ( ). In the patterns, the words in parentheses give specific information about the abbreviation or word that precedes them. For example, *V (present)* means that the verb in the pattern must be a present tense verb. *N (count)* means that the noun in the pattern must be a countable noun.

Alternatives. Alternatives are different ways to express the same idea. In the patterns, alternatives are written in a column. For example, in the following pattern, there are three alternatives:

had would have could have	participle

The alternatives are *had, would have,* and *could have.* Any one of the alternatives may be used with the participle. All three alternatives are correct.

TYPES OF PROBLEMS

Patterns and rules of style like those in this Review of Structure frequently appear on Section 2 of the TOEFL.

The emphasis that is placed on various patterns and style problems changes from year to year on the TOEFL. Research indicates that those problems shown in bold print in the reference list below are most frequently tested on current examinations.

To prepare for Section 2 of the TOEFL, study the problems in this chapter. Give special attention to the problems in bold print.

PATTERNS

Problems with Verbs

Problems with Main Verbs

1 Missing Main Verb

2 Verbs that Require an Infinitive in the Complement

3 Verbs that Require an *-ing* Form in the Complement

4 Verb Phrases that Require an *-ing* Form in the Complement

Problems with Tense

5 Irregular Past Forms

Problems with Conditionals

6 **Factual Conditionals—Absolute, Scientific Results**

7 Factual Conditionals—Probable Results for the Future

8 Contrary-to-Fact Conditionals—Change in Conditions *Unless*

Problems with Subjunctives

9 Importance—Subjunctive Verbs

10 Importance—Impersonal Expressions

Problems with Infinitives

11 Purpose—Infinitives

Problems with Passives

12 **Passives—Word Order**

13 **Belief and Knowledge—Anticipatory *It***

Problems with HAVE + Participle

14 Predictions—*Will Have* + Participle

Problems with Auxiliary Verbs

15 **Missing Auxiliary Verb—Active**

16 **Missing Auxiliary Verb—Passive**

Problems with Pronouns

17 Object Pronouns after Prepositions

18 Relative Pronouns that Refer to Persons and Things

Problems with Nouns

19 Count Nouns

20 Noncount Nouns

21 Nouns with Count and Noncount Meanings

22 Noncount Nouns that Are Count Nouns in Other Languages

23 Singular and Plural Expressions of Noncount Nouns

24 Infinitive and *-ing* Subjects

25 Nominal *That* Clause

STYLE

PATTERNS

Patterns are the parts of a sentence. In some books, *patterns* are called *structures*. In *patterns,* the words have the same order most of the time.

Some of the most important patterns are summarized in this review section. Remember, the generalizations in the charts and explanations for each pattern refer to the structure in the examples. There may be similar structures for which these generalizations are not appropriate.

Problems with Verbs

A *verb* is a word or phrase that expresses existence, action, or experience.

There are two kinds of verbs in English. They are the *main verb* and the *auxiliary verb.* In some grammar books, the *auxiliary verb* is called a *helping verb* because it is used with a *main verb.*

Every verb in English can be described by the following formula:

VERB = tense + (modal) + (have + participle) + (be + -ing) + verb word

Each of the parts of this formula will be summarized in one or more of the problems in this review. Don't spend time studying it now. Just refer to it as you progress through this review section.

PROBLEMS WITH MAIN VERBS

In English, a sentence must have a main verb. A sentence may or may not have an auxiliary verb.

1   Missing Main Verb

Remember that every English sentence must have a subject and a main verb.

S	V	
The sound of the dryer	bothers	my concentration

Avoid using an *-ing* form, an infinitive, an auxiliary verb, or another part of speech instead of a main verb.

EXAMPLES

INCORRECT: The prettiest girl in our class with long brown hair and brown eyes.
CORRECT: The prettiest girl in our class <u>has</u> long brown hair and brown eyes.

INCORRECT: In my opinion, too soon to make a decision.
CORRECT: In my opinion, <u>it is</u> too soon to make a decision.

INCORRECT: Do you know whether the movie that starts at seven?
CORRECT: Do you know whether the movie that starts at seven <u>is</u> good?

or

Do you know whether the movie <u>starts</u> at seven?

INCORRECT: Sam almost always a lot of fun.
CORRECT: Sam <u>is</u> almost always a lot of fun.

INCORRECT: The book that I lent you having a good bibliography.
CORRECT: The book that I lent you <u>has</u> a good bibliography.

EXERCISES

Part A: Choose the correct answer.

Arizona _____ a very dry climate.
   (A) has
   (B) being
   (C) having
   (D) with

Part B: Choose the incorrect word or phrase and correct it.

Venomous snakes <u>with</u> modified teeth connected to <u>poison glands</u> <u>in which</u> the venom <u>is secreted</u> and
            (A)   (B)   (C)   (D)

stored.

2   Verbs that Require an Infinitive in the Complement

Remember that the following verbs require an infinitive for a verb in the complement.

agree	*decide*	*hesitate*	*need*	*refuse*
appear	*demand*	*hope*	*offer*	*seem*
arrange	*deserve*	*intend*	*plan*	*tend*
ask	*expect*	*learn*	*prepare*	*threaten*
claim	*fail*	*manage*	*pretend*	*wait*
consent	*forget*	*mean*	*promise*	*want*

S	V	C (infinitive)	M
We	had planned	to leave	day before yesterday

Avoid using an *-ing* form after the verbs listed. Avoid using a verb word after *want*.

EXAMPLES

INCORRECT:	He wanted speak with Mr. Brown.
CORRECT:	He <u>wanted to speak</u> with Mr. Brown.
INCORRECT:	We demand knowing our status.
CORRECT:	We <u>demand to know</u> our status.
INCORRECT:	I intend the inform you that we cannot approve your application.
CORRECT:	I <u>intend to inform</u> you that we cannot approve your application.
INCORRECT:	They didn't plan buying a car.
CORRECT:	They didn't <u>plan</u> <u>to buy</u> a car.
INCORRECT:	The weather tends improving in May.
CORRECT:	The weather <u>tends to improve</u> in May.

EXERCISES

Part A: Choose the correct answer.

One of the least effective ways of storing information is learning _____ it.
(A) how repeat
(B) repeating
(C) to repeat
(D) repeat

Part B: Choose the incorrect word or phrase and correct it.

Representative democracy seemed <u>evolve</u> <u>simultaneously</u> <u>during</u> the eighteenth and nineteenth cen-
                            (A)   (B)   (C)
turies in Britain, Europe, and <u>the United States</u>.
                                      (D)

3   Verbs that Require an *-ing* Form in the Complement

Remember that the following verbs require an *-ing* form for a verb in the complement:

admit	*enjoy*	*recall*
appreciate	*finish*	*recommend*
avoid	*keep*	*regret*
complete	*mention*	*risk*
consider	*miss*	*stop*
delay	*postpone*	*suggest*
deny	*practice*	*tolerate*
discuss	*quit*	*understand*

S	V	C (-ing)	M
He	enjoys	traveling	by plane

Avoid using an infinitive after the verbs listed.

Forbid may be used with either an infinitive or an *-ing* complement, but *forbid from* is not idiomatic.

EXAMPLES

INCORRECT: She is considering not to go.
  CORRECT: She is <u>considering</u> not <u>going</u>.

INCORRECT: We enjoyed talk with your friend.
  CORRECT: We <u>enjoyed</u> <u>talking</u> with your friend.

INCORRECT: Hank completed the writing his thesis this summer.
  CORRECT: Hank <u>completed</u> <u>writing</u> his thesis this summer.

INCORRECT: I miss to watch the news when I am traveling.
  CORRECT: I <u>miss</u> <u>watching</u> the news when I am traveling.

INCORRECT: She mentions stop at El Paso in her letter.
  CORRECT: She <u>mentions</u> <u>stopping</u> at El Paso in her letter.

EXERCISES

Part A: Choose the correct answer.

Strauss finished _____ two of his published compositions before his tenth birthday.
  (A) written
  (B) write
  (C) to write
  (D) writing

Part B: Choose the incorrect word or phrase and correct it.

<u>Many</u> people have stopped <u>to smoke</u> <u>because</u> they are afraid that it <u>may be</u> harmful to their health.
  (A)   (B)   (C)   (D)

Verb Phrases that Require an *-ing* Form in the Complement

Remember that the following verb phrases require an *-ing* form for a verb in the complement:

approve of	*do not mind*	*keep on*
be better off	*forget about*	*look forward to*
can't help	*get through*	*object to*
count on	*insist on*	*think about*
		think of

S	V Ph	C (-ing)	M
She	forgot about	canceling	her appointment

Avoid using an infinitive after the verb phrases listed. Avoid using a verb word after *look forward to* and *object to.*

Remember that the verb phrase *BE likely* does not require an *-ing* form but requires an infinitive in the complement.

EXAMPLES

INCORRECT: She is likely knowing.
  CORRECT: She <u>is likely</u> <u>to know.</u>

INCORRECT: Let's go to the movie when you get through to study.
  CORRECT: Let's go to the movie when you <u>get through</u> <u>studying</u>.

INCORRECT: We can't help to wonder why she left.
  CORRECT: We <u>can't help</u> <u>wondering</u> why she left.

INCORRECT: I have been looking forward to meet you.
  CORRECT: I have been <u>looking forward to</u> <u>meeting</u> you.

INCORRECT: We wouldn't mind to wait.
  CORRECT: We <u>wouldn't mind</u> <u>waiting</u>.

EXERCISES

Part A: Choose the correct answer.

Many modern architects insist on _____ materials native to the region that will blend into the surrounding landscape.
   (A) use
   (B) to use
   (C) the use
   (D) using

Part B: Choose the incorrect word or phrase and correct it.

During Jackson's administration, those <u>who</u> did not approve of <u>permit</u> common people in the White
                                    (A)   (B)
House <u>were shocked</u> by the president's insistence that they <u>be invited</u> into the mansion.
             (C)   (D)

PROBLEMS WITH TENSE

Many grammar books list a large number of *tenses* in English, but the two basic tenses are present and past.

Auxiliary verbs are used with main verbs to express future and other special times.

5 Irregular Past Forms

Remember that past forms of the following irregular verbs are not the same as the participles:

Verb Word	Past Form	Participle
be	was/were	been
beat	beat	beaten
become	became	become
begin	began	begun
bite	bit	bitten
blow	blew	blown
break	broke	broken
choose	chose	chosen
come	came	come
do	did	done
draw	drew	drawn
drink	drank	drunk
drive	drove	driven
eat	ate	eaten
fall	fell	fallen
fly	flew	flown
forget	forgot	forgotten
forgive	forgave	forgiven
freeze	froze	frozen
get	got	gotten or got
give	gave	given
go	went	gone
grow	grew	grown
hide	hid	hidden
know	knew	known
ride	rode	ridden
run	ran	run
see	saw	seen
shake	shook	shaken
show	showed	shown
shrink	shrank	shrunk
sing	sang	sung
speak	spoke	spoken
steal	stole	stolen
swear	swore	sworn
swim	swam	swum
take	took	taken
tear	tore	torn
throw	threw	thrown
wear	wore	worn
weave	wove	woven
withdraw	withdrew	withdrawn
write	wrote	written

S	V (past)	M
The concert	began	at eight o'clock

Avoid using a participle instead of a past for simple past statements.

EXAMPLES

INCORRECT: They done it very well after they had practiced.
 CORRECT: They <u>did</u> it very well after they had practiced.

INCORRECT: Before she run the computer program, she had checked it out with her supervisor.
 CORRECT: Before she <u>ran</u> the computer program, she had checked it out with her supervisor.

INCORRECT: We eat dinner in Albuquerque on our vacation last year.
 CORRECT: We <u>ate</u> dinner in Albuquerque on our vacation last year.

INCORRECT: My nephew begun working for me about ten years ago.
 CORRECT: My nephew <u>began</u> working for me about ten years ago.

INCORRECT: I know that you been forty on your last birthday.
 CORRECT: I know that you <u>were</u> forty on your last birthday.

EXERCISES

Part A: Choose the correct answer.

Before the Angles and the Saxons _____ to England, the Iberians had lived there.
   (A) coming
   (B) come
   (C) came
   (D) did come

Part B: Choose the incorrect word or phrase and correct it.

When Columbus <u>seen</u> the New World, he <u>thought</u> that he <u>had reached</u> the East Indies <u>by way of</u> a
              (A)   (B)   (C)   (D)
Western route.

PROBLEMS WITH CONDITIONALS

Conditionals are statements with *if* or *unless.* They are opinions about the conditions (circumstances) that influence results, and opinions about the results.

There are two kinds of conditionals. In most grammar books, they are called *real* or *factual* conditionals and *unreal* or *contrary-to-fact* conditionals. *Factual conditionals* express absolute, scientific facts, probable results, or possible results. *Contrary-to-fact* conditionals express improbable or impossible results.

6 Factual Conditionals—Absolute, Scientific Results

Remember that *absolute conditionals* express scientific facts. *Will* and a verb word expresses the opinion that the result is absolutely certain.

CONDITION				RESULT		
If	S	V (present)	,	S	V (present)	
If	a catalyst	is used	,	the reaction	occurs	more rapidly

or

CONDITION				RESULT		
If	S	V (present)	,	S	will	verb word	
If	a catalyst	is used	,	the reaction	will	occur	more rapidly

Avoid using *will* and a verb word instead of the present verb in the clause beginning with *if*. Avoid using the auxiliary verbs *have*, *has*, *do*, and *does* with main verbs in the clause of result.

EXAMPLES

INCORRECT: If water freezes, it has become a solid.
 CORRECT: If <u>water freezes, it</u> becomes a solid.
  or
  If <u>water freezes, it will become</u> a solid.

INCORRECT: If children be healthy, they learn to walk at about eighteen months old.
 CORRECT: If <u>children are</u> healthy, <u>they learn</u> to walk at about eighteen months old.
  or
  If <u>children are</u> healthy, <u>they will learn</u> to walk at about eighteen months old.

INCORRECT: If orange blossoms are exposed to very cold temperatures, they withered and died.
 CORRECT: If <u>orange blossoms are exposed</u> to very cold temperatures, <u>they wither and die</u>.
  or
  If <u>orange blossoms are exposed</u> to very cold temperatures, <u>they will wither and die</u>.

INCORRECT: If the trajectory of a satellite will be slightly off at launch, it will get worse as the flight progresses.
 CORRECT: If <u>the trajectory</u> of a satellite <u>is</u> slightly off at launch, <u>it gets</u> worse as the flight progresses.
  or
  If <u>the trajectory</u> of a satellite <u>is</u> slightly off at launch, <u>it will get</u> worse as the flight progresses.

INCORRECT:	If light strikes a rough surface, it diffused.
CORRECT:	If <u>light</u> <u>strikes</u> a rough surface, <u>it</u> <u>diffuses.</u>
	or
	If <u>light</u> <u>strikes</u> a rough surface, <u>it</u> <u>will diffuse.</u>

EXERCISES

Part A: Choose the correct answer.

If water is heated to 212 degrees F. _____ as steam.
- (A) it will boil and escape
- (B) it is boiling and escaping
- (C) it boil and escape
- (D) it would boil and escape

Part B: Choose the incorrect word or phrase and correct it.

If a live sponge is <u>broken</u> into pieces, each piece <u>would turn</u> into a new sponge <u>like</u>
  (A)   (B)   (C)

<u>the original one</u>.
  (D)

PROBLEM 7

Factual Conditionals—Probable Results for the Future

Remember that *will* and a verb word expresses the opinion that the results are absolutely certain. In order of more to less probable, use the following modals: *will, can, may.*

If	S	V (present)		,	S	will can may	verb word	
If	we	find	her address	,	we	will	write	her

S	will can may	verb word		if	S	V (present)	
We	will	write	her	if	we	find	her address

Avoid using the present tense verb instead of a modal and a verb word in the clause of result.

EXAMPLES

INCORRECT: If you put too much water in rice when you cook it, it got sticky.
 CORRECT: <u>If</u> <u>you</u> <u>put</u> too much water in rice when you cook it, <u>it</u> <u>will get</u> sticky.
or
<u>It</u> <u>will get</u> sticky <u>if</u> <u>you</u> <u>put</u> too much water in rice when you cook it.

INCORRECT: If they have a good sale, I would have stopped by on my way home.
 CORRECT: <u>If</u> <u>they</u> <u>have</u> a good sale, <u>I</u> <u>will stop</u> by on my way home.
or
<u>I</u> <u>will stop</u> by on my way home <u>if</u> <u>they</u> <u>have</u> a good sale.

INCORRECT: We will wait if you wanted to go.
 CORRECT: <u>We</u> <u>will wait</u> <u>if</u> <u>you</u> <u>want</u> to go.
or
<u>If</u> <u>you</u> <u>want</u> to go, <u>we</u> <u>will wait</u>.

INCORRECT: If you listen to the questions carefully, you answer them easily.
 CORRECT: <u>If</u> <u>you</u> <u>listen</u> to the questions carefully, <u>you</u> <u>will answer</u> them easily.
or
<u>You</u> <u>will answer</u> them easily <u>if</u> <u>you</u> <u>listen</u> to the questions carefully.

INCORRECT: If we finished our work a little early today, we'll attend the lecture at the art museum.
 CORRECT: <u>If</u> <u>we</u> <u>finish</u> our work a little early today, <u>we'll attend</u> the lecture at the art museum.
or
<u>We'll attend</u> the lecture at the art museum <u>if</u> <u>we</u> <u>finish</u> our work a little early today.

EXERCISES

Part A: Choose the correct answer.

If services are increased, taxes _____.
    (A) will probably go up
    (B) probably go up
    (C) probably up
    (D) going up probably

Part B: Choose the incorrect word or phrase and correct it.

If you don't <u>register</u> before <u>the last day</u> of regular registration, you <u>paying</u> <u>a late fee</u>.
           (A)   (B)   (C)   (D)

PROBLEM 8

Contrary-to-Fact Conditionals—Change in Conditions *Unless*

Remember that there is a subject and verb that determines the change in conditions after the connector *unless*.

S	V	unless	S	V	
Luisa	won't return	unless	she	gets	a scholarship

Avoid deleting *unless* from the sentence; avoid deleting either the subject or the verb from the clause after *unless*.

EXAMPLES

INCORRECT: I can't go I don't get my work finished.
  CORRECT: I can't go <u>unless</u> <u>I</u> <u>get</u> my work finished.

INCORRECT: They are going to get a divorce unless he stopping drugs.
  CORRECT: They are going to get a divorce <u>unless</u> <u>he</u> <u>stops</u> taking drugs.

INCORRECT: You won't get well unless you are taking your medicine.
  CORRECT: You won't get well <u>unless</u> <u>you</u> <u>take</u> your medicine.

INCORRECT: Dean never calls his father unless needs money.
  CORRECT: Dean never calls his father <u>unless</u> <u>he</u> <u>needs</u> money.

INCORRECT: We can't pay the rent unless the scholarship check.
  CORRECT: We can't pay the rent <u>unless</u> <u>the scholarship check</u> <u>comes</u>.

EXERCISES

Part A: Choose the correct answer.

Football teams don't play in the Super Bowl championship _____ either the National or the American Conference.
  (A) unless they win
  (B) but they win
  (C) unless they will win
  (D) but to have won

Part B: Choose the incorrect word or phrase and correct it.

Usually <u>boys</u> cannot <u>become</u> Boy Scouts <u>unless completed</u> <u>the fifth grade</u>.
        (A)   (B)   (C)   (D)

PROBLEMS WITH SUBJUNCTIVES

Some verbs, nouns, and expressions require a subjunctive. A subjunctive is a change in the usual form of the verb. A subjunctive is often a verb word in English.

Importance—Subjunctive Verbs

Remember that the following verbs are used before *that* and the verb word clause to express importance.

ask	recommend
demand	request
desire	require
insist	suggest
prefer	urge
propose	

S	V	that	S	verb word	
Mr. Johnson	prefers	that	she	speak	with him personally

Avoid using a present or past tense verb instead of a verb word. Avoid using a modal before the verb word.

Note: The verb *insist* may be used in non-subjunctive patterns in the past tense. For example: *He* insisted *that I* was *wrong.*

EXAMPLES

INCORRECT: The doctor suggested that she will not smoke.
  CORRECT: The doctor <u>suggested</u> that she not <u>smoke.</u>

INCORRECT: I propose that the vote is secret ballot.
  CORRECT: I <u>propose</u> that the vote <u>be</u> secret ballot.

INCORRECT: The foreign student advisor recommended that she studied more English before enrolling at the university.
  CORRECT: The foreign student advisor <u>recommended</u> that she <u>study</u> more English before enrolling at the university.

INCORRECT: The law requires that everyone has his car checked at least once a year.
  CORRECT: The law <u>requires</u> that everyone <u>have</u> his car checked at least once a year.

INCORRECT: She insisted that they would give her a receipt.
  CORRECT: She <u>insisted</u> that they <u>give</u> her a receipt.

EXERCISES

Part A: Choose the correct answer.

Less moderate members of Congress are insisting that changes in the Social Security System _____ made.
    (A) will
    (B) are
    (C) being
    (D) be

Part B: Choose the incorrect word or phrase and correct it.

<u>Many</u> architects prefer that a dome <u>is used</u> to roof buildings that need <u>to conserve</u> <u>floor space</u>.
  (A)   (B)   (C)   (D)

PROBLEM 10 — Importance—Impersonal Expressions

Remember that the following adjectives are used in impersonal expressions.

essential
imperative
important
necessary

it is	adjective	infinitive	
It is	important	to verify	the data

or

it is	adjective	that	S	verb word	
It is	important	that	the data	be	verified

Avoid using a present tense verb instead of a verb word. Avoid using a modal before the verb word.

EXAMPLES

INCORRECT: It is not necessary that you must take an entrance examination to be admitted to an American university.

CORRECT: <u>It is not necessary to take</u> an entrance examination to be admitted to an American university.

                or

       <u>It is not necessary that you take</u> an entrance examination to be admitted to an American university.

INCORRECT:	It is imperative that you are on time.
CORRECT:	It is imperative <u>to be</u> on time.
	or
	It is imperative <u>that</u> <u>you</u> <u>be</u> on time.

INCORRECT:	It is important that I will speak with Mr. Williams immediately.
CORRECT:	It is important <u>to speak</u> with Mr. Williams immediately.
	or
	It is important <u>that</u> I <u>speak</u> with Mr. Williams immediately.

INCORRECT:	It is imperative that your signature appears on your identification card.
CORRECT:	It is imperative <u>to sign</u> your identification card.
	or
	It is imperative <u>that</u> <u>your signature</u> <u>appear</u> on your identification card.

INCORRECT:	It is essential that all applications and transcripts are filed no later than July 1.
CORRECT:	It is essential <u>to file</u> all applications and transcripts no later than July 1.
	or
	It is essential <u>that</u> <u>all applications and transcripts</u> <u>be</u> filed no later than July 1.

EXERCISES

Part A: Choose the correct answer.

It is necessary _____ the approaches to a bridge, the road design, and the alignment in such a way as to best accommodate the expected traffic flow over and under it.

(A) plan
(B) to plan
(C) planning
(D) the plan

Part B: Choose the incorrect word or phrase and correct it.

It is essential that vitamins <u>are</u> supplied either by foods <u>or</u> <u>by supplementary tablets</u> for normal
                            (A)   (B)   (C)

growth <u>to occur</u>.
      (D)

PROBLEMS WITH INFINITIVES

An infinitive is *to* + the verb word.

11 Purpose—Infinitives

Remember that an infinitive can express purpose. It is a short form of *in order to*.

S	V	C	infinitive (purpose)	
Laura She	jogs takes	vitamins	to stay to feel	fit better

Avoid expressing purpose without the word *to* in the infinitive. Avoid using *for* instead of *to*.

EXAMPLES

INCORRECT: Wear several layers of clothing for keep warm.
CORRECT: Wear several layers of clothing <u>to keep</u> warm.

INCORRECT: David has studied hard the succeed.
CORRECT: David has studied hard <u>to succeed.</u>

INCORRECT: Don't move your feet when you swing for play golf well.
CORRECT: Don't move your feet when you swing <u>to play</u> golf well.

INCORRECT: Virginia always boils the water twice make tea.
CORRECT: Virginia always boils the water twice <u>to make</u> tea.

INCORRECT: Wait until June plant those bulbs.
CORRECT: Wait until June <u>to plant</u> those bulbs.

EXERCISES

Part A: Choose the correct answer.

In the Morrill Act, Congress granted federal lands to the states _____ agricultural and mechanical arts colleges.
(A) for establish
(B) to establish
(C) establish
(D) establishment

Part B: Choose the incorrect word or phrase and correct it.

Papyrus <u>was used</u> <u>for to make</u> not only paper <u>but also</u> sails, baskets, <u>and</u> clothing.
    (A)   (B)   (C)   (D)

PROBLEMS WITH PASSIVES

A passive changes the emphasis of a sentence. Usually in a passive, the event or result is more important than the person who causes it to happen.

For example, *born*, *known as*, and *left* are participles. They are commonly used with BE in passive sentences. Why? Because the person born, the person known, and the person or thing left are the important parts of the sentences.

12 Passives—Word Order

Remember that in a passive sentence the actor is unknown or not important. The subject is not the actor.

Passive sentences are also common in certain styles of scientific writing.

S	BE	participle	
State University	is	located	at the corner of College and Third

Avoid using a participle without a form of the verb BE.

EXAMPLES

INCORRECT: My wedding ring made of yellow and white gold.
 CORRECT: My wedding ring <u>is made</u> of yellow and white gold.
         (It is the *ring*, not the person who made the ring, that is important.)

INCORRECT: If your brother invited, he would come.
 CORRECT: If your brother <u>were invited,</u> he would come.
         (It is your *brother*, not the person who invited him, that is important.)

INCORRECT: Mr. Wilson known as Willie to his friends.
 CORRECT: Mr. Wilson <u>is known</u> as Willie to his friends.
         (It is *Mr. Wilson*, not his friends, that is important.)

INCORRECT: References not used in the examination room.
 CORRECT: References <u>are not used</u> in the examination room.
         (It is *references*, not the persons using them, that are important.)

INCORRECT: Laura born in Iowa.
 CORRECT: Laura <u>was born</u> in Iowa.
         (It is *Laura*, not her mother who bore her, that is important.)

EXERCISES

Part A: Choose the correct answer.

In the stringed instruments, the tones _____ by playing a bow across a set of strings that may be made of wire or gut.
- (A) they produce
- (B) producing
- (C) are produced
- (D) that are producing

Part B: Choose the incorrect word or phrase and correct it.

<u>Work</u> <u>is</u> often <u>measure</u> in units <u>called</u> foot pounds.
 (A) (B)   (C)   (D)

13   Belief and Knowledge—Anticipatory *It*

Remember that an anticipatory *it* clause expresses belief or knowledge. Anticipatory means before. Some *it* clauses that go before main clauses are listed below:

It is believed
It is hypothesized
It is known
It is said
It is thought
It is true
It is written

Anticipatory *it*	that	S	V	
It is believed	that	all mammals	experience	dreams

Avoid using an *-ing* form, a noun, or an infinitive instead of a subject and verb after an anticipatory *it* clause.

EXAMPLES

INCORRECT: It is hypothesized that the subjects in the control group not to score as well.
  CORRECT: <u>It is hypothesized</u> that the <u>subjects</u> in the control group <u>will not score</u> as well.

INCORRECT: It is generally known that she leaving at the end of the year.
  CORRECT: <u>It is generally known</u> that <u>she</u> <u>is leaving</u> at the end of the year.

INCORRECT: It is said that a buried treasure near here.
  CORRECT: <u>It is said</u> that <u>a buried treasure</u> <u>was hidden</u> near here.

INCORRECT: It is believed that a horseshoe bringing good luck.
  CORRECT: <u>It is believed</u> that <u>a horseshoe</u> <u>brings</u> good luck.

INCORRECT: It is thought that our ancestors building this city.
  CORRECT: <u>It is thought</u> that <u>our ancestors</u> <u>built</u> this city.

EXERCISES

Part A: Choose the correct answer.

_____ Giant Ape Man, our biggest and probably one of our first human ancestors, was just about the size of a male gorilla.

(A) It is believed that
(B) That it is
(C) That is believed
(D) That believing

Part B: Choose the incorrect word or phrase and correct it.

<u>That it is believed</u> that <u>most of the earthquakes</u> in the world occur <u>near</u> <u>the youngest</u> mountain
    (A)   (B)   (C)   (D)
ranges—the Himalayas, the Andes, and the Sierra Nevadas.

PROBLEMS WITH HAVE + PARTICIPLE

Have, *has*, or *had* + participle express duration of time.

14   Predictions—*Will Have* + Participle

Remember that *will have* followed by a participle and a future adverb expresses a prediction for a future activity or event.

adverb (future)	Such as	will	have	participle	
By the year 2010,	researchers	will	have	discovered	a cure for cancer.

Avoid using *will* instead of *will have*.

EXAMPLES

INCORRECT:	You will finished your homework by the time the movie starts.
CORRECT:	You <u>will</u> <u>have</u> <u>finished</u> your homework <u>by the time the movie starts</u>.
INCORRECT:	Jan will left by five o'clock.
CORRECT:	Jan <u>will</u> <u>have</u> <u>left</u> by five o'clock.
INCORRECT:	Before school is out, I have returned all of my library books.
CORRECT:	<u>Before school is out</u>, I <u>will</u> <u>have</u> <u>returned</u> all of my library books.
INCORRECT:	We have gotten an answer to our letter by the time we have to make a decision.
CORRECT:	We <u>will</u> <u>have</u> <u>gotten</u> an answer to our letter <u>by the time we have to make a decision</u>.
INCORRECT:	Before we can tell them about the discount, they will bought the tickets.
CORRECT:	<u>Before we can tell them</u> about the discount, they <u>will</u> <u>have</u> <u>bought</u> the tickets.

EXERCISES

Part A: Choose the correct answer.

By the middle of the twenty-first century, the computer _____ a necessity in every home.
(A) became
(B) becoming
(C) has become
(D) will have become

Part B: Choose the incorrect word or phrase and correct it.

<u>It is believed</u> that <u>by 2010</u> immunotherapy <u>have succeeded</u> in <u>curing</u> a number of serious illnesses.
   (A)   (B)   (C)   (D)

PROBLEMS WITH AUXILIARY VERBS

Auxiliary verbs are additional verbs that may be used with main verbs to add meaning. For example, all of the forms of BE, HAVE, DO, and all modals are auxiliary verbs.

15 Missing Auxiliary Verb—Active

Remember that some main verbs require auxiliary verbs.

	BE	*-ing*	
Mom	is	watering	her plants

	HAVE	participle	
Mom	has	watered	her plants

	MODAL	verb word	
Mom	should	water	her plants

Avoid using *-ing* forms without BE, participles without HAVE, and verb words without modals when *-ing*, a participle, or a verb word function as a main verb.

EXAMPLES

INCORRECT:	The party is a surprise, but all of her friends coming.
CORRECT:	The party is a surprise, but all of her friends <u>are coming</u>.

INCORRECT:	She read it to you later tonight.
CORRECT:	She <u>will read</u> it to you later tonight.

INCORRECT:	The sun shining when we left this morning.
CORRECT:	The sun <u>was shining</u> when we left this morning.

INCORRECT:	We gone there before.
CORRECT:	We <u>have gone</u> there before.

INCORRECT:	I can't talk with you right now because the doorbell ringing.
CORRECT:	I can't talk with you right now because the doorbell <u>is ringing</u>.

EXERCISES

Part A: Choose the correct answer.

The giraffe survives in part because it _____ the vegetation in the high branches of trees where other animals have not grazed.

(A) to reach
(B) can reach
(C) reaching
(D) reach

Part B: Choose the incorrect word or phrase and correct it.

According to some scientists, the earth losing its outer atmosphere because of pollutants.
    (A)   (B) (C)   (D)

PROBLEM 16 Missing Auxiliary Verb—Passive

Remember that the passive requires an auxiliary BE verb.

S		BE	participle
The plants		are	watered
The plants	have	been	watered
The plants	should	be	watered

Avoid using a passive without a form of BE.

EXAMPLES

INCORRECT: The phone answered automatically.
CORRECT: The phone is answered automatically.

INCORRECT: They have informed already.
CORRECT: They have been informed already.

INCORRECT: These books should returned today.
CORRECT: These books should be returned today.

INCORRECT: The plane delayed by bad weather.
CORRECT: The plane was delayed by bad weather.

INCORRECT: My paper has not typed.
CORRECT: My paper has not been typed.

<u>EXERCISES</u>

Part A: Choose the correct answer.

Hydrogen peroxide_____as a bleaching agent because it effectively whitens a variety of fibers and surfaces.
   (A) used
   (B) is used
   (C) is using
   (D) that it uses

Part B: Choose the incorrect word or phrase and correct it.

If a rash <u>occurs</u> within twenty-four hours <u>after taking</u> a new <u>medication</u>, the treatment
                    (A)   (B)   (C)

<u>should discontinued</u>.
          (D)

Problems with Pronouns

You probably remember learning that "pronouns take the place of nouns." What this means is that pronouns often are used instead of nouns to avoid repetition of nouns.

A pronoun usually has a reference noun that has been mentioned before in conversation or in writing. The pronoun is used instead of repeating the reference noun. In some grammar books, the reference noun is called the "antecedent of the pronoun" because it has been mentioned before. "Ante" means "before." For example, in the following sentence, the word *them* is a pronoun that refers to the noun *secretaries*.

Many *secretaries* are using computers to help *them* work faster and more efficiently.

There are several different kinds of pronouns in English. Some of them are *personal* pronouns, which can be either subject or object pronouns; *possessive* pronouns; *relative* pronouns; *reflexive* pronouns; and *reciprocal* pronouns.

17 Object Pronouns after Prepositions

Remember that personal pronouns used as the object of a preposition should be object case pronouns.

	preposition	pronoun (object)
I would be glad to take a message	for	her

Remember that the following prepositions are commonly used with object pronouns:

among	of
between	to
for	with
from	

Avoid using a subject pronoun instead of an object pronoun after a proposition.

EXAMPLES

INCORRECT: The experiment proved to my lab partner and I that prejudices about the results of an investigation are often unfounded.

CORRECT: The experiment proved <u>to</u> my lab partner and <u>me</u> that prejudices about the results of an investigation are often unfounded.

INCORRECT: Of those who graduated with Betty and he, Ellen is the only one who has found a good job.

CORRECT: Of those who graduated <u>with</u> Betty and <u>him</u>, Ellen is the only one who has found a good job.

INCORRECT: Among we men, it was he who always acted as the interpreter.

CORRECT: <u>Among us</u> men, it was he who always acted as the interpreter.

INCORRECT: The cake is from Jan, and the flowers are from Larry and we.

CORRECT: The cake is from Jan, and the flowers are <u>from</u> Larry and <u>us</u>.

INCORRECT: Just between you and I, this isn't a very good price.

CORRECT: Just <u>between</u> you and <u>me</u>, this isn't a very good price.

EXERCISES

Part A: Choose the correct answer.

Since the Earth's crust is much thicker under the continents, equipment would have to be capable of drilling through 100,000 feet of rock to investigate the mantle _____ .
- (A) beneath them
- (B) beneath their
- (C) beneath its
- (D) beneath they

Part B: Choose the incorrect word or phrase and correct it.

According to Amazon legends, men <u>were forced</u> <u>to do</u> all of the household tasks for the women war-
                                      (A)   (B)

riors <u>who</u> governed and protected the cities <u>for they</u>.
   (C)   (D)

18   Relative Pronouns that Refer to Persons and Things

Remember that *who* is used to refer to persons, and *which* is used to refer to things.

	someone	who	
She is	the secretary	who	works in the international office

Avoid using *which* instead of *who* in reference to a person.

	something	which	
This is	the new typewriter	which	you ordered

Avoid using *who* instead of *which* in reference to a thing.

EXAMPLES

INCORRECT: The people which cheated on the examination had to leave the room.
CORRECT: The people <u>who</u> cheated on the examination had to leave the room.

INCORRECT: There is someone on line two which would like to speak with you.
CORRECT: There is <u>someone</u> on line two <u>who</u> would like to speak with you.

INCORRECT: Who is the man which asked the question?
CORRECT: Who is <u>the man</u> <u>who</u> asked the question?

INCORRECT: The person which was recommended for the position did not fulfill the minimum requirements.
CORRECT: <u>The person</u> <u>who</u> was recommended for the position did not fulfill the minimum requirements.

INCORRECT: The student which receives the highest score will be awarded a scholarship.
CORRECT: <u>The student</u> <u>who</u> receives the highest score will be awarded a scholarship.

EXERCISES

Part A: Choose the correct answer.

Charlie Chaplin was a comedian _____ was best known for his work in silent movies.
   (A) who
   (B) which
   (C) whose
   (D) what

Part B: Choose the incorrect word or phrase and correct it.

Absolute zero, the temperature at <u>whom</u> <u>all substances</u> have zero thermal energy and thus,
                                    (A)   (B)

<u>the lowest</u> possible temperatures, <u>is</u> unattainable in practice.
    (C)   (D)

Problems with Nouns

You have probably learned that "a noun is the name of a person, place, or thing." Nouns perform several functions in English, but "naming" is clearly the most important.

There are two basic classifications of nouns in English. In some grammar books, they are called *count nouns* and *noncount nouns*. In other grammar books, they are called *count nouns* and *mass nouns*. In still other grammar books, they are called *countable* and *uncountable* nouns.

All of these names are very confusing because, of course, everything can be counted. The problem is *how* to count it. And, in that respect, the two classifications of nouns are very different.

Count or countable nouns have both singular and plural forms. They are used in agreement with singular or plural verbs. In contrast, mass or noncount, uncountable nouns have only one form. They are used in agreement with singular verbs.

Often count or countable nouns are individual persons, places, or things that can be seen and counted individually. Often mass, noncount, or uncountable nouns are substances and ideas that are shapeless by nature and cannot be seen and counted individually.

But it is not always logic that determines whether a noun is count or noncount. Sometimes it is simply a grammatical convention—that is, a category that people agree to use in their language. Both beans and rice have small parts that would be difficult but not impossible to count. But beans is considered a count noun and rice is considered a noncount noun. Why? Because it is a grammatical convention.

19   Count Nouns

Remember that *count nouns* have both singular and plural forms. Plural numbers can precede *count nouns* but not *noncount* nouns.

There are several categories of *count nouns* that can help you organize your study. Some of them are listed here.

1. Names of persons, their relationships, and their occupations:
   one boy   two boys
   one friend   two friends
   one student   two students

2. Names of animals, plants, insects:
   one dog   two dogs
   one flower   two flowers
   one bee   two bees

3. Names of things with a definite, individual shape:

one car	*two cars*
one house	*two houses*
one room	*two rooms*

4. Units of measurement:

one inch	*two inches*
one pound	*two pounds*
one degree	*two degrees*

5. Units of classification in society:

one family	*two families*
one country	*two countries*
one language	*two languages*

6. Containers of noncount solids, liquids, pastes, and gases:

one bottle	*two bottles*
one jar	*two jars*
one tube	*two tubes*

7. A limited number of abstract concepts:

one idea	*two ideas*
one invention	*two inventions*
one plan	*two plans*

Number (plural)	Noun (count-plural)
sixty	years

Avoid using a singular *count noun* with a plural number.

EXAMPLES

INCORRECT:	We have twenty dollar left.
CORRECT:	We have <u>twenty</u> <u>dollars</u> left.
INCORRECT:	I hope that I can lose about five pound before summer.
CORRECT:	I hope that I can lose about <u>five</u> <u>pounds</u> before summer.
INCORRECT:	Several of the people in this class speak three or four language.
CORRECT:	Several of the people in this class speak <u>three or four</u> <u>languages</u>.
INCORRECT:	The temperature has risen ten degree in two hours.
CORRECT:	The temperature has risen <u>ten</u> <u>degrees</u> in two hours.
INCORRECT:	The teacher has ordered two book, but they aren't in at the bookstore.
CORRECT:	The teacher has ordered <u>two</u> <u>books,</u> but they aren't in at the bookstore.

EXERCISES

Part A: Choose the correct answer.

A desert receives less than twenty-five _____ of rainfall every year.
(A) centimeter
(B) a centimeter
(C) centimeters
(D) of centimeters

Part B: Choose the incorrect word or phrase and correct it.

In 1950 it was naively predicted that eight or ten computer would be sufficient to handle all of the
    (A)   (B)   (C)   (D)
scientific and business needs in the United States.

20   Noncount Nouns

Remember that *noncount* nouns have only one form. They are used in agreement with singular verbs. The word *the* does not precede them.

There are categories of *noncount* nouns that can help you organize your study. Some of them are listed here.

1. Food staples that can be purchased in various forms:
   bread
   meat
   butter

2. Construction materials that can change shape, depending on what is made:
   wood
   iron
   glass

3. Liquids that can change shape, depending on the shape of the container:
   oil
   tea
   milk

4. Natural substances that can change shape, depending on natural laws:
   steam, water, ice
   smoke, ashes
   oxygen

5. Substances with many small parts:
   rice
   sand
   sugar

6. Groups of things that have different sizes and shapes:

clothing	*(a coat, a shirt, a sock)*
furniture	*(a table, a chair, a bed)*
luggage	*(a suitcase, a trunk, a box)*

7. Languages:
Arabic
Japanese
Spanish

8. Abstract concepts, often with endings *-ness, -ance, -ence, -ity:*
beauty
ignorance
peace

9. Most *-ing* forms:
learning
shopping
working

noun (noncount)	verb (singular)	
Friendship	is	important

Avoid using *the* before a *noncount* noun. Avoid using a plural verb with a noncount noun.

EXAMPLES

INCORRECT:	The happiness means different things to different people.
CORRECT:	<u>Happiness</u> means different things to different people.
INCORRECT:	Toshi speaks the Japanese at home.
CORRECT:	Toshi speaks <u>Japanese</u> at home.
INCORRECT:	Bread are expensive in the grocery store on the corner.
CORRECT:	<u>Bread</u> <u>is</u> expensive in the grocery store on the corner.
INCORRECT:	I like my tea with the milk.
CORRECT:	I like my tea with <u>milk</u>.
INCORRECT:	If you open the door, airs will circulate better.
CORRECT:	If you open the door, <u>air</u> will circulate better.

EXERCISES

Part A: Choose the correct answer.

_____ at 212 degrees F. and freezes at 32 degrees F.
(A) Waters boils
(B) The water boils
(C) Water boils
(D) Waters boil

Part B: Choose the incorrect word or phrase and correct it.

The religion attempts to clarify mankind's relationship with a superhuman power.
   (A)   (B)   (C)   (D)

21   Nouns with Count and Noncount Meanings

Remember that some nouns may be used as *count* or as *noncount* nouns depending on their meanings. Materials and abstract concepts are *noncount* nouns, but they may be used as *count* nouns to express specific meanings.

Count noun	Specific meaning	Noncount noun	General meaning
an agreement agreements	an occasion or a document	agreement	abstract concept all agreements
a bone bones	a part of a skeleton	bone	construction material
a business businesses	a company	business	abstract concept all business transactions
a cloth cloths	a piece of cloth	cloth	construction material
a decision decisions	an occasion	decision	abstract concept all decisions
an education educations	a specific person's	education	abstract concept all education
a fire fires	an event	fire	material
a glass glasses	a container	glass	construction material

a history histories	a historical account	history	abstract concept all history
an honor honors	an occasion or an award	honor	abstract concept all honor
a language languages	a specific variety	language	abstract concept all languages
a life lives	a specific person's	life	abstract concept all life
a light lights	a lamp	light	the absence of darkness
a noise noises	a specific sound	noise	abstract concept all sounds
a pain pains	a specific occasion	pain	abstract concept all pain
a paper papers	a document or sheet	paper	construction material
a pleasure pleasures	a specific occasion	pleasure	abstract concept all pleasure
a silence silences	a specific occasion	silence	abstract concept all silence
a space spaces	a blank	space	the universe
a stone stones	a small rock	stone	construction material
a success successes	an achievement	success	abstract concept all success
a thought thoughts	an idea	thought	abstract concept all thought
a time times	a historical period or moment	time	abstract concept all time
a war wars	a specific war	war	the general act of war all wars
a work works	an artistic creation	work	employment abstract concept all work

	a document	
I have	a paper	due Monday

	construction material	
Let's use	paper	to make the present

Avoid using *count* nouns with specific meanings to express the general meanings of *noncount* nouns.

EXAMPLES

INCORRECT: Dr. Bradley will receive special honor at the graduation.
  CORRECT: Dr. Bradley will receive <u>a special honor</u> at the graduation.
  (an award)

INCORRECT: She needs to find a work.
  CORRECT: She needs to find <u>work</u>.
  (employment)

INCORRECT: My neighbor dislikes a noise.
  CORRECT: My neighbor dislikes <u>noise</u>.
  (all sounds)

INCORRECT: We need glass for the juice.
  CORRECT: We need <u>a glass</u> for the juice.
        or
  We need <u>glasses</u> for the juice.
  (containers)

INCORRECT: A war is as old as mankind.
  CORRECT: <u>War</u> is as old as mankind.
  (the act of war)

EXERCISES

Part A: Choose the correct answer.

It is generally believed that an M.B.A. degree is good preparation for a career in _____ .
  (A) a business
  (B) business
  (C) businesses
  (D) one business

Part B: Choose the incorrect word or phrase and correct it.

<u>A space</u> <u>is</u> the last frontier for <u>man</u> <u>to conquer</u>.
  (A) (B)   (C)   (D)

PROBLEM 22

Noncount Nouns that Are Count Nouns in Other Languages

Remember, many nouns that are *count* nouns in other languages may be *noncount* nouns in English. Some of the most troublesome have been listed for you on the following page.

advice	homework	money	poetry
anger	ignorance	music	poverty
courage	information	news	progress
damage	knowledge	patience	
equipment	leisure	permission	
fun	luck		

	Ø	Noun (noncount)
Did you do your		homework?

Avoid using *a* or *an* before *noncount* nouns.

EXAMPLES

INCORRECT: Do you have an information about it?
CORRECT: Do you have <u>information</u> about it?

INCORRECT: Counselors are available to give you an advice before you register for your classes.
CORRECT: Counselors are available to give you <u>advice</u> before you register for your classes.

INCORRECT: George had a good luck when he first came to State University.
CORRECT: George had good <u>luck</u> when he first came to State University.

INCORRECT: A news was released about the hostages.
CORRECT: <u>News</u> was released about the hostages.

INCORRECT: Did you get a permission to take the placement test?
CORRECT: Did you get <u>permission</u> to take the placement test?

EXERCISES

Part A: Choose the correct answer.

Fire-resistant materials are used to retard _____ of modern aircraft in case of accidents.
   (A) a damage to the passenger cabin
   (B) that damages to the passenger cabin
   (C) damage to the passenger cabin
   (D) passenger cabin's damages

Part B: Choose the incorrect word or phrase and correct it.

<u>A progress</u> <u>has been made</u> toward <u>finding</u> <u>a cure</u> for AIDS.
  (A)   (B)   (C) (D)

23 Singular and Plural Expressions of Noncount Nouns

Remember that the following singular and plural expressions are idiomatic:

a piece of advice	*two pieces of advice*
a piece of bread	*two pieces of bread*
a piece of equipment	*two pieces of equipment*
a piece of furniture	*two pieces of furniture*
a piece of information	*two pieces of information*
a piece of jewelry	*two pieces of jewelry*
a piece of luggage	*two pieces of luggage*
a piece of mail	*two pieces of mail*
a piece of music	*two pieces of music*
a piece of news	*two pieces of news*
a piece of toast	*two pieces of toast*
a loaf of bread	*two loaves of bread*
a slice of bread	*two slices of bread*
an ear of corn	*two ears of corn*
a bar of soap	*two bars of soap*
a bolt of lightning	*two bolts of lightning*
a clap of thunder	*two claps of thunder*
a gust of wind	*two gusts of wind*

	a	singular	of	noun (noncount)
A folk song is	a	piece	of	popular music

	number	plural	of	noun (noncount)
I ordered	twelve	bars	of	soap

Avoid using the noncount noun without the singular or plural idiom to express a singular or plural.

EXAMPLES

INCORRECT: A mail travels faster when the zip code is indicated on the envelope.
CORRECT: A piece of mail travels faster when the zip code is indicated on the envelope.

INCORRECT: There is a limit of two carry-on luggages for each passenger.
CORRECT: There is a limit of two pieces of carry-on luggage for each passenger.

INCORRECT: Each furniture in this display is on sale for half price.
CORRECT: Each piece of furniture in this display is on sale for half price.

INCORRECT: I'd like a steak, a salad, and a corn's ear with butter.
CORRECT: I'd like a steak, a salad, and an ear of corn with butter.

INCORRECT: The Engineering Department purchased a new equipment to simulate conditions in outer space.

CORRECT: The Engineering Department purchased <u>a new piece of equipment</u> to simulate conditions in outer space.

EXERCISES

Part A: Choose the correct answer.

Hybrids have one more _____ per plant than the other varieties.
   (A) corns
   (B) ear of corn
   (C) corn ears
   (D) corn's ears

Part B: Choose the incorrect word or phrase and correct it.

<u>A few</u> tiles on *Skylab* <u>were</u> the only <u>equipments</u> that failed <u>to perform</u> well in outer space.
   (A)   (B)   (C)   (D)

24   Infinitive and *-ing* Subjects

Remember that either an infinitive or an *-ing* form may be used as the subject of a sentence or a clause.

S (infinitive)	V	
To read a foreign language	is	even more difficult

S (*-ing*)	V	
Reading quickly and well	requires	practice

Avoid using a verb word instead of an infinitive or an *-ing* form in the subject. Avoid using *to* with an *-ing* form.

EXAMPLES

INCORRECT: To working provides people with personal satisfaction as well as money.
CORRECT: <u>To work</u> provides people with personal satisfaction as well as money.
            or
            <u>Working</u> provides people with personal satisfaction as well as money.

INCORRECT: The sneeze spreads germs.
CORRECT: <u>To sneeze</u> spreads germs.
            or
            <u>Sneezing</u> spreads germs.

INCORRECT:	Shoplift is considered a serious crime.
CORRECT:	<u>To shoplift</u> is considered a serious crime.
	or
	<u>Shoplifting</u> is considered a serious crime.

INCORRECT:	The rest in the afternoon is a custom in many countries.
CORRECT:	<u>To rest</u> in the afternoon is a custom in many countries.
	or
	<u>Resting</u> in the afternoon is a custom in many countries.

INCORRECT:	To exercising makes most people feel better.
CORRECT:	<u>To exercise</u> makes most people feel better.
	or
	<u>Exercising</u> makes most people feel better.

EXERCISES

Part A: Choose the correct answer.

_____ trees is a custom that many people engage in to celebrate Arbor Day.
(A) The plant
(B) Plant
(C) Planting
(D) To planting

Part B: Choose the incorrect word or phrase and correct it.

<u>Spell</u> <u>correctly</u> is easy with the aid of a number of <u>word processing</u> programs for personal <u>computers</u>.
 (A)   (B)   (C)   (D)

25   Nominal *That* Clause

Remember that sometimes the subject of a verb is a single noun. Other times it is a long noun phrase or a long noun clause.

One example of a long noun clause is the *nominal that* clause. Like all clauses, the *nominal that* clause has a subject and verb. The *nominal that* clause functions as the main subject of the main verb which follows it.

Nominal *that* clause S	V	
That vitamin C prevents colds	is	well known

EXAMPLES

| INCORRECT: | That it is that she has known him for a long time influenced her decision. |
| CORRECT: | <u>That she has known him for a long time</u> influenced her decision. |

| INCORRECT: | It is that we need to move is sure. |
| CORRECT: | <u>That we need to move</u> <u>is</u> sure. |

| INCORRECT: | Is likely that the library is closed. |
| CORRECT: | <u>That the library is closed</u> <u>is</u> likely. |

| INCORRECT: | She will win is almost certain. |
| CORRECT: | <u>That she will win</u> <u>is</u> almost certain. |

| INCORRECT: | That is not fair seems obvious. |
| CORRECT: | <u>That it is not fair</u> <u>seems</u> obvious. |

EXERCISES

Part A: Choose the correct answer.

_____ migrate long distances is well documented.
(A) That it is birds
(B) That birds
(C) Birds that
(D) It is that birds

Part B: Choose the incorrect word or phrase and correct it.

That <u>it is</u> the moon influences only <u>one kind</u> of tide is not <u>generally</u> <u>known</u>.
    (A)   (B)   (C)   (D)

Problems with Adjectives

Adjectives and adjective phrases describe nouns. They may be used to describe *quantity* (number or amount); *sufficiency* (number or amount needed); *consecutive order* (order in a sequence); *quality* (appearance); and *emphasis* (importance or force.)

Most adjectives and adjective phrases have only one form in English. They do not change forms to agree with the nouns they describe.

PROBLEMS WITH DETERMINERS

Determiners are a special kind of adjective. Like other adjectives, determiners describe nouns. But unlike other adjectives, determiners must agree with the nouns they describe. In other words, you must know whether the noun is a singular count noun, a plural count noun, or a noncount noun before you can choose the correct determiner. The noun *determines* which adjective form you use.

26   Noncount Nouns with Qualifying Phrases—*The*

Remember, *the* is used with count nouns. You have also learned that *the* can be used before an *-ing* noun that is followed by a qualifying phrase.

In addition, *the* can be used before a noncount noun with a qualifying phrase.

The	noncount noun	Qualifying Phrase	
The	art	of the Middle Ages	is on display

EXAMPLES

INCORRECT:	Poetry of Carl Sandburg is being read at the student union on Friday.
CORRECT:	<u>The poetry of Carl Sandburg</u> is being read at the student union on Friday.

INCORRECT:	Poverty of people in the rural areas is not as visible as that of people in the city.
CORRECT:	<u>The poverty of people</u> in the rural areas is not as visible as that of people in the city.

INCORRECT:	Science of genetic engineering is not very old.
CORRECT:	<u>The science of genetic engineering</u> is not very old.

INCORRECT:	History of this area is interesting.
CORRECT:	<u>The history of this area</u> is interesting.

INCORRECT:	Work of many people made the project a success.
CORRECT:	<u>The work of many people</u> made the project a success.

EXERCISES

Part A: Choose the correct answer.

_____ of Country-Western singers may be related to old English ballads.
(A) The music
(B) Music
(C) Their music
(D) Musics

Part B: Choose the incorrect word or phrase and correct it.

<u>Philosophy</u> of the ancient Greeks <u>has been preserved</u> in the <u>scholarly writing</u> of <u>Western civilization.</u>
   (A)   (B)   (C)   (D)

27   *No* Meaning *Not Any*

Remember that *no* means *not any*. It may be used with a singular or plural count noun or with a non-count noun.

no	noun (count singular) noun (count plural)	verb (singular) verb (plural)
No No	tree trees	grows above the tree line grow above the tree line

no	noun (noncount)	verb (singular)	
No	art	is	on display today

Avoid using the negatives *not* or *none* instead of *no*. Avoid using a singular verb with a plural count noun.

EXAMPLES

INCORRECT: There is not reason to worry.
  CORRECT: There is <u>no reason</u> to worry.

INCORRECT: None news is good news.
  CORRECT: <u>No news</u> is good news.

INCORRECT: We have not a file under the name Wagner.
  CORRECT: We have <u>no file</u> under the name Wagner.

INCORRECT: None of cheating will be tolerated.
  CORRECT: <u>No cheating</u> will be tolerated.

INCORRECT: Bill told me that he has none friends.
  CORRECT: Bill told me that he has <u>no friends</u>.

EXERCISES

Part A: Choose the correct answer.

At Woolworth's first five-and-ten-cent store, _____ more than a dime.
   (A) neither items cost
   (B) items not cost
   (C) items none costing
   (D) no item costs

Part B: Choose the incorrect word or phrase and correct it.

Some religions <u>have</u> <u>none</u> deity but <u>are</u> philosophies that function <u>instead of religions</u>.
          (A) (B)   (C)   (D)

28   *Almost All of the* and *Most of the*

Remember that *almost all of the* and *most of the* mean all except a few, but *almost all of the* includes more.

almost all (of the) most (of the)	noun (count—plural)	verb (plural)	
Almost all (of the) Most (of the)	trees in our yard trees	are are	oaks oaks

almost all (of the) most (of the)	noun (noncount)	verb (singular)
Almost all (of the) Most (of the)	art by R. C. Gorman art by R. C. Gorman	is expensive is expensive

Avoid using *almost* without *all* or *all of the*. Avoid using *most of* without *the*.

EXAMPLES

INCORRECT:	Almost the states have a sales tax.
CORRECT:	<u>Almost all of the</u> <u>states</u> have a sales tax.
	or
	<u>Almost all</u> <u>states</u> have a sales tax.
	or
	<u>Most of the</u> <u>states</u> have a sales tax.
	or
	<u>Most</u> <u>states</u> have a sales tax.
INCORRECT:	Most of teachers at State University care about their students' progress.
CORRECT:	<u>Almost all of the</u> <u>teachers</u> at State University care about their students' progress.
	or
	<u>Almost all</u> <u>teachers</u> at State University care about their students' progress.
	or
	<u>Most of the</u> <u>teachers</u> at State University care about their students' progress.
	or
	<u>Most</u> <u>teachers</u> at State University care about their students' progress.

INCORRECT: My cousin told me that most of people who won the lottery got only a few dollars, not the grand prize.

CORRECT: My cousin told me that <u>almost all of the</u> <u>people</u> who won the lottery got only a few dollars, not the grand prize.

or

My cousin told me that <u>almost all</u> <u>people</u> who won the lottery got only a few dollars, not the grand prize.

or

My cousin told me that <u>most of the</u> <u>people</u> who won the lottery got only a few dollars, not the grand prize.

or

My cousin told me that <u>most</u> <u>people</u> who won the lottery got only a few dollars, not the grand prize.

INCORRECT: Most the dictionaries have information about pronunciation.

CORRECT: <u>Almost all of the</u> <u>dictionaries</u> have information about pronunciation.

or

<u>Almost all</u> <u>dictionaries</u> have information about pronunciation.

or

<u>Most of the</u> <u>dictionaries</u> have information about pronunciation.

or

<u>Most</u> <u>dictionaries</u> have information about pronunciation.

INCORRECT: Is it true that most Americans watches TV every night?

CORRECT: It is true that <u>almost all of the</u> <u>Americans</u> watch TV every night?

or

Is it true that <u>almost all</u> <u>Americans</u> watch TV every night?

or

Is it true that <u>most of the</u> <u>Americans</u> watch TV every night?

or

Is it true that <u>most</u> <u>Americans</u> watch TV every night?

EXERCISES

Part A: Choose the correct answer.

_____ fuel that is used today is a chemical form of solar energy.

(A) Most of
(B) The most
(C) Most
(D) Almost the

Part B: Choose the incorrect word or phrase and correct it.

<u>Almost</u> the plants <u>known to us</u> are made up of <u>a great many cells,</u> specialized <u>to perform</u> different
  (A)   (B)   (C)   (D)
tasks.

PROBLEMS WITH OTHER ADJECTIVES

Besides determiners that express number and amount, there are adjectives and adjective-related structures that express *sufficiency*, *consecutive order*, *quality*, and *emphasis*.

Adjectives usually do not change to agree with the noun that they modify.

29 Nouns that Function as Adjectives

Remember that when two nouns occur together, the first noun describes the second noun; that is, the first noun functions as an adjective. Adjectives do not change form, singular or plural.

	noun	noun
All of us are foreign	language	teachers

Avoid using a plural form for the first noun even when the second noun is plural. Avoid using a possessive form for the first noun.

EXAMPLES

INCORRECT: May I borrow some notebooks paper?
CORRECT: May I borrow some <u>notebook paper</u>?

INCORRECT: All business' students must take the Graduate Management Admission Test.
CORRECT: All <u>business students</u> must take the Graduate Management Admission Test.

INCORRECT: I forgot their telephone's number.
CORRECT: I forgot their <u>telephone number</u>.

INCORRECT: There is a sale at the shoes store.
CORRECT: There is a sale at the <u>shoe store</u>.

INCORRECT: Put the mail on the hall's table.
CORRECT: Put the mail on the <u>hall table</u>.

EXERCISES

Part A: Choose the correct answer.

_____ is cheaper for students who maintain a B average because they are a better risk than average or below-average students.
(A) Automobile's insurance
(B) Insurance of automobiles
(C) Automobile insurance
(D) Insurance automobile

Part B: Choose the incorrect word or phrase and correct it.

<u>Sex's education</u> is instituted to help the student <u>understand</u> the process of maturation,
           (A)   (B)
<u>to eliminate anxieties</u> <u>related</u> to development, to learn values, and to prevent disease.
           (C)   (D)

30 Hyphenated Adjectives

Remember that it is common for a number to appear as the first in a series of hyphenated adjectives. Each word in a hyphenated adjective is an adjective and does not change form, singular or plural.

	a	adjective	—	adjective	noun
Agriculture 420 is	a	five	—	hour	class

a	adjective	—	adjective	—	adjective	noun	
A	sixty	—	year	—	old	employee	may retire

Avoid using a plural form for any of the adjectives joined by hyphens even when the noun that follows is plural.

EXAMPLES

INCORRECT: A three-minutes call anywhere in the United States costs less than a dollar when you dial it yourself.
  CORRECT: <u>A three-minute call</u> anywhere in the United States costs less than a dollar when you dial it yourself.

INCORRECT: They have a four-months-old baby.
  CORRECT: They have <u>a four-month-old baby</u>.

INCORRECT: Can you make change for a twenty-dollars bill?
  CORRECT: Can you make change for <u>a twenty-dollar bill</u>?

INCORRECT: A two-doors car is cheaper than a four-doors model.
  CORRECT: <u>A two-door car</u> is cheaper than <u>a four-door model</u>.

INCORRECT: I have to write a one-thousand-words paper this weekend.
  CORRECT: I have to write <u>a one-thousand-word paper</u> this weekend.

EXERCISES

Part A: Choose the correct answer.

The evolution of vertebrates suggests development from a very simple heart in fish to a _____ in man.

    (A) four-chamber heart
    (B) four-chambers heart
    (C) four-chamber hearts
    (D) four-chamber's heart

Part B: Choose the incorrect word or phrase and correct it.

The MX <u>is</u> <u>a four-stages</u> rocket with <u>an 8000</u>-mile range, <u>larger than</u> that of the Minuteman.
    (A)   (B)   (C)   (D)

PROBLEM 31   Cause-and-Result—*So*

Remember that *so* is used before an adjective or an adverb followed by *that*. The *so* clause expresses cause. The *that* clause expresses result.

CAUSE				RESULT			
S	V	so	adverb adjective	that	S	V	
She	got up	so	late	that	she	missed	her bus
The music	was	so	loud	that	we	couldn't talk	

Avoid using *as* or *too* instead of *so* in clauses of cause. Avoid using *as* instead of *that* in clauses of result.

EXAMPLES

INCORRECT: He is so slow as he never gets to class on time.
CORRECT: He is <u>so slow that</u> he never gets to class on time.

INCORRECT: This suitcase is as heavy that I can hardly carry it.
CORRECT: This suitcase is <u>so heavy that</u> I can hardly carry it.

INCORRECT: We arrived so late as Professor Baker had already called the roll.
CORRECT: We arrived <u>so late that</u> Professor Baker had already called the roll.

INCORRECT: He drives so fast as no one likes to ride with him.
CORRECT: He drives <u>so fast that</u> no one likes to ride with him.

INCORRECT: Preparing frozen foods is too easy that anyone can do it.
CORRECT: Preparing frozen foods is <u>so easy that</u> anyone can do it.

EXERCISES

Part A: Choose the correct answer.

Oil paints are _____ they have become the most popular painter's colors.
(A) so versatile and durable that
(B) so versatile and durable than
(C) such versatile and durable as
(D) such versatile and durable

Part B: Choose the incorrect word or phrase and correct it.

<u>By the mid-nineteenth century</u>, land was <u>such expensive</u> in large cities that architects began to
        (A)   (B)

<u>conserve</u> space <u>by designing</u> skyscrapers.
  (C)   (D)

Problems with Comparatives

Nouns may be compared for exact or general *similarity* or *difference.* They may also be compared for similar or different *qualities* or *degrees,* more or less, of specific qualities. In addition, they may be compared to *estimates.*

Exact Similarity—*the Same as* and *the Same*

Remember that *the same as* and *the same* have the same meaning, but *the same as* is used between the two nouns compared, and *the same* is used after the two nouns or a plural noun.

noun		the same as	noun
This coat	is	the same as	that one

noun		noun		the same
This coat	and	that one	are	the same

noun (plural)		the same
These coats	are	the same

Avoid using *to* and *like* instead of *as.* Avoid using *the same* between the two nouns compared.

EXAMPLES

INCORRECT:	That car is almost the same like mine.
CORRECT:	That car is almost <u>the same as</u> <u>mine</u>.
	or
	That car and mine are almost <u>the same</u>.

INCORRECT:	My briefcase is exactly the same that yours.
CORRECT:	My briefcase is exactly <u>the same as</u> <u>yours</u>.
	or
	My briefcase and yours are exactly <u>the same</u>.

INCORRECT:	Is your book the same to mine?
CORRECT:	Is your book <u>the same as</u> <u>mine</u>?
	or
	Are your book and mine <u>the same</u>?

INCORRECT:	Are this picture and the one on your desk same?
CORRECT:	Are this picture and the one on your desk <u>the same</u>?
	or
	Is this picture <u>the same as</u> <u>the one</u> on your desk?

INCORRECT:	The teacher gave Martha a failing grade on her composition because it was the same a composition he had already read.
CORRECT:	The teacher gave Martha a failing grade on her composition because it was <u>the same as</u> <u>a</u> <u>composition</u> he had already read.
	or
	The teacher gave Martha a failing grade on her composition because it and a composition he had already read were <u>the same</u>.

EXERCISES

Part A: Choose the correct answer.

Although we often use "speed" and "velocity" interchangeably, in a technical sense, "speed" is not always _____ "velocity."

(A) alike
(B) the same as
(C) similar
(D) as

Part B: Choose the incorrect word or phrase and correct it.

When two products are <u>basically</u> <u>the same as,</u> <u>advertising</u> can <u>influence</u> the public's choice.
                    (A)   (B)   (C)   (D)

33 General Similarity—*Like* and *Alike*

Remember that *like* and *alike* have the same meaning, but *like* is used between the two nouns compared, and *alike* is used after the two nouns or a plural noun.

noun		like	noun
This coat	is	like	that one

noun		noun		alike
This coat	and	that one	are	alike

noun (plural)		alike
These coats	are	alike

Avoid using *as* instead of *like*. Avoid using *like* after the two nouns compared.

EXAMPLES

INCORRECT: The weather feels as spring.
CORRECT: The weather feels <u>like</u> spring.

INCORRECT: These suits are like.
CORRECT: This suit is <u>like that suit</u>.
       or
   These suits are <u>alike</u>.

INCORRECT: Your recipe for chicken is like to a recipe that my mother has.
CORRECT: Your recipe for chicken is <u>like a recipe</u> that my mother has.
       or
   Your recipe for chicken and a recipe that my mother has are <u>alike</u>.

INCORRECT: I want to buy some shoes same like the ones I have on.
CORRECT: I want to buy some shoes <u>like the ones</u> I have on.
       or
   The shoes I want to buy and the shoes I have on are <u>alike</u>.

INCORRECT: Anthony and his brother don't look like.
CORRECT: Anthony doesn't look <u>like his brother</u>.
       or
   Anthony and his brother don't look <u>alike</u>.

EXERCISES

Part A: Choose the correct answer.

Although they are smaller, chipmunks are _____ most other ground squirrels.
(A) like to
(B) like as
(C) like
(D) alike

Part B: Choose the incorrect word or phrase and correct it.

The first living structures to appear on Earth thousands of years ago were alike viruses.
  (A)   (B)   (C)   (D)

34   General Difference—*to Differ from*

Remember that *differ* is a verb and must change forms to agree with the subject.

	DIFFER	from	
This one	differs	from	the rest

Avoid using BE with *differ*. Avoid using *than*, *of*, or *to* after *differ*.

EXAMPLES

INCORRECT: Sharon is different of other women I know.
  CORRECT: Sharon is different from other women I know.
                  or
             Sharon differs from other women I know.

INCORRECT: Do you have anything a little different to these?
  CORRECT: Do you have anything a little different from these?
                  or
             Do you have anything that differs a little from these?

INCORRECT: The campus at State University different from that of City College.
  CORRECT: The campus at State University differs from that of City College.
                  or
             The campus at State University is different from that of City College.

INCORRECT: Jayne's apartment is very differs from Bill's even though they are in the same building.
  CORRECT: Jayne's apartment is very different from Bill's even though they are in the same building.
                  or
             Jayne's apartment differs from Bill's even though they are in the same building.

INCORRECT: Customs differ one region of the country to another.
CORRECT: Customs <u>differ from</u> one region of the country to another.

         or

         Customs <u>are</u> <u>different from</u> one region of the country to another.

EXERCISES

Part A: Choose the correct answer.

Modern blimps like the famous Goodyear blimps _____ the first ones in that they are filled with helium instead of hydrogen.
    (A) differ from
    (B) different from
    (C) is different from
    (D) different

Part B: Choose the incorrect word or phrase and correct it.

<u>Crocodiles</u> <u>different from</u> alligators in that they have <u>pointed snouts</u> and long lower teeth that stick
  (A)   (B)   (C)

out when their mouths <u>are closed</u>.
                (D)

35 Comparative Estimates—Multiple Numbers

Remember that the following are examples of multiple numbers:

half	*four times*
twice	*five times*
three times	*ten times*

	multiple	as	much many	as	
Fresh fruit costs	twice	as	much	as	canned fruit
We have	half	as	many	as	we need

Avoid using *so* instead of *as* after a multiple. Avoid using *more than* instead of *as much as* or *as many as*. Avoid using the multiple after *as much* and *as many*.

EXAMPLES

INCORRECT: This one is prettier, but it costs twice more than the other one.
CORRECT: This one is prettier, but it costs <u>twice as much as</u> the other one.

INCORRECT: The rent at College Apartments is only half so much as you pay here.
CORRECT: The rent at College Apartments is only <u>half as much as</u> you pay here.

INCORRECT: Bob found a job that paid as much twice as he made working at the library.
  CORRECT: Bob found a job that paid <u>twice as much as</u> he made working at the library.

INCORRECT: The price was very reasonable; I would gladly have paid three times more than he asked.
  CORRECT: The price was very reasonable; I would gladly have paid <u>three times as much as</u> he asked.

INCORRECT: We didn't buy the car because they wanted as much twice as it was worth.
  CORRECT: We didn't buy the car because they wanted <u>twice as much as</u> it was worth.

EXERCISES

Part A: Choose the correct answer.

After the purchase of the Louisiana Territory, the United States had _____ it had previously owned.

   (A) twice more land than
   (B) two times more land than
   (C) twice as much land as
   (D) two times much land than

Part B: Choose the incorrect word or phrase and correct it.

With American prices for sugar at three times <u>as much</u> the world price, manufacturers <u>are</u> beginning
                                                    (A)   (B)
<u>to use</u> fructose blended with pure sugar, <u>or</u> sucrose.
   (C)   (D)

36

Comparative Estimates—*More Than* and *Less Than*

Remember that *more than* or *less than* is used before a specific number to express an estimate that may be a little more or a little less than the number.

	more than	number	
Steve has	more than	a thousand	coins in his collection

	less than	number	
Andy has	less than	a dozen	coins in his pocket

Avoid using *more* or *less* without *than* in estimates. Avoid using *as* instead of *than*.

EXAMPLES

INCORRECT:	More one hundred people came to the meeting.
CORRECT:	<u>More than one hundred</u> people came to the meeting.
INCORRECT:	We have lived in the United States for as less than seven years.
CORRECT:	We have lived in the United States for <u>less than seven</u> years.
INCORRECT:	The main library has more as one million volumes.
CORRECT:	The main library has <u>more than one million</u> volumes.
INCORRECT:	A new shopping center on the north side will have five hundred shops more than.
CORRECT:	A new shopping center on the north side will have <u>more than five hundred</u> shops.
INCORRECT:	There are most than fifty students in the lab, but only two computers.
CORRECT:	There are <u>more than fifty</u> students in the lab, but only two computers.

EXERCISES

Part A: Choose the correct answer.

In the Great Smoky Mountains, one can see _____ 150 different kinds of trees.
   (A) more than
   (B) as much as
   (C) up as
   (D) as many to

Part B: Choose the incorrect word or phrase and correct it.

Pelé scored <u>more as</u> 1280 goals <u>during his career</u>, <u>gaining</u> a reputation as <u>the best</u> soccer player of
       (A)   (B)   (C)   (D)

all time.

37   Comparative Estimates—*As Many As*

Remember that *as many as* is used before a specific number to express an estimate that does not exceed the number.

	as many as	number	
We should have	as many as	five hundred	applications

Avoid using *as many* instead of *as many as*. Avoid using *much* instead of *many* before a specific number.

Note: Comparative estimates with *as much as* are also used before a specific number that refers to weight, distance, or money. For example, *as much as* ten pounds, *as much as* two miles, or *as much as* twenty dollars.

EXAMPLES

INCORRECT:	We expect as much as thirty people to come.
CORRECT:	We expect <u>as many as</u> <u>thirty</u> people to come.
INCORRECT:	There are as many fifteen thousand students attending summer school.
CORRECT:	There are <u>as many as</u> <u>fifteen thousand</u> students attending summer school.
INCORRECT:	The children can see as much as twenty-five baby animals in the nursery at the zoo.
CORRECT:	The children can see <u>as many as</u> <u>twenty-five</u> baby animals in the nursery at the zoo.
INCORRECT:	Many as ten planes have sat in line waiting to take off.
CORRECT:	<u>As many as</u> <u>ten</u> planes have sat in line waiting to take off.
INCORRECT:	State University offers as much as two hundred major fields of study.
CORRECT:	State University offers <u>as many as</u> <u>two hundred</u> major fields of study.

EXERCISES

Part A: Choose the correct answer.

It has been estimated that _____ one hundred thousand men participated in the gold rush of 1898.

    (A) approximate
    (B) until
    (C) as many as
    (D) more

Part B: Choose the incorrect word or phrase and correct it.

It is generally accepted that the common cold <u>is caused</u> <u>by</u> <u>as much as</u> forty strains of viruses <u>that</u>
                                         (A)   (B)   (C)   (D)

may be present in the air at all times.

PROBLEM 38

Degrees of Comparison—Superlative Adjectives

Remember that superlatives are used to compare more than two.

		most (least) adjective (two + syllables) adjective -*est* (one syllable) adjective -*est* (two + syllables ending in -*y*)
	the	
An essay test is	the	most difficult
An essay test is	the	hardest
An essay test is	the	trickiest

Avoid using a comparative -*er* form when three or more are compared.

EXAMPLES

INCORRECT: She is more prettier than all of the girls in our class.
  CORRECT: She is <u>the prettiest</u> of all of the girls in our class.

INCORRECT: New York is the larger of all American cities.
  CORRECT: New York is <u>the largest</u> of all American cities.

INCORRECT: Of all of the candidates, Alex is probably the less qualified.
  CORRECT: Of all of the candidates, Alex is probably <u>the least</u> qualified.

INCORRECT: Although there are a number of interesting findings, a most significant results are in the abstract.
  CORRECT: Although there are a number of interesting findings, <u>the most</u> significant results are in the abstract.

INCORRECT: In my opinion, the more beautiful place in Oregon is Mount Hood.
  CORRECT: In my opinion, <u>the most</u> beautiful place in Oregon is Mount Hood.

EXERCISES

Part A: Choose the correct answer.

The blue whale is _____ known animal, reaching a length of more than one hundred feet.
  (A) thc large
  (B) the larger
  (C) the largest
  (D) most largest

Part B: Choose the incorrect answer and correct it.

The <u>more</u> important theorem of all in plane geometry <u>is</u> <u>the</u> Pythagorean Theorem.
(A)   (B)   (C)(D)

39 Degrees of Comparison—Irregular Adjectives

Remember that some very common adjectives have irregular forms. Some of them are listed here for you.

Adjective	Comparative— to compare two	Superlative— to compare three or more
bad	worse	the worst
far	farther	the farthest
	further	the furthest
good	better	the best
little	less	the least
many	more	the most
much	more	the most

	irregular comparative	than	
This ice cream is	better	than	the other brands

	irregular superlative	
This ice cream is	the best	of all

Avoid using a regular form instead of an irregular form for these adjectives.

EXAMPLES

INCORRECT: The lab is more far from the bus stop than the library.
CORRECT: The lab is <u>farther from</u> the bus stop than the library.
       or
The lab is <u>further from</u> the bus stop than the library.

INCORRECT: The badest accident in the history of the city occurred last night on the North Freeway.
CORRECT: The <u>worst</u> accident in the history of the city occurred last night on the North Freeway.

INCORRECT: These photographs are very good, but that one is the better of all.
CORRECT: These photographs are very good, but that one is <u>the best</u> of all.

INCORRECT: Please give me much sugar than you did last time.
CORRECT: Please give me <u>more</u> sugar than you did last time.

INCORRECT: This composition is more good than your last one.
CORRECT: This composition is <u>better</u> than your last one.

EXERCISES

Part A: Choose the correct answer.

_____ apples are grown in Washington State.
  (A) Best
  (B) The most good
  (C) The best
  (D) The better

Part B: Choose the incorrect word or phrase and correct it.

<u>Because</u> a felony is <u>more bad</u> than a misdemeanor, the punishment is <u>more severe</u>, and often in-
  (A)   (B)   (C)
cludes a jail sentence <u>as well as</u> a fine.
                (D)

40   Double Comparatives

Remember that when two comparatives are used together, the first comparative expresses cause and the second comparative expresses result. A comparative is *more* or *less* with an adjective, or an adjective with *-er*.

CAUSE				RESULT			
The	comparative	S	V,	the	comparative	S	V
The	more	you	review,	the	easier	the patterns	will be

Avoid using *as* instead of *the*. Avoid using the **incorrect** form *lesser*. Avoid omitting *the*. Avoid omitting *-er* from the adjective.

EXAMPLES

INCORRECT: The more you study during the semester, the lesser you have to study the week before exams.
  CORRECT: The more you study during the semester, the less you have to study the week before exams.

INCORRECT: The faster we finish, the soon we can leave.
  CORRECT: The faster we finish, the sooner we can leave.

INCORRECT: The less one earns, the lesser one must pay in income taxes.
  CORRECT: The less one earns, the less one must pay in income taxes.

INCORRECT: The louder he shouted, less he convinced anyone.
  CORRECT: The louder he shouted, the less he convinced anyone.

INCORRECT: The more you practice speaking, the well you will do it.
  CORRECT: The more you practice speaking, the better you will do it.

EXERCISES

Part A: Choose the correct answer.

It is generally true that the lower the stock market falls, _____ .
(A) higher the price of gold rises
(B) the price of gold rises high
(C) the higher the price of gold rises
(D) rises high the price of gold

Part B: Choose the incorrect word or phrase and correct it.

The higher the solar activity, the intense the auroras or polar light displays in the skies near
                       (A)   (B)   (C)
the Earth's geomagnetic poles.
    (D)

41 Illogical Comparatives—General Similarity and Difference

Remember that comparisons must be made with logically comparable nouns. You can't compare *the climate* in the North with *the South.* You must compare *the climate* in the North with *the climate* in the South.

Remember that *that of* and *those of* are used instead of repeating a noun to express a logical comparative. An example with *different from* appears below.

noun (singular)		different	from	that	
Football in the U.S.	is	different	from	that	in other countries

noun (plural)		different	from	those	
The rules	are	different	from	those	of soccer

Avoid omitting *that* and *those.* Avoid using *than* instead of *from* with *different.*

EXAMPLES

INCORRECT: The food in my country is very different than that in the United States.
CORRECT: The food in my country is very <u>different from that</u> in the United States.

INCORRECT: The classes at my university are very different from State University.
CORRECT: The classes at my university are very <u>different from those</u> at State University.

INCORRECT: The English that is spoken in Canada is similar to the United States.
CORRECT: The English that is spoken in Canada is <u>similar to that</u> of the United States.

INCORRECT: Drugstores here are not like at home.
CORRECT: Drugstores here are not <u>like those</u> at home.

INCORRECT: The time in New York City differs three hours from Los Angeles.
CORRECT: The time in New York City <u>differs</u> three hours <u>from that</u> of Los Angeles.

EXERCISES

Part A: Choose the correct answer.

One's fingerprints are _____ .
  (A) different from those of any other person
  (B) different from any other person
  (C) different any other person
  (D) differs from another person

Part B: Choose the incorrect word or phrase and correct it.

Perhaps the colonists were <u>looking for</u> a climate <u>like England</u>, when they decided <u>to settle</u> the North
                      (A)   (B)   (C)

American continent <u>instead of</u> the South American continent.
                         (D)

Problems with Prepositions

Prepositions are words or phrases that clarify relationships. Prepositions are usually followed by nouns and pronouns. Sometimes the nouns are *-ing* form nouns.

Prepositions are also used in idioms.

42

Addition—*Besides*

Remember that *besides* means *in addition to*. *Beside* means *near*.

besides	noun adjective	
Besides	our dog,	we have two cats and a canary
Besides	white,	we stock green and blue

	beside	noun
We sat	beside	the teacher

Avoid using *beside* instead of *besides* to mean *in addition*.

EXAMPLES

INCORRECT:	Beside Marge, three couples are invited.
CORRECT:	<u>Besides</u> Marge, three couples are invited.

INCORRECT:	Beside Domino's, four other pizza places deliver.
CORRECT:	<u>Besides</u> Domino's, four other pizza places deliver.

INCORRECT:	To lead a well-balanced life, you need to have other interests beside studying.
CORRECT:	To lead a well balanced life, you need to have other interests <u>besides</u> studying.

INCORRECT:	Beside taxi service, there isn't any public transportation in town.
CORRECT:	<u>Besides</u> taxi service, there isn't any public transportation in town.

INCORRECT: Janice has lots of friends beside her roommate.
  CORRECT: Janice has lots of friends <u>besides</u> her roommate.

EXERCISES

Part A: Choose the correct answer.

_____ a mayor, many city governments employ a city manager.
  (A) Beside
  (B) Besides
  (C) And
  (D) Also

Part B: Choose the incorrect word or phrase and correct it.

<u>To receive</u> a degree from an American university, one must take many courses <u>beside</u> <u>those</u> in <u>one's</u>
    (A)   (B)   (C)   (D)
major field.

43   Cause—*Because of* and *Because*

Remember that *because of* is a prepositional phrase. It introduces a noun or a noun phrase. *Because* is a conjunction. It introduces a clause with a subject and a verb.

	because	S	V
They decided to stay at home	because	the weather	was bad

or

	because of	noun
They decided to stay at home	because of	the weather

Avoid using *because of* before a subject and verb. Avoid using *because* before a noun which is not followed by a verb.

EXAMPLES

INCORRECT: Classes will be canceled tomorrow because a national holiday.
  CORRECT: Classes will be canceled tomorrow <u>because it is</u> a national holiday.
                    or
              Classes will be canceled tomorrow <u>because of a national holiday</u>.

INCORRECT:	She was absent because of her cold was worse.
CORRECT:	She was absent <u>because</u> <u>her cold was</u> worse.
	or
	She was absent <u>because of</u> <u>her cold</u>.

INCORRECT:	John's family is very happy because his being awarded a scholarship.
CORRECT:	John's family is very happy <u>because</u> <u>he has been awarded</u> a scholarship.
	or
	John's family is very happy <u>because of</u> <u>his being awarded</u> a scholarship.

INCORRECT:	She didn't buy it because of the price was too high.
CORRECT:	She didn't buy it <u>because</u> <u>the price was</u> too high.
	or
	She didn't buy it <u>because of</u> <u>the price</u>.

INCORRECT:	It was difficult to see the road clearly because the rain.
CORRECT:	It was difficult to see the road clearly <u>because</u> <u>it was raining</u>.
	or
	It was difficult to see the road clearly <u>because of</u> <u>the rain</u>.

EXERCISES

Part A: Choose the correct answer.

_____ in the cultivation of a forest, trees need more careful planning than any other crop does.

(A) Because the time and area involved
(B) For the time and area involving
(C) Because of the time and area involved
(D) As a cause of the time and area involved

Part B: Choose the incorrect word or phrase and correct it.

Many roads and railroads <u>were built</u> <u>in the 1880s</u> <u>because of</u> the industrial cities needed a network
                              (A)   (B)   (C)

<u>to link</u> them with sources of supply.
(D)

Problems with Conjunctions

Conjunctions are words or phrases that clarify relationships between clauses. "Conjoin" means "to join together."

PROBLEMS WITH CORRELATIVE CONJUNCTIONS

Correlative conjunctions are pairs that are used together. They often express inclusion or exclusion. Correlative conjunctions must be followed by the same grammatical structures; in other words, you must use parallel structures after correlative conjunctions.

44   Correlative Conjunctions—Inclusives *not only . . . but also*

Remember that *not only . . . but also* are correlative conjunctions. They are used together to include two parallel structures (two nouns, adjectives, verbs, adverbs).

	not only	parallel structure	but also	parallel structure
One should take	not only	cash	but also	traveler's checks
Checks are	not only	safer	but also	more convenient

Avoid using *only not* instead of *not only*. Avoid using *but* instead of *but also*.
Avoid using the incorrect pattern:

not only	parallel structure	but	parallel structure	also
not only	cash	but	traveler's checks	also
	safer	but	more convenient	also

EXAMPLES

INCORRECT: The program provides only not theoretical classes but also practical training.
  CORRECT: The program provides <u>not only</u> theoretical classes <u>but also</u> practical training.

INCORRECT: The new models are not only less expensive but more efficient also.
  CORRECT: The new models are <u>not only</u> less expensive <u>but also</u> more efficient.

INCORRECT: The objective is not to identify the problem but also to solve it.
  CORRECT: The objective is <u>not only</u> to identify the problem <u>but also</u> to solve it.

INCORRECT: Not only her parents but her brothers and sisters also live in Wisconsin.
  CORRECT: <u>Not only</u> her parents <u>but also</u> her brothers and sisters live in Wisconsin.

INCORRECT: To complete his physical education credits, John took not only swimming also golf.
  CORRECT: To complete his physical education credits, John took <u>not only</u> swimming <u>but also</u> golf.

EXERCISES

Part A: Choose the correct answer.

Amniocentesis can be used not only to diagnose fetal disorders _____ the sex of the unborn child with 95 percent accuracy.
  (A) but determining
  (B) but also determining
  (C) but to determine
  (D) but also to determine

Part B: Choose the incorrect word or phrase and correct it.

The deadbolt is <u>the best</u> lock for entry doors <u>because</u> it is <u>not only</u> inexpensive but <u>installation is easy.</u>
              (A)   (B)   (C)   (D)

PROBLEMS WITH OTHER CONJUNCTIONS

45   Future Result—*When*

Remember that *when* introduces a clause of condition for future result.

	RESULT		CONDITION	
S	V (present) V (will + verb word)	when	S	V (present)
The temperature The temperature	drops will drop	when when	the sun the sun	sets sets

Avoid using *will* instead of a present verb after *when*.

EXAMPLES

INCORRECT: I will call you when I will return from my country.
CORRECT: I will call you <u>when</u> I <u>return</u> from my country.

INCORRECT: Marilyn plans to work in her family's store when she will get her M.B.A.
CORRECT: Marilyn plans to work in her family's store <u>when</u> <u>she</u> <u>gets</u> her M.B.A.

INCORRECT: He will probably buy some more computer software when he will get paid.
CORRECT: He will probably buy some more computer software <u>when</u> <u>he</u> <u>gets</u> paid.

INCORRECT: She will feel a lot better when she will stop smoking.
CORRECT: She will feel a lot better <u>when</u> <u>she</u> <u>stops</u> smoking.

INCORRECT: When Gary will go to State University, he will be a teaching assistant.
CORRECT: <u>When</u> <u>Gary</u> <u>goes</u> to State University, he will be a teaching assistant.

EXERCISES

Part A: Choose the correct answer.

Bacterial spores germinate and sprout _____ favorable conditions of temperature and food supply.
   (A) when encountering of
   (B) when they encounter
   (C) when they will encounter
   (D) when the encounter of

Part B: Choose the incorrect word or phrase and correct it.

In <u>most states</u> insurance agents <u>must pass</u> an examination <u>to be licensed</u> when they <u>will complete</u>
        (A)   (B)   (C)   (D)
their training.

46 Indirect Questions

Remember that question words can be used as conjunctions. Question words introduce a clause of indirect question.

Question words include the following:

who	why
what	how
what time	how long
when	how many
where	how much

S	V	question word	S	V
I	don't remember	what	her name	is

V	S		question word	S	V
Do	you	remember	what	her name	is?

Avoid using *do, does,* or *did* after the question word. Avoid using the verb before the subject after the question word.

Examples

INCORRECT: I didn't understood what did he say.
  CORRECT: I didn't understand <u>what</u> he <u>said</u>.

INCORRECT: Do you know how much do they cost?
  CORRECT: Do you know <u>how much</u> <u>they</u> <u>cost</u>?

INCORRECT: I wonder when is her birthday.
  CORRECT: I wonder <u>when</u> <u>her birthday</u> <u>is</u>.

INCORRECT: Could you please tell me where is the post office?
  CORRECT: Could you please tell me <u>where</u> <u>the post office</u> <u>is</u>?

INCORRECT: Can they tell you what time does the movie start?
  CORRECT: Can they tell you <u>what time</u> <u>the movie</u> <u>starts</u>?

Exercises

Part A: Choose the correct answer.

Recently, there have been several outbreaks of disease like Legionnaire's syndrome, and doctors don't know _____.

   (A) what is the cause
   (B) the cause is what
   (C) is what the cause
   (D) what the cause is

Part B: Choose the incorrect word or phrase and correct it.

In Ground Control Approach, <u>the air traffic controller</u> <u>informs</u> the pilot how far <u>is the plane</u> from
                             (A)   (B)   (C)

<u>the touchdown point.</u>
    (D)

Problems with Adverbs and Adverb-Related Structures

Adverbs and adverb phrases add information to sentences. They add information about *manner*, that is, how something is done; *frequency* or how often; *time* and *date* or when; and *duration* of time or how long.

47   Negative Emphasis

Remember that negatives include phrases like *not one, not once, not until, never, never again, only rarely,* and *very seldom.* Negatives answer the question, *how often?* They are used at the beginning of a statement to express emphasis. Auxiliaries must agree with verbs and subjects.

negative	auxiliary	S	V	
Never	have	I	seen	so much snow

Avoid using a subject before the auxiliary in this pattern.

EXAMPLES

INCORRECT:	Never again they will stay in that hotel.
CORRECT:	Never again will they stay in that hotel.

INCORRECT:	Only rarely an accident has occurred.
CORRECT:	Only rarely has an accident occurred.

INCORRECT:	Very seldom a movie can hold my attention like this one.
CORRECT:	Very seldom can a movie hold my attention like this one.

INCORRECT:	Not one paper she has finished on time.
CORRECT:	Not one paper has she finished on time.

INCORRECT:	Not once Steve and Jan have invited us to their house.
CORRECT:	Not once have Steve and Jan invited us to their house.

EXERCISES

Part A: Choose the correct answer.

Not until the Triassic Period _____ .
  (A) the first primitive mammals did develop
  (B) did the first primitive mammals develop
  (C) did develop the first primitive mammals
  (D) the first primitive mammals develop

Part B: Chose the incorrect word or phrase and correct it.

Only rarely wins the same major league baseball team the World Series two years in a row.
  (A)   (B)   (C)   (D)

48   Duration—*For* and *Since*

Remember that *for* is used before a quantity of time. *For* expresses duration. *For* answers the question, *how long?* *Since* is used before a specific time. *Since* expresses duration too, but *since* answers the question, *beginning when?*

Remember that a quantity of time may be several days—a month, two years, etc. A specific time may be Wednesday, July, 1960, etc. You will notice that the structure *HAVE* and a participle is often used with adverbs of duration.

S	HAVE	participle		for	quantity of time
She	has	been	in the U.S.	for	six months

S	HAVE	participle		since	specific time
She	has	been	in the U.S.	since	June

Avoid using *for* before specific times. Avoid using *before* after HAVE and a participle.

EXAMPLES

INCORRECT: Mary has been on a diet since three weeks.
  CORRECT: Mary has been on a diet <u>for</u> <u>three weeks.</u>

INCORRECT: She has been living here before April.
  CORRECT: She has been living here <u>since</u> <u>April.</u>

INCORRECT: We haven't seen him since almost a year.
  CORRECT: We haven't seen him <u>for</u> <u>almost a year</u>.

INCORRECT: We have known each other before 1974.
  CORRECT: We have known each other <u>since</u> <u>1974</u>.

INCORRECT: He has studied English since five years.
  CORRECT: He has studied English <u>for</u> <u>five years</u>.

EXERCISES

Part A: Choose the correct answer.

Penguins, the most highly specialized of all aquatic birds, may live _____ twenty years.
  (A) before
  (B) since
  (C) for
  (D) from

Part B: Choose the incorrect word or phrase and correct it.

Because national statistics on crime have only been kept <u>for 1930,</u> <u>it</u> is not possible <u>to make</u> judg-
                                                              (A)   (B)   (C)

ments about crime <u>during the early years</u> of the nation.
                   (D)

Generalization—*As a Whole* and *Wholly*

Remember that *as a whole* means generally. *Wholly* means completely. *As a whole* is often used at the beginning of a sentence or a clause. *Wholly* is often used after the auxiliary or main verb.

generally as a whole	S	V	
As a whole	the news	is	correct

S	V	completely wholly	
The news	is	wholly	correct

Avoid using *wholly* instead of *as a whole* at the beginning of a sentence or clause to mean generally. Avoid using *as whole* instead of *as a whole*.

EXAMPLES

INCORRECT: Wholly, we are in agreement.
CORRECT: As a whole, we are in agreement.
(generally)

INCORRECT: The house and all of its contents was as a whole consumed by the fire.
CORRECT: The house and all of its contents was <u>wholly</u> consumed by the fire.
(completely)

INCORRECT: The teams are not rated equally, but, wholly, they are evenly matched.
CORRECT: The teams are not rated equally, but, <u>as a whole,</u> they are evenly matched.
(generally)

INCORRECT: Wholly, Dan's operation proved to be successful.
CORRECT: As a whole, Dan's operation proved to be successful.
(generally)

INCORRECT: As whole, people try to be helpful to tourists.
CORRECT: <u>As a whole,</u> people try to be helpful to tourists.
(generally)

EXERCISES

Part A: Choose the correct answer.

_____ the Gulf Stream is warmer than the ocean water surrounding it.
(A) Wholly
(B) Whole
(C) As a whole
(D) A whole as

Part B: Choose the incorrect word or phrase and correct it.

Although <u>there are</u> exceptions, <u>as whole,</u> the male of the bird species is <u>more</u> <u>brilliantly</u> colored.
        (A)   (B)   (C)   (D)

Problems with Sentences and Clauses

50   Sentences and Clauses

Remember that a main clause, also called an independent clause, can function as a separate sentence. A subordinate clause, also called a dependent clause, must be attached to a main clause. A dependent clause is often marked with the clause marker *that*.

SENTENCE		
Main Clause (Sentence)	Clause Marker - - - - - - - - - - - Dependent Clause	
We were glad	that	the box came

Avoid using the clause marker with dependent clauses as sentences. Avoid using the clause marker *that* with a sentence that has no dependent clause following it.

EXAMPLES

INCORRECT: Utensils and condiments that are found on the table by the door.
CORRECT: Utensils and condiments <u>are found</u> on the table by the door.

INCORRECT: During final exam week, that the library when opening all night.
CORRECT: During final exam week, <u>the library</u> <u>is open</u> all night.

INCORRECT: The weather that is very rainy this time of year.
CORRECT: <u>The weather</u> <u>is</u> very rainy this time of year.

INCORRECT: All of the dorms that are located on East Campus.
CORRECT: All of the <u>dorms</u> <u>are located</u> on East Campus.

INCORRECT: During our vacation, that we suspended the newspaper delivery.
CORRECT: During our vacation, <u>we</u> <u>suspended</u> the newspaper delivery.

EXERCISES

Part A: Choose the correct answer.

Of all the cities in Texas, _____.
   (A) that San Antonio is probably the most picturesque
   (B) San Antonio is probably the most picturesque
   (C) probably San Antonio the most picturesque
   (D) the most picturesque probably that San Antonio

Part B: Choose the incorrect word or phrase and correct it.

<u>Thunder</u> <u>that</u> is audible from distances as far away <u>as</u> ten <u>miles</u>.
 (A)   (B)   (C)   (D)

STYLE

Style is a general term that includes elements larger than a single grammatical pattern or structure. In most grammar books, *style* means *sentence structure*—that is, how the parts of a sentence relate to each other.

Some of the most important elements of style are summarized in this review section.

Problems with Point of View

Point of view means maintaining the correct sequence of verb tenses and time phrases in a sentence.

Point of View—Verbs

In all patterns, maintain a point of view, either present or past.
Avoid changing from present to past tense, or from past to present tense in the same sentence.

EXAMPLES

INCORRECT:	He was among the few who want to continue working on the project.
CORRECT:	He <u>is</u> among the few who <u>want</u> to continue working on the project.
	or
	He <u>was</u> among the few who <u>wanted</u> to continue working on the project.
INCORRECT:	It is an accepted custom for a man to open the door when he accompanied a woman.
CORRECT:	It <u>is</u> an accepted custom for a man to open the door when he <u>accompanies</u> a woman.
	or
	It <u>was</u> an accepted custom for a man to open the door when he <u>accompanied</u> a woman.
INCORRECT:	She closed the door and hurries away to class.
CORRECT:	She <u>closes</u> the door and <u>hurries</u> away to class.
	or
	She <u>closed</u> the door and <u>hurried</u> away to class.
INCORRECT:	We receive several applications a day and with them had been copies of transcripts and degrees.
CORRECT:	We <u>receive</u> several applications a day and with them <u>are</u> copies of transcripts and degrees.
	or
	We <u>received</u> several applications a day and with them <u>were</u> copies of transcripts and degrees.

INCORRECT: Mr. Davis tried to finish his research, but he found only part of the information that he needs.

CORRECT: Mr. Davis <u>tries</u> to finish his research, but he <u>finds</u> only part of the information that he <u>needs</u>.

or

Mr. Davis <u>tried</u> to finish his research, but he <u>found</u> only part of the information that he <u>needed</u>.

EXERCISES

Part A: Choose the correct answer.

The first transistor was basically a small chip made of germanium onto one surface of which two pointed wire contacts _____ side by side.

(A) are made
(B) made
(C) were made
(D) making

Part B: Choose the incorrect word or phrase and correct it.

<u>Because</u> early balloons were at the mercy of <u>shifting</u> winds, they <u>are</u> not considered a practical
  (A)   (B)   (C)

means of transportation <u>until the 1850s</u>.
                                  (D)

Point of View—Verbs and Adverbs

In all patterns, avoid using past adverbs with verbs in the present tense.

EXAMPLES

INCORRECT: Between one thing and another, Charles does not finish typing his paper last night.
CORRECT: Between one thing and another, Charles <u>did</u> not finish typing his paper <u>last</u> <u>night</u>.

INCORRECT: In 1990, according to statistics from the Bureau of Census, the population of the United States is 250,000,000.
CORRECT: <u>In 1990,</u> according to statistics from the Bureau of Census, the population of the United States <u>was</u> 250,000,000.

INCORRECT: We do not receive mail yesterday because it was a holiday.
CORRECT: We <u>did</u> not receive mail <u>yesterday</u> because it <u>was</u> a holiday.

INCORRECT: Mary does not finish her homework in time to go with us to the football game yesterday afternoon.
CORRECT: Mary <u>did</u> not finish her homework in time to go with us to the football game <u>yesterday</u> <u>afternoon</u>.

INCORRECT: Although there are only two hundred foreign students studying at State University in 1990, there are more than five hundred now.

CORRECT: Although there <u>were</u> only two hundred foreign students studying at State University <u>in 1990,</u> there are more than five hundred now.

EXERCISES

Part A: Choose the correct answer.

Iron _____ for weapons and tools in the Bronze Age following the Stone Age.
(A) is generally used
(B) generally used
(C) was generally used
(D) used generally

Part B: Choose the incorrect word or phrase and correct it.

<u>The Nineteenth Amendment</u> to the Constitution <u>gives</u> women the right <u>to vote</u> in <u>the elections</u> of
　　　　　　(A)　　　　　　　　　　　　　　(B)　　　　　　　　(C)　　　　(D)
1920.

Problems with Agreement

Agreement means selecting subjects that agree in person and number with verbs, and selecting pronouns that agree in person and number with reference nouns and other pronouns.

Agreement—Modified Subject and Verb

In all patterns, there must be agreement of subject and verb.
Avoid using a verb that agrees with the modifier of a subject instead of with the subject itself.

EXAMPLES

INCORRECT: His knowledge of languages and international relations aid him in his work.
CORRECT: His <u>knowledge</u> of languages and international relations <u>aids</u> him in his work.

INCORRECT: The facilities at the new research library, including an excellent microfilm file, is among the best in the country.
CORRECT: The <u>facilities</u> at the new research library, including an excellent microfilm file, <u>are</u> among the best in the country.

INCORRECT: All trade between the two countries were suspended pending negotiation of a new agreement.
CORRECT: All <u>trade</u> between the two countries <u>was</u> suspended pending negotiation of a new agreement.

INCORRECT:	The production of different kinds of artificial materials are essential to the conservation of our natural resources.
CORRECT:	The <u>production</u> of different kinds of artificial materials <u>is</u> essential to the conservation of our natural resources.

INCORRECT:	Since the shipment of supplies for our experiments were delayed, we will have to reschedule our work.
CORRECT:	Since the <u>shipment</u> of supplies for our experiments <u>was</u> delayed, we will have to reschedule our work.

EXERCISES

Part A: Choose the correct answer.

Groups of tissues, each with its own function, _____ in the human body.
    (A) it makes up the organs
    (B) make up the organs
    (C) they make up the organs
    (D) makes up the organs

Part B: Choose the incorrect word or phrase and correct it.

The Zoning Improvement Plan, <u>better known as</u> zip codes, <u>enable</u> postal clerks <u>to speed</u> the routing
                           (A)   (B)   (C)
of <u>an</u> ever-increasing volume of mail.
   (D)

4   Agreement—Subject with Appositive and Verb

Remember that there must be agreement of subject and verb. An appositive is a word or phrase that follows a noun and defines it. An appositive usually has a comma before it and a comma after it.

In all patterns, avoid using a verb that agrees with words in the appositive after a subject instead of with the subject itself.

EXAMPLES

INCORRECT:	The books, an English dictionary and a chemistry text, was on the shelf yesterday.
CORRECT:	<u>The books,</u> an English dictionary and a chemistry text, <u>were</u> on the shelf yesterday.

INCORRECT:	Three swimmers from our team, Paul, Ed, and Jim, is in competition for medals.
CORRECT:	<u>Three swimmers</u> from our team, Paul, Ed, and Jim, <u>are</u> in competition for medals.

INCORRECT:	Several pets, two dogs and a cat, needs to be taken care of while we are gone.
CORRECT:	<u>Several pets,</u> two dogs and a cat, <u>need</u> to be taken care of while we are gone.

INCORRECT:	State University, the largest of the state-supported schools, have more than 50,000 students on main campus.
CORRECT:	<u>State University,</u> the largest of the state-supported schools, <u>has</u> more than 50,000 students on main campus.

INCORRECT: This recipe, an old family secret, are an especially important part of our holiday celebrations.

CORRECT: <u>This recipe,</u> an old family secret, <u>is</u> an especially important part of our holiday celebrations.

EXERCISES

Part A: Choose the correct answer.

Cupid, one of the ancient Roman gods, _____.
(A) were a little winged child
(B) representing as a little winged child
(C) was represented as a little winged child
(D) a little winged child

Part B: Choose the incorrect word or phrase and correct it.

Columbus, Ohio, the capital of the state, <u>are</u> not only <u>the largest</u> city in Ohio <u>but also</u> a typical met-
                                  (A)   (B)   (C)
ropolitan area, often <u>used</u> in market research.
                (D)

5   Agreement—Verb-Subject Order

There and *here* introduce verb-subject order. The verb agrees with the subject following it.

there	V	S
There	are	the results of the election

here	V	S
Here	is	the result of the election

Avoid using a verb that does not agree with the subject.

EXAMPLES

INCORRECT: There was ten people in line already when we arrived.
CORRECT: There <u>were</u> <u>ten people</u> in line already when we arrived.

INCORRECT: There have been very little rain this summer.
CORRECT: There <u>has been</u> <u>very little rain</u> this summer.

INCORRECT: Here are their house.
CORRECT: Here <u>is</u> <u>their house</u>.

INCORRECT:	There has been several objections to the new policy.
CORRECT:	There <u>have been</u> <u>several objections</u> to the new policy.

INCORRECT:	I think that there were a problem.
CORRECT:	I think that there <u>was</u> <u>a problem</u>.

EXERCISES

Part A: Choose the correct answer.

In a suspension bridge _____ that carry one or more flexible cables firmly attached at each end.
   (A) there is two towers on it
   (B) there are two towers
   (C) two towers there are
   (D) towers there are two

Part B: Choose the incorrect word or phrase and correct it.

<u>There is</u> about 600 schools <u>in the United States</u> that <u>use</u> the Montessori method <u>to encourage</u> indi-
   (A)   (B)   (C)   (D)
vidual initiative.

6   Agreement—Noun and Pronoun

In all patterns, there must be agreement of noun and pronoun.
Avoid using a pronoun that does not agree in number with the noun to which it refers.

EXAMPLES

INCORRECT:	If you want to leave a message for Mr. and Mrs. Carlson, I will be glad to take them.
CORRECT:	If you want to leave <u>a message</u> for Mr. and Mrs. Carlson, I will be glad to take <u>it</u>.

INCORRECT:	Al is interested in mathematics and their applications.
CORRECT:	Al is interested in <u>mathematics</u> and <u>its</u> applications.

INCORRECT:	It is easier to talk about a problem than to resolve them.
CORRECT:	It is easier to talk about <u>a problem</u> than to resolve <u>it</u>.

INCORRECT:	Although their visas will expire in June, they can have it extended for three months.
CORRECT:	Although <u>their visas</u> will expire in June, they can have <u>them</u> extended for three months.

INCORRECT:	In spite of its small size, these cameras take very good pictures.
CORRECT:	In spite of <u>their</u> small size, <u>these cameras</u> take very good pictures.

EXERCISES

Part A: Choose the correct answer.

A college bookstore that sells used textbooks stocks _____ along with the new ones on the shelf under the course title.

- (A) its
- (B) their
- (C) a
- (D) them

Part B: Choose the incorrect word or phrase and correct it.

Magnesium, <u>the lightest</u> of our structural metals, has an important place <u>among</u> common
              (A)   (B)

engineering materials <u>because of</u> <u>their</u> weight.
                  (C)   (D)

7   Agreement—Subject and Possessive Pronouns

In all patterns, there must be agreement of subject pronoun and possessive pronouns that refer to the subject.

Subject Pronouns	Possessive Pronouns
I	*my*
you	*your*
he	*his*
she	*her*
it	*its*
we	*our*
you	*your*
they	*their*

Remember that *it* refers to a small baby. Avoid using *it's* instead of *its* as a possessive pronoun. *It's* means *it is*.

EXAMPLES

INCORRECT: Those of us who are over fifty years old should get their blood pressure checked regularly.

CORRECT: <u>Those of us</u> who are over fifty years old should get <u>our</u> blood pressure checked regularly.

INCORRECT: Our neighbors know that when they go on vacation, we will get its mail for them.

CORRECT: Our neighbors know that when <u>they</u> go on vacation, we will get <u>their</u> mail for them.

INCORRECT: A mother who works outside of the home has to prepare for emergencies when she cannot be there to take care of your sick child.

CORRECT: A mother who works outside of the home has to prepare for emergencies when <u>she</u> cannot be there to take care of <u>her</u> sick child.

INCORRECT: Wine tends to lose their flavor when it has not been properly sealed.

CORRECT: Wine tends to lose <u>its</u> flavor when <u>it</u> has not been properly sealed.

INCORRECT: Optional equipment on a car can add several hundred dollars to it's resale value when you trade it in.

CORRECT: Optional equipment on a car can add several hundred dollars to <u>its</u> resale value when you trade <u>it</u> in.

EXERCISES

Part A: Choose the correct answer.

The television programs we allow _____ to watch influence their learning.
(A) a children
(B) our children
(C) our child
(D) their childs

Part B: Choose the incorrect word or phrase and correct it.

Although maple trees are <u>among</u> the most colorful varieties <u>in the fall,</u> they lose <u>its</u> leaves

                             (A)   (B)   (C)

<u>sooner than</u> oak trees.
     (D)

Problems with Introductory Verbal Modifiers

Introductory verbal modifiers introduce and modify the subject and verb in the main clause of the sentence. They can be *-ing* forms, *-ed* forms, or infinitives. They are usually separated from the main clause by a comma.

Verbal Modifiers— *-ing* and *-ed* Forms

-ing forms and *-ed* forms may be used as verbals. Verbals function as modifiers.

An introductory verbal modifier with *-ing* or *-ed* should immediately precede the noun it modifies. Otherwise, the relationship between the noun and the modifier is unclear, and the sentence is illogical.

Avoid using a noun immediately after an introductory verbal phrase which may not be logically modified by the phrase.

EXAMPLES

INCORRECT: After graduating from City College, Professor Baker's studies were continued at State University, where he received his Ph.D. in English.

CORRECT: <u>After graduating</u> from City College, <u>Professor Baker</u> continued his studies at State University, where he received his Ph.D. in English.

INCORRECT:	Returning to her room, several pieces of jewelry were missing.
CORRECT:	<u>Returning</u> to her room, <u>she</u> found that several pieces of jewelry were missing.

INCORRECT:	Having been delayed by heavy traffic, it was not possible for her to arrive on time.
CORRECT:	<u>Having been delayed</u> by heavy traffic, <u>she</u> arrived late.

INCORRECT:	Accustomed to getting up early, the new schedule was not difficult for him to adjust to.
CORRECT:	<u>Accustomed to getting up</u> early, <u>he</u> had no difficulty adjusting to the new schedule.

INCORRECT:	After finishing his speech, the audience was invited to ask questions.
CORRECT:	<u>After finishing</u> his speech, <u>he</u> invited the audience to ask questions.

EXERCISES

Part A: Choose the correct answer.

_____ air traffic controllers guide planes through conditions of near zero visibility.
(A) They talk with pilots and watch their approach on radar,
(B) Talking with pilots and watching their approach on radar,
(C) Talk with pilots and watch their approach on radar,
(D) When they talked with pilots and watched their approach on radar,

Part B: Choose the incorrect word or phrase and correct it.

<u>Have designed</u> his own plane, *The Spirit of St. Louis,* Lindbergh <u>flew</u> from Roosevelt Field in New
  (A)   (B)
York across the ocean <u>to</u> Le Bourget Field <u>outside Paris</u>.
               (C)   (D)

PROBLEM 9

Verbal Modifiers—Infinitives of Purpose to Introduce Instructions

An infinitive that expresses purpose may be used as an introductory verbal modifier. Remember that a verb word follows the infinitive. The verb word expresses a manner to accomplish the purpose.

Avoid using a noun or *to* with an *-ing* form instead of the infinitive of purpose. Avoid using an *-ing* form or a passive construction after an introductory verbal modifier.

EXAMPLES

INCORRECT:	To protect yourself from dangerous exposure to the sun's rays, using a sunscreen.
CORRECT:	<u>To protect</u> yourself from dangerous exposure to the sun's rays, <u>use</u> a sunscreen.

INCORRECT:	Prepare for the TOEFL, study thirty minutes every day for several months.
CORRECT:	<u>To prepare</u> for the TOEFL, <u>study</u> thirty minutes every day for several months.

INCORRECT:	In order to take advantage of low air fares, to buy your tickets well in advance.
CORRECT:	In order <u>to take advantage</u> of low air fares, <u>buy</u> your tickets well in advance.

INCORRECT:	To taking action pictures, always use a high-speed film.
CORRECT:	<u>To take</u> action pictures, always <u>use</u> a high-speed film.

INCORRECT:	The send letters and packages from the United States overseas, use Global Mail or DHL Delivery.

CORRECT: <u>To send</u> letters and packages from the United States overseas, <u>use</u> Global Mail or
DHL Delivery.

EXERCISES

Part A: Choose the correct answer.

To relieve pressure in the skull, _____ into the blood.
(A) you will inject a strong solution of pure glucose
(B) to inject a strong solution of pure glucose
(C) a strong solution of glucose will inject purely
(D) inject a strong solution of pure glucose

Part B: Choose the incorrect word or phrase and correct it.

To estimate how much <u>it will cost</u> <u>to build</u> a home, <u>finding</u> the total square footage of the house and
                       (A)   (B)   (C)
multiply <u>by cost</u> per square foot.
        (D)

Problems with Parallel Structure

Parallel structure means expressing ideas of equal importance with the same grammatical
structures.

Parallel Structure—In a Series

In all patterns, ideas of equal importance should be expressed by the same grammatical structure.
Avoid expressing ideas in a series with different structures.

EXAMPLES

INCORRECT: Jane is young, enthusiastic, and she has talent.
CORRECT: Jane is <u>young, enthusiastic,</u> and <u>talented.</u>

INCORRECT: We learned to read the passages carefully and underlining the main ideas.
CORRECT: We learned <u>to read</u> the passages carefully and <u>to underline</u> the main ideas.

INCORRECT: The duties of the new secretary are to answer the telephone, to type letters, and bookkeeping.
CORRECT: The duties of the new secretary are <u>to answer</u> the telephone, <u>to type</u> letters, and <u>to do</u> the
bookkeeping.

INCORRECT: The patient's symptoms were fever, dizziness, and his head hurt.
CORRECT: The patient's symptoms were <u>fever, dizziness,</u> and <u>headaches</u>.

INCORRECT: Professor Williams enjoys teaching and to write.
CORRECT: Professor Williams enjoys <u>teaching</u> and <u>writing</u>.

EXERCISES

Part A: Choose the correct answer.

In a hot, sunny climate, man acclimatizes by eating less, drinking more liquids, wearing lighter clothing, and _____.

    (A) skin changes that darken

    (B) his skin may darken

    (C) experiencing a darkening of the skin

    (D) darkens his skin

Part B: Choose the incorrect word or phrase and correct it.

The aims of the European Economic Community <u>are</u> to eliminate tariffs between member countries;
                                                            (A)

<u>developing</u> common policies for agriculture, labor, welfare, trade, and <u>transportation</u>; and <u>to abolish</u>
  (B)   (C)   (D)

trusts and cartels.

11   Parallel Structure—After Correlative Conjunctions

Remember that ideas of equal importance are introduced by correlative conjunctions:

both...and
not only...but also

Avoid expressing ideas after correlative conjunctions with different structures.

EXAMPLES

INCORRECT: She is not only famous in the United States but also abroad.
 CORRECT: She is famous not only <u>in the United States</u> but also <u>abroad</u>.

INCORRECT: The exam tested both listening and to read.
 CORRECT: The exam tested both <u>listening</u> and <u>reading</u>.

INCORRECT: He is not only intelligent but also he is creative.
 CORRECT: He is not only <u>intelligent</u> but also <u>creative</u>.

INCORRECT: Flying is not only faster but also it is safer than traveling by car.
 CORRECT: Flying is not only <u>faster</u> but also <u>safer</u> than traveling by car.

INCORRECT: John registered for both Electrical Engineering 500 and to study Mathematics 390.
 CORRECT: John registered for both <u>Electrical Engineering</u> 500 and <u>Mathematics</u> 390.

<u>**EXERCISES**</u>

Part A: Choose the correct answer.

Both historically and _____, Ontario is the heartland of Canada.
  (A) in its geography
  (B) geographically
  (C) also its geography
  (D) geography

Part B: Choose the incorrect word or phrase and correct it.

The cacao bean <u>was cultivated</u> <u>by the Aztecs</u> not only to drink <u>but also</u> <u>currency</u>.
             (A)   (B)   (C)   (D)

Problems with Redundancy

Redundancy means using more words than necessary.

12 Redundancy—Unnecessary Phrases

In all patterns, prefer simple, direct sentences to complicated, indirect sentences. Find the Subject-Verb-Complement-Modifier, and determine whether the other words are useful or unnecessary.

S	V	C	M
Lee	learned	English	quickly

Avoid using an adjective with such phrases as *in character* or *in nature*.

Avoid using the redundant pattern instead of an adverb such as *quickly*.

in a	adjective	manner
in a	quick	manner

<u>**EXAMPLES**</u>

INCORRECT: The key officials who testified before the Senate committee responded in a manner that was evasive.
CORRECT: <u>The key officials</u> who testified before the Senate committee <u>responded</u> <u>evasively</u>.

INCORRECT: Mr. Davis knows a great deal in terms of the condition of the situation.
CORRECT: <u>Mr. Davis</u> <u>knows</u> <u>a great deal about the situation</u>.

INCORRECT: It was a problem which was very difficult in character and very delicate in nature.
CORRECT: <u>The problem</u> <u>was</u> <u>difficult and delicate</u>.

INCORRECT: The disease was very serious in the nature of it.
  CORRECT: <u>The disease was</u> very <u>serious.</u>

INCORRECT: Mary had always behaved in a responsible manner.
  CORRECT: <u>Mary had always behaved responsibly</u>.

EXERCISES

Part A: Choose the correct answer.

Waitresses and waiters who serve _____ deserve at least a 20 percent tip.
  (A) in a courteous manner
  (B) courteously
  (C) with courtesy in their manner
  (D) courteous

Part B: Choose the incorrect word or phrase and correct it.

Hummingbirds move <u>their</u> wings so <u>rapid a way</u> that they appear <u>to be hanging</u> <u>in the air</u>.
         (A)   (B)   (C)   (D)

13   Redundancy—Repetition of Words with the Same Meaning

In all patterns, avoid using words with the same meaning consecutively in a sentence.

EXAMPLES

INCORRECT: The money that I have is sufficient enough for my needs.
  CORRECT: The money that I have is <u>sufficient</u> for my needs.

INCORRECT: Bill asked the speaker to repeat again because he had not heard him the first time.
  CORRECT: Bill asked the speaker <u>to repeat</u> because he had not heard him the first time.

INCORRECT: The class advanced forward rapidly.
  CORRECT: The class <u>advanced</u> rapidly.

INCORRECT: She returned back to her hometown after she had finished her degree.
  CORRECT: She <u>returned</u> to her hometown after she had finished her degree.

INCORRECT: I am nearly almost finished with this chapter.
  CORRECT: I am <u>nearly</u> finished with this chapter.
                    or
             I am <u>almost</u> finished with this chapter.

EXERCISES

Part A: Choose the correct answer.

Famous for his _____ punctuation, typography, and language, Edward Estlin Cummings published his collected poems in 1954.

    (A) new innovations for
    (B) innovations in
    (C) newly approached
    (D) innovations newly approached in

Part B: Choose the incorrect word or phrase and correct it.

The idea of a submarine is <u>an old ancient one,</u> dating from <u>as early as</u> <u>the fifteenth century</u> when
                                (A)   (B)   (C)
Drebbel and Da Vinci <u>made</u> preliminary drawings.
                   (D)

14   Redundancy—Repetition of Noun by Pronoun

In all patterns, avoid using a noun and the pronoun that refers to it consecutively in a sentence. Avoid using a pronoun after the noun it refers to, and *that.*

EXAMPLES

INCORRECT: My teacher he said to listen to the news on the radio in order to practice listening comprehension.

CORRECT: <u>My teacher</u> <u>said</u> to listen to the news on the radio in order to practice listening comprehension.

INCORRECT: Steve he plans to go into business with his father.

CORRECT: <u>Steve</u> <u>plans</u> to go into business with his father.

INCORRECT: My sister she found a store that imported food from our country.

CORRECT: <u>My sister</u> <u>found</u> a store that imported food from our country.

INCORRECT: Hospitalization that it covers room, meals, nursing, and additional hospital expenses such as lab tests, X-rays, and medicine.

CORRECT: <u>Hospitalization</u> <u>covers</u> room, meals, nursing, and additional hospital expenses such as lab tests, X-rays, and medicine.

INCORRECT: Anne she wants to visit Washington, D.C., before she goes home.

CORRECT: <u>Anne</u> <u>wants</u> to visit Washington, D.C., before she goes home.

EXERCISES

Part A: Choose the correct answer.

A perennial is _____ for more than two years, such as trees and shrubs.
(A) any plant that it continues to grow
(B) any plant it continuing to grow
(C) any plant that continues to grow
(D) any plant continuing growth

Part B: Choose the incorrect word or phrase and correct it.

Advertising it provides most of the income for magazines, newspapers, radio, and television
        (A)   (B)   (C)
in the United States today.
      (D)

Problems with Word Choice

Word choice means choosing between similar words to express precise meanings.

15   Transitive and Intransitive Verbs—*Raise* and *Rise*

A transitive verb is a verb that takes a complement. An intransitive verb is a verb that does not take a complement.

The following pairs of verbs can be confusing. Remember that *raise* is a transitive verb; it takes a complement. *Rise* is an intransitive verb; it does not take a complement.

Transitive			Intransitive		
Verb word	*Past*	*Participle*	*Verb word*	*Past*	*Participle*
raise	raised	raised	rise	rose	risen

Remember that *to raise* means to move to a higher place or to cause to rise. *To rise* means to go up or to increase.

Raise and rise are also used as nouns. A *raise* means an increase in salary. A *rise* means an increase in price, worth, quantity, or degree.

S	RAISE	C	M
Heavy rain	raises	the water level of the reservoir	every spring
Heavy rain	raised	the water level of the reservoir	last week

S	RISE	C	M
The water level The water level	rises rose		when it rains every spring when it rained last week

EXAMPLES

INCORRECT: The cost of living has raised 3 percent in the past year.
  CORRECT: <u>The cost of living</u> <u>has risen</u> 3 percent in the past year.

INCORRECT: The flag is risen at dawn by an honor guard.
  CORRECT: <u>The flag</u> <u>is raised</u> at dawn <u>by an honor guard</u>.
             (An honor guard <u>raises</u> the flag.)

INCORRECT: Kay needs to rise her grades if she wants to get into graduate school.
  CORRECT: <u>Kay</u> <u>needs</u> <u>to raise</u> her grades if she wants to get into graduate school.

INCORRECT: The landlord has risen the rent.
  CORRECT: <u>The landlord</u> <u>has raised</u> the rent.

INCORRECT: The smoke that is raising from that oil refinery is black.
  CORRECT: The <u>smoke</u> that <u>is rising</u> from that oil refinery is black.

EXERCISES

Part A: Choose the correct answer.

The average elevation of the Himalayas is twenty thousand feet, and Mount Everest
_____ to more than twenty-nine thousand feet at its apex.

    (A) raises
    (B) rises
    (C) roses
    (D) arises

Part B: Choose the incorrect word or phrase and correct it.

When the temperature is <u>risen</u> to <u>the burning point</u> without a source of escape <u>for the heat</u>, sponta-
                (A)   (B)   (C)

neous combustion <u>occurs</u>.
      (D)

Transitive and Intransitive Verbs—*Lay* and *Lie*

Remember that *lay* is a transitive verb; it takes a complement. *Lie* is an intransitive verb; it does not
take a complement.

Transitive			**Intransitive**		
Verb word	*Past*	*Participle*	*Verb word*	*Past*	*Participle*
lay	laid	laid	lie	lay	lain

Remember that *to lay* means to put, to place, or to cause to lie. *To lie* means to recline or to occupy a place.

The past form of the verb *to lie* is *lay.*

S	LAY	C	M
The postman	lays	the mail	on the table every day
The postman	laid	the mail	on the table yesterday

S	LIE	C	M
He	lies		on the sofa to rest every day after work
He	lay		on the sofa to rest yesterday after work

EXAMPLES

INCORRECT: Her coat was laying on the chair.
CORRECT: Her coat was lying on the chair.

INCORRECT: I have lain your notebook on the table by the door so that you won't forget it.
CORRECT: I have laid your notebook on the table by the door so that you won't forget it.

INCORRECT: Key West lays off the coast of Florida.
CORRECT: Key West lies off the coast of Florida.

INCORRECT: Why don't you lay down for awhile?
CORRECT: Why don't you lie down for awhile?

INCORRECT: Linda always forgets where she lies her glasses.
CORRECT: Linda always forgets where she lays her glasses.

EXERCISES

Part A: Choose the correct answer.

The geographic position of North America, _____ in the early days of the European settlement.
    (A) laying between the Atlantic and the Pacific Oceans, isolating it
    (B) isolating it as it laid between the Atlantic and the Pacific Oceans
    (C) lying between the Atlantic and the Pacific Oceans, isolated it
    (D) isolating it between the Atlantic and the Pacific Oceans as it was layed

Part B: Choose the incorrect word or phrase and correct it.

Melanin, a pigment that <u>lays</u> under the skin, <u>is</u> responsible for skin color, including the varia-
                    (A)   (B)
tions that <u>occur</u> <u>among</u> different races.
      (C)   (D)

17 Transitive and Intransitive Verbs—*Set* and *Sit*

Remember that *set* is a transitive verb; it takes a complement. *Sit* is an intransitive verb; it does not take a complement.

Transitive			Intransitive		
Verb word	*Past*	*Participle*	*Verb word*	*Past*	*Participle*
set	set	set	sit	sat	sat

Remember that *to set* means to put, to place, or to cause to sit. *To sit* means to occupy a place on a chair or a flat surface.

S	SET	C	M
The students	set	the lab equipment	on the table every class
The students	set	the lab equipment	on the table last class period

S	SIT	C	M
The equipment	sits		on the table every class
The equipment	sat		on the table last class period

EXAMPLES

INCORRECT:	Please sit the telephone on the table by the bed.
CORRECT:	Please <u>set the telephone</u> on the table by the bed.

INCORRECT:	Won't you set down?
CORRECT:	Won't <u>you</u> <u>sit</u> down?

INCORRECT:	Their house sets on a hill overlooking a lake.
CORRECT:	Their <u>house</u> <u>sits</u> on a hill overlooking a lake.

INCORRECT:	Let's sit your suitcases out of the way.
CORRECT:	Let's <u>set your suitcases</u> out of the way.

INCORRECT:	Terry has set there waiting for us for almost an hour.
CORRECT:	<u>Terry</u> <u>has sat</u> there waiting for us for almost an hour.

EXERCISES

Part A: Choose the correct answer.

When Jacqueline Kennedy was first lady, she collected many beautiful antiques and _____ them among the original pieces in the White House.

    (A) sat
    (B) set
    (C) sit
    (D) sits

Part B: Choose the incorrect word or phrase and correct it.

Hyde Park, the family estate <u>of Franklin D. Roosevelt</u>, <u>sets</u> on top of a bluff <u>overlooking</u>
                            (A)   (B)   (C)
<u>the Hudson River.</u>
    (D)

PROBLEM 18   Similar Verbs—*Make* and *Do*

Verb word	Past	Participle	Verb word	Past	Participle
do	*did*	*done*	*make*	*made*	*made*

Remember that *to do* and *to make* have similar meanings, but *do* is often used before complements that describe work and chores. *To make* is often used before complements that are derived from verbs.

DO an assignment	MAKE an agreement	(to agree)
the dishes	an announcement	(to announce)
a favor	an attempt	(to attempt)
homework	a decision	(to decide)
the laundry	a discovery	(to discover)
a paper	an offer	(to offer)
research	a profit	(to profit)
work	a promise	(to promise)

S	DO	C	M
We	do	our homework	before class every day
We	did	our homework	before class yesterday

S	MAKE	C	M
We	make	an agreement	with each other every semester
We	made	an agreement	with each other last semester

EXAMPLES

INCORRECT:	I really don't mind making the homework for this class.
CORRECT:	I really don't mind <u>doing</u> the homework for this class.
INCORRECT:	Did you do a mistake?
CORRECT:	Did you <u>make</u> a mistake?
INCORRECT:	Please make me a favor.
CORRECT:	Please <u>do</u> me a favor.
INCORRECT:	Are they doing progress on the new road?
CORRECT:	Are they <u>making</u> <u>progress</u> on the new road?
INCORRECT:	Have you done any interesting discoveries while you were doing your research?
CORRECT:	Have you <u>made</u> any interesting <u>discoveries</u> while you were <u>doing</u> your <u>research?</u>

EXERCISES

Part A: Choose the correct answer.

The president usually _____ unless his press secretary approves it.
- (A) doesn't do a statement
- (B) doesn't make a statement
- (C) doesn't statement
- (D) no statement

Part B: Choose the incorrect word or phrase and correct it.

A <u>one hundred-horsepower tractor</u> <u>can</u> <u>make</u> the work of <u>a large number</u> of horses.
       (A)   (B) (C)   (D)

PROBLEM 19   Prepositional Idioms

Prefer these idioms	Avoid these errors
accede to	~~accede on, by~~
according to	~~according~~
approve of	~~approve for~~
ashamed of	~~ashamed with~~
bored with	~~bored of~~
capable of	~~capable to~~
compete with	~~compete together~~
composed of	~~composed from~~

Prefer these idioms	Avoid these errors
concerned with	concerned of
conscious of	conscious for
depend on	depend in, to
effects on	effects in
equal to	equal as
except for	excepting for
from now on	after now on
from time to time	for, when time to time
frown on	frown to
glance at, through	glance
incapable of	incapable to
in conflict	on conflict
inferior to	inferior with
in the habit of	in the habit to
in the near future	at the near future
knowledge of	knowledge on
near; next to	near to
of the opinion	in opinion
on top of	on top
opposite	opposite over
prior to	prior
regard to	regard of
related to	related with
respect for	respect of
responsible for	responsible
similar to	similar as
since	ever since
until	up until
with regard to	with regard of

EXAMPLES

INCORRECT: Excepting for the Gulf Coast region, most of the nation will have very pleasant weather tonight and tomorrow.

CORRECT: Except for the Gulf Coast region, most of the nation will have very pleasant weather tonight and tomorrow.

INCORRECT: In recent years, educators have become more concerned of bilingualism.
  CORRECT: In recent years, educators have become more <u>concerned with</u> bilingualism.

INCORRECT: He always does what he pleases, without regard of the rules and regulations.
  CORRECT: He always does what he pleases, without <u>regard to</u> the rules and regulations.

INCORRECT: The bank opposite over the university isn't open on Saturdays.
  CORRECT: The bank <u>opposite</u> the university isn't open on Saturdays.

INCORRECT: The customs of other countries are not inferior with those of our own country.
  CORRECT: The customs of other countries are not <u>inferior to</u> those of our own country.

EXERCISES

Part A: Choose the correct answer.

_____ discovery of insulin, it was not possible to treat diabetes.

(A) Prior to the
(B) Prior
(C) The prior
(D) To prior

Part B: Choose the incorrect word or phrase and correct it.

<u>The price</u> of gold <u>depends in</u> <u>several factors,</u> including supply and demand <u>in relation to</u> the value of
  (A)   (B)   (C)   (D)
the dollar.

20 Parts of Speech

Although it is usually very easy to identify the parts of speech, word families can be confusing. Word families are groups of words with similar meanings and spellings. Each word in the family is a different part of speech. For example, *agreement* is a noun; *agreeable* is an adjective; to *agree* is a verb.

The endings of words can help you identify the parts of speech.

Nouns Derived from Verbs

Verb	Ending	Noun
store	-age	storage
accept	-ance	acceptance
insist	-ence	insistence
agree	-ment	agreement
authorize	-sion/-tion	authorization

Nouns Derived from Adjectives

Adjective	Ending	Noun
convenient	-ce	convenience
redundant	-cy	redundancy
opposite	-tion	opposition
soft	-ness	softness
durable	-ty	durability

Adjectives Derived from Nouns

Noun	Ending	Adjective
possibility	-able/-ible	possible
intention	-al	intentional
distance	-ant	distant
frequency	-ent	frequent
juice	-y	juicy

Adverbs Derived from Adjectives

Adjective	Ending	Adverb
efficient	-ly	efficiently

EXAMPLES

INCORRECT: The agreeing is not legal unless everyone signs his name.
CORRECT: The <u>agreement</u> is not legal unless everyone signs his name.

INCORRECT: Even young children begin to show able in mathematics.
CORRECT: Even young children begin to show <u>ability</u> in mathematics.

INCORRECT: Arranging have been made for the funeral.
CORRECT: <u>Arrangements</u> have been made for the funeral.

INCORRECT: A free educating is guaranteed to every citizen.
CORRECT: A free <u>education</u> is guaranteed to every citizen.

INCORRECT: The develop of hybrids has increased yields.
CORRECT: The <u>development</u> of hybrids has increased yields.

EXERCISES

Part A: Choose the correct answer.

Unless protected areas are established, the Bengal tiger, the blue whale, and the California condor face _____ of extinction.

(A) possible
(B) the possibility
(C) to be possible
(D) possibly

Part B: Choose the incorrect word or phrase and correct it.

<u>Because</u> blood from different individuals may <u>different</u> in the type of antigen on the surface of the
  (A)   (B)

red cells and the type of antibody in the plasma, a dangerous reaction <u>can occur</u> between the donor
                                        (C)

<u>and</u> recipient in a blood transfusion.
(D)

TYPES OF QUESTIONS

Multiple-Choice Questions

All of the questions on both the Paper-Based TOEFL and the Computer-Based TOEFL are multiple-choice. There are no computer-assisted questions with special directions.

Although the structure questions in this book are numbered, and the answer choices are lettered A, B, C, and D, the same questions on the CD-ROM that is available to supplement the book are not numbered and lettered. You need the numbers and letters in the book to refer to the Answer Key, the Explanatory Answers, and the Transcript for the Listening section. On the CD-ROM, you can refer to other chapters by clicking on the screen. The questions on the CD-ROM are like those on the Computer-Based TOEFL.

Paper-Based TOEFL

1. If water is heated to 121 degrees F,
   _____ as steam.
   (A) it will boil and escape
   (B) it is boiling and escaping
   (C) it boil and escape
   (D) it would boil and escape

2. If <u>water</u> freezes, <u>it</u> <u>has become</u>
     (A)   (B)   (C)
   <u>a</u> solid.
   (D)

Computer-Based TOEFL

If water is heated to 121 degrees F,
_____ as steam.
  ● it will boil and escape
  ○ it is boiling and escaping
  ○ it boil and escape
  ○ it would boil and escape

If <u>water</u> freezes, <u>it</u> <u>has become</u>

<u>a</u> solid.

Answer Sheet

1. ● Ⓑ Ⓒ Ⓓ
2. Ⓐ Ⓑ ● Ⓓ

Computer Tutorial for the Structure Section

In order to succeed on the Computer-Based TOEFL, you must understand the computer vocabulary used for the test, and you must be familiar with the icons on the computer screens that you will see on the test. First, review the vocabulary that you learned in the Tutorial for Section 1 on page 75. The same vocabulary is used for Section 2. Then study the computer screens in this Tutorial.

Testing Tools: Review of Vocabulary, Icons, and Keys

The following words are from the list of general vocabulary for the Computer-Based TOEFL introduced in the previous chapter. Using the word list, fill in the blanks in the ten sentences.

Arrow	Help (Question mark)	Next
Click	Icon	Oval
Confirm Answer	Mouse	Time (Clock)
Dismiss Directions	Mouse Pad	

1. A _____ is a small control with a button on it.

2. A _____ is a rectangular pad where you move the mouse.

3. An _____ is a marker on the screen that shows you where you are moving on the computer.

4. To _____ is to depress the button on the mouse. You _____ the mouse to make changes on the screen.

5. An _____ is a small picture or word or phrase in a box. Move the arrow to the _____ to tell the computer what to do.

6. Click on _____ to remove the directions from the screen.

7. Click on an _____ to choose an answer to one of the multiple-choice questions.

8. Click on _____ , then click on _____ to see the next question.

9. Click on _____ to see a list of the icons and directions.

10. Click on _____ to hide or show the time you have left to finish the section of the test you are working on.

Computer Screens for Section 2

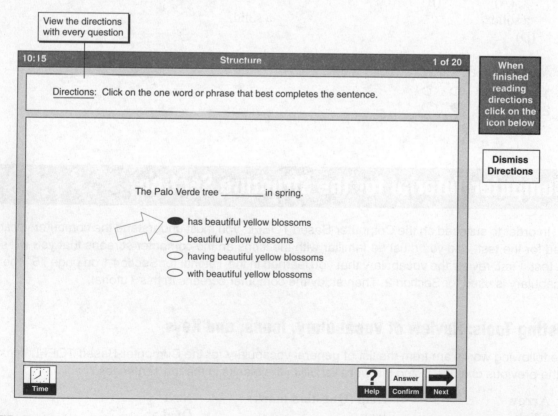

TIP: There are only two types of questions in Section 2. After you have read and understood the directions for both types of questions in this Tutorial, you will not need to read the top part of the screen every time.

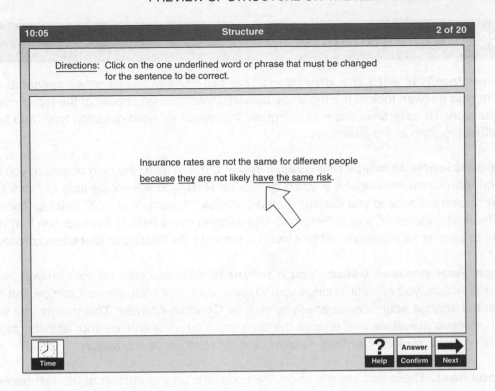

TIP: Be sure to click on **Next** before you click on **Answer Confirm.** If you do not click on these two icons in the correct order, the next question will not appear.

Simulations for Section 2

In order to prepare for the experience that you will have on the Computer-Based TOEFL, use the CD-ROM that supplements this book. Locate the Structure section on the Model Tests. The computer will simulate the Structure section on the Computer-Based TOEFL. These Model Tests are computer-assisted.

As part of your study plan, be sure to review all of the questions in all of the Model Tests. Use the Explanatory Answers on the CD-ROM or in Chapter 10. Refer to the Review of Structure on the CD-ROM or on pages 101–198 of this book. Finally, if you have the CD-ROM, take the Cumulative Model Test. This test is computer-adaptive, which means that the computer will select questions for you at your level of language proficiency.

If you do not have a computer, you can still simulate some of the features of the Computer-Based TOEFL. Section 2 in Model Tests 1–8 in Chapter 8 of this book presents both types of questions for the Structure section randomly. This is different from the Paper-Based TOEFL. You can become accustomed to making a quick decision about the kind of answer required—completion or correction.

Preview of Structure on the Next Generation TOEFL

There is no Structure Section on the Next Generation TOEFL. However, proficiency and accuracy in grammar are factored into the scores on the Speaking and Writing Sections.

Chapter 5 of this book is a grammar reference. The next edition of this book will include a new, revised Structure Chapter to help you identify the most common structure errors that students make when they speak and write in response to tasks on the Next Generation TOEFL.

Watch for *Barron's How to Prepare for the TOEFL, 12th Edition* to be published when the Next Generation TOEFL is introduced.

Advice for the Structure Section

Become familiar with the directions. The two types of questions will appear at random. If you forget how to answer, look at the top of the screen. Directions will appear at the top of every screen for each question. To save time, learn to recognize the format for each question type, and be ready to respond without looking at the directions.

Move efficiently through the questions. In order to go to the next question, you must click on **Next** and then **Confirm Answer**. If you only click on **Next**, you will not be able to move to the next question. A screen will remind you to return to the previous question. You must enter an answer before you go to the next question. Click on **Return to Question** to move back to the question that you did not answer. Try to answer all questions without being referred to the **Return to Question** screen.

Change your answer before you confirm it. After you click on your answer and see the dark oval or dark box, you can still change your answer. Just click on a different choice. But remember that you cannot change your answer after you click on **Confirm Answer**. This means that you cannot go back to previous questions and change the answers. You must choose your answer, click on your choice, click on **Next**, click on **Confirm Answer**, and move to the next question.

Do your best. The computer will select the questions on this section of the test based on your responses. You will begin with questions that are considered of average difficulty. You will receive easier questions if you are not able to answer the average questions. You will receive more difficult questions if you are able to answer the average questions. You receive more points for the more difficult questions. Just do your best, and you will receive the most points for your level of structure ability.

Understand the Help screen. The **Help** screen has a question mark on it. It is mostly designed to repeat directions. Be careful. You can waste a lot of time on this screen. If you click on **Help** and you want to go back to the question you were answering, look at the box in the bottom right corner. Click on **Return to Where I Was**.

Get help from the test administrator. If you think that your computer is not performing correctly, notify one of the test administrators immediately. There should be several in the room. They cannot help you with the answers on the TOEFL, but they can help you use the computer. That is why they are there. Tell the administrator, "Excuse me. My computer won't _____ ." Show the administrator the problem on the computer.

Stay focused. There is only one test question on the screen at any time. Focus on it. If you need to rest your eyes or your neck muscles, don't look around at other people. Look down at your lap with your eyes closed. Then look up at the ceiling with your eyes closed. Then return to the question. Remember that you cannot return to previous questions, so give each question your full attention while it is on the screen. Then, get ready to focus on the next question.

Advice for Success

Perspective means "the way you view experiences." Have you heard the story about the teacup? Two people sit down at a table. There is only enough tea for one cup so they each have half a cup of tea to drink. One person looks at the cup and says, "Oh my, the cup is half empty." The other person looks at the cup and says, "Oh look, the cup is half full." Which kind of person are you?

At this point in your review, it is easy to become discouraged. However, if you choose the "half full" perspective, you will have more energy to continue your studies. Yes, there is certainly a lot to review. If you know half of the problems, you have a choice. You can say, "Oh my, I know only half of this." Instead you can say, "Oh look, I already know half of this!" You choose.

My advice is *believe in yourself*. Don't look at the long distance yet to travel. Celebrate the long distance that you have already traveled. Then you will have the energy and the courage to keep going.

REVIEW OF READING

Overview of the Reading Section

**QUICK COMPARISON—READING
PAPER-BASED TOEFL,
COMPUTER-BASED TOEFL, AND NEXT GENERATION TOEFL**

Paper-Based TOEFL	*Computer-Based TOEFL*	*Next Generation TOEFL*
There are five reading passages with an average of 10 questions after each passage.	There are three to six reading passages with an average of 6 to 10 questions after each passage.	There are three reading passages with an average of 12–13 questions after each passage.
The passages are about 250–300 words in length.	The passages are about 350–450 words in length.	The passages are about 700–800 words in length.
Everyone taking the TOEFL answers the same questions.	You will have the same questions as others who take the same form of the test.	You will answer the same questions as others who take the same form of the test.
There are no pictures or visual cues.	There may be pictures in the text and questions that refer to the content of the reading passage.	There may be pictures in the text and questions that refer to the content of the reading passage.
All of the questions are multiple-choice.	Most of the questions are multiple-choice, but some of the questions have special directions on the screen.	Most of the questions are multiple-choice, but some of the questions have special directions.
Every question has only one answer.	Some of the questions have two or more answers.	Some of the questions have two or more answers.
You answer on a paper Answer Sheet, filling in ovals marked Ⓐ, Ⓑ, Ⓒ, and Ⓓ.	You click on the screen in the oval that corresponds to the answer you have chosen, or you follow the directions on the screen.	You click on the screen in the oval that corresponds to the answer you have chosen, or you follow the directions on the screen.
You can return to previous passages and questions, erase, and change answers on your answer sheet.	You can return to previous passages and questions, change answers, and answer questions you have left blank.	You can return to previous questions, change answers, and answer questions you have left blank, but you cannot return to a previous passage.
There is NO glossary.	There is NO glossary.	There may be a glossary of technical terms.
You may not take notes.	You may not take notes.	You may take notes while you read.

Directions and Example for Reading Questions

The Reading Section of the TOEFL tests your ability to understand written English as it is presented in textbooks and other academic materials in North America. This section is included in the Paper-Based TOEFL, the Computer-Based TOEFL, and the Next Generation TOEFL. The section is different for each of the three TOEFL formats.

Paper-Based TOEFL (PBT)

The directions for the Paper-Based TOEFL are reprinted with the permission of Educational Testing Service (ETS) from the official *Information Bulletin* for the Supplemental Paper-Based TOEFL.

Section 3 — Reading Comprehension

This section is designed to measure your ability to read and understand short passages similar in topic and style to those that students are likely to encounter in North American universities and colleges. This section contains reading passages and questions about the passages.

Directions: In this section you will read several passages. Each one is followed by a number of questions about it. You are to choose the **one** best answer, (A), (B), (C), or (D), to each question. Then, on your answer sheet, find the number of the question and fill in the space that corresponds to the letter of the answer you have chosen.

Answer all questions about the information in a passage on the basis of what is **stated** or **implied** in that passage.

Read the following passage:

The railroad was not the first institution to impose regularity on society, or to draw attention to the importance of precise timekeeping. For as long as merchants have set out their wares at *Line* daybreak and communal festivities have been celebrated, people
(5) have been in rough agreement with their neighbors as to the time of day. The value of this tradition is today more apparent than ever. Were it not for public acceptance of a single yardstick of time, social life would be unbearably chaotic: the massive daily transfers of goods, services, and information would proceed in fits and
(10) starts; the very fabric of modern society would begin to unravel.

Example I   **Sample Answer**

What is the main idea of the passage?   Ⓐ Ⓑ ● Ⓓ

- (A) In modern society we must make more time for our neighbors.
- (B) The traditions of society are timeless.
- (C) An accepted way of measuring time is essential for the smooth functioning of society.
- (D) Society judges people by the times at which they conduct certain activities.

The main idea of the passage is that societies need to agree about how time is to be measured in order to function smoothly. Therefore, you should choose answer (C).

Example II   **Sample Answer**

In line 6, the phrase "this tradition" refers to   Ⓐ Ⓑ Ⓒ ●

- (A) the practice of starting the business day at dawn
- (B) friendly relations between neighbors
- (C) the railroad's reliance on time schedules
- (D) people's agreement on the measurement of time

The phrase "this tradition" refers to the preceding clause, "people have been in rough agreement with their neighbors as to the time of day." Therefore, you should choose answer (D).

Computer-Based TOEFL (CBT)

The directions for the Computer-Based TOEFL are reprinted with the permission of Educational Testing Service (ETS) from the official *Information Bulletin* for the Computer-Based TOEFL.

This section measures the ability to read and understand short passages similar in topic and style to those that students are likely to encounter in North American universities and colleges. This section contains reading passages and questions about the passages. There are several different types of questions in this section.

In the Reading section, you will first have the opportunity to read the passage.

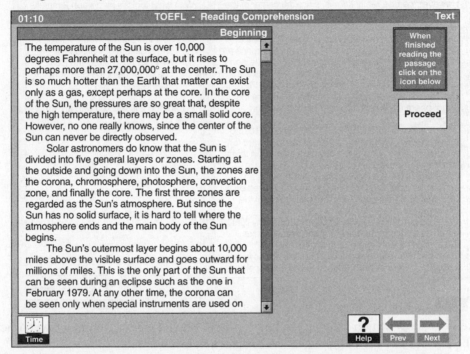

You will use the scroll bar to view the rest of the passage.

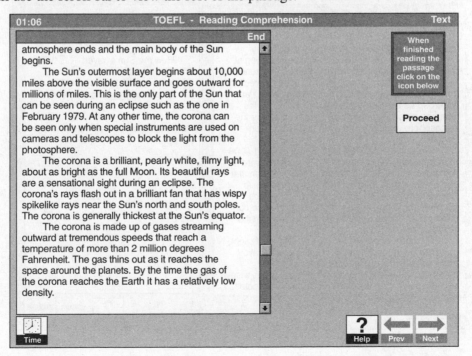

When you have finished reading the passage, you will use the mouse to click on **Proceed**. Then the questions about the passage will be presented. You are to choose the one best answer to each question. Answer all questions about the information in a passage on the basis of what is stated or implied in that passage.

Most of the questions will be multiple-choice questions. To answer these questions, you will click on a choice below the question. Here is an example.

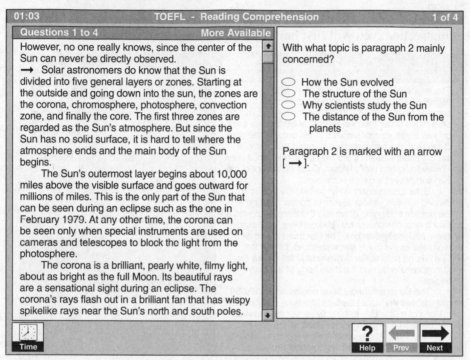

The oval darkens to show which answer you have chosen. To choose a different answer, click on a different oval. The correct answer is indicated on the screen below.

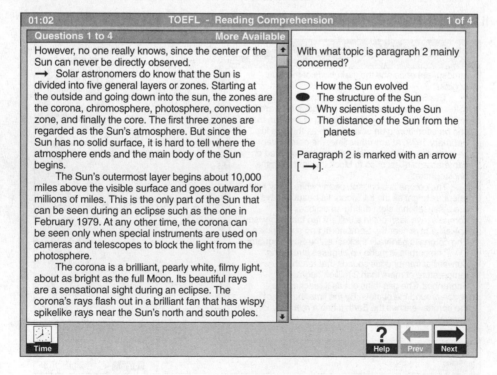

You will see the next question after you click on **Next**. To answer some questions, you will click on a word or phrase. Here is an example.

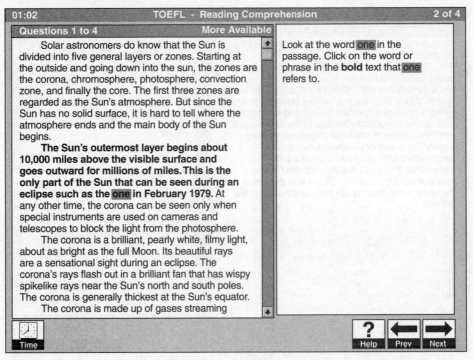

To answer, you can click on any part of the word or phrase in the passage. Your choice will darken to show which word you have chosen. The correct answer is indicated on the screen below.

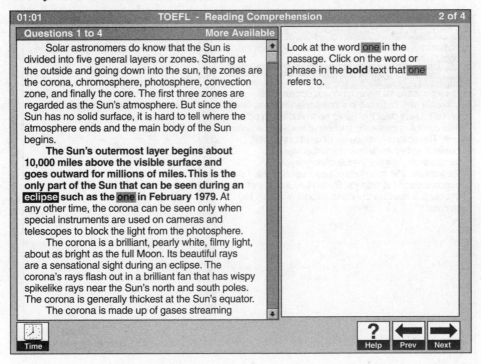

You will see the next question after you click on **Next**. To answer some questions, you will click on a sentence in the passage. Here is an example.

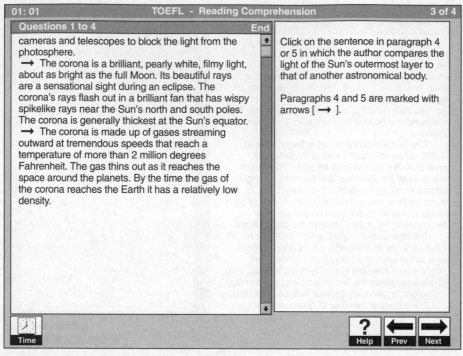

You can click on any part of the sentence in the passage. The sentence will darken to show which answer you have chosen. The correct answer is indicated below.

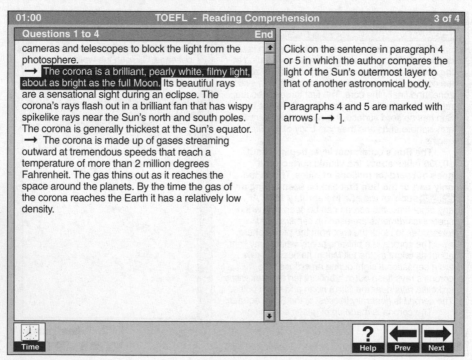

You will see the next question after you click on **Next**.

To answer some questions, you will click on a square to add a sentence to the passage.

Here is an example.

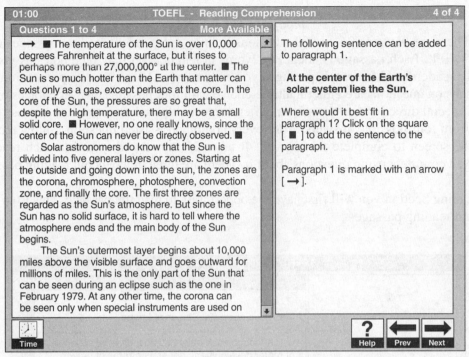

When you click on a square, the sentence will appear in the passage at the place you have chosen. You can see if this is the best place to add the sentence, and you can click on another square to change your answer.

The sentence will be added and shown in a dark box. The correct answer is indicated on the screen below.

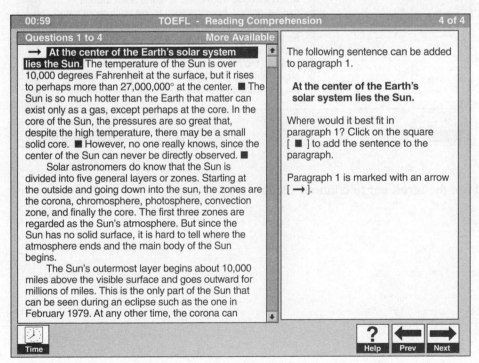

Next Generation TOEFL

There are two types of tasks included in the Reading Section: independent reading tasks and integrated reading tasks.

Independent Reading

Directions: There are between 36 and 39 questions in three independent reading passages on the Next Generation TOEFL. Each passage is about 800 words in length. You may take notes as you read. The topics are all academic. After each passage, you will answer 12 or 13 comprehension questions. The comprehension questions are either multiple-choice with four possible answer choices or computer-assisted with special directions on the screen. After every multiple-choice question, choose the best answer choice from four possible answers. After every computer-assisted question, follow the special directions on the screen to complete the answer. It takes 25 minutes to complete each reading and to answer 12 or 13 comprehension questions about it. There are three independent reading passages.

In the Reading Section you will first have the opportunity to read the passage. This is an example of an independent reading passage.

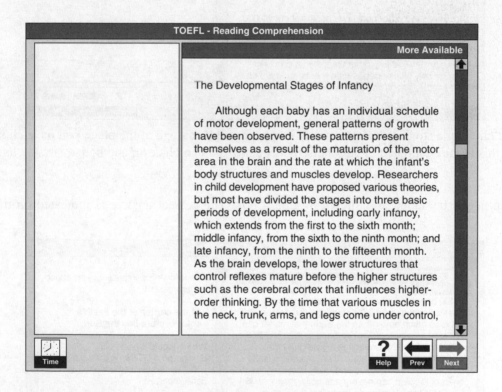

You will use the scroll bar to continue reading the passage.

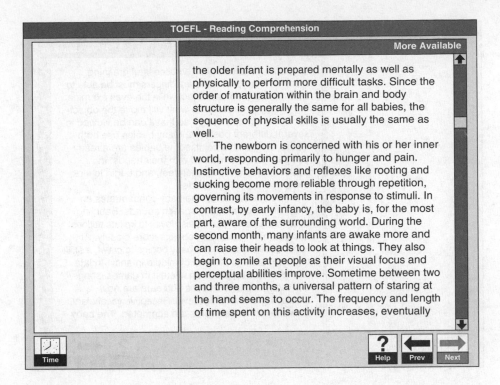

TOEFL - Reading Comprehension

More Available

the older infant is prepared mentally as well as physically to perform more difficult tasks. Since the order of maturation within the brain and body structure is generally the same for all babies, the sequence of physical skills is usually the same as well.

The newborn is concerned with his or her inner world, responding primarily to hunger and pain. Instinctive behaviors and reflexes like rooting and sucking become more reliable through repetition, governing its movements in response to stimuli. In contrast, by early infancy, the baby is, for the most part, aware of the surrounding world. During the second month, many infants are awake more and can raise their heads to look at things. They also begin to smile at people as their visual focus and perceptual abilities improve. Sometime between two and three months, a universal pattern of staring at the hand seems to occur. The frequency and length of time spent on this activity increases, eventually

Time   Help   Prev   Next

Continue to use the scroll bar to read the passage.

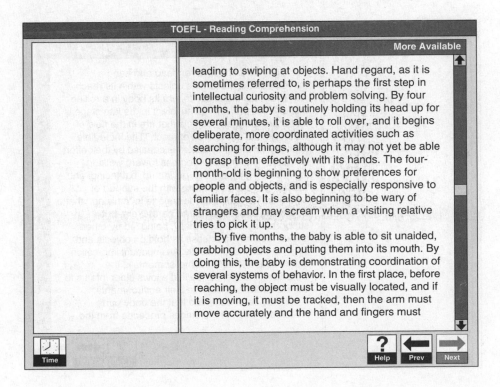

TOEFL - Reading Comprehension

More Available

leading to swiping at objects. Hand regard, as it is sometimes referred to, is perhaps the first step in intellectual curiosity and problem solving. By four months, the baby is routinely holding its head up for several minutes, it is able to roll over, and it begins deliberate, more coordinated activities such as searching for things, although it may not yet be able to grasp them effectively with its hands. The four-month-old is beginning to show preferences for people and objects, and is especially responsive to familiar faces. It is also beginning to be wary of strangers and may scream when a visiting relative tries to pick it up.

By five months, the baby is able to sit unaided, grabbing objects and putting them into its mouth. By doing this, the baby is demonstrating coordination of several systems of behavior. In the first place, before reaching, the object must be visually located, and if it is moving, it must be tracked, then the arm must move accurately and the hand and fingers must

Time   Help   Prev   Next

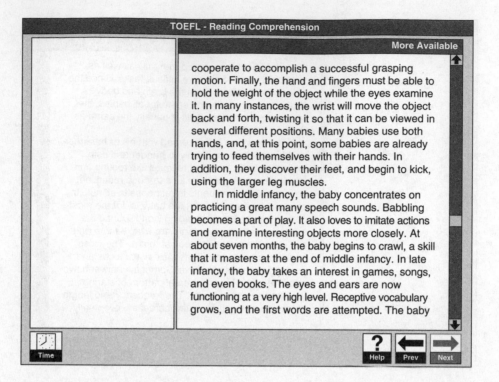

Continue to use the scroll bar to read the passage.

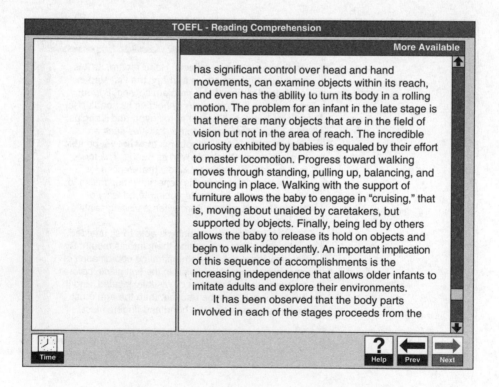

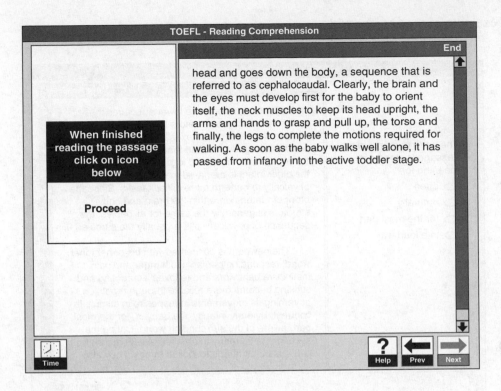

There may be a glossary to help you understand technical terms.

Glossary:
cephalocaudal: from the head to the tail
locomotion: ability to move from place to place

When you have finished reading the passage, you will click on **Proceed.** Then the questions about the passage will be presented. Follow the directions on the screen to answer the questions.

Here is an example of the passage with question references and questions:

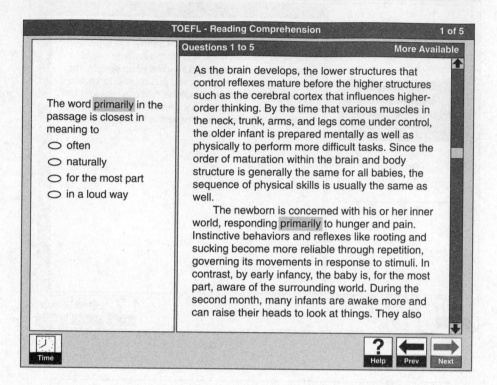

The correct answer is indicated below.

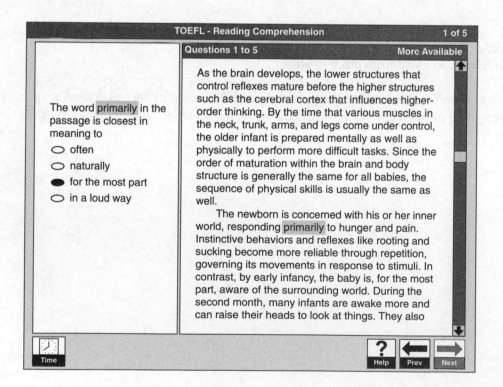

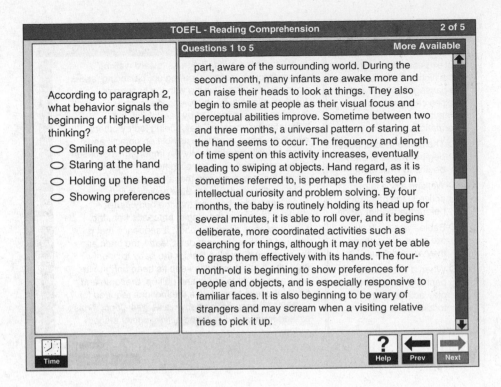

The correct answer is indicated below.

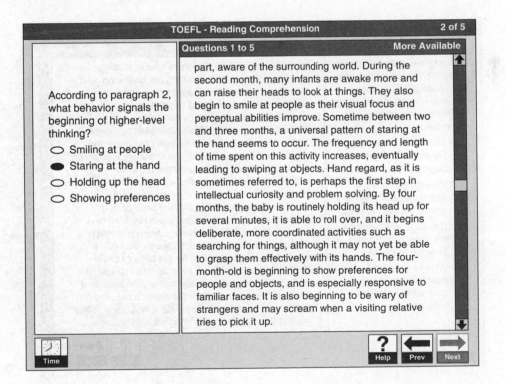

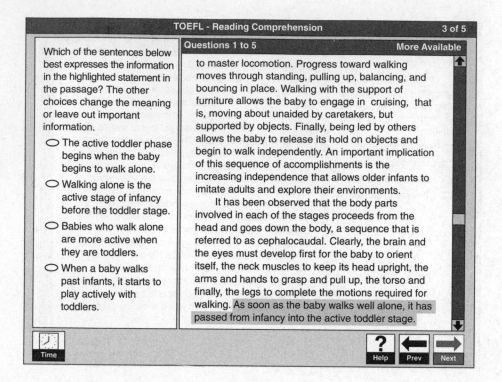

The correct answer is indicated below.

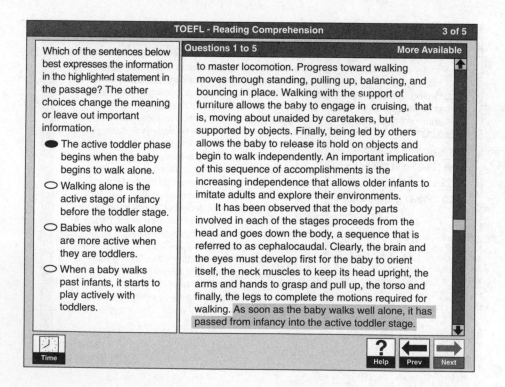

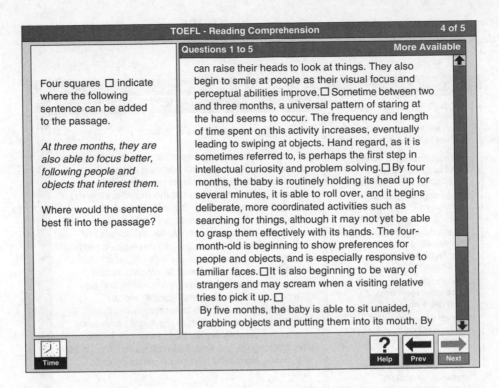

When you click on a square, the sentence will appear in the passage at the place you have chosen. The correct answer is indicated below.

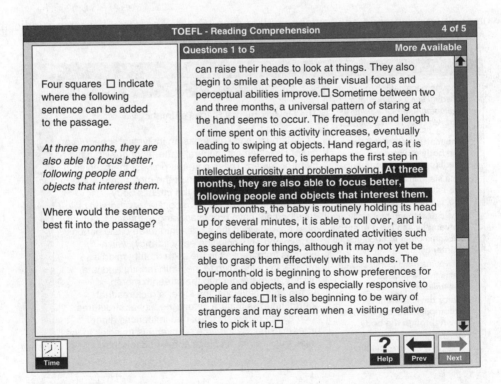

Complete a summary of the passage by choosing THREE answer choices that express the most important ideas.

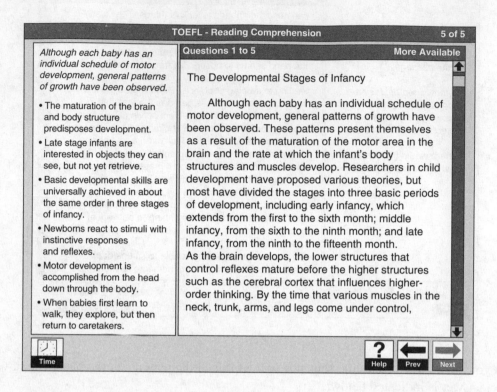

When you click on a sentence, the sentence will appear in bold. The correct answer is indicated below.

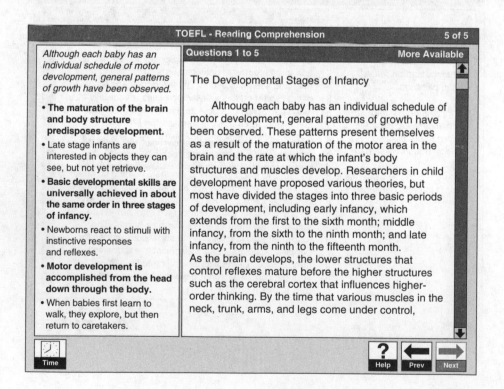

Integrated Reading

Directions: In the integrated reading tasks, you will read and respond to campus and textbook reading passages. You may take notes. After each reading, you will hear or see a question that requires you to respond by speaking or writing. Integrated examples are shown in the Directions and Examples for Speaking in Chapter 4 and the Directions and Examples for Writing in Chapter 7.

Review of Problems and Questions for the Reading Section

This Review can be used to prepare for the Paper-Based TOEFL, the Computer-Based TOEFL, and the Next Generation TOEFL. For the most part, the same types of problems are tested on all three formats. Most of the questions are multiple-choice.

Some of the questions on the Computer-Based TOEFL and the Next Generation TOEFL are computer-assisted. Although the computer-assisted questions in this book are numbered, and the answer choices are lettered A, B, C, and D, the same questions on the CD-ROM that supplements the book are not numbered and lettered. You need the numbers and letters in the book to refer to the Answer Key, the Explanatory Answers, and the Transcript for the Listening Section. On the CD-ROM, you can refer to other chapters by clicking on the screen. The computer-assisted questions have special directions on the screen.

TYPES OF PROBLEMS

Problems like those in this Review frequently appear on the Reading Section of the TOEFL.
To prepare for the Reading Section of the TOEFL, study the problems in this chapter.

Reading Comprehension

1 Previewing

2 Reading for Main Ideas

3 Using Contexts for Vocabulary

4 Scanning for Details

5 Making Inferences

6 Identifying Exceptions

7 Locating References

8 Referring to the Passage

9 Reading Faster

Previewing

Research shows that it is easier to understand what you are reading if you begin with a general idea of what the passage is about. Previewing helps you form a general idea of the topic in your mind.

To preview, read the first sentence of each paragraph and the last sentence of the passage. You should do this as quickly as possible. Remember, you are not reading for specific information, but for an impression of the *topic*.

EXERCISE

DIRECTIONS: Preview the following passage. Focus on the first sentence in each paragraph and the last sentence of the passage. Can you identify the topic? Check your answer using the key on page 485.

A black hole is a region of space created by the total gravitational collapse of matter. It is so intense that nothing, not even light or radiation, can escape. In other words, it is a one-way surface through which matter can fall inward but cannot emerge.

Some astronomers believe that a black hole may be formed when a large star collapses inward from its own weight. So long as they are emitting heat and light into space, stars support themselves against their own gravitational pull with the outward thermal pressure generated by heat from nuclear reactions deep in their interiors. But if a star eventually exhausts its nuclear fuel, then its unbalanced gravitational attraction could cause it to contract and collapse. Furthermore, it could begin to pull in surrounding matter, including nearby comets and planets, creating a black hole.

Reading for Main Ideas

By previewing, you can form a general idea of what a reading passage is about; that is, you identify the *topic.* By reading for main ideas, you identify the point of view of the author—that is, what the writer's *thesis* is. Specifically, what does the author propose to write about the topic? If you could reduce the reading to one sentence, what would it be?

Questions about the main idea can be worded in many ways. For example, the following questions are all asking for the same information: (1) What is the main idea? (2) What is the subject? (3) What is the topic? (4) What would be a good title?

EXERCISE

DIRECTIONS: The main idea usually occurs at the beginning of a reading passage. Look at the first two sentences in the following passage. Can you identify the main idea? What would be a good title for this passage? Check your answers using the key on page 485.

For more than a century, despite attacks by a few opposing scientists, Charles Darwin's theory of evolution by natural selection has stood firm. Now, however, some respected biologists are beginning to question whether the theory accounts for major developments such as the shift from water to land habitation. Clearly, evolution has not proceeded steadily but has progressed by radical advances. Recent research in molecular biology, particularly in the study of DNA, provides us with a new possibility. Not only environmental change but also genetic codes in the underlying structure of DNA could govern evolution.

3 Using Contexts for Vocabulary

Before you can use a context, you must understand what a context is. In English, a context is the combination of vocabulary and grammar that surrounds a word. Context can be a sentence or a paragraph or a passage. Context helps you make a general *prediction* about meaning. If you know the general meaning of a sentence, you also know the general meaning of the words in the sentence.

Making predictions from contexts is very important when you are reading a foreign language. In this way, you can read and understand the meaning of a passage without stopping to look up every new word in a dictionary. On an examination like the TOEFL, dictionaries are not permitted in the room.

EXERCISE

DIRECTIONS: Read the following passage, paying close attention to the underlined words. Can you understand their meanings from the context without using a dictionary? Check your answers using the key on page 485.

At the age of sixty-six, Harland Sanders had to underline auction off everything he owned in order to pay his debts. Once the successful underline proprietor of a large restaurant, Sanders saw his business suffer from the construction of a new freeway that bypassed his establishment and rerouted the traffic that had underline formerly passed.

With an income of only $105 a month in Social Security, he packed his car with a pressure cooker, some chickens, and sixty pounds of the seasoning that he had developed for frying chicken. He stopped at restaurants, where he cooked chicken for owners to underline sample. If they liked it, he offered to show them how to cook it. Then he sold them the seasoning and collected a underline royalty of four cents on each chicken they cooked. The rest is history. Eight years later, there were 638 Kentucky Fried Chicken franchises, and Colonel Sanders had sold his business again—this time for over two million dollars.

4 Scanning for Details

After reading a passage on the TOEFL, you will be expected to answer six to ten questions. Most of them are multiple-choice. First, read a question and find the important content words. Content words are usually nouns, verbs, or adjectives. They are called content words because they contain the content or meaning of a sentence.

Next, let your eyes travel quickly over the passage for the same content words or synonyms of the words. This is called *scanning.* By scanning, you can find a place in the reading passage where the answer to a question is found. Finally, read those specific sentences carefully and choose the answer that corresponds to the meaning of the sentences you have read.

EXERCISE

DIRECTIONS: First, read the following passage. Then, read the questions after the reading passage, and look for the content words. Finally, scan the passage for the same words or synonyms. Can you answer the questions? Check your answers using the key on pages 485–486.

To prepare for a career in engineering, a student must begin planning in high school. Mathematics and science should form the core curriculum. For example, in a school where sixteen credit hours are required for high school graduation, four should be in mathematics, one each in chemistry, biology, and physics. The remaining credits should include four in English and at least three in the humanities and social sciences. The average entering freshman in engineering should have achieved at least a 2.5 grade point average on a 4.0 scale in his or her high school. Although deficiencies can be corrected during the first year, the student who needs additional work should expect to spend five instead of four years to complete a degree.

1. What is the average grade point for an entering freshman in engineering?

2. When should a student begin planning for a career in engineering?

3. How can a student correct deficiencies in preparation?

4. How many credits should a student have in English?

5. How many credits are required for a high school diploma?

5 Making Inferences

Sometimes, in a reading passage, you will find a direct statement of fact. That is called evidence. But other times, you will not find a direct statement. Then you will need to use the evidence you have to make an inference. An *inference* is a logical conclusion based on evidence. It can be about the passage itself or about the author's viewpoint.

EXERCISE

DIRECTIONS: First, read the following passage. Then, read the questions after the passage, and make inferences. Can you find the evidence for your inference in the reading passage? Check your answers using the key on page 486.

When an acid is dissolved in water, the acid molecule divides into two parts, a hydrogen ion and another ion. An ion is an atom or a group of atoms that has an electrical charge. The charge can be either positive or negative. If hydrochloric acid is mixed with water, for example, it divides into hydrogen ions and chlorine ions.

A strong acid ionizes to a great extent, but a weak acid does not ionize so much. The strength of an acid, therefore, depends on how much it ionizes, not on how many hydrogen ions are produced. It is interesting that nitric acid and sulfuric acid become greatly ionized whereas boric acid and carbonic acid do not.

1. What kind of acid is sulfuric acid?

2. What kind of acid is boric acid?

6 Identifying Exceptions

After reading a passage on the TOEFL, you will be asked to select from four possible answers the one that is NOT mentioned in the reading.

Use your scanning skills to locate related words and phrases in the passage and the answer choices.

EXERCISE

DIRECTIONS: First, read the following passage. Then, read the question after the reading passage. Last, scan the passage again for related words and phrases. Try to eliminate three of the choices. Check your answer using the key on pages 486–487.

All music consists of two elements—expression and design. Expression is inexact and subjective and may be enjoyed in a personal or instinctive way. Design, on the other hand, is exact and must be analyzed objectively in order to be understood and appreciated. The folk song, for example, has a definite musical design that relies on simple repetition with a definite beginning and ending. A folk song generally consists of one stanza of music repeated for each stanza of verse.

Because of their communal, and usually uncertain origin, folk songs are often popular verse set to music. They are not always recorded and tend to be passed on in a kind of musical version of oral history. Each singer revises and perfects the song. In part as a consequence of this continuous revision process, most folk songs are almost perfect in their construction and design. A particular singer's interpretation of the folk song may provide an interesting expression, but the simple design that underlies the song itself is stable and enduring.

1. All of the following are true of a folk song EXCEPT
   (A) there is a clear start and finish
   (B) the origin is often not known
   (C) the design may change in the interpretation
   (D) simple repetition is characteristic of its design

7   Locating References

After reading a passage on the TOEFL, you will be asked to find the antecedent of a pronoun. An antecedent is a word or phrase to which a pronoun refers. Usually, you will be given a pronoun such as "it," "its," "them," or "their," and you will be asked to locate the reference word or phrase in the passage.

First, find the pronoun in the passage. Then read the sentence using the four answer choices in place of the pronoun. The meaning of the sentence in the context of the passage will not change when you substitute the correct antecedent.

EXERCISE

<u>DIRECTIONS</u>: First, find the pronoun in the following passage. Next, start reading several sentences before the sentence in which the pronoun is found, and continue reading several sentences after it. Then, substitute the words or phrases in the answer choices. Which one does not change the meaning of the sentence? Check your answer using the key on page 487.

> The National Road, also known as the Cumberland Road, was constructed in the early 1800s to provide transportation between the established commercial areas of the East and Northwest Territory. By 1818, the road had reached Wheeling, West Virginia, 130 miles from its point of origin in Cumberland, Maryland. The cost was a monumental thirteen thousand dollars per mile.
>
> Upon reaching the Ohio River, the National Road became one of the major trade routes to the western states and territories, providing Baltimore with a trade advantage over neighboring cities. In order to compete, New York state authorized the construction of the Erie Canal, and Philadelphia initiated a transportation plan to link it with Pittsburgh. Towns along the rivers, canals, and the new National Road became important trade centers.

1. The word its refers to
   (A) the Northwest Territory
   (B) 1818
   (C) the road
   (D) Wheeling, West Virginia

2. The word it refers to
   (A) plan
   (B) construction
   (C) canal
   (D) transportation

8   Referring to the Passage

After reading the passage on the TOEFL, you will be asked to find certain information in the passage, and identify it by line number or paragraph.

First, read the question. Then refer to the line numbers and paragraph numbers in the answer choices to scan for the information in the question.

EXERCISE

DIRECTIONS: First, read the following passage. Then, refer back to the passage. Can you find the correct reference? Check your answer using the key on page 487.

In September of 1929, traders experienced a lack of confidence in the stock market's ability to continue its phenomenal rise. Prices fell. For many inexperienced investors, the drop produced a panic. They had all their money tied up in the market, and they were pressed to sell before the prices fell even lower. Sell orders were coming in so fast that the ticker tape at the New York Stock Exchange could not accommodate all the transactions.

To try to reestablish confidence in the market, a powerful group of New York bankers agreed to pool their funds and purchase stock above current market values. Although the buy orders were minimal, they were counting on their reputations to restore confidence on the part of the smaller investors, thereby affecting the number of sell orders. On Thursday, October 24, Richard Whitney, the Vice President of the New York Stock Exchange and a broker for the J.P. Morgan Company, made the effort on their behalf. Initially, it appeared to have been successful, then, on the following Tuesday, the crash began again and accelerated. By 1932, stocks were worth only twenty percent of their value at the 1929 high. The results of the crash had extended into every aspect of the economy, causing a long and painful depression, referred to in American history as the Great Depression.

1. Where in the passage does the author refer to the reason for the stock market crash?

2. Where in the passage does the author suggest that there was a temporary recovery in the stock market?

Reading Faster

Read the following passage, using the skills you have learned. Preview, read for main ideas, and use contexts for vocabulary. To read faster, read phrases instead of words. Try to see an entire line of text when you focus your eyes on the passage. Scan for details and evidence. Make inferences.

The computer-based version of this reading passage is best viewed on the CD-ROM that supplements this book. Scroll through the passage, using the skills that you have learned. Check your answers on the screen. If you do not have a computer, then use the print version shown with the following computer-assisted questions.

> Jazz is an improvisational form of music that
> originated in the southern United States after the Civil War.
> Although its origins and history are somewhat vague, we know
> that it began as the musical expression of black people who
> had formerly been slaves, combining hymns, spirituals, and
> traditional work songs into something quite new. The style
> was a blend of the rhythms brought to America by the Africans
> *Line* who were imported as slave labor and the popular music of the
> (9) era that featured the ragtime piano. The term jazz itself is of
> obscure and possible nonmusical origin, but it was first used
> to describe this particular kind of musical expression in about 1915.
>
> A jazz band commonly includes four to twelve musicians
> with a relatively large proportion of the group in the rhythm section.
> Customarily, there are a drummer, a bass player, and a pianist.
> Often there is also a banjo player or guitarist. In traditional jazz,
> the clarinet, trumpet, and trombone carry the melody.
> In more modern jazz, the saxophone, violin, and flute may also
> be included in the melody section. Some jazz bands employ
> a blues singer. Most jazz is premised on the principle that
> an almost infinite number of variations can accommodate
> themselves to a progression of chords that can be repeated
> indefinitely to feature an improvisation by solo instruments or
> vocalists. For example, while the trumpet plays the melody,
> the clarinet might embellish and invent compatible melodies
> around the original theme. Such improvisation is a test of the
> jazz musician's skill and is referred to as tone color.
>
> Jazz first became popular outside the United States
> in the 1920s when jazz bands began to record, distribute, and
> even export their recordings to Europe. Since jazz is
> improvisational, it does not exist in the form of printed scores,
> and recorded performances were and still are the best way
> of preserving the music. A very basic library of recorded jazz
> would include work by such classic artists as Jelly Roll Morton,
> Louis Armstrong, Duke Ellington, Count Basie, and Billie Holiday.
> Theirs is probably America's most unique and most important
> contribution to the musical world, although a few
> contemporary artists are keeping the tradition alive.

TYPES OF QUESTIONS

Multiple-Choice Questions

Paper-Based TOEFL

1. Which of the following is the main topic of the passage?
   - Ⓐ A definition of jazz
   - Ⓑ Jazz musicians
   - Ⓒ Improvisation in jazz
   - Ⓓ Jazz bands

2. The new music of jazz was first heard
   - Ⓐ in Europe
   - Ⓑ in Africa
   - Ⓒ in South America
   - Ⓓ in North America

3. The word "blend" in the passage is closest in meaning to
   - Ⓐ mixture
   - Ⓑ rejection
   - Ⓒ imitation
   - Ⓓ variety

4. The author mentions all of the following as characteristics of jazz EXCEPT
   - Ⓐ a large number of percussion instruments
   - Ⓑ a printed score for the music
   - Ⓒ a melody played by the trumpet
   - Ⓓ a ragtime piano

Computer-Based TOEFL

Which of the following is the main topic of the passage?
   - ● A definition of jazz
   - ○ Jazz musicians
   - ○ Improvisation in jazz
   - ○ Jazz bands

The new music of jazz was first heard
   - ○ in Europe
   - ○ in Africa
   - ○ in South America
   - ● in North America

The word 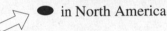 blend in the passage is closest in meaning to
   - ● mixture
   - ○ rejection
   - ○ imitation
   - ○ variety

The author mentions all of the following as characteristics of jazz EXCEPT
   - ○ a large number of percussion instruments
   - ● a printed score for the music
   - ○ a melody played by the trumpet
   - ○ a ragtime piano

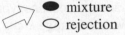

Answer Sheet

1. ● Ⓑ Ⓒ Ⓓ
2. Ⓐ Ⓑ Ⓒ ●
3. ● Ⓑ Ⓒ Ⓓ
4. Ⓐ ● Ⓒ Ⓓ

Computer-Assisted Questions

Location Questions

On some of the computer-assisted questions, you will be asked to locate information in the passage. These questions are like the multiple-choice questions on the Paper-Based TOEFL where you must locate information by identifying the line numbers in the passage. On the computer-assisted questions, you must click on the sentence or paragraph in the passage.

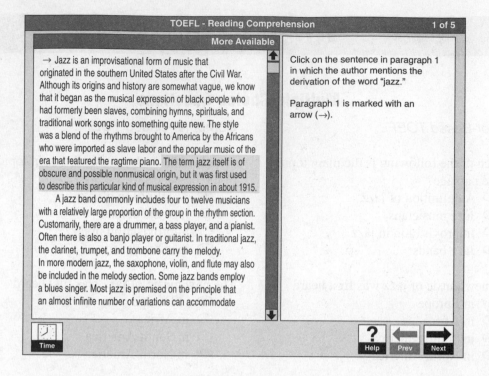

Synonyms

On some of the computer-assisted questions, you will be asked to locate synonyms in the reading passage. You must click on the word or phrase in the passage.

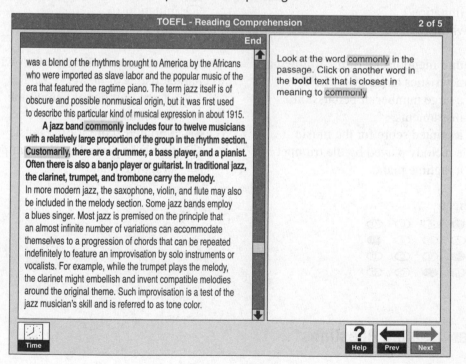

Paraphrased Sentences

On some of the computer-assisted questions, you will be asked to identify paraphrases of sentences in the passage.

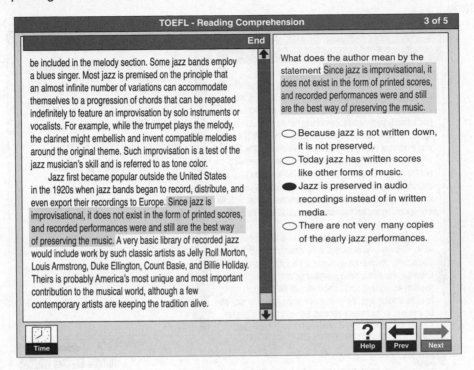

Reference Questions

On some of the computer-assisted questions, you will be asked to locate the nouns to which pronouns refer. These questions are like the multiple-choice questions on the Paper-Based TOEFL where you must choose the noun from four answer choices. On the computer-assisted questions, you must find the noun and click on it in the passage.

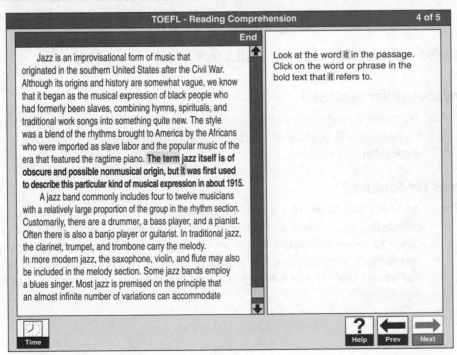

Sentence Insertion Questions

On some of the computer-assisted questions, you will be asked to locate the most logical place in the passage where a sentence could be inserted. You will have several options marked with a square (■) in the passage.

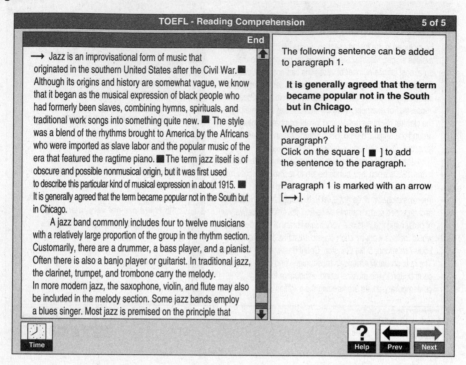

Computer Tutorial for the Reading Section

Testing Tools: Vocabulary, Icons, and Keys

Specific Vocabulary for Section 3

Scroll   To move through reading passages on a screen. If the reading passage is long, new sentences will appear at the bottom and sentences that you have already read will disappear at the top.

Specific Icons for Section 3

Scroll Bar   An *icon* used to move the reading passages on the screen so that you can see a long passage. First move the *arrow* to the top of the **scroll bar**; then hold the *mouse button* down to move the **scroll bar** from the beginning of the reading passage to the end. Remember, you can see the words *beginning*, *more available*, and *end* at the top of the **scroll bar**. These words show you the place in the passage that is displayed on the screen.

Proceed   An *icon* at the bottom of the screen with the reading passage. *Click* on **Proceed** after you have read the passage in order to see the first question. Remember, you cannot use **Proceed** until you have scrolled down to the end of the passage.

Previous   An *icon* at the bottom of the screen with the questions. *Click* on **Previous** to see the previous question.

Computer Screens for Section 3

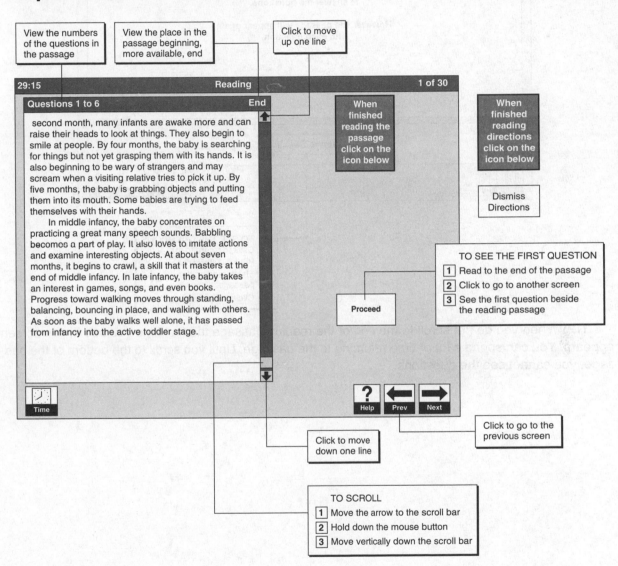

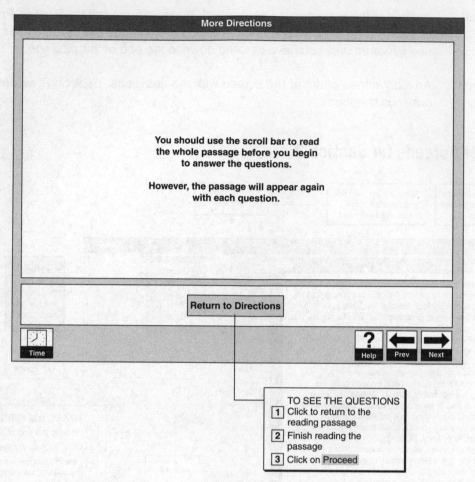

More Directions

You should use the scroll bar to read
the whole passage before you begin
to answer the questions.

However, the passage will appear again
with each question.

Return to Directions

Time   Help   Prev   Next

TO SEE THE QUESTIONS
1 Click to return to the
reading passage
2 Finish reading the
passage
3 Click on Proceed

TIP: When you do not scroll to the end of the reading passage the first time you see it, this screen appears. You can spend a lot of time returning to the passage. Until you scroll to the bottom of the passage, you cannot see the questions.

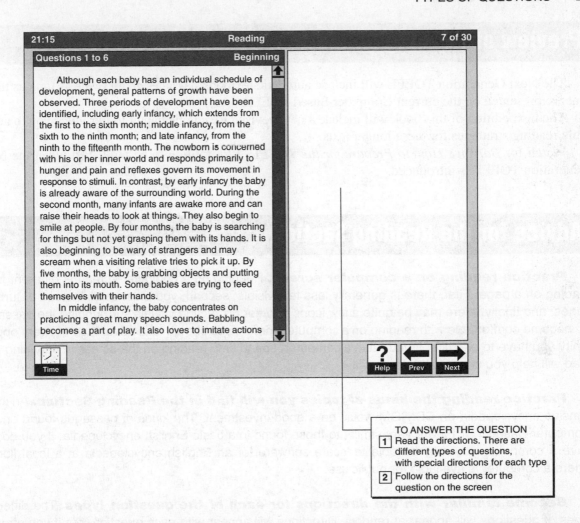

Questions 1 to 6   Beginning

Although each baby has an individual schedule of development, general patterns of growth have been observed. Three periods of development have been identified, including early infancy, which extends from the first to the sixth month; middle infancy, from the sixth to the ninth month; and late infancy, from the ninth to the fifteenth month. The newborn is concerned with his or her inner world and responds primarily to hunger and pain and reflexes govern its movement in response to stimuli. In contrast, by early infancy the baby is already aware of the surrounding world. During the second month, many infants are awake more and can raise their heads to look at things. They also begin to smile at people. By four months, the baby is searching for things but not yet grasping them with its hands. It is also beginning to be wary of strangers and may scream when a visiting relative tries to pick it up. By five months, the baby is grabbing objects and putting them into its mouth. Some babies are trying to feed themselves with their hands.

In middle infancy, the baby concentrates on practicing a great many speech sounds. Babbling becomes a part of play. It also loves to imitate actions

Time

? Help   ⬅ Prev   ➡ Next

TO ANSWER THE QUESTION
[1] Read the directions. There are different types of questions, with special directions for each type
[2] Follow the directions for the question on the screen

TIP: The answer to the question on the right side of the screen is always found in the part of the passage visible on the left side of the screen. You usually do not have to scroll through the passage to find the answer.

Simulations for Section 3

In order to prepare for the experience that you will have on the Computer-Based TOEFL, you can use the CD-ROM that supplements this book. Locate the Reading section on the Model Tests. The computer will simulate the Reading section on the Computer-Based TOEFL. These model tests are computer-assisted. The Reading section of the Computer-Based TOEFL is not computer-adaptive.

As part of your study plan, be sure to review all of the questions in all of the Model Tests. Use the Explanatory Answers on the CD-ROM or in Chapter 10.

If you do not have a computer, you can still simulate some of the features of the Computer-Based TOEFL. Section 3 of Model Tests 1–8 in Chapter 8 of this book is printed in two columns to give you the same kind of visual impression that you will have when you read from a computer screen. The on-screen directions for computer-assisted questions are also printed in the book.

Preview of Reading on the Next Generation TOEFL

The Next Generation TOEFL will include authentic textbook passages about twice as long as those that are presented on the current Computer-Based TOEFL.

The next edition of this book will include a new, revised Reading Chapter to introduce you to academic reading strategies for these longer texts.

Watch for *Barron's How to Prepare for the TOEFL, 12th Edition* to be published when the Next Generation TOEFL is introduced.

Advice for the Reading Section

Practice reading on a computer screen. Reading on a computer screen is different from reading on a page. First, there is generally less text visible; second, you must scroll instead of turning pages; and finally, there may be quite a few icons or other distracting visuals surrounding the passage. To become comfortable with reading on a computer screen, you should take advantage of every opportunity you have to practice. If you have a computer, spend time reading on the screen. Everything you read will help you improve this new skill.

Practice reading the kinds of topics you will find in the Reading Section. An inexpensive encyclopedia on CD-ROM would be a good investment. The kinds of passages found on the Computer-Based TOEFL are very similar to those found in a basic English encyclopedia. If you do not have a computer, you may be able to locate software for an English encyclopedia at a local library where a computer is available for public use.

Become familiar with the directions for each of the question types. The different types of questions will appear at random. Directions will appear with each question, but if you already recognize the type of question presented, and you are familiar with the directions, you will save time. The less time you have to spend reading directions, the more time you will have to read the passages.

Advice for Success

Why are you preparing for the TOEFL? What goal is motivating you to study and improve your score? Do you want to attend a university in the United States or Canada? Do you want to try for a scholarship from a sponsor in your country or region? Is the TOEFL required for graduation from your high school? Do you plan to apply for an assistantship at a graduate school? Do you need the score for a professional license in the United States?

Goals can be experienced as mental images. You can close your eyes and imagine everything, just like a movie. See yourself achieving your goal. Watch yourself as you attend school or practice your profession in your ideal environment. See other people congratulating you. Enjoy the success.

Understand that you cannot control reality with visualization. However, it does change your attitude, it helps you to focus, provides motivation, and reduces stress. Visualization is an excellent way to take a short break from studying.

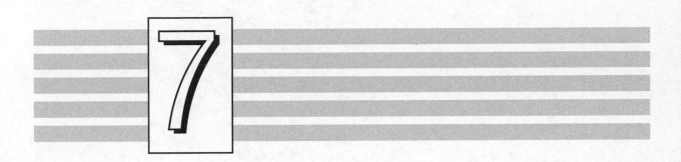

REVIEW OF WRITING

Overview of the Writing Section

**QUICK COMPARISON—WRITING
PAPER-BASED TOEFL,
COMPUTER-BASED TOEFL, AND NEXT GENERATION TOEFL**

Paper-Based TOEFL	*Computer-Based TOEFL*	*Next Generation TOEFL*
The essay, also called the Test of Written English (TWE), is offered five times each year. You must select a TOEFL test date when the TWE is scheduled if you need an essay score.	The essay is required as part of every TOEFL. You must write the essay as the last part of your TOEFL examination.	The Writing Section is required. It includes two essays.
When you register for the TOEFL on one of the dates when the TWE is offered, you are registered for the TWE at no additional cost.	When you register for the TOEFL, you are registered for the Writing Section at no additional cost.	When you register for the TOEFL, you are registered for the Writing Section at no additional cost.
There is only one topic for each essay.	There is only one topic for each essay.	There is only one topic for the independent writing task. A second topic is based on a lecture or a reading passage or both a lecture and a reading passage.
Everyone taking the TOEFL writes an essay about the same topic.	The computer selects a topic for you. It may not be the same topic that is selected for someone else taking the TOEFL that day.	Everyone taking the same form of the TOEFL will write about the same topics.
You do not know any of the topics for the essay before the test administration.	All of the topics for the essay are published in the *TOEFL Information Bulletin* for Computer-Based Testing free of charge from ETS. They are also listed on the ETS web site at *www.toefl.org*.	At this point, no writing topics have been published; however, the essay topics for the Computer-Based TOEFL on the ETS web site are good practice for the general-topic essay. Visit *www.toefl.org*.
Most of the topics ask you to agree or disagree with a statement or to express an opinion.	Most of the topics ask you to agree or disagree with a statement or to express an opinion.	The topic for the independent writing task asks you to agree or disagree with a statement or to express an opinion. The integrated task refers to topics from a lecture or a reading passage or both.
The topics are very general and do not require any specialized knowledge of the subject to answer them.	The topics are very general and do not require any specialized knowledge of the subject to answer them.	The independent topics are very general and do not require any specialized knowledge of the subject to answer them. Technical words are explained in the text or in a glossary for the integrated topics.

Paper-Based TOEFL	Computer-Based TOEFL	Next Generation TOEFL
You have 30 minutes to complete the essay.	You have 30 minutes to complete the essay.	You have 30 minutes to complete the independent writing task. You have 20 minutes to complete the writing sample that refers to a lecture or reading or both a lecture and a reading.
You handwrite your essay on paper provided in the test materials.	You can choose to handwrite your essay on paper or type it on the computer.	You should type your writing samples on the computer. If this is not possible, you can ask for special accommodations.
You have one page to organize your essay. This page is not graded. graded.	You have one page to organize your essay. This page is not graded.	You have paper to take notes and organize your writing. Your notes and outlines are not graded
Your essay will not be scored for neatness, but the readers must be able to understand what you have written.	Your essay will not be scored for neatness, but the readers must be able to understand what you have written.	Your writing will not be scored for neatness, but the readers must be able to understand what you have written.
You should write about 300 words, or three to five short paragraphs.	You should write about 300 words, or three to five short paragraphs.	You should write 300–350 words for the independent writing task, 200–250 words for the integrated writing sample.
A scale from 1 to 6 is used to grade the essay. The scale is explained on page 244.	A scale from 1 to 6 is used to grade the essay. The scale is explained on page 244.	A scale from 1 to 5 is planned to grade writing samples. Use the checklists on pages 246 and 249.
The score is reported separately from the TOEFL score. It is not included in the computation of the total TOEFL score and does not affect your score on the multiple-choice TOEFL.	The score is combined with the score on the Structure Section. It is factored in the section score at 50 percent.	The score is reported as a separate Writing Section score.

Directions and Examples for Writing Questions

The Writing Section of the TOEFL tests your ability to write in English on a variety of general and academic topics. This section is included in the Paper-Based TOEFL, the Computer-Based TOEFL, and the Next Generation TOEFL. The section is different for each of the three TOEFL formats.

Paper-Based TOEFL (PBT)

The Writing Section of the Paper-Based TOEFL is called the Test of Written English (TWE). There is one question on a general topic. You can use your personal experience and general knowledge to write an essay about the topic. The essay must be completed in 30 minutes. The score is calculated separately from the total score on the Paper-Based TOEFL.

The TWE test uses a variety of writing tasks that research has identified as typical of those required of college and university students. The following topics are examples from actual TWE tests. They are reprinted by permission of Educational Testing Service.

Topic One

Some people say that the best preparation for life is learning to work with others and be cooperative. Others take the opposite view and say that learning to be competitive is the best preparation. Discuss these positions, using specific examples of both. Tell which one you agree with and explain why.

Topic Two

Teachers should make learning enjoyable and fun for their students. Do you agree or disagree with the statement? Give reasons to support your opinion.

Computer-Based TOEFL

The directions for the Computer-Based TOEFL are reprinted with the permission of Educational Testing Service (ETS) from the official *Information Bulletin* for the Computer-Based TOEFL.

In this section, you will have an opportunity to demonstrate your ability to write in English. This includes the ability to generate and organize ideas, to support those ideas with examples or evidence, and to compose in standard written English in response to an assigned topic.

On the day of the test, an essay topic will be given to you. You will have 30 minutes to write your essay on that topic. Before the topic is presented, you must choose whether to type your essay on the computer or to handwrite your essay on the paper essay answer sheet provided.

Scratch paper will be given to you for making notes. However, only your response handwritten on the essay answer sheet or typed in the essay box on the computer will be scored.

The essay topic will be presented to you on the computer screen. The essay screen will be similar to this:

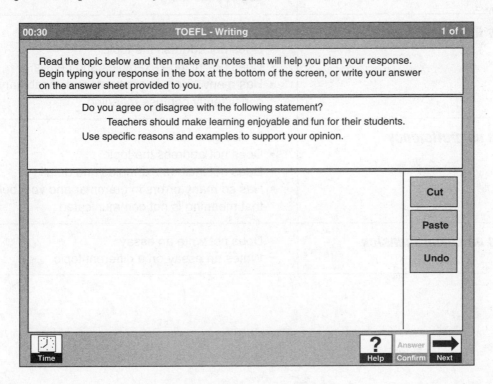

You can click on **Next** and **Confirm Answer** to end the Writing section at any time. At the end of 30 minutes the computer will automatically end the section. The score on the essay will be added to the score of the Structure section for a combined Structure/Essay score.

Scoring Scale for the Essay

The TWE and the Computer-Based TOEFL essay are scored on a scale of 1 to 6. A score between two points on the scale—5.5, 4.5, 3.5, 2.5, 1.5—can also be reported. The following guidelines are used by evaluators:

6 shows consistent proficiency	• Is well organized • Addresses the topic • Includes examples and details • Has few errors in grammar and vocabulary
5 shows inconsistent proficiency	• Is well organized • Addresses the topic • Includes fewer examples and details • Has more errors in grammar and vocabulary
4 shows minimal proficiency	• Is adequately organized • Addresses most of the topic • Includes some examples and details • Has errors in grammar and vocabulary that occasionally confuse meaning
3 shows developing proficiency	• Is inadequately organized • Addresses part of the topic • Includes few examples and details • Has many errors in grammar and vocabulary that confuse meaning
2 shows little proficiency	• Is disorganized • Does not address the topic • Does not include examples and details • Has many errors in grammar and vocabulary that consistently confuse meaning
1 shows no proficiency	• Is disorganized • Does not address the topic • Does not include examples and details • Has so many errors in grammar and vocabulary that meaning is not communicated
0 shows no comprehension	• Does not write an essay • Writes an essay on a different topic

Next Generation TOEFL

There are usually two questions in two parts on the Writing Section of the Next Generation TOEFL. The topics are both general and academic. There are two types of tasks included in the Writing Section: one independent writing task and one integrated writing task.

Independent Writing

Directions: In the independent writing task, you will read a question about a general topic. You can use your personal experience and common knowledge to answer. After each question, you have 30 minutes to prepare and write your essay. The essay should be about 300 words long.

This is an example of an independent writing question:

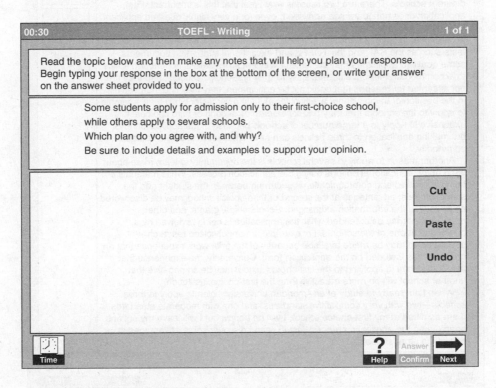

| 00:30 | TOEFL - Writing | 1 of 1 |

Read the topic below and then make any notes that will help you plan your response. Begin typing your response in the box at the bottom of the screen, or write your answer on the answer sheet provided to you.

Some students apply for admission only to their first-choice school, while others apply to several schools. Which plan do you agree with, and why? Be sure to include details and examples to support your opinion.

Cut

Paste

Undo

Time   Help   Answer Confirm   Next

You can click on **Next** and **Confirm Answer** to end the Writing Section at any time. At the end of 30 minutes the computer will automatically end the section.

Note: On the Next Generation TOEFL, the **Answer Confirm** button may appear as **OK** with a checkmark.

This is an example of an independent writing essay:

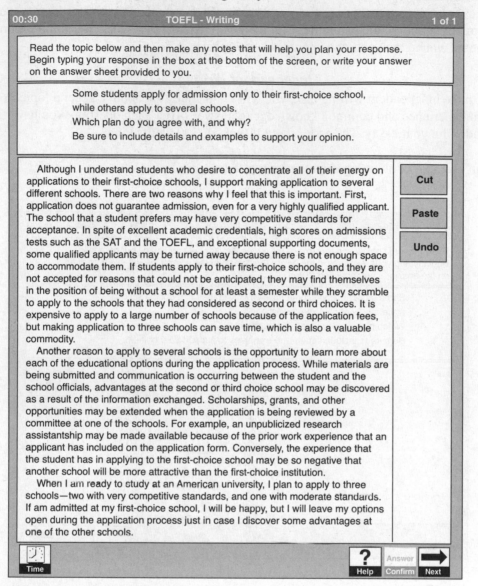

Checklist for Independent Writing

☑ The essay answers the topic question.

☑ The point of view or position is clear.

☑ The essay is direct and well-organized.

☑ The sentences are logically connected to each other.

☑ Details and examples support the main idea.

☑ The writer expresses complete thoughts.

☑ The meaning is easy for the reader to understand.

☑ A wide range of vocabulary is used.

☑ Various types of sentences are included.

☑ There are only minor errors in grammar and idioms.

☑ The general topic essay is within a range of 300–350 words.

Integrated Writing

Directions: In the integrated writing task, you will hear a lecture or read a passage, or listen to a lecture and read a related passage about an academic topic. You may take notes to prepare your answer. After each lecture or reading passage, you will read a question that requires you to answer by writing a short response. You will have 20 minutes to prepare and write the answer to the academic question. The answer should be 200–250 words long.

Here is an example of a reading passage for the integrated writing question:

The Birds of America was a work conceived and executed on a grand scale. It was finally published by subscription in eighty-seven parts between 1826 and 1838 in huge double-elephant folios containing 435 life-sized hand-colored engravings. The engravings were executed after John James Audubon's original watercolors by master engraver Robert Havell.

The plates represent 1,065 American birds, identified as 489 different species. The text that accompanies the plates was printed in a separate five-volume edition entitled *Ornithological Biography.* Based on field notes by Audubon, it was edited by the respected naturalist William MacGillvray.

Although the entire double-elephant folio edition was never republished, more than 100 plates were printed in a separate five-volume edition in 1860 after Audubon's death. Plates from either of the editions are considered collector's items and may be purchased separately through galleries and other art dealers. All of them were well-received upon publication and remain popular today, but the "Wild Turkey Cock" is perhaps his most requested plate.

Although he was a watercolorist, Audubon made copies of some of his birds in oil either to give to friends or to raise funds for his publications. His reputation, however, rests on the original watercolors of the bird series, more than four hundred of which may be found in the New York Historical Society. They continue to be greatly admired for their accurate detail and appreciated for their distinctive composition and presentation.

Audubon enjoys a unique place in American art. A genius who concentrated his talent on the representation of a highly specialized subject, he really cannot be compared with any other artist. His name has become synonymous with ornithology as well as watercolor. More importantly, the work has withstood the test of time.

This is an example of an integrated writing question:

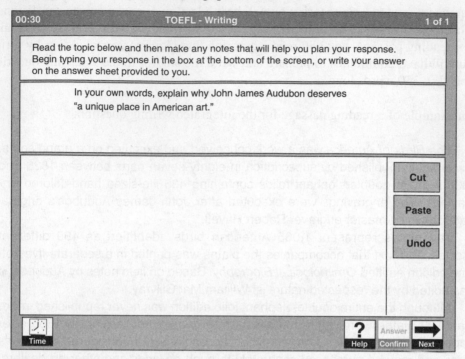

You can click on **Next** and **Confirm Answer** to end the Writing section at any time. At the end of 30 minutes the computer will automatically end the section.

This is an example of an integrated writing essay:

Notes on scratch paper:

Expertise as naturalist
    Specialized subject
    No comparison

Volume of work
    Five volumes
    435 life-sized engravings
    1,065 American birds

Timeless
    Still highly prized
    "Wild Turkey Cock"

Essay on computer:

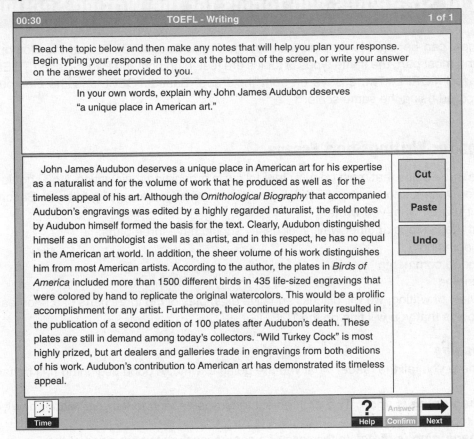

| 00:30 | TOEFL - Writing | 1 of 1 |

Read the topic below and then make any notes that will help you plan your response. Begin typing your response in the box at the bottom of the screen, or write your answer on the answer sheet provided to you.

In your own words, explain why John James Audubon deserves "a unique place in American art."

John James Audubon deserves a unique place in American art for his expertise as a naturalist and for the volume of work that he produced as well as for the timeless appeal of his art. Although the *Ornithological Biography* that accompanied Audubon's engravings was edited by a highly regarded naturalist, the field notes by Audubon himself formed the basis for the text. Clearly, Audubon distinguished himself as an ornithologist as well as an artist, and in this respect, he has no equal in the American art world. In addition, the sheer volume of his work distinguishes him from most American artists. According to the author, the plates in *Birds of America* included more than 1500 different birds in 435 life-sized engravings that were colored by hand to replicate the original watercolors. This would be a prolific accomplishment for any artist. Furthermore, their continued popularity resulted in the publication of a second edition of 100 plates after Audubon's death. These plates are still in demand among today's collectors. "Wild Turkey Cock" is most highly prized, but art dealers and galleries trade in engravings from both editions of his work. Audubon's contribution to American art has demonstrated its timeless appeal.

Cut

Paste

Undo

Time   Help   Confirm   Next

Checklist for Integrated Writing

☑ The essay answers the topic question.

☑ There are only minor inaccuracies in the content.

☑ The essay is direct and well-organized for the topic.

☑ The sentences are logically connected to each other.

☑ Details and examples support the main idea.

☑ The writer expresses complete thoughts.

☑ The meaning is easy for the reader to comprehend.

☑ A wide range of vocabulary is used.

☑ The writer paraphrases, using his or her own words.

☑ The writer credits the author with wording when necessary.

☑ There are only minor errors in grammar and idioms.

☑ The academic topic essay is within a range of 200–250 words.

Review of Strategies and Topics for the Writing Section

This Review can be used to prepare for both the Paper-Based TOEFL and the Computer-Based TOEFL. For the most part, the same types of topics are tested on both the Paper-Based TOEFL and the Computer-Based TOEFL. The essays on both the Paper-Based TOEFL and the Computer-Based TOEFL are scored using the same scale.

Three Steps for Writing Short Essays

There are three steps that most good writers follow in organizing their writing. You should use these steps when you write a short essay. First, tell your reader what you are going to write. Second, write it. Third, tell your reader what you wrote.

To look at these steps another way, your essay should have three parts:
1. A good beginning
2. Several good comments
3. A good ending

In this review of writing, we will discuss and give examples of the three parts of a short essay, using the types of topics that you will find on the TOEFL.

A Good Beginning

This is where you tell the reader what you are going to write. A good beginning has certain requirements.

A good beginning is short. Two or three sentences is enough to tell your reader how you plan to approach the topic.

A good beginning is direct. In the case of a comparison, state both sides of the argument in your first sentence. In a short composition, you don't have enough time for indirect approaches.

A good beginning is an outline. The second sentence usually outlines the organization. It gives the reader a general idea of your plan.

Good Comments

This is where you write.

Good comments include several points. A short essay may have between two and five points. Usually, the writer selects three. In the case of a comparison, three reasons is a standard argument.

Good comments are all related. All of the comments should relate to the general statement in the first sentence.

Good comments are logical. The points should be based on evidence. In the case of a comparison, the evidence should come from sources that can be cited, such as a television program that you have seen, an article that you have read in a magazine, a book that you have read, or a lecture that you have heard.

Good comments are not judgments. Opinions should be identified by phrases such as, "in my view," "in my opinion," or "it seems to me that." Furthermore, opinions should be based on evidence. Opinions that are not based on evidence are judgments. Judgments usually use words like "good" or "bad," "right" or "wrong." Judgments are not good comments.

A Good Ending

This is where you tell the reader what you wrote.

A good ending is a summary. The last sentence is similar to the first sentence. In a short essay, a good ending does not add new information. It does not introduce a new idea.

A good ending is not an apology. A good ending does not apologize for not having said enough, for not having had enough time, or for not using good English.

Example Essay

The following example essay would receive a score of 6. It is well organized, it addresses the topic, it includes examples and details, and it has some but not many errors in grammar and vocabulary.

Read and study this example essay before you complete the Model Tests.

Question:

Some students like to take distance-learning courses by computer. Other students prefer to study in traditional classroom settings with a teacher. Consider the advantages of both options, and make an argument for the way that students should organize their schedules.

Outline

Advantages distance-learning courses
- *Attend class at your convenience*
- *Complete assignments at own pace*
- *Repeat lectures*

Advantages traditional courses
- *Structured environment*
- *More personal relationship*
- *Immediate response to questions*
- *Study groups and friendships*

Example Essay

Both distance-learning classes and traditional classes provide important but different experiences for college students. On the one hand, there are many advantages to distance-learning courses. One of the most important benefits is the opportunity to

Line
(5) *attend class on your convenience. This is very important for students who hold full-time jobs since they can choose to take their classes on a schedule that allows them to continue working. Another advantage is the chance to complete assignments at your own pace. For students who can work more quick than their*

(10) *classmates, it is possible to earn more credits during the semester. A huge advantage to international students is the option of listen to lectures more than once.*

(15)
(20)

On the other hand, there are advantages to attending a traditional class. The structured environment is beneficial, especially for students who are not as highly motivating. In addition, it is more likely that you will develop a personal relationship with the teacher, an advantage not only for the course but also after the course when you need a recommendation. By seeing you and talking with you face-to-face, the teacher will remember you better. It is also easier to get an immediate response to questions because you only have to raise your hand instead sending e-mail and waiting for an answer. Last, the opportunity for study groups and friendships is different and more personal when you sit in the same room.

(25)
(30)
(35)

Given all the advantages of both types of courses, I think that students would be wise to register for distance-learning courses and traditional classroom courses during their college experiences. By participating in distance-learning courses, they can work independently in classes that may be more difficult for them, repeating the lectures on computer at convenient times. By attending traditional classes, they can get to know the teachers personally and will have good references when they need them. They will also make friends in the class. By sharing information with other students, they can organize their schedules for the following semester, chosing the best classes and including both distance-learning and traditional courses.

Evaluator's Comments

This writing sample is well-organized with a good topic sentence and good support statements. It addresses the question, and does not digress from the topic. There is a logical progression of ideas and excellent language proficiency, as evidenced by a variety of grammatical structures and appropriate vocabulary. There are only a few grammatical errors that have been corrected below:

Line 5	at your convenience
Line 9	more quickly
Line 11	the option of listening
Line 15	motivated
Line 21	instead of
Line 35	choosing

SCORE: 6

Computer Tutorial for the Writing Section

Testing Tools: Vocabulary, Icons, and Keys

Specific Vocabulary for the Essay

Text All printed material on the screen. **Text** can refer to a word, a sentence, a paragraph, several paragraphs, or an essay.

Cursor The line that shows you where you can begin typing. When you move the *mouse,* the **cursor** appears. You can move the **cursor** on your essay by moving the *mouse* on your *mouse pad.*

Blinking Flashing on and off. The *cursor* is usually **blinking** to help you see it.

Highlight To select *text* in your essay that you want to edit. To **highlight**, move the *cursor* to the beginning of the place in your essay that you want to change. Hold down the mouse button and move to the end of the place in your essay that you want to change. Release the mouse button. The **highlighted** *text* should be shaded.

Keys The individual buttons on the keyboard used for typing and editing your essay.

Keys for the Essay

Arrow Keys Keys that let you move around in your essay. There is an **up arrow, down arrow, left arrow,** and **right arrow**. They are found between the letters and the numbers on the keyboard. Use the **arrow keys** to move up, down, left, or right.

Page Up, Keys that let you see your essay if it is longer than the screen. The **Page Up** and
Page Down **Page Down** keys are above the *arrow keys* on the keyboard. Use **Page Up** to scroll to the beginning of your essay. Use **Page Down** to scroll to the end of your essay.

Backspace A key that moves you back one space at a time. Use the **Backspace** key to erase *text* from right to left.

Space Bar The long key at the bottom of the keyboard. Use the **Space Bar** two or three times to indent a paragraph. Remember, the *Tab* key does not function on your keyboard.

Icons for the Essay

Cut An example of an *icon*. After you *highlight* the text you want to delete or move, click on **Cut**. The text will disappear. Use the **Cut** icon to delete text or as the first step in moving text.

Paste An example of an *icon*. After you *cut* text, you can move the *cursor* to the place in the essay where you want to insert the text, and click on **Paste**. The text you *highlighted* will appear. Use the **Paste** icon as the second step in moving text.

Undo   An example of an *icon*. It lets you change your mind. For example, if you move a sentence, and then you want to move it back to the original place in your essay, click on **Undo**. **Undo** will return whatever you did last back to the way it looked before you made the change. Remember, **Undo** will only return your last change, not several changes.

Keyboard for the Essay

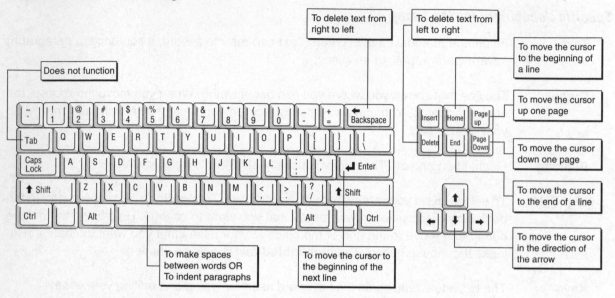

TIP: If you click the mouse, you can delete text. You may even delete your essay! If this happens, click on **Undo** immediately.

Computer Screen for the Essay

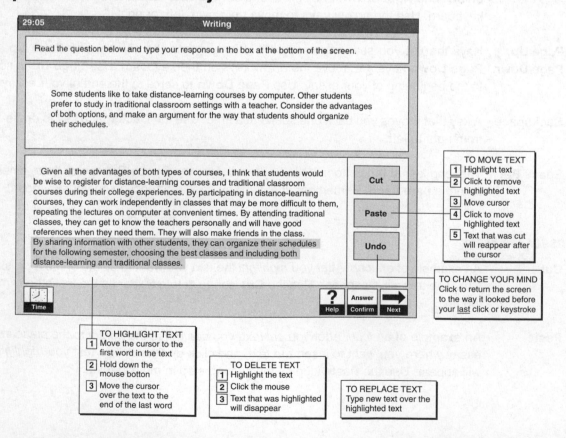

TIP: Be sure that you have completed the essay to your satisfaction before you click on **Answer Confirm.** After you click on **Answer Confirm**, you cannot continue writing or editing your essay.

Simulations for the Essay

In order to simulate the experience that you will have on the Computer-Based TOEFL, type the Model Test essays using the word processing program on the CD-ROM that supplements this book. If you do not have a computer, handwrite the Model Test essays on paper. Be sure to complete your essay in thirty minutes.

As part of your study plan, it is a good idea to have an English teacher score your essays using the guidelines on page 244 of this book.

Preview of Writing on the Next Generation TOEFL

The Next Generation TOEFL will include content essays as well as personal opinion topics like those on the Computer-Based TOEFL and the Test of Written English (TWE). Summarizing an academic lecture or a textbook passage is the skill you will need to develop in order to respond to the new content-based writing tasks on the Next Generation TOEFL.

The next edition of this book will include a new, revised Writing Chapter to help you improve this important skill.

Watch for *Barron's How to Prepare for the TOEFL, 12th Edition* to be published when the Next Generation TOEFL is introduced.

Advice for the Writing Section

Become familiar with the writing topics. All of the topics from the official TOEFL Writing Section are listed in the *TOEFL Information Bulletin* for Computer-Based Testing, available free from Educational Testing Service. Read through the questions and think about how you would respond to each of the topics. Since most of them require you to state an opinion, it is helpful to form a general opinion on each topic.

Decide whether you will handwrite or type your essay. The word processing program for the computer is very simple. If you know how to use Windows, it should be easy for you to adjust. But if you feel uncomfortable using the computer to write the essay, you may choose to handwrite it. By making your decision before you take the TOEFL, you will not waste time thinking about the way you will complete your test. You can use every minute to organize and write the essay.

Write on the topic you are assigned. If you write on a topic other than the one you have been assigned, your test will not be scored.

Get help from the test administrator. If you are having a problem with the word processing program, notify one of the test administrators immediately. There should be several in the room. They cannot help you with the answers on the TOEFL, but they can help you use the computer. That is why they are there. Tell the administrator, "Excuse me. I am trying to _____. What should I do?"

Advice for Success

Supportive people in our lives help us to do our best and be our best. Negative people steal our energy and bring us down with them. If negative people like that are in your life, you may not be able to avoid them completely, but you should consider spending less time with them, at least until you achieve your goal. You can spend the additional time with positive, supportive people who encourage you and energize you.

If you have even one negative person in your study group, he or she will affect the progress of the entire group. If you continue to associate with negative people, they will make it more difficult for you to act on the advice for success in this book. Associate with positive people. This decision will increase your confidence, motivation, and energy. Stay on track with the support of positive family members, teachers, and friends.

TOEFL
MODEL TESTS

There are three types of Model Tests to help you prepare for the TOEFL. The questions on Model Tests 1–8 in this book are like those that frequently appear on the Computer-Based TOEFL. The questions on the Cumulative Model Test on the CD-ROM that supplements this book are also like those that frequently appear on the Computer-Based TOEFL.

The difference between Model Tests 1–8 and the Cumulative Model Test is that Model Tests 1–8 are simulations of a Computer-Based TOEFL. A simulation is an experience that is similar, but not exactly the same. On these Model Tests, you will see the same types of questions, and you will answer them in the same way that you will on the actual Computer-Based TOEFL that you take, but the computer will not be selecting questions for you at your level of language proficiency. These Model Tests are computer-assisted, but not computer-adaptive. On the Cumulative Model Test, you will see the same types of questions, and you will answer them in the same way that you will on the actual Computer-Based TOEFL. In addition, the computer will be selecting questions for you at your level of language proficiency. This Model Test is computer-adaptive.

The third type of Model Test is a simulation of the Next Generation TOEFL. It appears as Model Test 9 in this book and on the CD-ROM that supplements this book.

How to Answer Questions for Model Tests

If you use the CD-ROM to take the Model Tests, you will not need to write in your book. If you do not have access to a computer, mark your responses directly on the tests in the book.

For multiple-choice questions that require you to choose one answer, fill in the oval of the letter that corresponds to the answer you have chosen.

The Palo Verde tree _____ in spring.

  Ⓐ has beautiful yellow blossoms
  Ⓑ beautiful yellow blossoms
  Ⓒ having beautiful yellow blossoms
  Ⓓ with beautiful yellow blossoms

The Palo Verde tree _____ in spring.

  ● has beautiful yellow blossoms
  Ⓑ beautiful yellow blossoms
  Ⓒ having beautiful yellow blossoms
  Ⓓ with beautiful yellow blossoms

For questions that require you to choose two answers, mark an X in the squares that correspond to the answers you have chosen.

According to the professor, what was the Hemingway style?
  Click on two answers

  Ⓐ Powerful descriptions
  Ⓑ Imaginative details
  Ⓒ Short sentences
  Ⓓ Difficult symbolism

According to the professor, what was the Hemingway style?
  Click on two answers

  ☒ Powerful descriptions
  Ⓑ Imaginative details
  ☒ Short sentences
  Ⓓ Difficult symbolism

For questions that require you to click on sentences to move them into categories on charts, write letters on the charts that correspond to the sentences you have chosen.

How did Hemingway use his experience in different novels?
  Click on the sentence.
Then click on the space where it belongs.
  Use each sentence only once.

  Ⓐ He was fishing in the Gulf of Mexico.
  Ⓑ He was driving an ambulance in Italy.
  Ⓒ He was working as a newspaper reporter in Paris.

How did Hemingway use his experience in different novels?
  Click on the sentence.
Then click on the space where it belongs.
  Use each sentence only once.

  Ⓐ He was fishing in the Gulf of Mexico.
  Ⓑ He was driving an ambulance in Italy.
  Ⓒ He was working as a newspaper reporter in Paris.

The Sun Also Rises	A Farewell to Arms	The Old Man and the Sea

The Sun Also Rises	A Farewell to Arms	The Old Man and the Sea
C	B	A

For questions that require you to put events in order, write letters in the numbered boxes that correspond to the sequence you have chosen.

The professor briefly describes Hemingway's life as an author. Summarize the biographical data by putting the events in order.

Click on the sentence.
Then click on the space where it belongs.
Use each sentence only once.

[A] Hemingway wrote about his experiences as an ambulance driver during the war.
[B] Hemingway received the Nobel Prize for literature.
[C] Hemingway published *The Old Man and the Sea*.
[D] Hemingway was a newspaper reporter in Paris.

1 [   ]

2 [   ]

3 [   ]

4 [   ]

The professor briefly describes Hemingway's life as an author. Summarize the biographical data by putting the events in order.

Click on the sentence.
Then click on the space where it belongs.
Use each sentence only once.

[A] Hemingway wrote about his experiences as an ambulance driver during the war.
[B] Hemingway received the Nobel Prize for literature.
[C] Hemingway published *The Old Man and the Sea*.
[D] Hemingway was a newspaper reporter in Paris.

1 [**D**   ]

2 [**A**   ]

3 [**C**   ]

4 [**B**   ]

For questions that require you to click on a word or phrase, circle the word or phrase in the passage.

Look at the word one in the passage.
Click on the word or phrase in the bold
text that one refers to.

> Solar astronomers do know that the sun is divided into five general layers or zones. Starting at the outside and going down into the sun, the zones are the corona, chromosphere, photosphere, convection zone, and finally the core. The first three zones are regarded as the sun s atmosphere. But since the sun has no solid surface, it is hard to tell where the atmosphere ends and the main body of the sun begins.
> **The sun s outermost layer begins about 10,000 miles above the visible surface and goes outward for millions of miles. This is the only part of the sun that can be seen during an eclipse such as the one in February 1979.** At any other time, the corona can be seen only when special instruments are used on cameras and telescopes to block the light from the photosphere.
> The corona is a brilliant, pearly white, filmy light, about as bright as the full moon. Its beautiful rays are a sensational sight during an eclipse. The corona s rays flash out in a brilliant fan that has wispy spikelike rays near the sun s north and south poles. The corona is generally thickest at the sun s equator.
> The corona is made up of gases streaming

Look at the word one in the passage.
Click on the word or phrase in the bold
text that one refers to.

> Solar astronomers do know that the sun is divided into five general layers or zones. Starting at the outside and going down into the sun, the zones are the corona, chromosphere, photosphere, convection zone, and finally the core. The first three zones are regarded as the sun s atmosphere. But since the sun has no solid surface, it is hard to tell where the atmosphere ends and the main body of the sun begins.
> **The sun s outermost layer begins about 10,000 miles above the visible surface and goes outward for millions of miles. This is the only part of the sun that can be seen during an (eclipse) such as the one in February 1979.** At any other time, the corona can be seen only when special instruments are used on cameras and telescopes to block the light from the photosphere.
> The corona is a brilliant, pearly white, filmy light, about as bright as the full moon. Its beautiful rays are a sensational sight during an eclipse. The corona s rays flash out in a brilliant fan that has wispy spikelike rays near the sun s north and south poles. The corona is generally thickest at the sun s equator.
> The corona is made up of gases streaming

For questions that require you to click on a sentence, circle the sentence in the passage.

Click on the sentence in paragraph 4 or 5
in which the author compares the light of
the sun's outermost layer to that of another
astronomical body.

Paragraphs 4 and 5 are marked
with arrows [→]

> cameras and telescopes to block the light from the photosphere.
> → The corona is a brilliant, pearly white, filmy light, about as bright as the full moon. Its beautiful rays are a sensational sight during an eclipse. The corona's rays flash out in a brilliant fan that has wispy spikelike rays near the sun's north and south poles. The corona is generally thickest at the sun's equator.
> → The corona is made up of gases streaming outward at tremendous speeds that reach a temperature of more than 2 million degrees Fahrenheit. The gas thins out as it reaches the space around the planets. By the time the gas of the corona reaches the Earth it has a relatively low density.

Click on the sentence in paragraph 4 or 5
in which the author compares the light of
the sun's outermost layer to that of another
astronomical body.

Paragraphs 4 and 5 are marked
with arrows [→]

> cameras and telescopes to block the light from the photosphere.
> → The corona is a brilliant, pearly white, filmy light, about as bright as the full moon. Its beautiful rays are a sensational sight during an eclipse. The corona's rays flash out in a brilliant fan that has wispy spikelike rays near the sun's north and south poles. The corona is generally thickest at the sun's equator.
> → The corona is made up of gases streaming outward at tremendous speeds that reach a temperature of more than 2 million degrees Fahrenheit. The gas thins out as it reaches the space around the planets. By the time the gas of the corona reaches the Earth it has a relatively low density.

For questions that require you to add a sentence, circle the square [■] where the sentence is to be inserted.

The following sentence can be added to paragraph 1.

At the center of the Earth's solar system lies the sun.

Where would it best fit in paragraph 1? Click on the square [■] to add the sentence to the paragraph.

Paragraph 1 is marked with an arrow [→].

→ ■ The temperature of the sun is over 10,000 degrees Fahrenheit at the surface, but it rises to perhaps more than 27,000,000° at the center. ■The sun is so much hotter than the Earth that matter can exist only as a gas, except perhaps at the core. In the core of the sun, the pressures are so great that, despite the high temperature, there may be a small solid core. ■However, no one really knows, since the center of the sun can never be directly observed. ■

Solar astronomers do know that the sun is divided into five general layers or zones. Starting at the outside and going down into the sun, the zones are the corona, chromosphere, photosphere, convection zone, and finally the core. The first three zones are regarded as the sun's atmosphere. But since the sun has no solid surface, it is hard to tell where the atmosphere ends and the main body of the sun begins.

The sun's outermost layer begins about 10,000 miles above the visible surface and goes outward for millions of miles. This is the only part of the sun that can be seen during an eclipse such as the one in

The following sentence can be added to paragraph 1.

At the center of the Earth's solar system lies the sun.

Where would it best fit in paragraph 1? Click on the square [■] to add the sentence to the paragraph.

Paragraph 1 is marked with an arrow [→].

→Ⓢ The temperature of the sun is over 10,000 degrees Fahrenheit at the surface, but it rises to perhaps more than 27,000,000° at the center. ■The sun is so much hotter than the Earth that matter can exist only as a gas, except perhaps at the core. In the core of the sun, the pressures are so great that, despite the high temperature, there may be a small solid core. ■However, no one really knows, since the center of the sun can never be directly observed. ■

Solar astronomers do know that the sun is divided into five general layers or zones. Starting at the outside and going down into the sun, the zones are the corona, chromosphere, photosphere, convection zone, and finally the core. The first three zones are regarded as the sun's atmosphere. But since the sun has no solid surface, it is hard to tell where the atmosphere ends and the main body of the sun begins.

The sun's outermost layer begins about 10,000 miles above the visible surface and goes outward for millions of miles. This is the only part of the sun that can be seen during an eclipse such as the one in

Model Test 1
Computer-Assisted TOEFL

Section 1:
Listening

The Listening Section of the test measures the ability to understand conversations and talks in English. You will use headphones to listen to the conversations and talks. While you are listening, pictures of the speakers or other information will be presented on your computer screen. There are two parts to the Listening Section, with special directions for each part.

On the day of the test, the amount of time you will have to answer all of the questions will appear on the computer screen. The time you spend listening to the test material will not be counted. The listening material and questions about it will be presented only one time. You will not be allowed to take notes or have any paper at your computer. You will both see and hear the questions before the answer choices appear. You can take as much time as you need to select an answer; however, it will be to your advantage to answer the questions as quickly as possible. You may change your answer as many times as you want before you confirm it. After you have confirmed an answer, you will not be able to return to the question.

Before you begin working on the Listening Section, you will have an opportunity to adjust the volume of the sound. You may not be able to change the volume after you have started the test.

QUESTION DIRECTIONS — Part A

In Part A of the Listening Section, you will hear short conversations between two people. In some of the conversations, each person speaks only once. In other conversations, one or both of the people speak more than once. Each conversation is followed by one question about it.

Each question in this part has four answer choices. You should click on the best answer to each question. Answer the questions on the basis of what is stated or implied by the speakers.

1. What is the man's problem?

   Ⓐ He doesn't mind the traffic.
   Ⓑ He takes the bus to school.
   Ⓒ He has to stand on the bus if he takes it to school.
   Ⓓ He wants to ride to school with the woman.

2. What does the man mean?

   Ⓐ The woman should not consider her advisor in the decision.
   Ⓑ The woman should not take Dr. Sullivan's section.
   Ⓒ The woman's advisor will not be offended.
   Ⓓ The woman should not take a physics course.

3. What does the woman imply?

   Ⓐ She is not interested in the man.
   Ⓑ She does not like lectures.
   Ⓒ She would go out with the man on another occasion.
   Ⓓ She would rather stay at home.

4. What does the woman mean?

   Ⓐ The bike is in good condition.
   Ⓑ The man needs to replace the bike.
   Ⓒ The bike is missing.
   Ⓓ It is a new bike.

5. What does the man want to drink?

   Ⓐ Something cold.
   Ⓑ Coffee.
   Ⓒ Tea.
   Ⓓ Both coffee and tea.

6. What does the man suggest the woman do?

   Ⓐ Ask directions.
   Ⓑ Walk to the shopping center.
   Ⓒ Take a taxi.
   Ⓓ Wait for the bus.

7. What can be inferred about the woman?

   Ⓐ She does not plan to study.
   Ⓑ She has a very busy schedule.
   Ⓒ She is lost.
   Ⓓ She has not registered yet.

8. What does the man mean?

   Ⓐ He does not want to listen to the radio.
   Ⓑ He has changed his opinion about turning on the radio.
   Ⓒ The radio will not bother him.
   Ⓓ The radio is not working very well.

9. What does the woman suggest Anna do?

   Ⓐ Stop worrying.
   Ⓑ Go out more.
   Ⓒ Talk to a friend.
   Ⓓ Get counseling.

10. What does the man mean?

   Ⓐ He prefers to talk another time.
   Ⓑ He wants the woman to go away.
   Ⓒ He would like the woman to continue.
   Ⓓ He doesn't know what to think.

11. What will the man probably do?

   Ⓐ Accept the woman's apology.
   Ⓑ Allow the woman to go ahead of him.
   Ⓒ Apologize to the woman.
   Ⓓ Go to the front of the line.

12. What does the woman imply?

   Ⓐ The neighbors have parties often.
   Ⓑ She does not like her neighbors.
   Ⓒ The neighbors' party is disturbing her.
   Ⓓ She will not be invited to the neighbors' party.

13. What had the man assumed?

   Ⓐ Dr. Franklin is not very understanding.
   Ⓑ The extension was a very bad idea.
   Ⓒ He is surprised that the woman was denied her request.
   Ⓓ The professor does not have a policy.

14. What problem do the man and woman have?

   Ⓐ They do not have a telephone.
   Ⓑ They are late.
   Ⓒ They have been left.
   Ⓓ They got lost.

15. What is the woman probably going to do?

   Ⓐ Pay the rent for half a month.
   Ⓑ Help the man move.
   Ⓒ Stay where she is living until the 15th.
   Ⓓ Move out of the apartment.

16. What had the man assumed about MaryAnne?

   Ⓐ She had already taken the test.
   Ⓑ She did not want to take classes.
   Ⓒ She had not taken the placement test.
   Ⓓ She would take the math classes later.

17. What does the man mean?

   Ⓐ The plan is to remain in the class.
   Ⓑ It is not comfortable in the classroom.
   Ⓒ He has been absent because he was sick.
   Ⓓ The weather has been very bad.

QUESTION DIRECTIONS — Part B

In Part B of the Listening Section, you will hear several longer conversations and talks. Each conversation or talk is followed by several questions. The conversations, talks, and questions will not be repeated.

The conversations and talks are about a variety of topics. You do not need special knowledge of the topics to answer the questions correctly. Rather, you should answer each question on the basis of what is stated or implied by the speakers in the conversations or talks.

For most of the questions, you will need to click on the best of four possible answers. Some questions will have special directions. The special directions will appear in a box on the computer screen.

18. What is Mike's problem?

   Ⓐ He was late arriving at registration.
   Ⓑ He needs an advisor's signature on a course request form.
   Ⓒ He is not doing well in the class because it is so large.
   Ⓓ He must have the permission of the instructor to enroll in a class.

19. What does Mike want Professor Day to do?

   Ⓐ Help him with the class.
   Ⓑ Explain some technical vocabulary.
   Ⓒ Give him special permission to take the class.
   Ⓓ Take a form to the registration area.

20. What does Mike say about graduation?

   Ⓐ He has planned to graduate in the fall.
   Ⓑ He has to take Professor Day's class in order to graduate.
   Ⓒ He needs the professor to sign his application for graduation.
   Ⓓ He does not have enough credits for graduation.

21. What does Professor Day decide to do?

   Ⓐ Enroll Mike in the class next year.
   Ⓑ Allow Mike to take the class this term.
   Ⓒ Give Mike permission to graduate without the class.
   Ⓓ Register Mike for another class.

22. What is MUZAK?

   Ⓐ A slow, soft song.
   Ⓑ Music in restaurants.
   Ⓒ Background music.
   Ⓓ A pleasant addition to the environment.

23. What is the average increase in productivity when MUZAK is introduced?

   Ⓐ Thirteen percent.
   Ⓑ Five to ten percent.
   Ⓒ One hundred percent.
   Ⓓ Thirty percent.

24. What is stimulus progression?

   Ⓐ Background music that is low in stimulus value.
   Ⓑ Upbeat music that stimulates sales.
   Ⓒ Music engineered to reduce stress.
   Ⓓ Music that starts slow and gets faster at times of the day when people get tired.

25. How does MUZAK influence sales in supermarkets?

   Ⓐ It can cause shoppers to go through the line faster.
   Ⓑ It can cause shoppers to buy thirty percent more or less.
   Ⓒ It can cause shoppers to walk slower and buy more.
   Ⓓ It does not influence sales.

26. What is this announcement mainly about?

   Ⓐ The "Sun-Up Semester" program.
   Ⓑ The Community College campus.
   Ⓒ Video telecourses.
   Ⓓ Technology for distance learning.

27. Why does the speaker mention the "Sun-Up Semester"?

   Ⓐ To clarify how to register.
   Ⓑ To advertise the college.
   Ⓒ To provide a listing of courses.
   Ⓓ To give students an alternative to video tapes.

28. How can students register for a course?

    Ⓐ They should come to campus.
    Ⓑ They can call the Community College.
    Ⓒ They must contact the instructor.
    Ⓓ They can use computers.

29. How can students contact the instructor?

    Ⓐ By using e-mail.
    Ⓑ By calling KCC7-TV.
    Ⓒ By writing letters.
    Ⓓ By making video tapes.

30. What is the main topic of this conversation?

    Ⓐ The woman's health.
    Ⓑ The woman's grades.
    Ⓒ The man's joke.
    Ⓓ The man's stress.

31. What was the woman's problem?

    Ⓐ She was taking too many classes.
    Ⓑ She was very tired because she studied too late.
    Ⓒ She had been ill last semester.
    Ⓓ She may have to withdraw from school this semester.

32. Why is mono called the "college disease"?

    Ⓐ Many students get mono while they are in college.
    Ⓑ If one student gets mono, the whole college becomes infected.
    Ⓒ It is a joke about college students that the woman tells.
    Ⓓ The disease was first identified on a college campus.

33. What advice does the woman give the man?

    Ⓐ Drop out of school for a semester and return later.
    Ⓑ Study harder to learn all the lessons this semester.
    Ⓒ Take fewer hours each semester and add one semester to the program.
    Ⓓ Add extra classes to the program even if it requires another semester.

34. What central theme does the lecture examine?

    Ⓐ The relationship between language and culture.
    Ⓑ The culture of Hopi society.
    Ⓒ Native American cultures.
    Ⓓ The life of Benjamin Lee Whorf.

35. Which languages did Whorf use in his research?

    Ⓐ European languages.
    Ⓑ South American languages.
    Ⓒ Native American languages.
    Ⓓ Computer languages.

36. According to the lecturer, what is linguistic relativity?

    Ⓐ All languages are related.
    Ⓑ All Native American languages are related.
    Ⓒ Language influences the manner in which an individual understands reality.
    Ⓓ Language and culture are not related.

37. What is another name for linguistic relativity?

    Ⓐ The Sapir Hypothesis.
    Ⓑ The Sapir-Whorf Hypothesis.
    Ⓒ The Sapir-Whorf-Boas Hypothesis.
    Ⓓ The American Indian Model of the Universe.

38. What is the topic of this discussion?

    Ⓐ Air pollution.
    Ⓑ Acid rain.
    Ⓒ Fossil fuels.
    Ⓓ The Great Lakes.

39. What is acid rain?

    Ⓐ Precipitation that is polluted by sulfuric acid and nitric acid.
    Ⓑ Rain that falls after a long period of severe drought.
    Ⓒ Large concentrations of acid in the soil around the Great Lakes.
    Ⓓ Water vapor that is mixed with a high concentration of sulfur.

40. In which two ways has the environment been damaged along the Great Lakes?

Click on 2 answers.

A The air now contains dangerous levels of carbon monoxide.
B Weather patterns have been disturbed.
C Water resources have been polluted.
D The soil has been depleted of nutrients.

41. What are the conditions of the Air Quality Accord?

Ⓐ Companies in the United States must control pollution that could affect Canadian resources.
Ⓑ There are limits placed on the quantity of acidic deposits that can cross the border.
Ⓒ Governments and agencies will regulate automobile emissions.
Ⓓ Fuels cannot contain any sulfur near the border.

42. What is the topic of this lecture?

Ⓐ Three major types of bacteria.
Ⓑ How microscopic organisms are measured.
Ⓒ How bacteria is used for research in genetics.
Ⓓ Diseases caused by bacteria.

43. Which two characteristics are common in bacteria?

Click on 2 answers.

A They have one cell.
B They are harmful to humans.
C They reproduce quickly.
D They die when exposed to air.

44. Which of the following slides contain cocci bacteria?

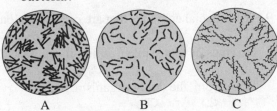

A   B   C

45. Why are bacteria being used in the research study at the University?

Ⓐ Bacteria have unusual cell formations.
Ⓑ Bacteria live harmlessly on the skin, mouth, and intestines.
Ⓒ Bacteria are similar to other life forms.
Ⓓ Bacteria cause many diseases in humans.

46. What is the purpose of this conversation?

Ⓐ The man needs help changing his schedule.
Ⓑ The man is looking for a job in the morning.
Ⓒ The man is trying to get a student loan.
Ⓓ The man is changing his major to sociology.

47. Why does the man need to take at least twelve hours?

Ⓐ He wants to graduate as soon as possible.
Ⓑ He must be a full-time student to qualify for his loan.
Ⓒ His advisor insists that he study full time.
Ⓓ All the courses are required.

48. Why does the man prefer Sociology 560?

Ⓐ It is a required course.
Ⓑ It is offered in the afternoon.
Ⓒ It is taught by Dr. Brown.
Ⓓ It is a sociology class.

49. What will Dr. Kelly do?

Ⓐ Help the man withdraw from school.
Ⓑ Change the man's class schedule.
Ⓒ Give the man a student loan.
Ⓓ Change the man's major.

50. What will the man probably do after the conversation?

Ⓐ Go to Dr. Brown's office.
Ⓑ See Dr. Brown in class.
Ⓒ Call Dr. Brown.
Ⓓ Send the form to Dr. Brown.

Section 2: Structure

This section measures the ability to recognize language that is appropriate for standard written English. There are two types of questions in this section.

In the first type of question, there are incomplete sentences. Beneath each sentence, there are four words or phrases. You will choose the one word or phrase that best completes the sentence. Clicking on a choice darkens the oval. After you click on **Next** and **Confirm Answer**, the next question will be presented.

The second type of question has four underlined words or phrases. You will choose the one underlined word or phrase that must be changed for the sentence to be correct. Clicking on an underlined word or phrase will darken it. After you click on **Next** and **Confirm Answer**, the next question will be presented.

1. Justice Sandra Day O'Connor was _____ to serve on the U.S. Supreme Court.

   Ⓐ the woman who first
   Ⓑ the first woman
   Ⓒ who the first woman
   Ⓓ the first and a woman

2. North Carolina is well known not only for the Great Smoky Mountains National Park _____ for the Cherokee settlements.

   Ⓐ also
   Ⓑ and
   Ⓒ but also
   Ⓓ because of

3. If biennials were planted this year, they

   will be likely to bloom next year.
     Ⓐ   Ⓑ   Ⓒ   Ⓓ

4. The value of the dollar declines as the rate of
           Ⓐ   Ⓑ Ⓒ

   inflation raises.
        Ⓓ

5. General Grant had General Lee _____ him at Appomattox to sign the official surrender of the Confederate forces.

   Ⓐ to meet
   Ⓑ met
   Ⓒ meet
   Ⓓ meeting

6. Anthropologists assert that many of the early

   Native Americans who lived on the Plains

   did not engage in planting crops but to hunt,
                     Ⓐ   Ⓑ

   living primarily on buffalo meat.
     Ⓒ   Ⓓ

7. The differential attractions of the sun and the

   moon have a direct effect in the rising and
        Ⓐ   Ⓑ   Ⓒ

   falling of the tides.
       Ⓓ

8. _____ both men and women have often achieved their career ambitions by midlife, many people are afflicted by at least a temporary period of dissatisfaction and depression.

   Ⓐ Because
   Ⓑ So
   Ⓒ A
   Ⓓ Who

9. With special enzymes that are call restriction
                        Ⓐ

   enzymes, it is possible to split off segments of
                   Ⓑ

   DNA from the donor organism.
        Ⓒ   Ⓓ

10. <u>Because of</u> the movement of a glacier,
   (A)

   <u>the form</u> <u>of</u> the Great Lakes was very <u>slow</u>.
   (B)   (C)   (D)

11. _____ small specimen of the embryonic
   fluid is removed from a fetus, it will be
   possible to determine whether the baby will
   be born with birth defects.

   (A) A
   (B) That a
   (C) If a
   (D) When it is a

12. To generate income, magazine publishers
   must decide whether to increase the subscription price or _____ .

   (A) to sell advertising
   (B) if they should sell advertising
   (C) selling advertising
   (D) sold advertising

13. <u>If</u> it receives <u>enough</u> rain at the proper time,
   (A)   (B)

   hay <u>will grow</u> quickly, <u>as</u> grass.
      (C)   (D)

14. *Psychology Today* <u>is</u> <u>interesting</u>, informative,
                     (A)   (B)

   and <u>it is</u> easy <u>to read</u>.
      (C)   (D)

15. <u>Before</u> she died, Andrew Jackson's daughter,
   (A)

   who <u>lives</u> in the family mansion, <u>used to take</u>
   (B) (C)   (D)

   tourists through her home.

16. If it _____ more humid in the desert of the
   Southwest, the hot temperatures would be
   unbearable.

   (A) be
   (B) is
   (C) was
   (D) were

17. _____ Java Man, who lived before the first
   Ice Age, is the first manlike animal.

   (A) It is generally believed that
   (B) Generally believed it is
   (C) Believed generally is
   (D) That is generally believed

18. It is essential that the temperature <u>is not</u>
                                        (A)

   elevated <u>to a point</u> where the substance
            (B)

   formed <u>may become</u> unstable and
          (C)

   decompose into <u>its</u> constituent elements.
                 (D)

19. John Philip Sousa, <u>who</u> <u>many</u> people consider
                      (A)   (B)

   the <u>greatest</u> composer of marches, wrote his
       (C)

   music during the era <u>known as</u> the Gay 90s.
                        (D)

20. For the investor who _____ money, silver
   or bonds are good options.

   (A) has so little a
   (B) has very little
   (C) has so few
   (D) has very few

21. Although <u>it</u> can be <u>derived from</u> oil, coal, and
            (A)   (B)

   tar, kerosene is usually <u>produced</u> <u>by refine</u> it
                            (C)   (D)

   from petroleum.

22. Aeronomy <u>is</u> <u>the study</u> of <u>the Earth's</u> upper
            (A) (B)   (C)

   atmosphere, which includes <u>their</u>
                              (D)

   composition, temperature, density, and

   chemical reactions.

23. The purpose <u>of</u> the United Nations,
                (A)

   <u>broad speaking,</u> <u>is</u> to maintain peace and
   (B)   (C)

   security and <u>to encourage</u> respect for
                (D)

   human rights.

24. Of all the cereals, rice is the one _____ food for more people than any of the other grain crops.

     Ⓐ it provides
     Ⓑ that providing
     Ⓒ provides
     Ⓓ that provides

25. Although Congressional representatives and senators may serve an unlimited number of term, the president is limited to two, for a total of eight years.
    Ⓐ   Ⓑ
    Ⓒ   Ⓓ

Section 3:
Reading

This section measures the ability to read and understand short passages similar in topic and style to those that students are likely to encounter in North American universities and colleges. This section contains reading passages and questions about the passages. There are several different types of questions in this section.

In the Reading Section, you will first have the opportunity to read the passage. You will use the scroll bar to view the rest of the passage.

When you have finished reading the passage, you will use the mouse to click on **Proceed**. Then the questions about the passage will be presented. You are to choose the one best answer to each question. Answer all questions about the information in a passage on the basis of what is stated or implied in that passage.

Most of the questions will be multiple-choice questions. To answer these questions you will click on a choice below the question.

To answer some questions, you will click on a word or phrase.
To answer some questions, you will click on a sentence in the passage.
To answer some questions, you will click on a square to add a sentence to the passage.

It has long been known that when the green parts of plants are exposed to light under suitable conditions of temperature and moisture, carbon dioxide is absorbed by the plant from the atmospheric CO_2, and oxygen is released into the air. This exchange of gases in plants is the opposite of the process that occurs in respiration. In this plant process, which is called photosynthesis, carbohydrates are synthesized in the presence of light from carbon dioxide and water by specialized structures in the cytoplasm of plant cells called chloroplasts. These chloroplasts contain not only two types of light-trapping green chlorophyll but also a vast array of protein substances called enzymes. In most plants, the water required by the photosynthesis process is absorbed from the soil by the roots and translocated through the xylem of the root and stem to the chlorophyll-laden leaves. Except for the usually small percentage used in respiration, the oxygen released in the process diffuses out of the leaf into the atmosphere through stomates. In simple terms, carbon dioxide is the fuel, and oxygen is the product of the chemical reaction. For each molecule of carbon dioxide used, one molecule of oxygen is released. Here is a summary chemical equation for photosynthesis:

$$6CO_2 + 6H_2O \rightarrow C_6H_{12}O_6 + 6O_2$$

As a result of this process, radiant energy from the sun is stored as chemical energy. In turn, the chemical energy is used to decompose carbon dioxide and water. The products of their decomposition are recombined into a new compound, which successively builds up into the more and more complex substances that comprise the plant. These organic substances, that is, the sugars, starches, and cellulose, all belong to the class of organic molecules. In other words, the process of photosynthesis can be understood as an enzyme-induced chemical change from carbon dioxide and water into the simple sugar glucose. This carbohydrate, in turn, is utilized by the plant to generate other forms of energy, such as the long chains of plant cells or polymers that comprise the cellular structures of starches or cellulose. Many intermediate steps are involved in the production of a simple sugar or starch. At the same time, a balance of gases is preserved in the atmosphere by the process of photosynthesis.

1. Which title best expresses the ideas in this passage?

   (A) A Chemical Equation
   (B) The Process of Photosynthesis
   (C) The Parts of Vascular Plants
   (D) The Production of Sugar

2. The combination of carbon dioxide and water to form sugar results in an excess of

   (A) water
   (B) oxygen
   (C) carbon
   (D) chlorophyll

3. Which process is the opposite of photosynthesis?

   (A) Decomposition
   (B) Synthesization
   (C) Diffusion
   (D) Respiration

4. In photosynthesis, energy from the sun is

   (A) changed to chemical energy
   (B) conducted from the xylem to the leaves of green plants
   (C) not necessary to the process
   (D) released one to one for each molecule of carbon dioxide used

5. Click on the sentence in paragraph 1 that describes how oxygen is released into the atmosphere.

Paragraph 1 is marked with an arrow (→).

Beginning

→ It has long been known that when the green parts of plants are exposed to light under suitable conditions of temperature and moisture, carbon dioxide is absorbed by the plant from the atmospheric CO_2, and oxygen is released into the air. This exchange of gases in plants is the opposite of the process that occurs in respiration. In this plant process, which is called photosynthesis, carbohydrates are synthesized in the presence of light from carbon dioxide and water by specialized structures in the cytoplasm of plant cells called chloroplasts. These chloroplasts contain not only two types of light-trapping green chlorophyll but also a vast array of protein substances called enzymes. In most plants, the water required by the photosynthesis process is absorbed from the soil by the roots and translocated through the xylem of the root and stem to the chlorophyll-laden leaves. Except for the usually small percentage used in respiration, the oxygen released in the process diffuses out of the leaf into the atmosphere through stomates. In simple terms, carbon dioxide is the fuel, and oxygen is the product of the chemical reaction. For each molecule of carbon dioxide

6. The word stored in paragraph 2 is closest in meaning to

   Ⓐ retained
   Ⓑ converted
   Ⓒ discovered
   Ⓓ specified

More Available

leaves. Except for the usually small percentage used in respiration, the oxygen released in the process diffuses out of the leaf into the atmosphere through stomates. In simple terms, carbon dioxide is the fuel, and oxygen is the product of the chemical reaction. For each molecule of carbon dioxide used, one molecule of oxygen is released. Here is a summary chemical equation for photosynthesis:

$$6CO_2 + 6H_2O \rightarrow C_6H_{12}O_6 + 6O_2$$

As a result of this process, radiant energy from the sun is stored as chemical energy. In turn, the chemical energy is used to decompose carbon dioxide and water. The products of their decomposition are recombined into a new compound, which successively builds up into the more and more complex substances that comprise the plant. These organic substances, that is, the sugars, starches, and cellulose, all belong to the class of organic molecules. In other words, the process of photosynthesis can be understood as an enzyme-induced chemical change from carbon dioxide and water into the simple sugar glucose. This carbohydrate, in turn, is utilized by the plant to generate other forms of

7. The word their in paragraph 2 refers to

   Ⓐ radiant energy and chemical energy
   Ⓑ carbon dioxide and water
   Ⓒ products
   Ⓓ complex substances

End

As a result of this process, radiant energy from the sun is stored as chemical energy. In turn, the chemical energy is used to decompose carbon dioxide and water. The products of their decomposition are recombined into a new compound, which successively builds up into the more and more complex substances that comprise the plant. These organic substances, that is, the sugars, starches, and cellulose, all belong to the class of organic molecules. In other words, the process of photosynthesis can be understood as an enzyme-induced chemical change from carbon dioxide and water into the simple sugar glucose. This carbohydrate, in turn, is utilized by the plant to generate other forms of energy, such as the long chains of plant cells or polymers that comprise the cellular structures of starches or cellulose. Many intermediate steps are involved in the production of a simple sugar or starch. At the same time, a balance of gases is preserved in the atmosphere by the process of photosynthesis.

8. The word successively in paragraph 2 is closest in meaning to

   Ⓐ with effort
   Ⓑ in a sequence
   Ⓒ slowly
   Ⓓ carefully

End

carbon dioxide and water. The products of their decomposition are recombined into a new compound, which successively builds up into the more and more complex substances that comprise the plant. These organic substances, that is, the sugars, starches, and cellulose, all belong to the class of organic molecules. In other words, the process of photosynthesis can be understood as an enzyme-induced chemical change from carbon dioxide and water into the simple sugar glucose. This carbohydrate, in turn, is utilized by the plant to generate other forms of energy, such as the long chains of plant cells or polymers that comprise the cellular structures of starches or cellulose. Many intermediate steps are involved in the production of a simple sugar or starch. At the same time, a balance of gases is preserved in the atmosphere by the process of photosynthesis.

9. Besides the manufacture of food for plants, what is another benefit of photosynthesis?

    Ⓐ It produces solar energy.
    Ⓑ It diffuses additional carbon dioxide into the air.
    Ⓒ It maintains a balance of gases in the atmosphere.
    Ⓓ It removes harmful gases from the air.

10. Which of the following is NOT true of the oxygen used in photosynthesis?

    Ⓐ Oxygen is absorbed by the roots.
    Ⓑ Oxygen is the product of photosynthesis.
    Ⓒ Oxygen is used in respiration.
    Ⓓ Oxygen is released into the atmosphere through the leaves.

Alfred Bernhard Nobel, a Swedish inventor and philanthropist, bequeathed most of his vast fortune to a trust that he designated as a fund from which annual prizes could be awarded to the individuals and organizations that had achieved through invention or discovery that which would have the greatest benefit to humanity in a particular year. According to the legend, Nobel's death had been erroneously reported in a newspaper, and the focus of the obituary was the fact that Nobel had invented dynamite. He rewrote his will in 1895, thereby establishing, with the original amount of nine million dollars, the Nobel Foundation as the legal owner and administering agent of the funds, and instituting the prizes that are named after him. Statutes to govern the awarding of the prizes were written, along with guidelines for operating procedures. Five years after Nobel's death, the first five prizes, worth about forty thousand dollars each, were to be awarded.

Originally the five classifications for outstanding contributions designated in Nobel's will included chemistry, physics, physiology or medicine, literature, and international peace. These prizes have been administered continually by the Nobel Foundation in Stockholm since they were first awarded in 1901. In 1969, a sixth prize, for accomplishments in the field of economics and endowed by the Central Bank of Sweden, was added. Candidates for the prizes must be nominated in writing by February 1 of each year by a qualified and recognized authority in each of the fields of competition. Recipients in physics, chemistry, and economics are selected by the Royal Swedish Academy, whereas recipients in peace are chosen by the Norwegian Nobel Committee appointed by Norway's parliament. With the King of Sweden officiating, the prizes are usually presented in Stockholm on December 10, the anniversary of Nobel's death. The value, fame, and prestige of the Nobel Prizes have continued to grow. Today the prize includes a medal, a diploma, and a cash award of about one million dollars.

11. What does this passage mainly discuss?

   Ⓐ Alfred Bernhard Nobel
   Ⓑ The Nobel Prizes
   Ⓒ Great contributions to mankind
   Ⓓ Swedish philanthropy

12. Why were the prizes named for Alfred Bernhard Nobel?

   Ⓐ He left money in his will to establish a fund for the prizes.
   Ⓑ He won the first Nobel Prize for his work in philanthropy.
   Ⓒ He is now living in Sweden.
   Ⓓ He serves as chairman of the committee to choose the recipients of the prizes.

13. The word will in paragraph 1 refers to

   Ⓐ Nobel's wishes
   Ⓑ a legal document
   Ⓒ a future intention
   Ⓓ a free choice

14. How often are the Nobel Prizes awarded?

   Ⓐ Five times a year
   Ⓑ Once a year
   Ⓒ Twice a year
   Ⓓ Once every two years

15. The following sentence can be added to the passage.

   When he read this objective summary of his life, the great chemist, it is said, decided that he wanted his name to be remembered for something more positive and humanitarian than inventing an explosive that was a potential weapon.

Where would it best fit in the passage?

Click on the square (■) to add the sentence to the passage.

Scroll the passage to see all of the choices.

More Available

particular year. According to the legend, Nobel's death had been erroneously reported in a newspaper, and the focus of the obituary was the fact that Nobel had invented dynamite. He rewrote his will in 1895, thereby establishing, with the original amount of nine million dollars, the Nobel Foundation as the legal owner and administering agent of the funds, and instituting the prizes that are named after him. Statutes to govern the awarding of the prizes were written, along with guidelines for operating procedures. Five years after Nobel's death, the first five prizes, worth about forty thousand dollars each, were to be awarded.

Originally the five classifications for outstanding contributions designated in Nobel's will included chemistry, physics, physiology or medicine, literature, and international peace. These prizes have been administered continually by the Nobel Foundation in Stockholm since they were first awarded in 1901. In 1969, a sixth prize, for accomplishments in the field of economics and endowed by the Central Bank of Sweden, was added. Candidates for the prizes must be

More Available

particular year. According to the legend, Nobel's death had been erroneously reported in a newspaper, and the focus of the obituary was the fact that Nobel had invented dynamite. ■ He rewrote his will in 1895, thereby establishing, with the original amount of nine million dollars, the Nobel Foundation as the legal owner and administering agent of the funds, and instituting the prizes that are named after him. ■ Statutes to govern the awarding of the prizes were written, along with guidelines for operating procedures. ■ Five years after Nobel's death, the first five prizes, worth about forty thousand dollars each, were to be awarded. ■

Originally the five classifications for outstanding contributions designated in Nobel's will included chemistry, physics, physiology or medicine, literature, and international peace. These prizes have been administered continually by the Nobel Foundation in Stockholm since they were first awarded in 1901. In 1969, a sixth prize, for accomplishments in the field of economics and endowed by the Central Bank of Sweden, was added. Candidates for the prizes must be

16. The word outstanding in paragraph 2 could best be replaced by

   Ⓐ recent
   Ⓑ unusual
   Ⓒ established
   Ⓓ exceptional

More Available

awarding of the prizes were written, along with guidelines for operating procedures. Five years after Nobel's death, the first five prizes, worth about forty thousand dollars each, were to be awarded.

Originally the five classifications for outstanding contributions designated in Nobel's will included chemistry, physics, physiology or medicine, literature, and international peace. These prizes have been administered continually by the Nobel Foundation in Stockholm since they were first awarded in 1901. In 1969, a sixth prize, for accomplishments in the field of economics and endowed by the Central Bank of Sweden, was added. Candidates for the prizes must be nominated in writing by February 1 of each year by a qualified and recognized authority in each of the fields of competition. Recipients in physics, chemistry, and economics are selected by the Royal Swedish Academy, whereas recipients in peace are chosen by the Norwegian Nobel Committee appointed by Norway's parliament. With the King of Sweden officiating, the prizes are usually presented in Stockholm on December 10,

---

17. A Nobel Prize would NOT be given to

   Ⓐ an author who wrote a novel
   Ⓑ a doctor who discovered a vaccine
   Ⓒ a composer who wrote a symphony
   Ⓓ a diplomat who negotiated a peace settlement

18. What does the author mean by the statement These prizes have been administered continually by the Nobel Foundation in Stockholm since they were first awarded in 1901?

   Ⓐ The Nobel Foundation oversees the management of the money and the distribution of the prizes.
   Ⓑ The Nobel Foundation selects the recipients of the prizes.
   Ⓒ The Nobel Foundation solicits applications and recommendations for the prizes.
   Ⓓ The Nobel Foundation recommends new prize classifications.

End

Originally the five classifications for outstanding contributions designated in Nobel's will included chemistry, physics, physiology or medicine, literature, and international peace. These prizes have been administered continually by the Nobel Foundation in Stockholm since they were first awarded in 1901. In 1969, a sixth prize, for accomplishments in the field of economics and endowed by the Central Bank of Sweden, was added. Candidates for the prizes must be nominated in writing by February 1 of each year by a qualified and recognized authority in each of the fields of competition. Recipients in physics, chemistry, and economics are selected by the Royal Swedish Academy, whereas recipients in peace are chosen by the Norwegian Nobel Committee appointed by Norway's parliament. With the King of Sweden officiating, the prizes are usually presented in Stockholm on December 10, the anniversary of Nobel's death. The value, fame, and prestige of the Nobel Prizes have continued to grow. Today the prize includes a medal, a diploma, and a cash award of about one million dollars.

19. Why are the awards presented on December 10?

    Ⓐ It is a tribute to the King of Sweden.
    Ⓑ Alfred Bernhard Nobel died on that day.
    Ⓒ That date was established in Alfred Nobel's will.
    Ⓓ The Central Bank of Sweden administers the trust.

20. Look at the word `prize` in the passage. Click on the word or phrase in the **bold** text that is closest in meaning to `prize` .

End

by a qualified and recognized authority in each of the fields of competition. Recipients in physics, chemistry, and economics are selected by the Royal Swedish Academy, whereas recipients in peace are chosen by the Norwegian Nobel Committee appointed by Norway's parliament. **With the King of Sweden officiating, the prizes are usually presented in Stockholm on December 10, the anniversary of Nobel's death. The value, fame, and prestige of the Nobel Prizes have continued to grow. Today the prize includes a medal, a diploma, and a cash award of about one million dollars.**

Although stage plays have been set to music since the era of the ancient Greeks, when the dramas of Sophocles and Aeschylus were accompanied by lyres and flutes, the usually accepted date for the beginning of opera as we know it is 1600. As a part of the celebration of the marriage of King Henry IV of France to the Italian aristocrat Maria de Medici, the Florentine composer Jacopo Perí produced his famous *Euridice*, generally considered to be the first opera. Following his example, a group of Italian musicians, poets, and noblemen called the Camerata began to revive the style of musical story that had been used in Greek tragedy. The Camerata took most of the plots for their operas from Greek and Roman history and mythology, beginning the process of creating an opera by writing a libretto or drama that could be used to establish the framework for the music. They called their compositions *opera in musica* or musical works. It is from this phrase that the word "opera" was borrowed and abbreviated.

For several years, the center of opera was Florence in northern Italy, but gradually, during the baroque period, it spread throughout Italy. By the late 1600s, operas were being written and performed in many places throughout Europe, especially in England, France, and Germany. However, for many years, the Italian opera was considered the ideal, and many non-Italian composers continued to use Italian librettos. The European form deemphasized the dramatic aspect of the Italian model. New orchestral effects and even ballet were introduced under the guise of opera. Composers gave in to the demands of singers, writing many operas that were little more than a succession of brilliant tricks for the voice, designed to showcase the splendid voices of the singers who had requested them. It was thus that complicated arias, recitatives, and duets evolved. The aria, which is a long solo, may be compared to a song in which the characters express their thoughts and feelings. The recitative, which is also a solo of sorts, is a recitation set to music, the purpose of which is to continue the story line. The duet is a musical piece written for two voices, a musical device that may serve the function of either an aria or a recitative within the opera.

21. This passage is a summary of

   (A) opera in Italy
   (B) the Camerata
   (C) the development of opera
   (D) *Euridice*

22. Look at the word usually in the passage. Click on the word or phrase in the **bold** text that is closest in meaning to usually.

> **Beginning**
>
> **Although stage plays have been set to music since the era of the ancient Greeks, when the dramas of Sophocles and Aeschylus were accompanied by lyres and flutes, the usually accepted date for the beginning of opera as we know it is 1600. As a part of the celebration of the marriage of King Henry IV of France to the Italian aristocrat Maria de Medici, the Florentine composer Jacopo Perí produced his famous** *Euridice*, **generally considered to be the first opera.** Following his example, a group of Italian musicians, poets, and noblemen called the Camerata began to revive the style of musical story that had been used in Greek tragedy. The Camerata took most of the plots for their operas from Greek and Roman history and mythology, beginning the process of creating an opera by writing a libretto or drama that could be used to establish the framework for the music. They called their compositions *opera in musica* or musical works. It is from this phrase that the word "opera" was borrowed and abbreviated.
>   For several years, the center of opera was Florence in northern Italy, but gradually, during the

23. According to this passage, when did modern opera begin?

   (A) In the time of the ancient Greeks
   (B) In the fifteenth century
   (C) At the beginning of the sixteenth century
   (D) At the beginning of the seventeenth century

24. The word it in paragraph 1 refers to

   (A) opera
   (B) date
   (C) era
   (D) music

> **Beginning**
>
> Although stage plays have been set to music since the era of the ancient Greeks, when the dramas of Sophocles and Aeschylus were accompanied by lyres and flutes, the usually accepted date for the beginning of opera as we know it is 1600. As a part of the celebration of the marriage of King Henry IV of France to the Italian aristocrat Maria de Medici, the Florentine composer Jacopo Perí produced his famous *Euridice*, generally considered to be the first opera. Following his example, a group of Italian musicians, poets, and noblemen called the Camerata began to revive the style of musical story that had been used in Greek tragedy. The Camerata took most of the plots for their operas from Greek and Roman history and mythology, beginning the process of creating an opera by writing a libretto or drama that could be used to establish the framework for the music. They called their compositions *opera in musica* or musical works. It is from this phrase that the word "opera" was borrowed and abbreviated.
>   For several years, the center of opera was Florence in northern Italy, but gradually, during the

25. According to the author, what did Jacopo Perí write?

   (A) Greek tragedy
   (B) The first opera
   (C) The opera *Maria de Medici*
   (D) The opera *The Camerata*

26. The author suggests that *Euridice* was produced

   (A) in France
   (B) originally by Sophocles and Aeschylus
   (C) without much success
   (D) for the wedding of King Henry IV

27. What was the Camerata?

   (A) A group of Greek musicians
   (B) Musicians who developed a new musical drama based upon Greek drama
   (C) A style of music not known in Italy
   (D) The name given to the court of King Henry IV

28. The word revive in paragraph 1 could best be replaced by

   Ⓐ appreciate
   Ⓑ resume
   Ⓒ modify
   Ⓓ investigate

29. The word plots in paragraph 1 is closest in meaning to

   Ⓐ locations
   Ⓑ instruments
   Ⓒ stories
   Ⓓ inspiration

Beginning

    Although stage plays have been set to music since the era of the ancient Greeks, when the dramas of Sophocles and Aeschylus were accompanied by lyres and flutes, the usually accepted date for the beginning of opera as we know it is 1600. As a part of the celebration of the marriage of King Henry IV of France to the Italian aristocrat Maria de Medici, the Florentine composer Jacopo Perí produced his famous *Euridice*, generally considered to be the first opera. Following his example, a group of Italian musicians, poets, and noblemen called the Camerata began to revive the style of musical story that had been used in Greek tragedy. The Camerata took most of the plots for their operas from Greek and Roman history and mythology, beginning the process of creating an opera by writing a libretto or drama that could be used to establish the framework for the music. They called their compositions opera in musica or musical works. It is from this phrase that the word "opera" was borrowed and abbreviated.

    For several years, the center of opera was Florence in northern Italy, but gradually, during the

More Available

know it is 1600. As a part of the celebration of the marriage of King Henry IV of France to the Italian aristocrat Maria de Medici, the Florentine composer Jacopo Perí produced his famous *Euridice*, generally considered to be the first opera. Following his example, a group of Italian musicians, poets, and noblemen called the Camerata began to revive the style of musical story that had been used in Greek tragedy. The Camerata took most of the plots for their operas from Greek and Roman history and mythology, beginning the process of creating an opera by writing a libretto or drama that could be used to establish the framework for the music. They called their compositions *opera in musica* or musical works. It is from this phrase that the word "opera" was borrowed and abbreviated.

    For several years, the center of opera was Florence in northern Italy, but gradually, during the baroque period, it spread throughout Italy. By the late 1600s, operas were being written and performed in many places throughout Europe, especially in England, France, and Germany. However, for many years, the Italian opera was

30. From what did the term "opera" derive?

   Ⓐ Greek and Roman history and mythology
   Ⓑ Non-Italian composers
   Ⓒ The Italian phrase that means "musical works"
   Ⓓ The ideas of composer Jacopo Perí

31. Look at the word them in the passage. Click on the word or phrase in the **bold** text that them refers to.

End ↑

However, for many years, the Italian opera was considered the ideal, and many non-Italian composers continued to use Italian librettos. The European form deemphasized the dramatic aspect of the Italian model. **New orchestral effects and even ballet were introduced under the guise of opera. Composers gave in to the demands of singers, writing many operas that were little more than a succession of brilliant tricks for the voice, designed to showcase the splendid voices of the singers who had requested them. It was thus that complicated arias, recitatives, and duets evolved. The aria, which is a long solo, may be compared to a song in which the characters express their thoughts and feelings. The recitative, which is also a solo of sorts, is a recitation set to music, the purpose of which is to continue the story line. The duet is a musical piece written for two voices, a musical device that may serve the function of either an aria or a recitative within the opera.**

↓

32. Look at the word function in the passage. Click on the word or phrase in the **bold** text that is closest in meaning to function.

End ↑

aspect of the Italian model. New orchestral effects and even ballet were introduced under the guise of opera. Composers gave in to the demands of singers, writing many operas that were little more than a succession of brilliant tricks for the voice, designed to showcase the splendid voices of the singers who had requested them. **It was thus that complicated arias, recitatives, and duets evolved. The aria, which is a long solo, may be compared to a song in which the characters express their thoughts and feelings. The recitative, which is also a solo of sorts, is a recitation set to music, the purpose of which is to continue the story line. The duet is a musical piece written for two voices, a musical device that may serve the function of either an aria or a recitative within the opera.**

↓

According to the controversial sunspot theory, great storms or eruptions on the surface of the sun hurl streams of solar particles into space and eventually into the atmosphere of our planet, causing shifts in the weather on the Earth and interference with radio and television communications.

A typical sunspot consists of a dark central umbra, a word derived from the Latin word for shadow, which is surrounded by a lighter penumbra of light and dark threads extending out from the center like the spokes of a wheel. Actually, the sunspots are cooler than the rest of the photosphere, which may account for their apparently darker color. Typically, the temperature in a sunspot umbra is about 4000 K, whereas the temperature in a penumbra registers 5500 K, and the granules outside the spot are 6000 K.

Sunspots range in size from tiny granules to complex structures with areas stretching for billions of square miles. About 5 percent of all sunspots are large enough so that they can be seen from Earth without instruments; consequently, observations of sunspots have been recorded for thousands of years.

Sunspots have been observed in arrangements of one to more than one hundred spots, but they tend to occur in pairs. There is also a marked tendency for the two spots of a pair to have opposite magnetic polarities. Furthermore, the strength of the magnetic field associated with any given sunspot is closely related to the spot's size. Sunspots have also been observed to occur in cycles, over a period of eleven years. At the beginning of a cycle, the storms occur between 20 and 40 degrees north and south of the equator on the sun. As the cycle continues, some of the storms move closer to the equator. As the cycle diminishes, the number of sunspots decreases to a minimum and they cluster between 5 and 15 degrees north and south latitude.

Although there is no theory that completely explains the nature and function of sunspots, several models show scientists' attempts to relate the phenomenon to magnetic field lines along the lines of longitude from the north and south poles of the sun.

33. What is the author's main purpose in the passage?

    Ⓐ To propose a theory to explain sunspots
    Ⓑ To describe the nature of sunspots
    Ⓒ To compare the umbra and the penumbra in sunspots
    Ⓓ To argue for the existence of magnetic fields in sunspots

34. The word controversial in paragraph 1 is closest in meaning to

    Ⓐ widely accepted
    Ⓑ open to debate
    Ⓒ just introduced
    Ⓓ very complicated

> **Beginning**
>
> According to the controversial sunspot theory, great storms or eruptions on the surface of the sun hurl streams of solar particles into space and eventually into the atmosphere of our planet, causing shifts in the weather on the Earth and interference with radio and television communications.
>
> A typical sunspot consists of a dark central umbra, a word derived from the Latin word for shadow, which is surrounded by a lighter penumbra of light and dark threads extending out from the center like the spokes of a wheel. Actually, the sunspots are cooler than the rest of the photosphere, which may account for their apparently darker color. Typically, the temperature in a sunspot umbra is about 4000 K, whereas the temperature in a penumbra registers 5500 K, and the granules outside the spot are 6000 K.
>
> Sunspots range in size from tiny granules to complex structures with areas stretching for billions of square miles. About 5 percent of all sunspots are large enough so that they can be seen from Earth without instruments; consequently, observations of sunspots have been recorded for thousands of years.

35. Solar particles are hurled into space by

    Ⓐ undetermined causes
    Ⓑ disturbances of wind
    Ⓒ small rivers on the surface of the sun
    Ⓓ changes in the Earth's atmosphere

36. The word particles in paragraph 1 refers to

    Ⓐ gas explosions in the atmosphere
    Ⓑ light rays from the sun
    Ⓒ liquid streams on the sun
    Ⓓ small pieces of matter from the sun

> **Beginning**
>
> According to the controversial sunspot theory, great storms or eruptions on the surface of the sun hurl streams of solar particles into space and eventually into the atmosphere of our planet, causing shifts in the weather on the Earth and interference with radio and television communications.
>
> A typical sunspot consists of a dark central umbra, a word derived from the Latin word for shadow, which is surrounded by a lighter penumbra of light and dark threads extending out from the center like the spokes of a wheel. Actually, the sunspots are cooler than the rest of the photosphere, which may account for their apparently darker color. Typically, the temperature in a sunspot umbra is about 4000 K, whereas the temperature in a penumbra registers 5500 K, and the granules outside the spot are 6000 K.
>
> Sunspots range in size from tiny granules to complex structures with areas stretching for billions of square miles. About 5 percent of all sunspots are large enough so that they can be seen from Earth without instruments; consequently, observations of sunspots have been recorded for thousands of years.

37. How can we describe matter from the sun that enters the Earth's atmosphere?

    Ⓐ Very small
    Ⓑ Very hot
    Ⓒ Very bright
    Ⓓ Very hard

38. What does the author mean by the statement Actually, the sunspots are cooler than the rest of the photosphere, which may account for their apparently darker color ?

   Ⓐ Neither sunspots nor the photosphere is hot.

   Ⓑ Sunspots in the photosphere do not have any color.

   Ⓒ The color of sunspots could be affected by their temperature.

   Ⓓ The size of a sunspot affects its temperature.

More Available

of light and dark threads extending out from the center like the spokes of a wheel. Actually, the sunspots are cooler than the rest of the photosphere, which may account for their apparently darker color. Typically, the temperature in a sunspot umbra is about 4000 K, whereas the temperature in a penumbra registers 5500 K, and the granules outside the spot are 6000 K.

Sunspots range in size from tiny granules to complex structures with areas stretching for billions of square miles. About 5 percent of all sunspots are large enough so that they can be seen from Earth without instruments; consequently, observations of sunspots have been recorded for thousands of years.

Sunspots have been observed in arrangements of one to more than one hundred spots, but they tend to occur in pairs. There is also a marked tendency for the two spots of a pair to have opposite magnetic polarities. Furthermore, the strength of the magnetic field associated with any given sunspot is closely related to the spot's size. Sunspots have also been observed to occur in cycles, over a period of eleven years. At the

---

39. Look at the word tiny in the passage. Click on the word or phrase in the **bold** text that is opposite in meaning to tiny .

More Available

color. Typically, the temperature in a sunspot umbra is about 4000 K, whereas the temperature in a penumbra registers 5500 K, and the granules outside the spot are 6000 K.

Sunspots range in size from tiny granules to complex structures with areas stretching for billions of square miles. About 5 percent of all sunspots are large enough so that they can be seen from Earth without instruments; consequently, observations of sunspots have been recorded for thousands of years.

Sunspots have been observed in arrangements of one to more than one hundred spots, but they tend to occur in pairs. There is also a marked tendency for the two spots of a pair to have opposite magnetic polarities. Furthermore, the strength of the magnetic field associated with any given sunspot is closely related to the spot's size. Sunspots have also been observed to occur in cycles, over a period of eleven years. At the beginning of a cycle, the storms occur between 20 and 40 degrees north and south of the equator on the sun. As the cycle continues, some of the storms move closer to the equator. As the cycle

---

40. The word they in paragraph 3 refers to

   Ⓐ structures

   Ⓑ spots

   Ⓒ miles

   Ⓓ granules

More Available

color. Typically, the temperature in a sunspot umbra is about 4000 K, whereas the temperature in a penumbra registers 5500 K, and the granules outside the spot are 6000 K.

Sunspots range in size from tiny granules to complex structures with areas stretching for billions of square miles. About 5 percent of all sunspots are large enough so that they can be seen from Earth without instruments; consequently, observations of sunspots have been recorded for thousands of years.

Sunspots have been observed in arrangements of one to more than one hundred spots, but they tend to occur in pairs. There is also a marked tendency for the two spots of a pair to have opposite magnetic polarities. Furthermore, the strength of the magnetic field associated with any given sunspot is closely related to the spot's size. Sunspots have also been observed to occur in cycles, over a period of eleven years. At the beginning of a cycle, the storms occur between 20 and 40 degrees north and south of the equator on the sun. As the cycle continues, some of the storms move closer to the equator. As the cycle

41. The word consequently in paragraph 3
    could best be replaced by

    Ⓐ as a result
    Ⓑ nevertheless
    Ⓒ without doubt
    Ⓓ in this way

More Available

color. Typically, the temperature in a sunspot
umbra is about 4000 K, whereas the temperature
in a penumbra registers 5500 K, and the granules
outside the spot are 6000 K.

Sunspots range in size from tiny granules to
complex structures with areas stretching for
billions of square miles. About 5 percent of all
sunspots are large enough so that they can
be seen from Earth without instruments;
consequently, observations of sunspots have
been recorded for thousands of years.

Sunspots have been observed in
arrangements of one to more than one hundred
spots, but they tend to occur in pairs. There is also
a marked tendency for the two spots of a pair to
have opposite magnetic polarities. Furthermore,
the strength of the magnetic field associated with
any given sunspot is closely related to the spot's
size. Sunspots have also been observed to occur
in cycles, over a period of eleven years. At the
beginning of a cycle, the storms occur between 20
and 40 degrees north and south of the equator on
the sun. As the cycle continues, some of the
storms move closer to the equator. As the cycle

---

42. In which configuration do sunspots usually
    occur?

    Ⓐ In one spot of varying size
    Ⓑ In a configuration of two spots
    Ⓒ In arrangements of one hundred or more
       spots
    Ⓓ In groups of several thousand spots

43. How are sunspots explained?

    Ⓐ Sunspots appear to be related to
       magnetic fields on the Earth.
    Ⓑ Sunspots may be related to magnetic
       fields that follow longitudinal lines on
       the sun.
    Ⓒ Sunspots are explained by storms that
       occur on the Earth.
    Ⓓ Sunspots have no theory or model to
       explain them.

44. Click on the paragraph that discusses the
    visibility of sunspots.

    Scroll the passage to see all of the
    paragraphs.

45. The sunspot theory is

    Ⓐ not considered very important
    Ⓑ widely accepted
    Ⓒ subject to disagreement
    Ⓓ relatively new

To check your answers for Model Test 1,
refer to the Answer Key on page 488. For
an explanation of the answers, refer to the
Explanatory Answers for Model Test 1 on
pages 501–520.

Writing Section:
Model Test 1

When you take a Model Test, you should use one sheet of paper, both sides. Time each Model Test carefully. After you have read the topic, you should spend 30 minutes writing. For results that would be closest to the actual testing situation, it is recommended that an English teacher score your test, using the guidelines on page 244 of this book.

Many people enjoy participating in sports for recreation; others enjoy participating in the arts. Give the benefits of each, take a position, and defend it.

Notes

To check your essay, refer to the Checklist on page 488. For an Example Essay, refer to the Explanatory Answers for Model Test 1 on page 520.

Model Test 2
Computer-Assisted TOEFL

Section 1:
Listening

The Listening Section of the test measures the ability to understand conversations and talks in English. You will use headphones to listen to the conversations and talks. While you are listening, pictures of the speakers or other information will be presented on your computer screen. There are two parts to the Listening Section, with special directions for each part.

On the day of the test, the amount of time you will have to answer all of the questions will appear on the computer screen. The time you spend listening to the test material will not be counted. The listening material and questions about it will be presented only one time. You will not be allowed to take notes or have any paper at your computer. You will both see and hear the questions before the answer choices appear. You can take as much time as you need to select an answer; however, it will be to your advantage to answer the questions as quickly as possible. You may change your answer as many times as you want before you confirm it. After you have confirmed an answer, you will not be able to return to the question.

Before you begin working on the Listening Section, you will have an opportunity to adjust the volume of the sound. You may not be able to change the volume after you have started the test.

QUESTION DIRECTIONS — Part A

In Part A of the Listening Section, you will hear short conversations between two people. In some of the conversations, each person speaks only once. In other conversations, one or both of the people speak more than once. Each conversation is followed by one question about it.

Each question in this part has four answer choices. You should click on the best answer to each question. Answer the questions on the basis of what is stated or implied by the speakers.

1. What had the man assumed?

   Ⓐ The woman was not truthful.
   Ⓑ Fewer students would attend.
   Ⓒ There would be a large group.
   Ⓓ Only foreign students would come.

2. What does the woman imply that the man should do?

   Ⓐ Knock on the door.
   Ⓑ Come back later.
   Ⓒ See Dr. Smith.
   Ⓓ Look at the sign.

3. What is the woman probably going to do?

   Ⓐ Take a class from Professor Wilson.
   Ⓑ Help the man with his class.
   Ⓒ Take an extra class.
   Ⓓ Do a project for her class.

4. What does the woman say about Paul?

   Ⓐ That he wants something to eat.
   Ⓑ That he will tell them if there is a problem.
   Ⓒ That he is not hungry.
   Ⓓ That he is angry.

5. What does the woman mean?

   Ⓐ Good grades are not that important to her.
   Ⓑ She did not get an A on the exam either.
   Ⓒ Two students got higher grades than she did.
   Ⓓ Besides hers, there were several other A grades.

6. What problem does the woman have?

   Ⓐ There is no time to finish.
   Ⓑ She cannot do it quickly.
   Ⓒ She has to study.
   Ⓓ She doesn't know what time it is.

7. What does the woman mean?

   Ⓐ She does not agree with the man.
   Ⓑ She thinks that it is better to wait.
   Ⓒ She thinks that it is better to drive at night.
   Ⓓ She does not think that the man made a wise decision.

8. What is the man going to do?

   Ⓐ Go to class.
   Ⓑ See a movie.
   Ⓒ Study at the library.
   Ⓓ Make an appointment.

9. What does the man mean?

   Ⓐ The message was not clear.
   Ⓑ There was no message on the machine.
   Ⓒ It was his intention to return the woman's call.
   Ⓓ He did not hear the woman's message.

10. What does the woman mean?

   Ⓐ They do not have as many people working as usual.
   Ⓑ The machine is broken.
   Ⓒ The man is next to be served.
   Ⓓ There is usually a long line.

11. What does the woman suggest that the man do?

   Ⓐ Get directions to the Math Department.
   Ⓑ Speak with the secretary.
   Ⓒ Go into Dr. Davis's office.
   Ⓓ Take the elevator to the fourth floor.

12. What can be inferred about Tom?

   Ⓐ He has finished the class.
   Ⓑ He has been sick.
   Ⓒ He does not have to take the final exam.
   Ⓓ He is not very responsible.

13. What does the man mean?

   Ⓐ He cannot find the woman's house.
   Ⓑ He has to change their plans.
   Ⓒ He will be happy to see the woman.
   Ⓓ He wants to know whether they have a date.

14. What will the woman probably do?

   Ⓐ Register for Dr. Collin's class.
   Ⓑ Graduate at a later date.
   Ⓒ Enroll in the section marked "staff."
   Ⓓ Find out who is teaching the other section of the class.

15. What does the woman think that the man should do?

   Ⓐ Wait for the results to be mailed.
   Ⓑ Call about the score.
   Ⓒ Take the test.
   Ⓓ Show more concern.

16. What does the woman mean?

   Ⓐ They have more time to travel.
   Ⓑ They are taking advantage of travel opportunities.
   Ⓒ They travel more than the man does.
   Ⓓ They spend most of their time traveling.

17. What does the man mean?

   Ⓐ The tickets are lost.
   Ⓑ Judy was responsible for getting the tickets.
   Ⓒ There were no tickets available.
   Ⓓ He does not have the tickets yet.

QUESTION DIRECTIONS — Part B

In Part B of the Listening Section, you will hear several longer conversations and talks. Each conversation or talk is followed by several questions. The conversations, talks, and questions will not be repeated.

The conversations and talks are about a variety of topics. You do not need special knowledge of the topics to answer the questions correctly. Rather, you should answer each question on the basis of what is stated or implied by the speakers in the conversations or talks.

For most of the questions, you will need to click on the best of four possible answers. Some questions will have special directions. The special directions will appear in a box on the computer screen.

18. What are the man and woman talking about?

    (A) A chapter in their textbook.
    (B) An experiment referred to in a group presentation.
    (C) A lecture in class.
    (D) A program on television.

19. Why is the moon an ideal environment for the experiment?

    (A) There is no air resistance on the moon.
    (B) There is no gravitational acceleration on the moon.
    (C) The gravity on the moon affects vertical motion.
    (D) There is no horizontal resistance for motions like pushing.

20. Why was it easier to lift the hammer on the moon?

    (A) The moon's gravitational acceleration was lower.
    (B) The hammer fell when it was released.
    (C) The surface of the moon encouraged motion.
    (D) The hammer was created for that environment.

21. How did the woman feel about the presentation?

    (A) She was surprised by it.
    (B) She was not interested in it.
    (C) She was impressed by it.
    (D) She was confused about it.

22. What was the video about?

    (A) The national health.
    (B) Stress.
    (C) Heart attacks.
    (D) Health care for women.

23. What did the students learn about women?

    (A) They are under more stress than men.
    (B) They have more heart attacks than men.
    (C) They do not get the same level of care as men.
    (D) They have fewer serious heart attacks than men.

24. How did the man feel about the video?

    (A) He did not see it.
    (B) He thought it was interesting.
    (C) He would not recommend it.
    (D) He was not surprised by it.

25. What will the woman probably do?

    (A) Discuss the video with the man.
    (B) Go to the library to see the video.
    (C) Check the video out of the library.
    (D) Get ready for class.

26. What is the main topic of this lecture?

    (A) Poet laureates.
    (B) The Victorian period.
    (C) Love poems in the English language.
    (D) Elizabeth Barrett Browning.

27. According to the lecturer, what was one reason that Elizabeth Barrett was considered for the title of Poet Laureate?

    (A) Because her husband was a famous poet.
    (B) Because of her publication, *Sonnets from the Portuguese*.
    (C) Because the monarch was a woman.
    (D) Because of her friendship with William Wordsworth.

28. Where did Elizabeth and Robert Browning live after their elopement?

    (A) In Spain.
    (B) In Italy.
    (C) In Portugal.
    (D) In England.

29. When did Elizabeth Barrett Browning die?

    (A) In 1843.
    (B) In 1849.
    (C) In 1856.
    (D) In 1861.

30. What is the main topic of this lecture?

    (A) The history of medicine in Greece.
    (B) The contributions of biology to medicine.
    (C) The scientific method.
    (D) Medical advances in the twentieth century.

31. What was Hippocrates' greatest contribution to medicine?

    (A) The classification of plants on the basis of body structure.
    (B) The sterilization of surgical instruments.
    (C) The scientific recording of symptoms and treatments.
    (D) The theory that disease was caused by the gods.

32. Who is known as the father of biology?

    (A) Hippocrates.
    (B) Aristotle.
    (C) Dioscorides.
    (D) Edward Jenner.

33. What was the contribution made to medicine by William Harvey?

    (A) The theory of germs and bacteria.
    (B) The discovery of a vaccine against smallpox.
    (C) The discovery of a mechanism for the circulation of the blood.
    (D) The *Materia Medica*.

34. What was surprising about Thrasher's study?

    (A) The size of the study, which included 1300 gangs.
    (B) The excellent summary by the student who located the research.
    (C) The changes that were reported in the history of gangs in the United States.
    (D) The fact that gang activity has been prevalent for many years.

35. According to the study by Moore, what causes gang activity?

    (A) Cliques that form in high school.
    (B) Normal feelings of insecurity that teenagers experience.
    (C) Dangerous neighborhoods and schools.
    (D) Loyalty to friends and family.

36. In which two ways are gang members identified by law enforcement authorities?

    Click on 2 answers.

    [A] By their tattoos.
    [B] By their clothing.
    [C] By maps of their territories.
    [D] By research studies.

37. What is the role of women in gangs?

    (A) Women are full members of the gangs.
    (B) Women are protected by the gangs.
    (C) Women are a support system for the gangs.
    (D) Women do not have any contact with the gangs.

38. What is Mary's problem?

  Ⓐ She does not want to work for Dr. Brown.
  Ⓑ She has a schedule conflict.
  Ⓒ She has been late to work too often.
  Ⓓ She needs to obtain a work-study position.

39. When is Mary's class next semester?

  Ⓐ Every day in the afternoon.
  Ⓑ Three hours a day, three times a week.
  Ⓒ Ten-thirty on Monday.
  Ⓓ Nine o'clock, three times a week.

40. How does Dr. Brown resolve the problem?

  Ⓐ He changes her work hours.
  Ⓑ He has her work fewer hours.
  Ⓒ He finds a different job for her.
  Ⓓ He gives her permission to arrive late.

41. What is a work-study employee?

  Ⓐ A person who works on campus.
  Ⓑ A new employee who is being trained.
  Ⓒ A student who can study at work after the job is complete.
  Ⓓ A part-time student with a full-time job.

42. What is the topic of this lecture?

  Ⓐ Reinforced concrete in buildings.
  Ⓑ Shear walls in earthquakes.
  Ⓒ Earthquake-resistant buildings.
  Ⓓ Understanding construction sites.

43. Which technique is used to reinforce walls?

  Ⓐ Cross-bracing.
  Ⓑ Shear cores.
  Ⓒ Bolts.
  Ⓓ Base isolators.

44. Which two materials are used in base isolators?

  Click on 2 answers.

  Ⓐ Rubber.
  Ⓑ Steel.
  Ⓒ Concrete.
  Ⓓ Soil.

45. What happens to fill dirt during an earthquake?

  Ⓐ It allows the building to sway.
  Ⓑ It reduces earthquake damage.
  Ⓒ It collapses.
  Ⓓ It creates shock waves.

46. Which two types represent the most common vein patterns in leaves?

  Click on 2 answers.

  Ⓐ Needle leaves.
  Ⓑ Parallel leaves.
  Ⓒ Palmate leaves.
  Ⓓ Pinnate leaves.

47. According to the lecturer, what is a midrib?

  Ⓐ One of the major classifications of veins in plants.
  Ⓑ The large vein that extends down the middle of a pinnate leaf.
  Ⓒ The central vein in a parallel leaf.
  Ⓓ The stem of a plant.

48. How does the lab assistant help students remember the palmate classification?

  Ⓐ She shows them a visual.
  Ⓑ She explains it carefully.
  Ⓒ She compares it to her hand.
  Ⓓ She refers them to their lab manual.

49. Match the leaves with their vein patterns.

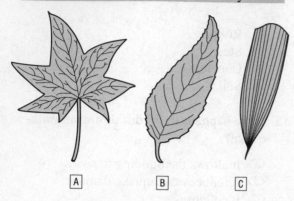

Click on the leaf. Then click on the empty box in the correct row. Use each leaf only once.

Pinnate	
Palmate	
Parallel	

50. What will the students probably do after the short lecture?

Ⓐ Classify leaves.
Ⓑ Take a lab quiz.
Ⓒ Read fifty-two pages in their manuals.
Ⓓ Discuss the lecture.

Section 2:
Structure

This section measures the ability to recognize language that is appropriate for standard written English. There are two types of questions in this section.

In the first type of question, there are incomplete sentences. Beneath each sentence, there are four words or phrases. You will choose the one word or phrase that best completes the sentence. Clicking on a choice darkens the oval. After you click on **Next** and **Confirm Answer**, the next question will be presented.

The second type of question has four underlined words or phrases. You will choose the one underlined word or phrase that must be changed for the sentence to be correct. Clicking on an underlined word or phrase will darken it. After you click on **Next** and **Confirm Answer**, the next question will be presented.

1. One of the most effective vegetable protein substitutes is the soybean _____ used to manufacture imitation meat products.

    Ⓐ which can be
    Ⓑ it can be
    Ⓒ who can be
    Ⓓ can be

2. _____ 1000 species of finch have been identified.

    Ⓐ As many as
    Ⓑ As many
    Ⓒ As much as
    Ⓓ Much as

3. The first electric lamp had two carbon rods
       Ⓐ
    from which vapor serves to conduct the
        Ⓑ   Ⓒ   Ⓓ
    current across the gap.

4. A thunderhead, dense clouds that rise high
    Ⓐ   Ⓑ Ⓒ
    into the sky in huge columns, produce hail,
                           Ⓓ
    rain, or snow.

5. According to the economic laws, the greater the demand, _____ the price.

    Ⓐ higher
    Ⓑ high
    Ⓒ the higher
    Ⓓ the high

6. Although no country has exactly the same
            Ⓐ
    folk music like that of any other, it is
              Ⓑ   Ⓒ
    significant that similar songs exist among

    widely separated people.
    Ⓓ

7. Despite of the Taft-Hartley Act which forbids
    Ⓐ   Ⓑ
    unfair union practices, some unions such as
                              Ⓒ
    the air traffic controllers have voted to strike
                                Ⓓ
    even though this action might endanger the

    national security.

8. The Continental United States is _____ that there are four time zones.

    Ⓐ much big
    Ⓑ too big
    Ⓒ so big
    Ⓓ very big

9. Benjamin West contributed a great deal to American art: _____ .

    Ⓐ painting, teaching, and lecturing
    Ⓑ painting, as a teacher and lecturer
    Ⓒ painting, teaching, and as a lecturer
    Ⓓ painting, a teacher, and a lecturer

10. Operant conditioning involves rewarding or

    punishing certain <u>behave</u> <u>to reinforce</u>
              Ⓐ   Ⓑ

    <u>or extinguish</u> <u>its</u> occurrence.
      Ⓒ   Ⓓ

11. <u>There is</u> an unresolved controversy as to
      Ⓐ

    <u>whom</u> <u>is</u> the real author of the Elizabethan
     Ⓑ Ⓒ

    plays <u>commonly</u> credited to William
          Ⓓ

    Shakespeare.

12. A catalytic agent <u>such</u> platinum may be used
            Ⓐ

    <u>so</u> that the chemical reaction <u>advances</u> more
    Ⓑ   Ⓒ

    <u>rapidly</u>.
    Ⓓ

13. Upon hatching, _____ .

    Ⓐ young ducks know how to swim
    Ⓑ swimming is known by young ducks
    Ⓒ the knowledge of swimming is in young ducks
    Ⓓ how to swim is known in young ducks

14. The observation deck at the World Trade Center _____ in New York.

    Ⓐ was highest than any other one
    Ⓑ was higher than any other one
    Ⓒ was highest that any other one
    Ⓓ was higher that any other one

15. When a patient's blood pressure is <u>much</u>
                        Ⓐ

    higher <u>than it</u> <u>should be</u>, a doctor usually
         Ⓑ   Ⓒ

    insists that he <u>will not</u> smoke.
            Ⓓ

16. <u>It</u> <u>was</u> <u>the invent</u> of the hand-held electronic
    Ⓐ Ⓑ   Ⓒ

    calculator that provided the original

    technology for <u>the present</u> generation of
              Ⓓ

    small but powerful computers.

17. _____ is necessary for the development of strong bones and teeth.

    Ⓐ It is calcium
    Ⓑ That calcium
    Ⓒ Calcium
    Ⓓ Although calcium

18. Located <u>in</u> the cranial cavity in the skull,
         Ⓐ

    <u>the brain</u> is the <u>larger</u> mass of nerve tissue
     Ⓑ   Ⓒ

    in the <u>human body</u>.
         Ⓓ

19. <u>Alike</u> other forms of energy, natural gas
    Ⓐ

    <u>may be used</u> <u>to heat</u> homes, cook food, and
     Ⓑ   Ⓒ

    even <u>run</u> automobiles.
       Ⓓ

20. An organ <u>is</u> a group <u>of tissues</u> capable
          Ⓐ   Ⓑ

    <u>to perform</u> some special function, as,
    Ⓒ

    <u>for example,</u> the heart, the liver, or the lungs.
      Ⓓ

21. _____ withstands testing, we may not conclude that it is true, but we may retain it.

    Ⓐ If a hypothesis
    Ⓑ That a hypothesis
    Ⓒ A hypothesis
    Ⓓ Hypothesis

22. <u>Insulin, it is</u> used <u>to treat</u> diabetes and <u>is</u>
      Ⓐ   Ⓑ   Ⓒ

    secured <u>chiefly</u> from the pancreas of cattle
         Ⓓ

    and hogs.

23. Not until a monkey is several years old _____ to exhibit signs of independence from its mother.

    Ⓐ it begins
    Ⓑ does it begin
    Ⓒ and begin
    Ⓓ beginning

24. Since Elizabeth Barrett Browning's father never approved of _____ Robert Browning, the couple eloped to Italy, where they lived and wrote.

   Ⓐ her to marry
   Ⓑ her marrying
   Ⓒ she marrying
   Ⓓ she to marry

25. In autumn, brilliant yellow, orange, and red
    Ⓐ
leaves are commonly to both the Sweet
          Ⓑ   Ⓒ
Gum tree and the Maple.
      Ⓓ

Section 3:
Reading

This section measures the ability to read and understand short passages similar in topic and style to those that students are likely to encounter in North American universities and colleges. This section contains reading passages and questions about the passages. There are several different types of questions in this section.

In the Reading Section, you will first have the opportunity to read the passage. You will use the scroll bar to view the rest of the passage.

When you have finished reading the passage, you will use the mouse to click on **Proceed**. Then the questions about the passage will be presented. You are to choose the one best answer to each question. Answer all questions about the information in a passage on the basis of what is stated or implied in that passage.

Most of the questions will be multiple-choice questions. To answer these questions you will click on a choice below the question.

To answer some questions, you will click on a word or phrase.
To answer some questions, you will click on a sentence in the passage.
To answer some questions, you will click on a square to add a sentence to the passage.

Recent technological advances in manned and unmanned undersea vehicles, along with breakthroughs in satellite technology and computer equipment, have overcome some of the limitations of divers and diving equipment for scientists doing research on the great oceans of the world. Without a vehicle, divers often became sluggish, and their mental concentration was severely limited. Because undersea pressure affects their speech organs, communication among divers has always been difficult or impossible. But today, most oceanographers avoid the use of vulnerable human divers, preferring to reduce the risk to human life and make direct observations by means of instruments that are lowered into the ocean, from samples taken from the water, or from photographs made by orbiting satellites. Direct observations of the ocean floor can be made not only by divers but also by deep-diving submarines in the water and even by the technology of sophisticated aerial photography from vantage points above the surface of the water. Some submarines can dive to depths of more than seven miles and cruise at depths of fifteen thousand feet. In addition, radio-equipped buoys can be operated by remote control in order to transmit information back to land-based laboratories via satellite. Particularly important for ocean study are data about water temperature, currents, and weather. Satellite photographs can show the distribution of sea ice, oil slicks, and cloud formations over the ocean. Maps created from satellite pictures can represent the temperature and the color of the ocean's surface, enabling researchers to study the ocean currents from laboratories on dry land. Furthermore, computers help oceanographers to collect, organize, and analyze data from submarines and satellites. By creating a model of the ocean's movement and characteristics, scientists can predict the patterns and possible effects of the ocean on the environment.

Recently, many oceanographers have been relying more on satellites and computers than on research ships or even submarine vehicles because they can supply a greater range of information more quickly and more effectively. Some of humankind's most serious problems, especially those concerning energy and food, may be solved with the help of observations made possible by this new technology.

1. With what topic is the passage primarily concerned?

    Ⓐ Technological advances in oceanography
    Ⓑ Communication among divers
    Ⓒ Direct observation of the ocean floor
    Ⓓ Undersea vehicles

2. The word sluggish in paragraph 1 is closest in meaning to

    Ⓐ nervous
    Ⓑ confused
    Ⓒ slow moving
    Ⓓ very weak

Beginning

Recent technological advances in manned and unmanned undersea vehicles, along with breakthroughs in satellite technology and computer equipment, have overcome some of the limitations of divers and diving equipment for scientists doing research on the great oceans of the world. Without a vehicle, divers often became sluggish, and their mental concentration was severely limited. Because undersea pressure affects their speech organs, communication among divers has always been difficult or impossible. But today, most oceanographers avoid the use of vulnerable human divers, preferring to reduce the risk to human life and make direct observations by means of instruments that are lowered into the ocean, from samples taken from the water, or from photographs made by orbiting satellites. Direct observations of the ocean floor can be made not only by divers but also by deep-diving submarines in the water and even by the technology of sophisticated aerial photography from vantage points above the surface of the water. Some submarines can dive to depths of more than seven miles and cruise at

3. Divers have had problems in communicating underwater because

    Ⓐ the pressure affected their speech organs
    Ⓑ the vehicles they used have not been perfected
    Ⓒ they did not pronounce clearly
    Ⓓ the water destroyed their speech organs

4. This passage suggests that the successful exploration of the ocean depends upon

    Ⓐ vehicles as well as divers
    Ⓑ radios that divers use to communicate
    Ⓒ controlling currents and the weather
    Ⓓ the limitations of diving equipment

5. Undersea vehicles

 Ⓐ are too small for a man to fit inside
 Ⓑ are very slow to respond
 Ⓒ have the same limitations that divers have
 Ⓓ make direct observations of the ocean floor

6. The word cruise in paragraph 1 could best be replaced by

 Ⓐ travel at a constant speed
 Ⓑ function without problems
 Ⓒ stay in communication
 Ⓓ remain still

More Available

affects their speech organs, communication among divers has always been difficult or impossible. But today, most oceanographers avoid the use of vulnerable human divers, preferring to reduce the risk to human life and make direct observations by means of instruments that are lowered into the ocean, from samples taken from the water, or from photographs made by orbiting satellites. Direct observations of the ocean floor can be made not only by divers but also by deep-diving submarines in the water and even by the technology of sophisticated aerial photography from vantage points above the surface of the water. Some submarines can dive to depths of more than seven miles and cruise at depths of fifteen thousand feet. In addition, radio-equipped buoys can be operated by remote control in order to transmit information back to land-based laboratories via satellite. Particularly important for ocean study are data about water temperature, currents, and weather. Satellite photographs can show the distribution of sea ice, oil slicks, and cloud formations over the ocean. Maps created from satellite pictures can represent

---

7. How is a radio-equipped buoy operated?

 Ⓐ By operators inside the vehicle in the part underwater
 Ⓑ By operators outside the vehicle on a ship
 Ⓒ By operators outside the vehicle on a diving platform
 Ⓓ By operators outside the vehicle in a laboratory on shore

8. Look at the word information in the passage. Click on the word or phrase in the **bold** text that is closest in meaning to information .

End

important for ocean study are data about water temperature, currents, and weather. Satellite photographs can show the distribution of sea ice, oil slicks, and cloud formations over the ocean. Maps created from satellite pictures can represent the temperature and the color of the ocean's surface, enabling researchers to study the ocean currents from laboratories on dry land. **Furthermore, computers help oceanographers to collect, organize, and analyze data from submarines and satellites. By creating a model of the ocean's movement and characteristics, scientists can predict the patterns and possible effects of the ocean on the environment.**

 Recently, many oceanographers have been relying more on satellites and computers than on research ships or even submarine vehicles because they can supply a greater range of information more quickly and more effectively. Some of humankind's most serious problems, especially those concerning energy and food, may be solved with the help of observations made possible by this new technology.

---

9. Which of the following are NOT shown in satellite photographs?

 Ⓐ The temperature of the ocean's surface
 Ⓑ Cloud formations over the ocean
 Ⓒ A model of the ocean's movements
 Ⓓ The location of sea ice

10. Look at the word those in the passage. Click on the word or phrase in the **bold** text that those refers to.

End

important for ocean study are data about water temperature, currents, and weather. Satellite photographs can show the distribution of sea ice, oil slicks, and cloud formations over the ocean. Maps created from satellite pictures can represent the temperature and the color of the ocean's surface, enabling researchers to study the ocean currents from laboratories on dry land. Furthermore, computers help oceanographers to collect, organize, and analyze data from submarines and satellites. By creating a model of the ocean's movement and characteristics, scientists can predict the patterns and possible effects of the ocean on the environment.

Recently, many oceanographers have been relying more on satellites and computers than on research ships or even submarine vehicles because they can supply a greater range of information more quickly and more effectively. Some of humankind's most serious problems, especially those concerning energy and food, may be solved with the help of observations made possible by this new technology.

---

11. Click on the paragraph in the passage that discusses problems that new technology might help eliminate.

Scroll the passage to see all of the paragraphs.

Although speech is generally accepted as the most advanced form of communication, there are many ways of communicating without using words. In every known culture, signals, signs, symbols, and gestures are commonly utilized as instruments of communication. There is a great deal of agreement among communication scientists as to what each of these methods is and how each differs from the others. For instance, the basic function of any signal is to impinge upon the environment in such a way that it attracts attention, as, for example, the dots and dashes that can be applied in a telegraph circuit. Coded to refer to speech, the potential for communication through these dots and dashes—short and long intervals as the circuit is broken—is very great. Less adaptable to the codification of words, signs also contain agreed upon meaning; that is, they convey information in and of themselves. Two examples are the hexagonal red sign that conveys the meaning of *stop*, and the red and white swirled pole outside a shop that communicates the meaning of *barber*.

Symbols are more difficult to describe than either signals or signs because of their intricate relationship with the receiver's cultural perceptions. In some cultures, applauding in a theater provides performers with an auditory symbol of approval. In other cultures, if done in unison, applauding can be a symbol of the audience's discontent with the performance. Gestures such as waving and handshaking also communicate certain cultural messages.

Although signals, signs, symbols, and gestures are very useful, they also have a major disadvantage in communication. They usually do not allow ideas to be shared without the sender being directly adjacent to the receiver. Without an exchange of ideas, interaction comes to a halt. As a result, means of communication intended to be used across long distances and extended periods must be based upon speech. To radio, television, and the telephone, one must add fax, paging systems, electronic mail, and the Internet, and no one doubts but that there are more means of communication on the horizon.

12. Which of the following would be the best title for the passage?

　　Ⓐ Signs and Signals
　　Ⓑ Gestures
　　Ⓒ Communication
　　Ⓓ Speech

13. What does the author say about speech?

　　Ⓐ It is the only true form of communication.
　　Ⓑ It is dependent upon the advances made by inventors.
　　Ⓒ It is necessary for communication to occur.
　　Ⓓ It is the most advanced form of communication.

14. Click on the sentence in paragraph 1 that defines the function of a signal.

Paragraph 1 is marked with an arrow (→).

> **Beginning**
>
> → Although speech is generally accepted as the most advanced form of communication, there are many ways of communicating without using words. In every known culture, signals, signs, symbols, and gestures are commonly utilized as instruments of communication. There is a great deal of agreement among communication scientists as to what each of these methods is and how each differs from the others. For instance, the basic function of any signal is to impinge upon the environment in such a way that it attracts attention, as, for example, the dots and dashes that can be applied in a telegraph circuit. Coded to refer to speech, the potential for communication through these dots and dashes—short and long intervals as the circuit is broken—is very great. Less adaptable to the codification of words, signs also contain agreed upon meaning; that is, they convey information in and of themselves. Two examples are the hexagonal red sign that conveys the meaning of *stop*, and the red and white swirled pole outside a shop that communicates the meaning of *barber*.
>
> Symbols are more difficult to describe than

15. The phrase impinge upon in paragraph 1 is closest in meaning to

　　Ⓐ intrude
　　Ⓑ improve
　　Ⓒ vary
　　Ⓓ prohibit

> **Beginning**
>
> Although speech is generally accepted as the most advanced form of communication, there are many ways of communicating without using words. In every known culture, signals, signs, symbols, and gestures are commonly utilized as instruments of communication. There is a great deal of agreement among communication scientists as to what each of these methods is and how each differs from the others. For instance, the basic function of any signal is to impinge upon the environment in such a way that it attracts attention, as, for example, the dots and dashes that can be applied in a telegraph circuit. Coded to refer to speech, the potential for communication through these dots and dashes—short and long intervals as the circuit is broken—is very great. Less adaptable to the codification of words, signs also contain agreed upon meaning; that is, they convey information in and of themselves. Two examples are the hexagonal red sign that conveys the meaning of *stop*, and the red and white swirled pole outside a shop that communicates the meaning of *barber*.
>
> Symbols are more difficult to describe than

16. The word it in paragraph 1 refers to

    Ⓐ function
    Ⓑ signal
    Ⓒ environment
    Ⓓ way

17. The word potential in paragraph 1 could best be replaced by

    Ⓐ range
    Ⓑ advantage
    Ⓒ organization
    Ⓓ possibility

Beginning

    Although speech is generally accepted as the most advanced form of communication, there are many ways of communicating without using words. In every known culture, signals, signs, symbols, and gestures are commonly utilized as instruments of communication. There is a great deal of agreement among communication scientists as to what each of these methods is and how each differs from the others. For instance, the basic function of any signal is to impinge upon the environment in such a way that it attracts attention, as, for example, the dots and dashes that can be applied in a telegraph circuit. Coded to refer to speech, the potential for communication through these dots and dashes—short and long intervals as the circuit is broken—is very great. Less adaptable to the codification of words, signs also contain agreed upon meaning; that is, they convey information in and of themselves. Two examples are the hexagonal red sign that conveys the meaning of *stop*, and the red and white swirled pole outside a shop that communicates the meaning of *barber*.

    Symbols are more difficult to describe than

Beginning

    Although speech is generally accepted as the most advanced form of communication, there are many ways of communicating without using words. In every known culture, signals, signs, symbols, and gestures are commonly utilized as instruments of communication. There is a great deal of agreement among communication scientists as to what each of these methods is and how each differs from the others. For instance, the basic function of any signal is to impinge upon the environment in such a way that it attracts attention, as, for example, the dots and dashes that can be applied in a telegraph circuit. Coded to refer to speech, the potential for communication through these dots and dashes—short and long intervals as the circuit is broken—is very great. Less adaptable to the codification of words, signs also contain agreed upon meaning; that is, they convey information in and of themselves. Two examples are the hexagonal red sign that conveys the meaning of *stop*, and the red and white swirled pole outside a shop that communicates the meaning of *barber*.

    Symbols are more difficult to describe than

18. Look at the word themselves in the passage. Click on the word or phrase in the **bold** text that themselves refers to.

> **More Available**
>
> scientists as to what each of these methods is and how each differs from the others. For instance, the basic function of any signal is to impinge upon the environment in such a way that it attracts attention, as, for example, the dots and dashes that can be applied in a telegraph circuit. **Coded to refer to speech, the potential for communication through these dots and dashes—short and long intervals as the circuit is broken—is very great. Less adaptable to the codification of words, signs also contain agreed upon meaning; that is, they convey information in and of themselves. Two examples are the hexagonal red sign that conveys the meaning of** *stop,* **and the red and white swirled pole outside a shop that communicates the meaning of** *barber.*
>
> Symbols are more difficult to describe than either signals or signs because of their intricate relationship with the receiver's cultural perceptions. In some cultures, applauding in a theater provides performers with an auditory symbol of approval. In other cultures, if done in unison, applauding can be a symbol of the audience's discontent with the performance. Gestures such as waving and

19. The word intricate in paragraph 2 could best be replaced by which of the following?

- Ⓐ inefficient
- Ⓑ complicated
- Ⓒ historical
- Ⓓ uncertain

> **More Available**
>
> also contain agreed upon meaning; that is, they convey information in and of themselves. Two examples are the hexagonal red sign that conveys the meaning of *stop,* and the red and white swirled pole outside a shop that communicates the meaning of *barber.*
>
> Symbols are more difficult to describe than either signals or signs because of their intricate relationship with the receiver's cultural perceptions. In some cultures, applauding in a theater provides performers with an auditory symbol of approval. In other cultures, if done in unison, applauding can be a symbol of the audience's discontent with the performance. Gestures such as waving and handshaking also communicate certain cultural messages.
>
> Although signals, signs, symbols, and gestures are very useful, they also have a major disadvantage in communication. They usually do not allow ideas to be shared without the sender being directly adjacent to the receiver. Without an exchange of ideas, interaction comes to a halt. As a result, means of communication intended to be used across long distances and extended periods

20. Applauding was cited as an example of

- Ⓐ a signal
- Ⓑ a sign
- Ⓒ a symbol
- Ⓓ a gesture

21. The following sentence can be added to the passage.

> **A loud smacking of the lips after a meal can be either a kinesthetic and auditory symbol of approval and appreciation, or simply a rude noise.**

Where would it best fit in the passage?

Click on the square (■) to add the sentence to the passage.

Scroll the passage to see all of the choices.

> **More Available**
>
> also contain agreed upon meaning; that is, they convey information in and of themselves. ■ Two examples are the hexagonal red sign that conveys the meaning of *stop,* and the red and white swirled pole outside a shop that communicates the meaning of *barber.*
>
> ■ Symbols are more difficult to describe than either signals or signs because of their intricate relationship with the receiver's cultural perceptions. In some cultures, applauding in a theater provides performers with an auditory symbol of approval. In other cultures, if done in unison, applauding can be a symbol of the audience's discontent with the performance. ■ Gestures such as waving and handshaking also communicate certain cultural messages.
>
> Although signals, signs, symbols, and gestures are very useful, they also have a major disadvantage in communication. ■ They usually do not allow ideas to be shared without the sender being directly adjacent to the receiver. Without an exchange of ideas, interaction comes to a halt. As a result, means of communication intended to be used across long distances and extended periods

22. Why were the telephone, radio, and TV invented?

- Ⓐ People were unable to understand signs, symbols, and signals.
- Ⓑ People wanted to communicate across long distances.
- Ⓒ People believed that signs, signals, and symbols were obsolete.
- Ⓓ People wanted new forms of entertainment.

23. Look at the word communication in the passage. Click on the word or phrase in the **bold** text that is closest in meaning to communication .

In some cultures, applauding in a theater provides performers with an auditory symbol of approval. In other cultures, if done in unison, applauding can be a symbol of the audience's discontent with the performance. Gestures such as waving and handshaking also communicate certain cultural messages.

Although signals, signs, symbols, and gestures are very useful, they also have a major disadvantage in communication. They usually do not allow ideas to be shared without the sender being directly adjacent to the receiver. Without an exchange of ideas, interaction comes to a halt. As a result, means of communication intended to be used across long distances and extended periods must be based upon speech. To radio, television, and the telephone, one must add fax, paging systems, electronic mail, and the Internet, and no one doubts but that there are more means of communication on the horizon.

Fertilizer is any substance that can be added to the soil to provide chemical elements essential for plant nutrition so that the yield can be increased. Natural substances such as animal droppings, ashes from wood fires, and straw have been used as fertilizers in fields for thousands of years, and lime has been used since the Romans introduced it during the Empire. It was not until the nineteenth century, however, that chemical fertilizers became widely accepted as normal agricultural practice. Today, both natural and synthetic fertilizers are available in a variety of forms.

A complete fertilizer is usually marked with a formula consisting of three numbers, such as 4-8-2 or 6-6-4, which designate the percentage of content of nitrogen, phosphoric acid, and potash in the order stated. Synthetic fertilizers, produced by factories, are available in either solid or liquid form. Solids, in the shape of chemical granules, are in demand because they are not only easy to store but also easy to apply. Recently, liquids have shown an increase in popularity, accounting for about 20 percent of the nitrogen fertilizer used throughout the world. Formerly, powders were also used, but they were found to be less convenient than either solids or liquids.

Fertilizers have no harmful effects on the soil, the crop, or the consumer as long as they are used according to recommendations based on the results of local research. Occasionally, however, farmers may use more fertilizer than necessary, in which case the plants do not need, and therefore do not absorb, the total amount of fertilizer applied to the soil. The surplus of fertilizer thus can damage not only the crop but also the animals or human beings that eat the crop. Furthermore, fertilizer that is not used in the production of a healthy plant is leached into the water table. Accumulations of chemical fertilizer in the water supply accelerate the growth of algae and, consequently, may disturb the natural cycle of life, contributing to the death of fish. Too much fertilizer on grass can cause digestive disorders in cattle and in infants who drink cow's milk. Fertilizer must be used with great attention to responsible use or it can harm the environment.

24. With which of the following topics is the passage primarily concerned?

   Ⓐ Local research and harmful effects of fertilizer
   Ⓑ Advantages and disadvantages of liquid fertilizer
   Ⓒ A formula for the production of fertilizer
   Ⓓ Content, form, and effects of fertilizer

25. The word essential in paragraph 1 could best be replaced by which of the following?

   Ⓐ limited
   Ⓑ preferred
   Ⓒ anticipated
   Ⓓ required

> **Beginning**
>
> Fertilizer is any substance that can be added to the soil to provide chemical elements essential for plant nutrition so that the yield can be increased. Natural substances such as animal droppings, ashes from wood fires, and straw have been used as fertilizers in fields for thousands of years, and lime has been used since the Romans introduced it during the Empire. It was not until the nineteenth century, however, that chemical fertilizers became widely accepted as normal agricultural practice. Today, both natural and synthetic fertilizers are available in a variety of forms.
>
> A complete fertilizer is usually marked with a formula consisting of three numbers, such as 4-8-2 or 6-6-4, which designate the percentage of content of nitrogen, phosphoric acid, and potash in the order stated. Synthetic fertilizers, produced by factories, are available in either solid or liquid form. Solids, in the shape of chemical granules, are in demand because they are not only easy to store but also easy to apply. Recently, liquids have shown an increase in popularity, accounting for about 20 percent of the nitrogen fertilizer used throughout the world. Formerly, powders were

26. Which of the following has the smallest percentage content in the formula 4-8-2?

   Ⓐ Nitrogen
   Ⓑ Phosphorus
   Ⓒ Acid
   Ⓓ Potash

27. What is the percentage of nitrogen in a 5-8-7 formula fertilizer?

   Ⓐ 3 percent
   Ⓑ 5 percent
   Ⓒ 7 percent
   Ⓓ 8 percent

28. The word designate in paragraph 2 could be replaced by

   Ⓐ modify
   Ⓑ specify
   Ⓒ limit
   Ⓓ increase

> **Beginning**
>
> Fertilizer is any substance that can be added to the soil to provide chemical elements essential for plant nutrition so that the yield can be increased. Natural substances such as animal droppings, ashes from wood fires, and straw have been used as fertilizers in fields for thousands of years, and lime has been used since the Romans introduced it during the Empire. It was not until the nineteenth century, however, that chemical fertilizers became widely accepted as normal agricultural practice. Today, both natural and synthetic fertilizers are available in a variety of forms.
>
> A complete fertilizer is usually marked with a formula consisting of three numbers, such as 4-8-2 or 6-6-4, which designate the percentage of content of nitrogen, phosphoric acid, and potash in the order stated. Synthetic fertilizers, produced by factories, are available in either solid or liquid form. Solids, in the shape of chemical granules, are in demand because they are not only easy to store but also easy to apply. Recently, liquids have shown an increase in popularity, accounting for about 20 percent of the nitrogen fertilizer used throughout the world. Formerly, powders were

29. Which of the following statements about fertilizer is true?

   Ⓐ Powders are more popular than ever.
   Ⓑ Solids are difficult to store.
   Ⓒ Liquids are increasing in popularity.
   Ⓓ Chemical granules are difficult to apply.

30. The word they in paragraph 2 refers to

    Ⓐ powders
    Ⓑ solids
    Ⓒ liquids
    Ⓓ fertilizer

31. The word convenient in paragraph 2 is closest in meaning to

    Ⓐ effective
    Ⓑ plentiful
    Ⓒ easy to use
    Ⓓ cheap to produce

More Available

content of nitrogen, phosphoric acid, and potash in the order stated. Synthetic fertilizers, produced by factories, are available in either solid or liquid form. Solids, in the shape of chemical granules, are in demand because they are not only easy to store but also easy to apply. Recently, liquids have shown an increase in popularity, accounting for about 20 percent of the nitrogen fertilizer used throughout the world. Formerly, powders were also used, but they were found to be less convenient than either solids or liquids.

Fertilizers have no harmful effects on the soil, the crop, or the consumer as long as they are used according to recommendations based on the results of local research. Occasionally, however, farmers may use more fertilizer than necessary, in which case the plants do not need, and therefore do not absorb, the total amount of fertilizer applied to the soil. The surplus of fertilizer thus can damage not only the crop but also the animals or human beings that eat the crop. Furthermore, fertilizer that is not used in the production of a healthy plant is leached into the water table. Accumulations of chemical fertilizer in the water

32. Click on the sentence in paragraph 3 that describes the effect of an accumulation of fertilizer in the water supply.

Paragraph 3 is marked with an arrow (→).

```
                                        End

→ Fertilizers have no harmful effects on the soil,
the crop, or the consumer as long as they are
used according to recommendations based on the
results of local research. Occasionally, however,
farmers may use more fertilizer than necessary, in
which case the plants do not need, and therefore
do not absorb, the total amount of fertilizer applied
to the soil. The surplus of fertilizer thus can
damage not only the crop but also the animals or
human beings that eat the crop. Furthermore,
fertilizer that is not used in the production of a
healthy plant is leached into the water table.
Accumulations of chemical fertilizer in the water
supply accelerate the growth of algae and,
consequently, may disturb the natural cycle of
life, contributing to the death of fish. Too much
fertilizer on grass can cause digestive disorders
in cattle and in infants who drink cow's milk.
Fertilizer must be used with great attention to
responsible use or it can harm the environment.
```

33. Look at the word harm in the passage. Click on the word or phrase in the **bold** text that is closest in meaning to harm .

```
                                        End

   Fertilizers have no harmful effects on the soil,
the crop, or the consumer as long as they are
used according to recommendations based on the
results of local research. Occasionally, however,
farmers may use more fertilizer than necessary, in
which case the plants do not need, and therefore
do not absorb, the total amount of fertilizer applied
to the soil. **The surplus of fertilizer thus can
damage not only the crop but also the animals or
human beings that eat the crop. Furthermore,
fertilizer that is not used in the production of a
healthy plant is leached into the water table.
Accumulations of chemical fertilizer in the water
supply accelerate the growth of algae and,
consequently, may disturb the natural cycle of
life, contributing to the death of fish. Too much
fertilizer on grass can cause digestive disorders
in cattle and in infants who drink cow's milk.
Fertilizer must be used with great attention to
responsible use or it can harm the environment.**
```

34. The following sentence can be added to the passage.

One objection to powders was their propensity to become solid chunks if the bags got damp.

Where would it best fit in the passage?

Click on the square (■) to add the sentence to the passage.

Scroll the passage to see all of the choices.

```
                              More Available

content of nitrogen, phosphoric acid, and potash
in the order stated. Synthetic fertilizers, produced
by factories, are available in either solid or liquid
form. Solids, in the shape of chemical granules,
are in demand because they are not only easy to
store but also easy to apply. ■ Recently, liquids
have shown an increase in popularity, accounting
for about 20 percent of the nitrogen fertilizer used
throughout the world. ■ Formerly, powders were
also used, but they were found to be less
convenient than either solids or liquids. ■
   Fertilizers have no harmful effects on the soil,
the crop, or the consumer as long as they are
used according to recommendations based on the
results of local research. ■ Occasionally, however,
farmers may use more fertilizer than necessary, in
which case the plants do not need, and therefore
do not absorb, the total amount of fertilizer applied
to the soil. The surplus of fertilizer thus can
damage not only the crop but also the animals or
human beings that eat the crop. Furthermore,
fertilizer that is not used in the production of a
healthy plant is leached into the water table.
Accumulations of chemical fertilizer in the water
```

The development of the horse has been recorded from the beginning through all of its evolutionary stages to the modern form. It is, in fact, one of the most complete and well-documented chapters of paleontological history. Fossil finds provide us not only with detailed information about the horse itself but also with valuable insights into the migration of herds, and even evidence for speculation about the climatic conditions that could have instigated such migratory behavior.

Geologists believe that the first horses appeared on Earth about sixty million years ago as compared with two million years ago for the appearance of human beings. There is evidence of early horses on both the American and European continents, but it has been documented that, almost twelve million years ago at the beginning of the Pliocene Age, a horse about midway through its evolutionary development crossed a land bridge where the Bering Strait is now located, from Alaska into the grasslands of Asia, and traveled all the way to Europe. This early horse was a hipparion, about the size of a modern-day pony with three toes and specialized cheek teeth for grazing. In Europe, the hipparion encountered another less advanced horse called the anchitheres, which had previously invaded Europe by the same route, probably during the Miocene Period. Less developed and smaller than the hipparion, the anchitheres was eventually completely replaced by it.

By the end of the Pleistocene Age, both the anchitheres and the hipparion had become extinct in North America where they had originated, as fossil evidence clearly indicates. In Europe, they evolved into the larger and stronger animal that is very similar to the horse as we know it today. For many years, the horse was probably hunted for food by early tribes of human beings. Then the qualities of the horse that would have made it a good servant were noted—mainly its strength and speed. It was time for the horse to be tamed, used as a draft animal at the dawning of agriculture, and then ridden as the need for transportation increased. It was the descendant of this domesticated horse that was brought back to the Americas by European colonists.

35. What is this passage mainly about?

Ⓐ The evolution of the horse
Ⓑ The migration of horses
Ⓒ The modern-day pony
Ⓓ The replacement of the anchitheres by the hipparion

36. According to the author, fossils are considered valuable for all of the following reasons EXCEPT

Ⓐ they suggest how the climate may have been
Ⓑ they provide information about migration
Ⓒ they document the evolution of the horse
Ⓓ they maintain a record of life prior to the Miocene Age

37. The word instigated in paragraph 1 could best be replaced by

Ⓐ explained
Ⓑ caused
Ⓒ improved
Ⓓ influenced

Beginning

The development of the horse has been recorded from the beginning through all of its evolutionary stages to the modern form. It is, in fact, one of the most complete and well-documented chapters of paleontological history. Fossil finds provide us not only with detailed information about the horse itself but also with valuable insights into the migration of herds, and even evidence for speculation about the climatic conditions that could have instigated such migratory behavior.

Geologists believe that the first horses appeared on Earth about sixty million years ago as compared with two million years ago for the appearance of human beings. There is evidence of early horses on both the American and European continents, but it has been documented that, almost twelve million years ago at the beginning of the Pliocene Age, a horse about midway through its evolutionary development crossed a land bridge where the Bering Strait is now located, from Alaska into the grasslands of Asia, and traveled all the way to Europe. This early horse was a hipparion, about the size of a modern-day pony with three toes and specialized

38. What does the author mean by the statement Geologists believe that the first horses appeared on Earth about sixty million years ago as compared with two million years ago for the appearance of human beings?

Ⓐ Horses appeared long before human beings according to the theories of geologists.

Ⓑ Both horses and human beings appeared several million years ago, if we believe geologists.

Ⓒ The geological records for the appearance of horses and human beings are not very accurate.

Ⓓ Horses and human beings cannot be compared by geologists because they appeared too long ago.

Beginning

The development of the horse has been recorded from the beginning through all of its evolutionary stages to the modern form. It is, in fact, one of the most complete and well-documented chapters of paleontological history. Fossil finds provide us not only with detailed information about the horse itself but also with valuable insights into the migration of herds, and even evidence for speculation about the climatic conditions that could have instigated such migratory behavior.

Geologists believe that the first horses appeared on Earth about sixty million years ago as compared with two million years ago for the appearance of human beings. There is evidence of early horses on both the American and European continents, but it has been documented that, almost twelve million years ago at the beginning of the Pliocene Age, a horse about midway through its evolutionary development crossed a land bridge where the Bering Strait is now located, from Alaska into the grasslands of Asia, and traveled all the way to Europe. This early horse was a hipparion, about the size of a modern-day pony with three toes and specialized

---

39. Which of the following conclusions may be made on the basis of information in the passage?

Ⓐ The hipparions migrated to Europe to feed in developing grasslands.

Ⓑ There are no fossil remains of either the anchitheres or the hipparion.

Ⓒ There were horses in North America when the first European colonists arrived.

Ⓓ Very little is known about the evolution of the horse.

---

40. According to this passage, the hipparions were

Ⓐ five-toed animals

Ⓑ not as highly developed as the anchitheres

Ⓒ larger than the anchitheres

Ⓓ about the size of a small dog

41. The word it in paragraph 2 refers to

Ⓐ anchitheres

Ⓑ hipparion

Ⓒ Miocene Period

Ⓓ route

More Available

appearance of human beings. There is evidence of early horses on both the American and European continents, but it has been documented that, almost twelve million years ago at the beginning of the Pliocene Age, a horse about midway through its evolutionary development crossed a land bridge where the Bering Strait is now located, from Alaska into the grasslands of Asia, and traveled all the way to Europe. This early horse was a hipparion, about the size of a modern-day pony with three toes and specialized cheek teeth for grazing. In Europe, the hipparion encountered another less advanced horse called the anchitheres, which had previously invaded Europe by the same route, probably during the Miocene Period. Less developed and smaller than the hipparion, the anchitheres was eventually completely replaced by it.

By the end of the Pleistocene Age both the anchitheres and the hipparion had become extinct in North America, where they had originated, as fossil evidence clearly indicates. In Europe, they evolved into the larger and stronger animal that is very similar to the horse as we know it today. For

42. The word extinct in paragraph 3 is closest in meaning to

    Ⓐ familiar
    Ⓑ widespread
    Ⓒ nonexistent
    Ⓓ tame

End

cheek teeth for grazing. In Europe, the hipparion encountered another less advanced horse called the anchitheres, which had previously invaded Europe by the same route, probably during the Miocene Period. Less developed and smaller than the hipparion, the anchitheres was eventually completely replaced by it.

By the end of the Pleistocene Age both the anchitheres and the hipparion had become extinct in North America, where they had originated, as fossil evidence clearly indicates. In Europe, they evolved into the larger and stronger animal that is very similar to the horse as we know it today. For many years, the horse was probably hunted for food by early tribes of human beings. Then the qualities of the horse that would have made it a good servant were noted—mainly its strength and speed. It was time for the horse to be tamed, used as a draft animal at the dawning of agriculture, and then ridden as the need for transportation increased. It was the descendant of this domesticated horse that was brought back to the Americas by European colonists.

---

43. Click on the paragraph that refers to the potential for conclusions from the evidence supplied by fossil remains.

Scroll the passage to see all of the paragraphs.

44. Look at the word domesticated in the passage. Click on the word or phrase in the **bold** text that is closest in meaning to domesticated .

End

By the end of the Pleistocene Age both the anchitheres and the hipparion had become extinct in North America, where they had originated, as fossil evidence clearly indicates. In Europe, they evolved into the larger and stronger animal that is very similar to the horse as we know it today. **For many years, the horse was probably hunted for food by early tribes of human beings. Then the qualities of the horse that would have made it a good servant were noted—mainly its strength and speed. It was time for the horse to be tamed, used as a draft animal at the dawning of agriculture, and then ridden as the need for transportation increased. It was the descendant of this domesticated horse that was brought back to the Americas by European colonists.**

---

45. It can be concluded from this passage that the

    Ⓐ Miocene Period was prior to the Pliocene
    Ⓑ Pleistocene Period was prior to the Miocene
    Ⓒ Pleistocene Period was prior to the Pliocene
    Ⓓ Pliocene Period was prior to the Miocene

To check your answers for Model Test 2, refer to the Answer Key on page 489. For an explanation of the answers, refer to the Explanatory Answers for Model Test 2 on pages 521–541.

Writing Section:
Model Test 2

When you take a Model Test, you should use one sheet of paper, both sides. Time each Model Test carefully. After you have read the topic, you should spend 30 minutes writing. For results that would be closest to the actual testing situation, it is recommended that an English teacher score your test, using the guidelines on page 244 of this book.

Read and think about the following statement:

Pets should be treated like family members.

Do you agree or disagree with the statement? Give reasons to support your opinion.

Notes

To check your essay, refer to the Checklist on page 489. For an Example Essay, refer to the Explanatory Answers for Model Test 2 on page 541.

Model Test 3
Computer-Assisted TOEFL

Section 1:
Listening

The Listening Section of the test measures the ability to understand conversations and talks in English. You will use headphones to listen to the conversations and talks. While you are listening, pictures of the speakers or other information will be presented on your computer screen. There are two parts to the Listening Section, with special directions for each part.

On the day of the test, the amount of time you will have to answer all of the questions will appear on the computer screen. The time you spend listening to the test material will not be counted. The listening material and questions about it will be presented only one time. You will not be allowed to take notes or have any paper at your computer. You will both see and hear the questions before the answer choices appear. You can take as much time as you need to select an answer; however, it will be to your advantage to answer the questions as quickly as possible. You may change your answer as many times as you want before you confirm it. After you have confirmed an answer, you will not be able to return to the question.

Before you begin working on the Listening Section, you will have an opportunity to adjust the volume of the sound. You may not be able to change the volume after you have started the test.

QUESTION DIRECTIONS — Part A

In Part A of the Listening Section, you will hear short conversations between two people. In some of the conversations, each person speaks only once. In other conversations, one or both of the people speak more than once. Each conversation is followed by one question about it.

Each question in this part has four answer choices. You should click on the best answer to each question. Answer the questions on the basis of what is stated or implied by the speakers.

1. What does the woman mean?

   Ⓐ She will not go home for spring vacation.
   Ⓑ She has not taken a vacation for a long time.
   Ⓒ She does not plan to graduate.
   Ⓓ She does not want to go home after graduation in May.

2. What are the speakers talking about?

   Ⓐ The class.
   Ⓑ The weekend.
   Ⓒ Homework.
   Ⓓ Books.

3. What does the man mean?

   Ⓐ He should have prepared more.
   Ⓑ He is very worried.
   Ⓒ He has been studying a lot.
   Ⓓ He needs a few more days.

4. What will the man probably do?

   Ⓐ Buy a textbook.
   Ⓑ Come back later.
   Ⓒ Go to the bookstore.
   Ⓓ Drop his English class.

5. What does the woman mean?

   Ⓐ She does not like the class.
   Ⓑ Her classmates are really great.
   Ⓒ The professor is not very nice.
   Ⓓ The class is interesting.

6. What will the woman probably do?

   (A) Make an appointment with Dr. Peterson's T.A.
   (B) Cancel her appointment with the T.A.
   (C) Postpone her appointment with Dr. Peterson's T.A.
   (D) See the T.A. more often.

7. What does the man mean?

   (A) He would rather have American food.
   (B) He has always liked American food.
   (C) He is accustomed to eating American food.
   (D) He ate American food more in the past.

8. What does the man mean?

   (A) He should go to bed.
   (B) He did not know the time.
   (C) He is trying to bring his work up to date.
   (D) He is not sleepy yet.

9. What is the woman going to do?

   (A) Spend some time with the man.
   (B) Make a list of the names.
   (C) Pass out the names.
   (D) Let someone else call the names.

10. What does the man mean?

    (A) The woman has missed the deadline.
    (B) He will investigate the situation.
    (C) The deadline has been canceled.
    (D) An exception might be possible.

11. What does the man mean?

    (A) The book is confusing.
    (B) He is doing well in the class.
    (C) The teacher is not very clear.
    (D) The lectures are from the book.

12. What does the woman mean?

    (A) She wants to submit her paper early.
    (B) The answers on the paper are all correct.
    (C) The deadline has passed for the paper.
    (D) The paper is not quite finished.

13. What does the woman say about the class?

    (A) She does not like the class.
    (B) It is not a required class.
    (C) She has already taken the class.
    (D) The man will have to take the class.

14. What did the T.A. suggest the students do?

    (A) Study together.
    (B) Prepare for an oral final.
    (C) Review the quizzes.
    (D) Take the professor's advice.

15. What is the woman going to do?

    (A) Make an appointment.
    (B) Give the man a pen.
    (C) Sign the form for the man.
    (D) Wait for the man.

16. What is the woman going to do?

    (A) Revise her work.
    (B) Close the window.
    (C) Copy from the man.
    (D) Hand in the work.

17. What had the man assumed about the loan payment?

    (A) The computer made an error.
    (B) The payment is due on the fifth of every month.
    (C) The loan must be paid by the first of the month.
    (D) The loan had already been paid in full.

QUESTION DIRECTIONS — Part B

In Part B of the Listening Section, you will hear several longer conversations and talks. Each conversation or talk is followed by several questions. The conversations, talks, and questions will not be repeated.

The conversations and talks are about a variety of topics. You do not need special knowledge of the topics to answer the questions correctly. Rather, you should answer each question on the basis of what is stated or implied by the speakers in the conversations or talks.

For most of the questions, you will need to click on the best of four possible answers. Some questions will have special directions. The special directions will appear in a box on the computer screen.

18. Why did Betty see Professor Hayes?

   Ⓐ To enroll in a class.
   Ⓑ To ask his opinion about a university.
   Ⓒ To find out who is chair of the selection committee.
   Ⓓ To get a letter for graduate school.

19. What does Professor Hayes think about Betty?

   Ⓐ She might need to take his seminar.
   Ⓑ She should do well in graduate school.
   Ⓒ She had better go to another university.
   Ⓓ She needs to apply before the end of April.

20. Who will decide whether Betty is accepted to the program?

   Ⓐ The chair of the selection committee.
   Ⓑ The entire selection committee.
   Ⓒ Professor Hayes.
   Ⓓ Dr. Warren.

21. When does Betty need to submit all her materials?

   Ⓐ On May 1.
   Ⓑ In three days.
   Ⓒ Before the April 30th deadline.
   Ⓓ Today.

22. Who is the speaker?

   Ⓐ A professor of religion.
   Ⓑ A professor of history.
   Ⓒ A guest lecturer in a drama class.
   Ⓓ A guest lecturer in a writing class.

23. According to the speaker, how did England control trade in the eighteenth century?

   Ⓐ By threatening to go to war.
   Ⓑ By competing with farmers.
   Ⓒ By keeping manufacturing processes secret.
   Ⓓ By stealing plans from the colonies.

24. What did Samuel Slater do?

   Ⓐ He kept designs for English machinery from being used in the colonies.
   Ⓑ He prevented Moses Brown from opening a mill.
   Ⓒ He committed designs for English machinery to memory.
   Ⓓ He smuggled drawings for English machines into the United States.

25. What happened as a result of the Slater-Brown partnership?

   Ⓐ A change from agriculture to industry began to occur in the United States.
   Ⓑ A rise in prices for English goods was evidenced.
   Ⓒ Many small farmers began to send their products to England.
   Ⓓ Americans had to keep their manufacturing processes secret.

26. What is the purpose of this conversation?

   Ⓐ The man wants to reserve textbooks for the following semester.
   Ⓑ The man is complaining about not having his books this semester.
   Ⓒ The woman needs to order enough books for the class.
   Ⓓ The woman is helping the man register for his courses.

27. What was the man's problem last semester?

    Ⓐ The bookstore was closed for three weeks.

    Ⓑ His books did not arrive before the semester began.

    Ⓒ He did not have any books this semester.

    Ⓓ He did not understand how to order his books.

28. How can the man order books?

    Ⓐ The teacher will order books for the class.

    Ⓑ He could fill out a form and pay for the books now.

    Ⓒ He must wait until the semester begins.

    Ⓓ He has to register for the classes, and the books will be ordered for him.

29. How will the man know that the books have arrived?

    Ⓐ He will receive a form in the mail.

    Ⓑ He will get a phone call.

    Ⓒ He will stop by the bookstore at the beginning of the semester.

    Ⓓ He will receive the books from his teacher in class.

30. What is the instructor defining?

    Ⓐ The term "essay."

    Ⓑ Prose writing.

    Ⓒ Personal viewpoint.

    Ⓓ Brainstorming.

31. What is the main point of the talk?

    Ⓐ The work of Alexander Pope.

    Ⓑ The difference between prose and poetry.

    Ⓒ The general characteristics of essays.

    Ⓓ The reason that the phrase "personal essay" is redundant.

32. According to the talk, which of the characteristics are NOT true of an essay?

    Ⓐ It is usually short.

    Ⓑ It can be either prose or poetry.

    Ⓒ It expresses a personal point of view.

    Ⓓ It discusses one topic.

33. What will the students probably do as an assignment?

    Ⓐ They will prepare for a quiz.

    Ⓑ They will write their first essay.

    Ⓒ They will read works by Pope.

    Ⓓ They will review their notes.

34. What is the main purpose of this talk?

    Ⓐ To provide an overview of U.S. history from 1743 to 1826.

    Ⓑ To discuss Jefferson's contribution to the American Revolution.

    Ⓒ To analyze Jefferson's presidency.

    Ⓓ To summarize Jefferson's life.

35. Jefferson was a member of which political group?

    Ⓐ Monarchist.

    Ⓑ Federalist.

    Ⓒ Republican.

    Ⓓ Democrat.

36. How did Jefferson become president?

    Ⓐ He received the most votes.

    Ⓑ Congress approved him.

    Ⓒ Aaron Burr withdrew from the race.

    Ⓓ As vice president, he automatically became president.

37. According to the lecturer, what was it that Jefferson was NOT?

    Ⓐ An effective public speaker.

    Ⓑ An architect.

    Ⓒ A literary draftsman.

    Ⓓ A diplomat.

38. What are the two most common places where fossils may be found?

Click on 2 answers.

    Ａ Ice.

    Ｂ Mud.

    Ｃ Sand.

    Ｄ Water.

39. The professor briefly explains a process. Summarize the process by putting the events in order.

> Click on a sentence. Then click on the space where it belongs. Use each sentence only once.

A A mold of the organism preserves the shape of the organism.
B Water soaks into the organism.
C Organisms are buried in mud or sand.
D Minerals in the water dissolve the original organism.

1 [   ]

2 [   ]

3 [   ]

4 [   ]

40. What is lost in the process of replacement?

- Ⓐ The fine shapes of fragile structures.
- Ⓑ The internal features of the plant or animal.
- Ⓒ The minerals in the deposit.
- Ⓓ The original fossil mold.

41. Why are the layers of sedimentary rock important to the fossil record?

- Ⓐ The ages of the fossils may be determined by their location in the layers of rock.
- Ⓑ The shapes of the fossils may be preserved in the layers of rock.
- Ⓒ The rock protects the fossils from the mineral water that dissolves them.
- Ⓓ Plants and animals that are formed at the same time are buried in different layers of rock.

42. Why didn't the man apply for graduation?

- Ⓐ He wasn't sure that he had completed the requirements.
- Ⓑ He did not have enough credit hours.
- Ⓒ He did not have a program of study.
- Ⓓ He did not understand that it was necessary.

43. How did the man select his courses?

- Ⓐ By reading the catalog.
- Ⓑ By consulting with the woman.
- Ⓒ By referring to his signed program of study.
- Ⓓ By making an appointment with his advisor.

44. What does the woman suggest?

- Ⓐ The man should take the required courses for graduation.
- Ⓑ The man should see an academic advisor to help him.
- Ⓒ The man should read the requirements in the college catalog.
- Ⓓ The man should bring her a copy of his transcript.

45. What is the man's problem?

- Ⓐ He may not have enough credit hours to graduate.
- Ⓑ He may not have taken the correct classes to graduate.
- Ⓒ He may not be able to see an academic advisor before graduation.
- Ⓓ He may not have time to take the rest of the required courses.

46. In which class would this discussion probably take place?

- Ⓐ Sociology.
- Ⓑ Education.
- Ⓒ Linguistics.
- Ⓓ Geography.

47. According to the discussion, what is the definition of a standard dialect?

- Ⓐ The dialect that is selected by the government.
- Ⓑ The dialect that is of a higher value than the others.
- Ⓒ The dialect that is able to express everything necessary.
- Ⓓ The dialect that is the model taught in schools.

48. What is the linguistic perspective put forward in the articles that were assigned?

   Ⓐ Some accents are not permitted in schools.

   Ⓑ There is only one standard accent in the United States.

   Ⓒ There is one major dialect in the United States.

   Ⓓ All dialects are of equal value.

49. Which two linguistic components are included in a dialect?

       Click on 2 answers.

   Ⓐ Grammar.

   Ⓑ Pronunciation.

   Ⓒ Vocabulary.

   Ⓓ Spelling.

50. What do sociologists tell us about accents?

   Ⓐ Some accents are more prestigious because they are spoken by the upper classes.

   Ⓑ Because they are more comprehensible, some accents are inherently better than others.

   Ⓒ One of the purposes of schools is to teach the accents that are considered most important.

   Ⓓ In general, accents are not as important as dialects because there is no standard for them.

Section 2: Structure

This section measures the ability to recognize language that is appropriate for standard written English. There are two types of questions in this section.

In the first type of question, there are incomplete sentences. Beneath each sentence, there are four words or phrases. You will choose the one word or phrase that best completes the sentence. Clicking on a choice darkens the oval. After you click on **Next** and **Confirm Answer**, the next question will be presented.

The second type of question has four underlined words or phrases. You will choose the one underlined word or phrase that must be changed for the sentence to be correct. Clicking on an underlined word or phrase will darken it. After you click on **Next** and **Confirm Answer**, the next question will be presented.

1. In simple animals, _____ reflex movement or involuntary response to stimuli.

   Ⓐ behavior mostly
   Ⓑ most is behavior
   Ⓒ most behavior is
   Ⓓ the most behavior

2. Although the weather in Martha's Vineyard isn't _____ to have a year-round tourist season, it has become a favorite summer resort.

   Ⓐ goodly enough
   Ⓑ good enough
   Ⓒ good as enough
   Ⓓ enough good

3. A swarm of locusts <u>is responsible</u> the
          Ⓐ
   consumption of <u>enough plant material</u>
                        Ⓑ
   <u>to feed</u> a million <u>and a half</u> people.
       Ⓒ   Ⓓ

4. Oyster <u>farming</u> has been <u>practice</u> in <u>most</u>
                Ⓐ   Ⓑ   Ⓒ
   parts of the world <u>for</u> many years.
                        Ⓓ

5. <u>It</u> was Shirley Temple Black <u>which</u>
    Ⓐ   Ⓑ
   <u>represented</u> her country in the United
       Ⓒ
   Nations and <u>later</u> became an ambassador.
                  Ⓓ

6. According to the wave theory, _____ population of the Americas may have been the result of a number of separate migrations.

   Ⓐ the
   Ⓑ their
   Ⓒ that
   Ⓓ whose

7. It is presumed that rules governing the sharing of food influenced _____ that the earliest cultures evolved.

   Ⓐ that the way
   Ⓑ is the way
   Ⓒ the way
   Ⓓ which way

8. The prices <u>at</u> chain stores <u>are</u> as reasonable,
                Ⓐ   Ⓑ
   <u>if not more</u> reasonable, <u>as</u> those at discount
       Ⓒ   Ⓓ
   stores.

9. <u>Historically</u> <u>there</u> <u>has been</u> <u>only</u> two major
       Ⓐ   Ⓑ   Ⓒ   Ⓓ
   factions in the Republican Party—the

   liberals and the conservatives.

10. Whitman wrote *Leaves of Grass* as a tribute

    to the Civil War soldiers who <u>had laid</u> on the
                                     Ⓐ
    battlefields and <u>whom</u> he <u>had seen</u>
                        Ⓑ   Ⓒ
    <u>while serving</u> as an army nurse.
        Ⓓ

11. Calculus, _____ elegant and economical symbolic system, can reduce complex problems to simple terms.

  Ⓐ it is an
  Ⓑ that an
  Ⓒ an
  Ⓓ is an

12. Canada does not require that U.S. citizens obtain passports to enter the country, and _____ .

  Ⓐ Mexico does neither
  Ⓑ Mexico doesn't either
  Ⓒ neither Mexico does
  Ⓓ either does Mexico

13. The Chinese were the first and large ethnic
       Ⓐ   Ⓑ
    group to work on the construction of the
             Ⓒ   Ⓓ
    transcontinental railroad system.

14. The range of plant life on a mountainside

    is a results of differences in temperature and
    Ⓐ   Ⓑ   Ⓒ
    precipitation at varying altitudes.
                      Ⓓ

15. The poet _____ just beginning to be recognized as an important influence at the time of his death.

  Ⓐ being Walt Whitman
  Ⓑ who was Walt Whitman
  Ⓒ Walt Whitman
  Ⓓ Walt Whitman was

16. _____ the formation of the sun, the planets, and other stars began with the condensation of an interstellar cloud.

  Ⓐ It accepted that
  Ⓑ Accepted that
  Ⓒ It is accepted that
  Ⓓ That is accepted

17. The more the relative humidity reading rises,
                                            Ⓐ
    the worst the heat affects us.
    Ⓑ   Ⓒ   Ⓓ

18. Because correlations are not causes,
                               Ⓐ
    statistical data which are extremely easy
                  Ⓑ   Ⓒ
    to misuse.
    Ⓓ

19. As a general rule, the standard of living _____ by the average output of each person in society.

  Ⓐ is fixed
  Ⓑ fixed
  Ⓒ has fixed
  Ⓓ fixes

20. Despite of many attempts to introduce a
    Ⓐ   Ⓑ   Ⓒ
    universal language, notably Esperanto and

    Idiom Neutral, the effort has met with very

    little success.
    Ⓓ

21. The *Consumer Price Index* lists _____ .

  Ⓐ how much costs every car
  Ⓑ how much does every car cost
  Ⓒ how much every car costs
  Ⓓ how much are every car cost

22. As every other nation, the United States
    Ⓐ   Ⓑ
    used to define its unit of currency, the dollar,
    Ⓒ   Ⓓ
    in terms of the gold standard.

23. The Ford Theater where Lincoln was shot _____ .

  Ⓐ must restore
  Ⓑ must be restoring
  Ⓒ must have been restored
  Ⓓ must restored

24. John Dewey thought that children <u>will learn</u>

(A)

<u>better</u> through participating in experiences

(B)

<u>rather than</u> through <u>listening to</u> lectures.

(C)   (D)

25. <u>Some</u> methods <u>to prevent</u> soil erosion <u>are</u>

(A)   (B)   (C)

plowing parallel with the slopes of hills,

<u>to plant</u> trees on unproductive land, and

(D)

rotating crops.

Section 3:
Reading

This section measures the ability to read and understand short passages similar in topic and style to those that students are likely to encounter in North American universities and colleges. This section contains reading passages and questions about the passages. There are several different types of questions in this section.

In the Reading Section, you will first have the opportunity to read the passage. You will use the scroll bar to view the rest of the passage.

When you have finished reading the passage, you will use the mouse to click on **Proceed**. Then the questions about the passage will be presented. You are to choose the one best answer to each question. Answer all questions about the information in a passage on the basis of what is stated or implied in that passage.

Most of the questions will be multiple-choice questions. To answer these questions you will click on a choice below the question.

To answer some questions, you will click on a word or phrase.
To answer some questions, you will click on a sentence in the passage.
To answer some questions, you will click on a square to add a sentence to the passage.

Few men have influenced the development of American English to the extent that Noah Webster did. Born in West Hartford, Connecticut, in 1758, Webster graduated from Yale in 1778. He was admitted to the bar in 1781 and thereafter began to practice law in Hartford. Later, when he turned to teaching, he discovered how inadequate the available schoolbooks were for the children of a new and independent nation. In response to the need for truly American textbooks, Webster published *A Grammatical Institute of the English Language,* a three-volume work that consisted of a speller, a grammar, and a reader. The first volume, which was generally known as *The American Spelling Book,* was so popular that eventually it sold more than 80 million copies and provided him with a considerable income for the rest of his life. While teaching, Webster began work on the *Compendious Dictionary of the English Language,* which was published in 1806, and was also very successful.

In 1807, Noah Webster began his greatest work, *An American Dictionary of the English Language.* In preparing the manuscript, he devoted ten years to the study of English and its relationship to other languages, and seven more years to the writing itself. Published in two volumes in 1828, *An American Dictionary of the English Language* has become the recognized authority for usage in the United States. Webster's purpose in writing it was to demonstrate that the American language was developing distinct meanings, pronunciations, and spellings from those of British English. He is responsible for advancing simplified spelling forms: *develop* instead of *develope; plow* instead of *plough; jail* instead of *gaol; theater* and *center* instead of *theatre* and *centre; color* and *honor* instead of *colour* and *honour.*

Webster was the first author to gain copyright protection in the United States by being awarded a copyright for his *American Speller.* He continued, for the next fifty years, to lobby for improvements in the protection of intellectual properties, that is, authors' rights. In 1840 Webster brought out a second edition of his dictionary, which included 70,000 entries instead of the original 38,000. The name Webster has become synonymous with American dictionaries. This edition served as the basis for the many revisions that have been produced by others, ironically, under the uncopyrighted Webster name.

1. Which of the following would be the best title for the passage?

   Ⓐ Webster's Work
   Ⓑ Webster's Dictionaries
   Ⓒ Webster's School
   Ⓓ Webster's Life

2. The word inadequate in paragraph 1 could best be replaced by

   Ⓐ unavailable
   Ⓑ expensive
   Ⓒ difficult
   Ⓓ unsatisfactory

Beginning

Few men have influenced the development of American English to the extent that Noah Webster did. Born in West Hartford, Connecticut, in 1758, Webster graduated from Yale in 1778. He was admitted to the bar in 1781 and thereafter began to practice law in Hartford. Later, when he turned to teaching, he discovered how inadequate the available schoolbooks were for the children of a new and independent nation. In response to the need for truly American textbooks, Webster published *A Grammatical Institute of the English Language,* a three-volume work that consisted of a speller, a grammar, and a reader. The first volume, which was generally known as *The American Spelling Book,* was so popular that eventually it sold more than 80 million copies and provided him with a considerable income for the rest of his life. While teaching, Webster began work on the *Compendious Dictionary of the English Language,* which was published in 1806, and was also very successful.

In 1807, Noah Webster began his greatest work, *An American Dictionary of the English Language.* In preparing the manuscript, he devoted

3. Why did Webster write *A Grammatical Institute of the English Language*?

   Ⓐ He wanted to supplement his income.
   Ⓑ There were no books available after the Revolutionary War.
   Ⓒ He felt that British books were not appropriate for American children.
   Ⓓ The children did not know how to spell.

4. From which publication did Webster earn a lifetime income?

Ⓐ *Compendious Dictionary of the English Language*
Ⓑ *An American Dictionary of the English Language*
Ⓒ *An American Dictionary of the English Language: Second Edition*
Ⓓ *The American Spelling Book*

5. Look at the word popular in the passage. Click on the word or phrase in the **bold** text that is closest in meaning to popular .

> **Beginning**
>
> Few men have influenced the development of American English to the extent that Noah Webster did. Born in West Hartford, Connecticut, in 1758, Webster graduated from Yale in 1778. He was admitted to the bar in 1781 and thereafter began to practice law in Hartford. Later, when he turned to teaching, he discovered how inadequate the available schoolbooks were for the children of a new and independent nation. **In response to the need for truly American textbooks, Webster published *A Grammatical Institute of the English Language,* a three-volume work that consisted of a speller, a grammar, and a reader. The first volume, which was generally known as *The American Spelling Book*, was so popular that eventually it sold more than 80 million copies and provided him with a considerable income for the rest of his life. While teaching, Webster began work on the *Compendious Dictionary of the English Language,* which was published in 1806, and was also very successful.**
>
> In 1807, Noah Webster began his greatest work, *An American Dictionary of the English Language*. In preparing the manuscript, he devoted ten years to

6. The word considerable in paragraph 1 most nearly means

Ⓐ large
Ⓑ prestigious
Ⓒ steady
Ⓓ unexpected

> **Beginning**
>
> Few men have influenced the development of American English to the extent that Noah Webster did. Born in West Hartford, Connecticut, in 1758, Webster graduated from Yale in 1778. He was admitted to the bar in 1781 and thereafter began to practice law in Hartford. Later, when he turned to teaching, he discovered how inadequate the available schoolbooks were for the children of a new and independent nation. In response to the need for truly American textbooks, Webster published *A Grammatical Institute of the English Language,* a three-volume work that consisted of a speller, a grammar, and a reader. The first volume, which was generally known as *The American Spelling Book*, was so popular that eventually it sold more than 80 million copies and provided him with a considerable income for the rest of his life. While teaching, Webster began work on the *Compendious Dictionary of the English Language,* which was published in 1806, and was also very successful.
>
> In 1807, Noah Webster began his greatest work, *An American Dictionary of the English Language*. In preparing the manuscript, he devoted ten years to

7. When was *An American Dictionary of the English Language* published?

Ⓐ 1817
Ⓑ 1807
Ⓒ 1828
Ⓓ 1824

8. The word **it** in paragraph 2 refers to

   Ⓐ language
   Ⓑ usage
   Ⓒ authority
   Ⓓ dictionary

9. Click on the sentence in paragraph 2 that explains Webster's purpose for writing an American dictionary.

   Paragraph 2 is marked with an arrow (→).

More Available

American Spelling Book, was so popular that eventually it sold more than 80 million copies and provided him with a considerable income for the rest of his life. While teaching, Webster began work on the *Compendious Dictionary of the English Language,* which was published in 1806, and was also very successful.

In 1807, Noah Webster began his greatest work, *An American Dictionary of the English Language.* In preparing the manuscript, he devoted ten years to the study of English and its relationship to other languages, and seven more years to the writing itself. Published in two volumes in 1828, *An American Dictionary of the English Language* has become the recognized authority for usage in the United States. Webster's purpose in writing **it** was to demonstrate that the American language was developing distinct meanings, pronunciations, and spellings from those of British English. He is responsible for advancing simplified spelling forms: *develop* instead of *develope; plow* instead of *plough; jail* instead of *gaol; theater* and *center* instead of *theatre* and *centre; color* and *honor* instead of *colour* and *honour.*

More Available

American Spelling Book, was so popular that eventually it sold more than 80 million copies and provided him with a considerable income for the rest of his life. While teaching, Webster began work on the *Compendious Dictionary of the English Language,* which was published in 1806, and was also very successful.
→ In 1807, Noah Webster began his greatest work, *An American Dictionary of the English Language.* In preparing the manuscript, he devoted ten years to the study of English and its relationship to other languages, and seven more years to the writing itself. Published in two volumes in 1828, *An American Dictionary of the English Language* has become the recognized authority for usage in the United States. Webster's purpose in writing **it** was to demonstrate that the American language was developing distinct meanings, pronunciations, and spellings from those of British English. He is responsible for advancing simplified spelling forms: *develop* instead of *develope; plow* instead of *plough; jail* instead of *gaol; theater* and *center* instead of *theatre* and *centre; color* and *honor* instead of *colour* and *honour.*

10. The word distinct in paragraph 2 is closest in meaning to

   (A) new
   (B) simple
   (C) different
   (D) exact

More Available

American Spelling Book, was so popular that eventually it sold more than 80 million copies and provided him with a considerable income for the rest of his life. While teaching, Webster began work on the *Compendious Dictionary of the English Language,* which was published in 1806, and was also very successful.

   In 1807, Noah Webster began his greatest work, *An American Dictionary of the English Language.* In preparing the manuscript, he devoted ten years to the study of English and its relationship to other languages, and seven more years to the writing itself. Published in two volumes in 1828, *An American Dictionary of the English Language* has become the recognized authority for usage in the United States. Webster's purpose in writing it was to demonstrate that the American language was developing distinct meanings, pronunciations, and spellings from those of British English. He is responsible for advancing simplified spelling forms: *develop* instead of *develope; plow* instead of *plough; jail* instead of *gaol; theater* and *center* instead of *theatre* and *centre; color* and *honor* instead of *colour* and *honour.*

---

11. According to this passage, which one of the following spellings would Webster have approved in his dictionaries?

   (A) *Develope*
   (B) *Theatre*
   (C) *Color*
   (D) *Honour*

The San Andreas Fault line is a fracture at the congruence of two major plates of the Earth's crust, one of which supports most of the North American continent, and the other of which underlies the coast of California and part of the ocean floor of the Pacific Ocean. The fault originates about six hundred miles south of the Gulf of California, runs north in an irregular line along the western coast to San Francisco, and continues north for about two hundred more miles before angling off into the ocean. In places, the trace of the fault is marked by a trench, or, in geological terms, a rift, and small ponds called sag ponds dot the landscape. Its western side always moves north in relation to its eastern side. The total net slip along the San Andreas Fault and the length of time it has been active are matters of conjecture, but it has been estimated that, during the past fifteen million years, coastal California along the San Andreas Fault has moved about 190 miles in a northwesterly direction with respect to the North American plate. Although the movement along the fault averages only a few inches a year, it is intermittent and variable. Some segments of the fault do not move at all for long periods of time, building up tremendous pressure that must be released. For this reason, tremors are not unusual along the San Andreas Fault, some of which are classified as major earthquakes. Also for this reason, small tremors are interpreted as safe, since they are understood to be pressure that releases without causing much damage.

   It is worth noting that the San Andreas Fault passes uncomfortably close to several major metropolitan areas, including Los Angeles and San Francisco. In addition, the San Andreas Fault has created smaller fault systems, many of which underlie the smaller towns and cities along the California coast. For this reason, Californians have long anticipated the recurrence of what they refer to as the "Big One," a chain reaction of destructive earthquakes that would measure near 8 on the Richter scale, similar in intensity to those that occurred in 1857 and 1906. Such a quake would wreak devastating effects on the life and property in the region. Unfortunately, as pressure continues to build along the fault, the likelihood of such an earthquake increases substantially.

12. What is the author's main purpose in the passage?

  Ⓐ To describe the San Andreas Fault
  Ⓑ To give a definition of a fault
  Ⓒ To explain the reason for tremors and earthquakes
  Ⓓ To classify different kinds of faults

13. How does the author define the San Andreas Fault?

  Ⓐ A plate that underlies the North American continent
  Ⓑ A crack in the Earth's crust between two plates
  Ⓒ Occasional tremors and earthquakes
  Ⓓ Intense pressure that builds up

14. The word originates in paragraph 1 could best be replaced by

  Ⓐ gets wider
  Ⓑ changes direction
  Ⓒ begins
  Ⓓ disappears

15. In which direction does the western side of the fault move?

  Ⓐ West
  Ⓑ East
  Ⓒ North
  Ⓓ South

16. The word it in paragraph 1 refers to

  Ⓐ total
  Ⓑ net
  Ⓒ side
  Ⓓ fault

Beginning

The San Andreas Fault line is a fracture at the congruence of two major plates of the Earth's crust, one of which supports most of the North American continent, and the other of which underlies the coast of California and part of the ocean floor of the Pacific Ocean. The fault originates about six hundred miles south of the Gulf of California, runs north in an irregular line along the western coast to San Francisco, and continues north for about two hundred more miles before angling off into the ocean. In places, the trace of the fault is marked by a trench, or, in geological terms, a rift, and small ponds called sag ponds dot the landscape. Its western side always moves north in relation to its eastern side. The total net slip along the San Andreas Fault and the length of time it has been active are matters of conjecture, but it has been estimated that, during the past fifteen million years, coastal California along the San Andreas Fault has moved about 190 miles in a northwesterly direction with respect to the North American plate. Although the movement along the fault averages only a few inches a year, it is intermittent and variable. Some

Beginning

The San Andreas Fault line is a fracture at the congruence of two major plates of the Earth's crust, one of which supports most of the North American continent, and the other of which underlies the coast of California and part of the ocean floor of the Pacific Ocean. The fault originates about six hundred miles south of the Gulf of California, runs north in an irregular line along the western coast to San Francisco, and continues north for about two hundred more miles before angling off into the ocean. In places, the trace of the fault is marked by a trench, or, in geological terms, a rift, and small ponds called sag ponds dot the landscape. Its western side always moves north in relation to its eastern side. The total net slip along the San Andreas Fault and the length of time it has been active are matters of conjecture, but it has been estimated that, during the past fifteen million years, coastal California along the San Andreas Fault has moved about 190 miles in a northwesterly direction with respect to the North American plate. Although the movement along the fault averages only a few inches a year, it is intermittent and variable. Some

17. The word intermittent in paragraph 1 could best be replaced by which of the following?

   Ⓐ dangerous
   Ⓑ predictable
   Ⓒ uncommon
   Ⓓ occasional

Beginning

The San Andreas Fault line is a fracture at the congruence of two major plates of the Earth's crust, one of which supports most of the North American continent, and the other of which underlies the coast of California and part of the ocean floor of the Pacific Ocean. The fault originates about six hundred miles south of the Gulf of California, runs north in an irregular line along the western coast to San Francisco, and continues north for about two hundred more miles before angling off into the ocean. In places, the trace of the fault is marked by a trench, or, in geological terms, a rift, and small ponds called sag ponds dot the landscape. Its western side always moves north in relation to its eastern side. The total net slip along the San Andreas Fault and the length of time it has been active are matters of conjecture, but it has been estimated that, during the past fifteen million years, coastal California along the San Andreas Fault has moved about 190 miles in a northwesterly direction with respect to the North American plate. Although the movement along the fault averages only a few inches a year, it is intermittent and variable. Some

---

18. Along the San Andreas Fault, tremors are

   Ⓐ small and insignificant
   Ⓑ rare, but disastrous
   Ⓒ frequent events
   Ⓓ very unpredictable

19. The phrase "the Big One" refers to which of the following?

   Ⓐ A serious earthquake
   Ⓑ The San Andreas Fault
   Ⓒ The Richter scale
   Ⓓ California

20. Look at the word destructive in the passage. Click on the word or phrase in the **bold** text that is closest in meaning to destructive.

End

It is worth noting that the San Andreas Fault passes uncomfortably close to several major metropolitan areas, including Los Angeles and San Francisco. In addition, the San Andreas Fault has created smaller fault systems, many of which underlie the smaller towns and cities along the California coast. **For this reason, Californians have long anticipated the recurrence of what they refer to as the "Big One," a chain reaction of destructive earthquakes that would measure near 8 on the Richter scale, similar in intensity to those that occurred in 1857 and 1906. Such a quake would wreak devastating effects on the life and property in the region. Unfortunately, as pressure continues to build along the fault, the likelihood of such an earthquake increases substantially.**

---

21. Look at the word those in the passage. Click on the word or phrase in the **bold** text that those refers to.

End

It is worth noting that the San Andreas Fault passes uncomfortably close to several major metropolitan areas, including Los Angeles and San Francisco. In addition, the San Andreas Fault has created smaller fault systems, many of which underlie the smaller towns and cities along the California coast. For this reason, Californians have long anticipated the recurrence of what they refer to as the "Big One," a chain reaction of destructive earthquakes that would measure near 8 on the Richter scale, similar in intensity to those that occurred in 1857 and 1906. Such a quake would wreak devastating effects on the life and property in the region. Unfortunately, as pressure continues to build along the fault, the likelihood of such an earthquake increases substantially.

22. Which of the following words best describes the San Andreas Fault?

Ⓐ Straight
Ⓑ Deep
Ⓒ Wide
Ⓓ Rough

The body of an adult insect is subdivided into three sections, including a head, a three-segment thorax, and segmented abdomen. Ordinarily, the thorax bears three pairs of legs and a single or double pair of wings. The vision of most adult insects is specialized through two large compound eyes and multiple simple eyes.

Features of an insect's mouth parts are used in classifying insects into types. Biting mouth parts, called mandibles, such as the mouth parts found in grasshoppers and beetles, are common among insects. Behind the mandibles are located the maxillae, or lower jaw parts, which serve to direct food into the mouth between the jaws. A labrum above and one below are similar to another animal's upper and lower lips. In an insect with a sucking mouth function, the mandibles, maxillae, labrum, and labium are modified in such a way that they constitute a tube through which liquid such as water, blood, or flower nectar can be drawn. In a butterfly or moth, this coiled drinking tube is called the proboscis because of its resemblance, in miniature, to the trunk of an elephant or a very large nose. Composed chiefly of modified maxillae fitted together, the insect's proboscis can be flexed and extended to reach nectar deep in a flower. In mosquitoes or aphids, mandibles and maxillae are modified to sharp stylets with which the insect can drill through surfaces like human or vegetable skin membranes to reach juice. In a housefly, the expanding labium forms a spongelike mouth pad that it can use to stamp over the surface of food, sopping up food particles and juices.

Insects, the most numerous creatures on our planet, are also the most adaptable. They require little food because they are small. They easily find shelter and protection in small crevices in trees and surface geological formations. Species of insects can evolve quickly because of their rapid reproduction cycle; they live in every climate, some making their homes in the frozen Arctic regions and many others choosing the humid, warm, and nutrient-rich rain forest environment. An active part of the natural food cycle, insects provide nutrition for animals and devour waste products of other life forms.

23. What is the best title for this passage?

    Ⓐ An Insect's Environment
    Ⓑ The Structure of an Insect
    Ⓒ Grasshoppers and Beetles
    Ⓓ The Stages of Life of an Insect

24. Look at the word subdivided in the passage. Click on the word or phrase in the **bold** text that is closest in meaning to subdivided.

Beginning

The body of an adult insect is subdivided into three sections, including a head, a three-segment thorax, and segmented abdomen. Ordinarily, the thorax bears three pairs of legs and a single or double pair of wings. The vision of most adult insects is specialized through two large compound eyes and multiple simple eyes.

Features of an insect's mouth parts are used in classifying insects into types. Biting mouth parts, called mandibles, such as the mouth parts found in grasshoppers and beetles, are common among insects. Behind the mandibles are located the maxillae, or lower jaw parts, which serve to direct food into the mouth between the jaws. A labrum above and one below are similar to another animal's upper and lower lips. In an insect with a sucking mouth function, the mandibles, maxillae, labrum, and labium are modified in such a way that they constitute a tube through which liquid such as water, blood, or flower nectar can be drawn. In a butterfly or moth, this coiled drinking tube is called tho proboscis because of its resemblance, in miniature, to the trunk of an elephant or a very large nose. Composed chiefly

---

25. How are insects classified?

    Ⓐ By the environment in which they live
    Ⓑ By the food they eat
    Ⓒ By the structure of the mouth
    Ⓓ By the number and type of wings

26. The word common in paragraph 2 is closest in meaning to

    Ⓐ normal
    Ⓑ rare
    Ⓒ important
    Ⓓ necessary

Beginning

The body of an adult insect is subdivided into three sections, including a head, a three-segment thorax, and segmented abdomen. Ordinarily, the thorax bears three pairs of legs and a single or double pair of wings. The vision of most adult insects is specialized through two large compound eyes and multiple simple eyes.

Features of an insect's mouth parts are used in classifying insects into types. Biting mouth parts, called mandibles, such as the mouth parts found in grasshoppers and beetles, are common among insects. Behind the mandibles are located the maxillae, or lower jaw parts, which serve to direct food into the mouth between the jaws. A labrum above and one below are similar to another animal's upper and lower lips. In an insect with a sucking mouth function, the mandibles, maxillae, labrum, and labium are modified in such a way that they constitute a tube through which liquid such as water, blood, or flower nectar can be drawn. In a butterfly or moth, this coiled drinking tube is called the proboscis because of its resemblance, in miniature, to the trunk of an elephant or a very large nose. Composed chiefly

---

27. The author compares labrum and labium to

    Ⓐ an upper and lower lip
    Ⓑ mandibles
    Ⓒ maxillae
    Ⓓ jaws

28. What is the proboscis?

    Ⓐ Nectar
    Ⓑ A tube constructed of modified maxillae
    Ⓒ A kind of butterfly
    Ⓓ A kind of flower

29. Which of the following have mandibles and maxillae that have been modified to sharp stylets?

    Ⓐ Grasshoppers
    Ⓑ Butterflies
    Ⓒ Mosquitoes
    Ⓓ Houseflies

30. The phrase drill through in paragraph 2 could best be replaced by

   Ⓐ penetrate
   Ⓑ saturate
   Ⓒ explore
   Ⓓ distinguish

31. The word it in paragraph 2 refers to

   Ⓐ pad
   Ⓑ food
   Ⓒ housefly
   Ⓓ mouth

More Available

the maxillae, or lower jaw parts, which serve to direct food into the mouth between the jaws. A labrum above and one below are similar to another animal's upper and lower lips. In an insect with a sucking mouth function, the mandibles, maxillae, labrum, and labium are modified in such a way that they constitute a tube through which liquid such as water, blood, or flower nectar can be drawn. In a butterfly or moth, this coiled drinking tube is called the proboscis because of its resemblance, in miniature, to the trunk of an elephant or a very large nose. Composed chiefly of modified maxillae fitted together, the insect's proboscis can be flexed and extended to reach nectar deep in a flower. In mosquitoes or aphids, mandibles and maxillae are modified to sharp stylets with which the insect can drill through surfaces like human or vegetable skin membranes to reach juice. In a housefly, the expanding labium forms a spongelike mouth pad that it can use to stamp over the surface of food, sopping up food particles and juices.

Insects, the most numerous creatures on our planet, are also the most adaptable. They require

More Available

the maxillae, or lower jaw parts, which serve to direct food into the mouth between the jaws. A labrum above and one below are similar to another animal's upper and lower lips. In an insect with a sucking mouth function, the mandibles, maxillae, labrum, and labium are modified in such a way that they constitute a tube through which liquid such as water, blood, or flower nectar can be drawn. In a butterfly or moth, this coiled drinking tube is called the proboscis because of its resemblance, in miniature, to the trunk of an elephant or a very large nose. Composed chiefly of modified maxillae fitted together, the insect's proboscis can be flexed and extended to reach nectar deep in a flower. In mosquitoes or aphids, mandibles and maxillae are modified to sharp stylets with which the insect can drill through surfaces like human or vegetable skin membranes to reach juice. In a housefly, the expanding labium forms a spongelike mouth pad that it can use to stamp over the surface of food, sopping up food particles and juices.

Insects, the most numerous creatures on our planet, are also the most adaptable. They require

32. The following sentence can be added to the passage.

Although some insects, like the cockroach, have remained essentially unchanged for eons, most insects adapt readily to changing environmental conditions.

Where would it best fit in the passage?

Click on the square (■) to add the sentence to the passage.

Scroll the passage to see all of the choices.

End

proboscis can be flexed and extended to reach nectar deep in a flower. In mosquitoes or aphids, mandibles and maxillae are modified to sharp stylets with which the insect can drill through surfaces like human or vegetable skin membranes to reach juice. In a housefly, the expanding labium forms a spongelike mouth pad that it can use to stamp over the surface of food, sopping up food particles and juices.

■Insects, the most numerous creatures on our planet, are also the most adaptable. They require little food because they are small. ■ They easily find shelter and protection in small crevices in trees and surface geological formations. ■ Species of insects can evolve quickly because of their rapid reproduction cycle; they live in every climate, some making their homes in the frozen Arctic regions and many others choosing the humid, warm, and nutrient-rich rain forest environment. An active part of the natural food cycle, insects provide nutrition for animals and devour waste products of other life forms. ■

33. What is the purpose of this passage?

Ⓐ To complain
Ⓑ To persuade
Ⓒ To entertain
Ⓓ To inform

The protozoans, minute aquatic creatures, each of which consists of a single cell of protoplasm, constitute a classification of the most primitive forms of animal life. The very name *protozoan* indicates the scientific understanding of the animals. *Proto-* means first or primitive, and *zoa* refers to animal. They are fantastically diverse, but three major groups may be identified on the basis of their motility. The Mastigophora have one or more long tails that they use to propel themselves forward. The Ciliata, which use the same basic means for locomotion as the Mastigophora, have a larger number of short tails. The Sarcodina, which include amoebae, float or row themselves about on their crusted bodies.

In addition to their form of movement, several other features discriminate among the three groups of protozoans. For example, at least two nuclei per cell have been identified in the Ciliata, usually a large nucleus that regulates growth but decomposes during reproduction, and a smaller one that contains the genetic code necessary to generate the large nucleus.

Chlorophyll, which is the green substance encountered in plants, is found in the bodies of some protozoans, enabling them to make some of their own food from water and carbon dioxide. Protozoans are not considered plants but animals, because unlike pigmented plants to which some protozoans are otherwise almost identical, they do not live on simple organic compounds. Their cell demonstrates all of the major characteristics of the cells of higher animals, such as eating, breathing, and reproducing.

Many species of protozoans collect into colonies, physically connected to one another and responding uniformly to outside stimulae. Current research into this phenomenon along with investigations carried out with advanced microscopes may necessitate a redefinition of what constitutes protozoans, even calling into question the basic premise that they have only one cell. Nevertheless, with the current data available, almost 40,000 species of protozoans have been identified. No doubt, as technology improves methods of observation, better models of classification of these simple single cells will be proposed.

34. With what topic is the passage primarily concerned?

    Ⓐ Colonies of protozoans
    Ⓑ Mastigophora
    Ⓒ Motility in protozoans
    Ⓓ Characteristics of protozoans

35. The word minute in paragraph 1 could best be replaced by

    Ⓐ very common
    Ⓑ very fast
    Ⓒ very old
    Ⓓ very small

37. Look at the word motility in the passage. Click on the word or phrase in the **bold** text that is closest in meaning to motility .

> **Beginning**
>
>   The protozoans, minute aquatic creatures, each of which consists of a single cell of protoplasm, constitute a classification of the most primitive forms of animal life. The very name *protozoan* indicates the scientific understanding of the animals. *Proto-* means first or primitive, and *zoa* refers to animal. **They are fantastically diverse, but three major groups may be identified on the basis of their motility. The Mastigophora have one or more long tails that they use to propel themselves forward. The Ciliata, which use the same basic means for locomotion as the Mastigophora, have a larger number of short tails. The Sarcodina, which include amoebae, float or row themselves about on their crusted bodies.**
>
>   In addition to their form of movement, several other features discriminate among the three groups of protozoans. For example, at least two nuclei per cell have been identified in the Ciliata, usually a large nucleus that regulates growth but decomposes during reproduction, and a smaller one that contains the genetic code necessary to generate the large nucleus.
>
>   Chlorophyll, which is the green substance

> **Beginning**
>
>   The protozoans, minute aquatic creatures, each of which consists of a single cell of protoplasm, constitute a classification of the most primitive forms of animal life. The very name *protozoan* indicates the scientific understanding of the animals. *Proto-* means first or primitive, and *zoa* refers to animal. They are fantastically diverse, but three major groups may be identified on the basis of their motility. The Mastigophora have one or more long tails that they use to propel themselves forward. The Ciliata, which use the same basic means for locomotion as the Mastigophora, have a larger number of short tails. The Sarcodina, which include amoebae, float or row themselves about on their crusted bodies.
>
>   In addition to their form of movement, several other features discriminate among the three groups of protozoans. For example, at least two nuclei per cell have been identified in the Ciliata, usually a large nucleus that regulates growth but decomposes during reproduction, and a smaller one that contains the genetic code necessary to generate the large nucleus.
>
>   Chlorophyll, which is the green substance

36. What is protoplasm?

    Ⓐ A class of protozoan
    Ⓑ The substance that forms the cell of a protozoan
    Ⓒ A primitive animal similar to a protozoan
    Ⓓ An animal that developed from a protozoan

38. What does the author mean by the statement They are fantastically diverse, but three major groups may be identified on the basis of their motility?

    Ⓐ The three major groups are unique in that they all move in the same manner.
    Ⓑ Everything we know about the protozoans is tied into their manner of movement.
    Ⓒ The manner of movement is critical when classifying the three major groups of protozoa.
    Ⓓ Mobility in the protozoans is insignificant.

41. Why are protozoans classified as animals?

    Ⓐ They do not live on simple organic compounds.
    Ⓑ They collect in colonies.
    Ⓒ They respond uniformly to outside stimulae.
    Ⓓ They may have more than one cell.

42. The word they in paragraph 4 refers to

    Ⓐ protozoans
    Ⓑ microscopes
    Ⓒ investigations
    Ⓓ colonies

Beginning

The protozoans, minute aquatic creatures, each of which consists of a single cell of protoplasm, constitute a classification of the most primitive forms of animal life. The very name *protozoan* indicates the scientific understanding of the animals. *Proto-* means first or primitive, and *zoa* refers to animal. They are fantastically diverse, but three major groups may be identified on the basis of their motility. The Mastigophora have one or more long tails that they use to propel themselves forward. The Ciliata, which use the same basic means for locomotion as the Mastigophora, have a larger number of short tails. The Sarcodina, which include amoebae, float or row themselves about on their crusted bodies.

In addition to their form of movement, several other features discriminate among the three groups of protozoans. For example, at least two nuclei per cell have been identified in the Ciliata, usually a large nucleus that regulates growth but decomposes during reproduction, and a smaller one that contains the genetic code necessary to generate the large nucleus.

Chlorophyll, which is the green substance

More Available

In addition to their form of movement, several other features discriminate among the three groups of protozoans. For example, at least two nuclei per cell have been identified in the Ciliata, usually a large nucleus that regulates growth but decomposes during reproduction, and a smaller one that contains the genetic code necessary to generate the large nucleus.

Chlorophyll, which is the green substance encountered in plants, is found in the bodies of some protozoans, enabling them to make some of their own food from water and carbon dioxide. Protozoans are not considered plants but animals, because unlike pigmented plants to which some protozoans are otherwise almost identical, they do not live on simple organic compounds. Their cell demonstrates all of the major characteristics of the cells of higher animals, such as eating, breathing, and reproducing.

Many species of protozoans collect into colonies, physically connected to one another and responding uniformly to outside stimulae. Current research into this phenomenon along with investigations carried out with advanced microscopes may necessitate a redefinition of what constitutes protozoans, even calling into question the basic premise that they have only one cell. Nevertheless, with the current data available, almost 40,000 species of protozoans have been identified. No doubt, as technology improves methods of observation, better models of classification of these simple single cells will be proposed.

---

39. To which class of protozoans do the amoebae belong?

    Ⓐ Mastigophora
    Ⓑ Ciliata
    Ⓒ Sarcodina
    Ⓓ Motility

40. What is the purpose of the large nucleus in the Ciliata?

    Ⓐ It generates the other nucleus.
    Ⓑ It contains the genetic code for the small nucleus.
    Ⓒ It regulates growth.
    Ⓓ It reproduces itself.

43. Click on the sentence in paragraph 4 that brings into question the current belief that protozoans are single celled.

    Paragraph 4 is marked with an arrow (→).

> **End**
>
> some protozoans, enabling them to make some of their own food from water and carbon dioxide. Protozoans are not considered plants but animals, because unlike pigmented plants to which some protozoans are otherwise almost identical, they do not live on simple organic compounds. Their cell demonstrates all of the major characteristics of the cells of higher animals, such as eating, breathing, and reproducing.
> → Many species of protozoans collect into colonies, physically connected to one another and responding uniformly to outside stimulae. Current research into this phenomenon along with investigations carried out with advanced microscopes may necessitate a redefinition of what constitutes protozoans, even calling into question the basic premise that they have only one cell. Nevertheless, with the current data available, almost 40,000 species of protozoans have been identified. No doubt, as technology improves methods of observation, better models of classification of these simple single cells will be proposed.

44. The word uniformly in paragraph 4 is closest in meaning to

    Ⓐ in the same way
    Ⓑ once in a while
    Ⓒ all of a sudden
    Ⓓ in the long run

> **End**
>
> some protozoans, enabling them to make some of their own food from water and carbon dioxide. Protozoans are not considered plants but animals, because unlike pigmented plants to which some protozoans are otherwise almost identical, they do not live on simple organic compounds. Their cell demonstrates all of the major characteristics of the cells of higher animals, such as eating, breathing, and reproducing.
> Many species of protozoans collect into colonies, physically connected to one another and responding uniformly to outside stimulae. Current research into this phenomenon along with investigations carried out with advanced microscopes may necessitate a redefinition of what constitutes protozoans, even calling into question the basic premise that they have only one cell. Nevertheless, with the current data available, almost 40,000 species of protozoans have been identified. No doubt, as technology improves methods of observation, better models of classification of these simple single cells will be proposed.

45. Which of the following statements is NOT true of protozoans?

    Ⓐ There are approximately 40,000 species.
    Ⓑ They are the most primitive forms of animal life.
    Ⓒ They have a large cell and a smaller cell.
    Ⓓ They are difficult to observe.

To check your answers for Model Test 3, refer to the Answer Key on page 490. For an explanation of the answers, refer to the Explanatory Answers for Model Test 3 on pages 542–561.

Writing Section:
Model Test 3

When you take a Model Test, you should use one sheet of paper, both sides. Time each Model Test carefully. After you have read the topic, you should spend 30 minutes writing. For results that would be closest to the actual testing situation, it is recommended that an English teacher score your test, using the guidelines on page 244 of this book.

Many people have learned a foreign language in their own country; others have learned a foreign language in the country in which it is spoken. Which is better? Give the advantages of each and support your viewpoint.

Notes

To check your essay, refer to the Checklist on page 490. For an Example Essay, refer to the Explanatory Answers for Model Test 3 on page 561.

Model Test 4
Computer-Assisted TOEFL

Section 1:
Listening

The Listening Section of the test measures the ability to understand conversations and talks in English. You will use headphones to listen to the conversations and talks. While you are listening, pictures of the speakers or other information will be presented on your computer screen. There are two parts to the Listening Section, with special directions for each part.

On the day of the test, the amount of time you will have to answer all of the questions will appear on the computer screen. The time you spend listening to the test material will not be counted. The listening material and questions about it will be presented only one time. You will not be allowed to take notes or have any paper at your computer. You will both see and hear the questions before the answer choices appear. You can take as much time as you need to select an answer; however, it will be to your advantage to answer the questions as quickly as possible. You may change your answer as many times as you want before you confirm it. After you have confirmed an answer, you will not be able to return to the question.

Before you begin working on the Listening Section, you will have an opportunity to adjust the volume of the sound. You may not be able to change the volume after you have started the test.

QUESTION DIRECTIONS — Part A

In Part A of the Listening Section, you will hear short conversations between two people. In some of the conversations, each person speaks only once. In other conversations, one or both of the people speak more than once. Each conversation is followed by one question about it.

Each question in this part has four answer choices. You should click on the best answer to each question. Answer the questions on the basis of what is stated or implied by the speakers.

1. What will the woman probably do?

   Ⓐ Have a party.
   Ⓑ Attend the International Students' Association.
   Ⓒ Go to work.
   Ⓓ Get some rest.

2. What will the speakers probably do?

   Ⓐ Leave immediately.
   Ⓑ Watch the game on TV.
   Ⓒ Start to play.
   Ⓓ Eat a sandwich.

3. What did the man do after he lost his passport?

   Ⓐ He went to see the foreign student advisor.
   Ⓑ He went to Washington.
   Ⓒ He wrote to the Passport Office.
   Ⓓ He reported it to the Passport Office.

4. What does the woman suggest the man do?

   Ⓐ Ask Dr. Tyler to clarify the assignment.
   Ⓑ Show a preliminary version to Dr. Tyler.
   Ⓒ Let her see the first draft before Dr. Tyler sees it.
   Ⓓ Talk to some of the other students in Dr. Tyler's class.

5. What does the woman mean?

   Ⓐ Dr. Clark is a good teacher.
   Ⓑ Statistics is a boring class.
   Ⓒ Two semesters of statistics are required.
   Ⓓ The students do not like Dr. Clark.

6. What are the speakers discussing?

   Ⓐ A teacher.
   Ⓑ A textbook.
   Ⓒ An assignment.
   Ⓓ A movie.

7. What had the man assumed about the woman?

   Ⓐ She was Sally Harrison's cousin.
   Ⓑ She was Sally Harrison's sister.
   Ⓒ She was Sally Harrison's friend.
   Ⓓ She was Sally Harrison.

8. What is the woman's problem?

   Ⓐ The desk drawer won't open.
   Ⓑ The pen is out of ink.
   Ⓒ She cannot find her pen.
   Ⓓ She is angry with the man.

9. What does the man imply about John?

   Ⓐ John is usually late.
   Ⓑ John will be there at eight-thirty.
   Ⓒ John will not show up.
   Ⓓ John is usually on time.

10. What does the man mean?

   Ⓐ The results of the tests are not available.
   Ⓑ The experiment had unexpected results.
   Ⓒ He has not completed the experiment yet.
   Ⓓ It is taking a lot of time to do the experiment.

11. What does the man imply about Barbara?

   Ⓐ She does not put much effort in her studies.
   Ⓑ She is very likable.
   Ⓒ She prefers talking to the woman.
   Ⓓ She has a telephone.

12. What does the man suggest the woman do?

   Ⓐ See the doctor.
   Ⓑ Get another job.
   Ⓒ Go to the counter.
   Ⓓ Buy some medicine.

13. What does the woman mean?

   Ⓐ She will try her best.
   Ⓑ She has to save her money.
   Ⓒ She is still undecided.
   Ⓓ She needs an application.

14. What does the woman mean?

   Ⓐ The man must stop working.
   Ⓑ There is a little more time.
   Ⓒ The test is important.
   Ⓓ It is time for the test.

15. What does the man imply?

   Ⓐ The woman's roommate took a different class.
   Ⓑ The book is very expensive.
   Ⓒ The textbook may have been changed.
   Ⓓ The course is not offered this semester.

16. What does the woman imply?

   Ⓐ Sally may get a bike for Christmas.
   Ⓑ Sally already has a bike like that one.
   Ⓒ Sally likes riding a bike.
   Ⓓ Sally may prefer a different gift.

17. What does the woman suggest that the man do?

   Ⓐ Take a break.
   Ⓑ Go to work.
   Ⓒ Do the other problems.
   Ⓓ Keep trying.

QUESTION DIRECTIONS — Part B

In Part B of the Listening Section, you will hear several longer conversations and talks. Each conversation or talk is followed by several questions. The conversations, talks, and questions will not be repeated.

The conversations and talks are about a variety of topics. You do not need special knowledge of the topics to answer the questions correctly. Rather, you should answer each question on the basis of what is stated or implied by the speakers in the conversations or talks.

For most of the questions, you will need to click on the best of four possible answers. Some questions will have special directions. The special directions will appear in a box on the computer screen.

18. What is the topic under discussion?

    Ⓐ Whether to introduce the metric system in the United States.
    Ⓑ How the metric system should be introduced in the United States.
    Ⓒ Which system is better—the English system or the metric system.
    Ⓓ How to convert measurements from the English system to the metric system.

19. What changes in measurement in the United States have the students observed?

    Ⓐ Now the weather on radio and TV is reported exclusively in metrics.
    Ⓑ Road signs have miles marked on them, but not kilometers.
    Ⓒ Both the English system and the metric system are being used on signs, packages, and in weather reports.
    Ⓓ Grocery stores use only metrics for their packaging.

20. What was Professor Baker's opinion?

    Ⓐ He thought that a gradual adoption would be better for everyone.
    Ⓑ He thought that only metrics should be used.
    Ⓒ He thought that only the English system should be used.
    Ⓓ He thought that adults should use both systems, but that children should be taught only the metric system.

21. Which word best describes Professor Baker's attitude toward his students?

    Ⓐ Unfriendly.
    Ⓑ Patronizing.
    Ⓒ Uninterested.
    Ⓓ Cooperative.

22. What is the talk mainly about?

    Ⓐ Private industry.
    Ⓑ Advances in medicine.
    Ⓒ Space missions.
    Ⓓ Technological developments.

23. Which of the advances listed are NOT mentioned as part of the technology developed for space missions?

    Ⓐ Contact lenses.
    Ⓑ Cordless tools.
    Ⓒ Food packaging.
    Ⓓ Ultrasound.

24. According to the speaker, why did NASA develop ultrasound?

    Ⓐ To monitor the condition of astronauts in spacecraft.
    Ⓑ To evaluate candidates who wanted to join the space program.
    Ⓒ To check the health of astronauts when they returned from space.
    Ⓓ To test spacecraft and equipment for imperfections.

25. Why does the speaker mention archeology?

    Ⓐ Archaeologists and astronauts were compared.
    Ⓑ Astronauts made photographs of the earth later used by archaeologists.
    Ⓒ Archaeologists have used advances in medical technology developed for astronauts.
    Ⓓ Space missions and underwater missions are very similar.

26. Why did the student want to see the professor?

    Ⓐ To give her a note from another student.
    Ⓑ To ask for an excused absence from class.
    Ⓒ To get notes from a class that she had missed.
    Ⓓ To make an appointment for help in a class.

27. What is the student's problem?

    Ⓐ She cannot see the slides and videos from her seat.
    Ⓑ Her friend's notes are difficult to read.
    Ⓒ She has been absent from class too often.
    Ⓓ Her family needs her help next week.

28. What does the professor offer to do?

    Ⓐ Ask another student to take notes for the woman.
    Ⓑ Meet with the woman to clarify the classes she will miss.
    Ⓒ Make an appointment for the woman with another professor.
    Ⓓ Repeat the lecture for the woman.

29. What is the professor's attitude in this conversation?

    Ⓐ Disinterested.
    Ⓑ Helpful.
    Ⓒ Appreciative.
    Ⓓ Confused.

30. What is the main purpose of this talk?

    Ⓐ Transportation on the Pacific Coast.
    Ⓑ History of California.
    Ⓒ Orientation to San Francisco.
    Ⓓ Specifications of the Golden Gate Bridge.

31. According to the speaker, what was the settlement called before it was renamed San Francisco?

    Ⓐ Golden Gate.
    Ⓑ San Francisco de Asis Mission.
    Ⓒ Military Post Seventy-six.
    Ⓓ Yerba Buena.

32. According to the speaker, what happened in 1848?

    Ⓐ Gold was discovered.
    Ⓑ The Transcontinental Railroad was completed.
    Ⓒ The Golden Gate Bridge was constructed.
    Ⓓ Telegraph communications were established with the East.

33. How long is the Golden Gate Bridge?

    Ⓐ Eighteen miles.
    Ⓑ 938 feet.
    Ⓒ One mile.
    Ⓓ Between five and six miles.

34. What does the lecturer mainly discuss?

    Ⓐ Transcendentalism.
    Ⓑ Puritanism.
    Ⓒ Ralph Waldo Emerson.
    Ⓓ Nature.

35. During which century did the literary movement develop?

    Ⓐ Seventeenth century.
    Ⓑ Eighteenth century.
    Ⓒ Nineteenth century.
    Ⓓ Twentieth century.

36. According to the speaker, what did the Puritans do?

    Ⓐ They stressed the importance of the individual.
    Ⓑ They supported the ideals of the Transcendental Club.
    Ⓒ They believed that society was more important than the individual.
    Ⓓ They established a commune at Brook Farm.

37. What is *Walden*?

    Ⓐ A book by Emerson.
    Ⓑ A history of Puritanism.
    Ⓒ A novel by Nathaniel Hawthorne.
    Ⓓ A book by Thoreau.

38. What is the purpose of this conversation?

    Ⓐ The man is looking for help with his research.
    Ⓑ The man is applying for a teaching position.
    Ⓒ The man is being trained to give library orientation.
    Ⓓ The man is interviewing for a job in the library.

39. Who is the man?

    Ⓐ A teacher.
    Ⓑ A librarian.
    Ⓒ A graduate student.
    Ⓓ A computer programmer.

40. What does the man need to do when he is not working?

    Ⓐ Take a few days off.
    Ⓑ Begin his own research.
    Ⓒ Write his dissertation.
    Ⓓ Take classes.

41. When would the man be available?

    Ⓐ After he graduates.
    Ⓑ When he completes his dissertation.
    Ⓒ After work and on his days off.
    Ⓓ Immediately.

42. Which two requirements are considered when mounting a solar collector on a roof?

    Click on 2 answers.

    Ⓐ The angle of the collector.
    Ⓑ The thickness of the glass.
    Ⓒ The direction of the exposure.
    Ⓓ The temperature of the air.

43. Identify the fan in the solar heating system.
    Click on a letter.

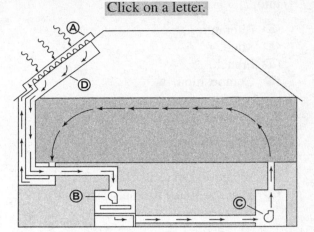

44. What problem does the professor point out?

    Ⓐ Solar heating is very expensive.
    Ⓑ The sun may not be available every day.
    Ⓒ Solar storage systems are too small.
    Ⓓ The sun does not supply enough energy without other power sources.

45. Why does the professor mention the project to place solar modules in orbit?

    Ⓐ It has the potential to generate cheap power.
    Ⓑ It is a research project that he is working on.
    Ⓒ It is the same basic principle he has been explaining.
    Ⓓ It is an example of a very complex model of a solar heating system.

46. What is the purpose of this conversation?

    Ⓐ The man wants to apply for a tutoring position.
    Ⓑ The man needs to arrange for tutoring.
    Ⓒ The man is looking for a friend who works at the Tutoring Center.
    Ⓓ The woman is tutoring the man.

47. For which course does the man want a tutor?

    Ⓐ Literature.
    Ⓑ Math.
    Ⓒ French.
    Ⓓ Composition.

48. How much will the tutoring cost?

    Ⓐ Five dollars an hour.
    Ⓑ Four dollars a session.
    Ⓒ Whatever the student can afford.
    Ⓓ There is no fee for the sessions.

49. When will the tutoring session begin?

    Ⓐ Tuesday morning.
    Ⓑ Thursday morning.
    Ⓒ Tuesday afternoon.
    Ⓓ Thursday afternoon.

50. What should the man bring to his tutoring session?

    Ⓐ A check for five dollars.
    Ⓑ Books and notes.
    Ⓒ His class schedule.
    Ⓓ A composition.

Section 2: Structure

This section measures the ability to recognize language that is appropriate for standard written English. There are two types of questions in this section.

In the first type of question, there are incomplete sentences. Beneath each sentence, there are four words or phrases. You will choose the one word or phrase that best completes the sentence. Clicking on a choice darkens the oval. After you click on **Next** and **Confirm Answer**, the next question will be presented.

The second type of question has four underlined words or phrases. You will choose the one underlined word or phrase that must be changed for the sentence to be correct. Clicking on an underlined word or phrase will darken it. After you click on **Next** and **Confirm Answer**, the next question will be presented.

1. Based on the premise that light was composed of color, the Impressionists came to the conclusion _____ not really black.

    Ⓐ which was that shadows
    Ⓑ was shadows which
    Ⓒ were shadows
    Ⓓ that shadows were

2. _____ a parliamentary system, the prime minister must be appointed on the basis of the distribution of power in the parliament.

    Ⓐ The considered
    Ⓑ To be considered
    Ⓒ Considering
    Ⓓ Considers

3. Interest <u>in</u> automatic data processing has
         Ⓐ
   <u>grown</u> <u>rapid</u> <u>since</u> the first large calculators
    Ⓑ   Ⓒ   Ⓓ
   were introduced in 1950.

4. Vaslav Nijinsky <u>achieved</u> world recognition
                        Ⓐ
   <u>as</u> both <u>a dancer</u> <u>as well as</u> a choreographer.
    Ⓑ   Ⓒ   Ⓓ

5. _____ of the play *Mourning Becomes Electra* introduces the cast of characters and hints at the plot.

    Ⓐ The act first
    Ⓑ Act one
    Ⓒ Act first
    Ⓓ First act

6. The plants that <u>they</u> <u>belong to</u> the family of
                        Ⓐ   Ⓑ
   ferns <u>are</u> quite varied in <u>their</u> size and
            Ⓒ   Ⓓ
   structure.

7. As soon as _____ with an acid, salt, and sometimes water, is formed.

    Ⓐ a base will react
    Ⓑ a base reacts
    Ⓒ a base is reacting
    Ⓓ the reaction of a base

8. Columbus Day <u>is celebrated</u> <u>on</u> the <u>twelve</u> of
                     Ⓐ   Ⓑ   Ⓒ
   October <u>because</u> on that day in 1492,
              Ⓓ
   Christopher Columbus first landed in the

   Americas.

9. One of <u>the most</u> <u>influence</u> newspapers in the
              Ⓐ   Ⓑ
   U.S. <u>is</u> *The New York Times,* which is
          Ⓒ
   <u>widely distributed</u> throughout the world.
          Ⓓ

10. Weathering _____ the action whereby surface rock is disintegrated or decomposed.

    Ⓐ it is
    Ⓑ is that
    Ⓒ is
    Ⓓ being

11. Coastal and inland waters <u>are inhabited</u>
    Ⓐ

    <u>not only</u> by fish but also by <u>such</u> <u>sea creature</u>
    Ⓑ   Ⓒ   Ⓓ

    as shrimps and clams.

12. Economists have tried <u>to discourage</u> <u>the use</u>
    Ⓐ   Ⓑ

    of the phrase "underdeveloped nation" and

    <u>encouraging</u> <u>the more</u> accurate phrase
    Ⓒ   Ⓓ

    "developing nation" in order to suggest an

    ongoing process.

13. A gas <u>like</u> propane will <u>combination</u> with
    Ⓐ   Ⓑ

    water molecules in a saline solution <u>to form</u>
    Ⓒ

    a solid <u>called</u> a hydrate.
    Ⓓ

14. The people of Western Canada have been
    considering _____ themselves from the
    rest of the provinces.

    Ⓐ to separate
    Ⓑ separated
    Ⓒ separate
    Ⓓ separating

15. Although <u>it</u> cannot <u>be proven</u>, <u>presumable</u>
    Ⓐ   Ⓑ   Ⓒ

    the expansion of the universe will slow

    down as <u>it approaches</u> a critical radius.
    Ⓓ

16. A City University professor reported that he

    <u>discovers</u> a vaccine <u>that</u> has been 80 percent
    Ⓐ   Ⓑ

    effective <u>in reducing</u> the instances of tooth
    Ⓒ

    decay <u>among</u> small children.
    Ⓓ

17. When they <u>have been</u> <u>frightened</u>, as, for
    Ⓐ   Ⓑ

    example, <u>by</u> an electrical storm, dairy cows
    Ⓒ

    may refuse <u>giving</u> milk.
    Ⓓ

18. Although Margaret Mead had several assistants during her long investigations of Samoa, the bulk of the research was done by _____ alone.

    Ⓐ herself
    Ⓑ she
    Ⓒ her
    Ⓓ hers

19. Miami, Florida, is <u>among</u> the few cities in the
    Ⓐ

    United States <u>that</u> <u>has been awarded</u> official
    Ⓑ   Ⓒ

    status <u>as</u> bilingual municipalities.
    Ⓓ

20. Fertilizers <u>are used</u> <u>primarily</u> to enrich <u>soil</u>
    Ⓐ   Ⓑ   Ⓒ

    and <u>increasing</u> yield.
    Ⓓ

21. _____ war correspondent, Hemingway used his experiences for some of his most powerful novels.

    Ⓐ But a
    Ⓑ It is a
    Ⓒ While
    Ⓓ A

22. If the ozone gases of the atmosphere

    <u>did not filter out</u> the ultraviolet rays of the
    Ⓐ

    sun, life <u>as</u> we know <u>it</u> would not have
    Ⓑ   Ⓒ

    evolved <u>on Earth</u>.
    Ⓓ

23. Thirty-eight national sites are known as parks, another eighty-two as monuments, and _____ .

    Ⓐ the another one hundred seventy-eight as historical sites
    Ⓑ the other one hundred seventy-eight as historical sites
    Ⓒ seventy-eight plus one hundred more as historical sites
    Ⓓ as historical sites one hundred seventy-eight

24. When he <u>was</u> a little boy, Mark Twain
Ⓐ

    <u>would walk</u> along the piers, <u>watch</u> the river
      Ⓑ   Ⓒ

    boats, <u>swimming</u> and fish in the Mississippi,
           Ⓓ

    much like his famous character, Tom Sawyer.

25. <u>Almost all</u> books have a few errors in them
Ⓐ

    <u>in spite of</u> the care <u>taken</u> to check <u>its</u> proof
      Ⓑ   Ⓒ   Ⓓ

    pages before the final printing.

Section 3:
Reading

This section measures the ability to read and understand short passages similar in topic and style to those that students are likely to encounter in North American universities and colleges. This section contains reading passages and questions about the passages. There are several different types of questions in this section.

In the Reading Section, you will first have the opportunity to read the passage. You will use the scroll bar to view the rest of the passage.

When you have finished reading the passage, you will use the mouse to click on **Proceed**. Then the questions about the passage will be presented. You are to choose the one best answer to each question. Answer all questions about the information in a passage on the basis of what is stated or implied in that passage.

Most of the questions will be multiple-choice questions. To answer these questions you will click on a choice below the question.

To answer some questions, you will click on a word or phrase.
To answer some questions, you will click on a sentence in the passage.
To answer some questions, you will click on a square to add a sentence to the passage.

Precipitation, commonly referred to as rainfall, is a measure of the quantity of atmospheric water in the form of rain, hail, or snow that reaches the ground. The average annual precipitation over the whole of the United States is thirty-six inches per year. It should be understood, however, that all precipitation is not measured equally. For example, a foot of snow does not equal a foot of precipitation. According to the general formula for computing the precipitation of snowfall, ten inches of snow equals one inch of precipitation. In upper New York State, for example, where there is typically a large amount of snowfall every winter, a hundred inches of snow in one year would be recorded as only ten inches of precipitation. On the other hand, rain is rain. Forty inches of rain would be recorded as forty inches of precipitation. The total annual precipitation for an area with forty inches of rain and one hundred inches of snow would be recorded as fifty inches of precipitation.

The amount of precipitation that an area receives is a combined result of several factors, including location, altitude, proximity to the sea, and the direction of prevailing winds. Most of the precipitation in the United States is brought originally by prevailing winds from the Pacific Ocean, the Gulf of Mexico, the Atlantic Ocean, and the Great Lakes. Because these prevailing winds generally come from the west, the Pacific Coast receives more annual precipitation than the Atlantic Coast. Along the Pacific Coast itself, however, altitude causes some diversity in rainfall. The mountain ranges of the United States, especially the Rocky Mountain Range and the Appalachian Mountain Range, influence the amount of precipitation in the areas to the windward and leeward sides of these ranges. East of the Rocky Mountains, the annual precipitation is substantially less than that west of the Rocky Mountains. The precipitation north of the Appalachian Mountains averages 40 percent less than that south of the Appalachian Mountains. As air currents from the oceans move over land, the air must rise to pass over the mountains. The air cools, and the water that is held in the clouds falls as rain or snow on the ascending side of the mountains. The air, therefore, is much drier on the other side of the mountains.

1. What does this passage mainly discuss?

   Ⓐ Precipitation
   Ⓑ Snowfall
   Ⓒ New York State
   Ⓓ A general formula

2. Which of the following is another word that is often used in place of precipitation?

   Ⓐ Humidity
   Ⓑ Wetness
   Ⓒ Rainfall
   Ⓓ Rain-snow

3. The term *precipitation* includes

   Ⓐ only rainfall
   Ⓑ rain, hail, and snow
   Ⓒ rain, snow, and humidity
   Ⓓ rain, hail, and humidity

4. What is the average annual rainfall in inches in the United States?

   Ⓐ Thirty-six inches
   Ⓑ Thirty-eight inches
   Ⓒ Forty inches
   Ⓓ Forty-two inches

5. If a state has 40 inches of snow in a year, by how much does this increase the annual precipitation?

   Ⓐ By two feet
   Ⓑ By four inches
   Ⓒ By four feet
   Ⓓ By 40 inches

6. The phrase proximity to in paragraph 2 is closest in meaning to

   Ⓐ communication with
   Ⓑ dependence on
   Ⓒ nearness to
   Ⓓ similarity to

More Available

The total annual precipitation for an area with forty inches of rain and one hundred inches of snow would be recorded as fifty inches of precipitation. The amount of precipitation that an area receives is a combined result of several factors, including location, altitude, proximity to the sea, and the direction of prevailing winds. Most of the precipitation in the United States is brought originally by prevailing winds from the Pacific Ocean, the Gulf of Mexico, the Atlantic Ocean, and the Great Lakes. Because these prevailing winds generally come from the west, the Pacific Coast receives more annual precipitation than the Atlantic Coast. Along the Pacific Coast itself, however, altitude causes some diversity in rainfall. The mountain ranges of the United States, especially the Rocky Mountain Range and the Appalachian Mountain Range, influence the amount of precipitation in the areas to the windward and leeward sides of these ranges. East of the Rocky Mountains, the annual precipitation is substantially less than that west of the Rocky Mountains. The precipitation north of the Appalachian Mountains averages 40 percent less than that south of the

---

7. Click on the sentence in paragraph 2 that identifies the origins of most of the precipitation in the United States.

Paragraph 2 is marked with an arrow (→).

More Available

The total annual precipitation for an area with forty inches of rain and one hundred inches of snow would be recorded as fifty inches of precipitation. → The amount of precipitation that an area receives is a combined result of several factors, including location, altitude, proximity to the sea, and the direction of prevailing winds. Most of the precipitation in the United States is brought originally by prevailing winds from the Pacific Ocean, the Gulf of Mexico, the Atlantic Ocean, and the Great Lakes. Because these prevailing winds generally come from the west, the Pacific Coast receives more annual precipitation than the Atlantic Coast. Along the Pacific Coast itself, however, altitude causes some diversity in rainfall. The mountain ranges of the United States, especially the Rocky Mountain Range and the Appalachian Mountain Range, influence the amount of precipitation in the areas to the windward and leeward sides of these ranges. East of the Rocky Mountains, the annual precipitation is substantially less than that west of the Rocky Mountains. The precipitation north of the Appalachian Mountains averages 40 percent less than that south of the

---

8. Where is the annual precipitation highest?

   Ⓐ The Atlantic Coast
   Ⓑ The Great Lakes
   Ⓒ The Gulf of Mexico
   Ⓓ The Pacific Coast

9. Which of the following was NOT mentioned as a factor in determining the amount of precipitation that an area will receive?

   Ⓐ Mountains
   Ⓑ Latitude
   Ⓒ The sea
   Ⓓ Wind

10. The word substantially in paragraph 2 could best be replaced by

   Ⓐ fundamentally
   Ⓑ slightly
   Ⓒ completely
   Ⓓ apparently

End

The mountain ranges of the United States, especially the Rocky Mountain Range and the Appalachian Mountain Range, influence the amount of precipitation in the areas to the windward and leeward sides of these ranges. East of the Rocky Mountains, the annual precipitation is substantially less than that west of the Rocky Mountains. The precipitation north of the Appalachian Mountains averages 40 percent less than that south of the Appalachian Mountains. As air currents from the oceans move over land, the air must rise to pass over the mountains. The air cools, and the water that is held in the clouds falls as rain or snow on the ascending side of the mountains. The air, therefore, is much drier on the other side of the mountains.

11. The word **that** in paragraph 2 refers to

Ⓐ decreases
Ⓑ precipitation
Ⓒ areas
Ⓓ mountain ranges

End

The mountain ranges of the United States, especially the Rocky Mountain Range and the Appalachian Mountain Range, influence the amount of precipitation in the areas to the windward and leeward sides of these ranges. East of the Rocky Mountains, the annual precipitation is substantially less than that west of the Rocky Mountains. The precipitation north of the Appalachian Mountains averages 40 percent less than **that** south of the Appalachian Mountains. As air currents from the oceans move over land, the air must rise to pass over the mountains. The air cools, and the water that is held in the clouds falls as rain or snow on the ascending side of the mountains. The air, therefore, is much drier on the other side of the mountains.

During the nineteenth century, women in the United States organized and participated in a large number of reform movements, including movements to reorganize the prison system, improve education, ban the sale of alcohol, grant rights to people who were denied them, and, most importantly, free slaves. Some women saw similarities in the social status of women and slaves. Women like Elizabeth Cady Stanton and Lucy Stone were not only feminists who fought for the rights of women but also fervent abolitionists who fought to do away with slavery. These brave people were social leaders who supported the rights of both women and blacks. They were fighting against a belief that voting should be tied to land ownership, and because land was owned by men, and in some cases by their widows, only those who held the greatest stake in government, that is the male landowners, were considered worthy of the vote. Women did not conform to the requirements.

A number of male abolitionists, including William Lloyd Garrison and Wendell Phillips, also supported the rights of women to speak and to participate equally with men in antislavery activities. Probably more than any other movement, abolitionism offered women a previously denied entry into politics. They became involved primarily in order to better their living conditions and improve the conditions of others. However, they gained the respect of those they convinced and also earned the right to be considered equal citizens.

When the civil war between the North and the South ended in 1865, the Fourteenth and Fifteenth Amendments to the Constitution adopted in 1868 and 1870 granted citizenship and suffrage to blacks but not to women. Discouraged but resolved, feminists worked tirelessly to influence more and more women to demand the right to vote. In 1869, the Wyoming Territory had yielded to demands by feminists, but the states on the East Coast resisted more stubbornly than before. A women's suffrage bill had been presented to every Congress since 1878, but it continually failed to pass until 1920, when the Nineteenth Amendment granted women the right to vote.

12. With what topic is the passage primarily concerned?

   Ⓐ The Wyoming Territory
   Ⓑ The Fourteenth and Fifteenth Amendments
   Ⓒ Abolitionists
   Ⓓ Women's suffrage

13. The word ban in paragraph 1 most nearly means to

   Ⓐ encourage
   Ⓑ publish
   Ⓒ prohibit
   Ⓓ limit

Beginning

During the nineteenth century, women in the United States organized and participated in a large number of reform movements, including movements to reorganize the prison system, improve education, ban the sale of alcohol, grant rights to people who were denied them, and, most importantly, free slaves. Some women saw similarities in the social status of women and slaves. Women like Elizabeth Cady Stanton and Lucy Stone were not only feminists who fought for the rights of women but also fervent abolitionists who fought to do away with slavery. These brave people were social leaders who supported the rights of both women and blacks. They were fighting against a belief that voting should be tied to land ownership, and because land was owned by men, and in some cases by their widows, only those who held the greatest stake in government, that is the male landowners, were considered worthy of the vote. Women did not conform to the requirements.

A number of male abolitionists, including William Lloyd Garrison and Wendell Phillips, also supported the rights of women to speak and to

---

14. Click on the sentence in paragraph 1 that explains the relationship between voting and property.

Paragraph 1 is marked with an arrow (→).

Beginning

→ During the nineteenth century, women in the United States organized and participated in a large number of reform movements, including movements to reorganize the prison system, improve education, ban the sale of alcohol, grant rights to people who were denied them, and, most importantly, free slaves. Some women saw similarities in the social status of women and slaves. Women like Elizabeth Cady Stanton and Lucy Stone were not only feminists who fought for the rights of women but also fervent abolitionists who fought to do away with slavery. These brave people were social leaders who supported the rights of both women and blacks. They were fighting against a belief that voting should be tied to land ownership, and because land was owned by men, and in some cases by their widows, only those who held the greatest stake in government, that is the male landowners, were considered worthy of the vote. Women did not conform to the requirements.

A number of male abolitionists, including William Lloyd Garrison and Wendell Phillips, also supported the rights of women to speak and to

---

15. The word primarily in paragraph 2 is closest in meaning to

   Ⓐ above all
   Ⓑ somewhat
   Ⓒ finally
   Ⓓ always

More Available

the rights of women but also fervent abolitionists who fought to do away with slavery. These brave people were social leaders who supported the rights of both women and blacks. They were fighting against a belief that voting should be tied to land ownership, and because land was owned by men, and in some cases by their widows, only those who held the greatest stake in government, that is the male landowners, were considered worthy of the vote. Women did not conform to the requirements.

A number of male abolitionists, including William Lloyd Garrison and Wendell Phillips, also supported the rights of women to speak and to participate equally with men in antislavery activities. Probably more than any other movement, abolitionism offered women a previously denied entry into politics. They became involved primarily in order to better their living conditions and improve the conditions of others. However, they gained the respect of those they convinced and also earned the right to be considered equal citizens.

When the civil war between the North and the

16. Look at the word **improve** in the passage. Click on the word or phrase in the **bold** text that is closest in meaning to **improve**.

> More Available
>
> rights of both women and blacks. They were fighting against a belief that voting should be tied to land ownership, and because land was owned by men, and in some cases by their widows, only those who held the greatest stake in government, that is the male landowners, were considered worthy of the vote. Women did not conform to the requirements.
>
> A number of male abolitionists, including William Lloyd Garrison and Wendell Phillips, also supported the rights of women to speak and to participate equally with men in antislavery activities. **Probably more than any other movement, abolitionism offered women a previously denied entry into politics. They became involved primarily in order to better their living conditions and improve the conditions of others. However, they gained the respect of those they convinced and also earned the right to be considered equal citizens.**
>
> When the civil war between the North and the South ended in 1865, the Fourteenth and Fifteenth Amendments to the Constitution adopted in 1868 and 1870 granted citizenship and suffrage to

17. What had occurred shortly after the Civil War?

   Ⓐ The Wyoming Territory was admitted to the Union.
   Ⓑ A women's suffrage bill was introduced in Congress.
   Ⓒ The eastern states resisted the end of the war.
   Ⓓ Black people were granted the right to vote.

18. The word **suffrage** in paragraph 3 could best be replaced by which of the following?

   Ⓐ pain
   Ⓑ citizenship
   Ⓒ freedom from bondage
   Ⓓ the right to vote

> End
>
> abolitionism offered women a previously denied entry into politics. They became involved primarily in order to better their living conditions and improve the conditions of others. However, they gained the respect of those they convinced and also earned the right to be considered equal citizens.
>
> When the civil war between the North and the South ended in 1865, the Fourteenth and Fifteenth Amendments to the Constitution adopted in 1868 and 1870 granted citizenship and suffrage to blacks but not to women. Discouraged but resolved, feminists worked tirelessly to influence more and more women to demand the right to vote. In 1869, the Wyoming Territory had yielded to demands by feminists, but the states on the East Coast resisted more stubbornly than before. A women's suffrage bill had been presented to every Congress since 1878, but it continually failed to pass until 1920, when the Nineteenth Amendment granted women the right to vote.

19. The word it in paragraph 3 refers to

Ⓐ bill
Ⓑ Congress
Ⓒ Nineteenth Amendment
Ⓓ vote

End

abolitionism offered women a previously denied entry into politics. They became involved primarily in order to better their living conditions and improve the conditions of others. However, they gained the respect of those they convinced and also earned the right to be considered equal citizens.

When the civil war between the North and the South ended in 1865, the Fourteenth and Fifteenth Amendments to the Constitution adopted in 1868 and 1870 granted citizenship and suffrage to blacks but not to women. Discouraged but resolved, feminists worked tirelessly to influence more and more women to demand the right to vote. In 1869, the Wyoming Territory had yielded to demands by feminists, but the states on the East Coast resisted more stubbornly than before. A women's suffrage bill had been presented to every Congress since 1878, but it continually failed to pass until 1920, when the Nineteenth Amendment granted women the right to vote.

---

20. What does the Nineteenth Amendment guarantee?

Ⓐ Voting rights for blacks
Ⓑ Citizenship for blacks
Ⓒ Voting rights for women
Ⓓ Citizenship for women

21. When were women allowed to vote throughout the United States?

Ⓐ After 1866
Ⓑ After 1870
Ⓒ After 1878
Ⓓ After 1920

The *Acacia*, a genus of trees and shrubs of the *mimosa* family that originated in Australia, has long been used there in building simple mud and stick structures. The *acacia* is called a wattle in Australia, and the structures are said to be made of daub and wattle. The *acacia* is actually related to the family of plants known as *legumes* that includes peas, beans, lentils, peanuts, and pods with beanlike seeds. Some *acacias* actually produce edible crops. Other *Acacia* varieties are valued for the sticky resin, called gum arabic or gum acacia, used widely in medicines, foods, and perfumes, for the dark dense wood prized for making pianos, or for the bark, rich in tannin, a dark, acidic substance used to cure the hides of animals, transforming them into leather.

Nearly five hundred species of *Acacia* have been analyzed, identified, categorized, and proven capable of survival in hot and generally arid parts of the world; however, only a dozen of the three hundred Australian varieties thrive in the southern United States. Most *acacia* imports are low spreading trees, but of these, only three flower, including the *Bailey Acacia* with fernlike silver leaves and small, fragrant flowers arranged in rounded clusters, the *Silver Wattle*, similar to the *Bailey Acacia*, which grows twice as high, and the squat *Sydney Golden Wattle*, bushy with broad, flat leaves, showy bright yellow blossoms, and sharp spined twigs. Another variety, the *Black Acacia,* also called the *Blackwood,* has dark green foliage and unobtrusive blossoms. Besides being a popular ornamental tree, the *Black Acacia* is considered valuable for its dark wood, which is used in making furniture, as well as highly prized musical instruments.

The *Acacia's* unusual custom of blossoming in February has been commonly attributed to its Australian origins, as if the date and not the quality of light made the difference for a tree in its flowering cycle. In the Southern Hemisphere, the seasons are reversed, and February, which is wintertime in the United States, is summertime in Australia. Actually, however, the pale, yellow blossoms appear in August in Australia. Whether growing in the Northern or Southern Hemisphere, the lovely *acacia* blossoms in winter.

22. With which of the following topics is the passage primarily concerned?

  Ⓐ The *Black Acacia*
  Ⓑ Characteristics and varieties of the *Acacia*
  Ⓒ Australian varieties of the *Acacia*
  Ⓓ The use of *Acacia* wood in ornamental furniture

23. Look at the word prized in the passage. Click on the word or phrase in the **bold** text that is closest in meaning to prized .

> **More Available**
>
> includes peas, beans, lentils, peanuts, and pods with beanlike seeds. Some *acacias* actually produce edible crops. **Other *Acacia* varieties are valued for the sticky resin, called gum arabic or gum acacia, used widely in medicines, foods, and perfumes, for the dark dense wood prized for making pianos, or for the bark, rich in tannin, a dark, acidic substance used to cure the hides of animals, transforming them into leather.**
>
> **Nearly five hundred species of *Acacia* have been analyzed, identified, categorized, and proven capable of survival in hot and generally arid parts of the world; however, only a dozen of the three hundred Australian varieties thrive in the southern United States.** Most *acacia* imports are low spreading trees, but of these, only three flower, including the *Bailey Acacia* with fernlike silver leaves and small, fragrant flowers arranged in rounded clusters, the *Silver Wattle*, similar to the *Bailey Acacia*, which grows twice as high, and the squat *Sydney Golden Wattle*, bushy with broad, flat leaves, showy bright yellow blossoms, and sharp spined twigs. Another variety, the *Black Acacia*, also called the *Blackwood*, has dark green

24. How many species of *Acacia* grow well in the southern United States?

  Ⓐ Five hundred
  Ⓑ Three hundred
  Ⓒ Twelve
  Ⓓ Three

25. The word thrive in paragraph 2 is closest in meaning to which of the following?

  Ⓐ grow well
  Ⓑ are found
  Ⓒ were planted
  Ⓓ can live

> **More Available**
>
> includes peas, beans, lentils, peanuts, and pods with beanlike seeds. Some *acacias* actually produce edible crops. Other *Acacia* varieties are valued for the sticky resin, called gum arabic or gum acacia, used widely in medicines, foods, and perfumes, for the dark dense wood prized for making pianos, or for the bark, rich in tannin, a dark, acidic substance used to cure the hides of animals, transforming them into leather.
>
> Nearly five hundred species of *Acacia* have been analyzed, identified, categorized, and proven capable of survival in hot and generally arid parts of the world; however, only a dozen of the three hundred Australian varieties thrive in the southern United States. Most *acacia* imports are low spreading trees, but of these, only three flower, including the *Bailey Acacia* with fernlike silver leaves and small, fragrant flowers arranged in rounded clusters, the *Silver Wattle*, similar to the *Bailey Acacia*, which grows twice as high, and the squat *Sydney Golden Wattle*, bushy with broad, flat leaves, showy bright yellow blossoms, and sharp spined twigs. Another variety, the *Black Acacia*, also called the *Blackwood*, has dark green

26. The word these in paragraph 2 refers to

    Ⓐ United States
    Ⓑ varieties
    Ⓒ species
    Ⓓ trees

28. In paragraph 2, the word flat most nearly means

    Ⓐ smooth
    Ⓑ pretty
    Ⓒ pointed
    Ⓓ short

More Available

includes peas, beans, lentils, peanuts, and pods with beanlike seeds. Some *acacias* actually produce edible crops. Other *Acacia* varieties are valued for the sticky resin, called gum arabic or gum acacia, used widely in medicines, foods, and perfumes, for the dark dense wood prized for making pianos, or for the bark, rich in tannin, a dark, acidic substance used to cure the hides of animals, transforming them into leather.

Nearly five hundred species of *Acacia* have been analyzed, identified, categorized, and proven capable of survival in hot and generally arid parts of the world; however, only a dozen of the three hundred Australian varieties thrive in the southern United States. Most *acacia* imports are low spreading trees, but of these, only three flower, including the *Bailey Acacia* with fernlike silver leaves and small, fragrant flowers arranged in rounded clusters, the *Silver Wattle*, similar to the *Bailey Acacia*, which grows twice as high, and the squat *Sydney Golden Wattle*, bushy with broad, flat leaves, showy bright yellow blossoms, and sharp spined twigs. Another variety, the *Black Acacia*, also called the *Blackwood*, has dark green

---

27. According to this passage, the *Silver Wattle*

    Ⓐ is squat and bushy
    Ⓑ has unobtrusive blossoms
    Ⓒ is taller than the *Bailey Acacia*
    Ⓓ is used for making furniture

More Available

includes peas, beans, lentils, peanuts, and pods with beanlike seeds. Some *acacias* actually produce edible crops. Other *Acacia* varieties are valued for the sticky resin, called gum arabic or gum acacia, used widely in medicines, foods, and perfumes, for the dark dense wood prized for making pianos, or for the bark, rich in tannin, a dark, acidic substance used to cure the hides of animals, transforming them into leather.

Nearly five hundred species of *Acacia* have been analyzed, identified, categorized, and proven capable of survival in hot and generally arid parts of the world; however, only a dozen of the three hundred Australian varieties thrive in the southern United States. Most *acacia* imports are low spreading trees, but of these, only three flower, including the *Bailey Acacia* with fernlike silver leaves and small, fragrant flowers arranged in rounded clusters, the *Silver Wattle*, similar to the *Bailey Acacia*, which grows twice as high, and the squat *Sydney Golden Wattle*, bushy with broad, flat leaves, showy bright yellow blossoms, and sharp spined twigs. Another variety, the *Black Acacia*, also called the *Blackwood*, has dark green

29. The word showy in paragraph 2 could best be replaced by

    Ⓐ strange
    Ⓑ elaborate
    Ⓒ huge
    Ⓓ fragile

More Available

includes peas, beans, lentils, peanuts, and pods with beanlike seeds. Some *acacias* actually produce edible crops. Other *Acacia* varieties are valued for the sticky resin, called gum arabic or gum acacia, used widely in medicines, foods, and perfumes, for the dark dense wood prized for making pianos, or for the bark, rich in tannin, a dark, acidic substance used to cure the hides of animals, transforming them into leather.

   Nearly five hundred species of *Acacia* have been analyzed, identified, categorized, and proven capable of survival in hot and generally arid parts of the world; however, only a dozen of the three hundred Australian varieties thrive in the southern United States. Most *acacia* imports are low spreading trees, but of these, only three flower, including the *Bailey Acacia* with fernlike silver leaves and small, fragrant flowers arranged in rounded clusters, the *Silver Wattle*, similar to the *Bailey Acacia*, which grows twice as high, and the squat *Sydney Golden Wattle*, bushy with broad, flat leaves, showy bright yellow blossoms, and sharp spined twigs. Another variety, the *Black Acacia*, also called the *Blackwood*, has dark green

---

30. Which of the following *Acacias* has the least colorful blossoms?

    Ⓐ *Bailey Acacia*
    Ⓑ *Sydney Golden Wattle*
    Ⓒ *Silver Wattle*
    Ⓓ *Black Acacia*

31. Which of the following would most probably be made from a *Black Acacia* tree?

    Ⓐ A flower arrangement
    Ⓑ A table
    Ⓒ A pie
    Ⓓ Paper

32. When do *Acacia* trees bloom in Australia?

    Ⓐ February
    Ⓑ Summer
    Ⓒ August
    Ⓓ Spring

33. The following sentence can be added to the passage.

Some *acacias* are popular in landscaping because of their graceful shapes, lacey foliage, and fragrant blossoms.

Where would it best fit in the passage?

Click on the square (■) to add the sentence to the passage.

Scroll the passage to see all of the choices.

Beginning

   The *Acacia*, a genus of trees and shrubs of the *mimosa* family that originated in Australia, has long been used there in building simple mud and stick structures. ■ The acacia is called a wattle in Australia, and the structures are said to be made of daub and wattle. ■ The acacia is actually related to the family of plants known as *legumes* that includes peas, beans, lentils, peanuts, and pods with beanlike seeds. Some *acacias* actually produce edible crops. ■ Other *Acacia* varieties are valued for the sticky resin, called gum arabic or gum acacia, used widely in medicines, foods, and perfumes, for the dark dense wood prized for making pianos, or for the bark, rich in tannin, a dark, acidic substance used to cure the hides of animals, transforming them into leather. ■

   Nearly five hundred species of *Acacia* have been analyzed, identified, categorized, and proven capable of survival in hot and generally arid parts of the world; however, only a dozen of the three hundred Australian varieties thrive in the southern United States. Most *acacia* imports are low spreading trees, but of these, only three flower, including the *Bailey Acacia* with fernlike silver

In 1626, Peter Minuit, governor of the Dutch settlements in North America known as New Amsterdam, negotiated with Canarsee chiefs for the purchase of Manhattan Island for merchandise valued at sixty guilders or about $24.12. He purchased the island for the Dutch West India Company.

The next year, Fort Amsterdam was built by the company at the extreme southern tip of the island. Because attempts to encourage Dutch immigration were not immediately successful, offers, generous by the standards of the era, were extended throughout Europe. Consequently, the settlement became the most heterogeneous of the North American colonies. By 1637, the fort had expanded into the village of New Amsterdam, other small communities had grown up around it, including New Haarlem and Stuyvesant's Bouwery, and New Amsterdam began to prosper, developing characteristics of religious and linguistic tolerance unusual for the times. By 1643, it was reported that eighteen different languages could be heard in New Amsterdam alone.

Among the multilingual settlers was a large group of English colonists from Connecticut and Massachusetts who supported the English King's claim to all of New Netherlands set out in a charter that gave the territory to his brother James, Duke of York. In 1644, when the English sent a formidable fleet of warships into the New Amsterdam harbor, Dutch governor Peter Stuyvesant surrendered without resistance.

When the English acquired the island, the village of New Amsterdam was renamed New York in honor of the Duke. By the onset of the Revolution, New York City was already a bustling commercial center. After the war, it was selected as the first capital of the United States. Although the government was eventually moved, first to Philadelphia and then to Washington, D.C., New York maintained its status. It became a haven for pirates who conspired with leading merchants to exchange supplies for their ships in return for a share in the plunder. As a colony, New York exchanged many agricultural products for English manufactured goods. In addition, trade with the West Indies prospered. Three centuries after his initial trade with the Native Americans, Minuit's tiny investment was worth more than seven billion dollars.

34. Which of the following would be the best title for this passage?

Ⓐ A History of New York City
Ⓑ An Account of the Dutch Colonies
Ⓒ A Biography of Peter Minuit
Ⓓ The First Capital of the United States

35. What did the Native Americans receive in exchange for their island?

Ⓐ Sixty Dutch guilders
Ⓑ $24.12 U.S.
Ⓒ Goods and supplies
Ⓓ Land in New Amsterdam

36. Where was New Amsterdam located?

Ⓐ In Holland
Ⓑ In North America
Ⓒ On the island of Manhattan
Ⓓ In India

37. What does the author mean by the statement Because attempts to encourage Dutch immigration were not immediately successful, offers, generous by the standards of the era, were extended throughout Europe?

    Ⓐ Other Europeans were given opportunities to immigrate to the new world after a slow response by the Dutch.

    Ⓑ Since the Dutch immigration was so successful, opportunities were provided for the Europeans to immigrate to the new world also.

    Ⓒ The Dutch took advantage of opportunities to immigrate to Europe instead of to the new world.

    Ⓓ Immigration to the new world required that the Dutch and other Europeans wait until opportunities were available.

> **Beginning**
>
> In 1626, Peter Minuit, governor of the Dutch settlements in North America known as New Amsterdam, negotiated with Canarsee chiefs for the purchase of Manhattan Island for merchandise valued at sixty guilders or about $24.12. He purchased the island for the Dutch West India Company.
>
> The next year, Fort Amsterdam was built by the company at the extreme southern tip of the island. Because attempts to encourage Dutch immigration were not immediately successful, offers, generous by the standards of the era, were extended throughout Europe. Consequently, the settlement became the most heterogeneous of the North American colonies. By 1637, the fort had expanded into the village of New Amsterdam, other small communities had grown up around it, including New Haarlem and Stuyvesant's Bouwery, and New Amsterdam began to prosper, developing characteristics of religious and linguistic tolerance unusual for the times. By 1643, it was reported that eighteen different languages could be heard in New Amsterdam alone.
>
> Among the multilingual settlers was a large

38. The word heterogeneous in paragraph 2 could best be replaced by

    Ⓐ liberal

    Ⓑ renowned

    Ⓒ diverse

    Ⓓ prosperous

> **Beginning**
>
> In 1626, Peter Minuit, governor of the Dutch settlements in North America known as New Amsterdam, negotiated with Canarsee chiefs for the purchase of Manhattan Island for merchandise valued at sixty guilders or about $24.12. He purchased the island for the Dutch West India Company.
>
> The next year, Fort Amsterdam was built by the company at the extreme southern tip of the island. Because attempts to encourage Dutch immigration were not immediately successful, offers, generous by the standards of the era, were extended throughout Europe. Consequently, the settlement became the most heterogeneous of the North American colonies. By 1637, the fort had expanded into the village of New Amsterdam, other small communities had grown up around it, including New Haarlem and Stuyvesant's Bouwery, and New Amsterdam began to prosper, developing characteristics of religious and linguistic tolerance unusual for the times. By 1643, it was reported that eighteen different languages could be heard in New Amsterdam alone.
>
> Among the multilingual settlers was a large

39. Why were so many languages spoken in New Amsterdam?

    Ⓐ The Dutch West India Company was owned by England.

    Ⓑ The Dutch West India Company allowed freedom of speech.

    Ⓒ The Dutch West India Company recruited settlers from many different countries in Europe.

    Ⓓ The Indians who lived there before the Dutch West India Company purchase spoke many languages.

40. Look at the word his in the passage. Click on the word or phrase in the **bold** text that his refers to.

> **More Available**
>
> extended throughout Europe. Consequently, the settlement became the most heterogeneous of the North American colonies. By 1637, the fort had expanded into the village of New Amsterdam, other small communities had grown up around it, including New Haarlem and Stuyvesant's Bouwery, and New Amsterdam began to prosper, developing characteristics of religious and linguistic tolerance unusual for the times. By 1643, it was reported that eighteen different languages could be heard in New Amsterdam alone.
>
> **Among the multilingual settlers was a large group of English colonists from Connecticut and Massachusetts who supported the English King's claim to all of New Netherlands set out in a charter that gave the territory to his brother James, Duke of York. In 1644, when the English sent a formidable fleet of warships into the New Amsterdam harbor, Dutch governor Peter Stuyvesant surrendered without resistance.**
>
> When the English acquired the island, the village of New Amsterdam was renamed New York in honor of the Duke. By the onset of the Revolution, New York City was already a bustling

41. The word formidable in paragraph 3 is closest in meaning to

    Ⓐ powerful

    Ⓑ modern

    Ⓒ expensive

    Ⓓ unexpected

> **More Available**
>
> extended throughout Europe. Consequently, the settlement became the most heterogeneous of the North American colonies. By 1637, the fort had expanded into the village of New Amsterdam, other small communities had grown up around it, including New Haarlem and Stuyvesant's Bouwery, and New Amsterdam began to prosper, developing characteristics of religious and linguistic tolerance unusual for the times. By 1643, it was reported that eighteen different languages could be heard in New Amsterdam alone.
>
> Among the multilingual settlers was a large group of English colonists from Connecticut and Massachusetts who supported the English King's claim to all of New Netherlands set out in a charter that gave the territory to his brother James, Duke of York. In 1644, when the English sent a formidable fleet of warships into the New Amsterdam harbor, Dutch governor Peter Stuyvesant surrendered without resistance.
>
> When the English acquired the island, the village of New Amsterdam was renamed New York in honor of the Duke. By the onset of the Revolution, New York City was already a bustling

42. Click on the paragraph that explains the reason for renaming New Amsterdam.

    Scroll the passage to see all of the paragraphs.

43. The word it in paragraph 4 refers to

    Ⓐ Revolution
    Ⓑ New York City
    Ⓒ the island
    Ⓓ the first capital

End

Massachusetts who supported the English King's claim to all of New Netherlands set out in a charter that gave the territory to his brother James, Duke of York. In 1644, when the English sent a formidable fleet of warships into the New Amsterdam harbor, Dutch governor Peter Stuyvesant surrendered without resistance.

When the English acquired the island, the village of New Amsterdam was renamed New York in honor of the Duke. By the onset of the Revolution, New York City was already a bustling commercial center. After the war, it was selected as the first capital of the United States. Although the government was eventually moved, first to Philadelphia and then to Washington, D.C., New York maintained its status. It became a haven for pirates who conspired with leading merchants to exchange supplies for their ships in return for a share in the plunder. As a colony, New York exchanged many agricultural products for English manufactured goods. In addition, trade with the West Indies prospered. Three centuries after his initial trade with the Indians, Minuit's tiny investment was worth more than seven billion dollars.

---

44. Which city was the first capital of the new United States?

    Ⓐ New Amsterdam
    Ⓑ New York
    Ⓒ Philadelphia
    Ⓓ Washington

45. On what date was Manhattan valued at $7 billion?

    Ⓐ 1626
    Ⓑ 1726
    Ⓒ 1656
    Ⓓ 1926

To check your answers for Model Test 4, refer to the Answer Key on page 491. For an explanation of the answers, refer to the Explanatory Answers for Model Test 4 on pages 561–579.

Writing Section: Model Test 4

When you take a Model Test, you should use one sheet of paper, both sides. Time each Model Test carefully. After you have read the topic, you should spend 30 minutes writing. For results that would be closest to the actual testing situation, it is recommended that an English teacher score your test, using the guidelines on page 244 of this book.

In your opinion, what is the best way to choose a marriage partner? Use specific reasons and examples why you think this approach is best.

Notes

To check your essay, refer to the Checklist on page 491. For an Example Essay, refer to the Explanatory Answers for Model Test 4 on page 580.

Model Test 5
Computer-Assisted TOEFL

Section 1:
Listening

The Listening Section of the test measures the ability to understand conversations and talks in English. You will use headphones to listen to the conversations and talks. While you are listening, pictures of the speakers or other information will be presented on your computer screen. There are two parts to the Listening Section, with special directions for each part.

On the day of the test, the amount of time you will have to answer all of the questions will appear on the computer screen. The time you spend listening to the test material will not be counted. The listening material and questions about it will be presented only one time. You will not be allowed to take notes or have any paper at your computer. You will both see and hear the questions before the answer choices appear. You can take as much time as you need to select an answer; however, it will be to your advantage to answer the questions as quickly as possible. You may change your answer as many times as you want before you confirm it. After you have confirmed an answer, you will not be able to return to the question.

Before you begin working on the Listening Section, you will have an opportunity to adjust the volume of the sound. You may not be able to change the volume after you have started the test.

QUESTION DIRECTIONS — Part A

In Part A of the Listening Section, you will hear short conversations between two people. In some of the conversations, each person speaks only once. In other conversations, one or both of the people speak more than once. Each conversation is followed by one question about it.

Each question in this part has four answer choices. You should click on the best answer to each question. Answer the questions on the basis of what is stated or implied by the speakers.

1. What is the man going to do?

   Ⓐ He will borrow some typing paper from the woman.
   Ⓑ He will lend the woman some typing paper.
   Ⓒ He will type the woman's paper.
   Ⓓ He will buy some typing paper for the woman.

2. What can be inferred about the man?

   Ⓐ He is a student at the university.
   Ⓑ He is not driving a car.
   Ⓒ He knows the woman.
   Ⓓ He needs to go to the drug store.

3. What does the man imply?

   Ⓐ He could not stay with his parents.
   Ⓑ He did not want to change his plans.
   Ⓒ He will not go to summer school.
   Ⓓ He has completed all the courses.

4. What are the speakers discussing?

   Ⓐ The telephone
   Ⓑ An apartment
   Ⓒ Utilities
   Ⓓ Furniture

5. What does the woman imply?

   Ⓐ She likes Dr. Taylor's class.
   Ⓑ She is not sure how Dr. Taylor feels.
   Ⓒ She did not get an A on the paper.
   Ⓓ She is not doing very well in the class.

6. What does the man suggest that the woman do?

   Ⓐ Pay ten dollars an hour
   Ⓑ Be a subject in an experiment
   Ⓒ Ask Sandy to participate
   Ⓓ Go to a psychologist

7. What can be inferred about the study group meeting?

   Ⓐ The speakers did not go to the study group meeting.
   Ⓑ The woman went to the study group meeting, but the man did not.
   Ⓒ The man went to the study group meeting, but the woman did not.
   Ⓓ Both speakers went to the study group meeting.

8. What does the man mean?

   Ⓐ The woman can borrow his pen.
   Ⓑ A pen might be a good gift.
   Ⓒ Her advisor would probably like a card.
   Ⓓ A gift is not necessary.

9. What does the woman mean?

   Ⓐ She does not want to leave.
   Ⓑ She must stay.
   Ⓒ She did not like the dorm.
   Ⓓ She is undecided.

10. What does the woman imply?

    Ⓐ The man may be taking on too much.
    Ⓑ The job is more important than school.
    Ⓒ The opportunity is very good.
    Ⓓ The contract may not be valid.

11. What does the man suggest the woman do?

    Ⓐ Call his family
    Ⓑ Write a letter
    Ⓒ Send postcards
    Ⓓ Buy presents

12. What are the speakers discussing?

    Ⓐ The length of time that it takes to get an answer from a university
    Ⓑ Where the woman will go to school
    Ⓒ States in the Midwest
    Ⓓ The University of Minnesota

13. What will the woman probably do?

    Ⓐ Buy a ticket
    Ⓑ Go to room 27
    Ⓒ Take a test in room 32
    Ⓓ Show the man her ticket

14. What can be inferred about the woman?

    Ⓐ She wasn't able to attend the reception.
    Ⓑ She is an honors student.
    Ⓒ She likes flowers very much.
    Ⓓ She is a teacher.

15. What does the woman suggest that Terry do?

    Ⓐ Try to be in class more often
    Ⓑ Try to get the work done
    Ⓒ Take the class twice
    Ⓓ Take the class next term

16. What does the man mean?

    Ⓐ He does not like English.
    Ⓑ Graduate school is easier than teaching.
    Ⓒ It is not surprising that the woman is doing well.
    Ⓓ The course is very interesting.

17. What problem do the students have?

    Ⓐ They are going to make a group presentation.
    Ⓑ They don't want to have Jane in their group.
    Ⓒ Carl does not want to be in their group.
    Ⓓ They are not good presenters.

QUESTION DIRECTIONS — Part B

In Part B of the Listening Section, you will hear several longer conversations and talks. Each conversation or talk is followed by several questions. The conversations, talks, and questions will not be repeated.

The conversations and talks are about a variety of topics. You do not need special knowledge of the topics to answer the questions correctly. Rather, you should answer each question on the basis of what is stated or implied by the speakers in the conversations or talks.

For most of the questions, you will need to click on the best of four possible answers. Some questions will have special directions. The special directions will appear in a box on the computer screen.

18. What problem do the speakers have?

   Ⓐ They do not have a syllabus.
   Ⓑ They do not understand the requirement for the research paper.
   Ⓒ They do not have an appointment with the professor.
   Ⓓ They do not know the professor's office hours.

19. How much does the research paper count toward the grade for the course?

   Ⓐ It is not clear from the syllabus.
   Ⓑ It is valued at half of the total points for the course.
   Ⓒ It is worth ten points.
   Ⓓ It will count thirty points.

20. What did the professor say last week?

   Ⓐ She mentioned presentations.
   Ⓑ She discussed the syllabus.
   Ⓒ She answered questions.
   Ⓓ She made appointments.

21. What will the students probably do?

   Ⓐ Prepare a presentation of the research
   Ⓑ Make an appointment to see the professor
   Ⓒ Ask questions about the assignment in class
   Ⓓ Go to see the professor during office hours

22. What is the main subject of this lecture?

   Ⓐ Captain Cook's life
   Ⓑ History of Hawaii
   Ⓒ Captain Cook's exploration of Hawaii
   Ⓓ Hawaiian culture

23. According to the lecturer, what were the two ships commanded by Captain Cook?

   Click on 2 answers.

   Ⓐ *The Third Voyage*
   Ⓑ *The Resolution*
   Ⓒ *The Discovery*
   Ⓓ *The England*

24. Why does the professor mention the name *Launo?*

   Ⓐ It was the original name for the Hawaiian Islands before Cook's arrival.
   Ⓑ It was the name of the king of Hawaii at the time of Cook's exploration.
   Ⓒ It was the name of the god that the islanders believed Cook embodied.
   Ⓓ It was the name of the welcome ceremony that the islanders gave Cook.

25. The professor briefly explains a sequence of events in the history of Hawaii.
Summarize the sequence by putting the events in order.

   Click on a sentence. Then click on the space where it belongs.

   Use each sentence only once.

   Ⓐ Captain Cook and four of his crew were killed.
   Ⓑ The islanders and the crew began to fight.
   Ⓒ The king was to be taken hostage.
   Ⓓ A small boat was stolen from the crew.

   1 ☐
   2 ☐
   3 ☐
   4 ☐

26. What is an alloy?

    Ⓐ Impure metals that occur accidentally
    Ⓑ Metals melted into liquid form
    Ⓒ A planned combination of metals for a specific purpose
    Ⓓ Industrial metals that do not have to be very pure

27. What does the speaker say about the properties of alloys?

    Click on 2 answers.

    Ⓐ They are chosen for a particular purpose.
    Ⓑ They are combined in specific proportions.
    Ⓒ They are difficult to determine because there is more than one metal involved.
    Ⓓ They occur accidentally in nature.

28. Why does the speaker use the example of the aircraft industry?

    Ⓐ To demonstrate how alloys can be used to solve industrial problems
    Ⓑ To emphasize the importance of the aviation industry
    Ⓒ To compare alloys and other mixtures
    Ⓓ To illustrate how metals can be used without alloying them

29. What is the difference between combinations of metals in nature and alloys?

    Ⓐ Mixtures of metals in nature are very pure.
    Ⓑ Combinations of metals do not occur in nature.
    Ⓒ Metals combined in nature are mixed in random proportion.
    Ⓓ Alloys are mixtures, but metals that occur in nature are not.

30. What do the speakers mainly discuss?

    Ⓐ British English pronunciation
    Ⓑ Spelling patterns
    Ⓒ British and American English
    Ⓓ Movies

31. How are the words referred to in the discussion?

    Click on a word. Then click on the empty box in the correct column.

    Use each word only once.

    Ⓐ color   Ⓑ theater
    Ⓒ centre   Ⓓ honour

American English spelling		British English spelling	

32. What can be inferred about the word *flat* in British English?

    Ⓐ It has a different spelling from that of American English.
    Ⓑ It has a different meaning from that of American English.
    Ⓒ The pronunciation is so different that it cannot be understood by Americans.
    Ⓓ It is really about the same in American English.

33. On what did the class agree?

    Ⓐ British English and American English are the same.
    Ⓑ British English and American English are so different that Americans cannot understand the English when they speak.
    Ⓒ British English and American English have different spelling and vocabulary but the same pronunciation.
    Ⓓ British English and American English have slightly different spelling, vocabulary, and pronunciation, but Americans and the English still understand each other.

34. What is the presentation mainly about?

    Ⓐ The National Department of Education
    Ⓑ School boards
    Ⓒ Public schools in the United States
    Ⓓ Local control of schools

35. What surprised the presenter about her research?

    Ⓐ Public schools are not the same throughout the United States.

    Ⓑ The school board members are not professional educators.

    Ⓒ The federal department is not the same as a department of education in many other countries.

    Ⓓ The members of the school board serve without pay.

36. How does each of the persons identified contribute to the operation of schools in the United States?

> Click on a word. Then click on the empty box in the correct row.
>
> Use each word only once.

    Ⓐ superintendent
    Ⓑ school board member
    Ⓒ resident of the district

governs the local school district	
carries out the policies of the governing board	
elects the members of the governing board	

37. According to the speaker, what is the function of the department of education in the United States?

> Click on 2 answers.

    Ⓐ To support research projects
    Ⓑ To organize a national curriculum
    Ⓒ To monitor national legislation for schools
    Ⓓ To appoint local school boards

38. What kind of meal plan does the man decide to buy?

> Click on 2 answers.

    Ⓐ Breakfast
    Ⓑ Lunch
    Ⓒ Dinner
    Ⓓ Supper

39. How much does the plan cost?

    Ⓐ Fourteen dollars a week
    Ⓑ Thirty dollars a week
    Ⓒ Thirty-six dollars a week
    Ⓓ Forty-two dollars a week

40. Why do most residents order a pizza or go out to eat on Sundays?

    Ⓐ Many of them live close enough to go home for the day.

    Ⓑ They are tired of the food in the dormitory.

    Ⓒ No meals are served on Sunday.

    Ⓓ Some of them have dates on the weekend.

41. How will the man pay for the meals?

    Ⓐ He will pay the woman in cash for the first quarter.

    Ⓑ He will use his credit card to pay the woman.

    Ⓒ He will wait to receive a bill from the dormitory.

    Ⓓ He will write a check on a form provided by the woman.

42. What will the man probably do?

    Ⓐ Pay the bill now
    Ⓑ Give the woman his credit card
    Ⓒ Fill out a form
    Ⓓ Think about his options

43. What is hydroponics?

    Ⓐ Growing plants without soil
    Ⓑ Mixing nutrients in water
    Ⓒ Finding the chemical composition of soil
    Ⓓ Solving problems in the water system

44. Why does the professor suggest that the students refer to their lab workbook?

    Ⓐ To see the diagram of the class experiment

    Ⓑ To read an experiment on plant growth

    Ⓒ To find a list of substances that plants need

    Ⓓ To locate the instructions for building a hydroponics tank

45. According to the speaker, why are roots important to plants?

    Click on 2 answers.

    A To absorb water and nutrients
    B To take in oxygen
    C To suspend the plants directly in the solution
    D To filter out toxins

46. Why was the pump attached to the tank in this experiment?

    Ⓐ It was needed to mix the nutrients in the solution.
    Ⓑ It was used to pump out harmful chemicals.
    Ⓒ It was required to pump oxygen into the solution.
    Ⓓ It was necessary to anchor the plants.

47. What does the professor want the students to do with the specimen of the nutrient solution?

    Ⓐ Take a taste of it
    Ⓑ Make a drawing of it
    Ⓒ Observe it and draw conclusions
    Ⓓ Put it in the tank

48. What are the speakers discussing?

    Ⓐ A class that the woman missed
    Ⓑ A book that they have both read
    Ⓒ A TV show that the man saw
    Ⓓ A video that they saw in class

49. Who was Harriet Tubman?

    Ⓐ She was one of the first freed slaves to work on the railroad.
    Ⓑ She was a slave who worked underground in the mines.
    Ⓒ She was a former slave who lived in Canada.
    Ⓓ She was a slave who escaped from her owners in Maryland during the Civil War.

50. What impressed the man about Harriet Tubman's story?

    Ⓐ She used the North Star to guide her to a free state.
    Ⓑ She returned to Maryland to help three hundred slaves escape.
    Ⓒ She founded the underground railroad.
    Ⓓ She was a slave for nineteen years.

Section 2: Structure

This section measures the ability to recognize language that is appropriate for standard written English. There are two types of questions in this section.

In the first type of question, there are incomplete sentences. Beneath each sentence, there are four words or phrases. You will choose the one word or phrase that best completes the sentence. Clicking on a choice darkens the oval. After you click on **Next** and **Confirm Answer**, the next question will be presented.

The second type of question has four underlined words or phrases. You will choose the one underlined word or phrase that must be changed for the sentence to be correct. Clicking on an underlined word or phrase will darken it. After you click on **Next** and **Confirm Answer**, the next question will be presented.

1. Gunpowder, in some ways the most effective
   ____A____   ____B____
   of all the explosive materials, were a mixture
   ___C___   __D__
   of potassium nitrate, charcoal, and sulfur.

2. As the demand increases, manufacturers who
   previously produced only a large, luxury car
   ___A___
   is compelled to make a smaller model in
   _B_   __C__ ____D____
   order to compete in the market.

3. There are twenty species of wild roses in
        _A_
   North America, all of which have prickly
                                  _B_
   stems, pinnate leaves, and large flowers,
   which usually smell sweetly.
   _C_   __D__

4. Professional people expect _____ when it
   is necessary to cancel an appointment.

   Ⓐ you to call them
   Ⓑ that you would call them
   Ⓒ your calling them
   Ⓓ that you are calling them

5. In a new culture, many embarrassing situations occur _____ a misunderstanding.

   Ⓐ for
   Ⓑ of
   Ⓒ because of
   Ⓓ because

6. Factoring is the process of finding two or
   ___A___   ___B___
   more expressions whose product is
                    __C__
   equal as the given expression.
   ___D___

7. Schizophrenia, a behavioral disorder
   typified by a fundamental break with reality,
   ___A___   _____B_____
   may be triggered by genetic predisposition,
   _____C_____
   stressful, drugs, or infections.
   ___D___

8. Sedimentary rocks are formed below the surface of the Earth _____ very high temperatures and pressures.

   Ⓐ where there are
   Ⓑ there are
   Ⓒ where are there
   Ⓓ there are where

9. If Grandma Moses <u>having</u> been able to
        Ⓐ

   continue <u>farming</u>, she may never have
               Ⓑ

   <u>begun</u> to <u>paint</u>.
    Ⓒ   Ⓓ

10. A computer is usually chosen because of
    its simplicity of operation and ease of
    maintenance _____ its capacity to store
    information.

    Ⓐ the same as
    Ⓑ the same
    Ⓒ as well as
    Ⓓ as well

11. Although the Red Cross <u>accepts</u> blood from
                            Ⓐ

    most donors, the nurses will not <u>leave</u> you
                                      Ⓑ

    <u>give</u> blood if you have just <u>had</u> a cold.
    Ⓒ   Ⓓ

12. _____ that gold was discovered at Sutter's
    Mill and that the California Gold Rush
    began.

    Ⓐ Because in 1848
    Ⓑ That in 1848
    Ⓒ In 1848 that it was
    Ⓓ It was in 1848

13. Frost occurs in valleys and on low grounds
    _____ on adjacent hills.

    Ⓐ more frequently as
    Ⓑ as frequently than
    Ⓒ more frequently than
    Ⓓ frequently than

14. The native people of the Americas <u>are called</u>
                                      Ⓐ

    Indians <u>because</u> when Columbus landed in
             Ⓑ

    the Bahamas <u>in 1492</u>, he thought that he
                  Ⓒ

    <u>has reached</u> the East Indies.
      Ⓓ

15. In the <u>relatively</u> short history of industrial
          Ⓐ

    <u>developing</u> <u>in the United States,</u> New York
       Ⓑ   Ⓒ

    City <u>has played</u> a vital role.
         Ⓓ

16. When a body enters the Earth's atmosphere,
    it travels _____ .

    Ⓐ very rapidly
    Ⓑ in a rapid manner
    Ⓒ fastly
    Ⓓ with great speed

17. Employers often require that candidates
    have not only a degree _____ .

    Ⓐ but two years experience
    Ⓑ also two years experience
    Ⓒ but also two years experience
    Ⓓ but more two years experience

18. The salary of a bus driver is much higher
    _____ .

    Ⓐ in comparison with the salary of a
       teacher
    Ⓑ than a teacher
    Ⓒ than that of a teacher
    Ⓓ to compare as a teacher

19. Farmers look forward to _____ every
    summer.

    Ⓐ participating in the county fairs
    Ⓑ participate in the county fairs
    Ⓒ be participating in the county fairs
    Ⓓ have participated in the county fairs

20. A turtle differs <u>from</u> all <u>other</u> reptiles in that
                     Ⓐ   Ⓑ

    its body is encased in a protective shell

    of <u>their</u> <u>own</u>.
       Ⓒ   Ⓓ

21. Excavations in a mound or village
    (A)
    often reveal an ancient community that
       (B)
    had been laying under later reconstructions
        (C)   (D)
    of the city.

22. One of the first and ultimately the most
                        (A)
    important purposeful of a reservoir was
              (B)
    to control flooding.
      (C)   (D)

23. After seeing a movie based on a novel,
    _____ .

    (A) the book is read by many people
    (B) the book made many people want to read it
    (C) many people want to read the book
    (D) the reading of the book interests many
        people

24. One of the world's best-selling authors,
              (A)
    Louis L'Amour said to have written 101
                   (B)   (C)
    books, mostly westerns.
             (D)

25. No other quality is more important for a
    (A)   (B)
    scientist to acquire as to observe carefully.
                        (C)   (D)

Section 3:
Reading

This section measures the ability to read and understand short passages similar in topic and style to those that students are likely to encounter in North American universities and colleges. This section contains reading passages and questions about the passages. There are several different types of questions in this section.

In the Reading Section, you will first have the opportunity to read the passage. You will use the scroll bar to view the rest of the passage.

When you have finished reading the passage, you will use the mouse to click on **Proceed**. Then the questions about the passage will be presented. You are to choose the one best answer to each question. Answer all questions about the information in a passage on the basis of what is stated or implied in that passage.

Most of the questions will be multiple-choice questions. To answer these questions you will click on a choice below the question.

To answer some questions, you will click on a word or phrase.
To answer some questions, you will click on a sentence in the passage.
To answer some questions, you will click on a square to add a sentence to the passage.

Perhaps it was his own lack of adequate schooling that inspired Horace Mann to work so hard to accomplish the important reforms in education that he advocated. While he was still a boy, his father and older brother died, and he became responsible for supporting his family. Like most of the children in his town, he attended school only two or three months a year. Later, with the help of several teachers, he was able to study law and become a member of the Massachusetts bar, but he never forgot those early struggles.

While serving in the Massachusetts legislature, he signed an historic education bill that set up a state board of education. Without regret, he gave up his successful legal practice and political career to become the first secretary of the board. There he exercised an enormous influence during the critical period of reconstruction that brought into existence the American graded elementary school as a substitute for the older district school system. Under his leadership, the curriculum was restructured, the school year was increased to a minimum of six months, and mandatory schooling was extended to age sixteen. Other important reforms that came into existence under Mann's guidance included the establishment of state normal schools for teacher training, institutes for inservice teacher education, and lyceums for adult education. He was also instrumental in improving salaries for teachers and creating school libraries.

Mann's ideas about school reform were developed and distributed in the twelve annual reports to the state of Massachusetts that he wrote during his tenure as secretary of education. Considered quite radical at the time, the Massachusetts reforms later served as a model for the nation's educational system. Mann was formally recognized as the father of public education.

During his lifetime, Horace Mann worked tirelessly to extend educational opportunities to agrarian families and the children of poor laborers. In one of his last speeches he summed up his philosophy of education and life: "Be ashamed to die until you have won some victory for humanity." Surely, his own life was an example of that philosophy.

1. Which of the following titles would best express the main topic of the passage?

  Ⓐ The Father of American Public Education
  Ⓑ Philosophy of Education
  Ⓒ The Massachusetts State Board of Education
  Ⓓ Politics of Educational Institutions

2. Why does the author mention Horace Mann's early life?

  Ⓐ As an example of the importance of an early education for success
  Ⓑ To make the biography more complete
  Ⓒ Because it served as the inspiration for his later work in education
  Ⓓ In tribute to the teachers who helped him succeed

3. The word struggles in paragraph 1 could best be replaced by

  Ⓐ valuable experiences
  Ⓑ happy situations
  Ⓒ influential people
  Ⓓ difficult times

Beginning

Perhaps it was his own lack of adequate schooling that inspired Horace Mann to work so hard to accomplish the important reforms in education that he advocated. While he was still a boy, his father and older brother died, and he became responsible for supporting his family. Like most of the children in his town, he attended school only two or three months a year. Later, with the help of several teachers, he was able to study law and become a member of the Massachusetts bar, but he never forgot those early struggles.

While serving in the Massachusetts legislature, he signed an historic education bill that set up a state board of education. Without regret, he gave up his successful legal practice and political career to become the first secretary of the board. There he exercised an enormous influence during the critical period of reconstruction that brought into existence the American graded elementary school as a substitute for the older district school system. Under his leadership, the curriculum was restructured, the school year was increased to a minimum of six months, and mandatory schooling was extended to age

4. The word there refers to

Ⓐ the Massachusetts legislature
Ⓑ the state board of education
Ⓒ Mann's legal practice
Ⓓ his political career

Beginning

Perhaps it was his own lack of adequate schooling that inspired Horace Mann to work so hard to accomplish the important reforms in education that he advocated. While he was still a boy, his father and older brother died, and he became responsible for supporting his family. Like most of the children in his town, he attended school only two or three months a year. Later, with the help of several teachers, he was able to study law and become a member of the Massachusetts bar, but he never forgot those early struggles.

While serving in the Massachusetts legislature, he signed an historic education bill that set up a state board of education. Without regret, he gave up his successful legal practice and political career to become the first secretary of the board. There he exercised an enormous influence during the critical period of reconstruction that brought into existence the American graded elementary school as a substitute for the older district school system. Under his leadership, the curriculum was restructured, the school year was increased to a minimum of six months, and mandatory schooling was extended to age

---

5. The word mandatory in paragraph 2 is closest in meaning to

Ⓐ required
Ⓑ equal
Ⓒ excellent
Ⓓ basic

Beginning

Perhaps it was his own lack of adequate schooling that inspired Horace Mann to work so hard to accomplish the important reforms in education that he advocated. While he was still a boy, his father and older brother died, and he became responsible for supporting his family. Like most of the children in his town, he attended school only two or three months a year. Later, with the help of several teachers, he was able to study law and become a member of the Massachusetts bar, but he never forgot those early struggles.

While serving in the Massachusetts legislature, he signed an historic education bill that set up a state board of education. Without regret, he gave up his successful legal practice and political career to become the first secretary of the board. There he exercised an enormous influence during the critical period of reconstruction that brought into existence the American graded elementary school as a substitute for the older district school system. Under his leadership, the curriculum was restructured, the school year was increased to a minimum of six months, and mandatory schooling was extended to age

---

6. Look at the word extended in the passage. Click on another word or phrase in the **bold** text that is closest in meaning to extended .

More available

law and become a member of the Massachusetts bar, but he never forgot those early struggles.

While serving in the Massachusetts legislature, he signed an historic education bill that set up a state board of education. Without regret, he gave up his successful legal practice and political career to become the first secretary of the board. There he exercised an enormous influence during the critical period of reconstruction that brought into existence the American graded elementary school as a substitute for the older district school system. Under his leadership, the curriculum was restructured, the school year was increased to a minimum of six months, and mandatory schooling was extended to age sixteen. Other important reforms that came into existence under Mann s guidance included the establishment of state normal schools for teacher training, institutes for inservice teacher education, and lyceums for adult education. He was also instrumental in improving salaries for teachers and creating school libraries.

Mann s ideas about school reform were developed and distributed in the twelve annual

---

7. Click on the paragraph that explains how the educational reforms were distributed.

Scroll the passage to see all of the paragraphs.

8. With which of the following statements would the author most probably agree?

   Ⓐ Horace Mann's influence on American education was very great.

   Ⓑ A small but important influence on American education was exerted by Horace Mann.

   Ⓒ Few educators fully understood Horace Mann's influence on American education.

   Ⓓ The influence on American education by Horace Mann was not accepted or appreciated.

9. Horace Mann advocated all of the following EXCEPT

   Ⓐ a state board of education

   Ⓑ a district school system

   Ⓒ classes for adults

   Ⓓ graded elementary schools

10. The reforms that Horace Mann achieved

   Ⓐ were not very radical for the time

   Ⓑ were used only by the state of Massachusetts

   Ⓒ were later adopted by the nation as a model

   Ⓓ were enforced by the Massachusetts bar

11. With which of the following statements would Horace Mann most probably agree?

   Ⓐ Think in new ways.

   Ⓑ Help others.

   Ⓒ Study as much as possible.

   Ⓓ Work hard.

Organic architecture—that is, natural architecture—may vary in concept and form, but it is always faithful to natural principles. The architect dedicated to the promulgation of organic architecture rejects outright all rules imposed by individual preference or mere aesthetics in order to remain true to the nature of the site, the materials, the purpose of the structure, and the people who will ultimately use it. If these natural principles are upheld, then a bank cannot be built to look like a Greek temple. Form does not follow function; rather, form and function are inseparably two aspects of the same phenomenon. In other words, a building should be inspired by nature's forms and constructed with materials that retain and respect the natural characteristics of the setting to create harmony between the structure and its natural environment. It should maximize people's contact with and utilization of the outdoors. Furthermore, the rule of functionalism is upheld; that is, the principle of excluding everything that serves no practical purpose.

Natural principles, then, are principles of design, not style, expressed by means and modes of construction that reflect unity, balance, proportion, rhythm, and scale. Like a sculptor, the organic architect views the site and materials as an innate form that develops organically from within. Truth in architecture results in a natural, spontaneous structure in total harmony with the setting. For the most part, these structures find their geometric shapes in the contours of the land and their colors in the surrounding palette of nature.

From the outside, an organic structure is so much a part of nature that it is often obscured by it. In other words, it may not be easy, or maybe not even possible, for the human eye to separate the artificial structure from the natural terrain. Natural light, air, and view permeate the whole structure, providing a sense of communication with the outdoors. From the inside, living spaces open into one another. The number of walls for separate rooms is reduced to a minimum, allowing the functional spaces to flow together. Moreover, the interiors are sparse. Organic architecture incorporates built-in architectural features such as benches and storage areas to take the place of furniture.

12. According to the passage, what is another name for organic architecture?

   Ⓐ Natural architecture
   Ⓑ Aesthetic architecture
   Ⓒ Principle architecture
   Ⓓ Varied architecture

13. Look at the word it in the passage. Click on the word or phrase in the **bold** text that it refers to.

> **Beginning**
>
> **Organic architecture—that is, natural architecture—may vary in concept and form, but it is always faithful to natural principles.** The architect dedicated to the promulgation of organic architecture rejects outright all rules imposed by individual preference or mere aesthetics in order to remain true to the nature of the site, the materials, the purpose of the structure, and the people who will ultimately use it. If these natural principles are upheld, then a bank cannot be built to look like a Greek temple. Form does not follow function; rather, form and function are inseparably two aspects of the same phenomenon. In other words, a building should be inspired by nature's forms and constructed with materials that retain and respect the natural characteristics of the setting to create harmony between the structure and its natural environment. It should maximize people's contact with and utilization of the outdoors. Furthermore, the rule of functionalism is upheld; that is, the principle of excluding everything that serves no practical purpose.
>
>   Natural principles, then, are principles of design, not style, expressed by means and modes

14. The word ultimately in paragraph 1 could best be replaced by

   Ⓐ fortunately
   Ⓑ eventually
   Ⓒ supposedly
   Ⓓ obviously

> **Beginning**
>
>   Organic architecture—that is, natural architecture—may vary in concept and form, but it is always faithful to natural principles. The architect dedicated to the promulgation of organic architecture rejects outright all rules imposed by individual preference or mere aesthetics in order to remain true to the nature of the site, the materials, the purpose of the structure, and the people who will ultimately use it. If these natural principles are upheld, then a bank cannot be built to look like a Greek temple. Form does not follow function; rather, form and function are inseparably two aspects of the same phenomenon. In other words, a building should be inspired by nature's forms and constructed with materials that retain and respect the natural characteristics of the setting to create harmony between the structure and its natural environment. It should maximize people's contact with and utilization of the outdoors. Furthermore, the rule of functionalism is upheld; that is, the principle of excluding everything that serves no practical purpose.
>
>   Natural principles, then, are principles of design, not style, expressed by means and modes

15. The word upheld in paragraph 1 is closest in meaning to

    Ⓐ invalidated
    Ⓑ disputed
    Ⓒ promoted
    Ⓓ perceived

Beginning

    Organic architecture—that is, natural architecture—may vary in concept and form, but it is always faithful to natural principles. The architect dedicated to the promulgation of organic architecture rejects outright all rules imposed by individual preference or mere aesthetics in order to remain true to the nature of the site, the materials, the purpose of the structure, and the people who will ultimately use it. If these natural principles are upheld, then a bank cannot be built to look like a Greek temple. Form does not follow function; rather, form and function are inseparably two aspects of the same phenomenon. In other words, a building should be inspired by nature's forms and constructed with materials that retain and respect the natural characteristics of the setting to create harmony between the structure and its natural environment. It should maximize people's contact with and utilization of the outdoors. Furthermore, the rule of functionalism is upheld; that is, the principle of excluding everything that serves no practical purpose.

    Natural principles, then, are principles of design, not style, expressed by means and modes

---

16. The following examples are all representative of natural architecture EXCEPT

    Ⓐ a bank that is built to look like a Greek temple
    Ⓑ a bank built so that the location is important to the structure
    Ⓒ a bank that is built to conform to the colors of the natural surroundings
    Ⓓ a bank that is built to be functional rather than beautiful

17. Why does the author compare an organic architect to a sculptor?

    Ⓐ To emphasize aesthetics
    Ⓑ To give an example of natural principles
    Ⓒ To make a point about the development of geometry
    Ⓓ To demonstrate the importance of style

18. The word obscured in paragraph 3 is closest in meaning to

    Ⓐ difficult to see
    Ⓑ in high demand
    Ⓒ not very attractive
    Ⓓ mutually beneficial

End

structure in total harmony with the setting. For the most part, these structures find their geometric shapes in the contours of the land and their colors in the surrounding palette of nature.

    From the outside, an organic structure is so much a part of nature that it is often obscured by it. In other words, it may not be easy, or maybe not even possible, for the human eye to separate the artificial structure from the natural terrain. Natural light, air, and view permeate the whole structure, providing a sense of communication with the outdoors. From the inside, living spaces open into one another. The number of walls for separate rooms is reduced to a minimum, allowing the functional spaces to flow together. Moreover, the interiors are sparse. Organic architecture incorporates built-in architectural features such as benches and storage areas to take the place of furniture.

19. Look at the word contours in the passage. Click on another word or phrase in the **bold** text that is closest in meaning to contours .

End ⬆

architect views the site and materials as an innate form that develops organically from within. Truth in architecture results in a natural, spontaneous structure in total harmony with the setting. **For the most part, these structures find their geometric shapes in the contours of the land and their colors in the surrounding palette of nature.**

From the outside, an organic structure is so much a part of nature that it is often obscured by it. In other words, it may not be easy, or maybe not even possible, for the human eye to separate the artificial structure from the natural terrain. Natural light, air, and view permeate the whole structure, providing a sense of communication with the outdoors. From the inside, living spaces open into one another. The number of walls for separate rooms is reduced to a minimum, allowing the functional spaces to flow together. Moreover, the interiors are sparse. Organic architecture incorporates built-in architectural features such as benches and storage areas to take the place of furniture.

⬇

---

20. Click on the sentence in paragraph 3 that describes the furnishings appropriate for natural architecture.

Paragraph 3 is marked with an arrow (→).

End ⬆

architect views the site and materials as an innate form that develops organically from within. Truth in architecture results in a natural, spontaneous structure in total harmony with the setting. For the most part, these structures find their geometric shapes in the contours of the land and their colors in the surrounding palette of nature.

→ From the outside, an organic structure is so much a part of nature that it is often obscured by it. In other words, it may not be easy, or maybe not even possible, for the human eye to separate the artificial structure from the natural terrain. Natural light, air, and view permeate the whole structure, providing a sense of communication with the outdoors. From the inside, living spaces open into one another. The number of walls for separate rooms is reduced to a minimum, allowing the functional spaces to flow together. Moreover, the interiors are sparse. Organic architecture incorporates built-in architectural features such as benches and storage areas to take the place of furniture.

⬇

---

21. With which of the following statements would the author most probably agree?

Ⓐ Form follows function.
Ⓑ Function follows form.
Ⓒ Function is not important to form.
Ⓓ Form and function are one.

22. Which of the following statements best describes the architect's view of nature?

Ⓐ Nature should be conquered.
Ⓑ Nature should not be considered.
Ⓒ Nature should be respected.
Ⓓ Nature should be improved.

Although its purpose and techniques were often magical, alchemy was, in many ways, the predecessor of the modern science of chemistry. The fundamental premise of alchemy derived from the best philosophical dogma and scientific practice of the time, and the majority of educated persons between 1400 and 1600 believed that alchemy had great merit.

The earliest authentic works on European alchemy are those of the English monk Roger Bacon and the German philosopher St. Albertus Magnus. In their treatises they maintained that gold was the perfect metal and that inferior metals such as lead and mercury were removed by various degrees of imperfection from gold. They further asserted that these base metals could be transmuted to gold by blending them with a substance more perfect than gold. This elusive substance was referred to as the "philosopher's stone." The process was called transmutation.

Most of the early alchemists were artisans who were accustomed to keeping trade secrets and often resorted to cryptic terminology to record the progress of their work. The term *sun* was used for gold, *moon* for silver, and the five known planets for base metals. This convention of substituting symbolic language attracted some mystical philosophers who compared the search for the perfect metal with the struggle of humankind for the perfection of the soul. The philosophers began to use the artisan's terms in the mystical literature that they produced. Thus, by the fourteenth century, alchemy had developed two distinct groups of practitioners—the laboratory alchemist and the literary alchemist. Both groups of alchemists continued to work throughout the history of alchemy, but, of course, it was the literary alchemist who was more likely to produce a written record; therefore, much of what is known about the science of alchemy is derived from philosophers rather than from the alchemists who labored in laboratories.

Despite centuries of experimentation, laboratory alchemists failed to produce gold from other materials. However, they gained wide knowledge of chemical substances, discovered chemical properties, and invented many of the tools and techniques that are used by chemists today. Many laboratory alchemists earnestly devoted themselves to the scientific discovery of new compounds and reactions and, therefore, must be considered the legitimate forefathers of modern chemistry. They continued to call themselves alchemists, but they were becoming true chemists.

23. Which of the following is the main point of the passage?

Ⓐ There were both laboratory and literary alchemists.
Ⓑ Base metals can be transmuted to gold by blending them with a substance more perfect than gold.
Ⓒ Roger Bacon and St. Albertus Magnus wrote about alchemy.
Ⓓ Alchemy was the predecessor of modern chemistry.

24. The word authentic in paragraph 2 could best be replaced by

Ⓐ valuable
Ⓑ genuine
Ⓒ complete
Ⓓ comprehensible

Beginning

Although its purpose and techniques were often magical, alchemy was, in many ways, the predecessor of the modern science of chemistry. The fundamental premise of alchemy derived from the best philosophical dogma and scientific practice of the time, and the majority of educated persons between 1400 and 1600 believed that alchemy had great merit.

The earliest authentic works on European alchemy are those of the English monk Roger Bacon and the German philosopher St. Albertus Magnus. In their treatises they maintained that gold was the perfect metal and that inferior metals such as lead and mercury were removed by various degrees of imperfection from gold. They further asserted that these base metals could be transmuted to gold by blending them with a substance more perfect than gold. This elusive substance was referred to as the "philosopher's stone." The process was called transmutation.

Most of the early alchemists were artisans who were accustomed to keeping trade secrets and often resorted to cryptic terminology to record the progress of their work. The term *sun* was used for

25. Look at the word those in the passage. Click on the word or phrase in the **bold** text that those refers to.

Although its purpose and techniques were often magical, alchemy was, in many ways, the predecessor of the modern science of chemistry. The fundamental premise of alchemy derived from the best philosophical dogma and scientific practice of the time, and the majority of educated persons between 1400 and 1600 believed that alchemy had great merit.

The earliest authentic works on European alchemy are those of the English monk Roger Bacon and the German philosopher St. Albertus Magnus. In their treatises they maintained that gold was the perfect metal and that inferior metals such as lead and mercury were removed by various degrees of imperfection from gold. They further asserted that these base metals could be transmuted to gold by blending them with a substance more perfect than gold. This elusive substance was referred to as the "philosopher's stone." The process was called transmutation.

Most of the early alchemists were artisans who were accustomed to keeping trade secrets and often resorted to cryptic terminology to record the progress of their work. The term *sun* was used for

26. According to the alchemists, what is the difference between base metals and gold?

  Ⓐ Perfection
  Ⓑ Chemical content
  Ⓒ Temperature
  Ⓓ Weight

27. Look at the word asserted in the passage. Click on the word or phrase in the **bold** text that is closest in meaning to asserted.

Although its purpose and techniques were often magical, alchemy was, in many ways, the predecessor of the modern science of chemistry. The fundamental premise of alchemy derived from the best philosophical dogma and scientific practice of the time, and the majority of educated persons between 1400 and 1600 believed that alchemy had great merit.

The earliest authentic works on European alchemy are those of the English monk Roger Bacon and the German philosopher St. Albertus Magnus. **In their treatises they maintained that gold was the perfect metal and that inferior metals such as lead and mercury were removed by various degrees of imperfection from gold. They further asserted that these base metals could be transmuted to gold by blending them with a substance more perfect than gold.** This elusive substance was referred to as the "philosopher's stone." The process was called transmutation.

Most of the early alchemists were artisans who were accustomed to keeping trade secrets and often resorted to cryptic terminology to record the progress of their work. The term *sun* was used for

28. According to the passage, what is the "philosopher's stone"?

  Ⓐ Lead that was mixed with gold
  Ⓑ An element that was never found
  Ⓒ Another name for alchemy
  Ⓓ A base metal

29. The word cryptic in paragraph 3 could be replaced by which of the following?

- Ⓐ scholarly
- Ⓑ secret
- Ⓒ foreign
- Ⓓ precise

> **More Available**
>
> further asserted that these base metals could be transmuted to gold by blending them with a substance more perfect than gold. This elusive substance was referred to as the "philosopher's stone." The process was called transmutation.
>
> Most of the early alchemists were artisans who were accustomed to keeping trade secrets and often resorted to cryptic terminology to record the progress of their work. The term *sun* was used for gold, *moon* for silver, and the five known planets for base metals. This convention of substituting symbolic language attracted some mystical philosophers who compared the search for the perfect metal with the struggle of humankind for the perfection of the soul. The philosophers began to use the artisan's terms in the mystical literature that they produced. Thus, by the fourteenth century, alchemy had developed two distinct groups of practitioners—the laboratory alchemist and the literary alchemist. Both groups of alchemists continued to work throughout the history of alchemy, but, of course, it was the literary alchemist who was more likely to produce a written record; therefore, much of what is known about the science

30. Why did the early alchemists use the terms *sun* and *moon*?

- Ⓐ To keep the work secret
- Ⓑ To make the work more literary
- Ⓒ To attract philosophers
- Ⓓ To produce a written record

31. Who were the first alchemists?

- Ⓐ Chemists
- Ⓑ Writers
- Ⓒ Artisans
- Ⓓ Linguists

32. In paragraph 3, the author suggests that we know about the history of alchemy because

- Ⓐ the laboratory alchemists kept secret notes
- Ⓑ the literary alchemists recorded it in writing
- Ⓒ the mystical philosophers were not able to hide the secrets of alchemy
- Ⓓ the historians were able to interpret the secret writings of the alchemists

Paragraph 3 is marked with an arrow (→).

> **More Available**
>
> further asserted that these base metals could be transmuted to gold by blending them with a substance more perfect than gold. This elusive substance was referred to as the "philosopher's stone." The process was called transmutation.
>
> → Most of the early alchemists were artisans who were accustomed to keeping trade secrets and often resorted to cryptic terminology to record the progress of their work. The term *sun* was used for gold, *moon* for silver, and the five known planets for base metals. This convention of substituting symbolic language attracted some mystical philosophers who compared the search for the perfect metal with the struggle of humankind for the perfection of the soul. The philosophers began to use the artisan's terms in the mystical literature that they produced. Thus, by the fourteenth century, alchemy had developed two distinct groups of practitioners—the laboratory alchemist and the literary alchemist. Both groups of alchemists continued to work throughout the history of alchemy, but, of course, it was the literary alchemist who was more likely to produce a written record; therefore, much of what is known about the science

33. With which of the following statements would the author most probably agree?

- Ⓐ Alchemy must be considered a complete failure.
- Ⓑ Some very important scientific discoveries were made by alchemists.
- Ⓒ Most educated people dismissed alchemy during the time that it was practiced.
- Ⓓ The literary alchemists were more important than the laboratory alchemists.

Human memory, formerly believed to be rather inefficient, is really much more sophisticated than that of a computer. Researchers approaching the problem from a variety of points of view have all concluded that there is a great deal more stored in our minds than has been generally supposed. Dr. Wilder Penfield, a Canadian neurosurgeon, proved that by stimulating their brains electrically, he could elicit the total recall of complex events in his subjects' lives. Even dreams and other minor events supposedly forgotten for many years suddenly emerged in detail.

The memory trace is the term for whatever forms the internal representation of the specific information about the event stored in the memory. Assumed to have been made by structural changes in the brain, the memory trace is not subject to direct observation but is rather a theoretical construct that is used to speculate about how information presented at a particular time can cause performance at a later time. Most theories include the strength of the memory trace as a variable in the degree of learning, retention, and retrieval possible for a memory. One theory is that the fantastic capacity for storage in the brain is the result of an almost unlimited combination of interconnections between brain cells, stimulated by patterns of activity. Repeated references to the same information support recall. Or, to say that another way, improved performance is the result of strengthening the chemical bonds in the memory.

Psychologists generally divide memory into at least two types, short-term and long-term memory, which combine to form working memory. Short-term memory contains what we are actively focusing on at any particular time, but items are not retained longer than twenty or thirty seconds without verbal rehearsal. We use short-term memory when we look up a telephone number and repeat it to ourselves until we can place the call. On the other hand, long-term memory can store facts, concepts, and experiences after we stop thinking about them. All conscious processing of information, as in problem solving for example, involves both short-term and long-term memory. As we repeat, rehearse, and recycle information, the memory trace is strengthened, allowing that information to move from short-term memory to long-term memory.

34. Which of the following is the main topic of the passage?

Ⓐ Wilder Penfield
Ⓑ Neurosurgery
Ⓒ Human memory
Ⓓ Chemical reactions

35. The word formerly in paragraph 1 could best be replaced by

Ⓐ in the past
Ⓑ from time to time
Ⓒ in general
Ⓓ by chance

Beginning

Human memory, formerly believed to be rather inefficient, is really much more sophisticated than that of a computer. Researchers approaching the problem from a variety of points of view have all concluded that there is a great deal more stored in our minds than has been generally supposed. Dr. Wilder Penfield, a Canadian neurosurgeon, proved that by stimulating their brains electrically, he could elicit the total recall of complex events in his subjects' lives. Even dreams and other minor events supposedly forgotten for many years suddenly emerged in detail.

The memory trace is the term for whatever forms the internal representation of the specific information about the event stored in the memory. Assumed to have been made by structural changes in the brain, the memory trace is not subject to direct observation but is rather a theoretical construct that is used to speculate about how information presented at a particular time can cause performance at a later time. Most theories include the strength of the memory trace as a variable in the degree of learning, retention, and retrieval possible for a memory. One theory is

36. Compared with a computer, human memory is

Ⓐ more complex
Ⓑ more limited
Ⓒ less dependable
Ⓓ less durable

37. Look at the word sophisticated in the passage. Click on the word in the **bold** text that is closest in meaning to sophisticated.

Human memory, formerly believed to be rather inefficient, is really much more sophisticated than that of a computer. **Researchers approaching the problem from a variety of points of view have all concluded that there is a great deal more stored in our minds than has been generally supposed. Dr. Wilder Penfield, a Canadian neurosurgeon, proved that by stimulating their brains electrically, he could elicit the total recall of complex events in his subjects' lives.** Even dreams and other minor events supposedly forgotten for many years suddenly emerged in detail.

The memory trace is the term for whatever forms the internal representation of the specific information about the event stored in the memory. Assumed to have been made by structural changes in the brain, the memory trace is not subject to direct observation but is rather a theoretical construct that is used to speculate about how information presented at a particular time can cause performance at a later time. Most theories include the strength of the memory trace as a variable in the degree of learning, retention, and retrieval possible for a memory. One theory is

38. Look at the word that in the passage. Click on the word or phrase in the **bold** text that that refers to.

Human memory, formerly believed to be rather inefficient, is really much more sophisticated than that of a computer. Researchers approaching the problem from a variety of points of view have all concluded that there is a great deal more stored in our minds than has been generally supposed. Dr. Wilder Penfield, a Canadian neurosurgeon, proved that by stimulating their brains electrically, he could elicit the total recall of complex events in his subjects' lives. Even dreams and other minor events supposedly forgotten for many years suddenly emerged in detail.

The memory trace is the term for whatever forms the internal representation of the specific information about the event stored in the memory. Assumed to have been made by structural changes in the brain, the memory trace is not subject to direct observation but is rather a theoretical construct that is used to speculate about how information presented at a particular time can cause performance at a later time. Most theories include the strength of the memory trace as a variable in the degree of learning, retention, and retrieval possible for a memory. One theory is

39. How did Penfield stimulate dreams and other minor events from the past?

- Ⓐ By surgery
- Ⓑ By electrical stimulation
- Ⓒ By repetition
- Ⓓ By chemical stimulation

40. According to the passage, the capacity for storage in the brain

- Ⓐ can be understood by examining the physiology of the brain
- Ⓑ is stimulated by patterns of activity
- Ⓒ has a limited combination of relationships
- Ⓓ is not influenced by repetition

41. The word bonds in paragraph 2 means

- Ⓐ promises
- Ⓑ agreements
- Ⓒ connections
- Ⓓ responsibilities

forms the internal representation of the specific information about the event stored in the memory. Assumed to have been made by structural changes in the brain, the memory trace is not subject to direct observation but is rather a theoretical construct that is used to speculate about how information presented at a particular time can cause performance at a later time. Most theories include the strength of the memory trace as a variable in the degree of learning, retention, and retrieval possible for a memory. One theory is that the fantastic capacity for storage in the brain is the result of an almost unlimited combination of interconnections between brain cells, stimulated by patterns of activity. Repeated references to the same information support recall. Or, to say that another way, improved performance is the result of strengthening the chemical bonds in the memory.

Psychologists generally divide memory into at least two types, short-term and long-term memory, which combine to form working memory. Short-term memory contains what we are actively focusing on at any particular time, but items are not retained longer than twenty or thirty seconds

42. Click on the sentence in paragraph 3 that defines working memory.

Paragraph 3 is marked with an arrow (→).

> **End**
>
> interconnections between brain cells, stimulated by patterns of activity. Repeated references to the same information support recall. Or, to say that another way, improved performance is the result of strengthening the chemical bonds in the memory. → Psychologists generally divide memory into at least two types, short-term and long-term memory, which combine to form working memory. Short-term memory contains what we are actively focusing on at any particular time, but items are not retained longer than twenty or thirty seconds without verbal rehearsal. We use short-term memory when we look up a telephone number and repeat it to ourselves until we can place the call. On the other hand, long-term memory can store facts, concepts, and experiences after we stop thinking about them. All conscious processing of information, as in problem solving for example, involves both short-term and long-term memory. As we repeat, rehearse, and recycle information, the memory trace is strengthened, allowing that information to move from short-term memory to long-term memory.

43. Why does the author mention looking up a telephone number?

   Ⓐ It is an example of short-term memory.
   Ⓑ It is an example of a weak memory trace.
   Ⓒ It is an example of an experiment.
   Ⓓ It is an example of how we move short-term memory to long-term memory.

44. All of the following are true of a memory trace EXCEPT that

   Ⓐ it is probably made by structural changes in the brain
   Ⓑ it is able to be observed directly by investigators
   Ⓒ it is a theoretical construct that we use to form hypotheses
   Ⓓ it is related to the degree of recall supported by repetition

45. With which of the following statements would the author most likely agree?

   Ⓐ The mind has a much greater capacity for memory than was previously believed.
   Ⓑ The physical basis for memory is clear.
   Ⓒ Different points of view are valuable.
   Ⓓ Human memory is inefficient.

To check your answers for Model Test 5, refer to the Answer Key on page 492. For an explanation of the answers, refer to the Explanatory Answers for Model Test 5 on pages 581–599.

Writing Section:
Model Test 5

When you take a Model Test, you should use one sheet of paper, both sides. Time each Model Test carefully. After you have read the topic, you should spend 30 minutes writing. For results that would be closest to the actual testing situation, it is recommended that an English teacher score your test, using the guidelines on page 244 of this book.

Some people believe that it is very important to make large amounts of money, while others are satisfied to earn a comfortable living. Analyze each viewpoint and take a stand. Give specific reasons for your position.

Notes

To check your essay, refer to the Checklist on page 492. For an Example Essay, refer to the Explanatory Answers for Model Test 5 on pages 599–600.

Model Test 6
Computer-Assisted TOEFL

Section 1:
Listening

The Listening Section of the test measures the ability to understand conversations and talks in English. You will use headphones to listen to the conversations and talks. While you are listening, pictures of the speakers or other information will be presented on your computer screen. There are two parts to the Listening Section, with special directions for each part.

On the day of the test, the amount of time you will have to answer all of the questions will appear on the computer screen. The time you spend listening to the test material will not be counted. The listening material and questions about it will be presented only one time. You will not be allowed to take notes or have any paper at your computer. You will both see and hear the questions before the answer choices appear. You can take as much time as you need to select an answer; however, it will be to your advantage to answer the questions as quickly as possible. You may change your answer as many times as you want before you confirm it. After you have confirmed an answer, you will not be able to return to the question.

Before you begin working on the Listening Section, you will have an opportunity to adjust the volume of the sound. You may not be able to change the volume after you have started the test.

QUESTION DIRECTIONS — Part A

In Part A of the Listening Section, you will hear short conversations between two people. In some of the conversations, each person speaks only once. In other conversations, one or both of the people speak more than once. Each conversation is followed by one question about it.

Each question in this part has four answer choices. You should click on the best answer to each question. Answer the questions on the basis of what is stated or implied by the speakers.

1. What does the woman mean?

   A She does not know how to play tennis.
   B She has to study.
   C She does not like the man.
   D She does not qualify to play.

2. What does the woman mean?

   A She has no attendance policy.
   B The attendance policy is not the same for undergraduates and graduate students.
   C The grade will be affected by absences.
   D This class is not for graduate students.

3. What does the woman say about Ali?

   A He is studying only at the American Language Institute.
   B He is taking three classes at the university.
   C He is a part-time student.
   D He is surprised.

4. What does the woman mean?

   A She will help the man.
   B She is not Miss Evans.
   C Dr. Warren has already gone.
   D The man should wait for Dr. Warren to answer the call.

5. What will the woman probably do?

   Ⓐ Return home
   Ⓑ Ask someone else about the shuttle
   Ⓒ Make a telephone call
   Ⓓ Board the bus

6. What does the woman mean?

   Ⓐ She will go to the bookstore.
   Ⓑ The books were too expensive.
   Ⓒ There weren't any math and English books left.
   Ⓓ She does not need any books.

7. What does the woman suggest the man do?

   Ⓐ Take a different route
   Ⓑ Leave earlier than planned
   Ⓒ Wait until seven to leave
   Ⓓ Stay at home

8. What does the woman mean?

   Ⓐ The class with the graduate assistant is very enjoyable.
   Ⓑ The students make a log of errors in the class.
   Ⓒ The graduate assistant ridicules his students.
   Ⓓ She is sorry that she took the class with the graduate assistant.

9. What does the man mean?

   Ⓐ He did not mean to insult the woman.
   Ⓑ What he said to Susan was true.
   Ⓒ The woman does not have an accent.
   Ⓓ Susan did not report the conversation accurately.

10. What does the woman agree to do for the man?

   Ⓐ Tell him the time
   Ⓑ Take care of his bag
   Ⓒ Help him find his books
   Ⓓ Go with him

11. What does the man mean?

   Ⓐ He has heard the woman talk about this often.
   Ⓑ He understands the woman's point of view.
   Ⓒ He is too tired to talk about it.
   Ⓓ He can hear the woman very well.

12. What does the woman imply?

   Ⓐ Mike does not have a car.
   Ⓑ Mike's brother is taking a break.
   Ⓒ Mike is in Florida.
   Ⓓ Mike is visiting his brother.

13. What does the woman advise the man to do?

   Ⓐ Get a job
   Ⓑ Finish the assignment
   Ⓒ Begin his project
   Ⓓ Pay his bills

14. What does the woman mean?

   Ⓐ She is not sure about going.
   Ⓑ She does not want to go to the show.
   Ⓒ She wants to know why the man asked her.
   Ⓓ She would like to go with the man.

15. What had the woman assumed about Bill and Carol?

   Ⓐ They would not get married.
   Ⓑ They were still away on their honeymoon.
   Ⓒ They didn't go on a honeymoon.
   Ⓓ They had not planned a large wedding.

16. What does the woman mean?

   Ⓐ She has already reviewed for the test.
   Ⓑ The test is important to her.
   Ⓒ The review session will not be helpful.
   Ⓓ The man does not understand her.

17. What will the man probably do?

   Ⓐ Telephone his sponsor
   Ⓑ Collect his check
   Ⓒ Help the woman to look for his check
   Ⓓ Ask the woman to look again

QUESTION DIRECTIONS — Part B

In Part B of the Listening Section, you will hear several longer conversations and talks. Each conversation or talk is followed by several questions. The conversations, talks, and questions will not be repeated.

The conversations and talks are about a variety of topics. You do not need special knowledge of the topics to answer the questions correctly. Rather, you should answer each question on the basis of what is stated or implied by the speakers in the conversations or talks.

For most of the questions, you will need to click on the best of four possible answers. Some questions will have special directions. The special directions will appear in a box on the computer screen.

18. What is Gary's problem?

    Ⓐ He is sick with the flu.
    Ⓑ He is in the hospital.
    Ⓒ He has missed some quizzes.
    Ⓓ He is behind in lab.

19. What does Gary want Margaret to do?

    Ⓐ Go to lab for him
    Ⓑ Let him copy her notes
    Ⓒ Help him study
    Ⓓ Be his lab partner

20. What does Margaret offer to do?

    Ⓐ Meet with him to clarify her notes
    Ⓑ Make a copy of the quizzes for him
    Ⓒ Read his notes before the next lab
    Ⓓ Show him how to do the lab experiments

21. What is Margaret's attitude in this conversation?

    Click on 2 answers.

    Ⓐ Helpful
    Ⓑ Worried
    Ⓒ Apologetic
    Ⓓ Friendly

22. What is the main topic of this lecture?

    Ⓐ Novelists of this century
    Ⓑ F. Scott Fitzgerald's work
    Ⓒ First novels by young authors
    Ⓓ Film versions of F. Scott Fitzgerald's novels

23. Why wasn't Fitzgerald more successful in his later life?

    Click on 2 answers.

    Ⓐ He had little natural talent.
    Ⓑ He was a compulsive drinker.
    Ⓒ The film versions of his books were not successful.
    Ⓓ He did not adjust to a changing world.

24. According to the lecturer, what do we know about the novels written by F. Scott Fitzgerald?

    Ⓐ They described the Jazz Age.
    Ⓑ They described the Deep South.
    Ⓒ They were based upon war experiences.
    Ⓓ They were written in stream-of-consciousness style.

25. What does the professor want the class to do after the lecture?

    Ⓐ Write a book report
    Ⓑ Read one of Fitzgerald's books
    Ⓒ Watch and discuss a video
    Ⓓ Research Fitzgerald's life

26. What is the main purpose of the talk?

    Ⓐ To explain chamber music
    Ⓑ To give examples of composers
    Ⓒ To congratulate the University Quartet
    Ⓓ To introduce madrigal singing

27. What is the origin of the term *chamber music*?

    Ⓐ A medieval musical instrument
    Ⓑ An old word that means small group
    Ⓒ A place where the music was played
    Ⓓ A name of one of the musicians who created it

28. According to the speaker, which instruments are the most popular for chamber music?

    Click on 2 answers.

    A   Piano
    B   Brass
    C   Strings
    D   Percussion

29. Why does the speaker mention Johann Sebastian Bach?

    Ⓐ He was a famous composer.
    Ⓑ He composed the pieces that will be performed.
    Ⓒ He wrote vocal chamber music.
    Ⓓ He wrote trio sonatas.

30. What will the listeners hear next?

    Ⓐ A discussion of music from the eighteenth century
    Ⓑ A concert by the University Quartet
    Ⓒ An introduction to religious music
    Ⓓ A history of music from the Elizabethan Period

31. Why did the man go to the Chemical Engineering Department?

    Ⓐ To make an appointment
    Ⓑ To cancel his appointment
    Ⓒ To change his appointment time
    Ⓓ To rearrange his schedule so that he could keep his appointment

32. What does the woman say about Dr. Benjamin?

    Ⓐ He is busy on Wednesday.
    Ⓑ He will not be in on Wednesday.
    Ⓒ He does not schedule appointments on Wednesday.
    Ⓓ He will be moving his Wednesday appointment to Thursday this week.

33. What did the secretary offer to do?

    Ⓐ Give him an appointment at three o'clock on Wednesday
    Ⓑ Give him an appointment at either four-thirty on Wednesday or ten o'clock on Thursday
    Ⓒ Give him an appointment at lunch time
    Ⓓ Give him a new appointment earlier on the same day as his original appointment

34. What did the man decide to do?

    Ⓐ Make a new appointment later
    Ⓑ Cancel his regular appointment
    Ⓒ Rearrange his schedule to keep his original appointment
    Ⓓ Call back later when Dr. Benjamin is in

35. What is the main topic of this lecture?

    Ⓐ Health food
    Ⓑ The processing of bread
    Ⓒ Organic gardens
    Ⓓ Poisons

36. Which term is used to identify foods that have not been processed or canned?

    Ⓐ Refined foods
    Ⓑ Natural foods
    Ⓒ Organic foods
    Ⓓ Unprocessed foods

37. What happens to food when it is processed?

    Click on 2 answers.

    A   Some toxic chemicals may be added.
    B   The food is cooked.
    C   Vitamins are added to the food.
    D   The vitamin content is reduced.

38. Which word best describes the speaker's attitude toward health foods?

    Ⓐ Uninformed
    Ⓑ Convinced
    Ⓒ Uncertain
    Ⓓ Humorous

39. How did the professor define the Stone Age?

    (A) The time when the first agricultural communities were established

    (B) The time when the glaciers from the last Ice Age receded

    (C) The time when prehistoric humans began to make tools

    (D) The time when metals were introduced as material for tools and weapons

40. According to the lecturer, which two occupations describe the Neanderthals?

    (A) Farmers

    (B) Hunters

    (C) Gatherers

    (D) Artisans

41. Identify the three time periods associated with the Stone Age.

> Click on a phrase. Then click on the empty box in the correct row.
>
> Use each phrase only once.

A **appearance of *Homo sapiens***
B **establishment of agricultural villages**
C **use of tools**

Old Stone Age	
Middle Stone Age	
Late Stone Age	

42. Why did tools change during the Late Stone Age?

    (A) They began to be used for domestic purposes.

    (B) They were not strong enough for the cold weather.

    (C) They were adapted as farm tools.

    (D) They were more complex as humans became more creative.

43. What marked the end of the Stone Age?

    (A) The introduction of farming

    (B) The preference for metal tools

    (C) The decline of Neanderthals

    (D) The onset of the Ice Age

44. What is a trap?

    (A) A man-made storage area for oil

    (B) Gas and water that collect near oil deposits

    (C) An underground formation that stops the flow of oil

    (D) Cracks and holes that allow the oil to move

45. Select the diagram of the anticline trap that was described in the lecture.

> Click on a diagram.

A

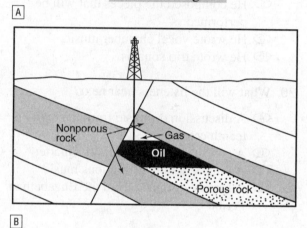

B

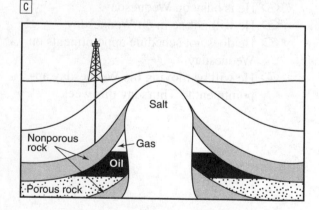

46. Identify the nonporous rock in the diagram.

Click on the letter.

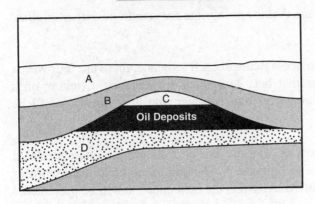

47. According to the speaker, how can geologists locate salt domes?

Ⓐ They look for a bulge in an otherwise flat area.

Ⓑ They look for an underground rock formation shaped like an arch.

Ⓒ They look for salt on the surface of the area.

Ⓓ They look for a large crack in the Earth.

48. What is the woman's problem?

Ⓐ She does not want to take the course.

Ⓑ She does not know which professor to choose.

Ⓒ She does not understand the course requirements.

Ⓓ She does not want to take the man's advice.

49. What do Dr. Perkins and Dr. Robinson have in common?

Ⓐ They teach two different sections of the same class.

Ⓑ They both use traditional teaching methods.

Ⓒ They have been teaching for a long time.

Ⓓ They are not considered very good teachers.

50. Why did the woman decide to take the class with Dr. Robinson?

Click on 2 answers.

A She has already taken classes with Dr. Robinson.

B She prefers to take lecture classes.

C She wants to take the class with the man.

D She likes a more traditional approach to teaching.

Section 2:
Structure

This section measures the ability to recognize language that is appropriate for standard written English. There are two types of questions in this section.

In the first type of question, there are incomplete sentences. Beneath each sentence, there are four words or phrases. You will choose the one word or phrase that best completes the sentence. Clicking on a choice darkens the oval. After you click on **Next** and **Confirm Answer**, the next question will be presented.

The second type of question has four underlined words or phrases. You will choose the one underlined word or phrase that must be changed for the sentence to be correct. Clicking on an underlined word or phrase will darken it. After you click on **Next** and **Confirm Answer**, the next question will be presented.

1. When friends insist on _____ expensive gifts, it makes most Americans uncomfortable.

    Ⓐ them to accept
    Ⓑ their accepting
    Ⓒ they accepting
    Ⓓ they accept

2. Gilbert Stuart is considered by most art critics _____ greatest portrait painter in the North American colonies.

    Ⓐ that he was
    Ⓑ as he was
    Ⓒ who was the
    Ⓓ the

3. The extent to which an individual is a
      Ⓐ
   product of either heredity or environment

   cannot proved, but several theories
        Ⓑ   Ⓒ
   have been proposed.
      Ⓓ

4. A child in the first grade tends to be _____ all of the other children in the class.

    Ⓐ the same old to
    Ⓑ the same age than
    Ⓒ as old like
    Ⓓ the same age as

5. The bird's egg is such an efficient structure for protecting the embryo inside _____ difficult for the hatchling to break.

    Ⓐ that is
    Ⓑ that
    Ⓒ and is
    Ⓓ that it is

6. Jane Addams had already established Hull
                        Ⓐ
   House in Chicago and began her work in
           Ⓑ   Ⓒ
   the Women's Suffrage Movement when she

   was awarded the Nobel Prize for peace.
        Ⓓ

7. The flag of the original first colonies may or
                     Ⓐ
   may not have been made by Betsy Ross
              Ⓑ   Ⓒ
   during the Revolution.
        Ⓓ

8. As a safety measure, the detonator for a nuclear device may be made of _____ , each of which is controlled by a different employee.

    Ⓐ two equipments
    Ⓑ two pieces of equipments
    Ⓒ two pieces of equipment
    Ⓓ two equipment pieces

9. _____ that the English settled in Jamestown.

    (A) In 1607 that it was
    (B) That in 1607
    (C) Because in 1607
    (D) It was in 1607

10. The most common form of treatment it is
        (A)   (B)   (C)

    mass inoculation and chlorination of

    water sources.
      (D)

11. An equilateral triangle is a triangle _____ and three angles of equal size.

    (A) that have three sides of equal length
    (B) it has three sides equally long
    (C) that has three sides of equal length
    (D) having three equal length sides in it

12. _____ are found on the surface of the moon.

    (A) Craters and waterless seas that
    (B) When craters and waterless seas
    (C) Craters and waterless seas
    (D) Since craters and waterless seas

13. Without alphabetical order, dictionaries
                            (A)

    would be impossibility to use.
       (B)   (C)   (D)

14. _____ two waves pass a given point simultaneously, they will have no effect on each other's subsequent motion.

    (A) So that
    (B) They are
    (C) That
    (D) If

15. The Pickerel Frog, native to southern
      (A)
    Canada and the eastern United States,

    should be avoided because their skin
         (B)   (C)
    secretions are lethal to small animals and

    irritating to humans.
      (D)

16. Staying in a hotel costs _____ renting a room in a dormitory for a week.

    (A) twice more than
    (B) twice as much as
    (C) as much twice as
    (D) as much as twice

17. Unlike most Europeans, many Americans _____ a bowl of cereal for breakfast every day.

    (A) used to eating
    (B) are used to eat
    (C) are used to eating
    (D) use to eat

18. Scientists had previously estimated that the
                    (A)

    Grand Canyon in Arizona is ten million
                     (B)

    years old, but now, by using a more modern
                   (C)

    dating method, they agree that the age is

    closer to six million years.
          (D)

19. Although jogging is a good way to lose
          (A)

    weight and improve one's physical

    condition, most doctors recommend that the
          (B)

    potential jogger begin in a correct manner
                   (C)

    by getting a complete checkup.
      (D)

20. Some conifers, that is, tree that have cones,
      (A)   (B) (C)
    are able to thrive on poor, thin soil.
    (D)

21. Fast-food restaurants have become popular because many working people want _____ .

    (A) to eat quickly and cheaply
    (B) eating quickly and cheaply
    (C) eat quickly and cheaply
    (D) the eat quickly and cheaply

22. Airports must be <u>located</u> <u>near to</u> major
               Ⓐ   Ⓑ

    population centers for the advantage of

    <u>air transportation</u> <u>to be retained</u>.
        Ⓒ   Ⓓ

23. On an untimed test, to answer accurately is
    more important than _____ .

    Ⓐ a quick finish
    Ⓑ to finish quickly
    Ⓒ finishing quickly
    Ⓓ you finish quickly

24. <u>It is</u> imperative that a graduate student
     Ⓐ

    <u>maintains</u> a grade point average <u>of</u> "B" in
       Ⓑ   Ⓒ

    <u>his</u> major field.
     Ⓓ

25. Dairying <u>is</u> concerned not only <u>with</u> the
            Ⓐ   Ⓑ

    production of milk, <u>but</u> with the manufac-
                     Ⓒ

    ture of milk products <u>such as</u> butter and
                        Ⓓ

    cheese.

Section 3:
Reading

This section measures the ability to read and understand short passages similar in topic and style to those that students are likely to encounter in North American universities and colleges. This section contains reading passages and questions about the passages. There are several different types of questions in this section.

In the Reading Section, you will first have the opportunity to read the passage. You will use the scroll bar to view the rest of the passage.

When you have finished reading the passage, you will use the mouse to click on **Proceed**. Then the questions about the passage will be presented. You are to choose the one best answer to each question. Answer all questions about the information in a passage on the basis of what is stated or implied in that passage.

Most of the questions will be multiple-choice questions. To answer these questions you will click on a choice below the question.

To answer some questions, you will click on a word or phrase.
To answer some questions, you will click on a sentence in the passage.
To answer some questions, you will click on a square to add a sentence to the passage.

A geyser is the result of underground water under the combined conditions of high temperatures and increased pressure beneath the surface of the Earth. Since temperature rises about 1°F for every sixty feet under the Earth's surface, and pressure increases with depth, water that seeps down in cracks and fissures until it reaches very hot rocks in the Earth's interior becomes heated to a temperature of approximately 290°F.

Water under pressure can remain liquid at temperatures above its normal boiling point, but in a geyser, the weight of the water nearer the surface exerts so much pressure on the deeper water that the water at the bottom of the geyser reaches much higher temperatures than does the water at the top of the geyser. As the deep water becomes hotter, and consequently lighter, it suddenly rises to the surface and shoots out of the surface in the form of steam and hot water. In turn, the explosion agitates all the water in the geyser reservoir, creating further explosions. Immediately afterward, the water again flows into the underground reservoir, heating begins, and the process repeats itself.

In order to function, then, a geyser must have a source of heat, a reservoir where water can be stored until the temperature rises to an unstable point, an opening through which the hot water and steam can escape, and underground channels for resupplying water after an eruption.

Favorable conditions for geysers exist in regions of geologically recent volcanic activity, especially in areas of more than average precipitation. For the most part, geysers are located in three regions of the world: New Zealand, Iceland, and the Yellowstone National Park area of the United States. The most famous geyser in the world is Old Faithful in Yellowstone Park. Old Faithful erupts every hour, rising to a height of 125 to 170 feet and expelling more than ten thousand gallons during each eruption. Old Faithful earned its name because, unlike most geysers, it has never failed to erupt on schedule even once in eighty years of observation.

1. Which of the following is the main topic of the passage?

   (A) The Old Faithful geyser in Yellowstone National Park
   (B) The nature of geysers
   (C) The ratio of temperature to pressure in underground water
   (D) Regions of geologically recent volcanic activity

2. In order for a geyser to erupt

   (A) hot rocks must rise to the surface of the Earth
   (B) water must flow underground
   (C) it must be a warm day
   (D) the earth must not be rugged or broken

3. Look at the word approximately in the passage. Click on another word or phrase in the **bold** text that is closest in meaning to approximately.

Beginning

A geyser is the result of underground water under the combined conditions of high temperatures and increased pressure beneath the surface of the Earth. **Since temperature rises about 1°F for every sixty feet under the Earth's surface, and pressure increases with depth, water that seeps down in cracks and fissures until it reaches very hot rocks in the Earth's interior becomes heated to a temperature of** approximately **290°F.**

Water under pressure can remain liquid at temperatures above its normal boiling point, but in a geyser, the weight of the water nearer the surface exerts so much pressure on the deeper water that the water at the bottom of the geyser reaches much higher temperatures than does the water at the top of the geyser. As the deep water becomes hotter, and consequently lighter, it suddenly rises to the surface and shoots out of the surface in the form of steam and hot water. In turn, the explosion agitates all the water in the geyser reservoir, creating further explosions. Immediately afterward, the water again flows into the underground reservoir, heating begins, and the process repeats itself.

4. The word it in paragraph 1 refers to

   Ⓐ water
   Ⓑ depth
   Ⓒ pressure
   Ⓓ surface

Beginning

    A geyser is the result of underground water under the combined conditions of high temperatures and increased pressure beneath the surface of the Earth. **Since temperature rises about 1°F for every sixty feet under the Earth's surface, and pressure increases with depth, water that seeps down in cracks and fissures until it reaches very hot rocks in the Earth's interior becomes heated to a temperature of approximately 290°F.**

    Water under pressure can remain liquid at temperatures above its normal boiling point, but in a geyser, the weight of the water nearer the surface exerts so much pressure on the deeper water that the water at the bottom of the geyser reaches much higher temperatures than does the water at the top of the geyser. As the deep water becomes hotter, and consequently lighter, it suddenly rises to the surface and shoots out of the surface in the form of steam and hot water. In turn, the explosion agitates all the water in the geyser reservoir, creating further explosions. Immediately afterward, the water again flows into the underground reservoir, heating begins, and the process repeats itself.

---

5. Click on the paragraph that explains the role of water pressure in an active geyser.

   Scroll the passage to see all of the paragraphs.

6. As depth increases

   Ⓐ pressure increases but temperature does not
   Ⓑ temperature increases but pressure does not
   Ⓒ both pressure and temperature increase
   Ⓓ neither pressure nor temperature increases

7. Why does the author mention New Zealand and Iceland in paragraph 4?

   Ⓐ To compare areas of high volcanic activity
   Ⓑ To describe the Yellowstone National Park
   Ⓒ To provide examples of areas where geysers are located
   Ⓓ To name the two regions where all geysers are found

Paragraph 4 is marked with an arrow (→).

End

Immediately afterward, the water again flows into the underground reservoir, heating begins, and the process repeats itself.

    In order to function, then, a geyser must have a source of heat, a reservoir where water can be stored until the temperature rises to an unstable point, an opening through which the hot water and steam can escape, and underground channels for resupplying water after an eruption.

→ Favorable conditions for geysers exist in regions of geologically recent volcanic activity, especially in areas of more than average precipitation. For the most part, geysers are located in three regions of the world: New Zealand, Iceland, and the Yellowstone National Park area of the United States. The most famous geyser in the world is Old Faithful in Yellowstone Park. Old Faithful erupts every hour, rising to a height of 125 to 170 feet and expelling more than ten thousand gallons during each eruption. Old Faithful earned its name because, unlike most geysers, it has never failed to erupt on schedule even once in eighty years of observation.

8. How often does Old Faithful erupt?

Ⓐ Every 10 minutes
Ⓑ Every 60 minutes
Ⓒ Every 125 minutes
Ⓓ Every 170 minutes

9. The word expelling in paragraph 4 is closest in meaning to

Ⓐ heating
Ⓑ discharging
Ⓒ supplying
Ⓓ wasting

End

Immediately afterward, the water again flows into the underground reservoir, heating begins, and the process repeats itself.

In order to function, then, a geyser must have a source of heat, a reservoir where water can be stored until the temperature rises to an unstable point, an opening through which the hot water and steam can escape, and underground channels for resupplying water after an eruption.

Favorable conditions for geysers exist in regions of geologically recent volcanic activity, especially in areas of more than average precipitation. For the most part, geysers are located in three regions of the world: New Zealand, Iceland, and the Yellowstone National Park area of the United States. The most famous geyser in the world is Old Faithful in Yellowstone Park. Old Faithful erupts every hour, rising to a height of 125 to 170 feet and expelling more than ten thousand gallons during each eruption. Old Faithful earned its name because, unlike most geysers, it has never failed to erupt on schedule even once in eighty years of observation.

---

10. What does the author mean by the statement Old Faithful earned its name because, unlike most geysers, it has never failed to erupt on schedule even once in eighty years of observation?

Ⓐ Old Faithful always erupts on schedule.
Ⓑ Old Faithful is usually predictable.
Ⓒ Old Faithful erupts predictably like other geysers.
Ⓓ Old Faithful received its name because it has been observed for many years.

11. According to the passage, what is required for a geyser to function?

Ⓐ A source of heat, a place for water to collect, an opening, and underground channels
Ⓑ An active volcano nearby and a water reservoir
Ⓒ Channels in the Earth and heavy rainfall
Ⓓ Volcanic activity, underground channels, and steam

This question has often been posed: Why were the Wright brothers able to succeed in an effort at which so many others had failed? Many explanations have been mentioned, but three reasons are most often cited. First, they were a team. Both men worked congenially and cooperatively, read the same books, located and shared information, talked incessantly about the possibility of manned flight, and served as a consistent source of inspiration and encouragement to each other. Quite simply, two geniuses are better than one.

Both were glider pilots. Unlike some other engineers who experimented with the theories of flight, Orville and Wilbur Wright experienced the practical aspects of aerodynamics by building and flying in kites and gliders. Each craft they built was slightly superior to the last, as they incorporated knowledge that they had gained from previous failures. They had realized from their experiments that the most serious challenge in manned flight would be stabilizing and maneuvering the aircraft once it was airborne. While others concentrated their efforts on the problem of achieving lift for take-off, the Wright brothers were focusing on developing a three-axis control for guiding their aircraft. By the time that the brothers started to build an airplane, they were already among the world's best glider pilots; they knew the problems of riding the air first hand.

In addition, the Wright brothers had designed more effective wings for the airplane than had been previously engineered. Using a wind tunnel, they tested more than two hundred different wing designs, recording the effects of slight variations in shape on the pressure of air on the wings. The data from these experiments allowed the Wright brothers to construct a superior wing for their aircraft.

In spite of these advantages, however, the Wright brothers might not have succeeded had they not been born at precisely the opportune moment in history. Attempts to achieve manned flight in the early nineteenth century were doomed because the steam engines that powered the aircrafts were too heavy in proportion to the power that they produced. But by the end of the nineteenth century, when the brothers were experimenting with engineering options, a relatively light internal combustion engine had already been invented, and they were able to bring the ratio of weight to power within acceptable limits for flight.

12. Which of the following is the main topic of the passage?

    Ⓐ The reasons why the Wright brothers succeeded in manned flight
    Ⓑ The advantage of the internal combustion engine in the Wright brothers' experiments
    Ⓒ The Wright brothers' experience as pilots
    Ⓓ The importance of gliders to the development of airplanes

13. The word cited in paragraph 1 is closest in meaning to which of the following?

    Ⓐ disregarded
    Ⓑ mentioned
    Ⓒ considered
    Ⓓ proven

Beginning

This question has often been posed: Why were the Wright brothers able to succeed in an effort at which so many others had failed? Many explanations have been mentioned, but three reasons are most often cited. First, they were a team. Both men worked congenially and cooperatively, read the same books, located and shared information, talked incessantly about the possibility of manned flight, and served as a consistent source of inspiration and encouragement to each other. Quite simply, two geniuses are better than one.

Both were glider pilots. Unlike some other engineers who experimented with the theories of flight, Orville and Wilbur Wright experienced the practical aspects of aerodynamics by building and flying in kites and gliders. Each craft they built was slightly superior to the last, as they incorporated knowledge that they had gained from previous failures. They had realized from their experiments that the most serious challenge in manned flight would be stabilizing and maneuvering the aircraft once it was airborne. While others concentrated their efforts on the problem of achieving lift for

14. The word incessantly in paragraph 1 could best be replaced by which of the following?

Ⓐ confidently
Ⓑ intelligently
Ⓒ constantly
Ⓓ optimistically

Beginning

This question has often been posed: Why were the Wright brothers able to succeed in an effort at which so many others had failed? Many explanations have been mentioned, but three reasons are most often cited. First, they were a team. Both men worked congenially and cooperatively, read the same books, located and shared information, talked incessantly about the possibility of manned flight, and served as a consistent source of inspiration and encouragement to each other. Quite simply, two geniuses are better than one.

Both were glider pilots. Unlike some other engineers who experimented with the theories of flight, Orville and Wilbur Wright experienced the practical aspects of aerodynamics by building and flying in kites and gliders. Each craft they built was slightly superior to the last, as they incorporated knowledge that they had gained from previous failures. They had realized from their experiments that the most serious challenge in manned flight would be stabilizing and maneuvering the aircraft once it was airborne. While others concentrated their efforts on the problem of achieving lift for

---

15. What kind of experience did the Wright brothers have that distinguished them from their competitors?

Ⓐ They were geniuses.
Ⓑ They were glider pilots.
Ⓒ They were engineers.
Ⓓ They were inventors.

16. Click on the sentence in paragraph 2 that explains the most serious problem that the Wright brothers anticipated in constructing a manned aircraft.

Paragraph 2 is marked with an arrow (→).

More Available

consistent source of inspiration and encouragement to each other. Quite simply, two geniuses are better than one.

→ Both were glider pilots. Unlike some other engineers who experimented with the theories of flight, Orville and Wilbur Wright experienced the practical aspects of aerodynamics by building and flying in kites and gliders. Each craft they built was slightly superior to the last, as they incorporated knowledge that they had gained from previous failures. They had realized from their experiments that the most serious challenge in manned flight would be stabilizing and maneuvering the aircraft once it was airborne. While others concentrated their efforts on the problem of achieving lift for take-off, the Wright brothers were focusing on developing a three-axis control for guiding their aircraft. By the time that the brothers started to build an airplane, they were already among the world's best glider pilots; they knew the problems of riding the air first hand.

In addition, the Wright brothers had designed more effective wings for the airplane than had been previously engineered. Using a wind tunnel,

---

17. Look at the word maneuvering in the passage. Click on the word or phrase in the **bold** text that is closest in meaning to maneuvering.

More Available

Both were glider pilots. Unlike some other engineers who experimented with the theories of flight, Orville and Wilbur Wright experienced the practical aspects of aerodynamics by building and flying in kites and gliders. Each craft they built was slightly superior to the last, as they incorporated knowledge that they had gained from previous failures. **They had realized from their experiments that the most serious challenge in manned flight would be stabilizing and maneuvering the aircraft once it was airborne. While others concentrated their efforts on the problem of achieving lift for take-off, the Wright brothers were focusing on developing a three-axis control for guiding their aircraft.** By the time that the brothers started to build an airplane, they were already among the world's best glider pilots; they knew the problems of riding the air first hand.

In addition, the Wright brothers had designed more effective wings for the airplane than had been previously engineered. Using a wind tunnel, they tested more than two hundred different wing designs, recording the effects of slight variations in shape on the pressure of air on the wings. The

18. Why does the author suggest that the experiments with the wind tunnel were important?

Ⓐ Because they allowed the Wright brothers to decrease the weight of their airplane to acceptable limits

Ⓑ Because they resulted in a three-axis control for their airplanc

Ⓒ Because they were important in the refinement of the wings for their airplane

Ⓓ Because they used the data to improve the engine for their airplane

19. The word they in paragraph 3 refers to

Ⓐ the Wright brothers

Ⓑ aircraft

Ⓒ engines

Ⓓ attempts

End

more effective wings for the airplane than had been previously engineered. Using a wind tunnel, they tested more than two hundred different wing designs, recording the effects of slight variations in shape on the pressure of air on the wings. The data from these experiments allowed the Wright brothers to construct a superior wing for their aircraft.

In spite of these advantages, however, the Wright brothers might not have succeeded had they not been born at precisely the opportune moment in history. Attempts to achieve manned flight in the early nineteenth century were doomed because the steam engines that powered the aircrafts were too heavy in proportion to the power that they produced. But by the end of the nineteenth century, when the brothers were experimenting with engineering options, a relatively light internal combustion engine had already been invented, and they were able to bring the ratio of weight to power within acceptable limits for flight.

---

20. The word doomed in paragraph 4 is closest in meaning to

Ⓐ destined to fail

Ⓑ difficult to achieve

Ⓒ taking a risk

Ⓓ not well planned

End

more effective wings for the airplane than had been previously engineered. Using a wind tunnel, they tested more than two hundred different wing designs, recording the effects of slight variations in shape on the pressure of air on the wings. The data from these experiments allowed the Wright brothers to construct a superior wing for their aircraft.

In spite of these advantages, however, the Wright brothers might not have succeeded had they not been born at precisely the opportune moment in history. Attempts to achieve manned flight in the early nineteenth century were doomed because the steam engines that powered the aircrafts were too heavy in proportion to the power that they produced. But by the end of the nineteenth century, when the brothers were experimenting with engineering options, a relatively light internal combustion engine had already been invented, and they were able to bring the ratio of weight to power within acceptable limits for flight.

21. In paragraph 4, the author suggests that the steam engines used in earlier aircraft had failed because

    Ⓐ They were too small to power a large plane.
    Ⓑ They were too light to generate enough power.
    Ⓒ They did not have internal combustion power.
    Ⓓ They did not have enough power to lift their own weight.

    Paragraph 4 is marked with an arrow (→).

    End ⬆

    more effective wings for the airplane than had been previously engineered. Using a wind tunnel, they tested more than two hundred different wing designs, recording the effects of slight variations in shape on the pressure of air on the wings. The data from these experiments allowed the Wright brothers to construct a superior wing for their aircraft.
    → In spite of these advantages, however, the Wright brothers might not have succeeded had they not been born at precisely the opportune moment in history. Attempts to achieve manned flight in the early nineteenth century were doomed because the steam engines that powered the aircrafts were too heavy in proportion to the power that they produced. But by the end of the nineteenth century, when the brothers were experimenting with engineering options, a relatively light internal combustion engine had already been invented, and they were able to bring the ratio of weight to power within acceptable limits for flight.

    ⬇
    ---

22. The passage discusses all of the following reasons that the Wright brothers succeeded EXCEPT

    Ⓐ They worked very well together.
    Ⓑ They both had practical experience building other aircraft.
    Ⓒ They made extensive tests before they completed the design.
    Ⓓ They were well funded.

The influenza virus is a single molecule composed of millions of individual atoms. Although bacteria can be considered a type of plant, secreting poisonous substances into the body of the organism they attack, viruses, like the influenza virus, are living organisms themselves. We may consider them regular chemical molecules since they have strictly defined atomic structure; but on the other hand, we must also consider them as being alive since they are able to multiply in unlimited quantities.

An attack brought on by the presence of the influenza virus in the body produces a temporary immunity, but, unfortunately, the protection is against only the type of virus that caused the influenza. Because the disease can be produced by any one of three types, referred to as A, B, or C, and many varieties within each type, immunity to one virus will not prevent infection by other types or strains. Protection from the influenza virus is also complicated by the fact that immunity to a specific virus persists for less than a year. Finally, because a virus may periodically change characteristics, the problem of mutation makes it difficult to carry out a successful immunization program. Vaccines are often ineffective against newly evolving strains.

Approximately every ten years, worldwide epidemics of influenza called pandemics occur. Thought to be caused by new strains of type-A virus, these pandemic viruses have spread rapidly, infecting millions of people.

Vaccines have been developed that have been found to be 70 to 90 percent effective for at least six months against either A or B types of the influenza virus, and a genetically engineered live-virus vaccine is under development. Currently, the United States Public Health Service recommends annual vaccination only for those at greatest risk of complications from influenza, including pregnant women and the elderly. Nevertheless, many other members of the general population request and receive flu shots every year, and even more are immunized during epidemic or pandemic cycles.

23. Which of the following is the main topic of the passage?

  Ⓐ The influenza virus
  Ⓑ Immunity to disease
  Ⓒ Bacteria
  Ⓓ Chemical molecules

24. According to this passage, bacteria are

  Ⓐ poisons
  Ⓑ very small
  Ⓒ larger than viruses
  Ⓓ plants

25. Look at the word themselves in the passage. Click on the word or phrase in the **bold** text that themselves refers to.

Beginning

The influenza virus is a single molecule composed of millions of individual atoms. **Although bacteria can be considered a type of plant, secreting poisonous substances into the body of the organism they attack, viruses, like the influenza virus, are living organisms themselves. We may consider them regular chemical molecules since they have strictly defined atomic structure;** but on the other hand, we must also consider them as being alive since they are able to multiply in unlimited quantities.

An attack brought on by the presence of the influenza virus in the body produces a temporary immunity, but, unfortunately, the protection is against only the type of virus that caused the influenza. Because the disease can be produced by any one of three types, referred to as A, B, or C, and many varieties within each type, immunity to one virus will not prevent infection by other types or strains. Protection from the influenza virus is also complicated by the fact that immunity to a specific virus persists for less than a year. Finally, because a virus may periodically change characteristics, the problem of mutation makes it difficult to carry out a successful immunization program. Vaccines are often ineffective

---

26. The word strictly in paragraph 1 could best be replaced by

  Ⓐ unusually
  Ⓑ completely
  Ⓒ broadly
  Ⓓ exactly

Beginning

The influenza virus is a single molecule composed of millions of individual atoms. Although bacteria can be considered a type of plant, secreting poisonous substances into the body of the organism they attack, viruses, like the influenza virus, are living organisms themselves. We may consider them regular chemical molecules since they have strictly defined atomic structure; but on the other hand, we must also consider them as being alive since they are able to multiply in unlimited quantities.

An attack brought on by the presence of the influenza virus in the body produces a temporary immunity, but, unfortunately, the protection is against only the type of virus that caused the influenza. Because the disease can be produced by any one of three types, referred to as A, B, or C, and many varieties within each type, immunity to one virus will not prevent infection by other types or strains. Protection from the influenza virus is also complicated by the fact that immunity to a specific virus persists for less than a year. Finally, because a virus may periodically change characteristics, the problem of mutation makes it difficult to carry out a successful immunization program. Vaccines are often ineffective

---

27. The atomic structure of viruses

  Ⓐ is variable
  Ⓑ is strictly defined
  Ⓒ cannot be analyzed chemically
  Ⓓ is more complex than that of bacteria

28. Why does the author say that viruses are alive?

  Ⓐ They have a complex atomic structure.
  Ⓑ They move.
  Ⓒ They multiply.
  Ⓓ They need warmth and light.

29. The word unlimited in paragraph 1 could best be replaced by which of the following?

    Ⓐ very small
    Ⓑ very large
    Ⓒ very similar
    Ⓓ very different

More Available

poisonous substances into the body of the organism they attack, viruses, like the influenza virus, are living organisms themselves. We may consider them regular chemical molecules since they have strictly defined atomic structure; but on the other hand, we must also consider them as being alive since they are able to multiply in unlimited quantities.

    An attack brought on by the presence of the influenza virus in the body produces a temporary immunity, but, unfortunately, the protection is against only the type of virus that caused the influenza. Because the disease can be produced by any one of three types, referred to as A, B, or C, and many varieties within each type, immunity to one virus will not prevent infection by other types or strains. Protection from the influenza virus is also complicated by the fact that immunity to a specific virus persists for less than a year. Finally, because a virus may periodically change characteristics, the problem of mutation makes it difficult to carry out a successful immunization program. Vaccines are often ineffective against newly evolving strains.

    Approximately every ten years, worldwide epidemics of influenza called pandemics occur.

---

30. Look at the word strains in the passage. Click on another word or phrase in the **bold** text that is closest in meaning to strains.

More Available

only the type of virus that caused the influenza. Because the disease can be produced by any one of three types, referred to as A, B, or C, and many varieties within each type, **immunity to one virus will not prevent infection by other types or strains. Protection from the influenza virus is also complicated by the fact that immunity to a specific virus persists for less than a year. Finally, because a virus may periodically change characteristics, the problem of mutation makes it difficult to carry out a successful immunization program.** Vaccines are often ineffective against newly evolving strains.

    Approximately every ten years, worldwide epidemics of influenza called pandemics occur. Thought to be caused by new strains of type-A virus, these pandemic viruses have spread rapidly, infecting millions of people.

    Vaccines have been developed that have been found to be 70 to 90 percent effective for at least six months against either A or B types of the influenza virus, and a genetically engineered live-virus vaccine is under development. Currently, the United States Public Health Service recommends annual vaccination only for those at greatest risk of complications from

---

31. The following sentence can be added to the passage.

    Epidemics or regional outbreaks have appeared on the average every two or three years for type-A virus, and every four or five years for type-B virus.

Where would it best fit into the passage?

Click on the square (■) to add the sentence to the passage.

Scroll the passage to see all of the choices.

End

mutation makes it difficult to carry out a successful immunization program. Vaccines are often ineffective against newly evolving strains.

    ■ Approximately every ten years, worldwide epidemics of influenza called pandemics occur. Thought to be caused by new strains of type-A virus, these pandemic viruses have spread rapidly, infecting millions of people.

    Vaccines have been developed that have been found to be 70 to 90 percent effective for at least six months against either A or B types of the influenza virus, and a genetically engineered live-virus vaccine is under development. ■Currently, the United States Public Health Service recommends annual vaccination only for those at greatest risk of complications from influenza, including pregnant women and the elderly. ■Nevertheless, many other members of the general population request and receive flu shots every year, and even more are immunized during epidemic or pandemic cycles.■

---

32. According to the passage, how does the body react to the influenza virus?

    Ⓐ It prevents further infection to other types and strains of the virus.
    Ⓑ It produces immunity to the type and strain of virus that invaded it.
    Ⓒ It becomes immune to types A, B, and C viruses, but not to various strains within the types.
    Ⓓ After a temporary immunity, it becomes even more susceptible to the type and strain that caused the influenza.

33. The passage discusses all of the following
    as characteristics of pandemics EXCEPT

    Ⓐ they spread very quickly
    Ⓑ they are caused by type-A virus
    Ⓒ they are regional outbreaks
    Ⓓ they occur once every ten years

The Federal Reserve System, as an independent agency of the United States government, is charged with overseeing the national banking system. Since 1913 the Federal Reserve System, commonly called the Fed, has served as the central bank for the United States. The system consists of twelve District Reserve Banks and their branch offices, along with several committees and councils. All national commercial banks are required by law to be members of the Fed, and all deposit-taking institutions like credit unions are subject to regulation by the Fed regarding the amount of deposited funds that must be held in reserve and that by definition, therefore, are not available for loans. The most powerful body is the seven-member Board of Governors in Washington, appointed by the President and confirmed by the Senate.

The System's primary function is to control monetary policy by influencing the cost and availability of money and credit through the purchase and sale of government securities. If the Federal Reserve provides too little money, interest rates tend to be high, borrowing is expensive, business activity slows down, unemployment goes up, and danger of recession is augmented. If there is too much money, interest rates decline, and borrowing can lead to excess demand, pushing up prices and fueling inflation.

The Fed has several responsibilities in addition to controlling the money supply. In collaboration with the U.S. Department of the Treasury, the Fed puts new coins and paper currency into circulation by issuing them to banks. It also supervises the activities of member banks abroad, and regulates certain aspects of international finance.

It has been said that the Federal Reserve is actually a fourth branch of the United States government because it is composed of national policy makers. However, in practice, the Federal Reserve does not stray from the financial policies established by the executive branch of the government. Although it is true that the Fed does not depend on Congress for budget allocations, and therefore is free from the partisan politics that influence most of the other governmental bodies, it is still responsible for frequent reports to the Congress on the conduct of monetary policies.

34. Which of the following is the most appropriate title for the passage?

    Ⓐ Banking
    Ⓑ The Federal Reserve System
    Ⓒ The Board of Governors
    Ⓓ Monetary Policies

35. The word overseeing in paragraph 1 is closest in meaning to

    Ⓐ supervising
    Ⓑ maintaining
    Ⓒ financing
    Ⓓ stimulating

Beginning

The Federal Reserve System, as an independent agency of the United States government, is charged with overseeing the national banking system. Since 1913 the Federal Reserve System, commonly called the Fed, has served as the central bank for the United States. The system consists of twelve District Reserve Banks and their branch offices, along with several committees and councils. All national commercial banks are required by law to be members of the Fed, and all deposit-taking institutions like credit unions are subject to regulation by the Fed regarding the amount of deposited funds that must be held in reserve and that by definition, therefore, are not available for loans. The most powerful body is the seven-member Board of Governors in Washington, appointed by the President and confirmed by the Senate.

The System's primary function is to control monetary policy by influencing the cost and availability of money and credit through the purchase and sale of government securities. If the Federal Reserve provides too little money, interest rates tend to be high, borrowing is expensive,

36. The word confirmed in paragraph 1 could best be replaced by

    Ⓐ modified
    Ⓑ considered
    Ⓒ examined
    Ⓓ approved

Beginning

The Federal Reserve System, as an independent agency of the United States government, is charged with overseeing the national banking system. Since 1913 the Federal Reserve System, commonly called the Fed, has served as the central bank for the United States. The system consists of twelve District Reserve Banks and their branch offices, along with several committees and councils. All national commercial banks are required by law to be members of the Fed, and all deposit-taking institutions like credit unions are subject to regulation by the Fed regarding the amount of deposited funds that must be held in reserve and that by definition, therefore, are not available for loans. The most powerful body is the seven-member Board of Governors in Washington, appointed by the President and confirmed by the Senate.

The System's primary function is to control monetary policy by influencing the cost and availability of money and credit through the purchase and sale of government securities. If the Federal Reserve provides too little money, interest rates tend to be high, borrowing is expensive,

37. According to the passage, the principal responsibility of the Federal Reserve System is

    Ⓐ to borrow money
    Ⓑ to regulate monetary policies
    Ⓒ to print government securities
    Ⓓ to appoint the Board of Governors

38. The word securities in paragraph 2 is intended to mean

  Ⓐ debts
  Ⓑ bonds
  Ⓒ protection
  Ⓓ confidence

More Available

Fed, and all deposit-taking institutions like credit unions are subject to regulation by the Fed regarding the amount of deposited funds that must be held in reserve and that by definition, therefore, are not available for loans. The most powerful body is the seven-member Board of Governors in Washington, appointed by the President and confirmed by the Senate.

The System's primary function is to control monetary policy by influencing the cost and availability of money and credit through the purchase and sale of government securities. If the Federal Reserve provides too little money, interest rates tend to be high, borrowing is expensive, business activity slows down, unemployment goes up, and danger of recession is augmented. If there is too much money, interest rates decline, and borrowing can lead to excess demand, pushing up prices and fueling inflation.

The Fed has several responsibilities in addition to controlling the money supply. In collaboration with the U.S. Department of the Treasury, the Fed puts new coins and paper currency into circulation by issuing them to banks. It also supervises the

---

39. What happens when the Federal Reserve provides too little money?

  Ⓐ Demand for loans increases.
  Ⓑ Unemployment slows down.
  Ⓒ Interest rates go up.
  Ⓓ Businesses expand.

40. In paragraph 2, the author suggests that inflation is caused by

  Ⓐ high unemployment rates
  Ⓑ too much money in the economy
  Ⓒ very high fuel prices
  Ⓓ a limited supply of goods

Paragraph 2 is marked with an arrow (→).

More Available

Fed, and all deposit-taking institutions like credit unions are subject to regulation by the Fed regarding the amount of deposited funds that must be held in reserve and that by definition, therefore, are not available for loans. The most powerful body is the seven-member Board of Governors in Washington, appointed by the President and confirmed by the Senate.

→ The System's primary function is to control monetary policy by influencing the cost and availability of money and credit through the purchase and sale of government securities. If the Federal Reserve provides too little money, interest rates tend to be high, borrowing is expensive, business activity slows down, unemployment goes up, and danger of recession is augmented. If there is too much money, interest rates decline, and borrowing can lead to excess demand, pushing up prices and fueling inflation.

The Fed has several responsibilities in addition to controlling the money supply. In collaboration with the U.S. Department of the Treasury, the Fed puts new coins and paper currency into circulation by issuing them to banks. It also supervises the

41. Look at the word them in the passage. Click on the word or phrase in the **bold** text that them refers to.

> **End**
>
> **The Fed has several responsibilities in addition to controlling the money supply. In collaboration with the U.S. Department of the Treasury, the Fed puts new coins and paper currency into circulation by issuing them to banks.** It also supervises the activities of member banks abroad, and regulates certain aspects of international finance.
>
> It has been said that the Federal Reserve is actually a fourth branch of the United States government because it is composed of national policy makers. However, in practice, the Federal Reserve does not stray from the financial policies established by the executive branch of the government. Although it is true that the Fed does not depend on Congress for budget allocations, and therefore is free from the partisan politics that influence most of the other governmental bodies, it is still responsible for frequent reports to the Congress on the conduct of monetary policies.

42. Click on the paragraph that outlines the responsibilities of the Fed to banks overseas.

    Scroll the passage to see all of the paragraphs.

43. What does the author mean by the statement However, in practice, the Federal Reserve does not stray from the financial policies established by the executive branch of the government?

    Ⓐ The Fed is more powerful than the executive branch of the government.
    Ⓑ The policies of the Fed and those of the executive branch of the government are not the same.
    Ⓒ The Fed tends to follow the policies of the executive branch of the government.
    Ⓓ The Fed reports to the executive branch of the government.

44. All of the following statements could be included in a summary of the passage EXCEPT:

    Ⓐ The Federal Reserve is an independent agency of the United States government.
    Ⓑ The Federal Reserve controls the flow of money and credit by buying and selling government securities.
    Ⓒ The Federal Reserve issues new coins and currency to banks.
    Ⓓ The Federal Reserve receives its yearly budget from Congress.

45. The following sentence can be added to the passage.

    > **In fact, the Fed is not confined by the usual checks and balances that apply to the three official branches of government—the executive, the legislative, and the judicial.**

    Where would it best fit in the passage?

    Click on the square (■) to add the sentence to the passage.

    Scroll the passage to see all of the choices.

> **End**
>
> The Fed has several responsibilities in addition to controlling the money supply. In collaboration with the U.S. Department of the Treasury, the Fed puts new coins and paper currency into circulation by issuing them to banks. It also supervises the activities of member banks abroad, and regulates certain aspects of international finance.
>
> ■It has been said that the Federal Reserve is actually a fourth branch of the United States government because it is composed of national policy makers. ■However, in practice, the Federal Reserve does not stray from the financial policies established by the executive branch of the government. ■Although it is true that the Fed does not depend on Congress for budget allocations, and therefore is free from the partisan politics that influence most of the other governmental bodies, it is still responsible for frequent reports to the Congress on the conduct of monetary policies. ■

To check your answers for Model Test 6, refer to the Answer Key on page 493. For an explanation of the answers, refer to the Explanatory Answers for Model Test 6 on pages 600–620.

Writing Section:
Model Test 6

When you take a Model Test, you should use one sheet of paper, both sides. Time each Model Test carefully. After you have read the topic, you should spend 30 minutes writing. For results that would be closest to the actual testing situation, it is recommended that an English teacher score your test, using the guidelines on page 244 of this book.

Advances in transportation and communication like the airplane and the telephone have changed the way that nations interact with each other in a global society. Choose another technological innovation that you think is important. Give specific reasons for your choice.

Notes

To check your essay, refer to the Checklist on page 493. For an Example Essay, refer to the Explanatory Answers for Model Test 6 on page 620.

Model Test 7
Computer-Assisted TOEFL

Section 1:
Listening

The Listening Section of the test measures the ability to understand conversations and talks in English. You will use headphones to listen to the conversations and talks. While you are listening, pictures of the speakers or other information will be presented on your computer screen. There are two parts to the Listening Section, with special directions for each part.

On the day of the test, the amount of time you will have to answer all of the questions will appear on the computer screen. The time you spend listening to the test material will not be counted. The listening material and questions about it will be presented only one time. You will not be allowed to take notes or have any paper at your computer. You will both see and hear the questions before the answer choices appear. You can take as much time as you need to select an answer; however, it will be to your advantage to answer the questions as quickly as possible. You may change your answer as many times as you want before you confirm it. After you have confirmed an answer, you will not be able to return to the question.

Before you begin working on the Listening Section, you will have an opportunity to adjust the volume of the sound. You may not be able to change the volume after you have started the test.

QUESTION DIRECTIONS — Part A

In Part A of the Listening Section, you will hear short conversations between two people. In some of the conversations, each person speaks only once. In other conversations, one or both of the people speak more than once. Each conversation is followed by one question about it.

Each question in this part has four answer choices. You should click on the best answer to each question. Answer the questions on the basis of what is stated or implied by the speakers.

1. What does the woman mean?

    Ⓐ The man should leave the dorm.
    Ⓑ The apartment would be noisy, too.
    Ⓒ The man should not find an apartment.
    Ⓓ The man is working too hard.

2. What can we assume from this conversation?

    Ⓐ The man and woman are eating lunch now.
    Ⓑ The man will call the woman to arrange for lunch.
    Ⓒ The man and woman have lunch at the same time.
    Ⓓ The woman does not want to have lunch with the man.

3. What will the woman probably do?

    Ⓐ Send two transcripts to San Diego State
    Ⓑ Prepare two transcripts
    Ⓒ Give two transcripts to the man, and send one to San Diego State
    Ⓓ Give the man three transcripts

4. What does the woman suggest the man do?

    Ⓐ Leave a note for the professor
    Ⓑ Give a note to the professor
    Ⓒ Wait to speak with the professor
    Ⓓ Go to the professor's class

5. What can be inferred about Susan?

    Ⓐ She will have two major fields of study.
    Ⓑ She prefers teaching.
    Ⓒ She does not talk with the woman very often.
    Ⓓ She cannot make up her mind.

6. What are the speakers talking about?

   Ⓐ The mail
   Ⓑ Grades for a class
   Ⓒ The newspaper
   Ⓓ The time of day

7. What had the woman assumed?

   Ⓐ The graduation list has an error on it.
   Ⓑ The man had already graduated.
   Ⓒ The man's name is the same as that of another student.
   Ⓓ The graduation will not be until next spring.

8. What does the woman mean?

   Ⓐ She did not apply yet.
   Ⓑ She is still not sure.
   Ⓒ She has decided to compete.
   Ⓓ She already has a scholarship.

9. What does the man imply?

   Ⓐ He does not like the woman.
   Ⓑ He does not usually study at the library.
   Ⓒ He has received a letter.
   Ⓓ He will not go to the library.

10. What are the speakers talking about?

   Ⓐ Toronto
   Ⓑ Plane fares
   Ⓒ Little towns
   Ⓓ The woman's vacation

11. How does the woman feel about the presentation?

   Ⓐ She wants to go to the bookstore.
   Ⓑ She prefers to do the presentation alone.
   Ⓒ She does not want a book.
   Ⓓ She is not interested in the presentation.

12. What do we learn about the two students in this conversation?

   Ⓐ Neither the man nor the woman was in class on Friday.
   Ⓑ The woman was at the airport while the man was in class.
   Ⓒ The man was with his mother while the woman was in class.
   Ⓓ The man and the woman were in New York together.

13. What does the man mean?

   Ⓐ Returning home is not very expensive.
   Ⓑ There hasn't been any time to think about the trip.
   Ⓒ The time has passed quickly.
   Ⓓ He expected to be more enthusiastic.

14. What does the woman mean?

   Ⓐ She always eats in the snack bar.
   Ⓑ She used to eat in the snack bar.
   Ⓒ She occasionally eats in the snack bar.
   Ⓓ She has never eaten in the snack bar.

15. What does the woman mean?

   Ⓐ The man should rest.
   Ⓑ The man's health has improved.
   Ⓒ The man worries too much.
   Ⓓ The man is very ill.

16. What does the man mean?

   Ⓐ He does not have an economics class.
   Ⓑ He likes to study economics.
   Ⓒ He used to take economics.
   Ⓓ He does not enjoy their economics class.

17. What does the man imply?

   Ⓐ He does not have a topic for his project yet.
   Ⓑ He needs more than thirty-five participants.
   Ⓒ He is discouraged about the research.
   Ⓓ He lost some data for his research project.

QUESTION DIRECTIONS — Part B

In Part B of the Listening Section, you will hear several longer conversations and talks. Each conversation or talk is followed by several questions. The conversations, talks, and questions will not be repeated.

The conversations and talks are about a variety of topics. You do not need special knowledge of the topics to answer the questions correctly. Rather, you should answer each question on the basis of what is stated or implied by the speakers in the conversations or talks.

For most of the questions, you will need to click on the best of four possible answers. Some questions will have special directions. The special directions will appear in a box on the computer screen.

18. What prompted this conversation?

    Ⓐ The student's final grade in a course
    Ⓑ The professor's error
    Ⓒ The student's midterm exam
    Ⓓ The professor's book

19. Where is this conversation taking place?

    Ⓐ In a doctor's office
    Ⓑ In a college professor's office
    Ⓒ In Rick's office
    Ⓓ At a driver's license center

20. What is the grade that Rick received for the course?

    Ⓐ B–
    Ⓑ C+
    Ⓒ D
    Ⓓ F

21. Why did Rick receive a lower grade?

    Ⓐ He did not do well on the midterm exam.
    Ⓑ He failed the final exam.
    Ⓒ He was often absent.
    Ⓓ The system was not fair.

22. Why does the professor call on Diane?

    Ⓐ She is a good student.
    Ⓑ She asks a lot of questions.
    Ⓒ She has young children.
    Ⓓ She is majoring in linguistics.

23. What are two characteristics of the language of toddlers?

    Click on 2 answers.

    Ⓐ They use a large number of commands.
    Ⓑ They repeat nouns and noun phrases.
    Ⓒ They delete the endings of verbs.
    Ⓓ They create one-word sentences.

24. What can be concluded about the phrase "We runned"?

    Ⓐ The child is probably about two years old.
    Ⓑ The child is learning regular verb endings now.
    Ⓒ The child is correcting previous errors.
    Ⓓ The child needs to be corrected.

25. By which age have most children learned the basic structures of language?

    Ⓐ Three years old
    Ⓑ Four years old
    Ⓒ Five years old
    Ⓓ Ten years old

26. What does the professor say about languages other than English?

    Ⓐ Basically, the stages for language acquisition are the same for all languages.
    Ⓑ The stages of learning a language discussed in this lecture are unique to English.
    Ⓒ The basic stages of language acquisition cannot be generalized across language groups.
    Ⓓ There is no evidence for the stages that children learn languages to compare language groups.

27. What suggestion does the professor make about the reading assignments?

    Ⓐ Read them before class
    Ⓑ Read them after the discussion
    Ⓒ Read them following the lecture
    Ⓓ Read them before the midterm

28. How are the points distributed for the course requirements?

    Click on the number of points. Then click on the empty box in the correct row. Use each number only once.

    Ⓐ 20 points   Ⓑ 30 points   Ⓒ 50 points

Final Examination	
Midterm Examination	
Final Project	

29. What are the choices for a project?

    Click on 2 answers.

    Ⓐ A book report to the class
    Ⓑ A thirty-minute presentation
    Ⓒ Readings on an assigned topic
    Ⓓ A paper on a topic to be chosen by the writer

30. According to the professor, what should students do if they must be absent?

    Ⓐ Call or send an e-mail to the professor
    Ⓑ Let the secretary know
    Ⓒ Do extra assignments
    Ⓓ Come in during office hours to make up the class

31. What is the main purpose of this lecture?

    Ⓐ To compare Earth with other planets
    Ⓑ To explain a theory of the formation of diamonds
    Ⓒ To introduce a group of astronomers from the University of Arizona
    Ⓓ To criticize Marvin Ross

32. Which planets are being discussed?

    Click on 2 answers.

    Ⓐ Earth
    Ⓑ Uranus
    Ⓒ Neptune
    Ⓓ Pluto

33. The professor briefly explains a process. Summarize the process by putting the events in order.

    Click on a sentence. Then click on the space where it belongs. Use each sentence only once.

    Ⓐ Methane separates into hydrogen and carbon.
    Ⓑ Diamonds are formed on the surface of the planet.
    Ⓒ High pressure squeezes the carbon atoms.
    Ⓓ Methane clouds cover the planet.

    1   ☐
    2   ☐
    3   ☐
    4   ☐

34. How does the speaker feel about the theory?

    Ⓐ He is studying it at the university.
    Ⓑ He agrees with it.
    Ⓒ He is interested in it.
    Ⓓ He thinks it is a joke.

35. What is the electoral college?

    Ⓐ A representative group of citizens
    Ⓑ The men who wrote the Constitution
    Ⓒ An organization of all the political parties
    Ⓓ All the candidates on the ballot

36. Why does the speaker mention Aaron Burr and Thomas Jefferson?

    Ⓐ To give an example of an election before the electoral college was formed
    Ⓑ To explain how candidates are nominated
    Ⓒ To illustrate why there is a separate vote for vice-president
    Ⓓ To demonstrate how well the system works

37. How are the people nominated for the electoral college?

   Ⓐ Each political party nominates electors.
   Ⓑ Congress chooses electors.
   Ⓒ Candidates select their party's electors.
   Ⓓ The people present names to the electoral college.

38. What is the popular vote?

   Ⓐ The people vote directly for the candidates.
   Ⓑ The electors vote for their party's candidate.
   Ⓒ The registered voters choose the electors.
   Ⓓ The Congress holds elections.

39. What is the man's problem?

   Ⓐ He did not attend class.
   Ⓑ He did not take notes.
   Ⓒ He did not understand the lecture.
   Ⓓ He did not read the book.

40. Which type of meteorite is the most common?

   Ⓐ The stone meteorite
   Ⓑ The iron meteorite
   Ⓒ The iron-metal meteorite
   Ⓓ The stony iron meteorite

41. How were most meteorites formed?

   Click on 2 answers.

   Ⓐ They were fragments of the Earth that escaped into space during the formation of the planet.
   Ⓑ They were fragments of large asteroids or comets that have broken loose.
   Ⓒ They were pieces of the moon or Mars that broke off during impact from an asteroid.
   Ⓓ They were small moons from planets that no longer exist in space.

42. What helped the woman follow the lecture?

   Ⓐ She took excellent notes during the lecture.
   Ⓑ She read the chapters in the book before class.
   Ⓒ She re-read the chapters in the book after class.
   Ⓓ She compared notes with the man after class.

43. What is the purpose of this talk?

   Ⓐ To summarize the history of the whaling industry
   Ⓑ To explain a folk art tradition
   Ⓒ To describe the life of sailors in the 1800s
   Ⓓ To discuss where scrimshaw may have gotten its name

44. Why does the lecturer mention the American Revolution and the Civil War?

   Ⓐ The dates of the war provide a time frame for the lecture.
   Ⓑ The lecturer is discussing art produced by soldiers during the wars.
   Ⓒ The history of military art is the topic of the lecture.
   Ⓓ In general, the designs on scrimshaw are battle scenes.

45. Identify the two techniques used to create scrimshaw.

   Click on 2 answers.

   Ⓐ Draw designs with ink on wood, stone, and bone.
   Ⓑ Carve bone into figures.
   Ⓒ Cut designs on bone and fill them with ink.
   Ⓓ Carve designs from wood and stone.

46. Select the object that is the best example of scrimshaw.

Click on a picture.

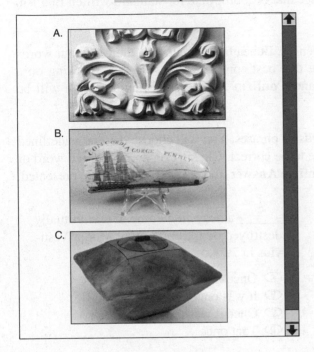

A.

B.

C.

47. Why has scrimshaw become so valuable?

- Ⓐ There are fewer artists who know the techniques.
- Ⓑ The art is very difficult and time consuming to produce.
- Ⓒ Many practical objects made in the 1800s have not survived.
- Ⓓ Few modern collectors are interested in purchasing it.

48. What is the man trying to decide?

- Ⓐ He may keep a zero balance on his credit card.
- Ⓑ He may apply for a new credit card.
- Ⓒ He may close his current credit card account.
- Ⓓ He may pay the balance on his credit card.

49. Why is the man interested in the credit card?

Click on 2 answers.

- Ⓐ The card does not require a credit check.
- Ⓑ The card has lower interest rates.
- Ⓒ The card has no annual fee.
- Ⓓ The card allows a $200 balance without interest.

50. Why does the man decide not to get the card?

- Ⓐ He already has a credit card and does not need another one.
- Ⓑ He is suspicious because everyone on campus received a letter.
- Ⓒ His roommate advises him not to send in the application.
- Ⓓ The card holder must maintain charges of at least $200 every month.

Section 2:
Structure

This section measures the ability to recognize language that is appropriate for standard written English. There are two types of questions in this section.

In the first type of question, there are incomplete sentences. Beneath each sentence, there are four words or phrases. You will choose the one word or phrase that best completes the sentence. Clicking on a choice darkens the oval. After you click on **Next** and **Confirm Answer**, the next question will be presented.

The second type of question has four underlined words or phrases. You will choose the one underlined word or phrase that must be changed for the sentence to be correct. Clicking on an underlined word or phrase will darken it. After you click on **Next** and **Confirm Answer**, the next question will be presented.

1. Besides rain, _____ is seldom pure.

   Ⓐ water naturally
   Ⓑ natural water
   Ⓒ water of nature
   Ⓓ the nature's water

2. Anyone <u>reproducing</u> copyrighted works
   　　　　　　Ⓐ

   without the permission of the holders of the

   copyrights <u>are</u> <u>breaking</u> <u>the law</u>.
   　　　　　Ⓑ　　Ⓒ　　　Ⓓ

3. Nitrogen <u>must be combine</u> with
   　　　　　　Ⓐ

   <u>another element</u> <u>such as</u> hydrogen or oxygen
   　　Ⓑ　　　　　Ⓒ

   <u>to be useful</u> in agriculture or industry.
   　Ⓓ

4. In the <u>sixteenth century</u>, François Vieta, a
   　　　　Ⓐ

   French mathematician, <u>used</u> the vowels
   　　　　　　　　　Ⓑ

   a, e, i, o, u <u>to represent</u> <u>a</u> unknown number.
   　　　　　Ⓒ　　　　Ⓓ

5. Burrowing animals provide paths for water
   in soil, and so do the roots of plants
   _____ .

   Ⓐ decaying and they dying
   Ⓑ when they die and decay
   Ⓒ they die and decay
   Ⓓ when they will die and decay

6. _____ a busy city, Pompeii was virtually
   destroyed by the eruption of Mount Vesuvius in 79 A.D.

   Ⓐ Once
   Ⓑ It was once
   Ⓒ Once it was
   Ⓓ That once

7. The FDA was set up in 1940 _____ that
   maintain standards for the sale of food and
   drugs.

   Ⓐ to enforce the laws
   Ⓑ to enforcing laws
   Ⓒ enforcing laws
   Ⓓ enforced the laws

8. Vasco da Gama, accompanied

   <u>by a large crew</u> and a fleet of twenty ships,
   　Ⓐ

   <u>were</u> trying <u>to establish</u> Portuguese
   　Ⓑ　　　　Ⓒ

   domination <u>in Africa and India</u> during the
   　　　　　　Ⓓ

   sixteenth century.

9. The bridge at <u>Niagara Falls</u> spans <u>the longer</u>
   　　　　　　Ⓐ　　　　　　Ⓑ

   unguarded border in the history of the world,

   symbolizing the peace and goodwill that

   <u>exist</u> <u>between</u> Canada and the United States.
   　Ⓒ　　Ⓓ

10. In ancient times and throughout the Middle

   Ages, many people believed that the Earth is
          Ⓐ   Ⓑ   Ⓒ Ⓓ

   motionless.

11. Doublestars orbit _____ .

   Ⓐ each to the other
   Ⓑ each other
   Ⓒ each other one
   Ⓓ other each one

12. With his father's guidance, Mozart begun
        Ⓐ   Ⓑ

   playing the clavier at the age of three and
   Ⓒ

   composing at the age of five.
   Ⓓ

13. Programs such as Head Start
              Ⓐ

   were developed to prepare children from
        Ⓑ   Ⓒ

   deprived situations to enter school

   without to experience unusual difficulties.
        Ⓓ

14. Almost poetry is more enjoyable when it is
    Ⓐ   Ⓑ   Ⓒ   Ⓓ

   read aloud.

15. All the cereal grains _____ grow on the
   prairies and plains of the United States.

   Ⓐ but rice
   Ⓑ except the rice
   Ⓒ but for rice
   Ⓓ excepting rice

16. Supersonic transport such the Concorde was
                              Ⓐ

   never widely accepted in part because of the
           Ⓑ   Ⓒ   Ⓓ

   problems of noise and atmospheric

   pollution.

17. Oscillatona, one of the few plants that can
   move about, _____ a wavy, gliding motion.

   Ⓐ having
   Ⓑ has
   Ⓒ being
   Ⓓ with

18. _____ a teacher in New England, Webster
   wrote the *Dictionary of the American
   Language.*

   Ⓐ It was while
   Ⓑ When
   Ⓒ When was
   Ⓓ While

19. A vine climbs from one tree to another,

   continuing to grow and support itself even
                Ⓐ   Ⓑ

   when the original supporting tree is
                        Ⓒ

   not longer alive.
   Ⓓ

20. Sometime ants keep smaller insects that
    Ⓐ   Ⓑ

   give off honeydew, milking them regularly
                                     Ⓒ

   and even building barns to shelter them.
                              Ⓓ

21. If a ruby is heated it _____ temporarily
   lose its color.

   Ⓐ would
   Ⓑ will
   Ⓒ does
   Ⓓ has

22. The neutron bomb provided the capable of a
                                   Ⓐ

   limited nuclear war in which buildings
   Ⓑ   Ⓒ

   would be preserved, but people would be
   Ⓓ

   destroyed.

23. <u>In</u> 1776 to 1800, <u>the population</u> of the U.S.
    Ⓐ   Ⓑ

    continued <u>to rise</u>, <u>reaching</u> five million
              Ⓒ   Ⓓ

    citizens by the turn of the century.

24. Not until a student has mastered algebra
    _____ the principles of geometry,
    trigonometry, and physics.

    Ⓐ he can begin to understand
    Ⓑ can he begin to understand
    Ⓒ he begins to understand
    Ⓓ begins to understand

25. <u>From space,</u> astronauts are <u>able</u> <u>to clearly see</u>
    Ⓐ   Ⓑ   Ⓒ

    the outline <u>of</u> the whole Earth.
                Ⓓ

Section 3:
Reading

This section measures the ability to read and understand short passages similar in topic and style to those that students are likely to encounter in North American universities and colleges. This section contains reading passages and questions about the passages. There are several different types of questions in this section.

In the Reading Section, you will first have the opportunity to read the passage. You will use the scroll bar to view the rest of the passage.

When you have finished reading the passage, you will use the mouse to click on **Proceed**. Then the questions about the passage will be presented. You are to choose the one best answer to each question. Answer all questions about the information in a passage on the basis of what is stated or implied in that passage.

Most of the questions will be multiple-choice questions. To answer these questions you will click on a choice below the question.

To answer some questions, you will click on a word or phrase.
To answer some questions, you will click on a sentence in the passage.
To answer some questions, you will click on a square to add a sentence to the passage.

Smallpox was the first widespread disease ever to be eliminated by human intervention. A highly contagious viral disease, it was endemic in Europe, causing the deaths of millions of people until the development of the vaccination by Edward Jenner around 1800. In many non-European nations, it remained a dreaded, often fatal illness until very recently. Its victims suffered high fever, vomiting, and painful, itchy pustules, pus-filled skin eruptions that left pits or pockmark scars. In villages and cities all over the world, scarred people showed that they had survived smallpox.

In May 1966, the World Health Organization (WHO), an agency of the United Nations, was authorized to initiate a global campaign to eradicate smallpox. The goal was to eliminate the disease in one decade. At the time, the disease posed a serious threat to people in thirty nations. More than 700 physicians, nurses, scientists, and other personnel from WHO joined about 200,000 health workers in the infected nations to battle the disease. Because similar projects for malaria and yellow fever had failed, few believed that a disease as widespread as smallpox could actually be eradicated, but eleven years after the initial organization of the anti-smallpox campaign, no cases were reported in the field.

The strategy that developed was to combat the disease at several levels. There was an education campaign, of course, so that the people in the threatened countries could be taught more about how the disease spread and become active participants in the fight against smallpox. Other strategies included not only providing mass vaccinations but also isolating patients with active smallpox in order to contain the spread of the disease, thus breaking the chain of human transmission. Monetary rewards for reporting smallpox assisted in motivating the public to aid health workers. One by one, each smallpox victim was sought out, removed from contact with others, and treated. At the same time, the entire village where the victim had lived was vaccinated.

By April of 1978, WHO officials announced that they had isolated the last known case of the disease, but health workers continued to search for new cases for two additional years to be completely sure. In May 1980, a formal statement was made to the global community. Today smallpox is no longer a threat to humanity. Routine vaccinations have been stopped worldwide.

1. Which of the following is the best title for the passage?

   Ⓐ The World Health Organization
   Ⓑ The Eradication of Smallpox
   Ⓒ Smallpox Vaccinations
   Ⓓ Infectious Diseases

2. Look at the word eradicate in the passage. Click on the word in the **bold** text that is closest in meaning to eradicate.

More Available

eruptions that left pits or pockmark scars. In villages and cities all over the world, scarred people showed that they had survived smallpox.

In May 1966, the World Health Organization (WHO), an agency of the United Nations, was authorized to initiate a global campaign to eradicate smallpox. The goal was to eliminate the disease in one decade. At the time, the disease posed a serious threat to people in thirty nations. More than 700 physicians, nurses, scientists, and other personnel from WHO joined about 200,000 health workers in the infected nations to battle the disease. Because similar projects for malaria and yellow fever had failed, few believed that a disease as widespread as smallpox could actually be eradicated, but eleven years after the initial organization of the anti-smallpox campaign, no cases were reported in the field.

The strategy that developed was to combat the disease at several levels. There was an education campaign, of course, so that the people in the threatened countries could be taught more about how the disease spread and become active participants in the fight against smallpox. Other

3. The word threat in paragraph 2 could best be replaced by

    Ⓐ debate
    Ⓑ humiliation
    Ⓒ risk
    Ⓓ bother

6. The word they in paragraph 4 refers to

    Ⓐ years
    Ⓑ officials
    Ⓒ victims
    Ⓓ cases

More Available

eruptions that left pits or pockmark scars. In villages and cities all over the world, scarred people showed that they had survived smallpox.

In May 1966, the World Health Organization (WHO), an agency of the United Nations, was authorized to initiate a global campaign to eradicate smallpox. The goal was to eliminate the disease in one decade. At the time, the disease posed a serious threat to people in thirty nations. More than 700 physicians, nurses, scientists, and other personnel from WHO joined about 200,000 health workers in the infected nations to battle the disease. Because similar projects for malaria and yellow fever had failed, few believed that a disease as widespread as smallpox could actually be eradicated, but eleven years after the initial organization of the anti-smallpox campaign, no cases were reported in the field.

The strategy that developed was to combat the disease at several levels. There was an education campaign, of course, so that the people in the threatened countries could be taught more about how the disease spread and become active participants in the fight against smallpox. Other

---

End

education campaign, of course, so that the people in the threatened countries could be taught more about how the disease spread and become active participants in the fight against smallpox. Other strategies included not only providing mass vaccinations but also isolating patients with active smallpox in order to contain the spread of the disease, thus breaking the chain of human transmission. Monetary rewards for reporting smallpox assisted in motivating the public to aid health workers. One by one, each smallpox victim was sought out, removed from contact with others, and treated. At the same time, the entire village where the victim had lived was vaccinated.

By April of 1978, WHO officials announced that they had isolated the last known case of the disease, but health workers continued to search for new cases for two additional years to be completely sure. In May 1980, a formal statement was made to the global community. Today smallpox is no longer a threat to humanity. Routine vaccinations have been stopped worldwide.

---

4. Click on the paragraph that explains the goal of the campaign against smallpox.

Scroll the passage to see all of the paragraphs.

5. According to the passage, what was the strategy used to eliminate the spread of smallpox?

    Ⓐ Vaccinations of entire villages
    Ⓑ Treatment of individual victims
    Ⓒ Isolation of victims and mass vaccinations
    Ⓓ Extensive reporting of outbreaks

7. The word isolated in paragraph 4 is closest in meaning to

Ⓐ restored
Ⓑ separated
Ⓒ attended
Ⓓ located

End ↑

education campaign, of course, so that the people in the threatened countries could be taught more about how the disease spread and become active participants in the fight against smallpox. Other strategies included not only providing mass vaccinations but also isolating patients with active smallpox in order to contain the spread of the disease, thus breaking the chain of human transmission. Monetary rewards for reporting smallpox assisted in motivating the public to aid health workers. One by one, each smallpox victim was sought out, removed from contact with others, and treated. At the same time, the entire village where the victim had lived was vaccinated.

By April of 1978, WHO officials announced that they had isolated the last known case of the disease, but health workers continued to search for new cases for two additional years to be completely sure. In May 1980, a formal statement was made to the global community. Today smallpox is no longer a threat to humanity. Routine vaccinations have been stopped worldwide.

↓

---

8. How was the public motivated to help the health workers?

Ⓐ By educating them
Ⓑ By rewarding them for reporting cases
Ⓒ By isolating them from others
Ⓓ By giving them vaccinations

9. Which one of the statements does NOT refer to smallpox?

Ⓐ Previous projects had failed.
Ⓑ People are no longer vaccinated for it.
Ⓒ The World Health Organization mounted a worldwide campaign to eradicate the disease.
Ⓓ It was a serious threat.

10. It can be inferred from the passage that

Ⓐ no new cases of smallpox have been reported this year
Ⓑ malaria and yellow fever have been reported this year
Ⓒ smallpox victims no longer die when they contract the disease
Ⓓ smallpox is not transmitted from one person to another

11. The following sentence can be added to the passage.

The number of smallpox-infected countries gradually decreased.

Where would it best fit in the passage?

Click on the square (■) to add the sentence to the passage.

Scroll the passage to see all of the choices.

End ↑

education campaign, of course, so that the people in the threatened countries could be taught more about how the disease spread and become active participants in the fight against smallpox. Other strategies included not only providing mass vaccinations but also isolating patients with active smallpox in order to contain the spread of the disease, thus breaking the chain of human transmission. Monetary rewards for reporting smallpox assisted in motivating the public to aid health workers. One by one, each smallpox victim was sought out, removed from contact with others, and treated. At the same time, the entire village where the victim had lived was vaccinated. ■

By April of 1978, WHO officials announced that they had isolated the last known case of the disease, but health workers continued to search for new cases for two additional years to be completely sure. ■ In May 1980, a formal statement was made to the global community. ■ Today smallpox is no longer a threat to humanity. ■ Routine vaccinations have been stopped worldwide.

↓

The nuclear family, consisting of a mother, father, and their children, may be more an American ideal than an American reality. Of course, the so-called traditional American family was always more varied than we had been led to believe, reflecting the very different racial, ethnic, class, and religious customs among different American groups, but today diversity is even more obvious.

The most recent government census statistics reveal that only about one third of all current American families fits the traditional mold of two parents and their children, and another third consists of married couples who either have no children or have none still living at home. An analysis of the remaining one third of the population reveals that about 20 percent of the total number of American households are single people, the most common descriptor being women over sixty-five years of age. A small percentage, about 3 percent of the total, consists of unmarried people who choose to live together; and the rest, about 7 percent, are single parents, with at least one child.

There are several easily identifiable reasons for the growing number of single-parent households. First, the sociological phenomenon of single-parent households reflects changes in cultural attitudes toward divorce and also toward unmarried mothers. A substantial number of adults become single parents as a result of divorce. In addition, the number of children born to unmarried women who choose to keep their children and rear them by themselves has increased dramatically. Finally, there is a small percentage of single-parent families that have resulted from untimely death. Today, these varied family types are typical and, therefore, normal.

In addition, because many families live far from relatives, close friends have become a more important part of family life than ever before. The vast majority of Americans claim that they have people in their lives whom they regard as family although they are not related. A view of family that only accepts the traditional nuclear arrangement not only ignores the reality of modern American family life, but also undervalues the familial bonds created in alternative family arrangements. Apparently, many Americans are achieving supportive relationships in family forms other than the traditional one.

12. Which of the following is the main topic of the passage?

  Ⓐ The traditional American family
  Ⓑ The nuclear family
  Ⓒ The current American family
  Ⓓ The ideal family

13. Look at the word reality in the passage. Click on the word or phrase in the **bold** text that is opposite in meaning to reality.

Beginning

The nuclear family, consisting of a mother, father, and their children, may be more an American ideal than an American reality. Of course, the so-called traditional American family was always more varied than we had been led to believe, reflecting the very different racial, ethnic, class, and religious customs among different American groups, but today diversity is even more obvious.

The most recent government census statistics reveal that only about one third of all current American families fits the traditional mold of two parents and their children, and another third consists of married couples who either have no children or have none still living at home. An analysis of the remaining one third of the population reveals that about 20 percent of the total number of American households are single people, the most common descriptor being women over sixty-five years of age. A small percentage, about 3 percent of the total, consists of unmarried people who choose to live together; and the rest, about 7 percent, are single parents, with at least one child.

There are several easily identifiable reasons

14. The word current in paragraph 2 could best be replaced by which of the following?

 Ⓐ typical
 Ⓑ present
 Ⓒ perfect
 Ⓓ traditional

Beginning

The nuclear family, consisting of a mother, father, and their children, may be more an American ideal than an American reality. Of course, the so-called traditional American family was always more varied than we had been led to believe, reflecting the very different racial, ethnic, class, and religious customs among different American groups, but today diversity is even more obvious.

The most recent government census statistics reveal that only about one third of all current American families fits the traditional mold of two parents and their children, and another third consists of married couples who either have no children or have none still living at home. An analysis of the remaining one third of the population reveals that about 20 percent of the total number of American households are single people, the most common descriptor being women over sixty-five years of age. A small percentage, about 3 percent of the total, consists of unmarried people who choose to live together; and the rest, about 7 percent, are single parents, with at least one child.

There are several easily identifiable reasons

---

15. The word none in paragraph 2 refers to

 Ⓐ parents
 Ⓑ children
 Ⓒ couples
 Ⓓ families

Beginning

The nuclear family, consisting of a mother, father, and their children, may be more an American ideal than an American reality. Of course, the so-called traditional American family was always more varied than we had been led to believe, reflecting the very different racial, ethnic, class, and religious customs among different American groups, but today diversity is even more obvious.

The most recent government census statistics reveal that only about one third of all current American families fits the traditional mold of two parents and their children, and another third consists of married couples who either have no children or have none still living at home. An analysis of the remaining one third of the population reveals that about 20 percent of the total number of American households are single people, the most common descriptor being women over sixty-five years of age. A small percentage, about 3 percent of the total, consists of unmarried people who choose to live together; and the rest, about 7 percent, are single parents, with at least one child.

There are several easily identifiable reasons

---

16. How many single people were identified in the survey?

 Ⓐ One third of the total surveyed
 Ⓑ One fourth of the total surveyed
 Ⓒ One fifth of the total surveyed
 Ⓓ Less than one tenth of the total surveyed

17. Who generally constitutes a one-person household?

 Ⓐ A single man in his twenties
 Ⓑ An elderly man
 Ⓒ A single woman in her late sixties
 Ⓓ A divorced woman

18. Look at the phrase the rest in the passage. Click on the word or phrase in the **bold** text that the rest refers to.

More Available

The most recent government census statistics reveal that only about one third of all current American families fits the traditional mold of two parents and their children, and another third consists of married couples who either have no children or have none still living at home. **An analysis of the remaining one third of the population reveals that about 20 percent of the total number of American households are single people, the most common descriptor being women over sixty-five years of age. A small percentage, about 3 percent of the total, consists of unmarried people who choose to live together; and the rest, about 7 percent, are single parents, with at least one child.**

There are several easily identifiable reasons for the growing number of single-parent households. First, the sociological phenomenon of single-parent households reflects changes in cultural attitudes toward divorce and also toward unmarried mothers. A substantial number of adults become single parents as a result of divorce. In addition, the number of children born to unmarried women who choose to keep their

19. Click on the sentence in paragraph 4 that refers to the way that most Americans feel about close friends.

    Paragraph 4 is marked with an arrow (→).

20. The word undervalues in paragraph 4 is closest in meaning to

    - ⒶⒶ does not appreciate
    - ⒷⒷ does not know about
    - ⒸⒸ does not include
    - ⒹⒹ does not understand

End

unmarried women who choose to keep their children and rear them by themselves has increased dramatically. Finally, there is a small percentage of single-parent families that have resulted from untimely death. Today, these varied family types are typical and, therefore, normal.
→ In addition, because many families live far from relatives, close friends have become a more important part of family life than ever before. The vast majority of Americans claim that they have people in their lives whom they regard as family although they are not related. A view of family that only accepts the traditional nuclear arrangement not only ignores the reality of modern American family life, but also undervalues the familial bonds created in alternative family arrangements. Apparently, many Americans are achieving supportive relationships in family forms other than the traditional one.

End

unmarried women who choose to keep their children and rear them by themselves has increased dramatically. Finally, there is a small percentage of single-parent families that have resulted from untimely death. Today, these varied family types are typical and, therefore, normal.

In addition, because many families live far from relatives, close friends have become a more important part of family life than ever before. The vast majority of Americans claim that they have people in their lives whom they regard as family although they are not related. A view of family that only accepts the traditional nuclear arrangement not only ignores the reality of modern American family life, but also undervalues the familial bonds created in alternative family arrangements. Apparently, many Americans are achieving supportive relationships in family forms other than the traditional one.

21. The passage discusses all of the following reasons for an increase in single-parent households EXCEPT

   Ⓐ a rising divorce rate
   Ⓑ death of one of the parents
   Ⓒ increased interest in parenting by fathers
   Ⓓ babies born to single women

22. With which of the following statements would the author most probably agree?

   Ⓐ There have always been a wide variety of family arrangements in the United States.
   Ⓑ Racial, ethnic, and religious groups have preserved the traditional family structure.
   Ⓒ The ideal American family is the best structure.
   Ⓓ Fewer married couples are having children.

Although noise, commonly defined as unwanted sound, is a widely recognized form of pollution, it is very difficult to measure because the discomfort experienced by different individuals is highly subjective and, therefore, variable. Exposure to lower levels of noise may be slightly irritating, whereas exposure to higher levels may actually cause hearing loss. Particularly in congested urban areas, the noise produced as a byproduct of our advancing technology causes physical and psychological harm but it also detracts from the quality of life for those exposed to it.

Unlike the eyes, which can be covered by the eyelids against strong light, the ear has no lid, and is, therefore, always open and vulnerable; noise penetrates without protection.

Noise causes effects that the hearer cannot control and to which the body never becomes accustomed. Loud noises instinctively signal danger to any organism with a hearing mechanism, including human beings. In response, heartbeat and respiration accelerate, blood vessels constrict, the skin pales, and muscles tense. In fact, there is a general increase in functioning brought about by the flow of adrenaline released in response to fear, and some of these responses persist even longer than the noise, occasionally as long as thirty minutes after the sound has ceased.

Because noise is unavoidable in a complex, industrial society, we are constantly responding in the same ways that we would respond to danger. Recently, researchers have concluded that noise and our response may be much more than an annoyance. It may be a serious threat to physical and psychological health and well-being, causing damage not only to the ear and brain but also to the heart and stomach. We have long known that hearing loss is America's number one nonfatal health problem, but now we are learning that some of us with heart disease and ulcers may be victims of noise as well. Fetuses exposed to noise tend to be overactive, they cry easily, and they are more sensitive to gastrointestinal problems after birth. In addition, the psychological effect of noise is very important. Nervousness, irritability, tension, and anxiety increase, affecting the quality of rest during sleep, and the efficiency of activities during waking hours, as well as the way that we interact with one another.

23. Which of the following is the author's main point?

    (A) Noise may pose a serious threat to our physical and psychological health.
    (B) Loud noises signal danger.
    (C) Hearing loss is America's number one nonfatal health problem.
    (D) The ear is not like the eye.

24. According to the passage, what is noise?

    (A) Unwanted sound
    (B) A byproduct of technology
    (C) Physical and psychological harm
    (D) Congestion

25. Why is noise difficult to measure?

    (A) It causes hearing loss.
    (B) All people do not respond to it in the same way.
    (C) It is unwanted.
    (D) People become accustomed to it.

26. The word congested in paragraph 1 could best be replaced by

    (A) hazardous
    (B) polluted
    (C) crowded
    (D) rushed

27. According to the passage, people respond to loud noises in the same way that they respond to

    (A) annoyance
    (B) danger
    (C) damage
    (D) disease

28. Look at the word accelerate in the passage. Click on the word or phrase in the **bold** text that is closest in meaning to accelerate .

More Available

eyelids against strong light, the ear has no lid, and is, therefore, always open and vulnerable; noise penetrates without protection.

    Noise causes effects that the hearer cannot control and to which the body never becomes accustomed. Loud noises instinctively signal danger to any organism with a hearing mechanism, including human beings. In response, heartbeat and respiration accelerate, blood vessels constrict, the skin pales, and muscles tense. **In fact, there is a general increase in functioning brought about by the flow of adrenaline released in response to fear, and some of these responses persist even longer than the noise, occasionally as long as thirty minutes after the sound has ceased.**

    Because noise is unavoidable in a complex, industrial society, we are constantly responding in the same ways that we would respond to danger. Recently, researchers have concluded that noise and our response may be much more than an annoyance. It may be a serious threat to physical and psychological health and well-being, causing damage not only to the ear and brain but also to the heart and stomach. We have long known that

---

Beginning

    Although noise, commonly defined as unwanted sound, is a widely recognized form of pollution, it is very difficult to measure because the discomfort experienced by different individuals is highly subjective and, therefore, variable. Exposure to lower levels of noise may be slightly irritating, whereas exposure to higher levels may actually cause hearing loss. Particularly in congested urban areas, the noise produced as a byproduct of our advancing technology causes physical and psychological harm but it also detracts from the quality of life for those exposed to it.

    Unlike the eyes, which can be covered by the eyelids against strong light, the ear has no lid, and is, therefore, always open and vulnerable; noise penetrates without protection.

    Noise causes effects that the hearer cannot control and to which the body never becomes accustomed. Loud noises instinctively signal danger to any organism with a hearing mechanism, including human beings. In response, heartbeat and respiration accelerate, blood vessels constrict, the skin pales, and muscles tense. In fact, there is a general increase in functioning brought about by

29. Look at the word it in the passage. Click on the word or phrase in the **bold** text that it refers to.

Although noise, commonly defined as unwanted sound, is a widely recognized form of pollution, it is very difficult to measure because the discomfort experienced by different individuals is highly subjective and, therefore, variable. Exposure to lower levels of noise may be slightly irritating, whereas exposure to higher levels may actually cause hearing loss. **Particularly in congested urban areas, the noise produced as a byproduct of our advancing technology causes physical and psychological harm but it also detracts from the quality of life for those exposed to it.**

Unlike the eyes, which can be covered by the eyelids against strong light, the ear has no lid, and is, therefore, always open and vulnerable; noise penetrates without protection.

Noise causes effects that the hearer cannot control and to which the body never becomes accustomed. Loud noises instinctively signal danger to any organism with a hearing mechanism, including human beings. In response, heartbeat and respiration accelerate, blood vessels constrict, the skin pales, and muscles tense. In fact, there is a general increase in functioning brought about by

30. The phrase as well in paragraph 4 is closest in meaning to which of the following?

- Ⓐ after all
- Ⓑ also
- Ⓒ instead
- Ⓓ regardless

Because noise is unavoidable in a complex, industrial society, we are constantly responding in the same ways that we would respond to danger. Recently, researchers have concluded that noise and our response may be much more than an annoyance. It may be a serious threat to physical and psychological health and well-being, causing damage not only to the ear and brain but also to the heart and stomach. We have long known that hearing loss is America's number one nonfatal health problem, but now we are learning that some of us with heart disease and ulcers may be victims of noise as well. Fetuses exposed to noise tend to be overactive, they cry easily, and they are more sensitive to gastrointestinal problems after birth. In addition, the psychological effect of noise is very important. Nervousness, irritability, tension, and anxiety increase, affecting the quality of rest during sleep, and the efficiency of activities during waking hours, as well as the way that we interact with one another.

31. It can be inferred from this passage that the eye

- Ⓐ responds to fear
- Ⓑ enjoys greater protection than the ear
- Ⓒ increases functions
- Ⓓ is damaged by noise

32. With which of the following statements would the author most probably agree?

- Ⓐ Noise is not a serious problem today.
- Ⓑ Noise is America's number-one problem.
- Ⓒ Noise is an unavoidable problem in an industrial society.
- Ⓓ Noise is a complex problem.

33. The following sentence can be added to the passage.

Investigations on human subjects have demonstrated that babies are affected by noise even before they are born.

Where would it best fit in the passage?

Click on the square (■) to add the sentence to the passage.

Scroll the passage to see all of the choices.

Because noise is unavoidable in a complex, industrial society, we are constantly responding in the same ways that we would respond to danger. Recently, researchers have concluded that noise and our response may be much more than an annoyance. ■ It may be a serious threat to physical and psychological health and well-being, causing damage not only to the ear and brain but also to the heart and stomach. ■ We have long known that hearing loss is America's number one nonfatal health problem, but now we are learning that some of us with heart disease and ulcers may be victims of noise as well. ■ Fetuses exposed to noise tend to be overactive, they cry easily, and they are more sensitive to gastrointestinal problems after birth. ■ In addition, the psychological effect of noise is very important. Nervousness, irritability, tension, and anxiety increase, affecting the quality of rest during sleep, and the efficiency of activities during waking hours, as well as the way that we interact with one another.

Very few people in the modern world obtain their food supply by hunting and gathering in the natural environment surrounding their homes. This method of harvesting from nature's provision, however, is not only the oldest known subsistence strategy, but also the one that has been practiced continuously in some parts of the world for at least the last two million years. It was, indeed, the only way to obtain food until rudimentary farming and very crude methods for the domestication of animals were introduced about 10,000 years ago.

Because hunter-gatherers have fared poorly in comparison with their agricultural cousins, their numbers have dwindled, and they have been forced to live in the marginal wastelands. In higher latitudes, the shorter growing season has restricted the availability of plant life. Such conditions have caused a greater dependence on hunting and, along the coasts and waterways, on fishing. The abundance of vegetation in the lower latitudes of the tropics, on the other hand, has provided a greater opportunity for gathering a variety of plants. In short, the environmental differences have restricted the diet and have limited possibilities for the development of subsistence societies.

Contemporary hunter-gatherers may help us understand our prehistoric ancestors. We know from observation of modern hunter-gatherers in both Africa and Alaska that a society based on hunting and gathering must be very mobile. Following the food supply can be a way of life. If a particular kind of wild herding animal is the basis of the food for a group of people, those people must move to stay within reach of those animals. For many of the native people of the great central plains of North America, following the buffalo, who were in turn following the growth of grazing foods, determined their way of life.

For gathering societies, seasonal changes mean a great deal. While the entire community camps in a central location, a smaller party harvests the food within a reasonable distance from the camp. When the food in the area is exhausted, the community moves on to exploit another site. We also notice a seasonal migration pattern evolving for most hunter-gatherers, along with a strict division of labor between the sexes. These patterns of behavior may be similar to those practiced by humankind during the Paleolithic Period.

34. Which of the following is the main topic of the passage?

    Ⓐ The Paleolithic Period
    Ⓑ Subsistence farming
    Ⓒ Hunter-gatherers
    Ⓓ Marginal environments

35. Which is the oldest subsistence strategy?

    Ⓐ Migrating
    Ⓑ Domesticating animals
    Ⓒ Farming
    Ⓓ Hunting and gathering

36. When was hunting and gathering introduced?

    Ⓐ Ten million years ago
    Ⓑ Two million years ago
    Ⓒ Ten thousand years ago
    Ⓓ Two thousand years ago

37. Look at the word rudimentary in the passage. Click on the word or phrase in the **bold** text that is closest in meaning to rudimentary .

Beginning

Very few people in the modern world obtain their food supply by hunting and gathering in the natural environment surrounding their homes. **This method of harvesting from nature's provision, however, is not only the oldest known subsistence strategy, but also the one that has been practiced continuously in some parts of the world for at least the last two million years. It was, indeed, the only way to obtain food until** rudimentary **farming and very crude methods for the domestication of animals were introduced about 10,000 years ago.**

Because hunter-gatherers have fared poorly in comparison with their agricultural cousins, their numbers have dwindled, and they have been forced to live in the marginal wastelands. In higher latitudes, the shorter growing season has restricted the availability of plant life. Such conditions have caused a greater dependence on hunting and, along the coasts and waterways, on fishing. The abundance of vegetation in the lower latitudes of the tropics, on the other hand, has provided a greater opportunity for gathering a variety of plants. In short, the environmental differences have restricted the diet and have limited possibilities for

38. The word dwindled in paragraph 2 is closest in meaning to

    Ⓐ disagreed
    Ⓑ decreased
    Ⓒ disappeared
    Ⓓ died

40. In paragraph 2, the author explains that hunters and gatherers in lower latitudes found

    Ⓐ more animals to hunt
    Ⓑ more coasts and waterways for fishing
    Ⓒ a shorter growing season
    Ⓓ a large variety of plant life

Paragraph 2 is marked with an arrow (→).

More Available

way to obtain food until rudimentary farming and very crude methods for the domestication of animals were introduced about 10,000 years ago.

Because hunter-gatherers have fared poorly in comparison with their agricultural cousins, their numbers have dwindled, and they have been forced to live in the marginal wastelands. In higher latitudes, the shorter growing season has restricted the availability of plant life. Such conditions have caused a greater dependence on hunting and, along the coasts and waterways, on fishing. The abundance of vegetation in the lower latitudes of the tropics, on the other hand, has provided a greater opportunity for gathering a variety of plants. In short, the environmental differences have restricted the diet and have limited possibilities for the development of subsistence societies.

Contemporary hunter-gatherers may help us understand our prehistoric ancestors. We know from observation of modern hunter-gatherers in both Africa and Alaska that a society based on hunting and gathering must be very mobile. Following the food supply can be a way of life. If a particular kind of wild herding animal is the basis

More Available

continuously in some parts of the world for at least the last two million years. It was, indeed, the only way to obtain food until rudimentary farming and very crude methods for the domestication of animals were introduced about 10,000 years ago.
→ Because hunter-gatherers have fared poorly in comparison with their agricultural cousins, their numbers have dwindled, and they have been forced to live in the marginal wastelands. In higher latitudes, the shorter growing season has restricted the availability of plant life. Such conditions have caused a greater dependence on hunting and, along the coasts and waterways, on fishing. The abundance of vegetation in the lower latitudes of the tropics, on the other hand, has provided a greater opportunity for gathering a variety of plants. In short, the environmental differences have restricted the diet and have limited possibilities for the development of subsistence societies.

Contemporary hunter-gatherers may help us understand our prehistoric ancestors. We know from observation of modern hunter-gatherers in both Africa and Alaska that a society based on hunting and gathering must be very mobile.

39. Look at the phrase such conditions in the passage. Click on the word or phrase in the **bold** text that such conditions refers to.

More Available

way to obtain food until rudimentary farming and very crude methods for the domestication of animals were introduced about 10,000 years ago.

Because hunter-gatherers have fared poorly in comparison with their agricultural cousins, their numbers have dwindled, and they have been forced to live in the marginal wastelands. **In higher latitudes, the shorter growing season has restricted the availability of plant life.** Such conditions **have caused a greater dependence on hunting and, along the coasts and waterways, on fishing. The abundance of vegetation in the lower latitudes of the tropics, on the other hand, has provided a greater opportunity for gathering a variety of plants.** In short, the environmental differences have restricted the diet and have limited possibilities for the development of subsistence societies.

Contemporary hunter-gatherers may help us understand our prehistoric ancestors. We know from observation of modern hunter-gatherers in both Africa and Alaska that a society based on hunting and gathering must be very mobile. Following the food supply can be a way of life. If a particular kind of wild herding animal is the basis

41. Why does the author mention contemporary hunter-gatherers in paragraph 3?

    Ⓐ Their seasonal migration patterns are important.

    Ⓑ Studying them gives us insights into the lifestyle of prehistoric people.

    Ⓒ There are very few examples of modern hunter-gatherer societies.

    Ⓓ Their societies are quite different from those of their ancestors.

Paragraph 3 is marked with an arrow (→).

More Available

the tropics, on the other hand, has provided a greater opportunity for gathering a variety of plants. In short, the environmental differences have restricted the diet and have limited possibilities for the development of subsistence societies.
→ Contemporary hunter-gatherers may help us understand our prehistoric ancestors. We know from observation of modern hunter-gatherers in both Africa and Alaska that a society based on hunting and gathering must be very mobile. Following the food supply can be a way of life. If a particular kind of wild herding animal is the basis of the food for a group of people, those people must move to stay within reach of those animals. For many of the native people of the great central plains of North America, following the buffalo, who were in turn following the growth of grazing foods, determined their way of life.

    For gathering societies, seasonal changes mean a great deal. While the entire community camps in a central location, a smaller party harvests the food within a reasonable distance from the camp. When the food in the area is exhausted, the community moves on to exploit

---

42. The word exploit in paragraph 4 is closest in meaning to

    Ⓐ use

    Ⓑ find

    Ⓒ take

    Ⓓ prepare

End

particular kind of wild herding animal is the basis of the food for a group of people, those people must move to stay within reach of those animals. For many of the native people of the great central plains of North America, following the buffalo, who were in turn following the growth of grazing foods, determined their way of life.

    For gathering societies, seasonal changes mean a great deal. While the entire community camps in a central location, a smaller party harvests the food within a reasonable distance from the camp. When the food in the area is exhausted, the community moves on to exploit another site. We also notice a seasonal migration pattern evolving for most hunter-gatherers, along with a strict division of labor between the sexes. These patterns of behavior may be similar to those practiced by humankind during the Paleolithic Period.

---

43. What does the author mean by the statement While the entire community camps in a central location, a smaller party harvests the food within a reasonable distance from the camp?

    Ⓐ Everyone is involved in hunting and gathering the food for the community.

    Ⓑ When the food has been harvested, the community has a celebration.

    Ⓒ A small group hunts and gathers food near the camp.

    Ⓓ The reason that the community harvests the food is that it is near the camp.

44. All of the patterns of behavior for hunter-gatherers are mentioned in the passage EXCEPT

    Ⓐ a small group plants food near the camp.
    Ⓑ the group moves when the food supply is low.
    Ⓒ men and women each have specific roles.
    Ⓓ the seasons dictate the movement of the group.

45. Which of the following sentences should NOT be included in a summary of the passage?

    Ⓐ Hunter-gatherers are mobile, tending to migrate seasonally.
    Ⓑ Hunter-gatherers share different responsibilities between the sexes.
    Ⓒ Hunter-gatherers camp in a central location.
    Ⓓ Hunter-gatherers have many social celebrations.

To check your answers for Model Test 7, refer to the Answer Key on page 494. For an explanation of the answers, refer to the Explanatory Answers for Model Test 7 on pages 621–640.

Writing Section:
Model Test 7

When you take a Model Test, you should use one sheet of paper, both sides. Time each Model Test carefully. After you have read the topic, you should spend 30 minutes writing. For results that would be closest to the actual testing situation, it is recommended that an English teacher score your test, using the guidelines on page 244 of this book.

Leaders like John F. Kennedy and Martin Luther King have made important contributions to humanity. Name another world leader you think is important. Give specific reasons for your choice.

Notes

To check your essay, refer to the Checklist on page 494. For an Example Essay, refer to the Explanatory Answers for Model Test 8 on page 640.

Model Test 8
Computer-Assisted TOEFL

Section 1:
Listening

The Listening Section of the test measures the ability to understand conversations and talks in English. You will use headphones to listen to the conversations and talks. While you are listening, pictures of the speakers or other information will be presented on your computer screen. There are two parts to the Listening Section, with special directions for each part.

On the day of the test, the amount of time you will have to answer all of the questions will appear on the computer screen. The time you spend listening to the test material will not be counted. The listening material and questions about it will be presented only one time. You will not be allowed to take notes or have any paper at your computer. You will both see and hear the questions before the answer choices appear. You can take as much time as you need to select an answer; however, it will be to your advantage to answer the questions as quickly as possible. You may change your answer as many times as you want before you confirm it. After you have confirmed an answer, you will not be able to return to the question.

Before you begin working on the Listening Section, you will have an opportunity to adjust the volume of the sound. You may not be able to change the volume after you have started the test.

QUESTION DIRECTIONS — Part A

In Part A of the Listening Section, you will hear short conversations between two people. In some of the conversations, each person speaks only once. In other conversations, one or both of the people speak more than once. Each conversation is followed by one question about it.

Each question in this part has four answer choices. You should click on the best answer to each question. Answer the questions on the basis of what is stated or implied by the speakers.

1. What can be inferred about the woman?

     Ⓐ She is not his advisor.
     Ⓑ She is not polite.
     Ⓒ She does not have a course request form.
     Ⓓ She will help the man.

2. What does the man mean?

     Ⓐ He is lost.
     Ⓑ He needs a different course.
     Ⓒ He will not withdraw from the class.
     Ⓓ He doesn't know what he will do.

3. What can be inferred about the man?

     Ⓐ He did not go to Dr. Peterson's class today.
     Ⓑ The man is a student in the class that the woman teaches.
     Ⓒ The man works in the same office as the woman.
     Ⓓ The man is a teaching assistant for Dr. Peterson.

4. What will the man and woman probably do?

     Ⓐ Get the man some glasses
     Ⓑ Sit together
     Ⓒ Move to the front of the room
     Ⓓ Have an argument

5. How did the man feel about Montreal?

Ⓐ He liked Montreal in the winter.
Ⓑ He liked Montreal spring, summer, and fall.
Ⓒ He liked Montreal all year round.
Ⓓ He did not like Montreal.

6. What does the man mean?

Ⓐ He will place a wager.
Ⓑ He will pay later for his purchases.
Ⓒ He will do more than the required assignments.
Ⓓ He will go to his job.

7. What did the woman suggest?

Ⓐ Use will power
Ⓑ Chew gum
Ⓒ Wear a nicotine patch
Ⓓ Join a support group

8. What does the man mean?

Ⓐ The class is too long.
Ⓑ The class is too small.
Ⓒ He does not like the subject.
Ⓓ He does not want to say.

9. What does the man mean?

Ⓐ He is asking where to go.
Ⓑ He is telling the woman to leave.
Ⓒ He is calling the woman a liar.
Ⓓ He is congratulating the woman.

10. What does the woman mean?

Ⓐ Her roommate got the assistantship.
Ⓑ She is not going to take a full load.
Ⓒ Teaching is more difficult than studying.
Ⓓ The man is correct.

11. What is the woman's problem?

Ⓐ Her back pack is too heavy.
Ⓑ She is not a very good student.
Ⓒ She cannot find her notebook.
Ⓓ She needs a ride home from class.

12. What does the woman mean?

Ⓐ She already has an ID card.
Ⓑ She does not need her picture taken.
Ⓒ She is ready to leave.
Ⓓ She does not know where to go.

13. What does the woman suggest?

Ⓐ The man should invite his friends to dinner.
Ⓑ The man's friends should come to his house.
Ⓒ The man could take a plant to his friends.
Ⓓ The man likes candy.

14. What will the woman probably do?

Ⓐ Go with the man
Ⓑ Look on the other side of the hall
Ⓒ Get a different room
Ⓓ Return to the front desk

15. What does the woman imply?

Ⓐ The application was lost.
Ⓑ The process takes about three weeks.
Ⓒ The response is probably in the mail.
Ⓓ The man should be patient.

16. What does the woman mean?

Ⓐ She wants to use her passport for ID.
Ⓑ She does not have a driver's license.
Ⓒ She prefers to pay with a credit card.
Ⓓ She does not have any checks.

17. What does the man mean?

Ⓐ He was polite to the committee.
Ⓑ The meeting went very well.
Ⓒ Additional members are needed for the committee.
Ⓓ The committee did not meet.

QUESTION DIRECTIONS — Part B

In Part B of the Listening Section, you will hear several longer conversations and talks. Each conversation or talk is followed by several questions. The conversations, talks, and questions will not be repeated.

The conversations and talks are about a variety of topics. You do not need special knowledge of the topics to answer the questions correctly. Rather, you should answer each question on the basis of what is stated or implied by the speakers in the conversations or talks.

For most of the questions, you will need to click on the best of four possible answers. Some questions will have special directions. The special directions will appear in a box on the computer screen.

18. Why is the student in the dean's office?

    Ⓐ Because he failed a class
    Ⓑ Because he needs some advice
    Ⓒ Because he was caught plagiarizing
    Ⓓ Because he stole a book

19. What is the student's excuse?

    Ⓐ He says he didn't understand.
    Ⓑ He says someone else did it.
    Ⓒ He says he is sorry.
    Ⓓ He says he needs a tutor.

20. How does the dean punish the student?

    Ⓐ By expelling him
    Ⓑ By giving him a failing grade in the course
    Ⓒ By warning him
    Ⓓ By sending him to the Learning Resources Center

21. What advice does the dean give the student?

    Ⓐ To come back to her office
    Ⓑ To get a tutor to help him
    Ⓒ To use his own ideas next time
    Ⓓ To go to another university

22. What is the woman trying to decide?

    Ⓐ Whether to go to graduate school
    Ⓑ If she wants to transfer or not
    Ⓒ Which job to accept
    Ⓓ What to do about her grades

23. What does she like about the college she is attending?

    Ⓐ The prestige of a large school
    Ⓑ The friends she has made
    Ⓒ The attitude of the teachers
    Ⓓ The opportunities for employment

24. How does the man respond to her problem?

    Ⓐ He is not interested.
    Ⓑ He gives her advice.
    Ⓒ He shares his plans.
    Ⓓ He just listens without comment.

25. What does the man plan to do?

    Ⓐ Go to a large graduate institution
    Ⓑ Continue his friendship with the woman
    Ⓒ Finish his degree at another school
    Ⓓ Schedule job interviews

26. What is the topic of this lecture?

    Ⓐ The role of fine arts in civilization
    Ⓑ A definition of culture in anthropology
    Ⓒ Customs of American society
    Ⓓ The study of complex societies

27. According to the speaker, what do most people mean when they use the word *culture* in ordinary conversation?

    Ⓐ Customs for a particular society
    Ⓑ Ethnic groups that share common experiences
    Ⓒ Values that are characteristic of society
    Ⓓ Familiarity with the arts

28. According to the speaker, what do anthropologists mean when they say a thought or activity is to be included as part of culture?

    Ⓐ It must be considered appropriate by small groups within society.
    Ⓑ It must be acquired by visiting museums, galleries, and theaters.
    Ⓒ It must be commonly shared by a group.
    Ⓓ It must be comprised of many diverse ethnic groups.

29. How does the professor explain American culture?

    Ⓐ Practices that are common to all Americans of diverse ethnicity
    Ⓑ The combination of diverse ethnic practices by different groups in America
    Ⓒ Diverse ethnic practices that are recognized but not practiced by all Americans
    Ⓓ Practices that the majority of Americans participate in

30. According to the speaker, what is a subculture?

    Ⓐ A museum or a gallery
    Ⓑ An informal culture
    Ⓒ A smaller group within the entire society
    Ⓓ The behaviors, beliefs, attitudes, and values of the majority society

31. How does the World Health Organization estimate compare with actual trends?

    Ⓐ The estimate is very accurate compared with the actual numbers.
    Ⓑ The estimate appears to be lower than the actual numbers.
    Ⓒ The estimate was much too high compared with the actual numbers.
    Ⓓ The estimate accounted for about two-thirds of the actual numbers.

32. The guest speaker briefly discusses a trend. Summarize the trend by putting the events in order.

    Click on a sentence. Then click on the space where it belongs.
    Use each sentence only once.

    Ⓐ Heterosexual contact accounted for most new infections.
    Ⓑ Many children were born with HIV.
    Ⓒ Rates of exposure and infection of women rose.
    Ⓓ The majority of AIDS victims were homosexual men.

    1 [   ]
    2 [   ]
    3 [   ]
    4 [   ]

33. Why are women so susceptible to the AIDS virus?

    Click on 2 answers.

    Ⓐ More women today tend to have multiple partners than they did in the past.
    Ⓑ Some cultures do not encourage the use of protection.
    Ⓒ Women are biologically more at risk for all sexually transmitted diseases.
    Ⓓ Traditionally, women have not been the partner responsible for protection.

34. Which segments of the population will probably constitute the majority of AIDS cases in the twenty-first century?

    Click on 2 answers.

    Ⓐ Children
    Ⓑ Teens
    Ⓒ Women
    Ⓓ Men

35. What causes jet lag?

    Ⓐ Adjustment to a longer or shorter day
    Ⓑ Air travel from west to east
    Ⓒ Different foods and drinks while traveling
    Ⓓ Lack of sleep during air travel

36. Who would suffer most from jet lag?

    Ⓐ A young person
    Ⓑ A person traveling west
    Ⓒ A person who has a regular routine
    Ⓓ A person who does not travel often

37. How can jet lag be minimized?

    Click on 2 answers.

    Ⓐ Eat a large meal on the plane
    Ⓑ Drink lots of water on the plane
    Ⓒ Arrive at your destination early in the evening
    Ⓓ Try not to sleep very much during the flight

38. How long does it take to adjust to a new time zone?

    Ⓐ One half day for every time zone
    Ⓑ Twenty-four hours after arrival
    Ⓒ One day for every time zone
    Ⓓ Three days after arrival

39. What is Elderhostel?

    Ⓐ A college program taught by retired professors
    Ⓑ A summer program for senior citizens
    Ⓒ An educational program for older adult students
    Ⓓ A travel program that includes inexpensive dormitory accommodations

40. Which of the statements is true of Elderhostel?

    Click on 2 answers.

    Ⓐ The courses are offered for credit.
    Ⓑ There are no final exams.
    Ⓒ Anyone may participate.
    Ⓓ College faculty teach the classes.

41. Which of the people in the picture would most probably be enrolled in an Elderhostel program?

    Click on a picture.

    A   B

    C   D

42. What should you do if you are interested in finding out more about Elderhostel?

    Ⓐ Write the national office
    Ⓑ Call your local college
    Ⓒ Listen to the radio station
    Ⓓ Attend an Elderhostel meeting

43. What problem does the lecturer point out?

    Ⓐ Pyrite looks like gold and is often mistaken for it.
    Ⓑ Pyrite is very flammable and can easily burst into flames.
    Ⓒ Pyrite is difficult to find in most parts of the world.
    Ⓓ Pyrite does not have an easily identifiable crystal formation.

44. What will the professor do with the specimen he has brought to class?

    Ⓐ He will return it to the museum.
    Ⓑ He will keep it in his office.
    Ⓒ He will use it for an experiment.
    Ⓓ He will put it in the mineral lab.

45. Select the specimen that is most similar to the one that the professor showed in class.

    Click on a picture.

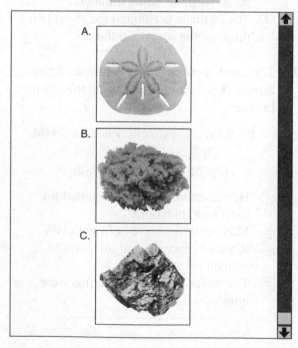

46. Identify the properties of pyrite.

Click on 2 answers.

A It is soft.
B It is brittle.
C It is flammable.
D It is rare.

47. What is an easy way to identify pyrite?

Ⓐ Heat the specimen
Ⓑ Put acid on the sample
Ⓒ Look for green and brown streaks
Ⓓ Smell the mineral

48. What prompted this conversation?

Ⓐ The man is studying for a test.
Ⓑ The man is looking for the Student Union.
Ⓒ The man has lost a book.
Ⓓ The man wants to meet the woman.

49. Where does the man think he left his book?

Ⓐ In class
Ⓑ At the Student Union
Ⓒ In the cafeteria
Ⓓ At the library

50. What does the woman suggest that the man do?

Click on 2 answers.

A Go to the Student Union immediately
B Study for his test
C Come back to see her tomorrow
D Check the lost and found tomorrow

Section 2:
Structure

This section measures the ability to recognize language that is appropriate for standard written English. There are two types of questions in this section.

In the first type of question, there are incomplete sentences. Beneath each sentence, there are four words or phrases. You will choose the one word or phrase that best completes the sentence. Clicking on a choice darkens the oval. After you click on **Next** and **Confirm Answer**, the next question will be presented.

The second type of question has four underlined words or phrases. You will choose the one underlined word or phrase that must be changed for the sentence to be correct. Clicking on an underlined word or phrase will darken it. After you click on **Next** and **Confirm Answer**, the next question will be presented.

1. The consistency of protoplasm and that of glue _____ .

   Ⓐ they are alike
   Ⓑ are similar to
   Ⓒ are similar
   Ⓓ the same

2. The decomposition of <u>microscopic animals</u>
   　　　　　　　　　　　　　　Ⓐ
   at the bottom of the sea <u>results</u> in
   　　　　　　　　　　　　　Ⓑ
   <u>an accumulation</u> <u>of the oil</u>.
   　Ⓒ　　　　　Ⓓ

3. Nerve impulses _____ to the brain at a speed of about one hundred yards per second.

   Ⓐ sending sensations
   Ⓑ to send sensations
   Ⓒ send sensations
   Ⓓ sensations

4. <u>A calorie</u> <u>is</u> the quantity of heat <u>required</u>
   　Ⓐ　　　Ⓑ　　　　　　　　　　Ⓒ
   <u>to rise</u> one gallon of water one degree
   　Ⓓ
   centrigrade at one atmospheric pressure.

5. The Supreme Court does not hear a case unless _____ , except those involving foreign ambassadors.

   Ⓐ a trial
   Ⓑ already tried
   Ⓒ it already trying
   Ⓓ it has already been tried

6. The yearly path of the sun around the heavens _____ .

   Ⓐ is known as the ecliptic
   Ⓑ known as the ecliptic
   Ⓒ it is known to be ecliptic
   Ⓓ knowing as the ecliptic

7. Before Alexander Fleming discovered penicillin, many people died _____ .

   Ⓐ infected with simple bacteria
   Ⓑ from simple bacterial infections
   Ⓒ infections were simple bacteria
   Ⓓ infecting of simple bacteria

8. <u>Wholly</u> the plow <u>is being displaced</u>
   　Ⓐ　　　　　　　　Ⓑ
   <u>by new techniques</u> that protect the land and
   　　Ⓒ
   <u>promise</u> more abundant crops.
   　Ⓓ

9. Although exact statistics vary because of political changes, _____ separate nation states are included in the official lists at any one time.

   Ⓐ more than two hundred
   Ⓑ as much as two hundred
   Ⓒ many as two hundred
   Ⓓ most that two hundred

10. Studies of job satisfaction are unreliable

    because there <u>is</u> so <u>many</u> variables and
                   Ⓐ   Ⓑ

    <u>because</u> the admission of dissatisfaction
      Ⓒ

    <u>may be viewed</u> as a personal failure.
        Ⓓ

11. _____ owe much of their success as a
    group to their unusual powers of migration.

    Ⓐ That birds
    Ⓑ A bird
    Ⓒ The bird
    Ⓓ Birds

12. _____ unknown quantities is the task of
    algebra.

    Ⓐ To found
    Ⓑ Find
    Ⓒ The find
    Ⓓ Finding

13. New synthetic materials <u>have</u> improved
                             Ⓐ

    <u>the construction</u> of artificial <u>body parts</u>
        Ⓑ   Ⓒ

    by <u>provide</u> both the power and the range of
       Ⓓ

    action for a natural limb.

14. <u>If</u> England had not <u>imposed</u> a tax on tea
    Ⓐ   Ⓑ

    over two hundred and twenty years <u>ago</u>, <u>will</u>
                                       Ⓒ   Ⓓ

    the United States have remained part of the

    British Commonwealth?

15. Research in the work place reveals that peo-
    ple work for many reasons _____ .

    Ⓐ money beside
    Ⓑ money besides
    Ⓒ beside money
    Ⓓ besides money

16. Both liquids and gases flow freely from a
    container because they have _____ .

    Ⓐ not definite shape
    Ⓑ none definite shape
    Ⓒ nothing definite shape
    Ⓓ no definite shape

17. A dolphin _____ a porpoise in that it has
    a longer nose.

    Ⓐ different
    Ⓑ differs
    Ⓒ different than
    Ⓓ differs from

18. Scientific fish farming, <u>known as</u>
                             Ⓐ

    aquaculture, has existed for <u>more than</u> 4000
                                 Ⓑ

    years, but scientists who <u>make</u> research in
                              Ⓒ

    this field are only recently providing the

    kind of information that growers need

    <u>to increase</u> production.
      Ⓓ

19. That most natural time units are not simple
    multiples of each other _____ in
    constructing a calendar.

    Ⓐ it is a primary problem
    Ⓑ is a primary problem
    Ⓒ a primary problem is
    Ⓓ a primary problem

20. The native people in the Americas were

    <u>referred to</u> as Indians because,
       Ⓐ

    <u>according to</u> the <u>believe</u> at the time,
       Ⓑ   Ⓒ

    Christopher Columbus <u>had reached</u> the
                           Ⓓ

    the East Indies.

21. Only after food has been dried or canned
    _____ .

    Ⓐ that it should be stored for later
      consumption
    Ⓑ should be stored for later consumption
    Ⓒ should it be stored for later consumption
    Ⓓ it should be stored for later consumption

22. Aging in most animals can be readily
    Ⓐ   Ⓑ

    modified when they will limit caloric intake.
    Ⓒ   Ⓓ

23. Although we are concerned about the
    Ⓐ

    problem of energy sources, we must not fail
    Ⓑ

    recognizing the need for environmental
    Ⓒ   Ⓓ

    protection.

24. _____, Carl Sandburg is also well known
    for his multivolume biography of Lincoln.

    Ⓐ An eminent American poet
    Ⓑ He is an eminent American poet
    Ⓒ An eminent American poet who is
    Ⓓ Despite an eminent American poet

25. The CBT will test your ability to understand
    Ⓐ

    spoken English, to read nontechnical
    Ⓑ

    language, and writing correctly.
    Ⓒ   Ⓓ

Section 3:
Reading

This section measures the ability to read and understand short passages similar in topic and style to those that students are likely to encounter in North American universities and colleges. This section contains reading passages and questions about the passages. There are several different types of questions in this section.

In the Reading Section, you will first have the opportunity to read the passage. You will use the scroll bar to view the rest of the passage.

When you have finished reading the passage, you will use the mouse to click on **Proceed**. Then the questions about the passage will be presented. You are to choose the one best answer to each question. Answer all questions about the information in a passage on the basis of what is stated or implied in that passage.

Most of the questions will be multiple-choice questions. To answer these questions you will click on a choice below the question.

To answer some questions, you will click on a word or phrase.
To answer some questions, you will click on a sentence in the passage.
To answer some questions, you will click on a square to add a sentence to the passage.

Seismologists have devised two scales of measurement to enable them to describe and record information about earthquakes in quantitative terms. The most widely known measurement is the Richter scale, a numerical logarithmic scale developed and introduced by American seismologist Charles R. Richter in 1935. The purpose of the scale is to measure the amplitude of the largest trace recorded by a standard seismograph one hundred kilometers from the epicenter of an earthquake. Tables have been formulated to demonstrate the magnitude of any earthquake from any seismograph. For example, a one-unit increase in magnitude translates into an increase of times thirty in released energy. To put that another way, each number on the Richter scale represents an earthquake ten times as strong as one of the next lower magnitude. Specifically, an earthquake of magnitude 6 is ten times as strong as an earthquake of magnitude 5.

On the Richter scale, earthquakes of 6.75 are considered great and 7.0 to 7.75 are considered major. An earthquake that reads 4 to 5.5 would be expected to have caused localized damage, and those of magnitude 2 may be felt.

The other earthquake-assessment scale, introduced by the Italian seismologist Giuseppe Mercalli, measures the intensity of shaking, using gradations from 1 to 12. Because the effects of such shaking dissipate with distance from the epicenter of the earthquake, the Mercalli rating depends on the site of the measurement. Earthquakes of Mercalli 2 or 3 are basically the same as those of Richter 3 or 4; measurements of 11 or 12 on the Mercalli scale can be roughly correlated with magnitudes of 8 or 9 on the Richter scale. In either case, the relative power or energy released by the earthquake can be understood, and the population waits to hear how bad the earthquake that just passed really was.

It is estimated that almost one million earthquakes occur each year, but most of them are so minor that they pass undetected. In fact, more than one thousand earthquakes of a magnitude of 2 or lower on the Richter scale occur every day.

1. Which of the following is the main topic of the passage?

   Ⓐ Earthquakes
   Ⓑ The Richter scale
   Ⓒ Charles F. Richter
   Ⓓ Seismography

2. According to information in the passage, what does the Richter scale record?

   Ⓐ The distance from the epicenter
   Ⓑ The amplitude of the largest trace
   Ⓒ The degree of damage
   Ⓓ The location of the epicenter

3. The word standard in paragraph 1 could be replaced by

   Ⓐ reliable
   Ⓑ complex
   Ⓒ conventional
   Ⓓ abandoned

Beginning

Seismologists have devised two scales of measurement to enable them to describe and record information about earthquakes in quantitative terms. The most widely known measurement is the Richter scale, a numerical logarithmic scale developed and introduced by American seismologist Charles R. Richter in 1935. The purpose of the scale is to measure the amplitude of the largest trace recorded by a standard seismograph one hundred kilometers from the epicenter of an earthquake. Tables have been formulated to demonstrate the magnitude of any earthquake from any seismograph. For example, a one-unit increase in magnitude translates into an increase of times thirty in released energy. To put that another way, each number on the Richter scale represents an earthquake ten times as strong as one of the next lower magnitude. Specifically, an earthquake of magnitude 6 is ten times as strong as an earthquake of magnitude 5.

On the Richter scale, earthquakes of 6.75 are considered great and 7.0 to 7.75 are considered major. An earthquake that reads 4 to 5.5 would be

4. What is the value of the tables?

   Ⓐ They allow us to interpret the magnitude of earthquakes.
   Ⓑ They help us to calculate our distance from earthquakes.
   Ⓒ They record all earthquakes.
   Ⓓ They release the energy of earthquakes.

5. How does each number on the Richter scale compare?

Ⓐ Each number is one hundred times as strong as the previous number.

Ⓑ Each magnitude is ten times stronger than the previous magnitude.

Ⓒ The strength of each magnitude is one less than the previous magnitude.

Ⓓ The scale decreases by five or six for each number.

6. Look at the word those in the passage. Click on the word or phrase in the **bold** text that those refers to.

More Available

released energy. To put that another way, each number on the Richter scale represents an earthquake ten times as strong as one of the next lower magnitude. Specifically, an earthquake of magnitude 6 is ten times as strong as an earthquake of magnitude 5.

On the Richter scale, earthquakes of 6.75 are considered great and 7.0 to 7.75 are considered major. An earthquake that reads 4 to 5.5 would be expected to have caused localized damage, and those of magnitude 2 may be felt.

The other earthquake-assessment scale, introduced by the Italian seismologist Giuseppe Mercalli, measures the intensity of shaking, using gradations from 1 to 12. Because the effects of such shaking dissipate with distance from the epicenter of the earthquake, the Mercalli rating depends on the site of the measurement. Earthquakes of Mercalli 2 or 3 are basically the same as those of Richter 3 or 4; measurements of 11 or 12 on the Mercalli scale can be roughly correlated with magnitudes of 8 or 9 on the Richter scale. In either case, the relative power or energy released by the earthquake can be

---

7. What does the author mean by the statement Because the effects of such shaking dissipate with distance from the epicenter of the earthquake, the Mercalli rating depends on the site of the measurement?

Ⓐ The Mercalli rating will vary depending on the location of the measurement.

Ⓑ The results of the Mercalli rating are less accurate at greater distances from the epicenter.

Ⓒ The stronger shaking of the earthquake at the center is not detected by the Mercalli rating.

Ⓓ The Mercalli rating is useful because it is taken farther away from the center of the earthquake.

8. Look at the word roughly in the passage. Click on the word or phrase in the **bold** text that is closest in meaning to the word roughly.

End

major. An earthquake that reads 4 to 5.5 would be expected to have caused localized damage, and those of magnitude 2 may be felt.

The other earthquake-assessment scale, introduced by the Italian seismologist Giuseppe Mercalli, measures the intensity of shaking, using gradations from 1 to 12. Because the effects of such shaking dissipate with distance from the epicenter of the earthquake, the Mercalli rating depends on the site of the measurement. **Earthquakes of Mercalli 2 or 3 are basically the same as those of Richter 3 or 4; measurements of 11 or 12 on the Mercalli scale can be roughly correlated with magnitudes of 8 or 9 on the Richter scale.** In either case, the relative power or energy released by the earthquake can be understood, and the population waits to hear how bad the earthquake that just passed really was.

It is estimated that almost one million earthquakes occur each year, but most of them are so minor that they pass undetected. In fact, more than one thousand earthquakes of a magnitude of 2 or lower on the Richter scale occur every day.

---

9. The word undetected in paragraph 4 is closest in meaning to

Ⓐ with no damage

Ⓑ with no notice

Ⓒ with no name

Ⓓ with no problem

End

major. An earthquake that reads 4 to 5.5 would be expected to have caused localized damage, and those of magnitude 2 may be felt.

The other earthquake-assessment scale, introduced by the Italian seismologist Giuseppe Mercalli, measures the intensity of shaking, using gradations from 1 to 12. Because the effects of such shaking dissipate with distance from the epicenter of the earthquake, the Mercalli rating depends on the site of the measurement. Earthquakes of Mercalli 2 or 3 are basically the same as those of Richter 3 or 4; measurements of 11 or 12 on the Mercalli scale can be roughly correlated with magnitudes of 8 or 9 on the Richter scale. In either case, the relative power or energy released by the earthquake can be understood, and the population waits to hear how bad the earthquake that just passed really was.

It is estimated that almost one million earthquakes occur each year, but most of them are so minor that they pass undetected. In fact, more than one thousand earthquakes of a magnitude of 2 or lower on the Richter scale occur every day.

10. With which of the following statements would the author most probably agree?

    Ⓐ Only the Richter scale describes earth-quakes in quantitative terms.
    Ⓑ Both the Richter scale and the Mercalli Scale measure earthquakes in the same way.
    Ⓒ Most earthquakes are measurable on either the Richter or the Mercalli scale.
    Ⓓ The Mercalli and the Richter scales are different but they can be compared.

11. The passage discusses all of the following in the explanation of the Richter scale EXCEPT

    Ⓐ It was introduced in 1935.
    Ⓑ It was developed by an American seis-mologist.
    Ⓒ It has a scale of 1 to 12.
    Ⓓ It measures the magnitude of earth-quakes.

Charles Ives, who is nowadays acclaimed as the first great American composer of the twentieth century, had to wait many years for the public recognition he deserved. Born to music as the son of a bandmaster, Ives played drums in his father's community band, and organ at the local church. He entered Yale University at twenty to study musical composition with Horatio Parker, but after graduation, he chose not to pursue a career in music. He suspected correctly that the public would not accept the music he wrote, for Ives did not follow the musical fashion of his times. While his contemporaries wrote lyrical songs, Ives transfigured music and musical form. He quoted, combined, insinuated, and distorted familiar hymns, marches, and battle songs, while experimenting with the effects of polytonality, or the simultaneous use of two or more keys, and dissonance, or the clash of keys with conflicting rhythms and time. Even when he could convince some musicians to show some interest in his compositions, after assessing them, conductors and performers said that they were essentially unplayable.

Instead, he became a successful insurance executive, building his company into the largest agency in the country in only two decades. Although he occasionally hired musicians to play one of his works privately for him, he usually heard his music only in his imagination.

After he recovered from a serious heart attack, he became reconciled to the fact that his ideas, especially the use of dissonance and special effects, were just too different for the musical mainstream to accept. Determined to share his music with the few people who might appreciate it, he published his work privately and distributed it free.

In 1939, when Ives was sixty-five, American pianist John Kirkpatrick played *Concord Sonata* in Town Hall. The reviews were laudatory. One reviewer proclaimed it "the greatest music composed by an American." By 1947, Ives was famous. His *Second Symphony* was presented to the public in a performance by the New York Philharmonic, fifty years after it had been written. The same year, Ives received the Pulitzer Prize. He was seventy-three.

12. Which of the following is the main topic of the passage?

  Ⓐ Modern musical composition
  Ⓑ Charles Ives' life
  Ⓒ The Pulitzer Prize
  Ⓓ Career choices

13. Why didn't the public appreciate Ives' music?

  Ⓐ It was not performed for a long time.
  Ⓑ It was very different from the music of the time.
  Ⓒ The performers did not play it well.
  Ⓓ He did not write it down.

14. Look at the word dissonance in the passage. Click on the word in the **bold** text that is closest in meaning to dissonance .

> **More Available**
>
> marches, and battle songs, **while experimenting with the effects of polytonality, or the simultaneous use of two or more keys, and dissonance, or the clash of keys with conflicting rhythms and time.** Even when he could convince some musicians to show some interest in his compositions, after assessing them, conductors and performers said that they were essentially unplayable.
>
> Instead, he became a successful insurance executive, building his company into the largest agency in the country in only two decades. Although he occasionally hired musicians to play one of his works privately for him, he usually heard his music only in his imagination.
>
> After he recovered from a serious heart attack, he became reconciled to the fact that his ideas, especially the use of dissonance and special effects, were just too different for the musical mainstream to accept. Determined to share his music with the few people who might appreciate it, he published his work privately and distributed it free.
>
> In 1939, when Ives was sixty-five, American pianist John Kirkpatrick played *Concord Sonata* in

15. The word they in paragraph 1 refers to

  Ⓐ conductors
  Ⓑ performers
  Ⓒ interest
  Ⓓ compositions

> **More Available**
>
> marches, and battle songs, while experimenting with the effects of polytonality, or the simultaneous use of two or more keys, and dissonance, or the clash of keys with conflicting rhythms and time. Even when he could convince some musicians to show some interest in his compositions, after assessing them, conductors and performers said that they were essentially unplayable.
>
> Instead, he became a successful insurance executive, building his company into the largest agency in the country in only two decades. Although he occasionally hired musicians to play one of his works privately for him, he usually heard his music only in his imagination.
>
> After he recovered from a serious heart attack, he became reconciled to the fact that his ideas, especially the use of dissonance and special effects, were just too different for the musical mainstream to accept. Determined to share his music with the few people who might appreciate it, he published his work privately and distributed it free.
>
> In 1939, when Ives was sixty-five, American pianist John Kirkpatrick played *Concord Sonata* in

16. How did Ives make a living for most of his life?

  Ⓐ He conducted a band.
  Ⓑ He taught musical composition.
  Ⓒ He owned an insurance company.
  Ⓓ He published music.

17. The phrase became reconciled to in paragraph 3 is closest in meaning to

Ⓐ accepted
Ⓑ repeated
Ⓒ disputed
Ⓓ neglected

More Available

marches, and battle songs, while experimenting with the effects of polytonality, or the simultaneous use of two or more keys, and dissonance, or the clash of keys with conflicting rhythms and time. Even when he could convince some musicians to show some interest in his compositions, after assessing them, conductors and performers said that they were essentially unplayable.

Instead, he became a successful insurance executive, building his company into the largest agency in the country in only two decades. Although he occasionally hired musicians to play one of his works privately for him, he usually heard his music only in his imagination.

After he recovered from a serious heart attack, he became reconciled to the fact that his ideas, especially the use of dissonance and special effects, were just too different for the musical mainstream to accept. Determined to share his music with the few people who might appreciate it, he published his work privately and distributed it free.

In 1939, when Ives was sixty-five, American pianist John Kirkpatrick played *Concord Sonata* in

---

18. According to the passage, Ives shared his music

Ⓐ by publishing free copies
Ⓑ by playing it himself
Ⓒ by hiring musicians to perform
Ⓓ by teaching at Yale

19. Which of the following characteristics is NOT true of the music of Charles Ives?

Ⓐ It included pieces of familiar songs.
Ⓑ It was very experimental.
Ⓒ It was difficult to play.
Ⓓ It was never appreciated.

20. How was the performance of *Concord Sonata* received?

Ⓐ There were no reviews.
Ⓑ The musicians felt it was unplayable.
Ⓒ The public would not accept it.
Ⓓ It established Ives as an important composer.

21. Look at the word it in the passage. Click on the word or phrase in the **bold** text that it refers to.

End

executive, building his company into the largest agency in the country in only two decades. Although he occasionally hired musicians to play one of his works privately for him, he usually heard his music only in his imagination.

After he recovered from a serious heart attack, he became reconciled to the fact that his ideas, especially the use of dissonance and special effects, were just too different for the musical mainstream to accept. Determined to share his music with the few people who might appreciate it, he published his work privately and distributed it free.

In 1939, when Ives was sixty-five, American pianist John Kirkpatrick played *Concord Sonata* in Town Hall. The reviews were laudatory. One reviewer proclaimed it "the greatest music composed by an American." By 1947, Ives was famous. His *Second Symphony* was presented to the public in a performance by the New York Philharmonic, fifty years after it had been written. The same year, Ives received the Pulitzer Prize. He was seventy-three.

22. The following sentence can be added to the passage.

> **Even during such a busy time in his career, he still dedicated himself to composing music in the evenings, on weekends, and during vacations.**

Where would it best fit in the passage?

Click on the square (■) to add the sentence to the passage.

Scroll the passage to see all of the choices.

More Available

marches, and battle songs, while experimenting with the effects of polytonality, or the simultaneous use of two or more keys, and dissonance, or the clash of keys with conflicting rhythms and time. Even when he could convince some musicians to show some interest in his compositions, after assessing them, conductors and performers said that they were essentially unplayable. ■

Instead, he became a successful insurance executive, building his company into the largest agency in the country in only two decades. ■ Although he occasionally hired musicians to play one of his works privately for him, he usually heard his music only in his imagination. ■

After he recovered from a serious heart attack, he became reconciled to the fact that his ideas, especially the use of dissonance and special effects, were just too different for the musical mainstream to accept. ■ Determined to share his music with the few people who might appreciate it, he published his work privately and distributed it free.

In 1939, when Ives was sixty-five, American pianist John Kirkpatrick played *Concord Sonata* in

---

Bats are not dirty, bloodthirsty monsters as portrayed in vampire films. These winged mammals groom themselves carefully like cats and only rarely carry rabies. Of the hundreds of species of bats, only three rely on blood meals. In fact, the majority eat fruit, insects, spiders, or small animals; some species gather nectar and pollen from flowers. The environmental benefits of bats are myriad. They consume an enormous number of pests, pollinate many varieties of plant life, and help reforest huge tracts of barren land by excreting millions of undigested seeds.

Bats also have served as models for sophisticated navigation systems in naval and airplane technology. Living models for radar and sonar, almost all bats use echolocation to navigate, especially at night. As they fly, they emit a series of high-pitched squeaks at the rate of about fifty per minute. As these signals bounce off objects in their path, an echo is detected by the bats' sensitive ears that informs them of the direction, distance, and nature of obstacles so that they can undertake corrective or evasive action. Echoes are used by bats but not because of physical limitations or impairments, for bats are not blind as widely assumed. In fact, all species of bats can see, probably about as well as human beings. Another myth, about bats being aggressive, intentionally entangling themselves in the hair of human beings, is also totally unfounded. It has been shown in studies not only that bats are timid, but also that they will assiduously avoid contact with larger creatures than themselves if possible.

Aggregation during the day may vary from small groups consisting of a single male and a dozen or more females to huge colonies of many thousands or even millions of individuals, hanging upside down in caves or in hollow trees, buildings, or other protected shelters. Within their social systems, bats assume specialized roles. Some guard the entrance to their caves, others scout for food, and still others warn the colony of approaching danger. An adult female bat usually gives birth to only one pup per year, tenderly caring for it, and a nursery colony within a larger colony may provide mother bats with a safe, supportive environment in which to rear their young.

23. With which of the following statements would the author most probably agree?

Ⓐ Bats are dirty and they carry rabies.
Ⓑ Bats are like the monsters in vampire films.
Ⓒ Bats are clean, helpful members of the animal world.
Ⓓ Bats are not very important in the animal world.

24. According to the passage, what do most bats eat?

Ⓐ Blood meals
Ⓑ Fruit and insects
Ⓒ Leaves and trees
Ⓓ Large animals

25. Look at the word enormous in the passage. Click on the word in the **bold** text that is closest in meaning to enormous.

Beginning

Bats are not dirty, bloodthirsty monsters as portrayed in vampire films. These winged mammals groom themselves carefully like cats and only rarely carry rabies. Of the hundreds of species of bats, only three rely on blood meals. In fact, the majority eat fruit, insects, spiders, or small animals; some species gather nectar and pollen from flowers. The environmental benefits of bats are myriad. **They consume an enormous number of pests, pollinate many varieties of plant life, and help reforest huge tracts of barren land by excreting millions of undigested seeds.**
Bats also have served as models for sophisticated navigation systems in naval and airplane technology. Living models for radar and sonar, almost all bats use echolocation to navigate, especially at night. As they fly, they emit a series of high-pitched squeaks at the rate of about fifty per minute. As these signals bounce off objects in their path, an echo is detected by the bats' sensitive ears that informs them of the direction, distance, and nature of obstacles so that they can undertake corrective or evasive action. Echoes are used by bats but not because of

---

26. How do bats help reforest the land?

Ⓐ By eating pests
Ⓑ By hanging upside down in trees at night
Ⓒ By excreting seeds
Ⓓ By taking evasive action

27. Which of the following is NOT characteristic of most bats?

Ⓐ They pollinate plants.
Ⓑ They have specialized roles in their colony.
Ⓒ They use echolocation.
Ⓓ They eat blood.

28. The word emit in paragraph 2 is closest in meaning to

Ⓐ send
Ⓑ continue
Ⓒ find
Ⓓ stop

Beginning

Bats are not dirty, bloodthirsty monsters as portrayed in vampire films. These winged mammals groom themselves carefully like cats and only rarely carry rabies. Of the hundreds of species of bats, only three rely on blood meals. In fact, the majority eat fruit, insects, spiders, or small animals; some species gather nectar and pollen from flowers. The environmental benefits of bats are myriad. They consume an enormous number of pests, pollinate many varieties of plant life, and help reforest huge tracts of barren land by excreting millions of undigested seeds.
Bats also have served as models for sophisticated navigation systems in naval and airplane technology. Living models for radar and sonar, almost all bats use echolocation to navigate, especially at night. As they fly, they emit a series of high-pitched squeaks at the rate of about fifty per minute. As these signals bounce off objects in their path, an echo is detected by the bats' sensitive ears that informs them of the direction, distance, and nature of obstacles so that they can undertake corrective or evasive action. Echoes are used by bats but not because of

---

29. According to the passage, how do bats navigate?

Ⓐ By responding to the echoes of their signals bouncing off objects
Ⓑ By warning the colony of approaching danger with high squeaks
Ⓒ By beating their wings fifty times per minute
Ⓓ By using their sensitive ears to hear the noises in their environment

30. The word them in paragraph 2 refers to

Ⓐ signals
Ⓑ objects
Ⓒ bats
Ⓓ squeaks

Beginning

Bats are not dirty, bloodthirsty monsters as portrayed in vampire films. These winged mammals groom themselves carefully like cats and only rarely carry rabies. Of the hundreds of species of bats, only three rely on blood meals. In fact, the majority eat fruit, insects, spiders, or small animals; some species gather nectar and pollen from flowers. The environmental benefits of bats are myriad. They consume an enormous number of pests, pollinate many varieties of plant life, and help reforest huge tracts of barren land by excreting millions of undigested seeds.

Bats also have served as models for sophisticated navigation systems in naval and airplane technology. Living models for radar and sonar, almost all bats use echolocation to navigate, especially at night. As they fly, they emit a series of high-pitched squeaks at the rate of about fifty per minute. As these signals bounce off objects in their path, an echo is detected by the bats' sensitive ears that informs them of the direction, distance, and nature of obstacles so that they can undertake corrective or evasive action. Echoes are used by bats but not because of

---

31. Click on the sentence in paragraph 2 that refers to the visual range of bats.

Paragraph 2 is marked with an arrow (→).

More Available

→ Bats also have served as models for sophisticated navigation systems in naval and airplane technology. Living models for radar and sonar, almost all bats use echolocation to navigate, especially at night. As they fly, they emit a series of high-pitched squeaks at the rate of about fifty per minute. As these signals bounce off objects in their path, an echo is detected by the bats' sensitive ears that informs them of the direction, distance, and nature of obstacles so that they can undertake corrective or evasive action. Echoes are used by bats but not because of physical limitations or impairments, for bats are not blind as widely assumed. In fact, all species of bats can see, probably about as well as human beings. Another myth, about bats being aggressive, intentionally entangling themselves in the hair of human beings, is also totally unfounded. It has been shown in studies not only that bats are timid, but also that they will assiduously avoid contact with larger creatures than themselves if possible.

Aggregation during the day may vary from small groups consisting of a single male and a dozen or more females to huge colonies of many

---

32. Look at the word Some in the passage. Click on the word or phrase in the **bold** text that Some refers to.

End

intentionally entangling themselves in the hair of human beings, is also totally unfounded. It has been shown in studies not only that bats are timid, but also that they will assiduously avoid contact with larger creatures than themselves if possible.

Aggregation during the day may vary from small groups consisting of a single male and a dozen or more females to huge colonies of many thousands or even millions of individuals, hanging upside down in caves or in hollow trees, buildings, or other protected shelters. **Within their social systems, bats assume specialized roles. Some guard the entrance to their caves, others scout for food, and still others warn the colony of approaching danger.** An adult female bat usually gives birth to only one pup per year, tenderly caring for it, and a nursery colony within a larger colony may provide mother bats with a safe, supportive environment in which to rear their young.

33. The following sentence can be added to the passage.

> **It is a little known fact that bats are highly social creatures.**

Where would it best fit in the passage?

Click on the square (■) to add the sentence to the passage.

Scroll the passage to see all of the choices.

End

intentionally entangling themselves in the hair of human beings, is also totally unfounded. It has been shown in studies not only that bats are timid, but also that they will assiduously avoid contact with larger creatures than themselves if possible. ■ Aggregation during the day may vary from small groups consisting of a single male and a dozen or more females to huge colonies of many thousands or even millions of individuals, hanging upside down in caves or in hollow trees, buildings, or other protected shelters. ■ Within their social systems, bats assume specialized roles. ■ Some guard the entrance to their caves, others scout for food, and still others warn the colony of approaching danger. ■ An adult female bat usually gives birth to only one pup per year, tenderly caring for it, and a nursery colony within a larger colony may provide mother bats with a safe, supportive environment in which to rear their young.

The fact that most Americans live in urban areas does not mean that they reside in the center of large cities. In fact, more Americans live in the suburbs of large metropolitan areas than in the cities themselves.

The Bureau of the Census regards any area with more than 2500 people as an urban area, and does not consider boundaries of cities and suburbs. According to the Bureau, the political boundaries are less significant than the social and economic relationships and the transportation and communication systems that integrate a locale. The term used by the Bureau for an integrated metropolis is an MSA, which stands for Metropolitan Statistical Area. In general, an MSA is any area that contains a city and its surrounding suburbs and has a total population of 50,000 or more.

At the present time, the Bureau reports more than 280 MSAs, which together account for 75 percent of the US population. In addition, the Bureau recognizes eighteen megapolises, that is, continuous adjacent metropolitan areas. One of the most obvious megapolises includes a chain of hundreds of cities and suburbs across ten states on the East Coast from Massachusetts to Virginia, including Boston, New York, and Washington, D.C. In the Eastern Corridor, as it is called, a population of 45 million inhabitants is concentrated. Another megapolis that is growing rapidly is the California coast from San Francisco through Los Angeles to San Diego.

34. Which of the following is the best title for the passage?

Ⓐ Metropolitan Statistical Areas
Ⓑ Types of Population Centers
Ⓒ The Bureau of the Census
Ⓓ Megapolises

35. According to the passage, where do most Americans live?

Ⓐ In the center of cities
Ⓑ In the suburbs surrounding large cities
Ⓒ In rural areas
Ⓓ In small towns

36. Look at the word reside in the passage. Click on the word in the **bold** text that is closest in meaning to reside.

Beginning

The fact that most Americans live in urban areas does not mean that they reside in the center of large cities. In fact, more Americans live in the suburbs of large metropolitan areas than in the cities themselves.

The Bureau of the Census regards any area with more than 2500 people as an urban area, and does not consider boundaries of cities and suburbs. According to the Bureau, the political boundaries are less significant than the social and economic relationships and the transportation and communication systems that integrate a locale. The term used by the Bureau for an integrated metropolis is an MSA, which stands for Metropolitan Statistical Area. In general, an MSA is any area that contains a city and its surrounding suburbs and has a total population of 50,000 or more.

At the present time, the Bureau reports more than 280 MSAs, which together account for 75 percent of the US population. In addition, the Bureau recognizes eighteen megapolises, that is, continuous adjacent metropolitan areas. One of the most obvious megapolises includes a chain of hundreds of cities and suburbs across ten states on the East Coast from Massachusetts to Virginia, including Boston, New

37. According to the Bureau of the Census, what is an urban area?

Ⓐ An area with 2500 people or more
Ⓑ An area with at least 50,000 people
Ⓒ The eighteen largest cities
Ⓓ A chain of adjacent cities

38. Which of the following are NOT considered important in defining an urban area?

Ⓐ Political boundaries
Ⓑ Transportation networks
Ⓒ Social relationships
Ⓓ Economic systems

39. The word integrate in paragraph 2 is closest in meaning to

Ⓐ benefit
Ⓑ define
Ⓒ unite
Ⓓ restrict

Beginning

The fact that most Americans live in urban areas does not mean that they reside in the center of large cities. In fact, more Americans live in the suburbs of large metropolitan areas than in the cities themselves.

The Bureau of the Census regards any area with more than 2500 people as an urban area, and does not consider boundaries of cities and suburbs. According to the Bureau, the political boundaries are less significant than the social and economic relationships and the transportation and communication systems that integrate a locale. The term used by the Bureau for an integrated metropolis is an MSA, which stands for Metropolitan Statistical Area. In general, an MSA is any area that contains a city and its surrounding suburbs and has a total population of 50,000 or more.

At the present time, the Bureau reports more than 280 MSAs, which together account for 75 percent of the US population. In addition, the Bureau recognizes eighteen megapolises, that is, continuous adjacent metropolitan areas. One of the most obvious megapolises includes a chain of hundreds of cities and suburbs across ten states on the East Coast from Massachusetts to Virginia, including Boston, New

40. Look at the word locale in the passage. Click on the word in the **bold** text that is closest in meaning to locale.

```
                                              End
According to the Bureau, the political boundaries are
less significant than the social and economic
relationships and the transportation and
communication systems that integrate a locale. The
term used by the Bureau for an integrated metropolis
is an MSA, which stands for Metropolitan Statistical
Area. In general, an MSA is any area that contains a
city and its surrounding suburbs and has a total
population of 50,000 or more.
    At the present time, the Bureau reports more than
280 MSAs, which together account for 75 percent of
the US population. In addition, the Bureau recognizes
eighteen megapolises, that is, continuous adjacent
metropolitan areas. One of the most obvious
megapolises includes a chain of hundreds of cities
and suburbs across ten states on the East Coast from
Massachusetts to Virginia, including Boston, New
York, and Washington, D.C. In the Eastern Corridor,
as it is called, a population of 45 million inhabitants is
concentrated. Another megapolis that is growing
rapidly is the California coast from San Francisco
through Los Angeles to San Diego.
```

41. The word its in paragraph 2 refers to

   Ⓐ the MSA's
   Ⓑ the area's
   Ⓒ the city's
   Ⓓ the population's

```
                                              End
According to the Bureau, the political boundaries are
less significant than the social and economic
relationships and the transportation and
communication systems that integrate a locale. The
term used by the Bureau for an integrated metropolis
is an MSA, which stands for Metropolitan Statistical
Area. In general, an MSA is any area that contains a
city and its surrounding suburbs and has a total
population of 50,000 or more.
    At the present time, the Bureau reports more than
280 MSAs, which together account for 75 percent of
the US population. In addition, the Bureau recognizes
eighteen megapolises, that is, continuous adjacent
metropolitan areas. One of the most obvious
megapolises includes a chain of hundreds of cities
and suburbs across ten states on the East Coast from
Massachusetts to Virginia, including Boston, New
York, and Washington, D.C. In the Eastern Corridor,
as it is called, a population of 45 million inhabitants is
concentrated. Another megapolis that is growing
rapidly is the California coast from San Francisco
through Los Angeles to San Diego.
```

42. Click on the paragraph that identifies the U.S. population now living in MSAs.

   Scroll the passage to see all of the paragraphs.

43. The word adjacent in paragraph 3 is closest in meaning to

   Ⓐ beside each other
   Ⓑ growing very fast
   Ⓒ the same size
   Ⓓ densely populated

```
                                              End
Area. In general, an MSA is any area that contains a
city and its surrounding suburbs and has a total
population of 50,000 or more.
    At the present time, the Bureau reports more than
280 MSAs, which together account for 75 percent of
the US population. In addition, the Bureau recognizes
eighteen megapolises, that is, continuous adjacent
metropolitan areas. One of the most obvious
megapolises includes a chain of hundreds of cities
and suburbs across ten states on the East Coast from
Massachusetts to Virginia, including Boston, New
York, and Washington, D.C. In the Eastern Corridor,
as it is called, a population of 45 million inhabitants is
concentrated. Another megapolis that is growing
rapidly is the California coast from San Francisco
through Los Angeles to San Diego.
```

44. According to the passage, what is a megapolis?

   Ⓐ One of the ten largest cities in the United States
   Ⓑ One of the eighteen largest cities in the United States
   Ⓒ One of the one hundred cities between Boston and Washington
   Ⓓ Any number of continuous adjacent cities and suburbs

45. Why does the author mention the Eastern Corridor and the California coast in paragraph 3?

    Ⓐ As examples of megapolises

    Ⓑ Because 75 percent of the population lives there

    Ⓒ To conclude the passage

    Ⓓ The Bureau of the Census is located there

Paragraph 3 is marked with an arrow (→).

End

Area. In general, an MSA is any area that contains a city and its surrounding suburbs and has a total population of 50,000 or more.

→ At the present time, the Bureau reports more than 280 MSAs, which together account for 75 percent of the US population. In addition, the Bureau recognizes eighteen megapolises, that is, continuous adjacent metropolitan areas. One of the most obvious megapolises includes a chain of hundreds of cities and suburbs across ten states on the East Coast from Massachusetts to Virginia, including Boston, New York, and Washington, D.C. In the Eastern Corridor, as it is called, a population of 45 million inhabitants is concentrated. Another megapolis that is growing rapidly is the California coast from San Francisco through Los Angeles to San Diego.

To check your answers for Model Test 8, refer to the Answer Key on page 495. For an explanation of the answers, refer to the Explanatory Answers for Model Test 8 on pages 641–660.

Writing Section:
Model Test 8

When you take a Model Test, you should use one sheet of paper, both sides. Time each Model Test carefully. After you have read the topic, you should spend 30 minutes writing. For results that would be closest to the actual testing situation, it is recommended that an English teacher score your test, using the guidelines on page 244 of this book.

Read and think about the following statement: The college years are the best time in a person's life. Do you agree or disagree with the statement? Give reasons to support your opinion.

Notes

To check your essay, refer to the Checklist on page 495. For an Example Essay, refer to the Explanatory Answers for Model Test 8 on pages 660–661.

Model Test 9
Next Generation TOEFL

Listening Section

This is the Listening Section of the Next Generation TOEFL Model Test. This section tests your ability to understand campus conversations and academic lectures. During the test, you will respond to two conversations and four lectures. You will hear each conversation and lecture one time. You may take notes while you listen. You may use your notes to answer the questions. After each conversation or lecture, you will have five or six questions to answer. Choose the best answer for multiple-choice questions. Follow the directions on the page or on the screen for computer-assisted questions. Click on **OK** and **Next** to go to the next question. You cannot return to previous questions. You have 25 minutes to answer all of the questions. A clock on the screen will show you how much time you have to complete your answers for the section. The clock does not count the time you are listening to the conversations and lectures.

Independent Listening 1: "Career Counseling"

Directions:
Choose the best answer for multiple-choice questions. Follow the directions on the page for computer-assisted questions.

1. What are the students mainly discussing?

   Ⓐ Group sessions in the Office of Career Development.
   Ⓑ The advantages of career counseling for the man.
   Ⓒ The woman's internship in the Office of Career Development.
   Ⓓ How to find employment in the field of career counseling.

2. What is the man's problem?

   Ⓐ He does not have time to see an advisor.
   Ⓑ He does not have an internship yet.
   Ⓒ He does not know which career to choose.
   Ⓓ He does not have a job offer after graduation.

3. Why does the woman tell the man about her experience?

   Ⓐ To demonstrate the benefits of going to the Office of Career Development.
   Ⓑ To encourage the man to talk with an advisor about an internship.
   Ⓒ To suggest that he change his major from math to library science.
   Ⓓ To give the man her opinion about his career decision.

4. What is the woman's attitude toward her internship?

   Ⓐ She would rather go to graduate school.
   Ⓑ She is looking forward to interning.
   Ⓒ She thinks that it is a very positive experience.
   Ⓓ She will be happy when she completes it.

5. What will the man probably do?

   Ⓐ He will make an appointment with his academic advisor.
   Ⓑ He will go to the Office of Career Development.
   Ⓒ He will apply for a job at the library.
   Ⓓ He will ask the woman to help him with his tests.

Independent Listening 2: "Admission"

Directions:

Choose the best answer for multiple-choice questions. Follow the directions on the page for computer-assisted questions.

6. Why does the student go to the admissions office?

    Ⓐ He is applying for financial aid.
    Ⓑ He is requesting an official transcript.
    Ⓒ He is transferring to another college.
    Ⓓ He is trying to enroll in classes.

7. What is missing from the student's file?

    Ⓐ A financial aid application.
    Ⓑ A transcript from County Community College.
    Ⓒ Grades from Regional College.
    Ⓓ An official copy of the application.

8. Listen again to part of the conversation. Then answer the question.

    "Oh, and you haven't been able to register for your courses here at State University because the computer shows that you are missing some of your application materials. Is that it?"

    Why does the woman say this:

    "Is that it?"

    Ⓐ She is asking the man to finish explaining the situation.
    Ⓑ She is confirming that she understands the problem.
    Ⓒ She is expressing impatience with the man's explanation.
    Ⓓ She is trying to comprehend a difficult question.

9. What does the woman suggest that the man do?

    Ⓐ Make a copy of his transcripts for his personal file.
    Ⓑ Complete all of the admissions forms as soon as possible.
    Ⓒ Change his provisional status to regular status before registering.
    Ⓓ Continue to request an official transcript from County Community College.

10. What will the student most probably do now?

    Ⓐ Return later in the day to see the woman in the Admissions Office.
    Ⓑ Go to the Office for Transfer Students to be assigned an advisor.
    Ⓒ Enter information in the computer to complete the application process.
    Ⓓ See the woman's superior to get a provisional admission to State University.

Independent Listening 3: "Groups"

Directions:
Choose the best answer for multiple-choice questions. Follow the directions on the page for computer-assisted questions.

11. What is the main topic of the talk?

    Ⓐ The problems inherent in group decisions.
    Ⓑ Ways that individuals become popular in groups.
    Ⓒ The influence of groups on individual behavior.
    Ⓓ The differences in social influence across cultures.

12. According to the professor, what two results were reported in the Asch and Abrams studies?

    Click on 2 answers.

    Ⓐ A larger group exerts significantly more pressure than a smaller group.
    Ⓑ Subjects conformed to group opinion in more than one-third of the trials.
    Ⓒ When the subject knows the group socially, there is greater pressure to conform.
    Ⓓ A majority opinion has as much influence as a unanimous opinion.

13. Listen again to part of the lecture. Then answer the question.

    "Later Asch manipulated the size of the control group . . . I'm sorry . . . the experimental group . . . to see whether group size would affect pressure, and it did, but probably less than you might expect."

    Why does the professor say this:

    "I'm sorry. The experimental group . . ."

    Ⓐ She regretted the result of the experiment.
    Ⓑ She knew that the students would not like the information.
    Ⓒ She needed to correct what she had said in a previous statement.
    Ⓓ She neglected to mention important facts.

14. What generally happens after a group makes a decision?

    Ⓐ Some group members regret their decision.
    Ⓑ At least one group member presents a new idea.
    Ⓒ As a whole, the group is even more united in its judgment.
    Ⓓ The popular group members compete for leadership.

15. Based on information in the lecture, indicate whether the statements describe the Asch study.

    For each sentence, click in the YES or NO column.

		YES	NO
A	Only one subject is being tested.		
B	The cards can be interpreted several ways.		
C	Some of the group collaborate with the experimenter.		

Independent Listening 4: "Photography"

Directions:
Choose the best answer for multiple-choice questions. Follow the directions on the page for computer-assisted questions.

16. What is the main topic of this lecture?

   Ⓐ The process of fixing a photograph.
   Ⓑ The problem of exposure time.
   Ⓒ The experiments by Louis Daguerre.
   Ⓓ The history of early photography.

17. According to the professor, what two limitations were noted in Daguerre's process for developing and fixing latent images?

   Click on 2 answers.

   Ⓐ The photograph disappeared after a few minutes.
   Ⓑ The images were very delicate and easily fell apart.
   Ⓒ Multiple images could not be made from the plate.
   Ⓓ The exposure time was still several hours long.

18. Listen again to part of the lecture. Then answer the question.

   "At first, he couldn't figure out why, but eventually, he concluded that this must have occurred as a result of mercury vapor from a broken thermometer that was also…enclosed in the cupboard. Supposedly, from this fortunate accident, he was able to invent a process for developing latent images on . . . exposed plates."

   Why does the professor say this:

   "Supposedly, from this fortunate accident, he was able to invent a process for developing latent images on . . . exposed plates."

   Ⓐ She is trying to generate interest in the topic.
   Ⓑ She makes reference to a story in the textbook.
   Ⓒ She is not certain that the account is true.
   Ⓓ She wants the students to use their imaginations.

19. What substance was first used to fix the images?

   Ⓐ Copper powder.
   Ⓑ Table salt.
   Ⓒ Mercury vapor.
   Ⓓ Hot water.

20. What can we assume about photographers in the 1800s?

   Ⓐ Most of them had originally been painters before they became interested in photography.
   Ⓑ Portrait photographers were in the highest demand since people wanted images of their families.
   Ⓒ There were only a few photographers who were willing to work in such a new profession.
   Ⓓ Some of them must have experienced health problems as a result of their laboratory work.

Independent Listening 5: "Authority"

Directions:
Choose the best answer for multiple-choice questions. Follow the directions on the page for computer-assisted questions.

21. What is the main purpose of this lecture?

    Ⓐ To discuss three types of authority.
    Ⓑ To distinguish between power and authority.
    Ⓒ To examine alternatives to Weber's model.
    Ⓓ To argue in favor of a legal rational system.

22. According to the professor, what two factors are associated with charismatic authority?

    Click on 2 answers.

    Ⓐ Sacred customs.
    Ⓑ An attractive leader.
    Ⓒ A social cause.
    Ⓓ Legal elections.

23. Listen again to part of the lecture. Then answer the question.

    "But what about power that is accepted by members of society as right and just, that is, legitimate power? Now we're talking about authority. And that is what I want to focus on today."

    Why does the professor say this:

    "But what about power that is accepted by members of society as right and just, that is, legitimate power?"

    Ⓐ He is asking the students to answer a question.
    Ⓑ He is introducing the topic of the lecture.
    Ⓒ He is expressing an opinion about the subject.
    Ⓓ He is reminding students of a previous point.

24. In an evolutionary model, how is rational legal authority viewed?

    Ⓐ The most modern form of authority.
    Ⓑ A common type of authority in the industrial age.
    Ⓒ Authority used by traditional leaders.
    Ⓓ A replacement for the three ideal types of authority.

25. What does the professor imply about the three types of authority?

    Ⓐ There is only one legitimate type of authority in modern societies.
    Ⓑ Sociologists do not agree about the development of the types of authority.
    Ⓒ Societies tend to select and retain one type of authority indefinitely.
    Ⓓ Weber's model explains why the social structure rejects power over time.

Independent Listening 6: "Mineral Exploitation"

Directions:

Choose the best answer for multiple-choice questions. Follow the directions on the page for computer-assisted questions.

26. What is the main topic of this lecture?

   Ⓐ How to exploit nonrenewable mineral resources.
   Ⓑ The exploitation of minerals in protected environments.
   Ⓒ Pollution as a by-product of mineral exploitation.
   Ⓓ The economic and environmental costs of exploiting minerals.

27. According to the professor, what are two problems that can be anticipated when roads are cut into an area for mining?

   Click on 2 answers.

   Ⓐ The labor is difficult to retain.
   Ⓑ The natural landscape is damaged.
   Ⓒ The roadbeds create waste piles.
   Ⓓ The ecosystem is disturbed.

28. Listen again to part of the lecture. Then answer the question.

   "And I was just thinking that in addition to the economic costs of the transportation for trucks and fuel and labor and everything, there could be, there might be some construction too, if there aren't any roads in and out of the area." "And that would mean . . ."

   Why does the professor say this:

   "And that would mean . . ."

   Ⓐ As encouragement for the student to give a more complete answer.
   Ⓑ Because he doesn't understand the student's answer.
   Ⓒ To give another student an opportunity to speak.
   Ⓓ For positive reinforcement of a correct answer.

29. What option is proposed as an alternative when all of the mineral resources in easily accessible locations have been depleted?

   Ⓐ Converting to nonrenewable resources.
   Ⓑ Concentrating on conservation of the resources.
   Ⓒ Developing synthetic resources to replace minerals.
   Ⓓ Using new technology to search the area again.

30. What does the professor imply about the environmental costs of mineral exploitation?

   Ⓐ He thinks that the environmental costs are less than the economic costs.
   Ⓑ He regrets that the environment is damaged during mineral exploitation.
   Ⓒ He opposes mineral exploitation when it is done close to urban areas.
   Ⓓ He believes in exploiting the reserves in national parks and historic reserves.

To check your answers for the Listening Section of Model Test 9, refer to the Answer Key on page 496. For an explanation of the answers, refer to the Explanatory Answers for Model Test 9 on pages 662–676.

Speaking Section

This is the Speaking Section of the Next Generation TOEFL Model Test. This section tests your ability to communicate in English in an academic context. During the test, you will respond to six speaking questions. You may take notes as you listen. You may use your notes to answer the questions. The reading passages and the questions are printed in the book, but most of the directions will be spoken. Your speaking will be evaluated on both the fluency of the language and the accuracy of the content. A clock on the screen will show you how much time you have to prepare your answer and how much time you have to record it.

Independent Speaking Question 1: "A Book"

Question:

Think about a book that you have enjoyed reading. Why did you like it? What was especially interesting about the book? Use specific details and examples to support your response.

Preparation Time: 15 seconds
Recording Time: 45 seconds

Independent Speaking Question 2: "Foreign Travel"

Question:

Some people think that it is better to travel as part of a tour group when they are visiting a foreign country. Other people prefer to make their own travel plans so that they can travel independently. Which approach do you think is better and why? Use specific reasons and examples to support your opinion.

Preparation Time: 15 seconds
Recording Time: 45 seconds

Integrated Speaking Question 3: "Old Main"

Reading Time: 45 seconds

Notice Concerning Old Main

The college will be celebrating the one-hundredth anniversary of the founding of the school by renovating Old Main, the original building. Two alternative plans are being considered. One plan would leave the outer structure intact and concentrate on electrical and plumbing upgrades as well as minor structural support. The other plan would demolish all of the building except the clock tower, which would form the centerpiece of a new structure. An open meeting is scheduled for Friday afternoon at three o'clock in the Old Main auditorium.

Question:

The professor expresses her opinion of the plan for the renovation of Old Main. Report her opinion and explain the reasons that she gives for having that opinion.

Preparation Time: 30 seconds
Recording Time: 60 seconds

Integrated Speaking Question 4: "Communication with Primates"

Reading Time: 45 seconds

Communication with Primates

Early experiments to teach primates to communicate with their voices failed because of the differences in their vocal organs, not their intellectual capacity. Dramatic progress was observed when researchers began to communicate by using American Sign Language. Some chimpanzees were able to learn several hundred signs that they put together to express a number of relationships similar to the initial language acquisition of children. In addition, success was achieved by using plastic symbols on a magnetic board, each of which represented a word. For example, a small blue triangle represented an apple. Chimpanzees were able to respond correctly to basic sequences and even to form some higher-level concepts by using the representative system.

Question:

Explain the importance of the Kanzi experiment in the context of research on primate communication.

Preparation Time: 30 seconds
Recording Time: 60 seconds

Integrated Speaking Question 5: "Headaches"

Question:
Describe the woman's problem and the two suggestions that her friend makes about how to handle it. What do you think the woman should do, and why?

Preparation Time: 20 seconds
Recording Time: 60 seconds

Integrated Speaking Question 6: "Fax Machines"

Question:
Using the main points and examples from the lecture, describe the three parts of a fax machine and then explain how the fax process works.

Preparation Time: 20 seconds
Recording Time: 60 seconds

To check your answers for the Speaking Section of Model Test 9, refer to the Checklists on page 496. For Example Answers, refer to the Explanatory Answers for Model Test 9 on pages 677–682.

Reading Section

This is the Reading Section of the Next Generation TOEFL Model Test. This section tests your ability to understand reading passages like those in college textbooks. There are three passages. After each passage, you will answer twelve or thirteen questions about it. Most questions are worth one point, but one question in each passage is worth more than one point. You will have 25 minutes to read each passage and answer the comprehension questions. You may take notes while you read. You may use your notes to answer the questions. Choose the best answer for multiple- choice questions. Follow the directions on the page or on the screen for computer-assisted questions. Click on **Next** to go to the next question. Click on **Back** to return to the previous question. You may return to previous questions in the same reading passage, but after you go to the next passage, you may not return to a previous passage. A clock on the screen will show you how much time you have to complete each passage.

Independent Reading 1: "Symbiotic Relationships"

Directions:
Choose the best answer for multiple-choice questions. Follow the directions on the page for computer-assisted questions.

Symbiosis is a close, long-lasting, physical relationship between two different species. In other words, the two species are usually in physical contact and at least one of them derives some sort of benefit from this contact. There are three different categories of symbiotic relationships: parasitism, commensalism, and mutualism.

Parasitism is a relationship in which one organism, known as the parasite, lives in or on another organism, known as the host, from which it derives nourishment. Generally, the parasite is much smaller than the host. Although the host is harmed by the interaction, it is generally not killed immediately by the parasite, and some host individuals may live a long time and be relatively little affected by their parasites. Some parasites are much more destructive than others, however. Newly established parasite/host relationships are likely to be more destructive than those that have a long evolutionary history. With a long-standing interaction between the parasite and the host, the two species generally evolve in such a way that they can accommodate one another. It is not in the parasite's best interest to kill its host. If it does, it must find another. Likewise, the host evolves defenses against the parasite, often reducing the harm done by the parasite to a level the host can tolerate.

Parasites that live on the surface of their hosts are known as **ectoparasites**. Fleas, lice, and some molds and mildews are examples of ectoparasites. Many other parasites, like tapeworms, malaria parasites, many kinds of bacteria, and some fungi are called **endoparasites** because they live inside the bodies of their hosts. A tapeworm lives in the intestines of its host where it is able to resist being digested and makes use of the nutrients in the intestine.

Even plants can be parasites. Mistletoe is a flowering plant that is parasitic on trees. It establishes itself on the surface of a tree when a bird transfers the seed to the tree. It then grows down into the water-conducting tissues of the tree and uses the water and minerals it obtains from these tissues to support its own growth.

If the relationship between organisms is one in which one organism benefits while the other is not affected, it is called **commensalism**. It is possible to visualize a parasitic relationship evolving into a commensal one. Since parasites generally evolve to do as little harm to their host as possible and the host is combating the negative effects of the parasite, they might eventually evolve to the point where the host is not harmed at all. There are many examples of commensal relationships. Many orchids use trees as a surface upon which to grow. The tree is not harmed or helped, but the orchid needs a surface upon which to establish itself and also benefits by being close to the top of the tree, where it can get more sunlight and rain. Some mosses, ferns, and many vines also make use of the surfaces of trees in this way.

In the ocean, many sharks have a smaller fish known as a remora attached to them. Remoras have a sucker on the top of their heads that they can use to attach to the shark. In this way, they can hitchhike a ride as the shark swims along. When the shark feeds, the remora frees itself and obtains small bits of food that the shark misses. Then, the remora reattaches. The shark does not appear to be positively or negatively affected by remoras.

Mutualism is another kind of symbiotic relationship and is actually beneficial to both species involved. In many mutualistic relationships, the relationship is obligatory; the species cannot live without each other. In others, the species can exist separately but are more successful when they are involved in a mutualistic relationship. Some species of *Acacia*, a thorny tree, provide food in the form of sugar solutions in little structures on their stems. Certain species of ants feed on the solutions and live in the tree, which they will protect from other animals by attacking any animal that begins to feed on the tree. Both organisms benefit; the ants receive food and a place to live, and the tree is protected from animals that would use it as food.

One soil nutrient that is usually a limiting factor for plant growth is nitrogen. Many kinds of plants, such as beans, clover, and alder trees, have bacteria that live in their roots in little nodules. The roots form these nodules when they are infected with certain kinds of bacteria. The bacteria do not cause disease but provide the plants with nitrogen-containing molecules that the plants can use for growth. The nitrogen-fixing bacteria benefit from the living site and nutrients that the plants provide, and the plants benefit from the nitrogen they receive.

Glossary:
sucker: an adaptation for sucking nourishment or sticking to a surface
nodules: growths in the form of knots

Question References: "Symbiotic Relationships"

Symbiosis is a close, long-lasting, physical relationship between two different species. In other words, the two species are usually in physical contact and at least one of them derives some sort of benefit from this contact. There are three different categories of symbiotic relationships: parasitism, commensalism, and mutualism.

Parasitism is a relationship in which one organism, known as the parasite, lives in or on another organism, known as the host, from which it derives nourishment. Generally, the parasite is much smaller than the host. Although the host is harmed by the interaction, it is generally not killed immediately by the parasite, and some host individuals may live a long time and be relatively little affected by their parasites. Some parasites are much more destructive than others, however. Newly established parasite/host relationships are likely to be more destructive than those that have a long evolutionary history. With a long-standing interaction between the parasite and the host, the two species generally evolve in such a way that they can accommodate one another. It is not in the parasite's best interest to kill its host. If it does, it must find another. Likewise, the host evolves defenses against the parasite, often reducing the harm done by the parasite to a level the host can tolerate.

Parasites that live on the surface of their hosts are known as **ectoparasites**. Fleas, lice, and some molds and mildews are examples of ectoparasites. [A] Many other parasites, like tapeworms, malaria parasites, many kinds of bacteria, and some fungi are called **endoparasites** because they live inside the bodies of their hosts. [B] A tapeworm lives in the intestines of its host where it is able to resist being digested and makes use of the nutrients in the intestine. [C]

Even plants can be parasites. Mistletoe is a flowering plant that is parasitic on trees. It establishes itself on the surface of a tree when a bird transfers the seed to the tree. It then grows down into the water-conducting tissues of the tree and uses the water and minerals it obtains from these tissues to support its own growth. [D]

If the relationship between organisms is one in which one organism benefits while the other is not affected, it is called **commensalism**. It is possible to visualize a parasitic relationship evolving into a commensal one. Since parasites generally evolve to do as little harm to their host as possible and the host is combating the negative effects of the parasite, they might eventually evolve to the point where the host is not harmed at all. There are many examples of commensal relationships. Many orchids use trees as a surface upon which to grow. The tree is not harmed or helped, but the orchid needs a surface upon which to establish itself and also benefits by being close to the top of the tree, where it can get more sunlight and rain. Some mosses, ferns, and many vines also make use of the surfaces of trees in this way.

In the ocean, many sharks have a smaller fish known as a remora attached to them. Remoras have a sucker on the top of their heads that they can use to attach to the shark. In this way, they can hitchhike a ride as the shark swims along. When the shark feeds, the remora frees itself and obtains small bits of food that the shark misses. Then, the remora reattaches. The shark does not appear to be positively or negatively affected by remoras.

Mutualism is another kind of symbiotic relationship and is actually beneficial to both species involved. In many mutualistic relationships, the relationship is obligatory; the species cannot live without each other. In others, the species can exist separately but are more successful when they are involved in a mutualistic relationship. Some species of *Acacia*, a thorny tree, provide food in the form of sugar solutions in little structures on their stems. Certain species of ants feed on the solutions and live in the tree, which they will protect from other animals by attacking any animal that begins to feed on the tree. Both organisms benefit; the ants receive food and a place to live, and the tree is protected from animals that would use it as food.

One soil nutrient that is usually a limiting factor for plant growth is nitrogen. Many kinds of plants, such as beans, clover, and alder trees, have bacteria that live in their roots in little nodules. The roots form these nodules when they are infected with certain kinds of bacteria. The bacteria do not cause disease but provide the plants with nitrogen-containing molecules that the plants can use for growth. The nitrogen-fixing bacteria benefit from the living site and nutrients that the plants provide, and the plants benefit from the nitrogen they receive.

Glossary:
sucker: an adaptation for sucking nourishment or sticking to a surface
nodules: growths in the form of knots

1. The word derives in the passage is closest in meaning to

   Ⓐ requests
   Ⓑ pursues
   Ⓒ obtains
   Ⓓ rejects

2. The word it in the passage refers to

   Ⓐ host
   Ⓑ organism
   Ⓒ parasite
   Ⓓ relationship

3. The word relatively in the passage is closest in meaning to

   Ⓐ comparatively
   Ⓑ routinely
   Ⓒ adversely
   Ⓓ frequently

4. Which of the sentences below best expresses the information in the highlighted statement in the passage? The other choices change the meaning or leave out important information.

   Ⓐ A parasite is less likely to destroy the host when it attaches itself at first.

   Ⓑ Parasites that have lived on a host for a long time have probably done a lot of damage.

   Ⓒ The most destructive phase for a host is when the parasite first invades it.

   Ⓓ The relationship between a parasite and a host will evolve over time.

5. The word tolerate in the passage is closest in meaning to

   Ⓐ permit

   Ⓑ oppose

   Ⓒ profit

   Ⓓ avoid

6. According to paragraph 3, how do ectoparasites survive?

   Ⓐ They live in mold and mildew on their hosts.

   Ⓑ They digest food in the intestines of their hosts.

   Ⓒ They live on the nutrients in their bacterial hosts.

   Ⓓ They inhabit the outside parts of their hosts.

7. Which of the following is mentioned as an example of a commensal relationship?

   Ⓐ Orchids

   Ⓑ Mistletoe

   Ⓒ Ants

   Ⓓ Fungus

8. The word actually in the passage is closest in meaning to

   Ⓐ frequently

   Ⓑ initially

   Ⓒ really

   Ⓓ usually

9. In paragraph 7, why does the author use the example of the *Acacia* tree?

   Ⓐ To demonstrate how ants survive by living in trees

   Ⓑ To explain how two species can benefit from contact

   Ⓒ To show the relationship between plants and animals

   Ⓓ To present a problem that occurs often in nature

10. How does bacteria affect beans and clover?

   Ⓐ It causes many of the plants to die.

   Ⓑ It limits the growth of young plants.

   Ⓒ It supplies nitrogen to the crops.

   Ⓓ It infects the roots with harmful nodules.

11. Four squares (☐) indicate where the following sentence can be added to the passage.

    They live on the feathers of birds or the fur of animals.

    Where would the sentence best fit into the passage?

12. In which of the following chapters would this passage most probably appear?

    Ⓐ Environment and Organisms
    Ⓑ Pollution and Policies
    Ⓒ Human Influences on Ecosystems
    Ⓓ Energy Resources

13. Complete a summary of the passage by choosing THREE answer choices that express the most important ideas. The other three sentences do not belong in the summary because they express ideas that are not in the passage or they are minor points that are not as important as the three major points. *This question is worth 2 points.*

    What are the categories of relationships between species?

    Ⓐ In commensalism, one species benefits, and the other is not affected.
    Ⓑ Mistletoe is a flowering plant that establishes a parasitic relationship on trees.
    Ⓒ A mutualistic relationship allows both species to benefit from their contact.
    Ⓓ Bacteria provides plants with nitrogen while deriving nutrients from the plants.
    Ⓔ Parasites live and feed in or on another organism referred to as a host.
    Ⓕ Sharks and remora enjoy a commensal relationship in which the shark is not harmed.

Independent Reading 2: "Civilization"

Directions:
Choose the best answer for multiple-choice questions. Follow the directions on the page for computer-assisted questions.

Between 4000 and 3000 B.C., significant technical developments began to transform the Neolithic towns. The invention of writing enabled records to be kept, and the use of metals marked a new level of human control over the environment and its resources. Already before 4000 B.C., craftspeople had discovered that metal-bearing rocks could be heated to liquefy metals, which could then be cast in molds to produce tools and weapons that were more useful than stone instruments. Although copper was the first metal to be utilized in producing tools, after 4000 B.C., craftspeople in western Asia discovered that a combination of copper and tin produced bronze, a much harder and more durable metal than copper. Its widespread use has led historians to speak of a Bronze Age from around 3000 to 1200 B.C., when bronze was increasingly replaced by iron.

At first, Neolithic settlements were hardly more than villages. But as their inhabitants mastered the art of farming, they gradually began to give birth to more complex human societies. As wealth increased, such societies began to develop armies and to build walled cities. By the beginning of the Bronze Age, the concentration of larger numbers of people in the river valleys of Mesopotamia and Egypt was leading to a whole new pattern for human life.

As we have seen, early human beings formed small groups that developed a simple culture that enabled them to survive. As human societies grew and developed greater complexity, a new form of human existence—called civilization—came into being. A civilization is a complex culture in which large numbers of human beings share a number of common elements. Historians have identified a number of basic characteristics of civilizations, most of which are evident in the Mesopotamian and Egyptian civilizations. These include (1) an urban revolution: cities became the focal points for political, economic, social, cultural, and religious development; (2) a distinct religious structure: the gods were deemed crucial to the community's success, and professional priestly classes, as stewards of the gods' property, regulated relations with the gods; (3) new political and military structures: an organized government bureaucracy arose to meet the administrative demands of the growing population while armies were organized to gain land and power; (4) a new social structure based on economic power: while kings and an upper class of priests, political leaders, and warriors dominated, there also existed a large group of free people (farmers, artisans, craftspeople) and at the very bottom, socially, a class of slaves; (5) the development of writing: kings, priests, merchants, and artisans used writing to keep records; and (6) new forms of significant artistic and intellectual activity, such as monumental architectural structures, usually religious, occupied a prominent place in urban environments.

Why early civilizations developed remains difficult to explain. Since civilizations developed independently in India, China, Mesopotamia, and Egypt, can general causes be identified that would explain why all of these civilizations emerged? A number of possible explanations of the beginning of civilization have been suggested. A theory of challenge and response maintains that challenges forced human beings to make efforts that resulted in the rise of civilization. Some scholars have adhered to a material explanation. Material forces, such as the growth of food surpluses, made possible the specialization of labor and development of large communities with bureaucratic organization. But the area of the Fertile Crescent, in which Mesopotamian civilization emerged, was not naturally conducive to agriculture. Abundant food could only be produced with a massive human effort to carefully manage the water, an effort that created the need for organization and bureaucratic control and led to civilized cities. Some historians have argued that nonmaterial forces, primarily religious, provided the sense of unity and purpose that made such organized activities possible. Finally, some scholars doubt that we are capable of ever discovering the actual causes of early civilization.

Question References: "Civilization"

Between 4000 and 3000 B.C., significant technical developments began to transform the Neolithic towns. The invention of writing enabled records to be kept, and the use of metals marked a new level of human control over the environment and its resources. Already before 4000 B.C., craftspeople had discovered that metal-bearing rocks could be heated to liquefy metals, which could then be cast in molds to produce tools and weapons that were more useful than stone instruments. Although copper was the first metal to be utilized in producing tools, after 4000 B.C., craftspeople in western Asia discovered that a combination of copper and tin produced bronze, a much harder and more durable metal than copper. Its widespread use has led historians to speak of a Bronze Age from around 3000 to 1200 B.C., when bronze was increasingly replaced by iron.

At first, Neolithic settlements were hardly more than villages. But as their inhabitants mastered the art of farming, they gradually began to give birth to more complex human societies. As wealth increased, such societies began to develop armies and to build walled cities. By the beginning of the Bronze Age, the concentration of larger numbers of people in the river valleys of Mesopotamia and Egypt was leading to a whole new pattern for human life.

As we have seen, early human beings formed small groups that developed a simple culture that enabled them to survive. As human societies grew and developed greater complexity, a new form of human existence—called civilization—came into being. A civilization is a complex culture in which large numbers of human beings share a number of common elements. Historians have identified a number of basic characteristics of civilizations, most of which are evident in the Mesopotamian and Egyptian civilizations. These include (1) an urban revolution: cities became the focal points for political, economic, social, cultural, and religious development; (2) a distinct religious structure: the gods were deemed crucial to the community's success, and professional priestly classes, as stewards of the gods' property, regulated relations with the gods; (3) new political and military structures: an organized government bureaucracy arose to meet the administrative demands of the growing population while armies were organized to gain land and power; (4) a new social structure based on economic power: while kings and an upper class of priests, political leaders, and warriors dominated, there also existed a large group of free people (farmers, artisans, craftspeople) and at the very bottom, socially, a class of slaves; (5) the development of writing: kings, priests, merchants, and artisans used writing to keep records; and (6) new forms of significant artistic and intellectual activity, such as monumental architectural structures, usually religious, occupied a prominent place in urban environments.

Why early civilizations developed remains difficult to explain. [A] Since civilizations developed independently in India, China, Mesopotamia, and Egypt, can general causes be identified that would explain why all of these civilizations emerged? [B] A number of possible explanations of the beginning of civilization have been suggested. C A theory of challenge and response maintains that challenges forced human beings to make efforts that resulted in the rise of civilization. Some scholars have adhered to a material explanation. D Material forces, such as the growth of food surpluses, made possible the specialization of labor and development of large communities with bureaucratic organization. But the area of the Fertile Crescent, in which Mesopotamian civilization emerged, was not naturally conducive to agriculture. Abundant food could only be produced with a massive human effort to carefully manage the water, an effort that created the need for organization and bureaucratic control and led to civilized cities. Some historians have argued that nonmaterial forces, primarily religious, provided the sense of unity and purpose that made such organized activities possible. Finally, some scholars doubt that we are capable of ever discovering the actual causes of early civilization.

1. Which of the following is the best definition of a civilization?

   Ⓐ Neolithic towns and cities
   Ⓑ Types of complex cultures
   Ⓒ An agricultural community
   Ⓓ Large population centers

2. The word its in the passage refers to

   Ⓐ copper
   Ⓑ bronze
   Ⓒ metal
   Ⓓ iron

3. According to paragraph 2, what happens as societies become more prosperous?

   Ⓐ More goods are produced.
   Ⓑ Walled cities are built.
   Ⓒ Laws are instituted.
   Ⓓ The size of families is increased.

4. The word hardly in the passage is closest in meaning to

   Ⓐ frequently
   Ⓑ likely
   Ⓒ barely
   Ⓓ obviously

5. Why does the author mention Neolithic towns?

   Ⓐ To give an example of a civilization
   Ⓑ To explain the invention of writing systems
   Ⓒ To argue that they should be classified as villages
   Ⓓ To contrast them with the civilizations that evolved

6. According to paragraph 3, how was the class system structured?

    Ⓐ There was an upper class and a lower class.
    Ⓑ There were slaves, free people, and a ruling class.
    Ⓒ There was a king, an army, and slaves.
    Ⓓ There were intellectuals and uneducated farmers and workers.

7. Which of the sentences below best expresses the information in the highlighted statement in the passage? The other choices change the meaning or leave out important information.

    Ⓐ Mesopotamian and Egyptian civilizations exhibit the majority of the characteristics identified by historians.
    Ⓑ The characteristics that historians have identified are not found in the Egyptian and Mesopotamian cultures.
    Ⓒ Civilizations in Mesopotamia and Egypt were identified by historians who were studying the characteristics of early cultures.
    Ⓓ The identification of most historical civilizations includes either Egypt or Mesopotamia on the list.

8. The word crucial in the passage is closest in meaning to

    Ⓐ fundamental
    Ⓑ arbitrary
    Ⓒ disruptive
    Ⓓ suitable

9. The word prominent in the passage is closest in meaning to

    Ⓐ weak
    Ⓑ important
    Ⓒ small
    Ⓓ new

10. According to paragraph 4, how can the independent development of civilization in different geographic regions be explained?

    Ⓐ Scholars agree that food surpluses encouraged populations to be concentrated in certain areas.
    Ⓑ There are several theories that explain the rise of civilization in the ancient world.
    Ⓒ The model of civilization was probably carried from one region to another along trade routes.
    Ⓓ Historians attribute the emergence of early cities at about the same time as a coincidence.

11. All of the following are cited as reasons why civilizations developed EXCEPT

    Ⓐ Religious practices unified the population.
    Ⓑ The management of water required organization.
    Ⓒ A major climate change made living in groups necessary.
    Ⓓ Extra food resulted in the expansion of population centers.

12. Four squares (☐) indicate where the following sentence can be added to the passage.

Some historians believe they can be established.

Where would the sentence best fit into the passage?

13. Complete a summary of the passage by choosing THREE answer choices that express the most important ideas. The other three sentences do not belong in the summary because they express ideas that are not in the passage or they are minor points that are not as important as the three major points. *This question is worth 2 points.*

What are some of the qualities that define a civilization?

Ⓐ Free citizens who work in professions for pay
Ⓑ Bureaucracies for the government and armies
Ⓒ Libraries to house art and written records
Ⓓ A strategic location near rivers or the sea
Ⓔ Organized religion, writing, and art
Ⓕ A densely populated group with a class structure

Independent Reading 3: "The Scientific Method"

Directions:
Choose the best answer for multiple-choice questions. Follow the directions on the page for computer-assisted questions.

In brief, the modern **scientific method** is an organized approach to explaining observed facts, with a model of nature, subject to the constraint that any proposed model must be testable and the provision that the model must be modified or discarded if it fails these tests.

In its most idealized form, the scientific method begins with a set of observed facts. A fact is supposed to be a statement that is objectively true. For example, we consider it a fact that the Sun rises each morning, that the planet Mars appeared in a particular place in our sky last night, and that the Earth rotates. Facts are not always obvious, as illustrated by the case of the Earth's rotation. For most of human history, the Earth was assumed to be stationary at the center of the universe. In addition, our interpretations of facts often are based on beliefs about the world that others might not share. For example, when we say that the Sun rises each morning, we assume that it is the same Sun day after day—an idea that might not have been accepted by ancient Egyptians, whose mythology held that the Sun died with every sunset and was reborn with every sunrise. Nevertheless, facts are the raw material that scientific models seek to explain, so it is important that scientists agree on the facts. In the context of science, a fact must therefore be something that anyone can verify for himself or herself, at least in principle.

Once the facts have been collected, a model can be proposed to explain them. A useful model must also make predictions that can be tested through further observations or experiments. Ptolemy's model of the universe was useful because it predicted future locations of the Sun, Moon, and planets in the sky. However, although the Ptolemaic model remained in use for nearly 1,500 years, eventually it became clear that its predictions didn't quite match actual observations—a key reason why the Earth-centered model of the universe finally was discarded.

In summary, the idealized scientific method proceeds as follows:

- *Observation*: The scientific method begins with the collection of a set of observed facts.
- *Hypothesis*: A model is proposed to explain the observed facts and to make new predictions. A proposed model is often called a **hypothesis**, which essentially means an *educated guess*.
- *Further observations/experiments*: The model's predictions are tested through further observations or experiments. When a prediction is verified, we gain confidence that the model truly represents nature. When a prediction fails, we recognize that the model is flawed, and we therefore must refine or discard the model.
- *Theory*: A model must be continually challenged with new observations or experiments by many different scientists. A model achieves the status of a scientific theory only after a broad range of its predictions has been repeatedly verified. Note that, while we can have great confidence that a scientific theory truly represents nature, we can never prove a theory to be true *beyond all doubt*. Therefore, even well-established theories must be subject to continuing challenges through further observations and experiments.

In reality, scientific discoveries rarely are made by a process as mechanical as the idealized scientific method described here. For example, Johannes Kepler, who discovered the laws of planetary motion in the early 1600s, tested his model against observations that had been made previously, rather than verifying new predictions based on his model. Moreover, like most scientific work, Kepler's work involved intuition, collaboration with others, moments of insight, and luck. Nevertheless, with hindsight we can look back at Kepler's theory and see that other scientists eventually made plenty of observations to verify the planetary positions predicted by his model. In that sense, the scientific method represents an ideal prescription for judging objectively whether a proposed model of nature is close to the truth.

Question References: "The Scientific Method"

In brief, the modern **scientific method** is an organized approach to explaining observed facts, with a model of nature, subject to the constraint that any proposed model must be testable and the provision that the model must be modified or discarded if it fails these tests.

In its most idealized form, the scientific method begins with a set of observed facts. ⟦A⟧ A fact is supposed to be a statement that is objectively true. For example, we consider it a fact that the Sun rises each morning, that the planet Mars appeared in a particular place in our sky last night, and that the Earth rotates. Facts are not always obvious, as illustrated by the case of the Earth's rotation. For most of human history, the Earth was assumed to be stationary at the center of the universe. ⟦B⟧ In addition, our interpretations of facts often are based on beliefs about the world that others might not share. For example, when we say that the Sun rises each morning, we assume that it is the same Sun day after day—an idea that might not have been accepted by ancient Egyptians, whose mythology held that the Sun died with every sunset and was reborn with every sunrise. [C] Nevertheless, facts are the raw material that scientific models seek to explain, so it is important that scientists agree on the facts. [D] In the context of science, a fact must therefore be something that anyone can verify for himself or herself, at least in principle.

Once the facts have been collected, a model can be proposed to explain them. A useful model must also make predictions that can be tested through further observations or experiments. Ptolemy's model of the universe was useful because it predicted future locations of the Sun, Moon, and planets in the sky. However, although the Ptolemaic model remained in use for nearly 1,500 years, eventually it became clear that its predictions didn't quite match actual observations—a key reason why the Earth-centered model of the universe finally was discarded.

In summary, the idealized scientific method proceeds as follows:

- *Observation*: The scientific method begins with the collection of a set of observed facts.
- *Hypothesis*: A model is proposed to explain the observed facts and to make new predictions. A proposed model is often called a **hypothesis**, which essentially means an *educated guess*.
- *Further observations/experiments*: The model's predictions are tested through further observations or experiments. When a prediction is verified, we gain confidence that the model truly represents nature. When a prediction fails, we recognize that the model is flawed, and we therefore must refine or discard the model.
- *Theory*: A model must be continually challenged with new observations or experiments by many different scientists. A model achieves the status of a scientific theory only after a broad range of its predictions has been repeatedly verified. Note that, while we can have great confidence that a scientific theory truly represents nature, we can never prove a theory to be true *beyond all doubt*. Therefore, even well-established theories must be subject to continuing challenges through further observations and experiments.

In reality, scientific discoveries rarely are made by a process as mechanical as the idealized scientific method described here. For example, Johannes Kepler, who discovered the laws of planetary motion in the early 1600s, tested his model against observations that had been made previously, rather than verifying new predictions based on his model. Moreover, like most scientific work, Kepler's work involved intuition, collaboration with others, moments of insight, and luck. Nevertheless, with hindsight we can look back at Kepler's theory and see that other scientists eventually made plenty of observations to verify the planetary positions predicted by his model. In that sense, the scientific method represents an ideal prescription for judging objectively whether a proposed model of nature is close to the truth.

1. The word obvious in the passage is closest in meaning to

    Ⓐ interesting
    Ⓑ clear
    Ⓒ simple
    Ⓓ correct

2. Why did the author give the example of the ancient Egyptians in paragraph 2?

    Ⓐ To explain the rotation of the Earth and the Sun
    Ⓑ To prove that facts may be interpreted differently across cultures
    Ⓒ To present a fact that can be verified by the reader
    Ⓓ To discard a model that was widely accepted

3. The word essentially in the passage is closest in meaning to

    Ⓐ obviously
    Ⓑ occasionally
    Ⓒ basically
    Ⓓ oddly

4. The word flawed in the passage is closest in meaning to

    Ⓐ not perfect
    Ⓑ not modern
    Ⓒ not routine
    Ⓓ not accepted

5. Which of the sentences below best expresses the information in the highlighted statement in the passage? The other choices change the meaning or leave out important information.

    Ⓐ An ideal form of the scientific method is explained in this passage.
    Ⓑ Making a discovery by using an ideal form of the scientific method is unusual.
    Ⓒ The description of the scientific method is a mechanical process.
    Ⓓ Here is an idealized description of the scientific process for scientific discovery.

6. According to paragraph 3, why was the Ptolemaic model replaced?

    Ⓐ The model was not useful in forecasting the movement of the Sun.
    Ⓑ The predictions did not conform to observations of the universe.
    Ⓒ The Ptolemaic model had been in use for about 1,500 years.
    Ⓓ Most scientists believed that the Earth was the center of the universe.

7. According to paragraph 4, theories that are generally accepted

    Ⓐ must still be verified
    Ⓑ have several models
    Ⓒ can be unscientific
    Ⓓ are very simple

8. According to paragraph 5, what did Kepler do to verify his theory of planetary motion?

    Ⓐ He made predictions based on the model.
    Ⓑ He asked other scientists to make predictions.
    Ⓒ He used prior observations to test the model.
    Ⓓ He relied on insight to verify the theory.

9. The word plenty in the passage is closest in meaning to

  Ⓐ broad
  Ⓑ reliable
  Ⓒ detailed
  Ⓓ numerous

10. All of the following statements are part of a definition of the term *fact* EXCEPT

  Ⓐ A fact is objectively true.
  Ⓑ A fact can be verified.
  Ⓒ A fact may be interpreted.
  Ⓓ A fact must be comprehensible.

11. It may be concluded from information in this passage that a model

  Ⓐ does not always reflect observations
  Ⓑ is not subject to change like theories are
  Ⓒ is considered true without doubt
  Ⓓ does not require further experimentation

12. Four squares (☐) indicate where the following sentence can be added to the passage.

  Clearly, cultural orientation will influence the way that scientists will explain their observations.

  Where would the sentence best fit into the passage?

13. Complete a summary of the passage by choosing THREE answer choices that express the most important ideas. The other three sentences do not belong in the summary because they express ideas that are not in the passage or they are minor points that are not as important as the three major points. ***This question is worth 2 points.***

  What are the three basic steps in the scientific method?

  Ⓐ Observational data collection
  Ⓑ Proof without question
  Ⓒ The testing of a hypothesis
  Ⓓ Intuitive discoveries
  Ⓔ A model that supports predictions
  Ⓕ The general approval of a paradigm

To check your answers for the Reading Section of Model Test 9, refer to the Answer Key on page 497. For an explanation of the answers, refer to the Explanatory Answers for Model Test 9 on pages 683–685.

Writing Section

This is the Writing Section of the Next Generation TOEFL Model Test. This section tests your ability to write essays in English. During the test, you will write two essays. The independent essay usually asks for your opinion about a familiar topic. The integrated essay asks for your response to an academic reading passage, a lecture, or both. You may take notes as you read and listen. You may use your notes to write the essays. If a lecture is included, it will be spoken, but the directions and the questions will be written. A clock on the screen will show you how much time you have to complete each essay.

<u>Independent Writing: "Study in the United States"</u>

Directions:
You have 30 minutes to plan, write, and revise your essay. Typically, a good response will require that you write a minimum of 300 words.

Question:
You are planning to study in the United States. What do you think you will like and dislike about this experience? Why? Use specific reasons and details to support your answer.

Notes

Use this space for essay notes only. Work done on this work sheet will *not* be scored.

Essay

Integrated Writing: "Problem Solving"

Directions:
You have 20 minutes to plan, write and revise your response to a reading passage and a lecture on the same topic. First, read the passage below and take notes. Then, listen to the lecture and take notes. Finally, write your response to the writing question. Typically, a good response will require that you write 200–250 words.

Solving a problem can be broken down into several steps. First, the problem must be identified correctly. Psychologists refer to this step as *problem representation*. For many problems, figuring out which information is relevant and which is extraneous can be difficult and can interfere with arriving at a good solution. Clearly, before a problem can be solved, it must be obvious what the problem is, however, this is not as easy as it might seem. One obstacle to efficient problem representation is *functional fixedness*, that is, allowing preconceived notions and even prejudices to color the facts. Most people tend to see objects and events in certain fixed ways, and by being inflexible in viewing the problem, they may be unable to notice the tools for the solution. Once the problem is identified accurately, however, the second step consists of considering the alternatives for a solution. A common way to evaluate alternatives is to write them down and then make a list of advantages and disadvantages for each solution. Here again, people may be limited by prior experiences. Often people adopt *mental sets* that lead them to the same problem-solving strategies that were successful for problems in the past. Although that can be helpful most of the time, sometimes a new situation requires a different strategy. In that case, the mental set must be abandoned, and new alternatives must be explored. This can be a difficult adjustment for some people.

After the alternatives have been compared, a strategy must be selected from among them. One way to avoid becoming mired in the options is to try the best option with a view to abandoning it for another if the results are unfavorable. This attitude allows many people to move on expeditiously to the next step—action. The strategy selected must be implemented and tested. If it solves the problem, no further action is necessary, but if not, then an unsuccessful solution may actually lead to a more successful option. If the solution is still not apparent, then the cycle begins again, starting with problem identification. By continuing to review the problem and repeat the problem-solving steps, the solution can be improved upon and refined.

Question:
Summarize the main points in the lecture, referring to the way that they relate to the reading passage.

Notes

Use this space for essay notes only. Work done on this work sheet will *not* be scored.

To check your answers for the Writing Section of Model Test 9, refer to the Answer Key on page 497. For Example Answers, refer to the Explanatory Answers for Model Test 9 on pages 685–687.

Essay

ANSWER KEYS

ANSWER KEYS

ANSWER KEY—EXERCISES FOR STRUCTURE

Patterns

Problem		Part A	Part B	Problem		Part A	Part B
Problem	1	(A)	(A) have	Problem	26	(A)	(A) The philosophy
Problem	2	(C)	(A) to evolve	Problem	27	(D)	(B) no
Problem	3	(D)	(B) smoking	Problem	28	(C)	(A) Most of *or*
Problem	4	(D)	(B) permitting				Almost all of
Problem	5	(C)	(A) saw	Problem	29	(C)	(A) Sex education
Problem	6	(A)	(B) turns *or* will turn	Problem	30	(A)	(B) four-stage
Problem	7	(A)	(C) will have to pay	Problem	31	(A)	(B) so expensive
			or may have to pay	Problem	32	(B)	(B) the same
Problem	8	(A)	(C) unless they	Problem	33	(C)	(D) like
			complete	Problem	34	(A)	(B) differ from *or* are
Problem	9	(D)	(B) be used				different from
Problem	10	(B)	(A) be	Problem	35	(C)	(A) as much as
Problem	11	(B)	(B) for making *or* to	Problem	36	(A)	(A) more than
			make	Problem	37	(C)	(C) as many as
Problem	12	(C)	(C) measured	Problem	38	(C)	(B) most
Problem	13	(A)	(A) It is believed	Problem	39	(C)	(B) worse
Problem	14	(D)	(C) will have	Problem	40	(C)	(A) the more intense
			succeeded	Problem	41	(A)	(B) like that of
Problem	15	(B)	(B) is losing				England
Problem	16	(B)	(D) should be	Problem	42	(B)	(B) besides
			discontinued	Problem	43	(C)	(C) because
Problem	17	(A)	(D) for them	Problem	44	(D)	(D) also easy to
Problem	18	(A)	(A) which				install
Problem	19	(C)	(C) eight or ten	Problem	45	(B)	(D) complete
			computers	Problem	46	(D)	(C) the plane is
Problem	20	(C)	(A) Religion	Problem	47	(B)	(B) does the same
Problem	21	(B)	(A) Space				major league
Problem	22	(C)	(A) Progress				baseball team
Problem	23	(B)	(C) pieces of				win
			equipment	Problem	48	(C)	(A) since 1930
Problem	24	(C)	(A) Spelling *or* To	Problem	49	(C)	(B) as a whole
			spell	Problem	50	(B)	(B) ~~that~~
Problem	25	(B)	(A) ~~it is~~				

Style

Problem		Part A	Part B
Problem	1	**(C)**	**(C)** were
Problem	2	**(C)**	**(B)** gave
Problem	3	**(B)**	**(B)** enables
Problem	4	**(C)**	**(A)** is
Problem	5	**(B)**	**(A)** There are
Problem	6	**(D)**	**(D)** its
Problem	7	**(B)**	**(C)** their
Problem	8	**(B)**	**(A)** Having designed
Problem	9	**(D)**	**(C)** find
Problem	10	**(C)**	**(B)** to develop
Problem	11	**(B)**	**(D)** to use as currency
Problem	12	**(B)**	**(B)** rapidly
Problem	13	**(B)**	**(A)** an old one *or* an ancient one
Problem	14	**(C)**	**(A)** ~~it~~
Problem	15	**(B)**	**(A)** raised
Problem	16	**(C)**	**(A)** lies
Problem	17	**(B)**	**(B)** sits
Problem	18	**(B)**	**(C)** do
Problem	19	**(A)**	**(B)** depends on
Problem	20	**(B)**	**(B)** differ

ANSWER KEY—EXERCISES FOR READING

Problem 1. Previewing

A black hole is a region of space created by the total gravitational collapse of matter. It is so intense that nothing, not even light or radiation, can escape. In other words, it is a one-way surface through which matter can fall inward but cannot emerge.

Some astronomers believe that a black hole may be formed when a large star collapses inward from its own weight. So long as they are emitting heat and light into space, stars support themselves against their own gravitational pull with the outward thermal pressure generated by heat from nuclear reactions deep in their interiors. But if a star eventually exhausts its nuclear fuel, then its unbalanced gravitational attraction could cause it to contract and collapse. Furthermore, it could begin to pull in surrounding matter, including nearby comets and planets, creating a black hole.

The topic is black holes.

Problem 2. Reading for Main Ideas

For more than a century, despite attacks by a few opposing scientists, Charles Darwin's theory of evolution by natural selection has stood firm. Now, however, some respected biologists are beginning to question whether the theory accounts for major developments such as the shift from water to land habitation. Clearly, evolution has not proceeded steadily but has progressed by radical advances. Recent research in molecular biology, particularly in the study of DNA, provides us with a new possibility. Not only environmental changes but also genetic codes in the underlying structure of DNA could govern evolution.

*The main idea is that biologists are beginning to question
Darwin's theory.
A good title would be "Questions about Darwin's Theory."*

Problem 3. Using Contexts for Vocabulary

1. *To auction* means to sell.

2. *Proprietor* means an owner.

3. *Formerly* means in the past.

4. *To sample* means to try or to taste.

5. *Royalty* means payment.

Problem 4. Scanning for Details

To prepare for a career in engineering, a student must begin planning in high school. Mathematics and science should form the core curriculum. For example, in a school where sixteen credit hours are required for high school graduation, four should be in mathematics, one each in chemistry, biology, and physics. The remaining credits should include four in English and at least three in the humanities and social sciences. The average entering freshman in engineering should have achieved at least a 2.5 grade point average on a 4.0 scale in his or her high school. Although deficiencies can be corrected during the first year, the student who needs additional work should expect to spend five instead of four years to complete a degree.

1. What is the average grade point for an entering freshman in engineering?

2.5

2. When should a student begin planning for a career in engineering?

in high school

3. How can a student correct deficiencies in preparation?

by spending five years

4. How many credits should a student have in English?

four

5. How many credits are required for a high school diploma?

sixteen

Problem 5. Making Inferences

When an acid is dissolved in water, the acid molecule divides into two parts, a hydrogen ion and another ion. An ion is an atom or a group of atoms which has an electrical charge. The charge can be either positive or negative. If hydrochloric acid is mixed with water, for example, it divides into hydrogen ions and chlorine ions.

A strong acid ionizes to a great extent, but a weak acid does not ionize so much. The strength of an acid, therefore, depends on how much it ionizes, not on how many hydrogen ions are produced. It is interesting that nitric acid and sulfuric acid become greatly ionized whereas boric acid and carbonic acid do not.

1. What kind of acid is sulfuric acid?

A strong acid ionizes to a great extent, and sulfuric acid becomes greatly ionized.
Conclusion: Sulfuric acid is a strong acid.

2. What kind of acid is boric acid?

A weak acid does not ionize so much and boric acid does not ionize greatly.
Conclusion: Boric acid is a weak acid.

Problem 6. Identifying Exceptions

All music consists of two elements—expression and design. Expression is inexact and subjective, and may be enjoyed in a personal or instinctive way. Design, on the other hand is exact and must be analyzed objectively in order to be understood and appreciated. The folk song, for example, has a definite musical design which relies on simple repetition with a definite beginning and ending. A folk song generally consists of one stanza of music repeated for each stanza of verse.

Because of their communal, and usually uncertain origin, folk songs are often popular verse set to music. They are not always recorded, and tend to be passed on in a kind of musical version of oral history. Each singer revises and perfects the song. In part as a consequence of this continuous revision process, most folk songs are almost perfect in their construction and design. A particular singer's interpretation of the folk song may provide an interesting expression, but the simple design that underlies the song itself is stable and enduring.

1. All of the following are true of a folk song EXCEPT

✓ There is a clear start and finish.
✓ The origin is often not known.
   The design may change in the interpretation.
✓ Simple repetition is characteristic of its design.

Problem 7. Locating References

The National Road, also known as the Cumberland Road, was constructed in the early 1800s to provide transportation between the established commercial areas of the East and Northwest Territory. By 1818, the road had reached Wheeling, West Virginia, 130 miles
Line from its point of origin in Cumberland, Maryland. The cost was a monumental thirteen thou-
(5) sand dollars per mile.

Upon reaching the Ohio River, the National Road became one of the major trade routes to the western states and territories, providing Baltimore with a trade advantage over neighboring cities. In order to compete, New York state authorized the construction of the Erie Canal, and Philadelphia initiated a transportation plan to link it with Pittsburgh. Towns along the
(10) rivers, canals, and the new National Road became important trade centers.

1. The word "its" in line 4 refers to *the road.*

2. The word "it" in line 9 refers to *the canal.*

Problem 8. Referring to the Passage

In September of 1929, traders experienced a lack of confidence in the stock market's ability to continue its phenomenal rise. Prices fell. For many inexperienced investors, the drop produced a panic. They had all their money tied up in the market, and they were pressed to
Line sell before the prices fell even lower. Sell orders were coming in so fast that the ticker tape at
(5) the New York Stock Exchange could not accommodate all the transactions.

To try to reestablish confidence in the market, a powerful group of New York bankers agreed to pool their funds and purchase stock above current market values. Although the buy orders were minimal, they were counting on their reputations to restore confidence on the part of the smaller investors, thereby affecting the number of sell orders. On Thursday, October
(10) 24, Richard Whitney, the Vice President of the New York Stock Exchange and a broker for the J.P. Morgan Company, made the effort on their behalf. Initially, it appeared to have been successful, then, on the following Tuesday, the crash began again and accelerated. By 1932, stocks were worth only twenty percent of their value at the 1929 high. The results of the crash had extended into every aspect of the economy, causing a long and painful depression,
(15) referred to in American history as the Great Depression.

1. Where in the passage does the author refer to the reason for the stock market crash? *Lines 1-3.*

2. Where in the passage does the author suggest that there was a temporary recovery in the stock market? *Lines 11-12.*

ANSWER KEY—MODEL TESTS

Model Test 1—Computer-Assisted TOEFL

Section 1: Listening

1. (C)	6. (B)	11. (B)	16. (C)	21. (B)	26. (C)	31. (C)	36. (C)	41. (B)	46. (A)
2. (A)	7. (D)	12. (A)	17. (C)	22. (C)	27. (D)	32. (A)	37. (B)	42. (A)	47. (B)
3. (C)	8. (C)	13. (C)	18. (D)	23. (B)	28. (B)	33. (C)	38. (B)	43.(A)(C)	48. (C)
4. (A)	9. (D)	14. (B)	19. (C)	24. (D)	29. (A)	34. (A)	39. (A)	44. (B)	49. (B)
5. (A)	10. (C)	15. (C)	20. (B)	25. (C)	30. (A)	35. (C)	40.(C)(D)	45. (C)	50. (B)

Section 2: Structure

1. (B)	5. (C)	9. (A)	13. (D)	17. (A)	21. (D)	25. (A)
2. (C)	6. (B)	10. (B)	14. (C)	18. (A)	22. (D)	
3. (A)	7. (B)	11. (C)	15. (C)	19. (A)	23. (B)	
4. (D)	8. (A)	12. (A)	16. (D)	20. (B)	24. (D)	

Section 3: Reading

1. (B)	10. (A)	17. (C)	27. (B)	37. (A)
2. (B)	11. (B)	18. (A)	28. (B)	38. (C)
3. (D)	12. (A)	19. (B)	29. (C)	39. large
4. (A)	13. (B)	20. award	30. (C)	40. (B)
5. sentence 6, paragraph 1	14. (B)	21. (C)	31. brilliant tricks	41. (A)
6. (A)	15. "…invented dynamite. When he read…"	22. generally	32. purpose	42. (B)
7. (B)		23. (D)	33. (B)	43. (B)
8. (B)		24. (A)	34. (B)	44. sentence 2, paragraph 3
9. (C)	16. (D)	25. (B)	35. (B)	
		26. (D)	36. (D)	45. (C)

Writing: Checklist for Essay

- ❑ The essay answers the topic question.
- ❑ The point of view or position is clear.
- ❑ The essay is direct and well-organized.
- ❑ The sentences are logically connected to each other.
- ❑ Details and examples support the main idea.
- ❑ The writer expresses complete thoughts.
- ❑ The meaning is easy for the reader to understand.
- ❑ A wide range of vocabulary is used.
- ❑ Various types of sentences are included.
- ❑ There are only minor errors in grammar and idioms.
- ❑ The general topic essay is within a range of 300–350 words.

Model Test 2—Computer-Assisted TOEFL

Section 1: Listening

1. (B)	7. (B)	13. (D)	19. (A)	25. (B)	31. (C)	37. (C)	43. (A)	49.(B)(A)(C)
2. (D)	8. (A)	14. (C)	20. (A)	26. (D)	32. (B)	38. (B)	44.(A)(B)	50. (A)
3. (D)	9. (C)	15. (A)	21. (C)	27. (C)	33. (C)	39. (D)	45. (C)	
4. (B)	10. (A)	16. (B)	22. (B)	28. (B)	34. (D)	40. (A)	46.(C)(D)	
5. (D)	11. (B)	17. (B)	23. (C)	29. (D)	35. (B)	41. (C)	47. (B)	
6. (A)	12. (D)	18. (B)	24. (B)	30. (B)	36.(A)(B)	42. (C)	48. (C)	

Section 2: Structure

1. (A)	5. (C)	9. (A)	13. (A)	17. (C)	21. (A)	25. (B)
2. (A)	6. (B)	10. (A)	14. (B)	18. (C)	22. (A)	
3. (C)	7. (A)	11. (B)	15. (D)	19. (A)	23. (B)	
4. (D)	8. (C)	12. (A)	16. (C)	20. (C)	24. (B)	

Section 3: Reading

1. (A)	12. (C)	21. "…a rude	29. (C)	37. (B)
2. (C)	13. (D)	noise.	30. (A)	38. (A)
3. (A)	14. sentence 4,	Gestures	31. (C)	39. (A)
4. (A)	paragraph 1	such as…"	32. sentence 5,	40. (C)
5. (D)	15. (A)	22. (B)	paragraph 3	41. (B)
6. (A)	16. (B)	23. interaction	33. damage	42. (C)
7. (D)	17. (D)	24. (D)	34. "…solids or	43. sentence 3,
8. data	18. signs	25. (D)	liquids. One	paragraph 1
9. (C)	19. (B)	26. (D)	objection…"	44. tamed
10. problems	20. (C)	27. (B)	35. (A)	45. (A)
11. sentence 2,		28. (B)	36. (D)	
paragraph 2				

Writing: Checklist for Essay

- ❑ The essay answers the topic question.
- ❑ The point of view or position is clear.
- ❑ The essay is direct and well-organized.
- ❑ The sentences are logically connected to each other.
- ❑ Details and examples support the main idea.
- ❑ The writer expresses complete thoughts.
- ❑ The meaning is easy for the reader to understand.
- ❑ A wide range of vocabulary is used.
- ❑ Various types of sentences are included.
- ❑ There are only minor errors in grammar and idioms.
- ❑ The general topic essay is within a range of 300–350 words.

Model Test 3—Computer-Assisted TOEFL

Section 1: Listening

1. (A)	8. (C)	15. (C)	22. (B)	29. (B)	36. (B)	42. (D)	49. (A)(C)
2. (C)	9. (D)	16. (A)	23. (C)	30. (A)	37. (A)	43. (A)	50. (A)
3. (C)	10. (B)	17. (B)	24. (C)	31. (C)	38. (B)(C)	44. (B)	
4. (A)	11. (A)	18. (D)	25. (A)	32. (B)	39. (C)(B)	45. (B)	
5. (A)	12. (A)	19. (B)	26. (A)	33. (B)	(D)(A)	46. (C)	
6. (A)	13. (D)	20. (B)	27. (B)	34. (D)	40. (B)	47. (D)	
7. (C)	14. (A)	21. (C)	28. (B)	35. (C)	41. (A)	48. (D)	

Section 2: Structure

1. (C)	5. (B)	9. (C)	13. (B)	17. (B)	21. (C)	25. (D)
2. (B)	6. (A)	10. (A)	14. (B)	18. (B)	22. (A)	
3. (A)	7. (C)	11. (C)	15. (D)	19. (A)	23. (C)	
4. (B)	8. (D)	12. (B)	16. (C)	20. (A)	24. (A)	

Section 3: Reading

1. (A)	10. (C)	21. earthquakes	32. "…other life	39. (C)
2. (D)	11. (C)	22. (D)	forms.	40. (C)
3. (C)	12. (A)	23. (B)	Although	41. (A)
4. (D)	13. (B)	24. segmented	some	42. (A)
5. very	14. (C)	25. (C)	insects…"	43. sentence 2,
successful	15. (C)	26. (A)	33. (D)	paragraph 4
6. (A)	16. (D)	27. (A)	34. (D)	44. (A)
7. (C)	17. (D)	28. (B)	35. (D)	45. (C)
8. (D)	18. (C)	29. (C)	36. (B)	
9. sentence 4,	19. (A)	30. (A)	37. locomotion	
paragraph 2	20. devastating	31. (C)	38. (C)	

Writing: Checklist for Essay

❑ The essay answers the topic question.

❑ The point of view or position is clear.

❑ The essay is direct and well-organized.

❑ The sentences are logically connected to each other.

❑ Details and examples support the main idea.

❑ The writer expresses complete thoughts.

❑ The meaning is easy for the reader to understand.

❑ A wide range of vocabulary is used.

❑ Various types of sentences are included.

❑ There are only minor errors in grammar and idioms.

❑ The general topic essay is within a range of 300–350 words.

Model Test 4—Computer-Assisted TOEFL

Section 1: Listening

1. (C)	6. (C)	11. (A)	16. (D)	21. (D)	26. (B)	31. (D)	36. (C)	41. (D)	46. (B)
2. (A)	7. (B)	12. (D)	17. (A)	22. (D)	27. (D)	32. (A)	37. (D)	42. (A)(C)	47. (D)
3. (A)	8. (C)	13. (A)	18. (B)	23. (A)	28. (B)	33. (C)	38. (D)	43. (B)	48. (D)
4. (B)	9. (A)	14. (A)	19. (C)	24. (D)	29. (B)	34. (A)	39. (C)	44. (B)	49. (C)
5. (D)	10. (B)	15. (C)	20. (D)	25. (B)	30. (C)	35. (C)	40. (C)	45. (C)	50. (B)

Section 2: Structure

1. (D)	5. (B)	9. (B)	13. (B)	17. (D)	21. (D)	25. (D)
2. (B)	6. (A)	10. (C)	14. (D)	18. (C)	22. (A)	
3. (C)	7. (B)	11. (D)	15. (C)	19. (C)	23. (B)	
4. (D)	8. (C)	12. (C)	16. (A)	20. (D)	24. (D)	

Section 3: Reading

1. (A)	11. (B)	21. (D)	32. (C)	40. the English
2. (C)	12. (D)	22. (B)	33. "...fragrant	King's
3. (B)	13. (C)	23. valued	blossoms.	41. (A)
4. (A)	14. sentence 5,	24. (C)	Other	42. sentence 1,
5. (B)	paragraph 1	25. (A)	*Acacia*..."	paragraph 4
6. (C)	15. (A)	26. (D)	34. (A)	43. (B)
7. sentence 2,	16. better	27. (C)	35. (C)	44. (B)
paragraph 2	17. (D)	28. (A)	36. (B)	45. (D)
8. (D)	18. (D)	29. (B)	37. (A)	
9. (B)	19. (A)	30. (D)	38. (C)	
10. (A)	20. (C)	31. (B)	39. (C)	

Writing: Checklist for Essay

- ❑ The essay answers the topic question.
- ❑ The point of view or position is clear.
- ❑ The essay is direct and well-organized.
- ❑ The sentences are logically connected to each other.
- ❑ Details and examples support the main idea.
- ❑ The writer expresses complete thoughts.
- ❑ The meaning is easy for the reader to understand.
- ❑ A wide range of vocabulary is used.
- ❑ Various types of sentences are included.
- ❑ There are only minor errors in grammar and idioms.
- ❑ The general topic essay is within a range of 300–350 words.

Model Test 5—Computer-Assisted TOEFL

Section 1: Listening

1. **(D)**	11. **(C)**	21. **(C)**	31. **(A)(B)(C)(D)**	41. **(C)**
2. **(B)**	12. **(B)**	22. **(C)**	32. **(B)**	42. **(C)**
3. **(C)**	13. **(B)**	23. **(B)(C)**	33. **(D)**	43. **(A)**
4. **(B)**	14. **(B)**	24. **(C)**	34. **(D)**	44. **(C)**
5. **(B)**	15. **(D)**	25. **(D)(C)(B)(A)**	35. **(A)**	45. **(A)(B)**
6. **(C)**	16. **(C)**	26. **(C)**	36. **(B)(A)(C)**	46. **(C)**
7. **(A)**	17. **(A)**	27. **(A)(B)**	37. **(A)(C)**	47. **(C)**
8. **(B)**	18. **(B)**	28. **(A)**	38. **(B)(C)**	48. **(C)**
9. **(D)**	19. **(D)**	29. **(C)**	39. **(C)**	49. **(D)**
10. **(A)**	20. **(A)**	30. **(C)**	40. **(C)**	50. **(B)**

Section 2: Structure

1. **(D)**	6. **(D)**	11. **(B)**	16. **(A)**	21. **(C)**
2. **(B)**	7. **(D)**	12. **(D)**	17. **(C)**	22. **(B)**
3. **(D)**	8. **(A)**	13. **(C)**	18. **(C)**	23. **(C)**
4. **(A)**	9. **(A)**	14. **(D)**	19. **(A)**	24. **(B)**
5. **(C)**	10. **(C)**	15. **(B)**	20. **(C)**	25. **(C)**

Section 3: Reading

1. **(A)**	10. **(C)**	20. **sentence 7,**	29. **(B)**	39. **(B)**
2. **(C)**	11. **(B)**	**paragraph 3**	30. **(A)**	40. **(B)**
3. **(D)**	12. **(A)**	21. **(D)**	31. **(C)**	41. **(C)**
4. **(B)**	13. **architecture**	22. **(C)**	32. **(B)**	42. **sentence 1,**
5. **(A)**	14. **(B)**	23. **(D)**	33. **(B)**	**paragraph 3**
6. **increased**	15. **(C)**	24. **(B)**	34. **(C)**	43. **(A)**
7. **sentence 1,**	16. **(A)**	25. **works**	35. **(A)**	44. **(B)**
paragraph 3	17. **(B)**	26. **(A)**	36. **(A)**	45. **(A)**
8. **(A)**	18. **(A)**	27. **maintained**	37. **complex**	
9. **(B)**	19. **shapes**	28. **(B)**	38. **the memory**	

Writing: Checklist for Essay

- ❑ The essay answers the topic question.
- ❑ The point of view or position is clear.
- ❑ The essay is direct and well-organized.
- ❑ The sentences are logically connected to each other.
- ❑ Details and examples support the main idea.
- ❑ The writer expresses complete thoughts.
- ❑ The meaning is easy for the reader to understand.
- ❑ A wide range of vocabulary is used.
- ❑ Various types of sentences are included.
- ❑ There are only minor errors in grammar and idioms.
- ❑ The general topic essay is within a range of 300–350 words.

Model Test 6—Computer-Assisted TOEFL

Section 1: Listening

1. **(B)**	11. **(B)**	21. **(A)(D)**	31. **(C)**	41. **(C)(A)(B)**
2. **(B)**	12. **(C)**	22. **(B)**	32. **(A)**	42. **(C)**
3. **(C)**	13. **(C)**	23. **(B)(D)**	33. **(B)**	43. **(B)**
4. **(C)**	14. **(D)**	24. **(A)**	34. **(C)**	44. **(C)**
5. **(C)**	15. **(A)**	25. **(C)**	35. **(A)**	45. **(B)**
6. **(C)**	16. **(C)**	26. **(A)**	36. **(B)**	46. **(B)**
7. **(B)**	17. **(A)**	27. **(C)**	37. **(A)(D)**	47. **(A)**
8. **(C)**	18. **(D)**	28. **(A)(C)**	38. **(B)**	48. **(B)**
9. **(A)**	19. **(B)**	29. **(B)**	39. **(C)**	49. **(A)**
10. **(B)**	20. **(A)**	30. **(B)**	40. **(B)(C)**	50. **(B)(D)**

Section 2: Structure

1. **(B)**	6. **(C)**	11. **(C)**	16. **(B)**	21. **(A)**
2. **(D)**	7. **(A)**	12. **(C)**	17. **(C)**	22. **(B)**
3. **(B)**	8. **(C)**	13. **(C)**	18. **(B)**	23. **(B)**
4. **(D)**	9. **(D)**	14. **(D)**	19. **(C)**	24. **(B)**
5. **(D)**	10. **(C)**	15. **(C)**	20. **(C)**	25. **(C)**

Section 3: Reading

1. **(B)**	11. **(A)**	21. **(D)**	31. **"...for type-**	39. **(C)**
2. **(B)**	12. **(A)**	22. **(D)**	**B virus. Ap-**	40. **(B)**
3. **about**	13. **(B)**	23. **(A)**	**proximately**	41. **coins and**
4. **(A)**	14. **(C)**	24. **(D)**	**every..."**	**paper**
5. **sentence 1,**	15. **(B)**	25. **the viruses**	32. **(B)**	**currency**
paragraph 2	16. **sentence 4,**	26. **(D)**	33. **(C)**	42. **sentence 3,**
6. **(C)**	**paragraph 2**	27. **(B)**	34. **(B)**	**paragraph 3**
7. **(C)**	17. **guiding**	28. **(C)**	35. **(A)**	43. **(C)**
8. **(B)**	18. **(C)**	29. **(B)**	36. **(D)**	44. **(D)**
9. **(B)**	19. **(C)**	30. **types**	37. **(B)**	45. **"...policy**
10. **(A)**	20. **(A)**		38. **(B)**	**makers.**
				In fact, the
				Fed..."

Writing: Checklist for Essay

- ❑ The essay answers the topic question.
- ❑ The point of view or position is clear.
- ❑ The essay is direct and well-organized.
- ❑ The sentences are logically connected to each other.
- ❑ Details and examples support the main idea.
- ❑ The writer expresses complete thoughts.
- ❑ The meaning is easy for the reader to understand.
- ❑ A wide range of vocabulary is used.
- ❑ Various types of sentences are included.
- ❑ There are only minor errors in grammar and idioms.
- ❑ The general topic essay is within a range of 300–350 words.

Model Test 7—Computer-Assisted TOEFL

Section 1: Listening

1. (A)	11. (D)	21. (C)	31. (B)	41. (B)(C)
2. (B)	12. (A)	22. (C)	32. (B)(C)	42. (B)
3. (C)	13. (D)	23. (A)(C)	33. (D)(A)(C)(B)	43. (B)
4. (A)	14. (C)	24. (B)	34. (C)	44. (A)
5. (B)	15. (A)	25. (C)	35. (A)	45. (B)(C)
6. (B)	16. (D)	26. (A)	36. (C)	46. (B)
7. (B)	17. (B)	27. (A)	37. (A)	47. (A)
8. (C)	18. (A)	28. (C)(B)(A)	38. (C)	48. (B)
9. (D)	19. (B)	29. (B)(D)	39. (C)	49. (B)(C)
10. (D)	20. (C)	30. (A)	40. (A)	50. (D)

Section 2: Structure

1. (B)	6. (A)	11. (B)	16. (A)	21. (B)
2. (B)	7. (A)	12. (B)	17. (B)	22. (A)
3. (A)	8. (B)	13. (D)	18. (D)	23. (A)
4. (D)	9. (B)	14. (A)	19. (D)	24. (B)
5. (B)	10. (D)	15. (A)	20. (A)	25. (C)

Section 3: Reading

1. (B)	11. "...was vaccinated. The number of..."	19. sentence 2, paragraph 4	30. (B)	38. (B)
2. eliminate		20. (A)	31. (B)	39. the shorter growing season
3. (C)		21. (C)	32. (C)	
4. sentence 2, paragraph 2	12. (C)	22. (A)	33. "...before they are born. Fetuses exposed..."	40. (D)
5. (C)	13. ideal	23. (A)		41. (B)
6. (B)	14. (B)	24. (A)		42. (A)
7. (B)	15. (B)	25. (B)		43. (C)
8. (B)	16. (C)	26. (C)	34. (C)	44. (A)
9. (A)	17. (C)	27. (B)	35. (D)	45. (D)
10. (A)	18. of the single people	28. increase	36. (B)	
		29. the noise	37. crude	

Writing: Checklist for Essay

☐ The essay answers the topic question.

☐ The point of view or position is clear.

☐ The essay is direct and well-organized.

☐ The sentences are logically connected to each other.

☐ Details and examples support the main idea.

☐ The writer expresses complete thoughts.

☐ The meaning is easy for the reader to understand.

☐ A wide range of vocabulary is used.

☐ Various types of sentences are included.

☐ There are only minor errors in grammar and idioms.

☐ The general topic essay is within a range of 300–350 words.

Model Test 8—Computer-Assisted TOEFL

Section 1: Listening

1. (A)	11. (C)	21. (B)	31. (B)	41. (C)
2. (C)	12. (C)	22. (B)	32. (D)(A)(C)(B)	42. (B)
3. (A)	13. (C)	23. (C)	33. (C)(D)	43. (A)
4. (C)	14. (B)	24. (C)	34. (A)(C)	44. (D)
5. (B)	15. (D)	25. (A)	35. (A)	45. (C)
6. (C)	16. (A)	26. (B)	36. (C)	46. (B)(C)
7. (C)	17. (B)	27. (D)	37. (B)(C)	47. (A)
8. (C)	18. (C)	28. (C)	38. (A)	48. (C)
9. (D)	19. (A)	29. (A)	39. (C)	49. (C)
10. (A)	20. (C)	30. (C)	40. (B)(D)	50. (A)(D)

Section 2: Structure

1. (C)	6. (A)	11. (D)	16. (D)	21. (C)
2. (D)	7. (B)	12. (D)	17. (D)	22. (D)
3. (C)	8. (A)	13. (D)	18. (C)	23. (C)
4. (D)	9. (A)	14. (D)	19. (B)	24. (A)
5. (D)	10. (A)	15. (D)	20. (C)	25. (C)

Section 3: Reading

1. (D)	13. (B)	22. "...in only	31. sentence 6,	38. (A)
2. (B)	14. clash of	two decades.	paragraph 2	39. (C)
3. (C)	keys...	Even during	32. bats	40. area
4. (A)	15. (D)	such..."	33. "...highly	41. (C)
5. (B)	16. (C)	23. (C)	social	42. sentence 1,
6. earthquakes	17. (A)	24. (B)	creatures.	paragraph 3
7. (A)	18. (A)	25. huge	Aggregation	43. (A)
8. basically	19. (D)	26. (C)	during..."	44. (D)
9. (B)	20. (D)	27. (D)	34. (B)	45. (A)
10. (D)	21. *Concord*	28. (A)	35. (B)	
11. (C)	*Sonata*	29. (A)	36. live	
12. (B)		30. (C)	37. (A)	

Writing: Checklist for Essay

- ❑ The essay answers the topic question.
- ❑ The point of view or position is clear.
- ❑ The essay is direct and well-organized.
- ❑ The sentences are logically connected to each other.
- ❑ Details and examples support the main idea.
- ❑ The writer expresses complete thoughts.
- ❑ The meaning is easy for the reader to understand.
- ❑ A wide range of vocabulary is used.
- ❑ Various types of sentences are included.
- ❑ There are only minor errors in grammar and idioms.
- ❑ The general topic essay is within a range of 300–350 words.

Model Test 9—Next Generation TOEFL

Listening: Independent Listening 1–6

1. **(B)**	11. **(C)**	21. **(A)**
2. **(C)**	12. **(B) (C)**	22. **(B) (C)**
3. **(A)**	13. **(C)**	23. **(B)**
4. **(C)**	14. **(C)**	24. **(A)**
5. **(B)**	15. **(A) YES (B) NO (C) YES**	25. **(B)**
6. **(D)**	16. **(D)**	26. **(D)**
7. **(B)**	17. **(B) (C)**	27. **(B) (D)**
8. **(B)**	18. **(C)**	28. **(A)**
9. **(D)**	19. **(B)**	29. **(C)**
10. **(B)**	20. **(D)**	30. **(B)**

Speaking: Checklist for Questions 1 and 2

☐ The talk answers the topic question.

☐ The point of view or position is clear.

☐ The talk is direct and well-organized.

☐ The sentences are logically connected to each other.

☐ Details and examples support the main idea.

☐ The speaker expresses complete thoughts.

☐ The meaning is easy for the listener to comprehend.

☐ A wide range of vocabulary is used.

☐ There are only minor errors in grammar and idioms.

☐ The talk is within a range of 100–150 words.

Speaking: Checklist for Questions 3, 4, 5, 6

☐ The talk answers the topic question.

☐ There are only minor inaccuracies in the content.

☐ The talk is direct and well-organized.

☐ The sentences are logically connected to each other.

☐ Details and examples support the main idea.

☐ The speaker expresses complete thoughts.

☐ The meaning is easy for the listener to comprehend.

☐ A wide range of vocabulary is used.

☐ The speaker paraphrases, using his or her own words.

☐ The speaker credits the lecturer with wording when necessary.

☐ There are only minor errors in grammar and idioms.

☐ The talk is within a range of 100–150 words.

Reading: Independent Reading 1

1. **(C)**
2. **(C)**
3. **(A)**
4. **(A)**
5. **(A)**
6. **(D)**
7. **(A)**
8. **(C)**
9. **(B)**
10. **(C)**
11. **(B)**
12. **(A)**
13. **(A) (C) (E)**

Reading: Independent Reading 2

1. **(B)**
2. **(B)**
3. **(B)**
4. **(C)**
5. **(D)**
6. **(B)**
7. **(A)**
8. **(A)**
9. **(B)**
10. **(B)**
11. **(C)**
12. **(B)**
13. **(B) (E) (F)**

Reading: Independent Reading 3

1. **(B)**
2. **(B)**
3. **(C)**
4. **(A)**
5. **(B)**
6. **(B)**
7. **(A)**
8. **(C)**
9. **(D)**
10. **(D)**
11. **(A)**
12. **(C)**
13. **(A) (C) (E)**

Writing: Checklist for Independent Writing

❑ The essay answers the topic question.
❑ The point of view or position is clear.
❑ The essay is direct and well-organized.
❑ The sentences are logically connected to each other.
❑ Details and examples support the main idea.
❑ The writer expresses complete thoughts.
❑ The meaning is easy for the reader to understand.
❑ A wide range of vocabulary is used.
❑ Various types of sentences are included.
❑ There are only minor errors in grammar and idioms.
❑ The general topic essay is within a range of 300–350 words.

Writing: Checklist for Integrated Writing

❑ The essay answers the topic question.
❑ There are only minor inaccuracies in the content.
❑ The essay is direct and well-organized for the topic.
❑ The sentences are logically connected to each other.
❑ Details and examples support the main idea.
❑ The writer expresses complete thoughts.
❑ The meaning is easy for the reader to comprehend.
❑ A wide range of vocabulary is used.
❑ The writer paraphrases, using his or her own words.
❑ The writer credits the author with wording when necessary.
❑ There are only minor errors in grammar and idioms.
❑ The academic topic essay is within a range of 200–250 words.

10

EXPLANATORY ANSWERS AND AUDIO SCRIPTS

NOTE

The Explanatory Answers include the transcript for the Listening Sections of the TOEFL Model Tests included in this book. Note that the Listening Sections always appear as Section 1 of the examinations.

When you take the Model Tests in this book as a preliminary step in your preparation for the actual examination, you should use either the CD-ROM, the compact disks, or the cassette tapes that supplement this book. If you use a CD-ROM, you will see visuals on your computer screen. If you use compact disks, you will hear the audio, but you will not see the visuals.

If you have someone read the TOEFL transcript to you, be sure that he or she understands the timing sequences. The reader should work with a stopwatch or with a regular watch with a second hand in order to keep careful track of the timed pauses between questions. The time for the pauses between questions is about 10 seconds. Be sure that the reader speaks clearly and at a moderately paced rate. For results that would be closest to the actual testing situation, it is recommended that three persons be asked to read, since some of the Listening Sections include dialogues.

Model Test 1—Computer-Assisted TOEFL

Section 1: Listening

The Listening Section of the test measures the ability to understand conversations and talks in English. On the actual TOEFL exam, you will use headphones to listen to the conversations and talks. While you are listening, pictures of the speakers or other information will be presented on your computer screen. There are two parts to the Listening Section, with special directions for each part.

On the day of the test, the amount of time you will have to answer all of the questions will appear on the computer screen. The time you spend listening to the test material will not be counted. The listening material and questions about it will be presented only one time. You will not be allowed to take notes or have any paper at your computer. You will both see and hear the questions before the answer choices appear. You can take as much time as you need to select an answer; however, it will be to your advantage to answer the questions as quickly as possible. You may change your answer as many times as you want before you confirm it. After you have confirmed an answer, you will not be able to return to the question.

Before you begin working on the Listening Section, you will have an opportunity to adjust the volume of the sound. You may not be able to change the volume after you have started the test.

QUESTION DIRECTIONS—Part A

In Part A of the Listening Section, you will hear short conversations between two people. In some of the conversations, each person speaks only once. In other conversations, one or both of the people speak more than once. Each conversation is followed by one question about it.

Each question in this part has four answer choices. You should click on the best answer to each question. Answer the questions on the basis of what is stated or implied by the speakers.

Audio

1. Woman: If I were you I'd take the bus to school. Driving in that rush-hour traffic is terrible.
   Man: But by the time the bus gets to my stop, there aren't any seats left.
   Narrator: What is the man's problem?

Answer

(C) Since the man says that there aren't any seats left, it must be concluded that he has to stand when he takes the bus to school. Choice (B) refers to the woman's suggestion, not to the man's response. Choices (A) and (D) are not mentioned and may not be concluded from information in the conversation.

Audio

2. Woman: I'd like to take Dr. Sullivan's section of Physics 100, but my advisor is teaching it too, and I don't want her to be offended.
   Man: Who cares?
   Woman: Well, I don't want to get on her bad side.
   Man: I wouldn't worry about it.
   Narrator: What does the man mean?

Answer

(A) *Who cares* means that it "isn't important" [that her advisor might be offended]. Choices (B), (C), and (D) are not mentioned and may not be concluded from information in the conversation.

Audio

3. Man: Let's go to the dance at the Student Center on Friday.
   Woman: Sounds great, but I'm going to a lecture. Thanks for asking me though.
   Narrator: What does the woman imply?

Answer

(C) Because the woman says that the invitation sounds "great" and she thanks the man for asking her, it must be concluded that she would go out with the man on another occasion. Choice (A) is not correct because she responds so positively while refusing the invitation. Choices (B) and (D) are not correct because she has plans to attend a lecture.

Audio

4. Man: That's a nice bike.
   Woman: I got it almost five years ago.
   Man: You did? It looks new.
   Woman :   Yes, it's still in really good shape.
   Narrator: What does the woman mean?

Answer

(A) *In good shape* is an idiomatic expression that means the item is "in good condition." Choice (B) is not correct because the man thinks the bike is new, and the woman says it is in good shape. Choice (C) is not correct because the speakers are talking about a bike that is able to be seen. Choice (D) is not correct because the woman got the bike almost five years ago.

Audio

5. Woman: Would you like some hot coffee or tea?
   Man: I like them both, but I'd rather have something cold.
   Narrator: What does the man want to drink?

Answer

(A) The man says that he would rather have something cold. Choices (B), (C), and (D) refer to what the man likes, not to what he wants.

Audio

6. Woman: How can I get to the shopping center from here? Not the one on campus. The one downtown.
   Man: You can take a bus or a taxi, but it isn't too far to walk.
   Narrator: What does the man suggest the woman do?

Answer

(B) "... it isn't too far to walk [to the shopping center]." Choice (A) is not correct because he is already giving the woman information about the shopping center. Choices (C) and (D) are alternative possibilities that the man mentions before making his suggestion.

Audio

7. Man: Have you found a class yet?
   Woman: I'm just checking the schedule now.
   Narrator: What can be inferred about the woman?

Answer

(D) Since the woman says that she is just checking the schedule now, it must be concluded that she has not registered yet. Choice (A) is not correct because she is checking the schedule for a class. Choices (B) and (C) are not mentioned and may not be concluded from information in the conversation.

Audio

8. Woman: Do you mind if I turn on the radio for a while?
   Man: No, I don't mind.
   Narrator: What does the man mean?

Answer

(C) To *not mind* is an idiomatic expression that means the speaker will "not be bothered" by an activity or situation. Choices (A), (B), and (D) are not paraphrases of the expression.

Audio

9. Man: I'm worried about Anna. She's really been depressed lately. All she does is stay in her room all day.
   Woman: That sounds serious. She'd better see someone at the Counseling Center.
   Narrator: What does the woman suggest Anna do?

Answer

(D) "She'd better see someone at the Counseling Center." Choices (A), (B), and (C) are not mentioned and may not be concluded from information in the conversation.

Audio

10. Woman: If you have a few minutes, I'd like to talk with you about my project.
    Man: Please go on.
    Narrator: What does the man mean?

Answer

(C) *Please go on* is an idiomatic expression that means the speaker wants the other person to "continue." Choices (A), (B), and (D) are not paraphrases of the expression.

Audio

11. Woman: Excuse me. I was in line here first.
     Man: Oh, I'm sorry. I didn't realize that you were waiting.
     Narrator: What will the man probably do?

Answer

(B) Since the man apologizes for going ahead of the woman in line, he will most probably allow her to go ahead of him. Choice (A) is not correct because it is the man, not the woman, who apologizes. Choice (C) is not correct because he has already apologized. Choice (D) is not mentioned and may not be concluded from information in the conversation.

Audio

12. Man: The neighbors are going to have another party.
     Woman: Not again!
     Narrator: What does the woman imply?

Answer

(A) *Not again* is an idiomatic expression that means the speaker is impatient with some kind of repeated behavior or activity. Choice (C) is not correct because she does not know about the party until the man informs her. Choices (B) and (D) are not mentioned and may not be concluded from information in the conversation.

Audio

13. Man: You mean Dr. Franklin said you couldn't have an extension?
     Woman: He said it was not his policy.
     Man: Really?
     Woman: Yes, so now I have to work over the holiday weekend.
     Narrator: What had the man assumed?

Answer

(C) Since the man says "Really?" it must be concluded that he is surprised by the professor's response to the woman's request. Choice (D) is not correct because the professor says it was not his policy. Choices (A) and (B) are not mentioned and may not be concluded from information in the conversation.

Audio

14. Man: We really should have left already.
     Woman: Maybe we ought to call and let them know.
     Narrator: What problem do the man and woman have?

Answer

(B) Since the man says that they should have left already, it must be concluded that they are late. Choice (A) is not likely because of the woman's suggestion that they make a call. Choices (C) and (D) are not mentioned and may not be concluded from information in the conversation.

Audio

15. Man: Have you moved out of your apartment yet?
     Woman: No. I'm paid up until the 15th.
     Narrator: What is the woman probably going to do?

Answer

(C) Since the woman says that she has her rent paid until the 15th, she will probably stay where she is living until the 15th. The reference to half a month in Choice (A) refers to the fact that the woman already has her rent paid until the 15th, not to what she will do. Choice (B) is not correct because the woman, not the man, is planning to move. Choice (D) is not correct because the woman mentions having her rent paid.

Audio

16. Woman: Mary Anne took the math placement test.
    Man: So, she *finally* did it!
    Narrator: What had the man assumed about Mary Anne?

Answer

(C) Since the man expresses surprise, it must be concluded that he thought she had not taken the placement test. Choice (A) is not correct because the man was surprised. Choices (B) and (D) are not mentioned and may not be concluded from information in the conversation.

Audio

17. Woman: Where have you been? I haven't seen you in class all week.
    Man: I caught cold, so I stayed in.
    Narrator: What does the man mean?

Answer

(C) To *catch cold* is an idiomatic expression that means to "get sick." Choices (A), (B), and (D) are not paraphrases of the expression and may not be concluded from information in the conversation.

QUESTION DIRECTIONS—Part B

In Part B of the Listening Section, you will hear several longer conversations and talks. Each conversation or talk is followed by several questions. The conversations, talks, and questions will not be repeated.

The conversations and talks are about a variety of topics. You do not need special knowledge of the topics to answer the questions correctly. Rather, you should answer each question on the basis of what is stated or implied by the speakers in the conversations or talks.

For most of the questions, you will need to click on the best of four possible answers. Some questions will have special directions. The special directions will appear in a box on the computer screen.

Audio Conversation

Narrator: Listen to a conversation with a professor.

Man: Professor Day, may I see you for a minute?
Woman: Sure. Come on in, Mike. What's the matter?
Man: I've got a problem.
Woman: Okay.
Man: I need your technical writing class. And, I knew I had to have it so I went early to registration, but by the time I got to the front of the line, it was closed. See, my advisor signed my course request and everything. I was just too far back in the line.
Woman: That's a big class already, Mike. If it's closed, that means I have fifty students in it.
Man: I'm not surprised. It's supposed to be a really good class.
Woman: Can't you take it next year? We offer it every fall.

Man:	Well, that's the problem. I'm supposed to be graduating this spring. But, of course, I can't graduate without your class.
Woman:	I see. In that case, I'll sign an override for you. It looks like there will be fifty-one. Take this form back to the registration area and they'll get you in.
Man:	Thanks, Professor Day. I really appreciate this!

> Now get ready to answer the questions

Audio

18. What is Mike's problem?

Answer

(D) "I need your technical writing class. . . . In that case, I'll sign an override for you." Choice (A) is not correct because he went early to registration. Choice (B) is not correct because his advisor signed his course request. Choice (C) is not correct because the course will not be taught until fall semester.

Audio

19. What does Mike want Professor Day to do?

Answer

(C) "...I'll sign an override. . . . Take this form back to the registration area and they'll get you in." Choice (D) refers to something that the professor tells Mike to do, not to something that Mike wants the professor to do. Choices (A) and (B) are not mentioned and may not be concluded from information in the conversation.

Audio

20. What does Mike say about graduation?

Answer

(B) "...I can't graduate without your class." Choice (A) is not correct because he plans to graduate in the spring. Choices (C) and (D) are not mentioned and may not be concluded from information in the conversation.

Audio

21. What does Professor Day decide to do?

Answer

(B) ". . . I'll sign an override for you." Choice (A) refers to the suggestion that the professor makes at the beginning of the conversation, not to what she actually decides to do. Choices (C) and (D) are not mentioned and may not be concluded from information in the conversation.

Audio Talk

Narrator: Listen to a talk by a business instructor.

Today's lecture is about the effects of background music on employee performance and retail sales. As you know, every day millions of people in offices and factories around the world do their work to the accompaniment of background music, more commonly known as MUZAK. But did you know that MUZAK is more than a pleasant addition to the environment? Studies show that this seemingly innocent background music can be engineered to control behavior. In fact, MUZAK can improve employee performance by reducing stress, boredom, and fatigue. In one survey, overall productivity increased by thirty percent, although five to ten percent is the average.

The key to MUZAK's success is something called stimulus progression, which means quite simply that the background music starts with a slow, soft song that is low in stimulus value and builds up gradually to an upbeat song that is high in stimulus value. The fastest, loudest sounds are programmed for about ten-thirty in the morning and two-thirty in the afternoon when people are generally starting to tire.

Besides employee performance, MUZAK can increase sales. In supermarkets, slow music can influence shoppers to walk slower and buy more. In restaurants, fast music can cause customers to eat quickly so that the same number of tables may be used to serve more people during peak times such as the lunch hour.

Now get ready to answer the questions

Audio

22. What is MUZAK?

Answer

(C) ". . . background music, more commonly known as MUZAK." Choice (A) is one kind of MUZAK, but it is not correct because MUZAK can be upbeat songs, too. Choice (B) is one place where MUZAK is played, but it is not correct because MUZAK can be played in the workplace and the supermarket, too. Choice (D) is not correct because MUZAK is more than a pleasant addition to the environment.

Audio

23. What is the average increase in productivity when MUZAK is introduced?

Answer

(B) "In one survey, overall productivity increased by thirty percent, although five to ten percent is the average." Choice (D) refers to one survey, not to the average. Choices (A) and (C) are not mentioned and may not be concluded from information in the talk.

Audio

24. What is stimulus progression?

Answer

(D) ". . . stimulus progression . . . starts with a slow, soft song . . . and builds up . . . to an upbeat song . . . programmed . . . when people are generally starting to tire." Choice (A) refers to the first stage of stimulus progression, not to the total progression. Choices (B) and (C) refer to varieties of MUZAK, not to stimulus progression.

Audio

25. How does MUZAK influence sales in supermarkets?

Answer

(C) "In supermarkets, slow music can influence shoppers to walk slower and buy more." Choice (D) is not correct because it can influence shoppers to buy more. Choices (A) and (B) are not mentioned and may not be concluded from information in the talk.

Audio Announcement

Narrator: Listen to a public service announcement.

Community College understands that everyone who wants to attend college will not be able to come to campus. So, as part of the Distance Learning Program, Community College offers a series of video telecourses to meet the needs of students who prefer to complete coursework in their homes, at their convenience.

These telecourses are regular college credit classes taught on videocassette tapes by a Community College professor. To use the materials for the course, you will need your own VHS-type VCR player. Some telecourses will also be broadcast on KCC7-TV's "Sun-Up Semester." This program airs from six o'clock in the morning to seven-thirty, Monday through Friday, and a complete listing of courses is printed in your regular television guide.

To register for a telecourse, phone the Community College Distance Learning Program at 782-6394. The course syllabus, books, and videotapes will be available at the Community College bookstore. During the first week of classes, your instructor will contact you to discuss the course and answer any questions you might have about the course requirements. Then, throughout the rest of the semester, you can use either an 800 telephone number or an e-mail address to contact your instructor.

> Now get ready to answer the questions

Audio

26. What is this announcement mainly about?

Answer

(C) " . . . Community College offers a series of video telecourses to meet the needs of students who prefer to complete coursework in their homes." Choices (A) and (B) are secondary themes used to develop the main theme of the talk. Choice (D) is not mentioned and may not be concluded from information in the conversation

Audio

27. Why does the speaker mention the "Sun-Up Semester"?

Answer

(D) "Some telecourses will also be broadcast on KCC7-TV's 'Sun-Up Semester.'" Choice (A) is not correct because students should call the Community College Distance Learning Program to register. Choice (C) is not correct because a listing of courses is printed in the television guide. Choice (B) is not mentioned and may not be concluded from information in the conversation.

Audio

28. How can students register for a course?

Answer

(B) "To register for a telecourse, phone the Community College . . . ." Choice (A) is not correct because the program is designed to meet the needs of students who are not able to come to campus. Choices (C) and (D) are not mentioned and may not be concluded from information in the conversation.

Audio

29. How can students contact the instructor?

Answer

(A) " . . . you can use either an 800 telephone number or an e-mail address to contact your instructor." Choices (B), (C), and (D) are not mentioned and may not be concluded from information in the conversation.

Audio Conversation

Narrator: Listen to part of a conversation between two friends on campus.

Donna: Hi, Bill.

Bill: Hi, Donna. Where have you been? I haven't seen you for weeks.

Donna: I know. I had to drop out last semester. I thought I had a cold, but it was mono.

Bill: I'm sorry to hear that. What is mono anyway?

Donna: It's a virus, actually, that attacks your immune system. You really become suscepti-ble to it when you stay up late, stress out, and get run down. It was my own fault. I just kept going, studying late. I didn't get enough rest. You know the story.

Bill: Wow! All too well. I'm surprised that we all don't have it.

Donna: A lot of college students do get it. In fact, it is jokingly called the "college disease." I can tell you though, it's no joke.

Bill: So how are you now?

Donna: I'm still tired. But I learned my lesson though. This semester I'm taking twelve hours, and I'm not pushing myself so hard.

Bill: Good for you. I'm taking twenty-one hours. Sometimes I just don't know why I put so much pressure on myself. If I took one more semester to finish my program, then I wouldn't be so overloaded.

Donna: Listen, if you get sick like I did, you'll have to drop out and you'll end up with an extra semester anyway. So you might as well slow down.

Bill: True. Well, it's something to think about. Take care of yourself, Donna.

Donna: I will. You, too.

> Now get ready to answer the questions

Audio

30. What is the main topic of this conversation?

Answer

(A) "I thought I had a cold, but it was mono. . . . It's a virus. . . ." The work *joke* in Choice (C) refers to the phrase *no joke,* which means something that "isn't funny." Choice (D) is mentioned but is not the main topic of the conversation. Choice (B) is not mentioned and may not be concluded from in-formation in the conversation.

Audio

31. What was the woman's problem?

Answer

(C) "I had to drop out last semester." Choices (A) and (B) are probably true, but they caused her problem; they were not the problem. Choice (D) is not correct because she had to withdraw last se-mester, not this semester.

Audio

32. Why is mono called the "college disease"?

Answer

(A) "A lot of college students get it [mono]." The work *joke* in Choice (C) refers to the phrase *no joke* which means something that "isn't funny." Choices (B) and (D) are not mentioned and may not be concluded from information in the conversation.

Audio

33. What advice does the woman give the man?

Answer

(C) ". . . if you get sick . . . you'll end up with an extra semester. . . . .So you might as well slow down." The woman warns the man that he will have to drop out of school if he gets sick, but she does not advise him to drop out as in Choice (A). Choices (B) and (D) are not correct because the woman suggests that the man slow down.

Audio Talk

Narrator: Listen to a talk by a college professor.

Now I would like to outline the development of the Sapir-Whorf Hypothesis concerning the relationship between language and culture.

When Edward Sapir was teaching at Yale, Benjamin Lee Whorf enrolled in his class. Whorf was recognized for his investigations of the Hopi language, including his authorship of a grammar book and a dictionary. Even in his early publications, it is clear that he was developing the theory that the very different grammar of Hopi might indicate a different manner of conceiving and perceiving the world on the part of the native speaker of Hopi.

In 1936, he wrote "An American Indian Model of the Universe," which explored the implications of the Hopi verb system with regard to the Hopi conception of space and time.

Whorf is probably best known for his article "The Relation of Habitual Thought and Behavior to Language" and for the three articles that appeared in 1941 in the *Technology Review*.

In these articles, he proposed what he called the principle of "linguistic relativity," which states, at least as a hypothesis, that the grammar of a language influences the manner in which the speaker understands reality and behaves with respect to it.

Since the theory did not emerge until after Whorf had begun to study with Sapir, and since Sapir had most certainly shared in the development of the idea, it came to be called the Sapir-Whorf Hypothesis.

> Now get ready to answer the questions

Audio

34. What central theme does the lecture examine?

Answer

(A) "Now I would like to outline the development of the Sapir-Whorf Hypothesis concerning the relationship between language and culture." Choices (B), (C), and (D) are secondary themes that are used to develop the main theme of the lecture.

Audio

35. Which languages did Whorf use in his research?

Answer

(C) "In 1936, he [Whorf] wrote 'An American Indian Model of the Universe,' which explored the implications of the Hopi verb system. . . ." Choice (A) refers to historical linguistics, not to the languages that Whorf used in his research. Choices (B) and (D) are not mentioned and may not be concluded from information in the talk.

Audio

36. According to the lecturer, what is linguistic relativity?

Answer

(C) ". . . 'linguistic relativity,' which states, at least as a hypothesis, that the grammar of a language influences the manner in which the speaker understands reality and behaves with respect to it." Choice (D) is not correct because grammar influences cultural behavior. Choices (A) and (B) are not mentioned and may not be concluded from information in the talk.

Audio

37. What is another name for linguistic relativity?

Answer

(B) ". . . it [linguistic relativity] came to be called the Sapir-Whorf Hypothesis." Choice (A) is incomplete because it does not include the name of Whorf. Choice (C) includes the name of Boas, who contributed to the hypothesis but was not named in it. Choice (D) refers to a paper written by Whorf regarding the Hopi verb system, not to linguistic relativity.

Audio Discussion

Narrator:	Listen to part of a class discussion in an environmental science class.
Dr. Green:	Let's begin our discussion today by defining acid rain. Joanne?
Joanne:	Acid rain is, uh, pollution that results when sulfur dioxide and nitrogen oxide mix with the water vapor in the atmosphere.
Dr. Green:	Good. But why do we call it acid rain, then?
Joanne:	Oh, well, sulfur dioxide and nitrogen oxide combine with water vapor and form sulfuric acid and nitric acid.
Dr. Green:	And the acid corrodes the environment?
Joanne:	It does. According to the book, acid reaches the Earth as rain, sleet, snow, fog, or even mist, but we call all of these various forms of pollution acid rain.
Dr. Green:	Exactly right. Now, who can explain how the sulfur dioxide and nitrogen oxide are introduced into the atmosphere in the first place? Ted?
Ted:	Fossil fuels, mostly. Right?
Dr. Green:	Right. Could you elaborate on that a little?
Ted:	Sure. The fossil fuels can be the result of natural events such as volcanic eruptions or forest fires, but most of the time, they are introduced into the atmosphere by industrial processes like the smelting of metals or the burning of oil, coal, and gas.
Dr. Green:	Anything else we should add to that? Yes, Joanne?
Joanne:	Dr. Green, I think it's important to mention the extent of the damage to areas like the Great Lakes.
Dr. Green:	Good point, Joanne. Acidity in the water and on the shorelines has all but eliminated some of the fish populations once found in the Great Lakes region along the United States-Canadian border. Any other damaging effects?
Ted:	I'm an agriculture major, Dr. Green, so I am more familiar with the large concentrations of acids that have been deposited in the soil around the Great Lakes.
Dr. Green:	And what has happened to the vegetation in that region?
Ted:	Well, the rain has caused a chemical change in the soil, which is absorbed by the roots of plants. The plants don't get the nutrients they need, and as a consequence, they die, and uh…
Dr. Green:	Yes?
Ted:	And it just occurred to me that acid rain is having an adverse effect not only on the environment but also on the economy, especially forestry and agriculture.

Dr. Green: Excellent deduction. Now, let me give you the good news. In the Great Lakes region that was mentioned in our book, an Air Quality Accord was signed by Canada and the United States about ten years ago to establish limits for the amount of acidic deposits that may flow across international boundaries. Since then, many companies on both sides of the border have installed equipment that limits sulfur dioxide emissions, and some have even changed to fuels that are lower in sulfur content.

Ted: Excuse me. Isn't it automobile emission that accounts for a high percentage of the nitrogen oxide?

Dr. Green: Yes, it is, Ted. And that problem presents a somewhat larger challenge to the governments and their agencies.

> Now get ready to answer the questions

Audio

38. What is the topic of this discussion?

Answer

(B) "Let's begin our discussion today by defining acid rain." Choices (A), (C), and (D) are all secondary points of discussion that are used to develop the main topic of the discussion.

Audio

39. What is acid rain?

Answer

(A) ". . . Acid rain is . . . sulfur dioxide and nitrogen oxide [that] combine with water vapor and form sulfuric acid and nitric acid." Choice (C) refers to the result of acid rain, not to a definition of it. Choice (D) is not correct because sulfur dioxide and nitrogen oxide, not just sulfur, combine with water vapor. Choice (B) is not mentioned and may not be concluded from information in the discussion.

Audio

40. In which two ways has the environment been damaged along the Great Lakes?

Answer

(C) (D) "Acidity…has all but eliminated . . . fish populations . . . in the Great Lakes . . . [and] rain has caused a chemical change in the soil. . . . Plants don't get the nutrients they need…." Choices (A) and (B) are not mentioned and may not be concluded from information in the discussion.

Audio

41. What are the conditions of the Air Quality Accord?

Answer

(B) ". . . Air Quality Accord . . . to establish limits for the amount of acidic deposits that may flow across international boundaries." Choice (A) refers to the result of the legislation, not to the conditions of it. Choice (C) is not correct because the problem of automobile emissions is a larger challenge to governments and their agencies. Choice (D) is not correct because the fuels are lower in sulfur, but some sulfur still remains in the fuels.

Audio Lecture
Narrator: Listen to part of a lecture in a microbiology class.

Bacteria is the common name for a very large group of one-celled microscopic organisms that, we believe, may be the smallest, simplest, and perhaps even the very first form of cellular life that evolved on Earth. Because they are so small, bacteria must be measured in microns, with one micron measuring about 0.00004 inches long. Most bacteria range from about 0.1 microns to 4 microns wide and 0.2 microns to 50 microns long. So you can understand that they are observable only under a microscope.

There are three main types of bacteria, which are classified according to their shape. The slides that I am going to show you are photographic enlargements of bacteria that I observed under the microscope in the lab earlier today. This slide is an example of bacilli.

The bacilli are a group of bacteria that occur in the soil and air. As you can see, they are shaped like rods, and if you were to see them in motion, they would be rolling or tumbling under the microscope. These bacilli are largely responsible for food spoilage.

The next slide is a very different shape of bacteria.

It is referred to as the cocci group, and it tends to grow in chains. This example is of the common streptococci that causes strep throat.

Finally, let's look at the spiral-shaped bacteria called the spirilla. They look a little like corkscrews, and they are responsible for a number of diseases in humans.

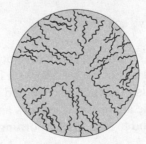

Some species of bacteria do cause diseases, but for the most part, bacteria live harmlessly on the skin, in the mouth, and in the intestines. In fact, bacteria are very helpful to researchers. Bacterial cells resemble the cells of other life forms in many ways, and may be studied to give us insights. For example, we have a major research project in genetics in progress here at the

University. Since bacteria reproduce very rapidly, we are using them to determine how certain characteristics are inherited.

> Now get ready to answer the questions

Audio

42. What is the topic of this lecture?

Answer

(A) "There are three main types of bacteria. . . . " Choices (B), (C), and (D) are all secondary points of discussion that are used to develop the main topic of discussion.

Audio

43. Which two characteristics are common in bacteria?

Answer

(A) (C) "Bacteria is the common name for a very large group of one-celled microscopic organisms. . . . Bacteria reproduce very rapidly. . . . " Choice (B) is not correct because, for the most part, bacteria live harmlessly on the skin, in the mouth, and in the intestines. Choice (D) is not mentioned and may not be concluded from information in the lecture.

Audio

44. Which of the following slides contain cocci bacteria?

Answer

(B) Visual B is the slide for the cocci bacteria. Visual A is the slide for the bacilli bacteria. Visual C is the slide for the spirilla bacteria.

Audio

45. Why are bacteria being used in the research study at the University?

Answer

(C) "Bacterial cells resemble the cells of other life forms. . . . " Choice (A) is not correct because bacteria cells resemble the cells of other life forms. Choices (B) and (D) are true, but they are not the reasons that bacteria are being used in research studies.

Audio Conversation

Narrator: Listen to part of a conversation between a student and an academic advisor on campus.

Man: Dr. Kelly, do you have a minute?
Dr. Kelly: Sure. Come in.
Man: Thanks. I need to talk with you about my sociology class.
Dr. Kelly: Let's see, that would be Sociology 530 with Dr. Brown.
Man: Right. The problem is that when I scheduled that class, it was supposed to be offered at three o'clock in the afternoon, Tuesdays and Thursdays, but for some reason the time has been changed to nine in the morning. Since I work mornings, I can't take it at that time.
Dr. Kelly: I see. Well, would you like to drop the class?
Man: Yes, but I also need to pick up another class. I have to be a full-time student in order to qualify for my student loan.
Dr. Kelly: So you need at least twelve hours. And you need afternoon classes.

Man:	That's right. Or evening classes.
Dr. Kelly:	Did you have anything in mind?
Man:	Yes. I was considering Sociology 560 or 570. I thought I'd get your opinion.
Dr. Kelly:	Either one will fit into your program since you are a Soc major, and they are both electives. Too bad you can't get a required course.
Man:	I know, but they all seem to be offered in the morning.
Dr. Kelly:	Okay, then. Which one is the most interesting to you?
Man:	I'm interested in both of them, but I was thinking since Dr. Brown teaches Soc 560, I might prefer that one. I've been trying to take a class with her because I hear that she is an excellent professor.
Dr. Kelly:	Good. The class is open, and I'll just sign that drop-add form for you to drop 530 and add 560. You can just tell Dr. Brown what happened when you see her in class.
Man:	Okay. Thanks a lot, Dr. Kelly. I really appreciate it.
Dr. Kelly:	Don't mention it.

> Now get ready to answer the questions

Audio

46. What is the purpose of this conversation?

Answer

(A) "It [the class] was supposed to be offered at three o'clock . . . the time has been changed. . . . " Choice (B) is not correct because the man has a job in the morning that conflicts with his class schedule. Choice (C) is not correct because the man has a student loan. Choice (D) is not correct because the man is already a sociology major.

Audio

47. Why does the man need to take at least twelve hours?

Answer

(B) "I have to be a full-time student in order to qualify for my student loan." Choice (D) is not correct because the courses are electives. Choices (A) and (C) are not mentioned and may not be concluded from information in the lecture.

Audio

48. Why does the man prefer Sociology 560?

Answer

(C) "Dr. Brown teaches Soc 560. . . . I've been trying to take a class with her. . . . " Choice (A) is not correct because it is an elective, not a required course. Choice (B) is not correct because it has been changed to nine in the morning. Choice (D) is not correct because both courses are sociology classes.

Audio

49. What will Dr. Kelly do?

Answer

(B) "...when I scheduled that class, it was supposed to be offered at three o'clock . . . but . . . the time has been changed. . . . " Choice (A) is not correct because the man is trying to register for classes. Choice (C) is not correct because the man already has a student loan. Choice (D) is not correct because the man is a sociology major, and he is trying to add a sociology class.

Audio

50. What will the man probably do after the conversation?

Answer

(B) ". . . tell Dr. Brown what happened when you see her in class." Choices (A), (C), and (D) are not correct because he will tell Dr. Brown what happened when he goes to her class.

Section 2: Structure

1. **(B)** A cardinal number is used after a noun. *The* is used with an ordinal number before a noun. Choice (A) is incomplete because there is no verb after *who*. Choices (C) and (D) are redundant.

2. **(C)** *But also* is used in correlation with the inclusive *not only*. Choice (B) would be used in correlation with *both*. Choices (A) and (D) are not used in correlation with another inclusive.

3. **(A)** A past form in the condition requires either *would* or *could* and a verb word in the result. Because the past form *planted* is used in the condition, *will* should be *would* in the result.

4. **(D)** In order to refer to an *increase* in the rate of inflation, *rises* should be used. *To raise* means to move to a higher place. *To rise* means to increase.

5. **(C)** A form of *have* with someone such as *General Lee* and a verb word expresses a causative. Choice (A) is an infinitive, not a verb word. Choice (B) is a participle. Choice (D) is an *-ing* form.

6. **(B)** Ideas after exclusives should be expressed by parallel structures. *To hunt* should be *in hunting* to provide for parallelism with the phrase *in planting*.

7. **(B)** *Effect on* is a prepositional idiom. *In* should be *on*.

8. **(A)** *Because* is used before a subject and verb to introduce cause. Choices (B), (C), and (D) are not accepted for statements of cause.

9. **(A)** The word order for a passive sentence is a form of BE followed by a participle. *Call* should be *called*.

10. **(B)** *Form* should be *formation*. Although both are nouns derived from verbs, the *-ation* ending is needed here. *Form* means the

structure. *Formation* means the process of forming over time.

11. **(C)** For scientific results, a present form in the condition requires a present or future form in the result. Choices (A), (B), and (D) are not conditional statements.

12. **(A)** Ideas in a series should be expressed by parallel structures. Only *to sell* in Choice (A) provides for parallelism with the infinitive *to increase*. Choices (B), (C), and (D) are not parallel.

13. **(D)** Because it is a prepositional phrase, *as grass* should be *like grass*. *As* functions as a conjunction. *Like* functions as a preposition.

14. **(C)** Ideas in a series should be expressed by parallel structures. *It is* should be deleted to provide for parallelism with the adjectives *interesting*, *informative*, and *easy*.

15. **(C)** Activities of the dead logically establish a point of view in the past. *Lives* should be *lived* in order to maintain the point of view.

16. **(D)** In contrary-to-fact clauses, *were* is the only accepted form of the verb BE. Choices (A), (B), and (C) are forms of the verb BE, but they are not accepted in contrary-to-fact clauses.

17. **(A)** The anticipatory clause *it is generally believed that* introduces a subject and verb, *Java Man...is*. In Choices (B) and (C) the verb *is* is repeated. Choice (D) may be used as a subject clause preceding a main verb, not preceding a subject and verb. "That it is generally believed that Java Man, who lived before the first Ice Age, is the first manlike animal *is* the result of entries in textbooks" would also be correct.

18. **(A)** A verb word must be used in a clause after an impersonal expression. *Is not* should be *not be* after the impersonal expression *it is essential*.

19. **(A)** *Who* should be *whom* because it is the complement of the clause *many people con-*

sider. Who functions as a subject. *Whom* functions as a complement.

20. **(B)** Only Choice (B) may be used with a noncount noun such as *money*. Choices (A), (C), and (D) may be used with count nouns.

21. **(D)** *By* expresses means before an *-ing* form. *Refine* should be *refining* after the preposition *by*.

22. **(D)** There must be agreement between pronoun and antecedent. *Their* should be *its* to agree with the singular antecedent *atmosphere*.

23. **(B)** Most adverbs of manner are formed by adding *-ly* to adjectives. *Broad* should be *broadly* to qualify the manner in which the speaking was done.

24. **(D)** An adjective clause modifies a noun in the main clause. *That provides food* modifies *the one*. Choice (A) is a subject and verb without the clause marker *that*. Choice (B) is a clause marker *that* with an *-ing* form, not a verb. Choice (C) is a verb without a clause marker.

25. **(A)** Plural count nouns are used after a number or a reference to a number of items. *Term* should be *terms*.

Section 3: Reading

1. **(B)** "The Process of Photosynthesis" is the best title because it states the main idea of the passage. The other choices are secondary ideas which are used to develop the main idea. Choice (A) describes the process in the form of an equation. In Choice (C), the parts of plants are named because of their roles in the process. Choice (D) is one of the products of the process.

2. **(B)** "…the green parts of plants use carbon dioxide from the atmosphere and release oxygen to it. Oxygen is the product of the reaction." The water referred to in Choice (A) and the carbon referred to in Choice (C) are used in photosynthesis, but neither one is mentioned as occurring in excess as a result of the process. Choice (D) refers to the natural substance in the chloroplasts of plants, not to a chemical combination of carbon dioxide and water.

3. **(D)** "These exchanges are the opposite of those that occur in respiration." Choices (A), (B), and (C) refer to processes which occur in photosynthesis, not to processes which are the opposite.

4. **(A)** "…radiant energy from the sun is stored as chemical energy." In Choice (B), it is water, not energy from the sun, which is conducted from the xylem to the leaves. Choice (C) is not correct because energy from the sun is the source of the chemical energy used in decomposing carbon dioxide and water. Choice (D) is not correct because it is oxygen, not energy, that is released one to one for each molecule of carbon dioxide used.

5. "Except for the usually small percentage used in respiration, the oxygen released in the process diffuses out of the leaf into the atmosphere through stomates." Quotation from sentence 6, paragraph 1.

6. **(A)** In the context of this passage, stored is closest in meaning to retained . Choices (B), (C), and (D) are not accepted definitions of the word.

7. **(B)** "The products of their decomposition [carbon dioxide and water] are recombined into a new compound, which is successively built up into more and more complex substances." Choices (A), (C), and (D) would change the meaning of the sentence.

8. **(B)** In the context of this passage, successively is closest in meaning to in a sequence . Choices (A), (C), and (D) are not accepted definitions of the word.

9. **(C)** "At the same time, a balance of gases is preserved in the atmosphere." Energy from the sun, referred to in Choice (A), and carbon dioxide, referred to in Choice (B), are used in the process of photosynthesis, not produced as a result of it. Choice (D) is not mentioned and may not be concluded from information in the passage.

10. **(A)** Choices (B), (C), and (D) are mentioned in sentences 6 and 7, paragraph 1. Water, not oxygen, is absorbed by the roots.

11. **(B)** The other choices are secondary ideas that are used to develop the main idea, "the Nobel Prizes." Choices (A), (C), and (D) are historically significant to the discussion.

12. **(A)** "The Nobel Prizes…were made available by a fund bequeathed for that purpose…by Alfred Bernhard Nobel." Because of the reference to *bequeath*, it must be concluded that Nobel left money in a will. In Choice (B), Nobel was the founder of the

prizes, not a recipient. Choice (C) refers to the place where Nobel was born, not to where he is living now. Since Nobel has bequeathed funds, it must be concluded that he is dead and could not serve as chairman of a committee as in Choice (D).

13. **(B)** In the context of this passage, will refers to a legal document Choices (A), (C), and (D) are not accepted definitions of the word in this context.

14. **(B)** "The Nobel Prizes, awarded annually …" Because of the reference to *annually*, it must be concluded that the prizes are awarded once a year. Choices (A), (C), and (D) are not mentioned and may not be concluded from information in the passage.

15. "According to the legend, Nobel's death had been erroneously reported in a newspaper, and the focus of the obituary was the fact that Nobel had invented dynamite. When he read this objective summary of his life [the obituary], the great chemist, it is said, decided that he wanted his name to be remembered for something more positive and humanitarian than inventing an explosive that was a potential weapon." The connection between these two sentences is the reference to "the obituary."

16. **(D)** In the context of this passage, outstanding could best be replaced by exceptional. Choices (A), (B), and (C) are not accepted definitions of the word.

17. **(C)** "The Nobel Prizes [are] awarded annually for distinguished work in chemistry, physics, physiology or medicine, literature, and international peace." Since there is no prize for music, a composer, in Choice (C) would not be eligible for an award. Choice (A) could be awarded a prize for literature. Choice (B) would be awarded a prize for medicine. Choice (D) could be awarded a prize for peace.

18. **(A)** Choice (A) is a restatement of the sentence referred to in the passage. To *administer* means to oversee or to manage. Choices (B), (C), and (D) would change the meaning of the original sentence.

19. **(B)** "The prizes are … presented … on December 10 … on the anniversary of his [Alfred Nobel's] death." Choice (A) is not correct because it is a tribute to Nobel, not to the King of Sweden. Choice (D) is not correct because the Nobel Foundation, not the Central Bank of Sweden, administers the trust. Choice (C) is not mentioned and may not be concluded from information in the passage.

20. In the context of this passage, the word award is closest in meaning to prize. No other words or phrases in the **bold** text are close to the meaning of the word prize.

21. **(C)** The other choices are secondary ideas that are used to develop the main idea, "the development of opera." Choices (A), (B), and (D) are historically significant to the discussion.

22. In the context of this passage, the word generally is closest in meaning to usually. No other words or phrases in the **bold** text are close to the meaning of the word usually.

23. **(D)** "The usually accepted date for the beginning of opera as we know it is 1600." Choice (A) refers to Greek tragedy, the inspiration for modern opera. Choices (B) and (C) are not mentioned and may not be concluded from information in the passage.

24. **(A)** "Although stage plays have been set to music since the era of the ancient Greeks, when the dramas of Sophocles and Aeschylus were accompanied by lyres and flutes, the usually accepted date for the beginning of opera as we know it [the opera] is 1600." Choices (B), (C), and (D) would change the meaning of the sentence.

25. **(B)** "…composer Jacopo Perí produced his famous *Euridice*, generally considered to be the first opera." Choice (A) refers to the form of musical story that inspired Perí, not to the opera that he wrote. Choice (C) refers to the wife of Henry IV for whose marriage the opera was written, not to the title of the opera. Choice (D) refers to the group of musicians who introduced the opera form, not to the title of an opera written by them.

26. **(D)** "As part of the celebration of the marriage of King Henry IV…Jacopo Perí produced his famous *Euridice*." Choice (A) is not correct because *Euridice* was produced in Florence, the native city of King Henry's wife and the place where the wedding was celebrated. Choice (B) refers to Greek tragedy, not to modern opera. Choice (C) is improbable because *Euridice* has become so famous.

27. **(B)** "…a group of Italian musicians called the Camerata began to revive the style of musical story that had been used in Greek

tragedy." In Choice (A), musicians in the Camerata were Italian, not Greek. Choice (C) is not correct because the center of the Camerata was Florence, Italy. King Henry IV referred to in Choice (D) was a patron of opera, but the name given to his court was not mentioned and may not be concluded from information in the passage.

28. **(B)** In the context of this passage, revive could best be replaced by resume . Choices (A), (C), and (D) are not accepted definitions of the word.

29. **(C)** In the context of this passage, plots is closest in meaning to stories . Choices (A), (B), and (D) are not accepted definitions of the word.

30. **(C)** "They called their compositions *opera in musica* or musical works. It is from this phrase that the word 'opera' is borrowed." Choice (A) refers to the origin of the plots for opera, not to the term. Choice (B) is not correct because the Camerata was a group of Italian musicians. Choice (D) refers to the composer of the first opera.

31. "Composers gave in to the demands of singers, writing many operas that were little more than a succession of brilliant tricks for the voice, designed to showcase the splendid voices of the singers who had requested them [brilliant tricks]." Other choices would change the meaning of the sentence.

32. In the context of this passage, the word purpose is closest in meaning to function . No other words or phrases in the **bold** text are close to the meaning of the word function .

33. **(B)** The author's main purpose is to describe the nature of sunspots. Choice (A) is not correct because there is no theory that completely explains sunspots. Choices (C) and (D) are important to the discussion, and provide details that support the main idea.

34. **(B)** In the context of this passage, controversial is closest in meaning to open to debate . Choices (A), (C), and (D) are not accepted definitions of the word.

35. **(B)** "...great storms on the surface of the sun hurl streams of solar particles into the atmosphere." *Storms* refer to disturbances of wind. Choice (A) is not correct because great storms have been identified as the cause of particles being hurled into space. In Choice (C), there are storms, not rivers on the surface of the sun. Choice (D) refers to what happens as a result of the particles being hurled into space.

36. **(D)** In the context of this passage, particles refers to small pieces of matter. Choices (A), (B), and (C) are not accepted definitions of the word.

37. **(A)** "...streams of solar particles [are hurled] into the atmosphere." Because of the reference to *particles*, it must be concluded that the matter is very small. Choices (B), (C), and (D) are not mentioned and may not be concluded from information in the passage.

38. **(C)** Choice (C) is a restatement of the sentence referred to in the passage. The fact that the cooler sunspots may account for their color means that the color could be affected by the cooler temperature.

39. In the context of this passage, the word large is most opposite in meaning to tiny . No other words or phrases in the **bold** text are opposite in meaning to the word tiny .

40. **(B)** "About five percent of the spots are large enough so that they [the spots] can be seen without instruments; consequently, observations of sunspots have been recorded for several thousand years." Choices (A), (C), and (D) would change the meaning of the sentence.

41. **(A)** In the context of this passage, consequently could best be replaced by as a result . Choices (B), (C), and (D) are not accepted definitions of the word.

42. **(B)** "Sunspots...tend to occur in pairs." Choices (A) and (C) refer to possibilities for arrangements, but not to the configuration in which sunspots usually occur. Choice (D) is not mentioned in the range of numbers for sunspots, from one to more than one hundred. The number *one thousand* refers to the number of years sunspots have been recorded, not to the number in a configuration.

43. **(B)** "...several models attempt to relate the phenomenon [of sunspots] to magnetic fields along the lines of longitude from the north and south poles of the sun." Choice (A) is not correct because the magnetic fields are on the sun, not the Earth. Choice (C) is not correct because the storms are on the sun, not on the Earth. Choice (D) is not correct because several models attempt to relate sunspots to magnetic fields.

44. "About 5 percent of all sunspots are large enough so that they can be seen from Earth without instruments; consequently, observations of sunspots have been recorded for thousands of years." Quotation from sentence 2, paragraph 3.

45. **(C)** "…the controversial sunspot theory." Because the theory is controversial, it must be concluded that it is subject to disagreement. Choice (B) is not correct because the theory is controversial. Choices (A) and (D) are not mentioned and may not be concluded from information in the passage.

Writing Section

Question

Many people enjoy participating in sports for recreation; others enjoy participating in the arts. Give the benefits of each, take a position, and defend it.

Outline

Benefits sports
- Group membership—teams
- Good health
- Life lessons—winning and losing

Benefits arts
- Creative outlet
- Cultural lessons—traditions
- Spiritual experience

Divide my time—balance
- Soccer
- Photography

Map

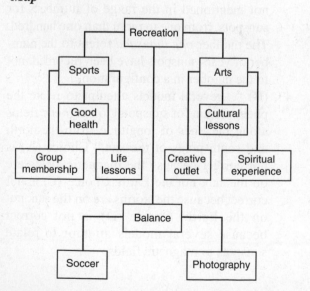

Example Essay

Many people enjoy participating in sports for recreation because it offers an opportunity to be part of a group. As a participant, you can join a team and enjoy all the benefits of membership—shared experiences, travel to other sites to play, and a feeling of belonging. In training for a sport, an exercise routine usually contributes to good health. Probably even more important than group identity and good health are the life lessons that participation in a sport provides. Setting a goal and working toward it, collaborating with others, and putting a plan into action are all good lessons that can be learned on the playing field. How to win graciously and lose gracefully are important not only in playing a game but also in being successful in life.

The arts offer another avenue for recreation. By spending time in artistic endeavors, you can explore your creativity and appreciate or make something beautiful—a picture, a song, or a floral arrangement. Besides the creative outlet, participating in the arts offers an opportunity to learn about the culture and traditions that infuse art with meaning. For some people, participating in or even viewing art can be a spiritual experience. To create and appreciate a beautiful environment is important not only for personal recreation but also because it makes the world a nicer place for everyone.

When I have time for recreational activities, I participate in both sports and the arts. By dividing my time between them, I can take advantage of all the benefits of both types of recreation. I enjoy playing soccer at school, which allows me to be part of a team. The training routine includes both physical and mental exercises. I also enjoy photography, which gives me a creative outlet. I find that alternating these activities provides balance in my life.

Model Test 2—Computer-Assisted TOEFL

Section 1: Listening

The Listening Section of the test measures the ability to understand conversations and talks in English. On the actual TOEFL exam, you will use headphones to listen to the conversations and talks. While you are listening, pictures of the speakers or other information will be presented on your computer screen. There are two parts to the Listening Section, with special directions for each part.

On the day of the test, the amount of time you will have to answer all of the questions will appear on the computer screen. The time you spend listening to the test material will not be counted. The listening material and questions about it will be presented only one time. You will not be allowed to take notes or have any paper at your computer. You will both see and hear the questions before the answer choices appear. You can take as much time as you need to select an answer; however, it will be to your advantage to answer the questions as quickly as possible. You may change your answer as many times as you want before you confirm it. After you have confirmed an answer, you will not be able to return to the question.

Before you begin working on the Listening Section, you will have an opportunity to adjust the volume of the sound. You may not be able to change the volume after you have started the test.

QUESTION DIRECTIONS—Part A

In Part A of the Listening Section, you will hear short conversations between two people. In some of the conversations, each person speaks only once. In other conversations, one or both of the people speak more than once. Each conversation is followed by one question about it.

Each question in this part has four answer choices. You should click on the best answer to each question. Answer the questions on the basis of what is stated or implied by the speakers.

Audio

1. Man: How many did you have for the orientation?
   Woman: Well, let me see. Fifty had registered, but everyone didn't show up. I believe that we had twenty-five from the Middle East and at least fifteen from Latin America.
   Man: You don't mean it!
   Narrator: What had the man assumed?

Answer

(B) *You don't mean it* is an idiomatic expression that means the speaker is surprised. Choice (C) is not correct because the man is surprised by the large turn out. Choices (A) and (D) are not mentioned and may not be concluded from information in the conversation.

Audio

2. Man: Excuse me. Could you tell me when Dr. Smith has office hours?
   Woman: Not really, but there's a sign on the door I think.
   Narrator: What does the woman imply that the man should do?

Answer

(D) Since the woman points out the sign on the door, she implies that the man should look at it. Choices (A), (B), and (C) are not mentioned and may not be concluded from information in the conversation.

Audio

3. Man: I heard that Professor Wilson will let you do a project for extra credit.
   Woman: That's great! I could use some.
   Narrator: What is the woman probably going to do?

Answer

(D) Since the woman expressed interest in and enthusiasm for the opportunity to do a project for extra credit, it must be concluded that she intends to do one. Choice (A) is not correct because the woman is already taking a class from Professor Wilson. Choice (C) is not correct because the reference to "extra" is to extra credit, not to an extra class. Choice (B) is not mentioned and may not be concluded from information in the conversation.

Audio

4. Man: Is Paul angry?
   Woman: If he were, he'd tell us.
   Narrator: What does the woman say about Paul?

Answer

(B) Listen carefully for the distinction between the words *angry* and *hungry*. Because the woman says that Paul would tell them if he were angry, it must be concluded that Paul would tell them if there were a problem. In Choices (A) and (C), the word *angry* is confused with the word *hungry*. Choice (B) refers to what the woman, not the man, thinks about Paul.

Audio

5. Man: I heard you got an A on the final exam. I think you're the only one who did!
   Woman: Not really. There were a couple of other As.
   Narrator: What does the woman mean?

Answer

(D) Since the woman says that there were a couple of As, it must be concluded that several other students received A grades. Choice (B) is not correct because she refers to other As, implying that she received one. Choices (A) and (C) are not mentioned and may not be concluded from information in the conversation.

Audio

6. Woman: Oh, no. It's five o'clock already and I haven't finished studying for the quiz in Dr. Taylor's class.
   Man: Don't worry. That clock is half an hour fast.
   Narrator: What problem does the woman have?

Answer
(C) Since the man says that the clock is fast, it must be concluded that the woman still has time to study. Choice (A) is not correct because a half hour is left. Choice (D) is not correct because the man knows the clock is fast. Choice (B) is not mentioned and may not be concluded from information in the conversation.

Audio
7. Man: It's much better to wait until tomorrow to go. Don't you agree?
   Woman: Yes. I couldn't agree more.
   Narrator: What does the woman mean?

Answer
(B) To *not agree more* means to "agree very much." Choices (A) and (D) misinterpret the phrase *couldn't agree more* as a negative. Choice (C) is not mentioned and may not be concluded from information in the conversation.

Audio
8. Man: I have to go to class because I have a test, but if I could, I'd go with you to the movie.
   Woman: That's too bad. I wish that you could come along.
   Narrator: What is the man going to do?

Answer
(A) The man says that he has to go to class. Choice (B) refers to what the woman, not the man, is going to do. Choices (C) and (D) are not mentioned and may not be concluded from information in the conversation.

Audio
9. Woman: I left a message on your answering machine a couple of days ago.
   Man: Yes. I've been meaning to get back with you.
   Narrator: What does the man mean?

Answer
(C) *Meaning to* is an idiomatic expression that means intention on the part of the speaker. To "get back with" someone means to return a call or otherwise communicate. Choice (B) is not correct because a message was left on the machine. Choice (D) is not correct because the man acknowledges the message. Choice (A) is not mentioned and may not be concluded from information in the conversation.

Audio
10. Man: I think it's my turn.
    Woman: Sorry you had to wait so long. One of the other secretaries is out today.
    Narrator: What does the woman mean?

Answer
(A) To be *out* is an idiomatic expression that means to be "absent." Choices (B), (C), and (D) are not paraphrases of the expression and may not be concluded from information in the conversation.

Audio

11. Man: Could you please tell me what room Dr. Robert Davis is in?
    Woman: Yes, he's in the Math Department on the fourth floor. Check with the secretary before going in, though.
    Narrator: What does the woman suggest that the man do?

Answer

(B) "Check with the secretary before going in . . ." Choice (A) is not correct because the woman has already given him directions to the Math Department. Choice (C) is not correct because the woman tells him to check with the secretary first. Choice (D) is not mentioned and may not be concluded from information in the conversation.

Audio

12. Man: Tom wasn't in class again today!
    Woman: I know. I wonder whether he'll show up for the final exam.
    Narrator: What can be inferred about Tom?

Answer

(D) Since Tom is often absent and there is doubt that he will be present for the final exam, it must be concluded that Tom is not very responsible. Choices (A), (B), and (C) are not mentioned and may not be concluded from information in the conversation.

Audio

13. Man: Hey, Kathy.
    Woman: Hi Ted. How are you doing?
    Man: Fine. Are we still on for tonight?
    Woman: I'm looking forward to it.
    Narrator: What does the man mean?

Answer

(D) *Are we still on* is an idiomatic expression that is used to confirm a date. Choice (C) refers to the woman's feelings, not to the man's feelings. Choices (A) and (B) are not mentioned and may not be concluded from information in the conversation.

Audio

14. Woman: So the course *is* closed. This is terrible! I have to have it to graduate.
    Man: You're okay. Just Dr. Collin's section is closed. There's another section that's still open, but nobody knows who's teaching it. It's marked "staff."
    Narrator: What will the woman probably do?

Answer

(C) Since the woman must have the course to graduate and Dr. Collin's section is closed, she will probably enroll in the section marked "staff." Choice (A) is not correct because Dr. Collin's section is closed. Choice (B) is not correct because the woman is distressed because she is planning to graduate soon. Choice (D) is not correct because she needs the course to graduate and is more interested in the course than in the instructor.

Audio

15. Woman: What's wrong?
    Man: I still haven't received my score on the GMAT test. Maybe I should call to check on it.
    Woman: Don't worry so much. It takes at least six weeks to receive your score.
    Narrator: What does the woman think that the man should do?

Answer

(A) Since the woman says that it takes six weeks to receive the score, she implies that the man should wait for the results to be mailed. Choice (B) refers to the man's plan, not to the woman's suggestion. Choice (C) is not correct because the man has already taken the test and is waiting for the score. Choice (D) is not correct because the woman tells him not to worry.

Audio

16. Man: You've been doing a lot of traveling, haven't you?
    Woman: Yes. We want to make the most of our time here.
    Narrator: What does the woman mean?

Answer

(B) To *make the most of* something is an idiomatic expression that means to "take advantage of" an opportunity. Choices (A), (C), and (D) are not paraphrases of the expression and may not be concluded from information in the conversation.

Audio

17. Woman: Did you get your tickets?
    Man: I talked to Judy about it, and she took care of it for me.
    Narrator: What does the man mean?

Answer

(B) To *take care of something* is an idiomatic expression that means to "be responsible" for it. Choices (A), (C), and (D) are not paraphrases of the expression and may not be concluded from information in the conversation.

QUESTION DIRECTIONS—Part B

In Part B of the Listening Section, you will hear several longer conversations and talks. Each conversation or talk is followed by several questions. The conversations, talks, and questions will not be repeated.

The conversations and talks are about a variety of topics. You do not need special knowledge of the topics to answer the questions correctly. Rather, you should answer each question on the basis of what is stated or implied by the speakers in the conversations or talks.

For most of the questions, you will need to click on the best of four possible answers. Some questions will have special directions. The special directions will appear in a box on the computer screen.

Audio Conversation

Narrator: Listen to part of a conversation between two classmates on a college campus.

Man: Did you understand that experiment that Bill mentioned in the group presentation?
Woman: The one about free fall?
Man: Right. The one that was conducted on the moon.
Woman: Sure. The astronaut held a hammer in one hand and a feather in the other. Then he dropped them at the same time…
Man: …and both of them hit the ground at the same time.
Woman: Yes. So that proves Galileo's theory that all objects fall at the same rate in the absence of air resistance.

Man:	Okay. That was the part that was missing for me. The part about air resistance.
Woman:	Oh. Well, since there is no air resistance on the moon, it is the ideal environment for the experiment.
Man:	That makes sense.
Woman:	Actually, the part that surprised me was how much easier it is to lift the hammer on the moon than it is on Earth because of the moon's lower rate of gravitational acceleration.
Man:	But didn't they say that it was just as difficult to push the hammer along the surface when it fell?
Woman:	Right again. Because gravity only governs vertical motion like lifting, but not horizontal motion like pushing.
Man:	Thanks for going over this with me.
Woman:	You're welcome. I really liked the presentation. I think the group did a good job.

> Now get ready to answer the questions

Audio

18. What are the man and woman talking about?

Answer

(B) "Did you understand that experiment that Bill mentioned in the group presentation?" Choices (A), (C), and (D) are not mentioned and may not be concluded from information in the discussion.

Audio

19. Why is the moon an ideal environment for the experiment?

Answer

(A) ". . . since there is no air resistance on the moon, it is the ideal environment for the experiment." Choice (B) refers to the fact that the moon has a lower gravitational acceleration, not that there is no gravitational acceleration. Choices (C) and (D) are true, but they are not the reason the moon is an ideal environment.

Audio

20. Why was it easier to lift the hammer on the moon?

Answer

(A) ". . . much easier . . . to lift the hammer on the moon…because of the moon's lower rate of gravitational acceleration." Choice (B) is true, but it is not the reason lifting the hammer on the moon is easier. Choices (C) and (D) are not mentioned and may not be concluded from information in the discussion.

Audio

21. How did the woman feel about the presentation?

Answer

(C) "I really liked the presentation." Choice (A) refers to information about the hammer, not to the entire presentation. Choice (B) is not correct because she liked the presentation. Choice (D) is not mentioned and may not be concluded from information in the discussion.

Audio Conversation

Narrator: Listen to a conversation between two college students.

Man: What did you think about the video we were supposed to watch for Professor Stephen's class?
Woman: I didn't see it. Was it good?
Man: Really it was. It was about stress.
Woman: How to relieve stress?
Man: Not really. More the effects of stress on the national health.
Woman: Oh.
Man: But it was interesting, though.
Woman: Really?
Man: Yes. I think they said that one out of nine women age forty-five through sixty-five will have a heart attack.
Woman: I'm surprised at that.
Man: I was, too. Oh, another thing. They said that women usually don't get the same level of care that men do, so the heart attack is likely to be more serious.
Woman: Why is that?
Man: Because many members of the medical profession still think of a heart attack as a male problem, so they don't recognize the symptoms in their women patients.
Woman: Well, it does sound like an interesting video. I'm going to try to see it before class next time so I'll be ready for the discussion.
Man: It's on reserve in the library, so you can't check it out, but you can use one of the viewing rooms. It's only an hour long.

> Now get ready to answer the questions

Audio
22. What was the video about?

Answer
(B) "It [the video] was about stress." Choices (A), (C), and (D) are secondary themes used to develop the main theme of the video.

Audio
23. What did the students learn about women?

Answer
(C) "They said that women usually don't get the same level of care that men do. . . ." Choice (D) is not correct because the heart attacks suffered by women are likely to be more serious. Choices (A) and (B) are not mentioned and may not be concluded from information in the conversation.

Audio
24. How did the man feel about the video?

Answer
(B) "Really it was [good]." Choice (A) is not correct because he explains the video to the woman. Choice (C) is not correct because he encourages the woman to view it. Choice (D) is not correct because he was surprised by the report on the number of women who have heart attacks.

Audio
25. What will the woman probably do?

Answer
(B) "It's on reserve in the library. . . . " Choice (A) refers to the fact that the man and woman have already discussed the video, not to what the woman will do. Choice (C) is not correct because tapes on reserve cannot be checked out. Choice (D) refers to what the woman will do after she sees the video.

Audio Lecture
Narrator: Listen to a lecture by an English intructor.

The romance and marriage of Elizabeth Barrett to Robert Browning inspired some of the greatest love poems written in the English language. Elizabeth, without a doubt the greatest woman poet of the Victorian period, was born in Durham County, England, in 1806. Her first important publication was *The Seraphim and Other Poems,* which appeared in 1838.

By 1843, she was so widely recognized that her name was suggested to replace the late Poet Laureate as the official national poet of England. In part because the sovereign was a woman, there was great support for a movement to break with the tradition of a male Poet Laureate. Nevertheless, she lost the competition to William Wordsworth.

A short time later, she married Robert Browning, himself a gifted poet, and they fled to Florence, Italy. A play, *The Barretts of Wimpole Street*, recounts their confrontation with Elizabeth's father and their eventual elopement against his wishes.

While living in Florence, their only son was born. A year later, in 1850, Elizabeth published her collected works, along with a volume of new poems entitled *Sonnets from the Portuguese*, so named because her husband often called her his "Portuguese." *Aurora Leigh*, her longest work, appeared in 1856, only five years before her death in Italy in 1861.

> Now get ready to answer the questions

Audio
26. What is the main topic of this lecture?

Answer
(D) Elizabeth Barrett Browning is the main topic of this lecture. Choices (A), (B), and (C) are secondary topics that are used to develop the main topic of the lecture.

Audio
27. According to the lecturer, what was one reason that Elizabeth Barrett was considered for the title of Poet Laureate?

Answer
(C) "In part because the sovereign was a woman, there was great support for a movement to break with the tradition of a male Poet Laureate." Choice (A) is not correct because Elizabeth Barrett was not married at the time that she was considered for the title of Poet Laureate. Choice (B) is not correct because *Sonnets from the Portuguese* was not published at the time that she was considered for the title. Choice (D) is not mentioned and may not be concluded from information in the talk.

Audio
28. Where did Elizabeth and Robert Browning live after their elopement?

Answer
(B) ". . . she married Robert Browning, himself a gifted poet, and they fled to Florence, Italy." The place in Choice (C) refers to the title of one of Elizabeth's most famous works, *Sonnets from the Portuguese,* not to a place where she lived. The place in Choice (D) refers to the country where she lived before, not after, her marriage. Choice (A) is not mentioned and may not be concluded from information in the talk.

Audio
29. When did Elizabeth Barrett Browning die?

Answer
(D) "*Aurora Leigh,* her longest work, appeared in 1856, only five years before her death in Italy in 1861." Choice (A) refers to the date when Elizabeth Barrett was suggested to replace the Poet Laureate, not to the date of her death. Choice (B) refers to the date when her son was born, one year before she published her collected works in 1850. Choice (C) refers to the date when *Aurora Leigh* was published, five years before her death.

Audio Lecture
Narrator: Listen to a lecture by a biology instructor.

Today's lecture will include the most outstanding achievements in biology as it relates to the medical sciences.

Early in Greek history, Hippocrates began to study the human body and to apply scientific method to the problems of diagnosis and the treatment of diseases. Unlike other physicians of his time, he discarded the theory that disease was caused by the gods. Instead, he kept careful records of symptoms and treatments, indicating the success or failure of the patient's cure. He has been recognized as the father of modern medicine.

About a century later, Aristotle began a scientific study of plants and animals, classifying more than five hundred types on the basis of body structure. Because of his great contribution to the field, Aristotle has been called the father of biology.

By the first century A.D., Dioscorides had collected a vast amount of information on plants, which he recorded in the now famous *Materia Medica,* a book that remained an authoritative reference among physicians for fifteen hundred years.

During the Middle Ages, scientific method was scorned in favor of alchemy. Thus, medicine and biology had advanced very little from the time of the ancients until the seventeenth century when the English physician and anatomist William Harvey discovered a mechanism for the circulation of the blood in the body.

> Now get ready to answer the questions

Audio
30. What is the main topic of this lecture?

Answer
(B) The contributions of biology to medicine are the main topic of this lecture. Choices (A), (C), and (D) are secondary topics that are used to develop the main topic of the lecture.

Audio

31. What was Hippocrates' greatest contribution to medicine?

Answer

(C) "Hippocrates began . . . to apply scientific method to the problems of diagnosis and the treatment of diseases. . . . He kept careful records of symptoms and treatments." Choice (A) refers to the work of Aristotle, not Hippocrates. Choice (D) refers to a theory that Hippocrates discarded in favor of the scientific method, not to his work. Choice (B) is not mentioned and may not be concluded from information in the lecture.

Audio

32. Who is known as the father of biology?

Answer

(B) "Because of his great contribution to the field, Aristotle has been called the father of biology." Choice (A) refers to the father of modern medicine, not to the father of biology. Choice (C) refers to the author of *Materia Medica*. Choice (D) is not mentioned and may not be concluded from information in the lecture.

Audio

33. What was the contribution made to medicine by William Harvey?

Answer

(C) ". . . the English physician and anatomist William Harvey discovered a mechanism for the circulation of the blood in the body." Choice (D) refers to a reference book that was a contribution by Dioscorides.

Audio Discussion

Narrator: Listen to part of a class discussion in a sociology class.

Dr. Jackson: Last class, I asked you to locate some articles about gang activity. Let's just go around the table and share what we found. Tracy, will you begin please?

Tracy: Okay. Actually, I did a search of sociological studies on gang activity, and I found that gangs have been prevalent for much longer than I had assumed. I was so surprised. For some reason, I thought that gang activity was a fairly recent phenomenon, but actually, one of the largest studies was carried out by Thrasher in 1936.

Dr. Jackson: Good. Good. I'm pleased that you did that. Thrasher's study is a classic research investigation. Can you summarize the findings?

Tracy: Sure. First, I should say that the study included more than 1300 gangs with more than 25,000 members. According to Thrasher, a gang is a group that may form spontaneously, but after that, will integrate through conflict and violence. Over time, a spirit of solidarity and an attachment to a local territory form. What is most interesting, besides the long history of gangs in the United States, is the fact that not much has changed over the years. And, oh yes, gang behavior seems pretty similar even across cultures.

Dr. Jackson: That is interesting.

Bill: Dr. Jackson, may I go next? I have just a brief comment that seems to fit in here.

Dr. Jackson: Please.

Bill: Well, another classic study, much later, about 1987 or 8, I think, by Joan Moore, indicated that gang behavior is probably caused by normal adolescent insecurities—the desire for peer approval, respect, support, acceptance, and, in some cases, protection, if the neighborhood is perceived as dangerous. It seems that gangs take the place of the more childish and acceptable cliques that develop in high schools.

Sandy:	Is it my turn? Well, I looked up the definitions of gang members by police departments and law enforcement agencies. According to the California Youth Gang Task Force, for example, a gang member will be recognizable because of gang-related tattoos, clothing, and paraphernalia like scarves and hats that identify a particular gang, and allow others to confirm that the wearer has a right to be on the gang's turf. And, to follow up on Tracy's comments about the history of gangs, these criteria have been in place for a long time.
Dr. Jackson:	Good job. So far, what I am hearing, though, refers to male gang membership. What about females? Did anyone find any research on their role in gang activity?
Bill:	I did. Although there are a few girl gangs, females are generally not considered members of the male-dominated gang. They are viewed as more of a support system, and an extended social group—friends and girlfriends to party with.
Sandy:	That's what I found, too.

> Now get ready to answer the questions

Audio

34. What was surprising about Thrasher's study?

Answer

(D) "...gangs have been prevalent for much longer than I had assumed. I was so surprised." The number in Choice (A) is true, but it was not what surprised the student. Choice (C) is not correct because not much has changed over the years. Choice (B) is not mentioned and may not be concluded from information in the discussion.

Audio

35. According to the study by Moore, what causes gang activity?

Answer

(B) ". . . Joan Moore, indicated that gang behavior is probably caused by normal adolescent insecurities. . . ." Choice (A) refers to a similar form of behavior but not to the cause of gang activity. Choice (C) refers to the neighborhoods where gang activity takes place, but they are not the cause of gang activity. Choice (D) is not mentioned and may not be concluded from information in the discussion.

Audio

36. In which two ways are gang members identified by law enforcement authorities?

Answer

(A) (B) ". . . a gang member will be recognizable because of gang-related tattoos, clothing. . . ." The phrase *research studies* in Choice (D) refers to the research reported in the discussion, not to ways that gang members are identified. Choice (C) is not mentioned and may not be concluded from information in the discussion.

Audio

37. What is the role of women in gangs?

Answer

(C) "They [women] are viewed as more of a support system. . . ." Choice (A) is not correct because women are not considered members of gangs. Choice (D) is not correct because women are part of the extended social group of a gang. Choice (B) is not mentioned and may not be concluded from information in the discussion.

Audio Conversation

Narrator:	Listen to part of a conversation between a student and a professor in the professor's office.
Mary:	Dr. Brown, could I speak with you for a minute?
Dr. Brown:	Sure, Mary. Come in.
Mary:	I'm afraid I have a problem.
Dr. Brown:	Oh?
Mary:	You see, I really like my job here.
Dr. Brown:	That's good. Because we really like having you here.
Mary:	Thank you. But the problem is I won't be able to work here next semester. You see, I have a problem with my schedule at school.
Dr. Brown:	Well, what exactly is the problem?
Mary:	I have a required class at nine o'clock on Monday, Wednesday, and Friday.
Dr. Brown:	Oh. Okay. Remind me what your hours are here.
Mary:	I work from nine to one every day. Which has been great, because I have been able to schedule all my classes in the afternoon, until now.
Dr. Brown:	I see. When does the class end?
Mary:	It's a three-hour class, so it meets for an hour three times a week.
Dr. Brown:	So you're finished at ten.
Mary:	Yes. And it would take me half an hour to get here after class, so you see, I would be an hour and a half late on those days.
Dr. Brown:	Well, we need someone four hours a day. But, how about this—you could come in at ten-thirty on Monday, Wednesday, and Friday, and work until two-thirty on those days. That would give you a fairly late lunch, but if that's not a problem for you, then we can do it.
Mary:	That would be great. So I'd just keep my regular hours on Tuesday and Thursday then.
Dr. Brown:	Right. Listen, Mary. You're a work-study employee, and that means that you have two responsibilities—to work and to study. We know that. As long as you put in the hours to get the job done, we expect to fit your work hours around your school schedule. And don't forget, you can study on the job as long as the work is done first.

> Now get ready to answer the questions

Audio

38. What is Mary's problem?

Answer

(B) "I have a problem with my schedule." Choice (A) is not correct because Mary really likes her job. Choice (D) is not correct because she is a work-study employee. Choice (C) is not mentioned and may not be concluded from information in the conversation.

Audio

39. When is Mary's class next semester?

Answer

(D) "I have a required class at nine o'clock on Monday, Wednesday, and Friday." The phrase *every day* in Choice (A) refers to her work schedule, not to her class schedule. The phrase *ten-thirty on Monday* in Choice (C) refers to the time she will report to work, not to the time for her class. Choice (B) is not mentioned and may not be concluded from information in the conversation.

Audio

40. How does Dr. Brown resolve the problem?

Answer

(A) "…you could come in at ten-thirty . . . and work until two-thirty. . . ." Choice (B) is not correct because she will continue to work four hours a day. Choice (D) is not correct because he changes her work schedule. Choice (C) is not mentioned and may not be concluded from information in the conversation.

Audio

41. What is a work-study employee?

Answer

(C) "You're a work-study employee, and that means . . . you can study on the job as long as the work is done first." Choice (A) is true, but it is not a complete definition of a work-study employee. Choices (B) and (D) are not mentioned and may not be concluded from information in the conversation.

Audio Lecture

Narrator: Listen to part of a lecture in an engineering class.

In recent years, we have developed several techniques for building more earthquake-resistant structures. For relatively small buildings, all we have to do is bolt the buildings to their foundations and provide some support walls.

These walls are referred to as shear walls in your textbook. They are made of reinforced concrete, and by that I mean concrete with steel rods embedded in it. This not only strengthens the structure but also diminishes the forces that tend to shake a building during a quake. In addition to the shear walls that surround a building, shear walls can be situated in the center of a building around an elevator shaft or a stairwell. This is really an excellent reinforcement. It is commonly known as a shear core, and it, too, contains reinforced concrete.

Walls can also be reinforced, using a technique called cross-bracing. Imagine steel beams that cross diagonally from the ceiling to the floor of each story in a building. Before the walls are finished, you can see a vertical row of steel x's on the structure.

Besides steel reinforcements, engineers have also devised base isolators, which are positioned below the building to absorb the shock of the sideways shaking that can undermine a building and cause it to collapse. Most of the base isolators that are currently being used are made of alternating layers of steel and synthetic rubber. The steel is for strength, but the rubber absorbs shock waves. In higher buildings, a moat of flexible materials allows the building to sway during seismic activity.

The combination of a reinforced structure and flexible materials has been proven to reduce earthquake damage. But even these engineering techniques are insufficient if the building has been constructed on filled ground. Soil used in fill dirt can lose its bearing strength when subjected to the shock waves of an earthquake, and the buildings constructed on it can literally disappear into the Earth.

In areas where earthquakes are known to occur, understanding the terrain and using the techniques we have discussed today can greatly reduce property damage, and can save lives as well.

> Now get ready to answer the questions

Audio
42. What is the topic of this lecture?

Answer
(C) ". . . we have developed several techniques for building more earthquake-resistant structures." Choices (A), (B), and (D) are all mentioned in the lecture, but they are secondary ideas used to develop the main topic of the lecture.

Audio
43. Which technique is used to reinforce walls?

Answer
(A) "Walls can also be reinforced, using . . . cross-bracing." Choice (B) refers to a structure in the center of a building. Choice (D) refers to a device positioned below the building. Choice (C) is not mentioned and may not be concluded from information in the lecture.

Audio
44. Which two materials are used in base isolators?

Answer
(A) (B) "Most . . . base isolators . . . are made of . . . layers of steel and synthetic rubber." Choice (C) refers to construction material but not to material used in base isolators. Choice (D) refers to fill dirt.

Audio
45. What happens to fill dirt during an earthquake?

Answer
(C) ". . . fill dirt can lose its bearing strength . . . and the buildings constructed on it can . . . disappear into the Earth." Choice (A) refers to the characteristics of a moat, not to those of fill dirt. Choice (B) refers to the techniques for building earthquake-resistant structures. The phrase *shock waves* in Choice (D) refers to the advantage of rubber, not to a characteristic of fill dirt.

Audio Lecture

Narrator: Listen to part of a lecture in a botany lab. The lab assistant is talking about leaves.

Food and water are carried throughout leaves by their veins. Today we will be looking at some examples of the main types of vein patterns in leaves. The most common are the pinnate and the palmate. This is a pinnate leaf, which is characteristic of trees like the beech and birch that you see outside this building on campus.

Remember that a pinnate leaf has one large central vein called the midrib, with large veins branching off on each side of it. The midrib extends the full length of the leaf.

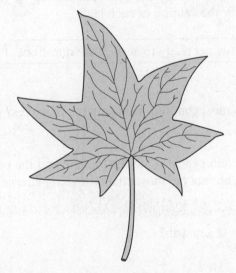

Notice how different this leaf is. This is an example of a palmate leaf from a maple tree. A good way to remember this classification is to think of the palm of your hand. In a palmate leaf, there are several main veins of about equal size that originate at the base of the leaf and extend out to the edge of the leaf like fingers.

A few very narrow leaves are neither pinnate nor palmate. This leaf of grass for example has a parallel pattern.

Several veins extend themselves from the base of the blade to the tip, as you can see here.

Needle leaves are so small that they only have one, or occasionally two, veins in the center of the needle. I don't have a good slide of a needle leaf, but there is a drawing in your lab manual for you to refer to.

Now, I'd like you to turn to chapter three in the manual, and use page fifty-two as a reference for your lab activity. You will find twenty leaves in a plastic bag on your lab table. Please work with your lab partner to classify the veining of each leaf.

> Now get ready to answer the questions

Audio
46. Which two types represent the most common vein patterns in leaves?

Answer
(C) (D) "The most common [vein patterns] are the pinnate and the palmate." Choices (A) and (B) refer to vein patterns, but they are not the most common vein patterns.

Audio
47. According to the lecturer, what is a midrib?

Answer
(B) ". . . a pinnate leaf has one large central vein called the midrib . . . [that] extends the full length of the leaf." Choice (A) is not correct because the pinnate leaf, not the midrib, is one of the major classifications. Choice (C) is not correct because the midrib is a central vein in the pinnate, not the parallel, leaf. Choice (D) is not mentioned and may not be concluded from information in the lecture.

Audio
48. How does the lab assistant help students remember the palmate classification?

Answer
(C) "A good way to remember this classification [palmate] is to think of the palm of your hand." Choices (A) and (B) are both true, but she did not use the visual or the explanation as a memory aid.

The phrase *lab manual* in Choice (D) refers to a reference for the lab activity, not to a way to remember the classification.

Audio

49. Match the leaves with their vein patterns.

Answer

(B) Pinnate **(A)** Palmate **(C)** Parallel

Audio

50. What will the students probably do after the short lecture?

Answer

(A) ". . . work with your lab partner to classify the veining of each leaf." The word *fifty-two* in Choice (C) refers to the page number in the lab manual, not to the number of pages to read. Choices (B) and (D) are not mentioned and may not be concluded from information in the lecture.

Section 2: Structure

1. **(A)** In some dependent clauses, the clause marker is the subject of the dependent clause. *Which* refers to *the soybeans* and is the subject of the verb *can be used.* Choices (B) and (D) do not have clause markers. Choice (C) is a clause marker that refers to a person, not to *soybeans.*

2. **(A)** Only Choice (A) may be used with a count noun like *species* and a number. Choices (C) and (D) may be used with noncount nouns. Choice (B) may be used with count nouns without a number. "As many species of finch have been identified" would also be correct.

3. **(C)** The verb *had* establishes a point of view in the past. *Serves* should be *served* in order to maintain the point of view.

4. **(D)** There must be agreement between subject and verb. *Produce* should be *produces* to agree with the singular subject *a thunderhead.*

5. **(C)** When the degree of one quality, *the price,* is dependent upon the degree of another quality, *the demand,* two comparatives are required, each of which must be preceded by *the.* Choice (A) is a comparative, but it is not preceded by *the.* Choices (B) and (D) are not accepted comparative forms.

6. **(B)** *The same like* is a combination of *the same as* and *like. Like* should be *as* in the phrase with *the same.*

7. **(A)** *Despite of* is a combination of *despite* and *in spite of.* Either *despite* or *in spite of* should be used.

8. **(C)** *So* is used with an adjective to express cause. Choice (A) may be used before a noun, not before an adjective such as *big.* Choices (B) and (D) may not be used to express cause before a clause of result such as *that there are four time zones.* "The United States is very big" would be correct without the clause of result.

9. **(A)** Ideas in a series should be expressed by parallel structures. Only Choice (A) has three parallel *-ing* forms. Choices (B), (C), and (D) are not parallel.

10. **(A)** *Behave* should be *behavior. Behave* is a verb. *Behavior* is a noun.

11. **(B)** *Whom* should be *who* because it is the subject of the verb *is. Whom* functions as a complement. *Who* functions as a subject.

12. **(A)** *Such as* is commonly used to introduce an example.

13. **(A)** An introductory verbal phrase should immediately precede the noun that it modifies. Only Choice (A) provides a noun that could be logically modified by the introductory verbal phrase *upon hatching. Swimming, the knowledge,* and *how to swim* could not logically *hatch* as would be implied by Choices (B), (C), and (D).

14. **(B)** Comparative forms are usually followed by *than. Highest* in Choices (A) and (C) may

be used to compare more than two decks. Choice (D) correctly compares *this deck* with *any other one*, but *that*, not *than*, follows the comparative.

15. **(D)** A verb word must be used in a clause after the verb *to insist. Will not smoke* should be *not smoke*.

16. **(C)** *Invent* should be *invention. Invent* is a verb. *Invention* is a noun.

17. **(C)** *Calcium* is the subject of the verb *is*. Choice (A) may be used with the word *that*. Choice (B) may be used as a subject clause preceding a main verb. Choice (D) may be used preceding a subject and verb. "It is calcium *that* is necessary for the development of strong bones and teeth." "That calcium is necessary for the development of strong bones and teeth *is* known," and "Although calcium is necessary for strong bones and teeth, *other minerals are* also important" would also be correct.

18. **(C)** *Larger* should be *largest*. Because there are more than two masses of nerve tissue in the human body, a superlative form must be used.

19. **(A)** *Like* is a preposition. *Alike* should be *like*.

20. **(C)** *Capable of* is a prepositional idiom. *To perform* should be *of performing*.

21. **(A)** For scientific results, a present form in the condition requires a present or future form in the result. Only Choice (A) introduces a conditional.

22. **(A)** Repetition of the subject by a subject pronoun is redundant. *It* should be deleted.

23. **(B)** A negative phrase introduces inverted order. *Not until* requires an auxiliary verb, subject, and main verb. In Choice (A) there is no auxiliary. In Choices (C) and (D), there is no subject and no auxiliary.

24. **(B)** The verb phrase *to approve of* requires an *-ing* form in the complement. *-Ing* forms are modified by possessive pronouns. Choices (A) and (D) are infinitives, not *-ing* forms. Choice (C) is an *-ing* form, but it is modified by a subject, not a possessive pronoun.

25. **(B)** *Commonly* should be *common. Commonly* is an adverb. *Common* is an adjective.

Section 3: Reading

1. **(A)** The other choices are secondary ideas that are used to develop the main idea, "Technological Advances in Oceanogra-phy." Choices (B), (C), and (D) are important to the discussion, and provide details that support the main idea.

2. **(C)** In the context of this passage, sluggish is closest in meaning to slow moving. Choices (A), (B), and (D) are not accepted definitions of the word.

3. **(A)** "Because of undersea pressure that affected their speech organs, communication among divers was difficult or impossible." Choices (B), (C), and (D) are not mentioned and may not be concluded from information in the passage.

4. **(A)** "Direct observations of the ocean floor are made not only by divers but also by deep-diving submarines." Choices (B), (C), and (D) are not correct because observations are made by deep-diving submarines as well as by divers.

5. **(D)** "Direct observations of the ocean floor are made … by deep-diving submarines." Choice (A) is not correct because some of the vehicles are manned. Choice (B) refers to the divers, not to the undersea vehicles. Choice (C) is not correct because undersea vehicles have overcome some of the limitations of divers.

6. **(A)** In the context of this passage, cruise could best be replaced by travel at a constant speed. Choices (B), (C), and (D) are not accepted definitions of the word.

7. **(D)** "Radio-equipped buoys can be operated by remote control in order to transmit information back to the land-based laboratories." Choices (A), (B), and (C) are not mentioned and may not be concluded from information in the passage.

8. In the context of this passage, the word data is closest in meaning to information. No other words or phrases in the **bold** text are close to the meaning of the word information.

9. **(C)** Choices (A), (B) and (D) are mentioned in sentences 8 and 9, paragraph 1. Choice (C) refers to computers, not to satellites.

10. "Some of humankind's most serious problems, especially those [problems] concerning energy and food, may be solved with the help of observations made possible by this new technology." Other choices would change the meaning of the sentence.

11. "Some of humankind's most serious problems, especially those concerning energy and food, may be solved with the help of observations made possible by this new technology." Quotation from sentence 2, paragraph 2.

12. **(C)** "Communication" is the best title because it states the main idea of the passage. The other choices are all examples of communication that provide details in support of the main idea.

13. **(D)** "Whereas speech is the most advanced form of communication...." Choice (A) is not correct because there are many ways to communicate without speech including signals, signs, symbols, and gestures. Choice (B) is not correct because the advances are dependent upon speech; speech is not dependent upon the advances. Choice (C) is not mentioned and may not be concluded from information in the passage.

14. "For instance, the function of any signal is to impinge upon the environment in such a way that it attracts attention, as for example, the dots and dashes that can be applied in a telegraph circuit." Quotation from sentence 4, paragraph 1.

15. **(A)** In the context of this passage, impinge upon is closest in meaning to intrude. Choices (B), (C), and (D) are not accepted definitions of the word.

16. **(B)** "The basic function of a signal is to impinge upon the environment in such a way that it [the signal] attracts attention, as, for example, the dots and dashes of a telegraph circuit." Choices (A), (C), and (D) would change the meaning of the sentence.

17. **(D)** In the context of this passage, potential could best be replaced by possibility. Choices (A), (B), and (C) are not accepted definitions of the word.

18. "Less adaptable to the codification of words, signs also contain agreed upon meaning; that is, they [signs] convey information in and of themselves [the signs]." Other choices would change the meaning of the sentence.

19. **(B)** In the context of this passage, intricate could best be replaced by complicated. Choices (A), (C), and (D) are not accepted definitions of the word.

20. **(C)** "...applauding in a theater provides performers with an auditory symbol." A telegraph circuit was cited as an example of Choice (A). A stop sign and a barber pole were cited as examples of Choice (B). Waving and handshaking were cited as examples of Choice (D).

21. "A loud smacking of the lips after a meal can be either a kinesthetic and auditory symbol of approval and appreciation, or simply a rude noise. Gestures such as waving and handshaking also communicate certain cultural messages." The connection between the two sentences is the reference to cultural symbols and cultural messages. The second sentence with the word *also* must be mentioned after the first sentence.

22. **(B)** "...means of communication intended to be used for long distances and extended periods are based upon speech. Radio, television, and telephone are only a few." Choices (A), (C), and (D) are not mentioned and may not be concluded from information in the passage.

23. In the context of this passage, the word interaction is closest in meaning to communication. No other words or phrases in the **bold** text are close to the meaning of the word communication.

24. **(D)** Choices (A), (B), and (C) are important to the discussion and provide details that support the primary topic, "the content, form, and effects of fertilizer."

25. **(D)** In the context of this passage, essential could best be replaced by required. Choices (A), (B), and (C) are not accepted definitions of the word.

26. **(D)** Since the last number in the formula represents the percentage content of potash, and since the last number is the smallest, it must be concluded that potash has the smallest percentage content. Choice (A) refers to the number 4 in the formula. Choices (B) and (C) are the substances found in phosphoric acid which refers to the number 8 in the formula.

27. **(B)** Since the content of nitrogen is represented by the first number in the formula, it must be concluded that there is 5 percent nitrogen in the fertilizer. The number in Choice (A) refers to the quantity of numbers in the formula. The percentage in Choice (C) refers to potash. The percentage in Choice (D) refers to phosphoric acid.

28. **(B)** In the context of this passage, designate could best be replaced by specify . Choices (A), (C), and (D) are not accepted definitions of the word.

29. **(C)** "Recently, liquids have shown an increase in popularity…." Choice (A) refers to a form of fertilizers that used to be used, but was found to be less convenient, not to a form that is more popular than ever. Choices (B) and (D) are not correct because solids in the shape of chemical granules are easy to store and apply.

30. **(A)** "Formerly, powders were also used, but these [powders] were found to be less convenient than either solids or liquids." Choices (B), (C), and (D) would change the meaning of the sentence.

31. **(C)** In the context of this passage, convenient is closest in meaning to easy to use . Choices (A), (B), and (D) are not accepted definitions of the word.

32. "Accumulations of chemical fertilizer in the water supply accelerate the growth of algae and, consequently, may disturb the natural cycle of life, contributing to the death of fish." Quotation from sentence 5, paragraph 3.

33. In the context of this passage, the word damage is closest in meaning to harm . No other words or phrases in the **bold** text are close to the meaning of the word harm .

34. "Formerly, powders were also used, but these were found to be less convenient than either solids or liquids. One objection to powders was their propensity to become solid chunks if the bags got damp." The connection between the two sentences is the reference to "powders." The first sentence is a general sentence, and the second sentence is an example.

35. **(A)** The other choices are secondary ideas that are used to develop the main idea, "the evolution of the horse." Choices (B), (C), and (D) are significant steps in the evolution.

36. **(D)** Choices (A), (B), and (C) are mentioned in sentence 3, paragraph 1. The Miocene Age is the earliest historical period mentioned in the passage.

37. **(B)** In the context of this passage, instigated could best be replaced by caused . Choices (A), (C), and (D) are not accepted definitions of the word.

38. **(A)** Choice (A) is a restatement of the sentence referred to in the passage. Since horses appeared 60 million years ago and humans appeared two million years ago, it must be concluded that horses appeared long before human beings.

39. **(A)** "…a horse crossed…from Alaska into the grasslands of Europe." Because of the reference to *grasslands*, it must be concluded that the hipparions migrated to Europe to feed in developing grasslands. Choice (B) is not correct because the European colonists brought horses to North America where the species had become extinct. Choice (D) is not correct because the evolution of the horse has been recorded from its beginnings through all of its evolutionary stages.

40. **(C)** "…smaller than the hipparion, the anchitheres was completely replaced by it." Choice (A) refers to the very early form of the horse, not to the hipparion. Choice (B) is not correct because the hipparion was a more highly evolved form than the anchitheres. Choice (D) is not correct because the hipparion was about the size of a small pony.

41. **(B)** "Less developed and smaller than the hipparion, the anchitheres was completely replaced by it [the hipparion]." Choices (A), (C), and (D) would change the meaning of the sentence.

42. **(C)** In the context of this passage, extinct is closest in meaning to nonexistent . Choices (A), (B), and (D) are not accepted definitions of the word.

43. "Fossil finds provide us not only with detailed information about the horse itself, but also with valuable insights into the migration of herds, and even evidence for speculation about the climatic conditions that could have instigated such migratory behavior." Quotation from sentence 3, paragraph 1.

44. In the context of this passage, tamed is closest in meaning to domesticated . No other words or phrases in the **bold** text are close to the meaning of the word domesticated .

45. **(A)** "At the beginning of the Pliocene Age, a horse…crossed…into the grasslands of Europe. The horse was the hipparion….The hipparion encountered…the anchitheres, which had previously invaded Europe… probably during the Miocene Period." Because the anchitheres invaded Europe during the Miocene and was already there when the hipparion arrived in the Pliocene, it must

be concluded that the Miocene Period was prior to the Pliocene Period. By the Pleistocene referred to in Choices (B) and (C), the anchitheres and the hipparion had become extinct. Therefore, the Pleistocene Period must have been after both the Miocene and the Pliocene.

Writing Section

Question:

Read and think about the following statement:

Pets should be treated like family members.

Do you agree or disagree with the statement? Give reasons to support your opinion.

Outline

Agree that pets should be treated like family members

- Children—learn how to care for brother, sister
- Couple—substitute for babies
- Disabled, elderly—help, caring like family members
- Every stage in life

Map

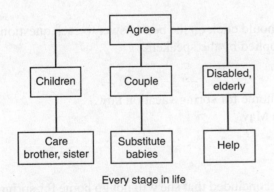

Every stage in life

Example Essay

Although the argument has been made that money spent on pets could better be directed to programs that provide assistance for needy people, I agree that pets should be treated like family members because they live in our homes and interact with us like family members do. Often parents allow children to have pets in order to teach them to be responsible. By feeding, walking, and grooming a dog, children learn to be dependable and kind. Parents expect their children to take care of the pets as if they were members of the family in order to learn these valuable lessons. For many children, a dog or a kitten is also a best friend and a wonderful way to learn how to treat a new brother or sister when the family expands.

Besides the friendship that children enjoy with animals, pets can substitute for the absence of other family members. Sometimes a couple who is unable to have children will adopt pets and treat them like babies. They shower the love on their cats that they might have provided a child and receive affection and companionship in return. Many people who are living alone enjoy the companionship of a pet instead of loved ones who are at a distance or have passed away. The pet becomes a family member for these people and deserves the same kind of treatment that a family member would receive.

Many articles have appeared in the popular press citing the benefits of pets to the disabled and the elderly. In addition to the usual services that pets may provide, such as bringing objects to their owners or helping a vision-impaired owner to walk in unfamiliar surroundings, there is evidence that pets actually extend the life expectancy of their owners. In a real sense, these pets are caring for their owners like family members would, and for this reason, they should be treated like family.

At every stage in life we interact with our pets in the same ways that we interact with family. Children, young married couples, and elderly people have reason to treat their pets like family members.

Model Test 3—Computer-Assisted TOEFL

Section 1: Listening

The Listening Section of the test measures the ability to understand conversations and talks in English. On the actual TOEFL exam, you will use headphones to listen to the conversations and talks. While you are listening, pictures of the speakers or other information will be presented on your computer screen. There are two parts to the Listening Section, with special directions for each part.

On the day of the test, the amount of time you will have to answer all of the questions will appear on the computer screen. The time you spend listening to the test material will not be counted. The listening material and questions about it will be presented only one time. You will not be allowed to take notes or have any paper at your computer. You will both see and hear the questions before the answer choices appear. You can take as much time as you need to select an answer; however, it will be to your advantage to answer the questions as quickly as possible. You may change your answer as many times as you want before you confirm it. After you have confirmed an answer, you will not be able to return to the question.

Before you begin working on the Listening Section, you will have an opportunity to adjust the volume of the sound. You may not be able to change the volume after you have started the test.

QUESTION DIRECTIONS—Part A

In Part A of the Listening Section, you will hear short conversations between two people. In some of the conversations, each person speaks only once. In other conversations, one or both of the people speak more than once. Each conversation is followed by one question about it.

Each question in this part has four answer choices. You should click on the best answer to each question. Answer the questions on the basis of what is stated or implied by the speakers.

Audio
1. Man: It doesn't make any sense for us to go home for spring vacation now.
   Woman: Especially since we'll be graduating in May.
   Narrator: What does the woman mean?

Answer
(A) Since the woman agrees with the man, it must be concluded that she will not go home for spring vacation. Choice (C) is not correct because she will be graduating in May. Choices (B) and (D) are not mentioned and may not be concluded from information in the conversation.

Audio

2. Man: Could you please explain the assignment for Monday, Miss Smith?

   Woman: Certainly. Read the next chapter in your textbook and come to class prepared to discuss what you've read.

   Narrator: What are the speakers talking about?

Answer

(C) From the reference to *the assignment for Monday*, it must be concluded that the speakers are talking about homework. Choices (A), (B), and (D) are all mentioned in the conversation in reference to the assignment.

Audio

3. Woman: Are you ready for this?

   Man: I should be. I've been cramming for the past three days.

   Narrator: What does the man mean?

Answer

(C) *Cramming* is an idiomatic expression that means "studying a lot," especially just before a test. Choices (A), (B), and (D) are not correct because the man is confident about being ready for the test.

Audio

4. Man: I need a book for English two-twenty-one.

   Woman: All of the textbooks are on the shelves in the back of the store.

   Narrator: What will the man probably do?

Answer

(A) Since the man says that he needs a book for an English course, it must be concluded that he will buy the textbook. Choice (C) is not correct because he is already in the bookstore. Choice (D) is not correct because he needs a book for the course. Choice (B) is not mentioned and may not be concluded from information in the conversation.

Audio

5. Man: You're in my economics class, aren't you?

   Woman: Yes. I'm not an economics major, though.

   Man: So, what do you think of Professor Collins?

   Woman: I think he's a great person, but the class just turns me off.

   Narrator: What does the woman mean?

Answer

(A) To *turn someone off* is an idiomatic expression that means the speaker "does not like" something or someone. Choice (D) is not correct because the woman does not like the class. Choice (C) is not correct because the woman thinks Professor Collins is a great person. Choice (B) is not mentioned and may not be concluded from information in the conversation.

Audio

6. Man: Have you made an appointment with Dr. Peterson's T.A. yet?

   Woman: No. And I really can't put it off anymore.

   Narrator: What will the woman probably do?

Answer

(A) To *not put off* is an idiomatic expression that means to "stop postponing." Choices (B) and (C) are not correct because the woman has not made an appointment yet. Choice (D) is not mentioned and may not be concluded from information in the conversation.

Audio

7. Woman: How do you like American food?
    Man: I'm used to it now.
    Narrator: What does the man mean?

Answer

(C) To be *used to something* is an idiomatic expression that means to be "accustomed to" something. Choices (A), (B), and (D) are not paraphrases of the expression and may not be concluded from information in the conversation.

Audio

8. Woman: Are you still studying? It's two o'clock in the morning.
    Man: I know. I just can't seem to get caught up.
    Narrator: What does the man mean?

Answer

(C) To *get caught up* is an idiomatic expression that means to "bring work or assignments up to date." Choice (B) is not correct because the man says he knows what time it is. Choices (A) and (D) are not mentioned and may not be concluded from information in the conversation.

Audio

9. Man: It's your turn to call the names on the list if you want to.
    Woman: I think I'll pass this time.
    Narrator: What is the woman going to do?

Answer

(D) To *pass* is an idiomatic expression that means to "agree to lose a turn." Choices (A), (B), and (C) are not paraphrases of the expression and may not be concluded from information in the conversation.

Audio

10. Woman: I'm pretty sure that the deadline for applications has passed.
    Man: Why don't you let me look into it for you?
    Narrator: What does the man mean?

Answer

(B) To *look into something* is an idiomatic expression that means to "investigate." Choice (A) refers to the woman's conclusion, not to the man's intention. Choices (C) and (D) are not mentioned and may not be concluded from information in the conversation.

Audio

11. Man: This is the first time I've had to get a tutor.
    Woman: What seems to be the problem?
    Man: Well, I understand the lectures but I get mixed up when I try to read the book.
    Narrator: What does the man mean?

Answer

(A) To *get mixed up* is an idiomatic expression that means to "become confused." Choice (C) is not correct because the man understands the lectures. Choices (B) and (D) are not mentioned and may not be concluded from information in the conversation.

Audio

12. Man: The paper isn't due until next week.

    Woman: Yes, I know. But I wanted to turn it in ahead of time if that's all right.

    Narrator: What does the woman mean?

Answer

(A) To *turn in* is an idiomatic expression that means to "submit." *Ahead of time* means "early." Choice (C) is not correct because she wants to turn in the paper before it is due. Choice (D) is not correct because she is ready to turn in the paper. Choice (B) is not mentioned and may not be concluded from information in the conversation.

Audio

13. Man: I can't stand this class!

    Woman: Well, you might as well get used to it. You have to take it in order to graduate.

    Narrator: What does the woman say about the class?

Answer

(D) "You have to take it [the class] in order to graduate." Choice (A) refers to the man's attitude, not to the woman's opinion. Choice (B) is not correct because the class is required for graduation. Choice (C) is not mentioned and may not be concluded from information in the conversation.

Audio

14. Woman: How are you going to get ready for an oral final?

    Man: The professor said we should study alone, but the T.A. said to get into a study group and quiz each other.

    Narrator: What did the T.A. suggest the students do?

Answer

(A) ". . . the T.A. said to get into a study group and quiz each other." Choice (B) refers to the type of exam that they will be given, not to the T.A.'s suggestion. Choice (C) refers to quizzes, but the T.A. suggests that they "quiz each other," which means to ask each other questions. Choice (D) is not correct because the professor recommends studying alone, not in a group.

Audio

15. Man: I need an advisor's signature on my course request form. Could I make an appointment, please?

    Woman: Oh, well, you don't need to make an appointment. Just wait here. I'll get a pen.

    Narrator: What is the woman going to do?

Answer

(C) Since the woman goes to get a pen, it must be concluded that she will sign the form. Choice (A) is not correct because the woman says he doesn't need an appointment. Choice (B) refers to the pen that the woman, not the man, will use. Choice (D) is not correct because the man is asked to wait for the woman.

Audio

16. Woman: Thanks for reading my paper.
    Man: Sure. This copy looks good. Why don't you just hand it in?
    Woman: No, I'd better make one more draft.
    Narrator: What is the woman going to do?

Answer

(A) "I'd better make one more draft." A "draft" is a revision of written work. Choice (D) refers to the man's suggestion, not to what the woman is going to do. Choices (B) and (C) are not mentioned and may not be concluded from information in the conversation.

Audio

17. Woman: Your loan payment is due on the first. Oh, sorry, the computer has you scheduled for the fifth.
    Man: That's good. That's what I thought.
    Narrator: What had the man assumed about the loan payment?

Answer

(B) "That's what I thought [that the computer . . . scheduled for the fifth]. Choice (C) refers to the woman's original statement, not to her final conclusion. Choice (D) is not correct because payments are still due. Choice (A) refers to an error made by the woman, not the computer.

QUESTION DIRECTIONS—Part B

In Part B of the Listening Section, you will hear several longer conversations and talks. Each conversation or talk is followed by several questions. The conversations, talks, and questions will not be repeated.

The conversations and talks are about a variety of topics. You do not need special knowledge of the topics to answer the questions correctly. Rather, you should answer each question on the basis of what is stated or implied by the speakers in the conversations or talks.

For most of the questions, you will need to click on the best of four possible answers. Some questions will have special directions. The special directions will appear in a box on the computer screen.

Audio Conversation

Narrator: Listen to a conversation between a student and a professor.

Woman: Hello, Professor Hayes. I'm Betty Peterson. I'm in your senior seminar this semester.
Man: Oh, yes, Betty. How are you?
Woman: Just fine, thanks. I'm here because I'm applying for graduate school, and I need three letters of recommendation. Would you be willing to write me one?
Man: Why yes, Betty. I'd be happy to. I think you are an excellent candidate for graduate school. Are you applying here or to another university?
Woman: Here. That's why I think your letter is so important. Everyone on the selection committee knows and respects you.
Man: Let's see, Dr. Warren is the chair of that committee, isn't she?
Woman: Yes. So, if you would just write the letter to her, that would be great.
Man: Okay. And when do you need this? I don't recall the deadline for applications.
Woman: The committee meets on April 30, so all the materials must be submitted before then.
Man: All right. I'll send it directly to her office.

Woman: Thank you. I really appreciate it.
Man: You're welcome. Glad to do it.

> Now get ready to answer the questions

Audio

18. Why did Betty see Professor Hayes?

Answer

(D) ". . . I need three letters of recommendation. Would you be willing to write me one?" Choice (A) is not correct because Betty is already in the professor's seminar class. Choice (C) refers to additional information that the professor gives to Betty, not to the purpose of her visit. Choice (B) is not mentioned and may not be concluded from information in the conversation.

Audio

19. What does Professor Hayes think about Betty?

Answer

(B) "I think you are an excellent candidate for graduate school." Choice (A) is not correct because Betty is already taking the seminar. Choice (D) is not correct because the professor does not recall the deadline for applications. Choice (C) is not mentioned and may not be concluded from information in the conversation.

Audio

20. Who will decide whether Betty is accepted to the program?

Answer

(B) "The committee meets on April 30." Choices (A) and (D) refer to the person who will receive the letter, not to who will make the decision. Choice (C) refers to the person who will make a recommendation.

Audio

21. When does Betty need to submit all her materials?

Answer

(C) "The committee meets on April 30, so all the materials must be submitted before then." Choice (A) is not correct because the materials must be submitted before April 30. Choices (B) and (D) are not mentioned and may not be concluded from information in the conversation.

Audio Lecture

Narrator: Listen to a lecture by a history professor.

I know that this is probably a digression from the topic of today's lecture, but it is worth noting that although England no longer ruled her former colonies after the eighteenth century, she controlled trade with them by selling products so cheaply that it was not possible for the new countries to manufacture and compete with English prices. To maintain this favorable balance of trade, England went to fantastic lengths to keep secret the advanced manufacturing processes upon which such a monopoly depended.

Enterprising Americans made all kinds of ingenious attempts to smuggle drawings for the most modern machines out of England, but it was an Englishman, Samuel Slater, who finally succeeded.

Although textile workers were forbidden to emigrate, Slater traveled to the United States in secret. Determined to take nothing in writing, he memorized the intricate designs for all the machines in an English textile mill, and in partnership with Moses Brown, a Quaker merchant, recreated the mill in Rhode Island.

Forty-five years later, in part as a result of the initial model by Slater and Brown, America had changed from a country of small farmers and craftsmen to an industrial nation in competition with England.

> Now get ready to answer the questions

Audio

22. Who is the speaker?

Answer

(B) Because the speaker is introduced as a professor of history and discusses trade during the eighteenth century, it must be concluded that she is a professor of history. It is not as probable that the lecturers mentioned in Choices (A), (C), and (D) would discuss this topic.

Audio

23. According to the speaker, how did England control trade in the eighteenth century?

Answer

(C) "To maintain this favorable balance of trade, England went to fantastic lengths to keep secret the advanced manufacturing processes. . . ." Choice (D) is not correct because the colony (America), not England, stole the plans. Choices (A) and (B) are not mentioned and may not be concluded from information in the talk.

Audio

24. What did Samuel Slater do?

Answer

(C) "Determined to take nothing in writing, he [Slater] memorized the intricate designs for all the machines in an English textile mill. . . ." Choices (A) and (B) are not correct because Slater, in partnership with Brown, opened a mill in the United States in the state of Rhode Island. Choice (D) is not correct because he took nothing in writing.

Audio

25. What happened as a result of the Slater-Brown partnership?

Answer

(A) ". . . in part as a result of Slater and Brown, America had changed from a country of small farmers and craftsmen to an industrial nation. . . ." Choices (B), (C), and (D) are not mentioned and may not be concluded from information in the talk.

Audio Conversation

Narrator: Listen to part of a conversation between a student and an employee in the bookstore on campus.

Man: Hi. I understand that I can reserve textbooks for next semester.

Woman: That's right. If you know what courses you will be taking, we can have your order waiting for you the week before classes start.

Man:	Great! This semester I couldn't get two of my books until three weeks into the semester because you ran out of them before I made it to the bookstore.
Woman:	That has been a problem for a lot of students, and that's why we are trying this system. If we know that you want them, we can order books right away instead of waiting until faculty members place their orders for the whole class.
Man:	What do I have to do?
Woman:	Just fill out one of these forms. Be sure that you include both the course number and the section number for each course because different instructors may not be using the same books. Then pay for your books at the register, and we'll place the order.
Man:	Then do I just stop by the bookstore at the beginning of the semester?
Woman:	There's a space for your phone number on the form. We'll call you as soon as they come in. Sometimes we get them before the end of the current semester.
Man:	That would be great. Then I could take them home with me over the break to get a head start on the reading.
Woman:	Quite a few students do that now.

> Now get ready to answer the questions

Audio

26. What is the purpose of this conversation?

Answer

(A) "I understand that I can reserve textbooks for next semester." Choice (B) is true, but it is a comment, not the purpose of the conversation. Choice (C) is not correct because the faculty member, not the woman, orders books for the whole class. Choice (D) is not mentioned and may not be concluded from information in the conversation.

Audio

27. What was the man's problem last semester?

Answer

(B) "This semester I couldn't get two of my books until three weeks into the semester. . . ." Choice (C) is not correct because he received his books three weeks after the semester started. Choice (D) refers to this semester, not last semester. Choice (A) is not mentioned and may not be concluded from information in the conversation.

Audio

28. How can the man order books?

Answer

(B) "Just fill out one of these forms. . . . Then pay for your books . . . and we'll place the order." Choice (A) is true but refers to ordering books for the whole class. Choices (C) and (D) are not mentioned and may not be concluded from information in the conversation.

Audio

29. How will the man know that the books have arrived?

Answer

(B) "We'll call you as soon as they [the books] come in." Choice (C) refers to the student's question about receiving his books but is not how he will know when the books arrive. The word *form* in Choice (A) refers to the system for ordering books, not to the way to know that books have arrived. Choice (D) is not mentioned and may not be concluded from information in the conversation.

Audio Talk

Narrator: Listen to a talk by a college instructor in an English class.

So many different kinds of writing have been called essays, it is difficult to define exactly what an essay is. Perhaps the best way is to point out four characteristics that are true of most essays. First, an essay is about one topic. It does not start with one subject and digress to another and another. Second, although a few essays are long enough to be considered a small book, most essays are short. Five hundred words is the most common length for an essay. Third, an essay is written in prose, not poetry. True, Alexander Pope did call two of his poems essays, but that word is part of a title, and after all, the "Essay on Man" and the "Essay on Criticism" really are not essays at all. They are long poems. Fourth, and probably most important, an essay is personal. It is the work of one person whose purpose is to share a thought, idea, or point of view. Let me also state here that since an essay is always personal, the term "personal essay" is redundant. Now, taking into consideration all of these characteristics, perhaps we can now define an essay as a short, prose composition that has a personal viewpoint that discusses one topic. With that in mind, let's brainstorm some topics for your first essay assignment.

> Now get ready to answer the questions

Audio

30. What is the instructor defining?

Answer

(A) "So many different kinds of writing have been called essays, it is difficult to define exactly what an essay is." Choices (B), (C), and (D) are secondary themes used to develop a definition of the essay.

Audio

31. What is the main point of the talk?

Answer

(C) ". . . four characteristics that are true of most essays." Choices (A), (B), and (D) are secondary themes used to develop the main theme of the talk.

Audio

32. According to the talk, which of the characteristics are NOT true of an essay?

Answer

(B) ". . . an essay [is] a short, prose composition with a personal viewpoint that discusses one topic." Choice (B) is not correct because an essay is written in prose, not poetry. Choices (A), (C), and (D) are all included in the definition.

Audio

33. What will the students probably do as an assignment?

Answer

(B) ". . . let's brainstorm some topics for your first essay assignment." Choices (A), (C), and (D) are not mentioned and may not be concluded from information in the conversation.

Audio Talk

Narrator: Listen to a talk by a guest speaker in a history class.

Thomas Jefferson was a statesman, a dipomat, an author, and an architect. Not a gifted public speaker, Thomas Jefferson was most talented as a literary draftsman. Sent to Congress by the Virginia Convention in 1775, he was elected to the committee to draft a declaration of independence from England. Although John Adams and Benjamin Franklin also served on the committee, the composition of the Declaration of Independence belongs indisputably to Jefferson. In 1779, Jefferson was elected governor of the state of Virginia, an office he held until Congress appointed him to succeed Franklin as U.S. minister to France. Upon returning to Washington, he accepted the position of secretary of state.

Although Jefferson was a Republican, he at first tried to cooperate with Alexander Hamilton, a Federalist who was first among President Washington's advisors. When he concluded that Hamilton was really in favor of a monarchy, hostility between the two men sharpened.

Having served as vice-president in John Adams' administration, Jefferson ran for president in the election of 1800. He and Federalist Aaron Burr received an identical vote, but the Republican Congress elected to approve Jefferson as president. The most outstanding accomplishment of his administration was the purchase of the Louisiana Territory from France in 1803. He was easily re-elected in 1804. When he left office four years later, he returned here to Monticello, where he promoted the formation of a liberal university for Virginia.

> Now get ready to answer the questions

Audio

34. What is the main purpose of this talk?

Answer

(D) The main purpose of this talk is to summarize Jefferson's life. Choices (A), (B), and (C) are secondary themes in the life of Jefferson.

Audio

35. Jefferson was a member of which political group?

Answer

(C) "Although Jefferson was a Republican, he at first tried to cooperate with Alexander Hamilton, a Federalist. . . ." Choice (A) refers to Jefferson's opinion of Hamilton's political affiliation. Choice (B) refers to Hamilton, not Jefferson. Choice (D) is not mentioned and may not be concluded from information in the talk.

Audio

36. How did Jefferson become president?

Answer

(B) "He [Jefferson] and Federalist Aaron Burr received an identical vote, but the Republican Congress elected to approve Jefferson as president." Choice (A) is not correct because Jefferson and Burr received an identical vote. Choices (C) and (D) are not mentioned and may not be concluded from information in the conversation.

Audio

37. According to the lecturer, what was it that Jefferson was NOT?

Answer

(A) "Thomas Jefferson was a statesman, a diplomat, an author, and an architect. . . . Not a gifted public speaker, he was most talented as a literary draftsman." Choices (B), (C), and (D) are all mentioned as attributes of Jefferson.

Audio Lecture

Narrator: Listen to part of a lecture on geology.

Fossils are the remains of organisms that have been preserved. Some of the most common fossils are shells, skeletons, leaves, and insects. They are occasionally preserved in ice, but most have been buried in mud or sand that collects at the bottom of bodies of water, especially lakes, swamps, and oceans. In order for fossils to form, the animals and plants must be buried quickly; otherwise, the organisms will disintegrate. If they are buried in loose sediment, the soft tissues will begin to decay. But the harder structures such as bones and shells will remain intact for much longer. After years of pressure from the layers of sediment above them, the lower layers of sediment turn into rock, encapsulating the organisms.

There are several different mineral processes that continue the fossilization of organisms in the sedimentary rocks. A few plants and animals become fossilized after mineral-rich water soaks into the pores and openings in the hard tissues of the plant or animal. In these fossils, the original body of the organism is strengthened by the infusion of mineral deposits, and every detail of the organism is preserved. But in most fossils, the minerals in the water dissolve the original organism, leaving a fossil mold. Minerals continue to be deposited in the mold at the same time, a process that results in the replacement of the living organism by a mineral deposit of exactly the same shape. In the casts of these molds, the internal features of the organism are not preserved, but the outer structure is accurate in every detail. Sometimes the fine shapes of even very fragile feathers and fur are preserved by mineral replacement.

Although the fossil record is incomplete, the composite of fossil findings chronicles the forms of life that existed at various periods in the past. In a sense, the fossil record is a history of life. The location of fossils in layers of undisturbed sedimentary rock shows not only which groups of organisms lived at approximately the same time but also indicates the order in which they were buried, that is, their relative ages. Plants and animals on the lower layers are presumed to be older than those buried after them in the layers above.

| Now get ready to answer the questions |

Audio

38. What are the two most common places where fossils may be found?

Answer

(B) (C) "They [fossils] are occasionally preserved in ice, but most have been buried in mud or sand . . . at the bottom . . . of water. . . . " Choice (A) refers to a place where fossils are occasionally preserved, not the most usual place. Choice (D) refers to the location of the mud and sand, under water.

Audio

39. The professor briefly explains a process. Summarize the process by putting the events in order.

Answer

(C) (B) (D) (A) ". . . animals and plants must be buried quickly . . . mineral-rich water soaks into the . . . plant or animal. . . . Minerals in the water dissolve the original organism, leaving a fossil mold."

Audio

40. What is lost in the process of replacement?

Answer

(B) ". . . the internal features of the organism are not preserved. . . ." Choice (A) is not correct because the shapes of fragile feathers and fur are preserved. The word *minerals* in Choice (C) refers to a part of the process, not to what is lost in the process. Choice (D) is not correct because the mold is left.

Audio

41. Why are the layers of sedimentary rock important to the fossil record?

Answer

(A) "The location of fossils in layers of . . . sedimentary rock shows . . . the order in which they were buried, that is, their relative ages." Choice (B) is true, but it is not the reason that the layers are important to the fossil record. Choice (C) is not correct because the mineral water dissolves the organisms. Choice (D) is not correct because plants and animals buried in the same layers of rock lived at approximately the same time.

Audio Conversation

Narrator: Listen to part of a conversation between a student and a secretary on campus.

Woman: Let me see if I understand this. You have completed all of your course work for graduation.

Man: Right.

Woman: But you didn't apply to graduate.

Man: Right.

Woman: But you want to graduate this semester.

Man: Yes, and I thought I would, automatically. I mean, I didn't understand that I had to do anything.

Woman: Who is your advisor?

Man: I'm not sure. I have been sort of advising myself.

Woman: You have?

Man: It's not that hard. The requirements are all spelled out in the catalog, and I have just been taking the required courses, and keeping track of all my grades. Here's my latest transcript, and as you can see, I've got all the credits I need.

Woman: So you don't even have a signed program of study.

Man: Not signed, no. But I have a program of study. I used the program in the catalog.

Woman: I know. But I am talking about a form that is filed by your advisor.

Man: No, I don't have that.

Woman: Okay. The first thing we need to do is to assign you an advisor to go over all your transcripts and help you create a program of study.

Man: How long will that take?

Woman: We'll try to get you in to see someone today. If you really have been able to take all the requirements, then there shouldn't be anything missing from the program and your advisor can sign it and also help you apply for graduation. But if you have misread the catalog or failed to take a critical course, then you may not be eligible for graduation. All I can tell you right now is that you have enough hours to graduate, but only an academic advisor can verify that you have completed the correct course work.

Man: Oh no. You mean I might not graduate?

Woman: I don't know. Let's make that appointment and go from there.

> Now get ready to answer the questions

Audio

42. Why didn't the man apply for graduation?

Answer

(D) ". . . I thought I would, [graduate] automatically." Choice (A) is not correct because the student believes he has completed all of the course work for graduation. Choice (B) is not correct because he has enough hours to graduate. Choice (C) is true but does not explain why the man did not apply for graduation.

Audio

43. How did the man select his courses?

Answer

(A) "The requirements are . . . in the catalog. . . ." Choice (B) is not correct because the man has to explain how he selected his courses. Choice (C) is not correct because the man did not have a program of study. Choice (D) is not correct because the man did not have an advisor.

Audio

44. What does the woman suggest?

Answer

(B) "The first thing we need to do is to assign you an advisor. . . ." Choice (A) is not correct because the man may have taken the required courses. Choice (C) is not correct because the man referred to the requirements in the catalog. Choice (D) is not correct because the man has his latest transcript with him.

Audio

45. What is the man's problem?

Answer

(B) ". . . if you . . . failed to take a critical course, then you may not be eligible for graduation." Choice (A) is not correct because the man is told that he has enough hours to graduate. Choice (C) is not correct because the woman will try to get the man in to see someone that day. Choice (D) is not mentioned and may not be concluded from information in the conversation.

Audio Discussion

Narrator: Listen to part of a class discussion about American English.

Dr. Wilson: Because the United States is so large, and has such a diverse population, several major dialect regions have been identified. The question is whether there is one universally acceptable standard of American English. Any thoughts?

Laura:	Dr. Wilson? I know that the two articles we read both argued that no dialect is inherently better than any other. Isn't that right?
Dr. Wilson:	Yes, I would say so. Since this is a linguistics class, the articles were written by linguists, and from a linguistic point of view, all dialects of a language are of equal value.
Laura:	Okay. And that is because all dialects can express everything that is necessary for a language community to communicate.
Dr. Wilson:	Precisely. But, I think you are going somewhere with this argument.
Laura:	I am. All dialects are linguistically equal, but are they equal socially? In other words, aren't some dialects more well-respected than others?
Dr. Wilson:	Interesting observation. In fact, your comment anticipates our assignment for the next class period when we will discuss standard dialects. For now, let me just say that, although there are several definitions of a standard dialect, the definition that we will use for our class is this: A standard dialect is the dialect that is selected as the educational model.
Laura:	Does that mean that the dialect of the schools is the standard?
Dr. Wilson:	Exactly.
Vicki:	Now I have a question.
Dr. Wilson:	Okay.
Vicki:	In different regions of the country, the pronunciation is very different, so the schools in each of these regions would have a different standard dialect. Isn't there a standard for the whole country?
Dr. Wilson:	Indeed, there is. Standard English has a common grammar and vocabulary. These are the basic building blocks of a dialect. The pronunciation is an accent, not a dialect. So the accent may be regional, but as long as the grammar and vocabulary are standard, the school is teaching the standard American English dialect with, let's say, a Southern accent or a New York accent.
Vicki:	So an accent is different from a dialect?
Dr. Wilson:	Technically, yes. However, certain accents tend to attach themselves to particular dialects.
Laura:	Oh, I see. So there is a standard accent, too, then.
Dr. Wilson:	Some linguists would say no, there isn't. But a number of sociologists would answer your question in a different way. Some accents are associated with a higher socioeconomic class and, therefore, tend to be the preferred standard accent in schools.
Laura:	I think I understand. There isn't anything inherently better about any dialect or accent, but the prestige of the social group that uses it makes some more desirable than others, so they are chosen for the language of the schools, and become the standard.
Dr. Wilson:	Well said.

> Now get ready to answer the questions

Audio

46. In which class would this discussion probably take place?

Answer

(C) "Since this is a linguistics class, the articles were written by linguists. . . ." Choices (A), (B), and (D) are subjects that are referred to in the discussion, but they are not the class in which the discussion takes place.

Audio

47. According to the discussion, what is the definition of a standard dialect?

Answer

(D) "A standard dialect is the dialect that is selected as the educational model." Choice (B) is not correct because all dialects of a language are of equal value. Choice (C) is true of all dialects, but it is not the definition of a standard dialect. Choice (A) is not mentioned and may not be concluded from information in the discussion.

Audio

48. What is the linguistic perspective put forward in the articles that were assigned?

Answer

(D) ". . . from a linguistic point of view, all dialects of a language are of equal value." Choice (A) is not correct because the accents taught with a standard grammar may be regional accents. Choice (B) is not correct because the school may teach a standard dialect with a regional accent. Choice (C) is not correct because several major dialect regions have been identified.

Audio

49. Which two linguistic components are included in a dialect?

Answer

(A) (C) "Standard English has a common grammar and vocabulary. These [grammar and vocabulary] are the basic building blocks of a dialect." Choice (B) refers to accent, not dialect. Choice (D) is not mentioned and may not be concluded from information in the discussion.

Audio

50. What do sociologists tell us about accents?

Answer

(A) "Some accents are associated with a higher socioeconomic class and, therefore, tend to be the preferred standard accent in schools." Choice (B) is not correct because the prestige of a social group makes a dialect more desirable. Choice (D) refers to the linguistic perspective of accents, not the sociological perspective. Choice (C) is not mentioned and may not be concluded from information in the discussion.

Section 2: Structure

1. **(C)** *Most* is used before a noncount noun to express a quantity that is larger than half the amount. A singular verb follows the noncount noun. Choice (A) does not have a verb. In Choice (B), the verb is before, not after the noun. In Choice (D), *the* is used before *most*.

2. **(B)** An adjective is used before *enough* to express sufficiency. In Choice (A), *goodly* is ungrammatical. The adverbial form of the adjective *good* is *well*. In Choice (C), *as* is unnecessary and incorrect. In Choice (D), the adjective is used after, not before *enough*.

3. **(A)** *Responsible for* is a prepositional idiom. *Responsible the* should be *responsible for the*.

4. **(B)** A form of BE is used with the participle in passive sentences. *Practice* should be *practiced*.

5. **(B)** There must be agreement between pronoun and antecedent. *Which* should be *who* to refer to the antecedent *Shirley Temple Black*. *Which* refers to things. *Who* refers to persons.

6. **(A)** *The* can be used before a noncount noun that is followed by a qualifying phrase. *Population* should be *the population* before the qualifying phrase *of the Americas*.

7. **(C)** An adjective clause modifies a noun in the main clause. *That the earliest cultures evolved* modifies *the way*. Choice (A) is a clause marker *that* and a noun. Choice (B) is a verb and a noun. Choice (D) is a clause marker *which* and a noun.

8. **(D)** Comparative forms are usually followed by *than*. After the comparative *more reasonable, as* should be *than*.

9. **(C)** *There* introduces inverted order, but there must still be agreement between subject and verb. *Has been* should be *have been* to agree with the plural subject *two major factions*.

10. **(A)** In order to refer to occupying a place on the battlefields, *lain* should be used. *To lay* means to put in a place, and the participle is *laid*. *To lie* means to occupy a place, and the participle is *lain*.

11. **(C)** A sentence has a subject and a verb. Choice (A) is redundant because the subject pronoun *it* is used consecutively with the subject *calculus*. Choice (B) has the marker *that* to introduce a main clause. Choice (D) is redundant because it has a verb that replaces the main verb *can reduce*.

12. **(B)** Subject-verb order and a negative verb with *either* expresses negative agreement. Negative agreement with *neither* requires verb-subject order and an affirmative verb. In Choice (A), verb-subject order is reversed. In Choice (C), verb-subject order is reversed, and *neither* is used at the beginning, not at the end of the clause. In Choice (D) *either*, not *neither*, is used with verb-subject order and an affirmative verb. "Neither does Mexico" would also be correct.

13. **(B)** *Large* should be *largest*. Because there were more than two ethnic groups, a superlative form must be used.

14. **(B)** The determiner *a* is used before a singular count noun. *Results* should be *result*.

15. **(D)** A sentence has a subject and a verb. Choice (A) does not have a verb. Choices (B) and (C) introduce a main clause subject and verb.

16. **(C)** The anticipatory clause *it is accepted that* introduces a subject and verb, *the formation...began*. Choices (A), (B), and (D) are incomplete and ungrammatical.

17. **(B)** When the degree of one quality, *the heat,* is dependent upon the degree of another quality, *the humidity,* two comparatives are used, each preceded by *the. The worst* should be *the worse* because it is a comparative.

18. **(B)** A dependent clause modifies an independent clause. *Which are* should be *are* to provide a verb for the subject *statistical data,* of the independent clause.

19. **(A)** The word order for a passive sentence is a form of BE followed by a participle. Only Choice (A) has the correct word order. Choice (B) does not have a BE form. Choice (C) has a HAVE, not a BE form. Choice (D) is a present tense verb, not BE followed by a participle.

20. **(A)** *Despite of* is a combination of *despite* and *in spite of*. Either *despite* or *in spite of* should be used.

21. **(C)** Subject-verb order is used in the clause after a question word connector such as *how much*. In Choice (A), subject-verb order is reversed. In Choice (B), the auxiliary *does* is unnecessary and incorrect. In Choice (D), the verb *are* is repetitive. "The Consumer Price Index lists how much every car *is*" would also be correct.

22. **(A)** Because it is a prepositional phrase, in a comparison *as every nation* should be *like every nation*. *As* functions as a conjunction. *Like* functions as a preposition.

23. **(C)** A logical conclusion about the past is expressed by *must have* and a participle. Choices (A), (B), and (D) are not logical because they imply that the theater will act to restore itself.

24. **(A)** The verb *thought* establishes a point of view in the past. *Will* should be *would* in order to maintain the point of view.

25. **(D)** Ideas in a series should be expressed by parallel structures. *To plant* should be *planting* to provide for parallelism with the *-ing* forms *plowing* and *rotating*.

Section 3: Reading

1. **(A)** "Webster's Work" is the best title because it states the main idea of the passage. Choice (B) is not correct because Webster's dictionaries represent only part of the work referred to in the passage. Choices (C) and (D) are mentioned briefly in the discussion, but are not the most important topics.

2. **(D)** In the context of this passage, inadequate could best be replaced by unsatisfactory Choices (A), (B), and (C) are not accepted definitions of the word.

3. **(C)** "...he discovered how inadequate the available schoolbooks were for the children of a new and independent nation.... In response to the need for truly American textbooks, Webster published *A Grammatical Institute of the English Language*." Choice (A) is a result of having written *A Grammatical Institute*, not a reason for writing it. Choice (B) is not correct because British books were available, but not appropriate. Choice (D) is not mentioned and may not be concluded from information in the passage.

4. **(D)** "...*The American Spelling Book*...provided him with a considerable income for the rest of his life." Choices (A), (B), and (C) are all publications by Webster, but the income afforded by each is not mentioned and may not be concluded from information in the passage.

5. In the context of this passage, popular is closest in meaning to the phrase very successful . No other words or phrases in the **bold** text are close to the meaning of the word popular .

6. **(A)** In the context of this passage, considerable is closest in meaning to large . Choices (B), (C), and (D) are not accepted definitions of the word.

7. **(C)** "Published...in 1828, *An American Dictionary of the English Language* has become the recognized authority for usage...." Choice (A) refers to the date that Webster finished his study of English and began writing the dictionary. Choice (B) refers to the date that Webster began work on the dictionary. Choice (D) refers to the date that Webster finished writing the dictionary, not to the date that it was published.

8. **(D)** "Webster's purpose in writing it [the dictionary] was to demonstrate that the American language was developing distinct meanings, pronunciations, and spellings from those of British English." Choices (A), (B), and (C) would change the meaning of the sentence.

9. "Webster's purpose in writing it [an American dictionary] was to demonstrate that the American language was developing distinct meanings, pronunciations, and spellings from those of British English." Quotation from sentence 4, paragraph 2.

10. **(C)** In the context of this passage, distinct is closest in meaning to different . Choices (A), (B), and (D) are not accepted definitions.

11. **(C)** "He [Webster] is responsible for advancing the form color...instead of colour." Choices (A), (B), and (D) are British English spellings.

12. **(A)** Choice (A) is the author's main purpose because the passage refers to the San Andreas Fault specifically. The general information referred to in Choices (B), (C), and (D) is not mentioned and may not be concluded from information in the passage.

13. **(B)** "The San Andreas Fault is a fracture at the congruence of two major plates of the Earth's crust." Choice (A) refers to the plates, not to the fracture. Choices (C) and (D) refer to the results of the movement along the fracture, not to the fault.

14. **(C)** In the context of this passage, originates could best be replaced by begins . Choices (A), (B), and (D) are not accepted definitions of the word.

15. **(C)** "Its western side always moves north in relation to its eastern side." Choices (A), (B), and (D) are not correct because the western side always moves north, not in any other direction.

16. **(D)** "The total net slip along the San Andreas Fault and the length of time it [the fault] has been active..." Choices (A), (B), and (C) would change the meaning of the sentence.

17. **(D)** Intermittent means occasional . Choices (A), (B), and (C) are not accepted definitions of the word.

18. **(C)** "Tremors are not unusual along the San Andreas Fault...." Choice (B) is not correct because tremors are not unusual. Choices (A) and (D) are not mentioned and may not be concluded from information in the passage.

19. **(A)** "Californians have long anticipated the recurrence of what they refer to as the 'Big One,' a chain reaction of destructive earthquakes...." Choices (B), (C), or (D) would change the meaning of the sentence.

20. In the context of this passage, devastating is closest in meaning to destructive . No other

words or phrases in the **bold** text are close to the meaning of the word destructive .

21. "Californians have long anticipated the re-currence of what they refer to as the 'Big One,' a chain reaction of destructive earth-quakes that would measure near 8 on the Richter scale, similar in intensity to those [earthquakes] that occurred in 1857 and 1906." Other choices would change the meaning of the sentence.

22. **(D)** "…the San Andreas Fault…runs north in an irregular line…." The word *uneven* in Choice (D) means irregular. Choice (A) is not correct because the line is irregular. Choices (B) and (C) are not mentioned and may not be concluded from information in the passage.

23. **(B)** "The Structure of an Insect" is the best title because it states the main idea of the passage. Choice (C) is a secondary idea that is used to develop the main idea. Choices (A) and (D) are not mentioned and may not be concluded from information in the passage.

24. In the context of this passage, the word segmented is closest in meaning to sub-divided . No other words or phrases in the **bold** text are close to the meaning of the word subdivided .

25. **(C)** "Features of the mouth parts are very helpful in classifying the many kinds of insects." Choices (A), (B), and (D) are dis-cussed, but not as a basis for classification.

26. **(A)** In the context of this passage, the word normal is closest in meaning to common . Choices (B), (C), and (D) are not accepted definitions of the word.

27. **(A)** "A labrum above and a labium below are similar to an upper and lower lip." Choice (B) is compared to Choice (D). Choice (C) is discussed, but not compared to anything.

28. **(B)** "…the coiled drinking tube…called the proboscis…[is] composed…of modified maxillae." Choice (A) refers to food, not to the proboscis that is used in reaching it. Choices (C) and (D) are not mentioned and may not be concluded from information in the passage.

29. **(C)** "In a mosquito or an aphid, mandibles and maxillae are modified to sharp stylets." The insect referred to in choice (A) has mandibles similar to jaws, not sharp stylets. The insect referred to in Choice (B) has a

proboscis. The insect referred to in Choice (D) has a spongelike mouth pad.

30. **(A)** In the context of this passage, drill through could best be replaced by pene-trate . Choices (B), (C), and (D) are not ac-cepted definitions of the phrase.

31. **(C)** "In a housefly, the expanding labium forms a spongelike mouth pad that it [the housefly] can use to stamp over the surface of food." Choices (A), (B), and (D) would change the meaning of the sentence.

32. "An active part of the natural food cycle, in-sects provide nutrition for animals and de-vour waste products of other life forms. Al-though some insects, like the cockroach, have remained essentially unchanged for eons, most insects adapt readily to changing environmental conditions." The connection between the two sentences occurs on the paragraph level. The first sentence in the paragraph introduces the idea that insects are adaptable, and the four sentences that follow provide examples. The inserted sentence is a conclusion that reinforces the first sentence.

33. **(D)** Because the passage is a statement of sci-entific facts written from an objective point of view, it must be concluded that the purpose is to inform. Choices (A) and (B) are improb-able because the passage is not written from a subjective point of view. Choice (C) is improbable because of the scientific content.

34. **(D)** The primary topic is the characteristics of protozoans. Choices (A), (B), and (C) are important to the discussion and provide details that support the primary topic.

35. **(D)** In the context of this passage, minute could best be replaced by very small . Choices (A), (B), and (C) are not accepted definitions of the word.

36. **(B)** "The protozoans…[consist] of a single cell of protoplasm…." Choices (A), (C), and (D) are not correct because the cell of a pro-tozoan is composed of protoplasm.

37. In the context of this passage, locomotion is closest in meaning to motility . No other words or phrases in the **bold** text are close to the meaning of the word motility .

38. **(C)** Choice (C) is a restatement of the sen-tence referred to in the passage. *Motility* means the manner of movement. Choices (A), (B), and (D) would change the meaning of the original sentence.

39. **(C)** "The Sarcodina, which include amoebae...." Choices (A) and (B) refer to two other groups of protozoans that do not include amoebae. Choice (D) refers to the basis of classification for the three major groups of protozoans.

40. **(C)** "...a large nucleus that regulates growth but decomposes during reproduction..." Choice (A) refers to the small, not the large, nucleus. Choice (B) is not correct because the small nucleus contains the genetic code for the large nucleus. Choice (D) is not correct because the large nucleus decomposes during reproduction.

41. **(A)** "Protozoans are considered animals because...they do not live on simple organic compounds." Choices (B) and (C) refer to characteristics of some protozoans, not to a reason why they are considered animals. Choice (D) is not correct because they have only one cell, although current research is calling that into question.

42. **(A)** "Current research into this phenomenon along with investigations carried out with advanced microscopes may necessitate a redefinition of what constitutes a protozoan, even calling into question the basic premise that they [protozoans] have only one cell." Choices (B), (C), and (D) would change the meaning of the sentence.

43. "They are fantastically diverse, but three major groups may be identified on the basis of their motility." Quotation from sentence 2, paragraph 4.

44. **(A)** In the context of this passage, uniformly is closest in meaning to in the same way. Choices (B), (C), and (D) are not accepted definitions of the word.

45. **(C)** Choice (A) is mentioned in sentence 3, paragraph 4. Choice (B) is mentioned in sentence 1, paragraph 1. Choice (D) is mentioned in sentence 4, paragraph 4. Protozoans consist of a single cell, although in the case of Ciliata, the cell may have a larger nucleus and a smaller nucleus.

Writing Section

Question:

Many people have learned a foreign language in their own country; others have learned a foreign language in the country in which it is spoken. Which is better? Give the advantages of each and support your viewpoint.

Outline

Advantages own country
- Teacher has similar experience—can use L1
- Cheaper than foreign travel
- Less stressful

Advantages foreign country
- Natural speech—accent + idioms
- Cultural context—behaviors
- Opportunities

My opinion—intermediate proficiency own country + advanced abroad

Map

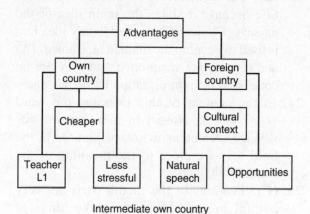

Intermediate own country
Advanced abroad

Example Essay

There are many advantages to learning a language in your own country. In the first place, it is quite a lot cheaper than it would be to travel to the country where the language is spoken. The cost of airfare, living accommodations, food, and tuition at a foreign school can be prohibitively high. In addition, there is less stress involved in learning in a familiar environment. Studying abroad requires that you speak the foreign language all the time to accomplish basic activities. Although it is an opportunity to use the language daily in a real setting, it can be very wearing. Finally, it is advantageous to have teachers who speak your native language because they have gone through the same stages of learning the foreign language that you are experiencing, and they know how to explain the new language by relating it to the native language.

Nevertheless, an argument can be made for learning a language in the country in which it is spoken. Only there can you truly hear the accent and idioms of natural speech. Being surrounded by the foreign language allows you to acquire nuances that elude the classroom. It is also beneficial to learn the language within the context of the culture so that you can learn the behaviors that accompany language. For example, learning how to order in a restaurant when you are right there with native speakers will also let you see how to behave in a restaurant in the foreign country. Finally, there are often opportunities that occur while you are in another country. Friendships can result in invitations to spend time with native speakers in their homes, and possibilities can present themselves for work or study in the foreign country.

In my opinion, the best way to learn a language is to achieve an intermediate level of proficiency in your own country and then to travel to the country where the language is spoken to make progress from the intermediate to the advanced level. By using this plan, you can benefit from the advantages of both options.

Model Test 4—Computer-Assisted TOEFL

Section 1: Listening

The Listening Section of the test measures the ability to understand conversations and talks in English. On the actual TOEFL exam, you will use headphones to listen to the conversations and talks. While you are listening, pictures of the speakers or other information will be presented on your computer screen. There are two parts to the Listening Section, with special directions for each part.

On the day of the test, the amount of time you will have to answer all of the questions will appear on the computer screen. The time you spend listening to the test material will not be counted. The listening material and questions about it will be presented only one time. You will not be allowed to take notes or have any paper at your computer. You will both see and hear the questions before the answer choices appear. You can take as much time as you need to select an answer; however, it will be to your advantage to answer the questions as quickly as possible. You may change your answer as many times as you want before you confirm it. After you have confirmed an answer, you will not be able to return to the question.

Before you begin working on the Listening Section, you will have an opportunity to adjust the volume of the sound. You may not be able to change the volume after you have started the test.

QUESTION DIRECTIONS—Part A

In Part A of the Listening Section, you will hear short conversations between two people. In some of the conversations, each person speaks only once. In other conversations, one or both of the people speak more than once. Each conversation is followed by one question about it.

Each question in this part has four answer choices. You should click on the best answer to each question. Answer the questions on the basis of what is stated or implied by the speakers.

Audio

1. Man: The International Students' Association is having a party Saturday night. Can you come or do you have to work at the hospital?

   Woman: I wish I could.

   Narrator: What will the woman probably do?

Answer

(C) *I wish I could* is an idiomatic expression that means the speaker "would like to but is not able to do" something. Choice (A) refers to a party that the association, not the woman, will have. Choice (B) refers to what the woman would like to do, not to what she will probably do. Choice (D) is not mentioned and may not be concluded from information in the conversation.

Audio

2. Woman: I think that the game starts at eight.

   Man: Good. We have just enough time to get there.

   Narrator: What will the speakers probably do?

Answer

(A) Since they have just enough time to get there, it must be concluded that they will leave immediately. Choices (B), (C), and (D) are not mentioned and may not be concluded from information in the conversation.

Audio

3. Woman: What did you do after you lost your passport?

   Man: I went to see the foreign student advisor, and he reported it to the Passport Office in Washington.

   Narrator: What did the man do after he lost his passport?

Answer

(A) The man said that he went to see the foreign student advisor. Choice (D) refers to what the advisor did, not to what the man did himself. The Passport Office is in Washington, D.C., but Choices (B) and (C) are not mentioned and may not be concluded from information in the conversation.

Audio

4. Man: I'm not sure what Dr. Tyler wants us to do.

   Woman: If I were you, I'd write a rough draft and ask Dr. Tyler to look at it.

   Narrator: What does the woman suggest the man do?

Answer

(B) "I'd write a rough draft and ask Dr. Tyler to look at it." A "rough draft" is a preliminary version. Choice (C) is not correct because the woman says to show the draft to Dr. Tyler, not to her. Choices (A) and (D) are not mentioned and may not be concluded from information in the conversation.

Audio

5. Man: Dr. Clark is the only one teaching statistics this term.

   Woman: You mean we have to put up with her for another semester?

   Narrator: What does the woman mean?

Answer

(D) To *put up with* is an idiomatic expression that means to "tolerate." It must be concluded that the students do not like Dr. Clark. Choices (A), (B), and (C) are not paraphrases of the expression and may not be concluded from information in the conversation.

Audio

6. Woman: Did we have an assignment for Monday? I don't have anything written down.

   Man: Nothing to read in the textbook, but we have to see a movie and write a paragraph about it.

   Narrator: What are the speakers discussing?

Answer

(C) The references to a *textbook* and a *movie* in Choices (B) and (D) relate to the assignment for the class. Choice (A) is not mentioned and may not be concluded from information in the conversation.

Audio

7. Man: Excuse me. Are you Sally Harrison's sister?

   Woman: No, I'm not. I'm her cousin.

   Narrator: What had the man assumed about the woman?

Answer

(B) Since the man asks whether the woman is Sally Harrison's sister, it must be concluded that he assumed the women were sisters. Choice (A) refers to who the woman is, not to the man's assumption. Choices (C) and (D) are not correct because the woman is Sally Harrison's cousin.

Audio

8. Woman: I can't find my pen. It was right here on the desk yesterday and now it's gone. Have you seen it?

   Man: Yes. I put it in the desk drawer.

   Narrator: What is the woman's problem?

Answer

(C) Since the woman says that she can't find her pen, it must be concluded that finding her pen is the problem. Choices (A), (B), and (D) are not mentioned and may not be concluded from information in the conversation.

Audio

9. Woman: When is John coming?

   Man: Well, he said he'd be here at eight-thirty, but if I know him, it will be at least nine o'clock.

   Narrator: What does the man imply about John?

Answer

(A) Because John agreed to arrive at eight-thirty but the man estimates that he won't arrive until nine o'clock, or one half-hour later, it must be concluded that John is usually late. Choice (B) refers to the time when John agreed to arrive, not to a conclusion that the man wants us to make. Choice (C) is not correct because John had agreed to come, and the man estimates John's arrival at nine o'clock. Choice (D) is not correct because the man estimates John's arrival one half-hour after he has agreed to arrive.

Audio
10. Woman: How is your experiment coming along?
    Man: It's finished, but it didn't turn out quite like I thought it would.
    Narrator: What does the man mean?

Answer
(B) ". . . it didn't turn out quite like I thought it would." Choice (A) is not correct because the man knows how it turned out. Choice (C) is not correct because the man says the experiment is finished. Choice (D) is not mentioned and may not be concluded from information in the conversation.

Audio
11. Woman: Barbara sure likes to talk on the phone.
    Man: If only she liked her classes as well!
    Narrator: What does the man imply about Barbara?

Answer
(A) Since the man expresses exasperation about the woman's attention to her classes, he implies that she does not put much effort in her studies. Choice (D) is true, but it is not what the man implies by his comment. Choices (B) and (C) are not mentioned and may not be concluded from information in the conversation.

Audio
12. Man: What's the matter?
    Woman: My allergies are really bothering me. I guess I'll have to go to the doctor.
    Man: If I were you, I'd try some over-the-counter medications first. They usually do the job.
    Narrator: What does the man suggest the woman do?

Answer
(D) ". . . I'd try some over-the-counter medications. . . ." Choice (A) refers to the woman's plan, not to the man's suggestion. Choice (B) refers to the idiom *do the job* which means to "cure." Choice (C) refers to the place to buy nonprescription (over-the-counter) medicine, not to the man's suggestion.

Audio
13. Man: What did you decide about the scholarship? Did you fill out the application?
    Woman: I'm going to give it all I've got.
    Narrator: What does the woman mean?

Answer
(A) To *give it all you've got* is an idiomatic expression that means to "try your best." Choices (B), (C), and (D) are not paraphrases of the expression and may not be concluded from information in the conversation.

Audio
14. Woman: Please pass your papers in.
    Man: Could I have a few more minutes to finish?
    Woman: I'm afraid not. It's a timed test.
    Narrator: What does the woman mean?

Answer

(A) Since the woman denies the man's request for a few more minutes, it must be concluded that the man must stop working on the test. Choice (B) is not correct because the man cannot have a few more minutes to finish. Choice (D) is not correct because the test is in progress, not about to start. Choice (C) is not mentioned and may not be concluded from information in the conversation.

Audio

15. Man: Dr. Taylor's class is supposed to be really good.
    Woman: The best part is I can use my roommate's book.
    Man: I'm not so sure about that. I think they're using a different book this semester.
    Narrator: What does the man imply?

Answer

(C) Since the man thinks they are using a different book this semester, he implies that the textbook may have been changed. Choice (D) is not correct because they are discussing plans for this semester. Choices (A) and (B) are not mentioned and may not be concluded from information in the conversation.

Audio

16. Man: I'm going to get Sally a bike for Christmas.
    Woman: Are you sure she'd like one?
    Narrator: What does the woman imply?

Answer

(D) Since the woman questions whether Sally would like a bike, she implies that Sally may prefer a different gift. Choice (A) refers to the man's idea, not to the woman's comment. Choices (B) and (C) are not mentioned and may not be concluded from information in the conversation.

Audio

17. Man: I just can't get the answer to this problem! I've been working on it for three hours.
    Woman: Maybe you should get some rest and try it again later.
    Narrator: What does the woman suggest that the man do?

Answer

(A) ". . . get some rest and try it again later." Choices (B) and (D) are not correct because the woman recommends rest. Choice (C) is not mentioned and may not be concluded from information in the conversation.

QUESTION DIRECTIONS—Part B

In Part B of the Listening Section, you will hear several longer conversations and talks. Each conversation or talk is followed by several questions. The conversations, talks, and questions will not be repeated.

The conversations and talks are about a variety of topics. You do not need special knowledge of the topics to answer the questions correctly. Rather, you should answer each question on the basis of what is stated or implied by the speakers in the conversations or talks.

For most of the questions, you will need to click on the best of four possible answers. Some questions will have special directions. The special directions will appear in a box on the computer screen.

Audio Discussion

Narrator: Listen to a class discussion.

Baker: It seems to me that the question is not whether the metric system should be introduced in the United States, but rather, how it should be introduced.

Woman: I think that it should be done gradually to give everyone enough time to adjust.

Man: Yes. Perhaps we could even have two systems for a while. I mean, we could keep
the English system and use metrics as an optional system.

Woman: That's what they seem to be doing. When you go to the grocery store, look at the
labels on the cans and packages. They are marked in both ounces and grams.

Man: Right. I've noticed that too. And the weather reporters on radio and TV give the
temperature readings in both degrees Fahrenheit and degrees Celsius now.

Woman: Some road signs have the distances marked in both miles and kilometers, especially on the interstate highways. What do you think, Professor Baker?

Baker: Well, I agree that a gradual adoption is better for those of us who have already been
exposed to the English system of measurement. But I would favor teaching only
metrics in the elementary schools.

Man: I see your point. It might be confusing to introduce two systems at the same time.

> Now get ready to answer the questions

Audio

18. What is the topic under discussion?

Answer

(B) ". . . the question is not whether the metric system should be introduced in the United States, but
rather, how it should be introduced." Choice (A) is not correct because the question is not whether
the metric system should be introduced. Choices (C) and (D) are not mentioned and may not be concluded from information in the discussion.

Audio

19. What changes in measurement in the United States have the students observed?

Answer

(C) "They [cans and packages] are marked in both ounces and grams. . . . And the weather reporters
on radio and TV give the temperature readings in both degrees Fahrenheit and degrees Celsius now.
. . . Some road signs have the distances marked in both miles and kilometers. . . . " Choice (A) is not
correct because the temperature readings are in both degrees Fahrenheit and degrees Celsius.
Choice (B) is not correct because the road signs have distances marked in both miles and kilometers. Choice (D) is not correct because cans and packages are marked in both ounces and grams.

Audio

20. What was Professor Baker's opinion?

Answer

(D) "I [Professor Baker] agree that a gradual adoption is better for those of us who have already
been exposed to the English system of measurement. But I would favor teaching only metrics in the
elementary schools." Choice (A) refers to the woman's suggestion, not to Professor Baker's opinion. The opinions expressed in Choices (B) and (C) are not mentioned and may not be concluded
from information in the discussion.

Audio
21. Which word best describes Professor Baker's attitude toward his students?

Answer
(D) Because Professor Baker invites a free exchange of ideas and does not criticize his students, it must be concluded that he is cooperative. The words in Choices (A), (B), and (C) do not describe Professor Baker's manner in the conversation.

Audio Lecture
Narrator: Listen to part of a lecture in a science class.

Since the National Aeronautics and Space Administration was established in 1961, NASA has been engaged in an extensive research effort, which, in cooperation with private industry, has transferred technology to the international marketplace. Hundreds of everyday products can be traced back to the space mission, including cordless electrical tools, airtight food packaging, water purification systems, and even scratch coating for eyeglasses.

In addition, many advances in medical technology can be traced back to NASA laboratories. First used to detect flaws in spacecraft, ultrasound is now standard equipment in almost every hospital for diagnosis and assessment of injuries and disease; equipment first used by NASA to transmit images from space to Earth is used to assist in cardiac imaging, and lasers first used to test satellites are now used in surgical procedures. Under-the-skin implants for the continuous infusion of drugs, and small pacemakers to regulate the heart were originally designed to monitor the physical condition of astronauts in space.

Finally, with the help of images that were obtained during space missions, and NASA technology, archaeologists have been able to explore the Earth. Cities lost under desert sands have been located and rediscovered, and the sea floor has been mapped using photographs from outer space.

> Now get ready to answer the questions

Audio
22. What is the talk mainly about?

Answer
(D) ". . . an extensive research effort, which, in cooperation with private industry, has transferred technology to the international marketplace." Choices (A), (B), and (C) are secondary themes used to develop the main theme of the talk.

Audio
23. Which of the advances listed are NOT mentioned as part of the technology developed for space missions?

Answer
(A) "Hundreds of everyday products can be traced back to the space mission, including cordless electric tools, airtight food packaging . . . ultrasound. . . ." Choice (A) is not mentioned and may not be concluded from information in the talk.

Audio
24. According to the speaker, why did NASA develop medical equipment?

Answer

(D) "First used to detect flaws in spacecraft, ultrasound is now standard equipment in almost every hospital. . . . " Choice (A) refers to implants and pacemakers, not to ultrasound. Choices (B) and (C) are not mentioned and may not be concluded from information in the conversation.

Audio

25. Why does the speaker mention archaeology?

Answer

(B) ". . . archaeologists have been able to explore the Earth. . . . cities…have been located. . . . and the sea floor has been mapped using photographs from outer space." Choices (A), (C), and (D) are not mentioned and may not be concluded from information in the conversation.

Audio Conversation

Narrator: Listen to part of a conversation between a student and a professor in the professor's office.

Beverly: Oh, Dr. Williams. I expected to leave you a note since this is not one of your office hours. But I would really appreciate a few minutes of your time. I'm Beverly Jackson, and I'm in your two o'clock political science class.

Dr. Williams: Yes, Beverly. I remember you. You always sit in the front.

Beverly: I do. I really like the class, and I want to be able to see all the slides and videos.

Dr. Williams: Good, so what can I do for you?

Beverly: I'm hoping you can help me. I have a family emergency, and I am needed at home for at least a week. That means I'll have to miss your Wednesday and Friday class, but I'm sure that I can be back by class on Monday.

Dr. Williams: Oh.

Beverly: I know that attendance is part of the evaluation, and I want to get a good grade in the class. Is there any way you could give me an excused absence or something so it won't bring my grade down? I would be happy to do extra work to make up the time.

Dr. Williams: Oh, don't worry about that, Beverly. You never miss class, and I'm sure you have a very good reason to be absent this time. I'll be glad to give you an excused absence for Wednesday and Friday. Is there anything else I can do?

Beverly: Not really. I have already arranged to get the notes from Gloria Hayes. She and I always study together.

Dr. Williams: Fine. Well, when you get back, and you read Gloria's notes, let me know if there is anything you don't understand. Sometimes it's hard to understand someone else's notes. If you need some clarification, I can meet with you for a few minutes before class on Monday.

Beverly: That's very nice of you, Dr. Williams. I'll call to set up an appointment, if I need to. But I think I'll be okay with the notes. Thanks for the excused absence.

Dr. Williams: You're very welcome. And I hope that everything goes well for you at home.

Beverly: Thank you, Dr. Williams. I really appreciate it.

Now get ready to answer the questions

Audio

26. Why did the student want to see the professor?

Answer

(B) "Is there any way you could give me an excused absence. . . ." The word *note* in Choice (A) refers to the notes that Beverly plans to borrow from her friend Gloria, not to a note she has for the professor. Choice (C) is not correct because she never misses class. Choice (D) is not mentioned and may not be concluded from information in the conversation.

Audio

27. What is the student's problem?

Answer

(D) "I have a family emergency, and I am needed at home for at least a week." Choice (A) is not correct because Beverly sits in front to see better. Choice (B) refers to the professor's concern, not to the student's problem. Choice (C) is not correct because the professor says she never misses class.

Audio

28. What does the professor offer to do?

Answer

(B) "If you need some clarification, I can meet with you for a few minutes before class on Monday." Choice (A) is not correct because the woman has already arranged to borrow notes from her friend, Gloria. Choices (C) and (D) are not mentioned and may not be concluded from information in the conversation.

Audio

29. What is the professor's attitude in this conversation?

Answer

(B) "You're very welcome. And I hope that everything goes well for you at home." Choice (A) is not correct because the professor spends so much time talking with Beverly. Choice (C) describes the woman's attitude, not that of the professor. The word *confused* in Choice (D) refers to the professor's comment about how difficult it can be to understand someone else's notes, not to her attitude.

Audio Talk

Narrator: Listen to part of a talk in a history class.

The first permanent settlement was made in San Francisco in 1776, when a Spanish military post was established on the end of that peninsula. During the same year, some Franciscan Fathers founded the Mission San Francisco de Asis on a hill above the post. A trail was cleared from the military post to the mission, and about halfway between the two, a station was established for travelers called *Yerba Buena*, which means "good herbs."

For thirteen years, the village had fewer than one hundred inhabitants. But in 1848, with the discovery of gold, the population grew to ten thousand. That same year, the name was changed from Yerba Buena to San Francisco.

By 1862, telegraph communications linked San Francisco with eastern cities, and by 1869, the first transcontinental railroad connected the Pacific coast with the Atlantic seaboard. Today San Francisco has a population of almost three million. It is the financial center of the West, and serves as the terminus for trans-Pacific steamship lines and air traffic. The port of San Francisco, which is almost eighteen miles long, handles between five and six million tons of cargo annually.

If you travel to San Francisco, you will see the most identifiable landmark, the Golden Gate Bridge. The bridge, which is more than one mile long, spans the harbor from San Francisco to Marin County and the Redwood Highway. It was completed in 1937 at a cost of thirty-two million dollars and is still one of the largest suspension bridges in the world.

| Now get ready to answer the questions |

Audio

30. What is the main purpose of this talk?

Answer

(C) The speaker discusses the history, economy, and landmarks of San Francisco. Choices (A), (B), and (D) are secondary themes used to support the main purpose of the talk, an orientation to the City of San Francisco.

Audio

31. According to the speaker, what was the settlement called before it was renamed San Francisco?

Answer

(D) ". . . the name was changed from Yerba Buena to San Francisco." Choice (A) refers to the name of the bridge, not a settlement. Choice (B) refers to a mission established before Yerba Buena was settled. Choice (C) refers to a military post established before the settlement of Yerba Buena.

Audio

32. According to the speaker, what happened in 1848?

Answer

(A) ". . . in 1848, with the discovery of gold, the population grew to ten thousand." Choice (B) refers to what happened in 1869, not 1848. Choice (C) refers to what happened in 1937. Choice (D) refers to what happened in 1862.

Audio

33. How long is the Golden Gate Bridge?

Answer

(C) "The bridge, which is more than one mile long, spans the harbor from San Francisco to Marin County. . . ." Choice (A) refers to the length of the port of San Francisco, not to the length of the Golden Gate Bridge. Choice (B) refers to the altitude of the city. The number in Choice (D) refers to the number of tons of cargo handled at the port of San Francisco every year.

Audio Talk

Narrator: Listen to a talk by an English professor.

Today we will discuss Transcendentalism, which is a philosophical and literary movement that developed in New England in the early nineteenth century. Transcendentalism began with the formation in 1836 of the Transcendental Club in Boston, Massachusetts, by a group of artists and writers. This group advanced a reaction against the rigid Puritanism of the period, especially insofar as it emphasized society at the expense of the individual.

One of the most distinguished members of the club was Ralph Waldo Emerson, who served as editor of the literary magazine *Dial*. His writing stressed the importance of the individual. In one of his best-known essays, "Self-Reliance," he appealed to intuition as a source of ethics, asserting that people should be the judge of their own actions, without the rigid restrictions of society.

From 1841 to 1843, Emerson entertained in his home the naturalist and author Henry David Thoreau, who also became a member of the Transcendental Club. Probably more than any other member, he demonstrated by his lifestyle the ideas that the group advanced. He preferred to go to jail rather than to pay taxes to the federal government for a war of which he did not approve.

Upon leaving Emerson's home, Thoreau built a small cabin along the shores of Walden Pond near Concord, Massachusetts, where he lived alone for two years. Devoting himself to the study of nature and to writing, he published an account of his experiences in *Walden*, a book that is generally acknowledged as the most original and sincere contribution to literature by the Transcendentalists.

> Now get ready to answer the questions

Audio
34. What does the lecturer mainly discuss?

Answer
(A) "Today we will discuss Transcendentalism...." Choices (B), (C), and (D) are secondary themes that are used to develop the main theme of the lecture.

Audio
35. During which century did this literary movement develop?

Answer
(C) "Today we will discuss Transcendentalism, which is a philosophical and literary movement that developed in New England in the early nineteenth century." Choices (A), (B), and (D) are not mentioned and may not be concluded from information in the talk.

Audio
36. According to the lecturer, what did the Puritans do?

Answer
(C) "This group [the Transcendental Club] advanced a reaction against the rigid Puritanism of the period, especially insofar as it emphasized society at the expense of the individual." Choices (A) and (D) refer to the Transcendental Club, not to the Puritans. Choice (B) is not correct because the Transcendental Club reacted against the Puritans.

Audio
37. What is *Walden?*

Answer
(D) "Thoreau built a small cabin along the shores of Walden Pond . . . he published an account of his experiences in *Walden*. . . ." Choices (A), (B), and (C) are not mentioned and may not be concluded from information in the talk.

Audio Conversation
Narrator: Listen to part of a conversation between a student and a librarian.

Woman: Do you have any experience working in a library?
Man: No, not as an employee. But I am working toward my doctorate at the University, and I have spent a great deal of time doing my own research in the library. I'm finishing my dissertation now.
Woman: So you are familiar with the electronic search equipment?
Man: Yes, I am. I used several databases for my review of the literature in my dissertation, and I know how to use most of the search equipment that you have here, because this is where I am doing most of my own research.
Woman: Good. Can you think of anything else that would qualify you for the job?

Man:	Yes. I like helping students. My undergraduate degree was in education, and I was a high school teacher for twelve years before I came back to school. The ad says that you want someone to show new students how to do computer searches for their term papers, and I think that my teaching experience would be very useful.
Woman:	Good, good. But what about the hours? If you are working on your dissertation, will you be able to work? This job requires twenty hours of your time per week, and the hours are not regular. You see, in addition to helping students one-on-one, we make appointments for faculty to bring their classes to the library for orientation before they make their first term paper assignments.
Man:	That sounds very interesting. I feel that I can handle a job now. I have most of my own research finished, and I'm writing my dissertation. I plan to do that after work and on my days off.
Woman:	So you aren't taking any classes now?
Man:	No. That's another advantage I have. I can schedule my time around the appointments.
Woman:	And if you are the successful candidate, when could you start?
Man:	Right away!

> Now get ready to answer the questions

Audio

38. What is the purpose of this conversation?

Answer

(D) "Do you have any experience working in a library?" Choice (A) is not correct because the man does his own research in the library and knows how to use most of the search equipment. The phrase *teaching position* in Choice (B) refers to a job that the man had before he came back to school, not to a position that he is applying for now. The phrase *library orientation* in Choice (C) refers to one of the responsibilities of the position that the man is applying for, not to training that he is receiving now.

Audio

39. Who is the man?

Answer

(C) "I am working toward my doctorate at the University. . . ." Choice (A) is not correct because he was a teacher before he came back to school, not now. Choice (B) is not correct because he has never been an employee in a library. The word *computer* in Choice (D) refers to the type of library searches that the students need to do for their term papers, not to the man's background.

Audio

40. What does the man need to do when he is not working?

Answer

(C) "I'm writing my dissertation. I plan to do that [write my dissertation] after work and on my days off." Choice (B) is not correct because he has most of his own research finished. Choice (D) is not correct because he is not taking any classes now. Choice (A) is not mentioned and may not be concluded from information in the conversation.

Audio

41. When would the man be available?

Answer

(D) ". . . when could you start? Right away!" Choices (A) and (B) are not correct because he will complete his dissertation after work and on his days off, and he will graduate after the dissertation is complete. Choice (C) refers to when he will write his dissertation, not to when he will be available for work.

Audio Lecture

Narrator: Listen to part of a lecture on solar heating.

   In general, solar heating requires a solar collector, a water or air distribution system, and a storage system. Most of the time, a solar collector is mounted on the roof of a building at a somewhat steep angle, positioned with a southern exposure. In the hot water system that I am going to show you, the collector is a glass plate with another plate under it, and an air space between the two, through which water can be pumped. I think it will make more sense when you see the model, so let's look at it now.

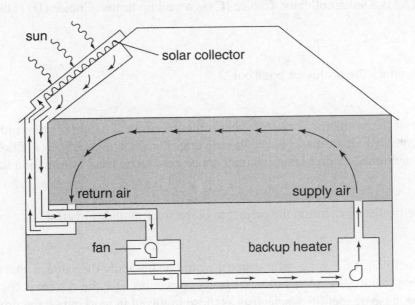

   Notice that water that has been heated by the sun is pumped in closely positioned tubes through the space between the plates. The hot water is then pumped to a storage tank, and warmed air is circulated to the other side of the building with a fan. You will also see a backup heater in this system, usually a conventional furnace, because only about 20 to 30 percent of the solar energy can actually be used in this design. The supply air moves across the space to be heated, and enters the return air exchanger where it rises and, with exposure to the sun, begins heating again to raise the temperature of the water in the tubes below. So, the process begins again.

   Of course, one of the problems with solar heat is the intermittent nature of solar radiation as an energy source. Especially in climates where the sun does not shine regularly, it just isn't a feasible option without large, and often complex, storage systems. However, scientists are now working on a project to place solar modules in orbit around the Earth, where energy generated by the sun could be converted to microwaves and beamed to antennas for conversion to electric power. It is estimated that such a system, although costly and somewhat cumbersome, could potentially generate as much power as five large nuclear power plants. The principle would be basically the same as that of the much simpler model that I showed you. A solar collector, an air distribution center, and a storage system would be required. So if you understand the model here, you can understand even the most complex solar heating unit.

$$\boxed{\text{Now get ready to answer the questions}}$$

Audio

42. Which two requirements are considered when mounting a solar collector on a roof?

Answer

(A) (C) ". . . a solar collector is mounted . . . at a . . . steep angle . . . with a southern exposure." Choices **(B)** and **(D)** are not mentioned and may not be concluded from information in the lecture.

Audio

43. Identify the fan in the solar heating system.

Answer

(B) Choice **(A)** is a solar collector. Choice **(C)** is a backup heater. Choice **(D)** is the space under the collector.

Audio

44. What problem does the professor point out?

Answer

(B) ". . . one of the problems with solar heat is the intermittent nature of solar radiation as an energy source. Especially in climates where the sun does not shine regularly. . . ." Choices **(A)**, **(C)**, and **(D)** are not mentioned as problems and may not be concluded from information in the lecture.

Audio

45. Why does the professor mention the project to place solar modules in orbit?

Answer

(C) "The principle [of the solar orbit system] would be basically the same as that of the much simpler model that I showed you." Choice **(A)** is not correct because the system is costly. Choice **(B)** is not correct because he identifies scientists as those involved in working on the project and does not include himself. Choice **(D)** is true, but it is not the reason that the professor mentioned the project.

Audio Conversation

Narrator: Listen to part of a conversation between a student and a secretary in the Tutoring Center.

Man: Excuse me, is this where I request a tutor?
Woman: Yes, it is. Which course do you need help in?
Man: English.
Woman: English language or literature?
Man: Composition really. I seem to have a hard time figuring out how to write my essays.
Woman: Oh. Well, we have some excellent tutors for that.
Man: My grades are really good in math and science, but I can't figure out how to organize my writing.

Woman:	When would you be able to come in for tutoring? Do you have classes in the afternoon?
Man:	Just on Monday, Wednesday, and Friday. I only have morning classes on Tuesday and Thursday.
Woman:	Good. Some of our best tutors for English work in the afternoon. I could set you up with Janine on Tuesdays and Thursdays at four o' clock if you want.
Man:	Is the tutoring session an hour long?
Woman:	Yes. You would be finishing up about five.
Man:	Okay. I could do that. And, uh, how much will that cost?
Woman:	Oh, I thought you knew. This is a free service for our students.
Man:	It is? No, I wasn't aware of that.
Woman:	Actually, a lot of students who receive tutoring come back and serve as tutors once they get squared away themselves.
Man:	That's really a great system.
Woman:	Janine needed some tutoring in math a few years ago, as I recall, and now she helps us in English composition and French.
Man:	So, should I just come back on Tuesday at four?
Woman:	Yes. I have your name down. Just check in with me when you get here, and I'll take you over to Janine's table. And, bring your books for the class that you need help in, along with a syllabus, your class notes, and anything that might help your tutor to understand the course requirements.
Man:	Thank you so much. I'll see you Tuesday, then.

> Now get ready to answer the questions

Audio
46. What is the purpose of this conversation?

Answer
(B) ". . . is this where I request a tutor?" Choice (A) is not correct because the man asks for a tutor, not for a position. Choice (D) is not correct because the woman is helping the man to arrange for tutoring. Choice (C) is not mentioned and may not be concluded from information in the conversation.

Audio
47. For which course does the man want a tutor?

Answer
(D) "Which course do you need help in? English . . . composition. . . ." The word *literature* in Choice (A) refers to a question that the woman asked, not to the course that the man needs help in. Choice (B) refers to the course that Janine was tutored for, not to the course for which the man needs a tutor. Choice (C) refers to the other course that Janine tutors in, not to the course that the man will receive tutoring in.

Audio
48. How much will the tutoring cost?

Answer
(D) "This is a free service. . . ." Choices (A), (B), and (C) are not correct because the tutoring is a free service.

Audio

49. When will the tutoring session begin?

Answer

(C) ". . . should I just come back on Tuesday at four? Yes." Choices (A) and (B) refer to the times for the man's classes. Choice (D) refers to one of the times for which the man scheduled tutoring but not the first session.

Audio

50. What should the man bring to his tutoring session?

Answer

(B) ". . . bring your books . . . a syllabus, your class notes. . . ." Choice (A) is not correct because the service is free. The word *composition* in Choice (D) refers to the course in which the man will receive tutoring, not to an essay that he should bring to his tutoring session. Choice (C) is not mentioned and may not be concluded from information in the conversation.

Section 2: Structure

1. **(D)** A dependent clause modifies an independent clause. Choice (A) has two clause markers, *which* and *that*. Choice (B) is a verb followed by a noun and a clause marker. Choice (C) does not have a clause marker.

2. **(B)** A passive infinitive is used to express purpose. Choice (A) is a noun. Choice (C) is an *-ing* form. Choice (D) is a present verb.

3. **(C)** Most adverbs of manner are formed by adding *-ly* to adjectives. *Rapid* should be *rapidly* to qualify the manner in which automatic data processing has grown.

4. **(D)** *As well as* should be *and*, which is used in correlation with *both*.

5. **(B)** A cardinal number is used after a noun. *The* is used with an ordinal number before a noun. In Choices (A) and (C), an ordinal number is used after, not before a noun. Choice (D) is incomplete because it does not include *the* before the ordinal number.

6. **(A)** Repetition of the subject by a subject pronoun is redundant. *They* should be deleted.

7. **(B)** *As soon as* is an idiom that introduces a limit of time. The phrase *as soon as* is followed by a noun and a simple present verb. Choice (A) is a modal and a verb word, not a simple present verb. Choice (D) is a noun. Choice (C) uses a present but not a simple present form.

8. **(C)** Because dates require ordinal numbers, *twelve* should be *twelfth*.

9. **(B)** *Influence* should be *influential*. *Influence* is a noun. *Influential* is an adjective.

10. **(C)** *Weathering* is the subject of the verb *is*. Choices (A) and (B) are redundant and indirect. Choice (D) is an *-ing* form, not a verb.

11. **(D)** *Such . . . as* introduces the example *shrimps and clams,* which must refer to a plural antecedent. *Sea creature* should be *sea creatures*.

12. **(C)** Ideas in a series should be expressed by parallel structures. *Encouraging* should be *to encourage* to provide for parallelism with the infinitive *to discourage*.

13. **(B)** *Combination* should be *combine*. *Combination* is a noun. *Combine* is a verb.

14. **(D)** The verb *to consider* requires an *-ing* form in the complement. Choice (A) is an infinitive, not an *-ing* form. Choice (B) is a participle. Choice (C) is a verb word.

15. **(C)** *Presumable* should be *presumably*. *Presumable* is an adjective. *Presumably* is an adverb.

16. **(A)** The verb *reported* establishes a point of view in the past. *Discovers* should be *discovered* in order to maintain the point of view.

17. **(D)** Because the verb *refuse* requires an infinitive in the complement, *giving* should be *to give*.

18. **(C)** Object pronouns are used after prepositions such as *by*. Choice (A) is a reflexive pronoun, not an object pronoun. Choices (B)

and (D) are possessive pronouns. "The work was done *by herself*" without the repetitive word *alone* would also be correct.

19. **(C)** There must be agreement between subject and verb. *Has* should be *have* to agree with the plural subject *the few cities*.

20. **(D)** Ideas in a series should be expressed by parallel structures. *Increasing* should be *to increase* to provide for parallelism with the infinitive *to enrich*.

21. **(D)** An appositive does not require connectors or an additional subject. Choices (A) and (C) include connecting conjunctions. Choice (B) is an anticipatory *it* clause, not an appositive.

22. **(A)** *Would have* and a participle in the result requires *had* and a participle in the condition. Because *would not have evolved* is used in the result, *did not filter out* should be *had not filtered out* in the condition.

23. **(B)** Consecutive order must be maintained, along with parallel structure.

24. **(D)** Ideas in a series should be expressed by parallel structures. *Swimming* should be *swim* to provide for parallelism with the verb words *walk, watch,* and *fish*.

25. **(D)** There must be agreement between pronoun and antecedent. *Its* should be *their* to agree with the plural antecedent *books*.

Section 3: Reading

1. **(A)** The other choices are secondary ideas that are used to develop the main idea, "precipitation." Choices (B), (C), and (D) provide details and examples.

2. **(C)** "Precipitation [is] commonly referred to as rainfall." Choices (A), (B), and (D) are not mentioned and may not be concluded from information in the passage.

3. **(B)** "Precipitation, commonly referred to as rainfall, is a measure of the quantity of water in the form of either rain, hail, or snow." Choice (A) is incomplete because it does not include hail and snow. Humidity referred to in Choices (C) and (D) is not mentioned and may not be concluded from information in the passage.

4. **(A)** "The average annual precipitation over the whole of the United States is thirty-six inches." Choice (B) refers to the formula for computing precipitation, not to the annual rainfall over the United States. Choice (C)

refers to the amount of rain recorded in New York State, not in the United States. Choice (D) refers to the total annual precipitation recorded in New York State.

5. **(B)** "A general formula for computing the precipitation of snowfall is that ten inches of snow is equal to one inch of precipitation." Forty inches of snow divided by 10 inches per one inch of precipitation is four inches, or one-third foot. Choices (A), (C), and (D) may not be computed on the basis of the formula in the passage.

6. **(C)** In the context of this passage, proximity to is closest in meaning to nearness to. Choices (A), (B), and (D) are not accepted definitions of the phrase.

7. "Most of the precipitation in the United States is brought originally by prevailing winds from the Pacific Ocean, the Gulf of Mexico, the Atlantic Ocean, and the Great Lakes." Quotation from sentence 2, paragraph 2.

8. **(D)** "…the Pacific Coast receives more annual precipitation than the Atlantic Coast." Choices (A), (B), and (C) refer to the prevailing winds, not to the highest annual precipitation.

9. **(B)** Choice (A) is mentioned in sentence 5, paragraph 1. Choices (C) and (D) are mentioned in sentence 1, paragraph 2. Choice (B) is not mentioned and may not be concluded from information in the passage.

10. **(A)** In the context of this passage, substantially could best be replaced by fundamentally. Choices (B), (C), and (D) are not accepted definitions of the word.

11. **(B)** "East of the Rocky Mountains, the annual precipitation decreases substantially from that [precipitation] west of the Rocky Mountains." Choices (A), (C), and (D) would change the meaning of the sentence.

12. **(D)** Choices (A), (B), and (C) are important to the discussion, and provide details that support the main topic, "women's suffrage."

13. **(C)** In the context of this passage, ban most nearly means to prohibit. Choices (A), (B), and (D) are not accepted definitions of the word.

14. "They were fighting against a belief that voting should be tied to land ownership, and because land was owned by men, and in some cases by their widows, only those who

held the greatest stake in government, that is the male landowners, were considered worthy of the vote." Quotation from sentence 5, paragraph 1.

15. **(A)** In the context of this passage, primarily is closest in meaning to above all . Choices (B), (C), and (D) are not accepted definitions of the word.

16. In the context of this passage, better is closest in meaning to improve . No other words or phrases in the **bold** text are close to the meaning of the word improve .

17. **(D)** "When the Civil War ended...the Fifteenth Amendment...granted...suffrage to blacks...." *Suffrage* means the right to vote. Choice (B) is not correct because the bill was presented to Congress in 1878, not immediately after the Civil War. Choice (C) refers to the fact that the eastern states resisted the women's suffrage bill, not the end of the Civil War. Choice (A) is not mentioned and may not be concluded from information in the passage.

18. **(D)** *Suffrage* means the right to vote; the exercise of such a right. Choice (A) is a definition of the word *suffering*, not *suffrage*. Choices (B) and (C) are related to the word *suffrage*, but they are not accepted definitions of it.

19. **(A)** "A women's suffrage bill had been presented to every Congress since 1878 but it [the bill] continually failed to pass until 1920, when the Nineteenth Amendment granted women the right to vote." Choices (B), (C), and (D) would change the meaning of the sentence.

20. **(C)** "...the Nineteenth Amendment granted women the right to vote." Choice (A) refers to the Fifteenth, not the Nineteenth Amendment. Choice (B) refers to the Fourteenth Amendment. Choice (D) is not mentioned and may not be concluded from information in the passage.

21. **(D)** "...1920 when the Nineteenth Amendment granted women the right to vote." Choice (A) refers to the date when the Civil War ended. Choice (B) refers to the date when the Fifteenth Amendment was adopted granting blacks, not women, the right to vote. Choice (C) refers to the date when the bill to grant women the right to vote was pre-

sented to Congress, not to the date that it was passed and became law.

22. **(B)** The other choices are secondary topics that are used to develop the primary topic, "characteristics and varieties of the *Acacia*." Choices (A), (C), and (D) are important details and examples.

23. In the context of this passage, valued is closest in meaning to prized . No other words or phrases in the **bold** text are close to the meaning of the word prized .

24. **(C)** "Only about a dozen of the three hundred Australian varieties grow well in the southern United States." Choice (A) refers to the number of species identified, not to the number that grow well in the United States. Choice (B) refers to the number of species that grow well in Australia, not in the southern United States. Choice (D) refers to the number of species that have flowers, not to the total number of species that grow well in the southern United States.

25. **(A)** In the context of this passage, thrive is closest in meaning to the phrase grow well . Choices (B), (C), and (D) are not accepted definitions of the word.

26. **(D)** "Most *acacia* imports are low spreading trees, but of these [trees], only three flower." Choices (A), (B), and (C) would change the meaning of the sentence.

27. **(C)** "The *Silver Wattle*, although very similar to the *Bailey Acacia*, grows twice as high." Choice (A) refers to the *Sydney Golden Wattle*, not to the *Silver Wattle*. Choices (B) and (D) refer to the *Black Acacia*.

28. **(A)** In the context of this passage, flat most nearly means smooth . Choices (B), (C), and (D) are not accepted definitions of the word.

29. **(B)** In the context of this passage, showy could best be replaced by elaborate . Choices (A), (C), and (D) are not accepted definitions of the word.

30. **(D)** "...the *Black Acacia* or *Blackwood*, has dark green leaves and unobtrusive blossoms." The species referred to in Choices (A), (B), and (C) have fragrant clusters of yellow flowers.

31. **(B)** "...the *Black Acacia* is valuable for its dark wood which is used in making cabinets and furniture." Choices (A), (C), and (D) are

not mentioned and may not be concluded from information in the passage.

32. **(C)** "...the pale yellow blossoms appear in August in Australia." Choice (A) refers to the month that the *Acacia* blooms in the United States, not in Australia. Choices (B) and (D) refer to the reversal of seasons in the northern and southern hemispheres, but not to the blossoming of the *Acacia*.

33. "Some acacias are popular in landscaping because of their graceful shapes, lacey foliage, and fragrant blossoms. Other *Acacia* varieties are valued for the sticky resin, called gum Arabic or gum acacia, used widely in medicines, foods, and perfumes, for the dark dense wood prized for making pianos, or for the bark, rich in tannin, a dark, acidic substance used to cure the hides of animals, transforming them into leather." The connection between the two sentences occurs in the first words—*Some* and *Other*, which determine consecutive order.

34. **(A)** "A History of New York City" is the best title because it states the main idea of the passage. Choices (C) and (D) are details used to develop the main idea. Choice (B) is not specific enough.

35. **(C)** "Peter Minuit...negotiated with Canarsee chiefs for the purchase of Manhattan Island for merchandise...." Choices (A) and (B) refer to the value of the merchandise, not to what the Native Americans received. Choice (D) refers to where the Dutch settlements were located.

36. **(B)** "...Dutch settlements in North America known as New Amsterdam...." Choice (C) refers to the location of the land that was purchased from the Native Americans. Choices (A) and (D) are not mentioned and may not be concluded from information in the passage.

37. **(A)** Choice (A) is a restatement of the sentence in the passage. Since offers were extended throughout Europe, it must be assumed that other Europeans were given opportunities to immigrate.

38. **(C)** In the context of this passage, heterogeneous could best be replaced by diverse. Choices (A), (B), and (D) are not accepted definitions of the word.

39. **(C)** "...offers, generous by the standards of the era, were extended throughout Europe. Consequently, the settlement became the most heterogeneous of the North American colonies." Choice (A) is not correct because it was New Amsterdam, not the Dutch West India Company, that the English acquired. Choices (B) and (D) are not mentioned and may not be concluded from information in the passage.

40. "Among the multilingual settlers was a large group of English colonists from Connecticut and Massachusetts who supported the English King's claim to all of New Netherlands set out in a charter that gave the territory to his [the English King's] brother James, Duke of York." Other choices would change the meaning of the sentence.

41. **(A)** In the context of this passage, formidable is closest in meaning to powerful. Choices (B), (C), and (D) are not accepted definitions of the word.

42. "When the English acquired the island, the village of New Amsterdam was renamed New York in honor of the Duke." Quotation from sentence 1, paragraph 4.

43. **(B)** "After the war, it [New York] was selected as the first capital of the United States." Choices (A), (C), and (D) would change the meaning of the sentence.

44. **(B)** "After the war, it [New York] was selected as the first capital of the United States." Choice (A) refers to the former name for New York, which had already been changed when it became the first capital. Choices (C) and (D) refer to cities that became the capital after New York.

45. **(D)** "Three centuries after his initial trade...Minuit's tiny investment was worth more than seven billion dollars." Choice (A) refers to the date that the Dutch purchased Manhattan Island from the Native Americans. Choice (B) refers to the date one century after the purchase. Choice (C) refers to the date three decades after the purchase.

Writing Section

Question:

In your opinion, what is the best way to choose a marriage partner? Use specific reasons and examples why you think this approach is best.

Outline

Old tradition—arranged marriage
• Family + intermediary

Modern—romantic love
• Media

Both
• Parents arrange meetings—wisdom
• Mutual attraction—romantic ideal

Map

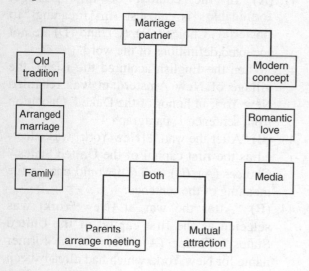

Example Essay

In my view, the best way to choose a marriage partner is to combine the old tradition of arranged marriage with the more modern concept of a love match. In my country, it is our custom to become engaged to a partner who has been selected by an intermediary. Usually, the families of the couple have made it known that they are interested in a union, and the intermediary makes the arrangements and negotiates the financial agreement that precedes the marriage ceremony. I agree with this way to choose a marriage partner because the marriages that have been arranged in my culture, for the most part, have been successful. Traditionally, this type of arrangement has been good because the families that agree to the marriage have maintained a long friendship, they know the parties involved very well, and they have the maturity and wisdom to select compatible partners. In addition, the families have a vested interest in the success of the marriage and tend to be very supportive of the young couple, both financially and emotionally.

Recently, however, young people have been influenced by the modern idea of romantic love that is presented in the media, and they want to participate in choosing their partners. Physical attraction and the meeting of minds is often unable to be anticipated, but it needs to be considered. Although it is expected that love will grow as the couple shares the experiences of marriage, a strong bond from the beginning is preferable.

Therefore, I advocate using both the traditional and the more modern ways of choosing a marriage partner. When I get married, I will ask my parents to arrange meetings with several women who come from families with whom my parents associate. I am sure that there will be a mutual attraction between one of the women and me. In this way, I will have the benefit of my family's wisdom without sacrificing my own romantic ideal.

Model Test 5—Computer-Assisted TOEFL

Section 1: Listening

The Listening Section of the test measures the ability to understand conversations and talks in English. On the actual TOEFL exam, you will use headphones to listen to the conversations and talks. While you are listening, pictures of the speakers or other information will be presented on your computer screen. There are two parts to the Listening Section, with special directions for each part.

On the day of the test, the amount of time you will have to answer all of the questions will appear on the computer screen. The time you spend listening to the test material will not be counted. The listening material and questions about it will be presented only one time. You will not be allowed to take notes or have any paper at your computer. You will both see and hear the questions before the answer choices appear. You can take as much time as you need to select an answer; however, it will be to your advantage to answer the questions as quickly as possible. You may change your answer as many times as you want before you confirm it. After you have confirmed an answer, you will not be able to return to the question.

Before you begin working on the Listening Section, you will have an opportunity to adjust the volume of the sound. You may not be able to change the volume after you have started the test.

QUESTION DIRECTIONS—Part A

In Part A of the Listening Section, you will hear short conversations between two people. In some of the conversations, each person speaks only once. In other conversations, one or both of the people speak more than once. Each conversation is followed by one question about it.

Each question in this part has four answer choices. You should click on the best answer to each question. Answer the questions on the basis of what is stated or implied by the speakers.

Audio

1. Woman: I'm out of typing paper. Will you lend me some?
   Man: I don't have any either, but I'll be glad to get you some when I go to the bookstore.
   Narrator: What is the man going to do?

Answer

(D) The man offers to get some paper at the bookstore. Choice (A) is not correct because the woman, not the man, wants to borrow some typing paper. Choice (B) is not correct because the man doesn't have any paper either. Choice (C) is not mentioned and may not be concluded from information in the conversation.

Audio

2. Man: Excuse me, Miss. Could you please tell me how to get to the University City Bank?
   Woman: Sure. Go straight for two blocks, then turn left and walk three more blocks until you get to the drugstore. It's right across the street.
   Narrator: What can be inferred about the man?

Answer

(B) ". . . walk three more blocks. . . ." Since the woman gives directions for walking, it must be concluded that the man is not driving a car. Choice (C) is not correct because the man calls the woman *Miss.* Choices (A) and (D) are not mentioned and may not be concluded from information in the conversation.

Audio

3. Woman: Are you still going to summer school at the university near your parent's house?
   Man: That plan kind of fell through because there weren't enough courses.
   Narrator: What does the man imply?

Answer

(C) To *fall through* is an idiomatic expression that means "not to happen as planned." Choice (D) is not correct because he planned to go to summer school. Choices (A) and (B) are not mentioned and may not be concluded from information in the conversation.

Audio

4. Man: How much is the rent for the apartment?
   Woman: It's six hundred and fifty dollars a month unfurnished or eight hundred dollars a month furnished. Utilities are seventy-five dollars extra, not including the telephone. It's expensive, but it's worth it because it's within walking distance from the university.
   Narrator: What are the speakers discussing?

Answer

(B) Choices (A), (C), and (D) are mentioned in reference to the main topic of discussion, the apartment.

Audio

5. Man: Dr. Taylor must have really liked your paper. You were about the only one who got an A.
   Woman: I know.
   Man: So why are you so down?
   Woman: He never seems to call on me in class.
   Narrator: What does the woman imply?

Answer

(B) Since the woman mentions that Dr. Taylor does not interact with her in class despite her good grades, she implies that she is not sure how Dr. Taylor feels. Choices (C) and (D) are not correct because she was the only one who received an A on her paper. Choice (A) is not mentioned and may not be concluded from information in the conversation.

Audio

6. Woman: Do you know anyone who would like to participate in a psychology experiment? It pays ten dollars an hour.
   Man: Have you asked Sandy?
   Woman: No. Do you think she would do it?
   Man: I think she would.
   Narrator: What does the man suggest that the woman do?

Answer

(C) Since the man inquires whether she has asked Sandy, he implies that she should ask her. Choice (A) refers to the payment for participation, not to the man's suggestion. Choice (B) refers to the woman's request, not to the man's suggestion. Choice (D) refers to the experiment in psychology, not to a person that the woman should see.

Audio

7. Woman: Didn't you go to the study group meeting last night either?
   Man: No. I had a slight headache.
   Narrator: What can be inferred about the study group meeting?

Answer

(A) Because *either* means that the speaker is including herself in her statement, it must be concluded that the woman did not go to the meeting. The man said that he did not go because of a headache. Choice (B) is not correct because of the use of the word *either* in the woman's question. Choice (C) is not correct because of the man's negative response to the question of whether he went to the meeting. Choice (D) is not correct because of both the use of the word *either* and the man's negative response.

Audio

8. Woman: I have a card, but now I need a farewell gift for my advisor.
   Man: How about a nice pen?
   Narrator: What does the man mean?

Answer

(B) "How about [buying] a nice pen?" Choice (C) refers to the card that the woman has already purchased, not to the man's idea. Choice (D) is not correct because the man offers a suggestion for a gift. Choice (A) is not mentioned and may not be concluded from information in the conversation.

Audio

9. Man: Are you going to move out of the dorm next semester?
   Woman: I just can't seem to make up my mind.
   Narrator: What does the woman mean?

Answer

(D) To *not make up one's mind* is an idiomatic expression that means to "be undecided." Choices (A) and (C) are not correct because she is still considering both alternatives. Choice (B) is not correct because she has a choice.

Audio

10. Man: I signed the contract.
    Woman: Do you really think you can work and go to school full time?
    Narrator: What does the woman imply?

Answer

(A) Since the woman asks whether the man can work and go to school, she implies that he may be taking on too much. Choices (B), (C), and (D) are not mentioned and may not be concluded from information in the conversation.

Audio

11. Woman: I owe everyone in my family a letter, but I really don't have time to sit down and write them and it's too expensive to call.
    Man: Why don't you just buy some postcards?
    Narrator: What does the man suggest the woman do?

Answer

(C) Since the man suggests that the woman buy postcards, it must be concluded that she should send postcards to her family. Choice (B) is not correct because she does not have time to write a letter. Choice (A) refers to the man's family, not to the woman's family. Choice (D) is not mentioned and may not be concluded from information in the conversation.

Audio

12. Man: Are you going to stay here for graduate school?

    Woman: I don't think so.

    Man: Have you heard from any schools yet?

    Woman: Yes, I was accepted at Kansas State, the University of Oklahoma, and the University
                    of Nebraska, but I'm going to wait until I hear one way or another from the
                    University of Minnesota.

    Narrator: What are the speakers discussing?

Answer

(B) Choices (A), (C), and (D) are all mentioned as they relate to the main topic of the conversation,
"where the woman will go to school."

Audio

13. Woman: I thought I was supposed to take the test in Room 32.

    Man: No. Ticket number 32 is in Room 27.

    Narrator: What will the woman probably do?

Answer

(B) Since the man says that ticket number 32 is in room 27, the woman will probably go to room 27.
Choice (A) is not correct because the woman already has a ticket. Choice (C) refers to the number
of the ticket, not to the number of the room. Choice (D) is not correct because the man has already
seen her ticket.

Audio

14. Man: Where did you get the flower?

    Woman: At the Honors Reception. The teachers gave them to all of the honors students.

    Narrator: What can be inferred about the woman?

Answer

(B) Since the teachers gave flowers to all of the honors students and the woman has a flower, it must
be concluded that she is an honors student. Choice (A) is not correct because she has a flower that
was presented at the reception. Choice (D) is not correct because she received a flower for students.
Choice (C) is not mentioned and may not be concluded from information in the conversation.

Audio

15. Man: Terry is really having trouble in Dr. Wise's class. She's missed too much to catch up.

    Woman: If I were Terry, I'd drop the course, and take it over next semester.

    Narrator: What does the woman suggest that Terry do?

Answer

(D) ". . . take it over next semester." Choices (B) and (C) are not correct because the woman says to
drop the class. Choice (A) is not mentioned and may not be concluded from information in the
conversation.

Audio

16. Woman: I used to teach English before I came back to graduate school.

    Man: No wonder you like this course!

    Narrator: What does the man mean?

Answer

(C) Since the woman used to teach English, the man is not surprised that she likes the course. *No wonder* is an idiomatic expression that means the information is logical. Choice (D) refers to the woman's interest, not to the course. Choices (A) and (B) are not mentioned and may not be concluded from information in the conversation.

Audio

17. Man: We should ask Carl to be in our group.
    Woman: We probably ought to ask Jane, too. She's really good at making presentations.
    Narrator: What problem do the students have?

Answer

(A) Since they are discussing potential group members and their value to a presentation, it must be concluded that they are planning to make a presentation. Choice (B) is not correct because the woman says they should ask Jane. Choices (C) and (D) are not mentioned and may not be concluded from information in the conversation.

QUESTION DIRECTIONS—Part B

In Part B of the Listening Section, you will hear several longer conversations and talks. Each conversation or talk is followed by several questions. The conversations, talks, and questions will not be repeated.

The conversations and talks are about a variety of topics. You do not need special knowledge of the topics to answer the questions correctly. Rather, you should answer each question on the basis of what is stated or implied by the speakers in the conversations or talks.

For most of the questions, you will need to click on the best of four possible answers. Some questions will have special directions. The special directions will appear in a box on the computer screen.

Audio Conversation

Narrator: Listen to part of a conversation between two students on campus.

Man: To tell the truth, I really don't know what Dr. Brown wants us to do. The assignment was pretty vague.

Woman: I know. I've already looked in the syllabus, but all it says under the course requirements is "Research paper, thirty points."

Man: Thirty points? I hadn't realized that it counted so much. That's almost one-third of the grade for the course.

Woman: That's why I'm so worried about it. At first I thought she wanted us to do library research, and write it up; then she started talking about presentations. Last week she said there would be time during the next to the last class for us to present.

Man: I was thinking about making an appointment to see her, or just stopping by during her office hours.

Woman: You could do that. But since so many of us are confused, maybe we should ask about it in class tomorrow. I bet we won't be the only ones with questions either.

Man: That's a good idea.

> Now get ready to answer the questions

Audio

18. What problem do the speakers have?

Answer

(B) "I really don't know what Dr. Brown wants us to do. . . . The assignment was pretty vague." Choice (A) is not correct because they looked in the syllabus. Choice (C) refers to the fact that the man was thinking of making an appointment with Dr. Brown to resolve the problem. Choice (D) is not correct because the man was considering stopping by Dr. Brown's office during her office hours.

Audio

19. How much does the research paper count toward the grade for the course?

Answer

(D) ". . . it says under the course requirements. . . . " Research paper, thirty points.'" Choice (A) is not correct because it says thirty points in the syllabus. Choice (B) is not correct because thirty points is one-third, not one-half, of the total grade. Choice (C) is not correct because it is thirty, not ten, points.

Audio

20. What did the professor say last week?

Answer

(A) ". . . then she started talking about presentations." Choice (C) refers to the fact that the students are planning to ask questions in the next class, not to questions that were asked last week. Choices (B) and (D) are not mentioned and may not be concluded from information in the conversation.

Audio

21. What will the students probably do?

Answer

(C) ". . . maybe we should ask about it in class tomorrow." Since the man agrees that she has a good idea, it must be concluded that they will ask questions about the assignment in class. Choices (B) and (D) were discussed earlier in the conversation before they decided to ask in class. Choice (A) is not correct because they do not understand the assignment.

Audio Lecture

Narrator: Listen to part of a lecture in a world history class. Today the professor will talk about exploration and discovery. She will focus on the Hawaiian Islands.

On his third exploratory voyage, as captain of two ships, the *Resolution* and the *Discovery*, Captain James Cook came upon a group of uncharted islands that he named the Sandwich Islands as a tribute to his friend, the Earl of Sandwich. Today the islands are known as the Hawaiian Islands.

Some historians contend that the islanders welcomed Cook, believing that he was the god Launo, protector of peace and agriculture. I have that name written on the board for you. Of course, it didn't take long for them to realize that Launo had not returned.

These islanders were short, strong people, with a well-organized social system. The men fished and raised crops, including taro, coconuts, sweet potatoes, and sugarcane. The women cared for the children and made clothing—loin cloths for the men and short skirts for the women. The natives were eager to exchange food and supplies for iron nails and tools, and Cook was easily able to restock his ship.

Because of a severe storm in which the *Resolution* was damaged, it was necessary to return to Hawaii. Now sure that Cook and his crew were men and not gods, the natives welcomed them less hospitably. Besides, diseases brought by the English had reached epidemic proportions. When a small boat was stolen from the *Discovery*, Cook demanded that the king be taken as a hostage until the boat was returned. In the fighting that followed, Cook and four crewmen were killed.

> Now get ready to answer the questions

Audio

22. What is the main subject of this lecture?

Answer

(C) "On his third exploratory voyage, as captain of two ships. . . . Captain James Cook came upon . . . the Hawaiian Islands." Choices (A), (B), and (D) are secondary themes used to develop the main theme of the talk.

Audio

23. According to the lecturer, what were the two ships commanded by Captain Cook?

Answer

(B) (C) ". . . as captain in charge of two ships, the *Resolution* and the *Discovery*, Captain James Cook came upon a group of uncharted islands. . . ." Choice (A) refers to the fact that this was Cook's third voyage to explore the Pacific Ocean, not to the name of his ship. *England* in Choice (D) refers to the country that commissioned Cook, not to the name of his ship.

Audio

24. Why does the professor mention the name *Launo*?

Answer

(C) "Some historians contend that the islanders welcomed Cook, believing that he was the god Launo, protector of peace and agriculture." Choices (A), (B), and (D) are not mentioned and may not be concluded from information in the lecture.

Audio

25. The professor briefly explains a sequence of events in the history of Hawaii. Summarize the sequence by putting the events in order.

Answer

(D) (C) (B) (A) ". . . Cook demanded that the king be taken as a hostage until the boat was returned. In the fighting that followed, Cook and four other crewmen were killed."

Audio Lecture

Narrator: Listen to part of a lecture in an engineering class. The professor will discuss alloys.

An alloy is a substance that is formed by combining a metal with other metals, or nonmetals. For example, brass is an alloy of the metals copper and zinc, and steel is an alloy of the metal iron with the nonmetal carbon.

The special characteristics of metals, such as hardness, strength, flexibility, and weight are called its properties. By the process of alloying, it is possible to create materials with the exact combinations of properties for a particular use. In the aircraft industry, there is a need for metals that are both strong and light. Steel is strong but too heavy, whereas aluminum is light but not strong. By alloying aluminum with copper and other metals, a material that is strong enough to withstand the stresses of flight, but light enough to reduce the cost of fuel to lift the craft is created. By alloying steel with nickel and chromium, the steel alloy that results is not only lighter but also stronger than solid steel.

Of course, there is an important difference between the alloys we have used in our examples and the combination of metals that occur accidentally as impure metals. Both are mixtures, but alloys are mixtures that have been deliberately combined in specific proportion for a definite purpose.

> Now get ready to answer the questions

Audio

26. What is an alloy?

Answer

(C) ". . . alloys are mixtures that have been deliberately combined in specific proportion for a definite purpose." Choice (A) refers to natural combinations of metals, not to alloys. Choice (B) is true but incomplete because it does not mention the specific purposes. Choice (D) is not mentioned and may not be concluded from information in the conversation.

Audio

27. What does the speaker say about the properties of alloys?

Answer

(A) (B) ". . . alloys are mixtures that have been deliberately combined in specific proportion for a definite purpose." Choice (D) refers to impure metals, not to alloys. Choice (C) is not mentioned and may not be concluded from information in the conversation.

Audio

28. Why does the speaker use the example of the aircraft industry?

Answer

(A) "In the aircraft industry, there is a need for metals that are both strong and light." Choice (D) is not correct because the metals referred to are alloys. Choices (B) and (C) are not mentioned and may not be concluded from information in the conversation.

Audio

29. What is the difference between combinations of metals in nature and alloys?

Answer

(C) "Both [alloys and combinations in nature] are mixtures, but alloys are mixtures that have been deliberately combined in specific proportion for a definite purpose." Choice (A) is not correct because metals that occur accidentally in nature are impure. Choice (B) is not correct because combinations of metals occur accidentally in nature. Choice (D) is not correct because both alloys and combinations of metals that occur in nature are mixtures.

Audio Discussion

Narrator: Listen to part of a discussion in an English class.

John: British English and American English are really about the same, aren't they?

Mary: I don't think so. It seems to me that some of the spellings are different.

Baker: You're right, Mary. Words like *theater* and *center* end in *re* in England instead of in *er*, the way that we spell them. Let me write that on the board. Can you think of any more examples?

Mary: The word *color*?

Baker: Good. In fact, many words that end in *or* in American English are spelled *our* in British English, like *color* and *honor*.

John: I'm still not convinced. I mean, if someone comes here from England, we can all understand what he's saying. The spelling doesn't really matter that much.

Baker: Okay. Are we just talking about spelling? Or are there some differences in pronunciation and meaning too?

Mary: Professor Baker?

Baker: Yes?

Mary: I remember seeing an English movie where the actors kept calling their apartment a *flat*. Half of the movie was over before I realized what they were talking about.

John: So there are slight differences in spelling and some vocabulary.

Mary: And pronunciation, too. You aren't going to tell me that you sound like Richard Burton.

John: Richard Burton wasn't English. He was Welsh.

Mary: Okay. Anyway, the pronunciation is different.

Baker: I think that what we are really disagreeing about is the extent of the difference. We all agree that British English and American English are different. Right?

Mary: Yes.

John: Sure.

Baker: But not so different that it prevents us from understanding each other.

John: Well, that's what I mean.

Mary: That's what I mean, too.

> Now get ready to answer the questions

Audio

30. What do the speakers mainly discuss?

Answer

(C) "We all agree that British English and American English are different. Right? . . .But not so different that it prevents us from understanding each other." Choices (A), (B), and (D) are secondary points of discussion that are used to develop the main topic of the discussion.

Audio

31. How are these words referred to in the discussion?

Answer

(A) (B) (C) (D) "Words like *theater* and *center* end in *re* in England instead of *er*, the way that we [Americans] spell them. . . . In fact, many words that end in *or* in American English are spelled *our* in British English, like *color* and *honor*."

Audio

32. What can be inferred about the word *flat* in British English?

Answer

(B) "I remember seeing an English movie where the actors kept calling their apartment a *flat*. Half of the movie was over before I realized what they were talking about." Choice (D) is not correct because the woman did not understand the word. Choices (A) and (C) are not mentioned and may not be concluded from information in the discussion.

Audio

33. On what did the class agree?

Answer

(D) "We all agree that British English and American English are different. . . . But not so different that it prevents us from understanding each other." Choice (A) refers to the man's opinion at the beginning of the discussion, not to the opinion of the class at the conclusion of the discussion. The opinions expressed in Choices (B) and (C) are not mentioned and may not be concluded from information in the discussion.

Audio Talk

Narrator: Listen to part of a talk in an education class. A student is giving a presentation about local control of schools.

My report is on local control of schools. First, I was surprised to learn that public schools in the United States are not the same in every state or even from community to community within the state. The reason for differences in organization, curriculum, and school policies is because each school district has a governing board, called the school board, that makes the decisions about the way the schools in their district will be run. Of course, a superintendent is selected by the board to carry out policies and the superintendent is usually a professional educator, but the board, often made up of community leaders who are not professional educators, must approve the recommendations of the superintendent.

There are two ways to organize a school board. In most communities, the board is elected by the residents in their local school district. And the members usually serve without pay for three to five years. But in some districts, the school board is appointed by the mayor.

Of course, the federal government has an interest in improving education on a national level, even though schools are controlled locally. But the function of the national department is very different from a department of education in many parts of the world. This national agency is primarily involved in collecting demographics, supporting research and projects, and supervising the compliance of schools with national legislation.

> Now get ready to answer the questions

Audio

34. What is the presentation mainly about?

Answer

(D) "My report is on local control of schools." Choices (A), (B), and (C) are secondary themes used to develop the main theme of the report.

Audio

35. What surprised the presenter about her research?

Answer

(A) ". . . I was surprised to learn that public schools in the United States are not the same in every state or even from community to community. . . . " Choices (B), (C), and (D) are all true, but they are not what surprised the presenter about her research.

Audio

36. How does each of the persons identified contribute to the operation of schools in the United States?

Answer

(B) (A) (C) ". . . a governing board, called the school board, that makes the decisions . . . a superintendent…to carry out policies. . . . In most communities, the board is elected by the residents in their local school district."

Audio

37. According to the speaker, what is the function of the department of education in the United States?

Answer

(A) (C) "The function of the national department is . . . supporting research and projects, and supervising the compliance of schools with national legislation." Choice (B) is not correct because the school board makes decisions about the curriculum in the local district. Choice (D) is not correct because local school boards are elected by the people or appointed by the mayor.

Audio Conversation

Narrator: Listen to part of a conversation between a student and a secretary in a college dormitory.

Man: I want to buy a meal ticket.
Woman: Okay. Which plan do you want?
Man: You mean there is more than one?
Woman: Sure. You can buy one meal a day, two meals a day, or three meals a day.
Man: Oh. If I buy two meals a day, can I choose which meals?
Woman: Not really. The two-meal plan includes lunch and dinner. No breakfast.
Man: Great. That's what I would have wanted anyway. How much is that?
Woman: It's thirty-six dollars a week, which works out to about three dollars a meal.
Man: Wait a minute. Fourteen meals at three dollars would be forty-two dollars, wouldn't it?
Woman: Yes, but we don't serve meals on Sunday.
Man: Oh.
Woman: Most residents order a pizza or go out to eat on Sundays. Of course, some students live close enough to go home for the day.
Man: Okay. I'll take the two-meal plan. Do I pay by the quarter or by the week?
Woman: By the quarter.
Man: Fine. Do you take credit cards?
Woman: Yes, but you don't have to pay now. Just fill out this form, and we'll bill you.

Now get ready to answer the questions

Audio

38. What kind of meal plan does the man decide to buy?

Answer

(B) (C) "The two-meal plan includes lunch and dinner." Choice (A) is not correct because there is no breakfast included. Choice (D) is not mentioned and may not be concluded from information in the conversation.

Audio

39. How much does the plan cost?

Answer

(C) "It's thirty-six dollars a week, which works out to about three dollars a meal." The number in Choice (A) refers to the number of meals that the man uses to calculate, not the cost. Choice (D) refers to the cost of two meals per day for seven days, not to the cost of a six-day plan. Choice (B) is not mentioned and may not be concluded from information in the conversation.

Audio

40. Why do most residents order a pizza or go out to eat on Sundays?

Answer

(C) ". . . we don't serve meals on Sunday." Choice (A) refers to the situation that some students have, but not to the reason that they eat out. Choices (B) and (D) are not mentioned and may not be concluded from information in the conversation.

Audio

41. How will the man pay for the meals?

Answer

(C) "Just fill out this form, and we'll bill you." Choice (B) refers to the man's question about credit cards, not to the way that he will pay. Choices (A) and (D) are not correct because the man will be billed.

Audio

42. What will the man probably do?

Answer

(C) "Just fill out this form, and we'll bill you." Choice (A) is not correct because the man does not have to pay now. Choice (B) refers to the man's offer, not to what he will probably do. Choice (D) is not mentioned and may not be concluded from information in the conversation.

Audio Lecture

Narrator: Listen to part of a lecture in a botany class. The professor is talking about hydroponics.

As you will recall, hydroponics is the science of growing plants without soil, using a solution of nutrients in water. Of course, good soil has the nutrients necessary for plant growth, but when plants are grown without soil, all the nutrients must be provided in another way. This solution contains potassium nitrate, ammonium sulfate, magnesium sulfate, monocalcium phosphate, and calcium sulfate. Don't try to write down all of that now. You can refer to your lab workbook for the list of substances and the proportions needed for proper plant growth.

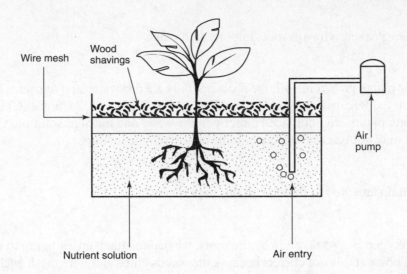

For now, let's look at the diagram that we worked on last time when we began our hydroponics experiment. Your drawing should look more or less like this one. As you know, for plants grown in soil, the roots not only absorb water and nutrients but also serve to anchor the plant. That is why the roots of our hydroponic plants are not placed directly in the water and nutrient solution. We used wood chips held in place by wire mesh to anchor the plants and allow us to suspend the roots in the tank below that contains the water and nutrient solution. Because oxygen is also taken in by the roots, we had to attach an air pump to mix oxygen into the solution. And you can see the way that the pump was attached to the tank.

During our break this morning, I'd like you to come over to the hydroponics area and examine the experiment close up. I'd also like you to take a closer look at this specimen of nutrient solution. What do you notice about this? What conclusions can you draw?

> Now get ready to answer the questions

Audio

43. What is hydroponics?

Answer

(A) ". . . hydroponics is the science of growing plants without soil. . . . " Choice (B) refers to the nutrients that are used in the solution in order to grow the plants, not to a definition of hydroponics. Choices (C) and (D) are not mentioned and may not be concluded from information in the lecture.

Audio

44. Why does the professor suggest that the students refer to the lab workbooks?

Answer

(C) "You can refer to your lab workbook for the list of substances and the proportions needed for proper plant growth." Choice (A) is not correct because the professor shows the diagram. Choice (D) is not correct because the hydroponics tank is already built and displayed in class. Choice (B) is not mentioned and may not be concluded from information in the lecture.

Audio

45. According to the speaker, why are roots important to plants?

Answer

(A) (B) ". . . for plants grown in soil, the roots not only absorb water and nutrients but also serve to anchor the plant. . . . Because oxygen is also taken in by the roots. . . . " Choice (C) is not correct because hydroponic plants are not placed directly in the water and nutrient solution. Choice (D) is not mentioned and may not be concluded from information in the lecture.

Audio

46. Why was the pump attached to the tank in this experiment?

Answer

(C) "Because oxygen is also taken in by the roots, we had to attach an air pump to mix oxygen into the solution." Choice (D) is not correct because the woods chips and wire mesh anchored the plants. Choices (A) and (B) are not mentioned and may not be concluded from information in the lecture.

Audio

47. What does the professor want the students to do with the specimen of the nutrient solution?

Answer

(C) "I'd also like you to take a closer look at this specimen of nutrient solution. . . . What conclusions can you draw?" Choice (B) confuses the word *draw* with the idiom *to draw conclusions*. Choices (A) and (D) are not mentioned and may not be concluded from information in the lecture.

Audio Conversation

Narrator: Listen to part of a conversation between two students on campus.

Man: Did you watch *American Biography* last night?
Woman: No, I had class. Did you?
Man: Yes. Actually, it was an assignment for my history class, and it was excellent.
            It featured Harriet Tubman.
Woman: Who is Harriet Tubman?
Man: Don't feel bad. I didn't know either until I watched the show. She was a member of
            the underground railroad. You know, the organization that helped runaway slaves
            escape to free states or to Canada in the mid eighteen hundreds, just before and
            during the Civil War.
Woman: Oh, I know who you mean. She had been a slave herself, hadn't she?
Man: Right. According to the program, when she escaped from her owners in Maryland,
            she felt for moss on the north side of trees, and followed the North Star until she got
            to Philadelphia.
Woman: No kidding.
Man: What really impressed me though was the fact that after she escaped, she went back
            to Maryland nineteen times to lead others to freedom. I think they said she freed
            more than three hundred slaves.
Woman: That sounds interesting. I'm sorry I missed it.
Man: Sometimes they rerun the biographies.
Woman: Well I'll watch for it then. Thanks for telling me about it.

Now get ready to answer the questions

Audio

48. What are the speakers discussing?

Answer

(C) "Did you watch *American Biography* last night?" Choice (A) is not correct because the woman had a class. Choice (B) is not correct because the man watched the show. Choice (D) is not correct because the program was scheduled last night, and may be rerun.

Audio

49. Who was Harriet Tubman?

Answer

(D) ". . . she escaped from her owners in Maryland. . . ." Tubman was a member of the underground railroad, but it was not mentioned whether she worked on the regular railroad or underground in a mine as in Choices (A) and (B). Choice (C) refers to the destination of many slaves who were helped by the underground railroad, not to Tubman's home.

Audio

50. What impressed the man about Harriet Tubman's story?

Answer

(B) "What really impressed me though was the fact that after she escaped, she went back to Maryland nineteen times . . . [and] freed more than three hundred slaves." Choice (A) is true, but it is not what impressed the man. The number *nineteen* in Choice (D) refers to the number of times that she returned to Maryland to help others, not to the number of years she spent in slavery. Choice (C) is not mentioned and may not be concluded from information in the conversation.

Section 2: Structure

1. **(D)** There must be agreement between subject and verb, not between the verb and words in the appositive after the subject. *Were* should be *was* to agree with the singular subject *gunpowder*.

2. **(B)** There must be agreement between subject and verb. *Is* should be *are* to agree with the plural subject *manufacturers*.

3. **(D)** Because adjectives are used after verbs of the senses, *sweetly* should be *sweet* after the verb *smell*. *Sweetly* is an adverb. *Sweet* is an adjective.

4. **(A)** The verb *to expect* requires an infinitive in the complement. Choices (B), (C), and (D) are not infinitives.

5. **(C)** *Because of* is used before nouns such as *a misunderstanding* to express cause. Choices (A) and (B) are not accepted for statements of cause. Choice (D) is used before a subject and verb, not a noun, to express cause.

6. **(D)** *Equal to* is a prepositional idiom. *As* should be *to*.

7. **(D)** Ideas in a series should be expressed by parallel structures. *Stressful* should be *stress* to provide for parallelism with the nouns *predisposition, drugs,* or *infection*.

8. **(A)** Subject-verb order is used in the clause after a question word connector such as *where*. In Choice (B), there is no question word connector. In Choice (C), the subject-verb order is reversed. In Choice (D), the question word connector is used after, not before, the subject and verb.

9. **(A)** *May* and a verb word in the result require a past form in the condition. Because *may have* is used in the result, *having* should be *had* in the condition.

10. **(C)** *As well as* is used in correlation with the inclusive *and*. Choices (A) and (B) would be used in clauses of comparison, not correlation. Choice (D) is incomplete because it does not include the final word *as*.

11. **(B)** In order to refer to nurses not allowing you to give blood, *let* should be used. *To leave* means to go. *To let* means to allow.

12. **(D)** The anticipatory clause *it was in 1848 that* introduces a subject and verb, *gold was discovered*. Choice (A) may be used preceding a subject and verb without *that*. Choice (B) may be used as a subject clause preceding a main verb. Choice (C) is redundant and indirect. "Because in 1848 gold was discovered at Sutter's Mill, the California Gold Rush began," and "That in 1848 gold was discovered at Sutter's Mill was the cause of the California Gold Rush" would also be correct.

13. **(C)** Comparative forms for three-syllable adverbs are usually preceded by *more* and followed by *than*. Choice (A) is followed by *as*. Choice (B) is preceded by *as*. Choice (D) is not preceded by *more*.

14. **(D)** The verb *thought* establishes a point of view in the past. *Has* should be *had* in order to maintain the point of view.

15. **(B)** *Developing* should be *development*. Although both are nouns derived from verbs, the *-ment* ending is preferred. *Developing* means progressing. *Development* means the act of developing or the result of developing.

16. **(A)** Most adverbs of manner are formed by adding *-ly* to adjectives. Choices (B) and (D) are redundant and indirect. Choice (C) is ungrammatical because the adverb *fast* does not have an *-ly* ending.

17. **(C)** *But also* is used in correlation with the inclusive *not only*. Choice (A) would be used in correlation with *not*, not in correlation with *not only*. Choices (B) and (D) are not used in correlation with another inclusive.

18. **(C)** Comparisons must be made with logically comparable nouns. Choices (A) and (D) are redundant and indirect. Choice (B) makes an illogical comparison of *a salary* with *a teacher*. Only Choice (C) compares two salaries.

19. **(A)** The verb phrase *to look forward to* requires an *-ing* form in the complement. Choices (B) and (D) are not *-ing* forms. Choice (C) is BE and an *-ing* form.

20. **(C)** There must be agreement between pronoun and antecedent. *Their* should be *its* to agree with the singular antecedent *a turtle*.

21. **(C)** In order to refer to a city which has been *occupying a place, lying* should be used. *To lay* means to put in a place. *To lie* means to occupy a place.

22. **(B)** *Purposeful* should be *purposes*. *Purposeful* is an adjective. *Purposes* is a noun.

23. **(C)** An introductory verbal phrase should immediately precede the noun that it modifies. Only Choice (C) provides a noun which could be logically modified by the introductory verbal phrase, *after seeing the movie*. Neither *the book* nor *the reading* could logically *see a movie* as would be implied by Choices (A), (B), and (D).

24. **(B)** A form of BE is used with the participle in passive sentences. *Said* should be *is said*.

25. **(C)** Comparative forms are usually followed by *than*. After the comparative *more important, as* should be *than*.

Section 3: Reading

1. **(A)** "The Father of American Public Education" is the best title because it states the main idea of the passage. Choice (C) is a detail used to develop the main idea. Choices (B) and (D) are not specific enough.

2. **(C)** "Perhaps it was his own lack of adequate schooling that inspired Horace Mann to work so hard for the important reforms in education that he accomplished." Choice (A) is not correct because Mann did not have benefit of an early education. Choice (B) is not correct because the biography is limited to Horace Mann's work as an educator. Choice (D) is not correct because the teachers are mentioned only briefly.

3. **(D)** In the context of this passage, struggles could best be replaced by difficult times. Choices (A), (C), and (B) are not accepted definitions of the word.

4. **(B)** "…to become first secretary of the board [of education]. There [at the board of education] he exercised an enormous influence…." Choices (A), (C), and (D) would change the meaning of the sentence.

5. **(A)** In the context of this passage, mandatory is closest in meaning to required. Choices (B), (C), and (D) are not accepted definitions of the word.

6. In the context of this passage, the word extended could best be replaced by increased. No other words or phrases in the **bold** text are close to the meaning of the word extended.

7. "Mann's ideas about school reform were developed and distributed in twelve annual reports to the state of Massachusetts...." Quotation from sentence 1, paragraph 3.

8. (**A**) "Mann was recognized as the father of public education." Choice (B) is not correct because Horace Mann exercised an enormous influence. Choices (C) and (D) are unlikely since his influence resulted in a change in the school system.

9. (**B**) "There he exercised an enormous influence during the critical period of reconstruction that brought into existence the American graded elementary school as a substitute for the older district school system." Choice (A) refers to "the historic education bill that set up a state board of education" and to the fact that Mann served as first secretary of the board. Choice (C) refers to "the lyceums for adult education," which he founded. Choice (D) refers to the new system that was brought into existence under Mann's influence.

10. (**C**) "...the Massachusetts reforms later served as a model for the nation." Choice (A) is not correct because the reforms were considered quite radical at the time. Choice (B) is not correct because they served as a model for the nation. Choice (D) is not mentioned and may not be concluded from information in the passage.

11. (**B**) "Be ashamed to die until you have won some victory for humanity." Choices (A), (C), and (D) are not mentioned specifically as part of Mann's philosophy.

12. (**A**) "Organic architecture, that is, natural architecture...." Choice (B) refers to the rule rejected by organic architecture, not to another name for it. Choices (C) and (D) refer to the fact that organic architecture may be varied but always remains true to natural principles. Neither principle architecture nor varied architecture was cited as another name for organic architecture, however.

13. "Organic architecture—that is, natural architecture—may be varied in concept and form, but it [the architecture] is always faithful to natural principles." Other choices would change the meaning of the sentence.

14. (**B**) In the context of this passage, ultimately could best be replaced by eventually. Choices (A), (C), and (D) are not accepted definitions of the word.

15. (**C**) In the context of this passage, upheld is closest in meaning to promoted. Choices (A), (B), and (D) are not accepted definitions of the word.

16. (**A**) "If these natural principles are upheld, then a bank cannot be built to look like a Greek temple." Choice (B) refers to the fact that natural principles require "total harmony with the setting." Choice (C) refers to the fact that the colors are taken from "the surrounding palette of nature." Choice (D) refers to the fact that "the rule of functionalism is upheld."

17. (**B**) "Natural principles then, are principles of design, not style.... Like a sculptor, the organic architect views the site and materials as an innate form that develops organically from within." Choice (C) refers to the geometric themes mentioned later in the passage. Choice (D) is not correct because the author emphasizes design, not style. Choice (A) is not mentioned and may not be concluded from information in the passage.

18. (**A**) In the context of this passage, obscured is closest in meaning to difficult to see. Choices (B), (C), and (D) are not accepted definitions of the word.

19. In the context of this passage, the word shapes is closest in meaning to contours. No other words or phrases in the **bold** text are close to the meaning of the word contours.

20. "Organic architecture incorporates built-in architectural features such as benches and storage areas to take the place of furniture." Quotation from sentence 7, paragraph 3.

21. (**D**) "Form does not follow function; form is inseparable from function." Choice (A) is not correct because form does not follow function. Choices (B) and (C) are not correct because form is inseparable from function.

22. (**C**) "...a building should...respect the natural characteristics of the setting to create harmony with its natural environment." Choices (A), (B), and (D) are not correct because nature should be respected.

23. (**D**) Choices (A), (B), and (C) are important to the discussion and provide details that support the main point that alchemy was the predecessor of modern chemistry.

24. **(B)** In the context of the passage, authentic could best be replaced by genuine. Choices (A), (C), and (D) are not accepted definitions of the word.

25. "The earliest authentic works on European alchemy are those [works] of the English monk Roger Bacon and the German philosopher St. Albertus Magnus." Other choices would change the meaning of the sentence.

26. **(A)** "…inferior metals such as lead and mercury were removed by various degrees of imperfection from gold." Choices (B), (C), and (D) are not mentioned and may not be concluded from information in the passage.

27. In the context of this passage, the word maintained is closest in meaning to asserted. No other words or phrases in the **bold** text are close to the meaning of the word asserted.

28. **(B)** "…base metals could be transmuted to gold by blending them with a substance even more perfect than gold. This elusive substance was referred to as the 'philosopher's stone.'" Choices (A) and (D) are not correct because the "philosopher's stone" was more perfect than gold. Choice (C) is not correct because the "philosopher's stone" was an element that alchemists were searching for, not another name for their art.

29. **(B)** In the context of this passage, cryptic could be replaced by secret. Choices (A), (C), and (D) are not accepted definitions of the word.

30. **(A)** Because the early alchemists were "artisans who were accustomed to keeping trade secrets," it must be concluded that early alchemists used cryptic terms like *sun* and *moon* to keep the work secret. Choices (B) and (C) refer to the fact that philosophers were attracted to alchemy and began to use the symbolic language in their literature, but they are not reasons why the alchemists used the terms. Choice (D) refers to the record of the progress of the work that was produced by alchemists, not to the reason for cryptic language.

31. **(C)** "Most of the early alchemists were artisans…." Choice (B) refers to the second group, not the first group, of alchemists. Choices (A) and (D) are not mentioned and may not be concluded from information in the passage.

32. **(B)** "…it was the literary alchemist who was most likely to produce a written record; therefore, much of what is known about the science of alchemy is derived from philosophers rather than from the alchemists who labored in laboratories." Choice (A) is true, but it is not the reason that we know about the history of alchemy. Choices (C) and (D) are not mentioned and may not be concluded from information in the passage.

33. **(B)** "…they [laboratory alchemists] did gain a wide knowledge of chemical substances, discovered chemical properties, and invented many of the tools and techniques that are still used by chemists today." Choice (A) is not correct because the alchemists made scientific discoveries and were considered the legitimate forefathers of modern chemistry. Choice (C) is not correct because the majority of educated persons in the period from 1400 to 1600 believed that alchemy had great merit. Although the author mentions the work of both laboratory and literary alchemists, Choice (D) is not mentioned and may not be concluded from information in the passage.

34. **(C)** The other choices are secondary ideas that are used to develop the main idea, "human memory." Choices (A), (B), and (D) are important to the discussion, but are not the main topic.

35. **(A)** In the context of this passage, formerly could best be replaced by in the past. Choices (B), (C), and (D) are not accepted definitions of the word.

36. **(A)** "Human memory…is really more sophisticated than that of a computer." Choice (B) is not correct because human memory is more sophisticated. Choices (C) and (D) are not mentioned and may not be concluded from information in the passage.

37. In the context of this passage, the word complex is closest in meaning to sophisticated. No other words or phrases in the **bold** text are close to the meaning of the word sophisticated.

38. "Human memory, formerly believed to be rather inefficient, is really more sophisticated than that [the memory] of a computer." Other choices would change the meaning of the sentence.

39. (**B**) "...by stimulating their brains electrically, he could elicit the total recall of complex events." Choice (A) refers to the fact that Penfield was a neurosurgeon, but he did not rely on surgery to elicit dreams. Choice (C) refers to the procedure for supporting recall. Choice (D) refers to the way that performance is improved in memory, not to the procedure for eliciting dreams.

40. (**B**) "...the...capacity for storage in the brain is the result of an almost unlimited combination of interconnections...stimulated by patterns of activity." Choice (A) is not correct because the physical basis for memory is not yet understood. Choice (C) is not correct because storage in the brain is the result of an almost unlimited combination of interconnections. Choice (D) is not correct because repeated references to the same information supports recall.

41. (**C**) Although Choices (A), (B), and (D) are definitions of the word bonds, the meaning in the context of the sentence is connections.

42. "Psychologists generally divide memory into at least two types, short-term and long-term, which combine to form working memory." Quotation from sentence 1, paragraph 3.

43. (**A**) "We use short-term memory when we look up a telephone number and repeat it to ourselves until we can place the call." Choices (B), (C), and (D) are not mentioned and may not be concluded from information in the passage.

44. (**B**) "The memory trace is...made by structural changes in the brain...is not subject to direct observation...is rather a theoretical construct.... Repeated references to the same information supports recall." Choices (A), (C), and (D) are all mentioned in the passage. Choice (B) is not correct because the memory trace is not subject to direct observation.

45. (**A**) "...there is a great deal more stored in our minds than has been generally supposed." Choice (B) is not correct because the physical basis of memory is not yet understood. Choice (C) refers to the fact that researchers have approached the problem from a variety of points of view, but it may not be concluded that different points of view are valuable. Choice (D) is not correct because memory was formerly believed to be inefficient, but is really sophisticated.

Writing Section

Question:

Some people believe that it is very important to make large amounts of money, while others are satisfied to earn a comfortable living. Analyze each viewpoint and take a stand. Give specific reasons for your position.

Outline

Comfortable living
* Healthy lifestyle—less pressured, less stress
* Time with family members

Large amounts of money
* Better standard of living for family
* More opportunities for charities

My experience
* Busy father
* Prefer time with my children

Map

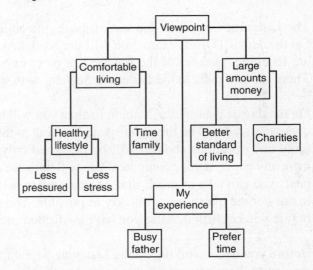

Example Essay

When we are considering options for a major field in college, the counselors often mention the amount of money that we can expect to earn if we make that career choice. Then it is up to us to decide whether it is important to make large amounts of money or whether we are satisfied to earn a comfortable living. Certainly, there are good reasons for both decisions.

If we make a lot of money, it will be possible to provide a better standard of living for our families. We can live in better homes, our children can go to more prestigious schools and partici-pate in activities or take lessons, we can go on vacations and have experiences that would be impossible without the financial resources that a high-paying job produces. We can enjoy what the material world has to offer because we can pay for it. Besides supporting our personal lifestyles, we can afford to give generously to charities.

In contrast, if we make a comfortable living, the advantages are less visible but nonetheless important. We can participate in a healthy lifestyle because we will be less pressured. A job that pays less may have a slower pace and fewer responsibilities. Less stress may allow us to sleep better. There may be fewer demands on our time so we can exercise more and have more meals at home, contributing to good health. The extra time can also be spent with family members in-stead of at the office. We can be at the ball game when our child hits the home run.

In making a personal decision, I am opting for a comfortable living instead of the high-powered job with a larger salary. As the son of a success-ful executive, I remember expensive vacations that my father paid for but did not participate in because he was too busy at work. I prefer to spend time with my children instead of spending money on them. I plan to be at the ball game.

Model Test 6—Computer-Assisted TOEFL

Section 1: Listening

The Listening Section of the test measures the ability to understand conversations and talks in English. On the actual TOEFL exam, you will use headphones to listen to the conversations and talks. While you are listening, pictures of the speakers or other information will be presented on your computer screen. There are two parts to the Listening Section, with special directions for each part.

On the day of the test, the amount of time you will have to answer all of the questions will appear on the computer screen. The time you spend listening to the test material will not be counted. The listening ma-terial and questions about it will be presented only one time. You will not be allowed to take notes or have any paper at your computer. You will both see and hear the questions before the answer choices ap-pear. You can take as much time as you need to select an answer; however, it will be to your advantage to answer the questions as quickly as possible. You may change your answer as many times as you want before you confirm it. After you have confirmed an answer, you will not be able to return to the question.

Before you begin working on the Listening Section, you will have an opportunity to adjust the volume of the sound. You may not be able to change the volume after you have started the test.

QUESTION DIRECTIONS—Part A

In Part A of the Listening Section, you will hear short conversations between two people. In some of the conversations, each person speaks only once. In other conversations, one or both of the people speak more than once. Each conversation is followed by one question about it.

Each question in this part has four answer choices. You should click on the best answer to each question. Answer the questions on the basis of what is stated or implied by the speakers.

Audio

1. Man: What are you going to do this weekend? Maybe we can play some tennis.
   Woman: Don't tempt me. I have to study for my qualifying examinations. I take them on Monday.
   Narrator: What does the woman mean?

Answer

(B) According to the woman, she has to study for her qualifying examinations. Choices (A) and (C) are not correct because the woman says she is tempted to go. Choice (D) is not correct because the woman is taking a qualifying examination for a degree. She is not trying to qualify in order to play tennis.

Audio

2. Woman: Any questions about the syllabus?
   Man: Yes. Does attendance count toward the grade in this class?
   Woman: No. I have an attendance requirement for undergraduates, but not for graduate students.
   Narrator: What does the woman mean?

Answer

(B) "I have an attendance requirement for undergraduates, but not for graduate students." Choice (A) is not correct because she has a policy for undergraduates. Choice (C) is not correct because the woman says "no" when she is asked whether attendance will count toward the grade. Choice (D) is not correct because the woman has an attendance requirement for undergraduates, but not for this class, which implies that it is a graduate course.

Audio

3. Man: Have you talked to Ali lately? I thought that he was studying at the American Language Institute, but yesterday I saw him going into the chemistry lab in the engineering building.
   Woman: That is not surprising. Ali is a part-time student this term. He is taking three classes at the Institute and one class at the university.
   Narrator: What does the woman say about Ali?

Answer

(C) The woman says that Ali is a part-time student this term. Choice (A) is incomplete because Ali is studying both at the university and the American Language Institute. The number in Choice (B) refers to the number of classes that Ali is taking at the Institute, not at the university. Choice (D) is not correct because it is the man in the conversation, not Ali, who is surprised. The woman says that Ali's situation is not surprising.

Audio

4. Man: Hello, Miss Evans? This is Paul Thompson. I would like to talk with Dr. Warren, please.
   Woman: Oh, Paul. You just missed her.
   Narrator: What does the woman mean?

Answer

(C) To *just miss* someone is an idiomatic expression that means that the person "has already left." Choices (A), (B), and (D) are not paraphrases of the expression and may not be concluded from information in the conversation.

Audio

5. Man: I am sorry. The last campus shuttle has already left.
   Woman: Oh. All right. Can you please tell me where I can find a telephone?
   Narrator: What will the woman probably do?

Answer

(C) Since the woman asks where she can find a telephone, she will probably make a phone call. Choice (D) is not correct because the shuttle has already departed. Choices (A) and (B) are not mentioned and may not be concluded from information in the conversation.

Audio

6. Man: Have you bought your books yet?
   Woman: I tried to, but the math and English books were sold out.
   Narrator: What does the woman mean?

Answer

(C) *Sold out* is an idiomatic expression that means there are "none left." Choice (A) is not correct because she has already tried to buy her books at the bookstore. Choice (D) is not correct because she tried to buy the books. Choice (B) is not mentioned and may not be concluded from information in the conversation.

Audio

7. Man: I don't have to be there until seven.
   Woman: The traffic is really bad though. You'd better leave a few minutes early.
   Narrator: What does the woman suggest the man do?

Answer

(B) "You'd better leave a few minutes early." Choice (C) refers to the time the man has to be there, not to the time he should leave. Choices (A) and (D) are not mentioned and may not be concluded from information in the conversation.

Audio

8. Man: You don't like the new graduate assistant, do you?
   Woman: No. He makes fun of his students' mistakes.
   Narrator: What does the woman mean?

Answer

(C) To *make fun of* is an idiomatic expression that means to "ridicule." Choices (A), (B), and (D) are not paraphrases of the expression and may not be concluded from information in the conversation.

Audio

9. Woman: Susan told me what you said about my accent.
   Man: I don't know what she told you, but I really didn't mean it as a put-down.
   Narrator: What does the man mean?

Answer

(A) A *put-down* is an idiomatic expression that means an "insult." Choices (B), (C), and (D) are not paraphrases of the expression and may not be concluded from information in the conversation.

Audio

10. Man: I'll be right back. Can you watch my book bag for a minute?

    Woman: Sure. I'll be glad to.

    Narrator: What does the woman agree to do for the man?

Answer

(B) "Can you watch my book bag?" Choice (D) is not correct because the man wants the woman to stay with his book bag. Choices (A) and (C) are not mentioned and may not be concluded from information in the conversation.

Audio

11. Woman: I'm really tired of spending every weekend studying.

    Man: I hear you.

    Narrator: What does the man mean?

Answer

(B) *I hear you* is an idiomatic expression that means the speaker "understands" the other person's point of view. Choices (A), (C), and (D) are not paraphrases of the expression and may not be concluded from information in the conversation.

Audio

12. Man: Is that Mike's car? I thought you said that Mike was spending spring break in Florida.

    Woman: That's Mike's brother. He's using the car while Mike's away.

    Narrator: What does the woman imply?

Answer

(C) Since Mike's brother is using the car while Mike is away, it must be concluded that Mike is in Florida as planned. Choice (A) is not correct because Mike's brother is using his car. Choice (B) refers to Mike, not to his brother. Choice (D) is not correct because Mike's brother is here and Mike is in Florida.

Audio

13. Woman: We turned in our project today.

    Man: You did? We haven't even started.

    Woman: Well, you'd better start working. It's due in a week.

    Man: I will. I'll get it done.

    Narrator: What does the woman advise the man to do?

Answer

(C) "You'd better start working [on that project]." Choice (B) is not correct because the man has not started yet. Choices (A) and (D) are not mentioned and may not be concluded from information in the conversation.

Audio

14. Man: Do you want to go to the International Talent Show?
    Woman: Sure. Why not?
    Narrator: What does the woman mean?

Answer

(D) *Why not?* is an idiomatic expression that means the speaker "agrees" with the other person's plan. Choices (A), (B), and (C) are not paraphrases of the expression and may not be concluded from information in the conversation.

Audio

15. Man: Did you know that Bill and Carol are back from their honeymoon?
    Woman: So they *did* get married after all.
    Narrator: What had the woman assumed about Bill and Carol?

Answer

(A) Since the woman registers surprise, it must be concluded that she thought the couple would not get married. Choices (B) and (C) are not correct because the woman made her comment about the wedding, not the honeymoon. The size of the wedding in Choice (D) is not mentioned and may not be concluded from information in the conversation.

Audio

16. Man: Are you going to the review session for the test?
    Woman: What's the point?
    Narrator: What does the woman mean?

Answer

(C) *What's the point?* is an idiomatic expression that means the speaker "does not believe that the suggestion will be helpful." Choices (A), (B), and (D) are not paraphrases of the expression and may not be concluded from information in the conversation.

Audio

17. Woman: Your check isn't here.
    Man: Oh no. What can I do?
    Woman: I suggest that you call your sponsor.
    Man: Okay. I'll be back.
    Narrator: What will the man probably do?

Answer

(A) Since the woman says, "I suggest that you call your sponsor," the man will probably do it. Choice (B) is not correct because the check isn't here. Choices (C) and (D) are not mentioned and may not be concluded from information in the conversation.

QUESTION DIRECTIONS—Part B

In Part B of the Listening Section, you will hear several longer conversations and talks. Each conversation or talk is followed by several questions. The conversations, talks, and questions will not be repeated.

The conversations and talks are about a variety of topics. You do not need special knowledge of the topics to answer the questions correctly. Rather, you should answer each question on the basis of what is stated or implied by the speakers in the conversations or talks.

For most of the questions, you will need to click on the best of four possible answers. Some questions will have special directions. The special directions will appear in a box on the computer screen.

Audio Conversation

Narrator: Listen to part of a conversation between two students on campus.

Woman: Where have you been? I've missed you in lab.

Man: I've been sick.

Woman: Nothing serious, I hope.

Man: Well, I stayed out of the hospital, but to tell the truth, I was in pretty bad shape. Some kind of flu.

Woman: That's too bad. Are you better now?

Man: Well enough to start thinking about school again. Now I'm worried about getting caught up.

Woman: Let's see, how many labs have you missed?

Man: Margaret, I got sick three weeks ago, so I am really behind.

Woman: Let me look at my notebook. I've got it right here.

Man: Oh, great. I was hoping you'd let me make a copy of your notes.

Woman: Sure. You can do that, Gary. And I have some good news for you. You haven't missed any quizzes. We haven't had any since you've been gone. Listen, after you have a chance to look at my notes, why don't we get together? If there's anything you don't understand, maybe I can explain it to you. It's hard trying to read someone else's notes.

Man: That would be perfect. I hate to bother you though.

Woman: No bother. I'm sure you'd do it for me.

> Now get ready to answer the questions

Audio

18. What is Gary's problem?

Answer

(D) "I've been sick. . . . Now I'm worried about getting caught up." Choice (A) refers to the fact that the man has been sick, but he is not sick now. Choice (B) is not correct because he stayed out of the hospital. Choice (C) is not correct because he has not missed any quizzes.

Audio

19. What does Gary want Margaret to do?

Answer

(B) "I was hoping you'd let me make a copy of your notes." Choice (C) refers to the offer that she makes, not to what Gary asks Margaret to do. Choices (A) and (D) are not mentioned and may not be concluded from information in the conversation.

Audio

20. What does Margaret offer to do?

Answer

(A) ". . . why don't we get together . . . [so that] I can explain it [my notes] to you." Choice (B) is not correct because he hasn't missed any quizzes. Choices (C) and (D) are not mentioned and may not be concluded from information in the conversation.

Audio

21. What is Margaret's attitude in this conversation?

Answer

(A) (D) Since Margaret agrees to let Gary borrow her notes, it must be concluded that she is helpful. Her attitude is positive and friendly. Choices (B) and (C) cannot be concluded from information in the conversation.

Audio Lecture

Narrator: Listen to part of a lecture in an American literature class. The professor is talking about American novelists in the twentieth century. He is focusing on F. Scott Fitzgerald.

There have been a number of important American novelists in this century, but I have chosen F. Scott Fitzgerald for our class because he is one of the more interesting ones. Born in 1896 and educated at Princeton, he wrote novels that describe the post-war American society, very much caught up in the rhythms of jazz.

In 1920, the same year that he published his first book, *This Side of Paradise*, he married Zelda Sayre, also a writer. His most famous book, *The Great Gatsby*, appeared in 1925.

Fitzgerald had a great natural talent, but unfortunately he became a compulsive drinker. A brilliant success in his youth, he never made the adjustments necessary to a maturing writer in a changing world. His later novels, *All the Sad Young Men, Tender Is the Night,* and *The Last Tycoon,* were less successful, so that when he died in 1940 his books were out of print and he had been almost forgotten. His reputation now is far greater than it was in his lifetime, especially since the film version of his novel *The Great Gatsby* was released.

Now, with that introduction, I am going to run the video version of *The Great Gatsby*, and then we'll divide up into groups to talk about it.

> Now get ready to answer the questions

Audio
22. What is the main topic of this lecture?

Answer
(B) The main topic of this talk is F. Scott Fitzgerald's work. The other topics are secondary themes used to develop the main topic.

Audio
23. Why wasn't Fitzgerald more successful in his later life?

Answer
(B) (D) "Fitzgerald had a great natural talent, but unfortunately he became a compulsive drinker. . . . He never made the adjustments necessary to a maturing writer in a changing world." Choice (A) is not correct because Fitzgerald had a great natural talent. Choice (C) is not correct because his reputation is greater since the film version of his novel *The Great Gatsby* was released.

Audio
24. According to the lecturer, what do we know about the novels written by F. Scott Fitzgerald?

Answer
(A) "He wrote novels that describe the post-war American society . . . caught up in the rhythms of jazz." Choice (C) is not correct because his novels describe post-war society, not war experiences. Choices (B) and (D) are not mentioned and may not be concluded from information in the talk.

Audio
25. What does the professor want the class to do after the lecture?

Answer
(C) ". . . I am going to run the video version of *The Great Gatsby*, and then we'll divide up into groups to talk about it." Choices (A), (B), and (D) are not mentioned and may not be concluded from information in the talk.

Audio Talk
Narrator: The university quartet has been invited to play for a music appreciation class. Listen to a talk by the director of the quartet.

Before the concert begins, let me tell you a little bit about chamber music. From medieval times through the eighteenth century, musicians in Europe had two options for employment—the church or the nobility. So when they were not performing at religious functions, they were playing in the chambers of stately homes. And they came to be known as chamber players.

Chamber music is written to be performed by a small group, more than one, but fewer than a dozen musicians. Pieces for more than eight players are unusual though, and it is rare to see a conductor. It may surprise you to know that any combination of instruments can be used for chamber music. The most popular are the piano, strings, and woodwinds, but chamber music has been written for other instruments as well.

Early chamber music, let's say the sixteenth and seventeenth centuries, was often written for the recorder, harpsichord, and viola. During the Elizabethan Period, there were many talented composers of chamber music, including William Byrd and Orlando Gibbons. And at that time, vocal chamber music, called madrigal singing, was very popular. Later, both Johann Sebastian

Bach and George Frederick Handel wrote trio sonatas for chamber groups. This evening the University Quartet will perform two of the later pieces by Bach.

Ladies and gentlemen, the University Quartet.

> Now get ready to answer the questions

Audio
26. What is the main purpose of the talk?

Answer
(A) ". . . let me tell you a little bit about chamber music." Choice (B) is a detail used to develop the main purpose of the talk. Choices (C) and (D) are not mentioned and may not be concluded from information in the talk.

Audio
27. What is the origin of the term *chamber music?*

Answer
(C) "So when they were not performing at religious functions, they were playing in the chambers of stately homes. And they came to be known as chamber players." The musical instrument in Choice (A) might be a recorder, harpsichord, or viola, not chamber music. The musicians in Choice (D) refer to Handel and Bach. Choice (B) is not mentioned and may not be concluded from information in the lecture.

Audio
28. According to the speaker, which instruments are the most popular for chamber music?

Answer
(A) (C) ". . . any combination of instruments can be used for chamber music. The most popular are the piano, strings, and woodwinds. . . . " Choices (B) and (D) are not mentioned and may not be concluded from information in the talk.

Audio
29. Why does the speaker mention Johann Sebastian Bach?

Answer
(B) "This evening the University Quartet will perform two of the later pieces by Bach." Choices (A) and (D) are true, but they are not the reason that the speaker mentions Bach. Choice (C) is not correct because Bach wrote music after vocal chamber music was popular.

Audio
30. What will the listeners hear next?

Answer
(B) "Ladies and Gentlemen, the University Quartet." Choices (A), (C), and (D) are mentioned earlier in the talk.

Audio Conversation

Narrator: Listen to part of a conversation between a student and a secretary in the chemical engineering department.

Woman: May I help you?

Man: Yes. My name is Bob Stephens and I have an appointment with Dr. Benjamin at three o'clock on Wednesday.

Woman: Three o'clock on Wednesday? Yes. I see it here on his calendar.

Man: Well, I was wondering whether he has an earlier appointment available on the same day.

Woman: I'm sorry, Mr. Stephens, but Dr. Benjamin is tied up in a meeting until noon, and he has two appointments scheduled before yours when he gets back from lunch.

Man: Oh.

Woman: There is a later appointment time open though, at four-thirty, if that would help you. Or you could see him Thursday morning at ten.

Man: Hmmm. No thank you. I think I'll just rearrange my own schedule so I can keep my regular appointment.

| Now get ready to answer the questions |

Audio

31. Why did the man go to the Chemical Engineering Department?

Answer

(C) ". . . I was wondering whether he has an earlier appointment available on the same day [as my regular appointment]." Choice (A) is not correct because he has an appointment at three o'clock on Wednesday. Choice (B) is not correct because he asked for an early appointment. Choice (D) refers to what the man ultimately decided to do, not to the purpose of his call.

Audio

32. What does the woman say about Dr. Benjamin?

Answer

(A) ". . . Dr. Benjamin is tied up in a meeting until noon, and he has two appointments scheduled before yours. . . . " Choices (B), (C), and (D) are not correct because Dr. Benjamin has a meeting and appointments on Wednesday.

Audio

33. What did the secretary offer to do?

Answer

(B) "There is a later appointment time open . . . at four-thirty . . . or . . . Thursday morning at ten." Choice (A) refers to the man's regular appointment time, not to the new appointment that the secretary offered to make. Choice (D) refers to what the man wanted to do, not to what the secretary offered to do. Choice (C) is not mentioned and may not be concluded from information in the conversation.

Audio

34. What did the man decide to do?

Answer

(C) "I think I'll just rearrange my own schedule so I can keep my regular appointment." Choices (A), (B), and (D) are not mentioned and may not be concluded from information in the conversation.

Audio Lecture

Narrator: Listen to part of a lecture in a health class. The professor will be talking about nutrition. She will focus on health food.

Health food is a general term applied to all kinds of foods that are considered more healthful than the types of foods widely sold in supermarkets. For example, whole grains, dried beans, and corn oil are health foods. A narrower classification of health food is natural food. This term is used to distinguish between types of the same food. Fresh fruit is a natural food, but canned fruit, with sugars and other additives, is not. The most precise term of all and the narrowest classification within health foods is organic food, used to describe food that has been grown on a particular kind of farm. Fruits and vegetables that are grown in gardens treated only with organic fertilizers, that are not sprayed with poisonous insecticides, and that are not refined after harvest are organic foods.

In choosing the type of food you eat, then, you have basically two choices: inorganic, processed foods, or organic, unprocessed foods. A wise decision should include investigation of the allegations that processed foods contain chemicals, some of which are proven to be toxic, and that vitamin content is greatly reduced in processed foods. My advice? Eat health foods, preferably the organic variety.

> Now get ready to answer the questions

Audio

35. What is the main topic of this lecture?

Answer

(A) "Health food is a general term applied to all kinds of foods that are considered more healthful than the types of food widely sold in supermarkets." Although Choices (B), (C), and (D) are all mentioned in the talk, they are secondary ideas used to develop the main idea.

Audio

36. Which term is used to identify foods that have not been processed or canned?

Answer

(B) "A narrower classification of health food is natural food. This term [natural food] is used to distinguish between types of the same food. Fresh fruit is a natural food, but canned fruit, with sugars and other additives, is not." Choice (A) refers to foods like refined sugar but is not mentioned as a term to distinguish between types of the same food. Choice (C) refers to food grown on a particular kind of farm. Choice (D) refers to organic foods that are not refined after harvest.

Audio

37. What happens to food when it is processed?

Answer

(A) (D) "…the allegations that processed foods contain chemicals, some of which are . . . toxic, and that vitamin content is greatly reduced in processed foods." Choice (C) is not correct because vitamin content is reduced. Choice (B) is not mentioned and may not be concluded from information in the talk.

Audio

38. Which word best describes the speaker's attitude toward health foods?

Answer

(B) "Eat health foods, preferably the organic variety." Choice (A) is not correct because the speaker has provided detailed information in the talk. Choice (C) is not correct because the speaker recommends eating health foods. Choice (D) may not be concluded from the manner in which the talk was delivered.

Audio Discussion

Narrator:	Listen to part of a class discussion in an anthropology class. The professor is talking about the Stone Age.
Professor:	So, as you will recall, the Stone Age is the time, early in the development of human cultures, before the introduction of metals, when prehistoric people started to make stone tools and weapons. Can anyone remember the exact dates for the Stone Age? Chuck?
Chuck:	Well, you said that the exact dates would vary for different parts of the world.
Professor:	That's exactly right. I did. But in general, the use of flint for tools was widespread about two million years ago. That was the beginning of the Paleolithic Period, which is also referred to as the Old Stone Age. What can you tell me about the humanoid creatures that were alive during this period? Yes, Beverly?
Beverly:	They were Neanderthals, and they were nomads. And they survived by hunting and gathering.
Professor:	Very good. Beverly, can you tell us anything about the tools that they made?
Beverly:	Yes, they were primarily general purpose tools such as axes, knives, and arrowheads that they used for hunting.
Professor:	Correct. But we have also found some interesting tools for specific domestic purposes as well. Bone implements were being introduced in the Old Stone Age, and we have reason to believe that they were actually making sewing needles. Any ideas on why that might be so? Chuck?
Chuck:	The Ice Age. They must have been cold.
Professor:	That's true. The last Ice Age was about 13000 B.C. which is at the end of the Paleolithic Period. Do you remember anything else about that time that is of particular importance? Beverly?
Beverly:	Neanderthal man began to decline, and *Homo sapiens* emerged.
Professor:	Right. This marks the end of the Old Stone Age and the beginning of the Middle Stone Age, or the Mesolithic Period. In fact, "Meso" means "middle." Now let's think about the changing climate and the emergence of *Homo sapiens*. How would this influence the kind of tools that would be produced? Any ideas, Chuck?
Chuck:	Well, with the more moderate climate, *Homo sapiens* didn't have to wander so far to hunt and gather. Wasn't it in the Middle Stone Age that agricultural villages started to develop?

Professor: Actually, it was during the Neolithic Period or the Late Stone Age, about 8000 B.C. But you are on the right track. Some of the tools previously used for hunting were adapted for rudimentary farming even during the Middle Stone Age before farming communities started to develop.

Chuck: So was it farming that marked the end of the Stone Age then?

Professor: It was influential. But the introduction of metals was usually considered the defining event that brought an end to the Stone Age. As metals started to challenge stone as the material of choice for tools, mankind entered a new era.

> Now get ready to answer the questions

Audio
39. How did the professor define the Stone Age?

Answer
(C) ". . . the Stone Age is the time . . . when prehistoric people started to make stone tools and weapons." Choice (A) refers to an event in the Late Stone Age, not to a defining feature of the Stone Age. Choice (D) is not correct because the introduction of metals marked the end of the Stone Age. Choice (B) is not mentioned and may not be concluded from information in the discussion.

Audio
40. According to the lecturer, which two occupations describe the Neanderthals?

Answer
(B) (C) "They were Neanderthals, and they were nomads. And they survived by hunting and gathering." Choice (A) is not correct because farming did not appear until the Middle Stone Age, after the decline of the Neanderthals. Choice (D) is not mentioned and may not be concluded from information in the lecture.

Audio
41. Name the three time periods associated with the Stone Age.

Answer
(C) (A) (B) ". . . the use of flint for tools . . . was the beginning of the Old Stone Age. . . . *Homo Sapiens* emerged . . . [which] marks . . . the beginning of the Middle Stone Age. . . . Actually it was during the . . . Late Stone Age [that agricultural villages started to develop]. . . . "

Audio
42. Why did tools change during the Late Stone Age?

Answer
(C) "Some of the tools previously used for hunting were adapted for rudimentary farming. . . . " Choice (A) is not correct because tools for domestic purposes were being used during the Old Stone Age. Choices (B) and (D) are not mentioned and may not be concluded from information in the discussion.

Audio

43. What marked the end of the Stone Age?

Answer

(B) ". . . the introduction of metals was usually considered the defining event that brought an end to the Stone Age." Choice (A) refers to Chuck's idea, not to the event that marked the end of the Stone Age. Choices (C) and (D) occurred much earlier.

Audio Lecture

Narrator: Listen to part of a lecture in a geology class. The professor is talking about oil deposits.

Most crude oil is found in underground formations called traps. In a trap, the oil collects in porous rocks, along with gas and water. Over time, the oil moves up toward the surface of the earth through cracks and holes in the porous rock until it reaches a nonporous rock deposit that will not allow it to continue moving. The oil becomes trapped under the nonporous rock deposit.

There are several different types of traps, but today we will talk about the three most common ones—the anticline trap, the salt dome trap, and the fault trap.

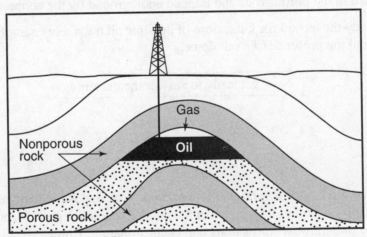

Look at this diagram. Here is an example of an anticline. As you can see, the oil is trapped under a formation of rock that resembles an arch. In this anticline, the petroleum is trapped under a formation of nonporous rock with a gas deposit directly over it. This is fairly typical of an anticline.

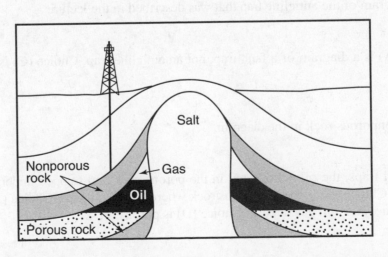

Now, let's look at a diagram of a salt dome. This salt dome shows how a cylinder-shaped salt deposit has pushed up through a layer of sedimentary rocks, causing them to arch and fracture. The oil deposits have collected along the sides of the salt dome.

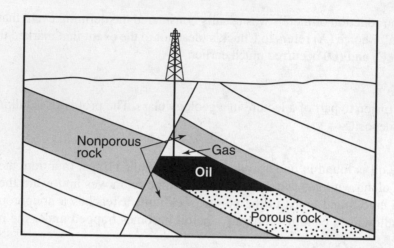

Finally, I want to show you a fault trap. This diagram represents a fracture in the Earth that has shifted a nonporous rock formation on top of a porous formation. Remember, as in all traps, the oil is collected in the porous rock and trapped underground by the nonporous rock.

Geologists study the terrain for indications of possible oil traps. For example, a bulge in a flat surface may signal the presence of a salt dome.

> Now get ready to answer the questions

Audio
44. What is a trap?

Answer
(C) ". . . oil moves up . . . until it reaches a nonporous rock deposit which will not allow it to continue moving. The oil becomes trapped under the nonporous rock deposit." Choice (A) is not correct because traps are underground formations that occur in nature. Choice (B) is true, but it is not the definition of a trap. Choice (D) is not correct because the trap stops the flow of oil through the cracks and holes.

Audio
45. Select the diagram of the anticline trap that was described in the lecture.

Answer
(B) Choice (A) is a diagram of a fault trap, not an anticline trap. Choice (C) is a diagram of a salt dome trap.

Audio
46. Identify the nonporous rock in the diagram.

Answer
(B) ". . . in all traps, the oil is collected in the porous rock and trapped underground by the nonporous rock." Choice (B) is the nonporous rock where the oil collects. Choice (A) is above ground. Choice (C) is a water and gas deposit. Choice (D) is porous rock.

Audio
47. According to the speaker, how can geologists locate salt domes?

Answer

(A) ". . . a bulge in a flat surface may signal the presence of a salt dome." Choice (B) refers to an anticline trap, not a salt dome. Choices (C) and (D) are not mentioned and may not be concluded from information in the lecture.

Audio Conversation

Narrator:	Listen to part of a conversation between two students on campus.
Man:	Who is teaching the class?
Woman:	Actually, I have a choice between Dr. Perkins and Dr. Robinson. Do you know anything about them?
Man:	Sure. I've taken classes with both of them.
Woman:	So what do you think?
Man:	They are both good in their own way. But it depends on how you learn best, because they approach the class from two entirely different points of view.
Woman:	I've heard that Robinson is very strict.
Man:	You could say that. I'd call it traditional. He lectures every day, gives quizzes every week, leading up to a comprehensive final exam, multiple-choice as I recall.
Woman:	How about Perkins?
Man:	More relaxed. Uses group discussion and projects instead of quizzes. And I'm pretty sure his final is short essay.
Woman:	Which one would you advise me to take?
Man:	I really can't say. If you like to listen to lectures and take notes, and if you do well on objective tests, I'd say Robinson. But if you enjoy working in groups, and you do better on essay exams, then I'd recommend Perkins.
Woman:	Thanks. That was helpful. I think I'll sign up for Robinson's class.

Now get ready to answer the questions

Audio
48. What is the woman's problem?

Answer

(B) ". . . I have a choice between Dr. Perkins and Dr. Robinson." Choice (D) is not correct because she asks for the man's advice and tells him that it was helpful. Choices (A) and (C) are not mentioned and may not be concluded from information in the conversation.

Audio
49. What do Dr. Perkins and Dr. Robinson have in common?

Answer

(A) Since the woman can choose between Dr. Perkins and Dr. Robinson, it must be concluded that they teach two different sections of the same class. Choice (B) refers to Dr. Robinson, not to Dr. Perkins. Choice (D) is not correct because the man says they are both good in their own way. Choice (C) is not mentioned and may not be concluded from information in the conversation.

Audio

50. Why did the woman decide to take the class with Dr. Robinson?

Answer

(B) (D) "I'd call [Robinson] traditional. . . . If you like to listen to lectures and take notes. . . . I'd say Robinson." Since the woman decides to take the class with Dr. Robinson, it must be concluded that she prefers lectures and a more traditional approach to teaching. Choice (A) is not correct because she does not know about either of the professors. Choice (C) is not correct because the man is re-calling information about the professor, which implies that he has already taken the class that the woman is going to take.

Section 2: Structure

1. **(B)** The verb phrase *to insist on* requires an *-ing* form in the complement. *-Ing* forms are modified by possessive pronouns. Choice (A) is an infinitive modified by an object pronoun. Choice (C) is an *-ing* form, but it is modified by a subject, not a possessive pronoun. Choice (D) is a verb word.

2. **(D)** *The* must be used with a superlative. Choices (A), (B), and (C) are wordy and ungrammatical.

3. **(B)** A form of BE is used with the participle in passive sentences. *Cannot proved* should be *cannot be proved*.

4. **(D)** *The same* is used with a quality noun such as *age*, and *as* in comparisons. *As* is used with a quality adjective such as *old*, and *as*. Choice (A) is a quality adjective, not a noun, with *to*. In Choice (B), *the same* is used with *than*, not *as*. "As old as" would also be correct.

5. **(D)** *Such* is used with a noun phrase to express cause before *that* and a subject and verb that expresses result. Choice (A) does not have a subject. Choice (B) does not have a subject or verb. Choice (C) is not a *that* clause.

6. **(C)** *Began* should be *begun* because the auxiliary *had* requires a participle. *Began* is a past form. *Begun* is a participle.

7. **(A)** Using words with the same meaning consecutively is repetitive. *First* should be deleted because *original* means *first*.

8. **(C)** Singular and plural expressions of non-count nouns such as *equipment* occur in idiomatic phrases, often *piece* or *pieces of*. Choices (A), (B), and (D) are not idiomatic.

9. **(D)** The anticipatory clause *it was in 1607 that* introduces a subject and verb, *the English settled*. Choice (A) is wordy and indirect. Choice (B) may be used as part of a subject clause preceding a main verb. Choice (C) may be used without *that* preceding a subject and verb. "That in 1607 the English settled in Jamestown *has changed* the history of the Americas," and "Because in 1607 the English settled in Jamestown, *the history* of the Americas *has changed*" would also be correct.

10. **(C)** Repetition of the subject by a subject pronoun is redundant. *It* should be deleted.

11. **(C)** There must be agreement between subject and verb. *Have* should be *has* to agree with the singular subject *triangle*.

12. **(C)** A sentence has a subject and a verb. Choice (A) is the subject, but there is no main clause verb. Choices (B) and (D) introduce a main clause subject and verb.

13. **(C)** *Impossibility* should be *impossible*. *Impossibility* is a noun. *Impossible* is an adjective.

14. **(D)** For scientific results, a present form in the condition requires a present or future form in the result. Only Choice (D) introduces a conditional.

15. **(C)** There must be agreement between pronoun and antecedent. *Their* should be *its* to refer to the singular antecedent *Pickerel Frog*.

16. **(B)** Multiple comparatives like *twice* are expressed by the multiple followed by the phrase *as much as*. Choice (A) is a multiple number followed by the phrase *more than*. Choices (C) and (D) reverse the order of the multiple number and the phrase.

17. **(C)** *Used to* requires a verb word. When preceded by a form of BE, *used to* requires an *-ing* form. In Choice (A), *used to* requires a verb word, not an *-ing* form. In Choice (B), *used to* preceded by a form of BE may be used with an *-ing* form, not an infinitive. Choice (D) uses the incorrect form, *use to*.

18. **(B)** The adverb *previously* establishes a point of view in the past. *Is* should be *was* in order to maintain the point of view.

19. **(C)** Redundant, indirect phrases should be avoided. *In a correct manner* is a redundant pattern. The adverb *correctly* is simple and more direct.

20. **(C)** The noun in the appositive must agree with the antecedent. *Tree* should be *trees* to agree with the antecedent *conifers*.

21. **(A)** The verb *to want* requires an infinitive complement. Choice (B) is an *-ing* form, not an infinitive. Choice (C) is a verb word. Choice (D) is ungrammatical.

22. **(B)** *Near* does not require a preposition. *Near to* should be *near*. *Nearby* would also be correct.

23. **(B)** Ideas in a series should be expressed by parallel structures. Only *to finish* in Choice (B) provides for parallelism with the infinitive *to answer*. Choices (A), (C), and (D) are not parallel.

24. **(B)** A verb word must be used in a clause after an impersonal expression. *Maintains* should be *maintain* after the impersonal expression *it is imperative*.

25. **(C)** *But* should be *but also*, which is used in correlation with the inclusive *not only*.

Section 3: Reading

1. **(B)** The other choices are secondary ideas used to develop the main idea, "the nature of geysers." Choices (A), (C), and (D) are subtopics that provide details and examples.

2. **(B)** "A geyser is the result of underground water under the combined conditions of high temperatures and increased pressure beneath the surface of the Earth." Choice (A) is not correct because water, not hot rocks, rises to the surface. Choice (C) is not correct because the hot rocks are in the Earth's interior, not on the surface. Choice (D) is not correct because the water seeps down in cracks and fissures in the Earth.

3. In the context of this passage, approximately could best be replaced by about. No other words or phrases in the **bold** text are close to the meaning of the word approximately.

4. **(A)** "Since temperature rises about 1° F for every sixty feet under the Earth's surface, and pressure increases with depth, water that seeps down in cracks and fissures until it [water] reaches very hot rocks in the Earth's interior becomes heated to a temperature of approximately 290° F." Choices (B), (C), and (D) would change the meaning of the sentence.

5. "Water under pressure ..." Quotation from sentence 1, paragraph 2.

6. **(C)** "Since temperature rises...and pressure increases with depth ..." Choices (A), (B), and (D) are not correct because both temperature and pressure increase with depth.

7. **(C)** "For the most part, geysers are located in three regions of the world: New Zealand, Iceland, and the Yellowstone National Park area of the United States." Choice (A) is not correct because no comparisons are made among the areas. Choice (B) is not correct because Yellowstone National Park is in the United States, not in New Zealand or Iceland. Choice (D) is not correct because geysers are also found in a third region, the Yellowstone National Park area of the United States.

8. **(B)** "Old Faithful erupts almost every hour." The number in Choice (A) refers to the number of thousand gallons of water that is expelled during an eruption, not to the number of minutes between eruptions. The numbers in Choices (C) and (D) refer to the number of feet to which the geyser rises during an eruption.

9. **(B)** In the context of this passage, expelling is closest in meaning to discharging. Choices (A), (C), and (D) are not accepted definitions of the word.

10. **(A)** Choice (A) is a restatement of the sentence referred to in the passage. *Never failed* means always. Choices (B), (C), and (D) would change the meaning of the original sentence.

11. **(A)** "...a geyser must have a source of heat, a reservoir where water can be stored...an

opening through which the hot water and steam can escape, and underground channels…. Favorable conditions for geysers exist in regions of geologically recent volcanic activity…in areas of more than average precipitation." Choice (C) includes some of, but not all, the necessary conditions. Choices (B) and (D) are not correct because the volcanic activity should be recent, but not active.

12. **(A)** Choice (A) is the author's main point because the reasons for success are referred to throughout the passage. Choices (B), (C), and (D) are each specific reasons for success.

13. **(B)** In the context of this passage, cited is closest in meaning to mentioned. Choices (A), (C), and (D) are not accepted definitions of the word.

14. **(C)** Incessantly means constantly. Choices (A), (B), and (D) are not accepted definitions of the word.

15. **(B)** "They were also both glider pilots. Unlike some other engineers who experimented with the theories of flight, [they] experienced the practical side…." Choices (A), (C), and (D) were all true of the Wright brothers, but these experiences were not different from those of their competitors.

16. "They had realized from their experiments that the most serious problems in manned flight would be stabilizing and maneuvering the aircraft once it was airborne." Quotation from sentence 4, paragraph 2.

17. In the context of this passage, the word guiding is closest in meaning to maneuvering. No other words or phrases in the **bold** text are close to the meaning of the word maneuvering.

18. **(C)** "The data from these experiments [using the wind tunnel] allowed the Wright brothers to construct a superior wing for their craft." Choice (A) is not correct because the light internal combustion engine had already been invented by someone else. Choice (B) is not correct because they developed a three-axis control while experimenting with gliders, not with the wind tunnel. Choice (D) is not correct because they used the data to improve the wings, not the engine for their airplane.

19. **(C)** "Attempts to achieve manned flight in the early nineteenth century were doomed

because the steam engines that powered the aircraft were too heavy in proportion to the power that they [the engines] produced." Choices (A), (B), and (D) would change the meaning of the sentence.

20. **(A)** In the context of this passage, doomed is closest in meaning to destined to fail. Choices (B), (C), and (D) are not accepted definitions of the word.

21. **(D)** "…they were able to bring the ratio of weight to power within acceptable limits for flight." From the reference to the ratio of weight to power and *acceptable limits*, it must be concluded that previous engines did not have acceptable limits of weight to power and, thus, did not have enough power to lift their own weight. Choice (B) is not correct because the engines were relatively heavy. Choice (C) is not correct because they were experimenting with internal combustion engines. The size in Choice (A) is not mentioned and may not be concluded from information in the passage.

22. **(D)** Choice (A) refers to the fact that the Wright brothers were "a team." Choice (B) refers to the fact that they were "among the best glider pilots in the world." Choice (C) refers to the "experiments [that] allowed the Wright brothers to construct a superior wing for their craft." Choice (D) is not mentioned and may not be concluded from information in the passage.

23. **(A)** The other choices are secondary ideas used to develop the main idea, "the influenza virus." Choices (B), (C), and (D) are subtopics that provide details and examples.

24. **(D)** "…bacteria can be considered a type of plant…." Choice (A) refers to the secretions of bacteria, not to the bacteria themselves. Although it may be true that bacteria are very small, as in Choice (B), or larger than viruses, as in Choice (C), this information is not mentioned and may not be concluded from reading the passage.

25. "…viruses, like the influenza virus, are living organisms [the viruses] themselves." Other choices would change the meaning of the sentence.

26. **(D)** In the context of this passage, strictly could best be replaced by exactly. Choices (A), (B), and (C) are not accepted definitions of the word.

27. **(B)** "…they [viruses] have strictly defined atomic structure…." Choice (A) is not correct because viruses have a strictly defined atomic structure. Choice (C) is not correct because we may consider them as regular chemical molecules. Although Choice (D) is implied, it may not be concluded from information in the passage.

28. **(C)** "…we must also consider them [viruses] as being alive since they are able to multiply in unlimited quantities." Choice (A) is the reason that we must consider them as regular chemical molecules, not the reason that we must consider them as being alive. Choices (B) and (D) are not mentioned and may not be concluded from information in the passage.

29. **(B)** Unlimited means without limits; very large. Choices (A), (C), and (D) are not accepted definitions of the word.

30. In the context of this passage, the word types is closest in meaning to strains. No other words or phrases in the **bold** text are close to the meaning of the word strains.

31. "Epidemics or regional outbreaks have appeared on the average every two or three years for type-A virus, and every four or five years for type-B virus. Approximately every ten years, worldwide epidemics of influenza called pandemics also occur." The connection between the two sentences is the reference to "epidemics" and the transition word "also." The second sentence with the word "also" must be mentioned after the first sentence.

32. **(B)** "…the protection is against only the type of virus that caused the influenza." Choices (A) and (C) are not correct because the protection is against only the one type of virus. Choice (D) is not mentioned and may not be concluded from information in the passage.

33. **(C)** "…every ten years…pandemics occur. Thought to be caused by new strains of type-A virus, these pandemics spread rapidly." Choices (A), (B), and (D) are all mentioned in the passage. Choice (C) refers to epidemics, not to pandemics.

34. **(B)** The other choices are secondary ideas that are used to develop the main idea, "The Federal Reserve System." Choices (A), (C), and (D) are important to the discussion as they relate to the Federal Reserve System.

35. **(A)** In the context of this passage, oversee is closest in meaning to supervise. Choices

(B), (C), and (D) are not accepted definitions of the word.

36. **(D)** In the context of this passage, confirmed could best be replaced by approved. Choices (A), (B), and (C) are not accepted definitions of the word.

37. **(B)** "The System's primary function is to control monetary policy by influencing the cost and availability of money and credit through the purchase and sale of government securities." Choice (A) refers to the effect of regulation on the public, not to the System's responsibility. Choice (D) is not correct because the Board of Governors is appointed by the President. Choice (C) is not mentioned and may not be concluded from information in the passage.

38. **(B)** Although Choices (A), (C), and (D) are definitions of the word securities, the meaning in the context of the sentence is bonds.

39. **(C)** "If the Federal Reserve provides too little money, interest rates tend to be high, borrowing is expensive, business activity slows down, unemployment goes up…." Choice (A) is not correct because interest rates are high and borrowing is expensive. Choice (B) is not correct because unemployment goes up. Choice (D) is not correct because business activity slows down.

40. **(B)** "If there is too much money, interest rates decline, and borrowing can lead to excess demand, pushing up prices and fueling inflation." Choice (A) is not correct because during times of too little money, unemployment goes up. Choice (C) misinterprets the word *fuel* to mean *oil*. Choice (D) is not mentioned and may not be concluded from information in the passage.

41. "In collaboration with the U.S. Department of the Treasury, the Fed puts new coins and paper currency into circulation by issuing them [coins and paper currency] to banks." Other choices would change the meaning of the sentence.

42. "It [the Fed] also supervises the activities of member banks abroad, and regulates certain aspects of international finance." Quotation from sentence 3, paragraph 3.

43. **(C)** Choice (C) is a restatement of the sentence referred to in the passage. *Not stray* means *follow*. Choices (A), (B), and (D) would change the meaning of the original sentence.

44. **(D)** Choice (A) refers to the fact that the "Federal Reserve System is an independent agency of the United States government that helps oversee the national banking system." Choice (B) refers to the fact that the Federal Reserve's "…primary function is to control monetary policy…through the purchase and sale of government securities." Choice (C) refers to the fact that "the Fed puts new coins and paper currency into circulation by issuing them to banks." Choice (D) is not correct because "the Fed does not depend on Congress for budget allocations" although it does send "frequent reports to the Congress."

45. "It has been said that the Federal Reserve is actually an informal branch of the United States government because it is composed of national policy makers. In fact, the Fed is not confined by the usual checks and balances that apply to the three official branches of government—the executive, the legislative, and the judicial." The connection between the two sentences is the reference to an "informal branch" in the first sentence and a reference to "the three official branches of government" in the second sentence.

Writing Section

Question:
Advances in transportation and communication like the airplane and the telephone have changed the way that nations interact with each other in a global society. Choose another technological innovation that you think is important. Give specific reasons for your choice.

Outline
Computer
- Mail
- Meetings + conferences
- Language
Cheaper, easier to exchange information

Map

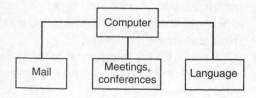

Cheaper, easier to exchange information

Example Essay
Without doubt, computers have changed the way that nations interact with each other in a global society. One type of communication that has been greatly affected by the computer is international mail. For example, prior to the widespread use of computers, a letter from the United States to my country would take weeks for delivery. I recall that the cost was almost $10 U.S. at a time when the same amount of money would buy groceries for a family for one week. Now mail can be delivered instantly at virtually no cost by electronic mail.

Another way that computers have affected international communication is in the way that people assemble in meetings and conferences. Before the introduction of computer technology, it was necessary to fly into a central location to conduct business or training. The time involved in travel was often ten times that of the actual meeting time. Now, through the miracle of teleconferencing, participants from many nations can meet in local sites and connect by means of satellite to a central conference facility. They can see each other on large screens and interact with each other from multiple sites around the world. After the initial investment in the equipment, a company can expect to save money because the travel budget can be adjusted down.

Finally, computers have influenced the language of communication around the world. Although English was a popular foreign language prior to the advent of the Internet, it is even more useful now. The computer keyboards in Roman letters are more efficient and, at least initially, the flood of information onto the "information highway" was often in the English language. To be connected in a global society increasingly means knowing English as a second language.

Computers have changed the way that nations interact with each other to send international mail, to attend world meetings and conferences, and to connect to the Internet. They have made it cheaper and easier to exchange information.

Model Test 7—Computer-Assisted TOEFL

Section 1: Listening

The Listening Section of the test measures the ability to understand conversations and talks in English. On the actual TOEFL exam, you will use headphones to listen to the conversations and talks. While you are listening, pictures of the speakers or other information will be presented on your computer screen. There are two parts to the Listening Section, with special directions for each part.

On the day of the test, the amount of time you will have to answer all of the questions will appear on the computer screen. The time you spend listening to the test material will not be counted. The listening material and questions about it will be presented only one time. You will not be allowed to take notes or have any paper at your computer. You will both see and hear the questions before the answer choices appear. You can take as much time as you need to select an answer; however, it will be to your advantage to answer the questions as quickly as possible. You may change your answer as many times as you want before you confirm it. After you have confirmed an answer, you will not be able to return to the question.

Before you begin working on the Listening Section, you will have an opportunity to adjust the volume of the sound. You may not be able to change the volume after you have started the test.

QUESTION DIRECTIONS—Part A

In Part A of the Listening Section, you will hear short conversations between two people. In some of the conversations, each person speaks only once. In other conversations, one or both of the people speak more than once. Each conversation is followed by one question about it.

Each question in this part has four answer choices. You should click on the best answer to each question. Answer the questions on the basis of what is stated or implied by the speakers.

Audio

1. Man: It's so noisy in the dorm I can't get anything done.
   Woman: I know. I used to live in a dorm myself.
   Man: I'll have to do something different next semester.
   Woman: Why not move into an apartment?
   Narrator: What does the woman mean?

Answer

(A) *Why not* means "you should." Choice (C) is not correct because the woman says to move into an apartment. Choices (B) and (D) are not mentioned and may not be concluded from information in the conversation.

Audio

2. Man: Hi Jan.
   Woman: Hi. Are you going to school here now?
   Man: Yes, I transferred from community college last term. Let's have lunch sometime.
   Woman: Sounds good. Give me a call.
   Narrator: What can we assume from this conversation?

Answer

(B) Because the man suggests that they have lunch and the woman responds that the idea sounds good, inviting him to call her, it must be concluded that the man will call the woman to arrange for lunch. Choice (A) is not correct because the invitation is for the future. Choice (D) is not correct because the woman invites that man to give her a call. Choice (C) is not mentioned and may not be concluded from information in the conversation.

Audio

3. Woman: How many transcripts do you want me to send to San Diego State?
   Man: Just one, but I want two for myself.
   Narrator: What will the woman probably do?

Answer

(C) Since the man needs one transcript for San Diego State and two for himself, the woman will probably send one to San Diego State and give two to him. Choice (A) is not correct because he only needs one for San Diego State. Choice (B) is not correct because he needs a total of three transcripts. Choice (D) refers to the total number of transcripts that the man requested, not to how many he wants to take himself.

Audio

4. Man: I ought to wait until Professor Bloom gets back from class.
   Woman: Not really. You can just leave a note. I'll give it to her.
   Narrator: What does the woman suggest the man do?

Answer

(A) "You can just leave a note." Choice (C) refers to the man's plan, not to the woman's suggestion. Choices (B) and (D) are not mentioned and may not be concluded from information in the conversation.

Audio

5. Woman: Susan told me she was really interested in social work.
   Man: Yes, but when she declared her major she chose education.
   Narrator: What can be inferred about Susan?

Answer

(B) Since Susan chose education for her major, it must be concluded that she prefers teaching. Choice (D) is not correct because she declared her major. Choices (A) and (C) are not mentioned and may not be concluded from information in the conversation.

Audio

6. Woman: I wonder whether the grades are posted yet?

   Man: I don't think so. It usually takes about three days, and we just turned in our papers yesterday.

   Narrator: What are the speakers talking about?

Answer

(B) From the reference to the *grades being posted*, it must be concluded that they are talking about grades. The verb *posted* does not refer to mail as in Choice (A), and the *papers* are assignments, not newspapers as in Choice (C). Choice (D) is not mentioned and may not be concluded from information in the conversation.

Audio

7. Woman: Congratulations! I saw your name on the graduation list.

   Man: Someone else must have the same name then. I'm not graduating until next spring.

   Narrator: What had the woman assumed?

Answer

(B) Since the woman saw the man's name on the graduation list, she had assumed that he had already graduated. Choice (C) refers to the man's explanation, not to the woman's assumption. Choice (D) refers to the man's plan for graduation. Choice (A) is not mentioned and may not be concluded from information in the conversation.

Audio

8. Man: Did you ever apply for that scholarship? You weren't sure whether you wanted to compete with all those applicants.

   Woman: I decided to go for it!

   Narrator: What does the woman mean?

Answer

(C) To *go for it* is an idiomatic expression that means to "compete." Choices (A) and (D) are not correct because she is competing now. Choice (B) is not correct because she has decided.

Audio

9. Woman: We're going to the library. Want to come along?

   Man: I'm waiting for the mail to come.

   Narrator: What does the man imply?

Answer

(D) Since the man says he is waiting for the mail to come, he implies that he will not go to the library with the woman. Choice (C) is not correct because he is waiting for the mail, which has not yet arrived. Choices (A) and (B) are not mentioned and may not be concluded from information in the conversation.

Audio

10. Man: How was your break? You went to Toronto, didn't you?
    Woman: I was going there, but I got a really great fare to Montreal, then I drove to Quebec and some of the little towns in the province.
    Narrator: What are the speakers talking about?

Answer

(D) "How was your break?" Choices (A), (B), and (C) are all mentioned as they relate to the main topic of the conversation, the woman's vacation.

Audio

11. Man: Do you want me to get anything else for our presentation while I'm at the bookstore?
    Woman: I couldn't care less.
    Narrator: How does the woman feel about the presentation?

Answer

(D) *I couldn't care less* is an idiomatic expression that means the speaker is "not interested." Choices (A), (B), and (C) are not paraphrases of the expression and may not be concluded from information in the conversation.

Audio

12. Man: Weren't you in class Friday either?
    Woman: No. I had to take my mother to the airport. She went back to New York.
    Narrator: What do we learn about the two students in this conversation?

Answer

(A) Since the man asks whether or not the woman was in class on Friday and uses the word *either*, it must be concluded that he was not in class on that day. Choice (B) is not correct because the man was not in class. Choice (C) is not correct because the woman was not in class. Choice (D) is not correct because the woman's mother, not the man and the woman, was in New York.

Audio

13. Woman: You must be so excited about going home after four years.
    Man: Not as much as I thought I would be.
    Narrator: What does the man mean?

Answer

(D) Since the man says that he is not as excited as he thought he would be, it must be concluded that he expected to be more enthusiastic. Choices (A), (B), and (C) are not mentioned and may not be concluded from information in the conversation.

Audio

14. Man: Do you usually bring your lunch?
    Woman: I eat in the snack bar now and then.
    Narrator: What does the woman mean?

Answer

(C) *Now and then* is an idiomatic expression that means "occasionally." Choices (A), (B), and (D) are not correct because the woman eats in the snack bar occasionally.

Audio

15. Woman: We were just talking about you.
    Man: Really? Why?
    Woman: I heard you were in the hospital.
    Man: I'm much better now. No need to worry.
    Woman: You'd better take it easy though, or you'll get sick again.
    Narrator: What does the woman mean?

Answer

(A) To *take it easy* is an idiomatic expression that means to "rest." Choice (B) refers to the man's comment, not to the woman's observation. Choice (C) is not correct because the man warns the woman not to worry. Choice (D) refers to the fact that the man was sick in the past, not that he is sick now.

Audio

16. Woman: I don't like our economics class.
    Man: Neither do I.
    Narrator: What does the man mean?

Answer

(D) Since the man says "neither do I" when the woman comments about not liking the class, it must be concluded that he does not enjoy the economics class either. Choice (A) is not correct because neither the man nor the woman enjoys the class. Choices (B) and (C) are not mentioned and may not be concluded from information in the conversation.

Audio

17. Woman: Did you find enough subjects for your research project?
    Man: Not yet. I have thirty-five though, so that's a good start.
    Narrator: What does the man imply?

Answer

(B) Since the man has thirty-five subjects and that is not enough, it must be concluded that he needs more than thirty-five participants. Choice (A) is not correct because he has started working on the project. Choice (C) is not correct because he feels he has a good start. Choice (D) is not mentioned and may not be concluded from information in the conversation.

QUESTION DIRECTIONS—Part B

In Part B of the Listening Section, you will hear several longer conversations and talks. Each conversation or talk is followed by several questions. The conversations, talks, and questions will not be repeated.

The conversations and talks are about a variety of topics. You do not need special knowledge of the topics to answer the questions correctly. Rather, you should answer each question on the basis of what is stated or implied by the speakers in the conversations or talks.

For most of the questions, you will need to click on the best of four possible answers. Some questions will have special directions. The special directions will appear in a box on the computer screen.

Audio Conversation

Narrator: Listen to part of a conversation between a student and his professor.

Rick: Thank you for seeing me today, Dr. Wilson. I want to talk with you about my final grade.

Dr. Wilson: Yes?

Rick: Well, I was surprised to get a D after doing so well on the midterm.

Dr. Wilson: Let's see. I'll just check my grade book here.

Rick: I got a B, Dr. Wilson. I brought my test with me.

Dr. Wilson: Yes, you did. I have it recorded here. And you passed the final with a C.

Rick: Then I should have gotten a C+ or a B–.

Dr. Wilson: Yes, you should have, but the problem was your attendance. Twenty-five percent of your grade was calculated on the basis of class participation, and Rick, you just didn't participate.

Rick: But I passed the exams.

Dr. Wilson: Yes, I know you did. And you passed the course. D is a passing grade.

Rick: But . . .

Dr. Wilson: I'm sorry, Rick. I gave you a syllabus on the first day of class and the grading system was outlined in it. You received an F in class participation because you missed too many days, and that brought your grade down.

| Now get ready to answer the questions |

Audio

18. What prompted this conversation?

Answer

(A) "I want to talk to you about my final grade." Choice (C) is mentioned as an argument for changing the grade. Choice (D) refers to the professor's grade book, not to what prompted the conversation. Choice (B) is not mentioned and may not be concluded from information in the conversation.

Audio

19. Where is this conversation taking place?

Answer

(B) From the reference to a *grade*, a *grade book*, a *test*, *exams*, a *course*, and *class*, it must be concluded that the conversation is taking place in a college professor's office. Choice (C) is not correct because Rick brought his test with him to the meeting. Choices (A) and (D) are not mentioned and may not be concluded from information in the conversation.

Audio

20. What is the grade that Rick received for the course?

Answer

(C) "Well, I was surprised to get a D. . . ." Choices (A) and (B) refer to the grades that Rick claims he should have gotten, not to the grade that he received. Choice (D) refers to the grade that Rick received in class participation, not to the grade that he received for the course.

Audio
21. Why did Rick receive a lower grade?

Answer

(C) "You received an F in class participation because you missed too many days, and that brought your grade down." Choice (A) is not correct because Rick got a B on the midterm exam. Choice (B) is not correct because Rick passed the final with a C. Choice (D) is not correct because Dr. Wilson gave Rick a syllabus on the first day of class and the grading system was outlined in it.

Audio Discussion

Narrator: Listen to a discussion in a linguistics class. The class has been discussing first language development in children.

Richards: Today we'll be talking about grammatical development in children. Does anyone here have any small children at home? Diane, you have young children at home, so you will be able to help us with a lot of examples. Let's start with the kind of language that we hear from twelve- to eighteen-month-old children who are just starting to use one-word sentences. What kind of words do we hear in those sentences?

Diane: "Water," "Mama," "book."

Richards: Those are very typical of one-word sentences, Diane. Your examples are all nouns. At this early stage, children are naming their world, and they need nouns to do that. But soon, by about eighteen months to two years of age, they are putting two-, three-, even four-word sentences together, and combining them in complex ways to produce a wide variety of structures. Can anyone think of any examples for this stage? Yes, Jerry.

Jerry: My son is two, and his favorite sentence right now is "Daddy up" when he wants me to carry him.

Richards: Good example. In addition to the statements that younger children use, toddlers are beginning to use commands appropriately. They also start using questions. I think one of the most interesting features of this stage is the omission of small words such as "is" and "the" as well as word endings like "I-N-G" on verbs.

Diane: Yes, I notice that my three-year-old is starting to put those endings on the verbs now, but sometimes they aren't perfect. He says things like "We runned fast" instead of "ran." All my children did that.

Richards: Good observation. What is actually happening there is that he is learning the regular verb endings and extending their use to irregular verbs. That is another very common characteristic of language acquisition in children. Perhaps the most important aspect of child grammar at age four is the active correction of previous errors. By age five, the grammar is not error-free, but there is evidence that children have learned the basic structures of their language, but, of course, recent research indicates that several grammatical constructions are still being acquired by children as old as ten or eleven. Did you have a question, Jerry?

Jerry: Yes. I was wondering if these stages are the same for children learning all languages or just English.

Richards: Excellent question, Jerry. There is evidence that the basic stages are the same for all languages.

Now get ready to answer the questions

Audio

22. Why does the professor call on Diane?

Answer

(C) "Diane, you have young children at home, so you will be able to help us with a lot of examples." Choice (B) is not correct because Diane does not ask any questions during the discussion. Choices (A) and (D) are not mentioned and may not be concluded from information in the discussion.

Audio

23. What are two charcteristics of the language of toddlers?

Answer

(A) (C) ". . . toddlers are beginning to use commands. . . . One of the most interesting features of this [toddler] stage is the omission of small words such as 'is' and 'the' as well as word endings like 'I-N-G' on verbs." Choices (B) and (D) refer to the pretoddler stage, not to the toddler stage.

Audio

24. What can be concluded about the phrase "We runned"?

Answer

(B) "What is actually happening there [when Diane's child is saying 'runned'] is that he is learning the regular verb endings. . . . " Choice (A) is not correct because the child is three, not two, years old. Choice (C) refers to language acquisition by a child four years old, not to the phrase "We runned." Choice (D) is not mentioned and may not be concluded from information in the discussion.

Audio

25. By which age have most children learned the basic structures of language?

Answer

(C) "By age five . . .there is evidence that children have learned the basic structures of their language. . . ." Choice (A) refers to the age when children are learning verb endings, not to the age when they have learned the basic structures of their language. Choice (B) refers to the age when children are correcting previous errors. Choice (D) refers to the age when children are still acquiring several grammatical structures.

Audio

26. What does the professor say about languages other than English?

Answer

(A) "There is evidence that the basic stages [of language acquisition] are the same for all languages." Choices (B), (C), and (D) contradict the professor's statement.

Audio Talk

Narrator: Listen to a professor talking with her class on the first day of the course. She will be clarifying the course syllabus.

Before we begin our discussion of today's topic, I'd like to point out a few important features on the syllabus. First, please look at the calendar. As you see, we will be meeting for fifteen weeks. The last week of November we will not meet because of the Thanksgiving holiday. But, all of the other dates are listed, along with the reading assignments in your textbook. In general, it is better to read the assigned pages before you come to class so that you will be prepared to participate in the discussion that follows the lecture.

Now, let's look at the course requirements. As you see, you have a midterm examination the last week of October, and a final examination the second week of December. The midterm is worth thirty points and the final is worth fifty points. That leaves twenty points for the project that you will be working on, and you have several choices to fulfill that requirement. You can either write a paper or make a half-hour presentation on a topic of your choice. We'll be talking a bit more about the projects in the next several weeks. Oh, yes, you will notice that I don't factor attendance into the grade, but I do expect you to be here. If you must miss class for whatever reason, please get in touch with me. My office hours are listed on the syllabus, along with my voice mail number and my e-mail address.

$$\boxed{\text{Now get ready to answer the questions}}$$

Audio

27. What suggestion does the professor make about the reading assignments?

Answer

(A) ". . . it is better to read the assigned pages before you come to class so that you will be prepared to participate in the discussion that follows the lecture." Choices (B) and (C) are not correct because the reading should be done before the lecture and discussion. Choice (D) is not mentioned and may not be concluded from information in the talk.

Audio

28. How are the points distributed for the course requirements?

Answer

(C) (B) (A) "The midterm is worth thirty points and the final is worth fifty points. That leaves twenty points for the project. . . ."

Audio

29. What are the choices for a project?

Answer

(B) (D) "You can either write a paper or make a half-hour presentation on a topic of your choice." Choices (A) and (C) are not mentioned and may not be concluded from information in the talk.

Audio

30. According to the professor, what should students do if they must be absent?

Answer

(A) "If you must miss class for whatever reason, please get in touch with me." Choices (B), (C), and (D) are not mentioned and may not be concluded from information in the talk.

Audio Lecture

Narrator: Listen to part of a lecture in an astronomy course. Today the professor will talk about distant planets. He will focus on Neptune and Uranus.

Today I'm going to share a rather interesting theory with you. As you already know from your reading material, many scientists believe that the atmosphere of the seventh and eighth planets from our sun, Uranus and Neptune, have an outer film of hydrogen and helium. The atmosphere of Neptune above its methane ice clouds is about 85 percent hydrogen and 15 percent helium, and beneath the clouds, methane concentrations increase to more than 1 percent. The atmosphere of Uranus consists mostly of hydrogen with 2 percent methane and 10 to 20 percent helium, with lesser amounts of ammonia. Because of this, the surfaces of these planets are probably covered with frozen ammonia and methane.

Now Marvin Ross of the Lawrence Livermore National Laboratory in California has postulated that the methane could have separated into the carbon and hydrogen atoms that form it, and furthermore, that at the high pressure common to those planets, the carbon atoms could have been squeezed into a layer of diamonds.

Astronomers at the University of Arizona in Tucson agree that the pressures on these planets, some 200,000 to 6 million times that of Earth's atmosphere, could set up conditions whereby diamonds might form. Moreover, since the two giant planets are each nearly four times the size of the Earth, and each is nearly one-fifth carbon, the quantities of diamonds could be huge.

Now get ready to answer the questions

Audio

31. What is the main purpose of this lecture?

Answer

(B) The main purpose of this lecture is to explain a theory of the formation of diamonds on Neptune and Uranus. Choices (A), (C), and (D) are mentioned during the explanation but are not central to the theory.

Audio

32. Which planets are being discussed?

Answer

(B) (C) ". . . the seventh and eighth planets from our sun, Uranus and Neptune. . . ." Choice (A) refers to the planet that is compared with Uranus and Neptune, not to one of the planets discussed in the lecture. Choice (D) is not mentioned and may not be concluded from information in the lecture.

Audio

33. The professor briefly explains a process. Summarize the process by putting the events in order.

Answer

(D) (A) (C) (B) ". . . Neptune [has] . . . methane ice clouds . . . [and] Uranus [has] . . . 2 percent methane. . . . [The] methane could have separated into the carbon and hydrogen atoms . . . [which at] high pressure . . . squeezed into a layer of diamonds. . . ."

Audio

34. How does the speaker feel about the theory?

Answer

(C) "Today I'm going to share a rather interesting theory with you." Choice (D) is not correct because he believes that the theory is interesting. Choices (A) and (B) are not mentioned and may not be concluded from information in the talk.

Audio Lecture

Narrator: Listen to part of a lecture in a political science class. The professor will talk about the electoral process.

In the United States, the people do not elect the president by direct vote. This is so because the men who wrote the Constitution in 1787 believed that ordinary citizens would not be informed enough to make such an important decision, and they created a system whereby a representative group of citizens called the electoral college would be responsible for making the choice. The candidate with the most votes became president, and the candidate receiving the next highest number of votes became vice-president. But in 1800, when Aaron Burr and Thomas Jefferson received an equal number of votes, the system had to be changed to provide for separate voting for president and vice-president.

Later, when political parties had become more influential, the parties nominated candidates and then chose electors to vote for them.

Look at this diagram. Today, each political party in the state nominates a slate of electors pledged to support the party's nominees for president and vice-president. Each state has the same number of electors in the college as it has members of Congress. On election day, registered voters go to the polls to choose the electors.

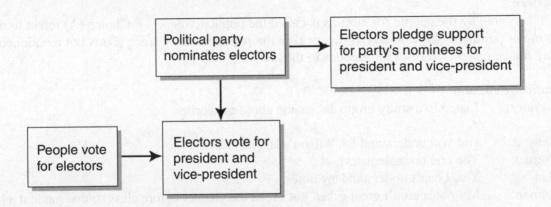

In most states, the ballots list only the names of the candidates for president and vice-president that the electors have pledged to support. This vote by the people for electors is called the popular vote, and the candidates who receive the most popular votes win all the electoral votes in a state.

> Now get ready to answer the questions

Audio

35. What is the electoral college?

Answer

(A) ". . . a system whereby a representative group of citizens called the electoral college would be responsible for making the choice." Choices (B), (C), and (D) are mentioned in the lecture but are not a definition of the electoral college.

Audio

36. Why does the speaker mention Aaron Burr and Thomas Jefferson?

Answer

(C) ". . . when Aaron Burr and Thomas Jefferson received an equal number of votes, the system had to be changed to provide for separate voting for president and vice-president." Choice (A) is not correct because the electoral college voted for Burr and Jefferson. Choice (D) is not correct because the system had to be changed. Choice (B) is not mentioned and may not be concluded from information in the talk.

Audio

37. How are the people nominated for the electoral college?

Answer

(A) ". . . the [political] parties nominated candidates and then chose electors. . . . " Choices (B), (C), and (D) are not correct because the parties make the nominations.

Audio

38. What is the popular vote?

Answer

(C) ". . . vote by the people for electors is called the popular vote. . . . " Choice (A) refers to direct vote, not popular vote. Choice (B) occurs after the popular vote. Choice (D) is not mentioned and may not be concluded from information in the talk.

Audio Discussion

Narrator:	Listen to a study group discussion about meteorites.
Man:	Did you understand Dr. Wilson's last lecture?
Woman:	The one on meteorites?
Man:	Yes. I can't understand my notes.
Woman:	My notes aren't great either, but I read the chapter before class so that made it a little easier to follow. Where did you get lost?
Man:	Well, he said that there were three basic types of meteorites, and that they were classified according to their composition.
Woman:	So far, so good.
Man:	But I only have two types written down—the iron meteorite that is mostly iron, with some trace metals like nickel and cobalt, and the stone meteorite that is mostly silicates and a wide variety of minerals.
Woman:	Oh, well, you are missing the stony iron meteorite that contains varying proportions of both iron and stone. He went over that one pretty fast, but he did say that the stony iron meteorite is very rare and represents only about 1 percent of the meteorites that fall to the Earth, so you might want to make a note of that.
Man:	Okay. The stone meteorite is the most common.
Woman:	Right. Stone meteorites account for almost 90 percent.
Man:	Great. Then what did he say about asteroids and comets right at the end of the lecture?
Woman:	Let's see. That was when he was talking about the formation of meteorites. And he said most meteorites are believed to be fragments of either asteroids or comets, but then he said that some stone meteorites may have dislodged themselves from the moon or from Mars during the impact from a large asteroid.

Man: That makes sense. Thanks a lot.

Woman: No problem. The book is really clear, too.

Man: It is. Maybe I should read the chapters before class like you do, instead of after the lecture like I have been.

Now get ready to answer the questions

Audio

39. What is the man's problem?

Answer

(C) Since the man asks whether the woman understood the last lecture and he tells her that he cannot understand his notes, it must be concluded that he did not understand the lecture. Choices (A) and (B) are not correct because the man cannot understand the notes that he took during the lecture. Choice (D) refers to the fact that the man reads the book after the lecture, not before the lecture, but reading the book is not the man's problem.

Audio

40. Which type of meteorite is the most common?

Answer

(A) "The stone meteorite is the most common. . . . Stone meteorites account for almost 90 percent." Choice (B) refers to the meteorite that accounts for 9 percent. Choice (D) refers to the meteorite that accounts for only about 1 percent of the total. Choice (C) is not mentioned and may not be concluded from information in the discussion.

Audio

41. How were most meteorites formed?

Answer

(B) (C) ". . . most meteorites are . . . fragments of either asteroids or comets, but…some stone meteorites may have dislodged themselves from the moon or from Mars during the impact from a large asteroid." Choices (A) and (D) are not mentioned and may not be concluded from information in the discussion.

Audio

42. What helped the woman follow the lecture?

Answer

(B) ". . . I read the chapter [in the book] before class so that made it a little easier to follow [the lecture]." Choice (A) is not correct because the woman says her notes aren't great either. Choice (D) is true, but it is not what helped the woman. Choice (C) is not mentioned and may not be concluded from information in the discussion.

Audio Lecture

Narrator: An artist from Alaska has been invited to talk about folk art to an art history class. She will be discussing scrimshaw. Listen to the beginning of the lecture.

In the period between the American Revolution and the Civil War, about 1775–1865, the hunting of whales was a major industry in America. In addition to the whale oil that was a primary item of trade, whale bones and even teeth became valuable for intricate carvings that the sailors made on them. This was called scrimshaw, although no one seems to know where it got the name.

There are two techniques for scrimshaw. One is to carve the bone into figures, in much the same way that wood or stone is carved. The other is to cut designs on the bone and then fill them with ink so that they are more visible.

This is an example of a scrimshaw from about 1800. As you can see, the results are quite beautiful, and even more impressive since the artist probably had no training at all and worked with only a pocket knife or a needle.

Like most folk artists, the sailors who practiced the art of scrimshaw tended to create practical objects such as tools, boxes, jewelry, and buttons. I have a number of examples here that I am going to pass around so that you can better appreciate the intricate details on the designs.

As you can imagine, because of the decline in whaling, there has also been a decline in the number of folk artists who produce scrimshaw. These pieces are quite rare and, as a result, quite valuable.

> Now get ready to answer the questions

Audio
43. What is the purpose of this talk?

Answer
(B) The purpose of this talk is to discuss scrimshaw, which is a folk art tradition. Choices (A), (C), and (D) are mentioned during the discussion but are secondary themes used to develop the main theme of the talk.

Audio
44. Why does the lecturer mention the American Revolution and the Civil War?

Answer
(A) "In the period between the American Revolution and the Civil War . . . the hunting of whales was a major industry . . . whale bones became valuable for intricate carvings. . . . ." Choice (B) is not correct because sailors, not soldiers, produced the art. Choice (C) is not correct because scrimshaw, not military art, is the topic of the lecture. Choice (D) is not correct because the examples are not battle scenes.

Audio
45. Identify the two techniques used to create scrimshaw.

Answer
(B) (C) "There are two techniques for scrimshaw. One is to carve the bone into figures. . . . The other is to cut designs on the bone and then fill them with ink. . . . " Choices (A) and (D) are not mentioned as techniques for scrimshaw.

Audio
46. Select the object that is the best example of scrimshaw.

Answer
(B) Choice (B) is the only example of scrimshaw. The other two pictures are examples of other kinds of folk art.

Audio
47. Why has scrimshaw become so valuable?

Answer
(A) ". . . because of the decline in whaling, there has also been a decline in the number of folk artists who produce scrimshaw." Choices (B), (C), and (D) are not mentioned and may not be concluded from information in the lecture.

Audio Conversation

Narrator:	Listen to part of a conversation between two students on campus.
Man:	Look. I got this in the mail, and I'm thinking about applying for a card.
Woman:	Oh, right. I got one, too. And so did a lot of people on campus.
Man:	So, what do you think? Are you going to do it?
Woman:	No. First of all, I already have a credit card, and I think one is enough for me right now.
Man:	Yeah, I have a credit card, too, but this one doesn't have an annual fee, and the interest charges are lower.
Woman:	Maybe. I'm not too sure, because I didn't look into it myself, but my roommate told me that you have to carry a $200 balance to keep the card . . .
Man:	So you can't pay it off every month?
Woman:	No, you can't. And that means you automatically have to pay interest. It's lower, but still, you can't avoid it by keeping a zero balance.
Man:	What happens if you don't carry a $200 balance?
Woman:	Well, first they send you a letter warning you that the account will be closed if activity doesn't pick up. Then, after a month or two, they close your account.
Man:	I see. Well, forget that. It doesn't sound like such a good deal after all.

Now get ready to answer the questions

Audio

48. What is the man trying to decide?

Answer

(B) "I'm thinking about applying for a [credit] card." The phrase "zero balance" in Choices (A) and (D) refers to the options that the woman mentions, not to the man's decision. Choice (C) is not mentioned and may not be concluded from information in the conversation.

Audio

49. Why is the man interested in the credit card?

Answer

(B) (C) ". . . this [credit card] doesn't have an annual fee, and the interest charges are lower." Choice (D) is not correct because you have to carry a $200 balance, which automatically accrues interest. Choice (A) is not mentioned and may not be concluded from information in the conversation.

Audio

50. Why does the man decide not to get the card?

Answer

(D) ". . . you have to carry a $200 balance . . . so you can't pay it off every month." Choice (A) is not correct because the man says he has a credit card while he is still considering the new card. The woman, not the man, thinks one credit card is enough. Choice (C) refers to the woman's, not the man's, roommate. Choice (B) is not mentioned and may not be concluded from information in the conversation.

Section 2: Structure

1. **(B)** When two nouns are used consecutively, the first often functions as an adjective. Choices (A), (C), and (D) are redundant and unidiomatic.

2. **(B)** There must be agreement between subject and verb. *Are* should be *is* to agree with the singular subject *anyone*.

3. **(A)** A form of BE is used with a participle in passive sentences. *Combine* should be *combined*.

4. **(D)** *A* should be *an* before the vowel sound *u* in *unknown*. *A* is used before consonant sounds. *An* is used before vowel sounds.

5. **(B)** A present tense verb is used after *when* to express future.

6. **(A)** *Once* means at one time in the past. *Once* is used in an introductory phrase with a *busy city* to modify the noun *Pompeii*.

7. **(A)** An infinitive is used to express purpose.

8. **(B)** There must be agreement between subject and verb. *Were* should be *was* to agree with the singular subject *Vasco da Gama*. The phrase of accompaniment, *accompanied by a large crew and a fleet of twenty ships*, is not the subject.

9. **(B)** *The longer* should be *the longest*. Because there are more than two unguarded borders in the history of the world, a superlative form must be used.

10. **(D)** The clause *many people believed* establishes a point of view in the past. *Is* should be *was* to maintain the point of view.

11. **(B)** *Each other* is used to express mutual acts. Choices (A), (C), and (D) are not idiomatic. "One another" would also be correct.

12. **(B)** *Begun* should be *began* because a past form is required to refer to Mozart's childhood. *Begun* is a participle. *Began* is a past form.

13. **(D)** *To experience* should be *experiencing* after the preposition *without*. *-Ing* nouns and noun forms are used after prepositions.

14. (**A**) *Almost* should be *most*. "Almost all of the poetry" would also be correct.

15. (**A**) *But* means except. "All of the cereal grains except rice" would also be correct.

16. (**A**) *Such* should be *such as*, which introduces the example *the Concorde*.

17. (**B**) Every sentence must have a main verb. Choices (A), (C), and (D) are not main verbs.

18. (**D**) *While* means at the same time. *While* is used in an introductory phrase with *a* to modify the noun *Webster*.

19. (**D**) *No longer* is an idiom that means *not any more*. *Not* should be *no* before *longer*.

20. (**A**) In order to refer to *occasionally, sometimes* should be used. *Sometimes* means occasionally. *Sometime* means at some time in the future.

21. (**B**) In scientific results, a present form in the condition requires a present or future form in the result. Choice (A) is a past, not future form. Choices (C) and (D) are present forms but they are auxiliary verbs.

22. (**A**) *Capable* should be *capability*. *Capable* is an adjective. *Capability* is a noun.

23. (**A**) *From* is used with *to* to express a time limit. *In* should be *From*.

24. (**B**) A negative phrase introduces inverted order. *Not until* requires an auxiliary verb, subject, and main verb. In Choice (A), the subject precedes the auxiliary. In Choice (C), there is no auxiliary. In Choice (D), there is no auxiliary and no subject.

25. (**C**) The two words in an infinitive should not be divided by an adverb of manner. *Clearly* should be placed at the end of the sentence.

Section 3: Reading

1. (**B**) "The Eradication of Smallpox" is the best title because it states the main idea of the passage. The other choices are secondary ideas that are used to develop the main idea. Choice (A) refers to the organization that initiated the campaign to eradicate smallpox. Choice (C) refers to one of the methods used to contain the spread of the disease. Choice (D) refers to the kind of disease that smallpox is.

2. In the context of this passage, the word eliminate is closest in meaning to eradicate. No other words or phrases in the **bold** text are close to the meaning of the word eradicate.

3. (**C**) In the context of this passage, threat could best be replaced by risk. Choices (A), (B), and (D) are not accepted definitions of the word.

4. "The goal was to eliminate the disease in one decade." Quotation from sentence 2, paragraph 2.

5. (**C**) "The strategy was not only to provide mass vaccinations but also to isolate patients...." Choice (A) refers to only one part of the strategy. It contradicts the fact that individual victims were treated. Choice (B) refers to only one part of the strategy. It contradicts the fact that entire villages were vaccinated. Choice (D) refers to a method to locate both villages and individuals for treatment.

6. (**B**) "By April of 1978, WHO officials announced that they [the officials] had isolated the last known case of the disease, but health workers continued to search for new cases for two additional years to be completely sure." Choices (A), (C), and (D) would change the meaning of the sentence.

7. (**B**) In the context of this passage, isolated is closest in meaning to separated. Choices (A), (C), and (D) are not accepted definitions of the word.

8. (**B**) "Rewards for reporting smallpox assisted in motivating the public." Choices (A), (C), and (D) refer to procedures for eliminating the spread of the disease, not to ways to motivate the public to help health workers.

9. (**A**) "...the World Health Organization...was authorized to initiate a global campaign to eradicate smallpox.... Today smallpox is no longer a threat [as it was in the past].... Routine vaccinations have been stopped...." Choices (B), (C), and (D) refer to smallpox. Choice (A) refers to malaria and yellow fever.

10. (**A**) "...eleven years after the initial organization of the campaign, no cases [of smallpox] were reported in the field." Choice (B) is not correct because similar projects for malaria and yellow fever had failed. Choice (C) is not correct because no cases are being reported. Choice (D) is not correct because patients had to be isolated to contain the spread of the disease.

11. "At the same time, the entire village where the victim had lived was vaccinated. The number of smallpox-infected countries gradually decreased." The connection between the two sentences is cause and result. The first sentence explains the strategy that caused the decrease referred to in the second sentence.

12. **(C)** The other choices are secondary ideas that are used to develop the main idea, "the current American family." Choices (A), (B), and (D) are classifications of families among those included in the current American family.

13. In the context of this passage, the word ideal is most opposite in meaning to reality. No other words or phrases in the **bold** text are opposite in meaning to the word reality.

14. **(B)** Current means present. Choices (A), (C), and (D) are not accepted definitions of the word.

15. **(B)** "The most recent government statistics reveal that only about one third of all current American families fit the traditional mold of two parents and their children, and another third consists of married couples who either have no children or have none [no children] still living at home." Choices (A), (C), and (D) would change the meaning of the sentence.

16. **(C)** "Of the final one third, about 20 percent of the total number of American households are single people...." Choice (A) refers to the final one third, not to the 20 percent who are single. Choices (B) and (D) are not correct because 20 percent equals one fifth.

17. **(C)** "...about 20 percent...are single people, usually women over sixty-five years of age." Choice (D) refers to 7 percent, not to the majority of one-person households. Choices (A) and (B) are not mentioned and may not be concluded from information in the passage.

18. "...about 20 percent of the total number of American households are single people, usually women over sixty-five years of age. A small percentage [of the single people]... consists of unmarried people who choose to live together; and the rest [of the single people]...are single parents, with at least one child." Other choices would change the meaning of the sentence.

19. "The vast majority of Americans claim that they have people in their lives whom they regard as family although they are not related." Quotation from sentence 2, paragraph 4.

20. **(A)** In the context of this passage, undervalues is closest in meaning to does not appreciate. Choices (B), (C), and (D) are not accepted definitions of the word.

21. **(C)** "...the number of births to unmarried women...divorce...deaths result in single-parent families." Choices (A), (B), and (D) are all mentioned in the reference to single-parent families. Choice (C) is not mentioned and may not be concluded from information in the passage.

22. **(A)** "...the so-called traditional American family was always more varied than we had been led to believe, reflecting the very different racial, ethnic, class, and religious customs among different American groups." Choice (B) is not correct because customs are different among these groups. Choices (C) and (D) are not mentioned and may not be concluded from information in the passage.

23. **(A)** The other choices are secondary ideas that are used to develop the main idea that "noise may pose a serious threat to our physical and psychological health." Choices (B), (C), and (D) are all true, but they are details, not the main idea.

24. **(A)** "Noise, commonly defined as unwanted sound ..." Choices (B) and (D) refer to the origins of noise, not to definitions of it. Choice (C) refers to the effects of noise.

25. **(B)** "...it [noise] is very difficult to measure because the discomfort experienced by different individuals is highly subjective and, therefore, variable." Choices (A), (C), and (D) are all mentioned in reference to noise, but are not the reason that noise is difficult to measure.

26. **(C)** In the context of this passage, congested could best be replaced by crowded. Choices (A), (B), and (D) are not accepted definitions of the word.

27. **(B)** "Loud noises instinctively signal danger...we are constantly responding [to noise] in the same ways that we would respond to danger." Choice (A) is not correct because noise and our response to it may be more

than an annoyance. Choices (C) and (D) refer to the results of our response to noise, not to the source of our response.

28. In the context of this passage, the word increase is closest in meaning to accelerate. No other words or phrases in the **bold** text are close to the meaning of the word accelerate.

29. "…the noise produced as a byproduct of our advancing technology causes physical and psychological harm, and detracts from the quality of life for those who are exposed to it [the noise]." Other choices would change the meaning of the sentence.

30. (B) In the context of this passage, as well is closest in meaning to also. Choices (A), (C), and (D) are not accepted definitions of the phrase.

31. (B) "Unlike the eyes [which have lids], the ear has no lid…therefore,…noise penetrates without protection." Choices (A), (C), and (D) are not mentioned and may not be concluded from information in the passage.

32. (C) "…noise is unavoidable in a complex industrial society…." Choice (A) is not correct because it [noise] is a serious threat to physical and psychological well-being. Choice (B) refers to hearing loss, which is America's number one nonfatal health problem, not to noise. Choice (D) refers to an industrial society, not to noise.

33. "Investigations on human subjects have demonstrated that babies are affected by noise even before they are born. Fetuses exposed to noise tend to be overactive, they cry easily, and they are more sensitive to gastrointestinal problems after birth." The connection between the two sentences is the reference to "babies…before they are born" and "fetuses." The first sentence is a general statement followed by examples in the second sentence.

34. (C) Choices (A), (B), and (D) are important to the discussion and provide details that support the main topic, "hunter-gatherers."

35. (D) "This method of harvesting from nature's provision [hunting and gathering] is the oldest known subsistence strategy." Choice (A) refers to a practice engaged in by hunter-gatherers in order to locate new sources of food, not to the subsistence strategy. Choices (B) and (C) refer to later strategies for subsistence.

36. (B) "This method [hunting and gathering] has been practiced for at least the last 2 million years." Choice (C) refers to the date when farming and the domestication of animals, not hunting and gathering, were introduced. Choices (A) and (D) are not mentioned and may not be concluded from information in the passage.

37. In the context of this passage, the word crude is closest in meaning to rudimentary. No other words or phrases in the **bold** text are close to the meaning of the word rudimentary.

38. (B) In the context of this passage, dwindled is closest in meaning to decreased. Choices (A), (C), and (D) are not accepted definitions of the word.

39. "In higher latitudes, the shorter growing season has restricted the availability of plant life. Such conditions [the shorter growing season] have caused a greater dependence on hunting…." Other choices would change the meaning of the sentence.

40. (D) "The abundance of vegetation in the lower latitudes…has provided a greater opportunity for gathering a variety of plants." Choices (A), (B), and (C) refer to the higher latitudes, not to the lower latitudes.

41. (B) "Contemporary hunter-gatherers may help us understand our prehistoric ancestors." Choices (A) and (C) may be true, but they are not mentioned as a reason to study contemporary hunter-gatherer societies. Choice (D) is not correct because the author believes the patterns of behavior of contemporary hunter-gatherers may be similar to those practiced by mankind during the Paleolithic Period.

42. (A) In the context of this passage, exploit is closest in meaning to use. Choices (B), (C), and (D) are not accepted definitions of the word.

43. (C) Choice (C) is a restatement of the sentence referred to in the passage. *Within a reasonable distance* means near. Choices (A), (B), and (D) would change the meaning of the original sentence.

44. (A) "It [hunting-gathering] was…the only way to obtain food until rudimentary farming and very crude methods for the domestication of animals were introduced…." Choice (A) refers to farming, not to patterns

of behavior for hunter-gatherers. The small group harvests the food by gathering it, not by planting it. Choices (B), (C), and (D) are all mentioned in paragraph 3.

45. **(D)** Choice (A) refers to the fact that a society based on hunting and gathering must be very mobile. Choice (B) refers to the fact that there is a strict division of labor between the sexes. Choice (C) refers to the fact that the camp is located near the food supply. Only Choice (D) is not mentioned and may not be concluded from information in the passage.

Writing Section

Question:

Leaders like John F. Kennedy and Martin Luther King have made important contributions to humanity. Name another world leader you think is important. Give specific reasons for your choice.

Outline

William Lyon Mackenzie King
- Offices
    Parliament
    Head Liberal Party
    Prime minister
- Longevity
    21 years P.M.
    50 years public service
- Accomplishments
    Unity French + English provinces
    Represented all Canadians

Map

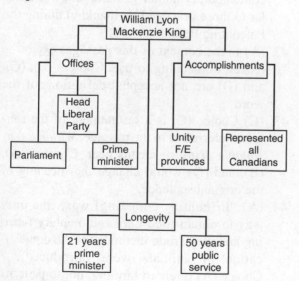

Example Essay

William Lyon Mackenzie King was a member of the Canadian parliament and head of the Liberal Party in the first half of the twentieth century. He held the office of prime minister for a total of twenty-one years, which is a longer period of time than that of any public servant in the history of Canada. Because his terms of office as prime minister were not consecutive, he held other positions of public service in many appointed and elected offices as well over a period of fifty years. Although it could be argued that he was an important world leader on the basis of longevity alone, I admire him because of his qualities of leadership. He was active in government during two world wars and the Great Depression and played a key role in guiding Canada during those very difficult years. He understood the importance of a unified nation and worked to bring various partisan groups together for the higher good of the country. Under his tenure in office, Canada became a participant in world affairs.

His three terms of office as prime minister were marked by compromise and often criticism, but he earned the respect of most Canadians for his political astuteness and his determination to unify Canada. In part because of his friendship with Wilfrid Laurier, he was able to preserve the unity between the French-speaking and English-speaking provinces, a negotiation that must be considered his greatest achievement. One biographer, John Moir of the University of Toronto, has identified a quality in King called "essential Canadianness." I understand this to mean that he was able to understand and represent all of the people of Canada.

King's methods were frustrating to some, but he was able to extend Canadian autonomy and maintain unity while acting within a difficult federal system. He did so for a very long time, even representing Canada in the international arena in his elder years. In my view, William Lyon Mackenzie King is worthy of being named in the company of John F. Kennedy and Martin Luther King as a world leader who made an important contribution to humanity.

Model Test 8—Computer-Assisted TOEFL

Section 1: Listening

The Listening Section of the test measures the ability to understand conversations and talks in English. On the actual TOEFL exam, you will use headphones to listen to the conversations and talks. While you are listening, pictures of the speakers or other information will be presented on your computer screen. There are two parts to the Listening Section, with special directions for each part.

On the day of the test, the amount of time you will have to answer all of the questions will appear on the computer screen. The time you spend listening to the test material will not be counted. The listening material and questions about it will be presented only one time. You will not be allowed to take notes or have any paper at your computer. You will both see and hear the questions before the answer choices appear. You can take as much time as you need to select an answer; however, it will be to your advantage to answer the questions as quickly as possible. You may change your answer as many times as you want before you confirm it. After you have confirmed an answer, you will not be able to return to the question.

Before you begin working on the Listening Section, you will have an opportunity to adjust the volume of the sound. You may not be able to change the volume after you have started the test.

QUESTION DIRECTIONS—Part A

In Part A of the Listening Section, you will hear short conversations between two people. In some of the conversations, each person speaks only once. In other conversations, one or both of the people speak more than once. Each conversation is followed by one question about it.

Each question in this part has four answer choices. You should click on the best answer to each question. Answer the questions on the basis of what is stated or implied by the speakers.

Audio
1. Man: Could you please sign my course request form?
   Woman: I'm sorry. You have to get your advisor's signature on that.
   Narrator: What can be inferred about the woman?

Answer
(A) Because the woman refuses to sign and tells the man that he has to get his advisor's signature, we must conclude that she is not the man's advisor. In Choice (B), although she says she is sorry, that is not the reason she cannot sign the form. Choice (C) is not correct because the man asks her to sign a course request form. In Choice (D), it is true that he needs his advisor's signature, but that is not the reason the woman cannot sign the form.

Audio

2. Woman: So what are you going to do? Drop the course?
   Man: No way!
   Narrator: What does the man mean?

Answer

(C) *No way* is an idiomatic expression that means "it is not going to happen." Choice (A) misinterprets the phrase *no way* to mean directions. Choice (B) is not correct because he will not withdraw from the course he is in. Choice (D) is not correct because he gives the woman a definitive answer to her question.

Audio

3. Man: Did Dr. Peterson pass back our tests today?
   Woman: No. She didn't have them all graded yet. But we can pick them up after Wednesday in her office if we don't want to wait until class next Monday.
   Narrator: What can be inferred about the man?

Answer

(A) Since the man is asking what happened in Dr. Peterson's class, it must be concluded that the man did not go to class. Choice (B) is not correct because the woman is in Dr. Peterson's class. Choices (C) and (D) are not mentioned and may not be concluded from information in the conversation.

Audio

4. Woman: It looks like Dr. Williams is going to show some slides.
   Man: You're right. Let's sit closer to the front. I can't see very well.
   Woman: That's a good idea.
   Narrator: What will the man and woman probably do?

Answer

(C) Since the man suggests that they sit closer to the front and the woman agrees, they will probably move to the front of the room. Choice (B) is not correct because they are already sitting together. Choice (D) is not correct because the woman agrees with the man. Choice (A) is not mentioned and may not be concluded from information in the conversation.

Audio

5. Woman: Did you like living in Montreal?
   Man: Yes. Most of the time. The weather was really cold in the winter, but the rest of the year was beautiful.
   Narrator: How did the man feel about Montreal?

Answer

(B) Because the man objected to the cold winter but said he liked Montreal the rest of the year, it must be concluded that he liked Montreal in the spring, summer, and fall. Choice (A) is not correct because the man objected to the cold winter. Choice (C) is not correct because the man liked Montreal most of the time. Choice (D) is not correct because the man said "yes" when he was asked if he liked living in Montreal.

Audio

6. Woman: Are you going to do the work for extra credit?
   Man: You bet!
   Narrator: What does the man mean?

Answer

(C) *You bet* is an idiomatic expression that means "certainly." Choice (A) misinterprets the word *bet* to mean a wager. Choices (B) and (D) are not mentioned and may not be concluded from information in the conversation.

Audio

7. Man: I've got to quit smoking. But how? I've tried chewing gum. I've joined a support group. My willpower only lasts about two weeks.
   Woman: It's hard. I smoked for almost ten years. Then I got one of those nicotine patches. Why don't you try it?
   Narrator: What did the woman suggest?

Answer

(C) The woman says she got a nicotine patch. Choices (A), (B), and (D) refer to the methods that the man has used to quit smoking in the past.

Audio

8. Man: You're in my American Lit class, aren't you?
   Woman: Yes, I am. How do you like the class so far?
   Man: Well, to tell the truth, I'm not too big on literature.
   Narrator: What does the man mean?

Answer

(C) To *not be too big on* something is an idiomatic expression that means to "not like it very much." Choice (D) is not correct because he responds to the woman's question. Choices (A) and (B) are not mentioned and may not be concluded from information in the conversation.

Audio

9. Woman: Can you believe it? I got an A on my final!
   Man: Way to go!
   Narrator: What does the man mean?

Answer

(D) *Way to go* is an idiomatic expression that means "congratulations." Choices (A), (B), and (C) misinterpret the meaning of the phrase *way to go*.

Audio

10. Man: Hey, I heard that you got an assistantship.
    Woman: You must be thinking of my roommate. I'm not going to try to teach next year while I'm studying full time.
    Narrator: What does the woman mean?

Answer

(A) "You must be thinking of my roommate [who got an assistantship]." Choice (B) is not correct because she will be studying full time. Choice (D) is not correct because the man has confused the woman with her roommate. Choice (C) is not mentioned and may not be concluded from information in the conversation.

Audio

11. Man: What did you do with your notebook?
    Woman: I wish I knew. I thought I had put it in my car so I wouldn't have to carry it around all day in my backpack.
    Narrator: What is the woman's problem?

Answer

(C) *I wish I knew* is an idiomatic expression that means the person "does not know." Choices (A), (B), and (D) are not paraphrases of the expression and may not be concluded from information in the conversation.

Audio

12. Man: You'd better hurry. They're only taking pictures for ID cards until five o'clock.
    Woman: I'm on my way.
    Narrator: What does the woman mean?

Answer

(C) To be *on one's way* is an idiomatic expression that means to "be ready to leave." Choices (A), (B), and (D) are not paraphrases of the expression and may not be concluded from information in the conversation.

Audio

13. Man: What is an appropriate gift to take to some friends who have invited you to their house for dinner? I was thinking maybe some candy.
    Woman: That sounds good. Or you could get a plant.
    Narrator: What does the woman suggest?

Answer

(C) ". . . you could get a plant." Choice (D) refers to the fact that the man considered taking candy to his friends, not to the woman's suggestion. Choices (A) and (B) are not mentioned and may not be concluded from information in the conversation.

Audio

14. Man: Are you lost?

    Woman: I'm afraid so. I can't find Dr. Warren's office. It's number 119.

    Man: Oh! The even numbers are on this side, so it must be on the other side.

    Narrator: What will the woman probably do?

Answer

(B) Since the woman's room number is 119 and the man points out that the odd numbers are on the other side, the woman will probably look on the other side of the hall. Choices (A), (C), and (D) are not mentioned and may not be concluded from information in the conversation.

Audio

15. Man: But I sent my application three weeks ago.

    Woman: Well that's why you haven't heard, then. It takes six weeks to process it.

    Narrator: What does the woman imply?

Answer

(D) Since the woman assures the man that it takes a long time to process the application, she implies that he should be patient. Choice (B) is not correct because it takes six weeks, not three weeks, to process. Choices (A) and (C) are not mentioned and may not be concluded from information in the conversation.

Audio

16. Man: If you want to cash a check at the Student Union, they'll need to see your driver's license and a major credit card.

    Woman: Even for a traveler's check? I have my passport.

    Narrator: What does the woman mean?

Answer

(A) Since the woman offers her passport, it must be concluded that she wants to use it for ID. Choice (C) refers to the method of payment, not to the identification required. Choice (D) is not correct because she is paying with a traveler's check. Choice (B) is not mentioned and may not be concluded from information in the conversation.

Audio

17. Woman: How did the meeting go with your doctoral committee?

    Man: I couldn't have been more pleased.

    Narrator: What does the man mean?

Answer

(B) *I couldn't have been more pleased* is an idiomatic expression that means the speaker was "very pleased." Choice (D) is not correct because the man was pleased with the meeting. Choices (A) and (C) were not mentioned and may not be concluded from information in the conversation.

QUESTION DIRECTIONS—Part B

In Part B of the Listening Section, you will hear several longer conversations and talks. Each conversation or talk is followed by several questions. The conversations, talks, and questions will not be repeated.

The conversations and talks are about a variety of topics. You do not need special knowledge of the topics to answer the questions correctly. Rather, you should answer each question on the basis of what is stated or implied by the speakers in the conversations or talks.

For most of the questions, you will need to click on the best of four possible answers. Some questions will have special directions. The special directions will appear in a box on the computer screen.

Audio Conversation

Narrator: Listen to part of a conversation between a student and the dean of students on campus.

Dean: You are here because you are accused of plagiarism. That is one of the most serious kinds of misconduct at the University. It is intellectual theft.

Student: But I didn't mean to steal.

Dean: Maybe not, but copying is stealing.

Student: I didn't copy.

Dean: Yes, you did. In this case, you copied from a book instead of from a friend. It's still copying. Look, if you want to use someone else's words, you must put them in quotation marks, and you must cite the source. You know that, don't you?

Student: Yes, but . . .

Dean: Even if you don't copy word for word, but you use someone else's ideas, if those ideas are not widely published, it can still be plagiarism to use them without a citation.

Student: That is what I don't understand, Dean Conners.

Dean: Mr. Farr, your professor already gave you a failing grade for the course, and in this case I feel that is punishment enough. I'm going to give you a warning this time. But if you ever come back to my office for a similar offense, I'll have you expelled. In the meantime, if you really don't know how to write a research paper, I suggest that you go over to the Learning Resources Center for some tutoring.

> Now get ready to answer the questions

Audio

18. Why is the student in the dean's office?

Answer

(C) "You are here because you are accused of plagiarism." Choice (A) refers to the fact that the professor gave him a failing grade, not to the reason why the student is in the dean's office. The dean gives the student some advice, but Choice (B) is not mentioned as a reason for his being in the dean's office. Choice (D) is incorrect because the dean refers to the fact that plagiarism is intellectual theft, not to the theft of a book.

Audio

19. What is the student's excuse?

Answer

(A) "That [using ideas with a citation] is what I don't understand." Choice (D) refers to the dean's suggestion that the student get a tutor, not to the student's excuse. Choices (B) and (C) are not mentioned and may not be concluded from information in the conversation.

Audio

20. How does the dean punish the student?

Answer

(C) "I'm going to give you a warning this time." Choice (A) refers to the dean's decision to expel the student if she ever sees him in her office for a similar offense. Choice (B) refers to the professor's, not the dean's, punishment of the student. Choice (D) refers to the advice, not the punishment, that the dean gave the student.

Audio

21. What advice does the dean give the student?

Answer

(B) "I suggest that you go over to the Learning Resources Center for some tutoring." Choices (A), (C), and (D) are not mentioned and may not be concluded from information in the conversation.

Audio Conversation

Narrator: Listen to part of a conversation on campus between two students.

Man: What's bothering you? You've been really quiet tonight.
Woman: I'm sorry. I'm trying to decide whether to stay here or to transfer to a larger school.
Man: Well, there are advantages to both, I suppose.
Woman: That's the problem. I keep thinking that eventually it will be better to have the degree from a larger, more prestigious college, but I really like it here.
Man: I know what you mean. At a small place like this, we have professors teaching our classes, not graduate students.
Woman: Exactly. And, besides that, your teachers know you, and they seem to really care about you. I'm not sure it would be like that in a huge university.
Man: True. So, you are basically happy here, but you are worried about the impression that you will make with a degree from such a small college.
Woman: Yes. I'm afraid I'll be in a job interview sometime, and the interviewer will say, "And just where *is* your alma mater?"
Man: I've thought about that myself.
Woman: And?
Man: Well, as you know, I'm planning to go to graduate school, so my plan is to get really good grades here and try to get into a well-known university for my master's degree. I think that will give me the best of both worlds.

> Now get ready to answer the questions

Audio

22. What is the woman trying to decide?

Answer

(B) "I'm trying to decide whether to stay here or to transfer to a larger school." Choices (A), (C), and (D) are not mentioned and may not be concluded from information in the conversation.

Audio

23. What does she like about the college she is attending?

Answer

(C) ". . . your teachers know you, and they really seem to care about you." Choices (A) and (D) refer to the advantages of a larger school, not to what she likes about the college she is attending. Choice (B) is not mentioned and may not be concluded from information in the conversation.

Audio

24. How does the man respond to her problem?

Answer

(C) ". . . I'm planning to go to graduate school, so my plan is to get really good grades here and try to get into a well-known university for my master's degree. Choice (A) is not correct because he listens to the woman. Choice (D) is not correct because he tries to understand her point of view and shares his plans. Choice (B) is not mentioned and may not be concluded from information in the conversation.

Audio

25. What does the man plan to do?

Answer

(A) ". . . try to get into a well-known university for my master's degree." Choice (C) is not correct because his plan is to get good grades in the undergraduate program at his current school. Choices (B) and (D) are not mentioned and may not be concluded from information in the conversation.

Audio Talk

Narrator: Listen to part of a talk in an anthropology class.

In informal conversation, the word *culture* refers to a desirable personal attribute that can be acquired by visiting museums and galleries and by attending concerts and theatrical performances. An educated person who has culture is familiar with the finer things produced in civilized society. And that's what most people think of when they hear the word culture. In anthropology, however, culture is defined in a very different way. To an anthropologist, culture refers to the complex whole of ideas and material objects produced by groups in their historical experience; that is, the learned behaviors, beliefs, attitudes, and values that are characteristic of a particular society. For a thought or activity to be included as part of a culture, it must be commonly shared by or considered appropriate for the group.

Even in a complex society like that of the United States, which comprises many diverse ethnic groups, there are practices common to all Americans, and these practices constitute American culture. In addition, the smaller groups within the larger society have shared customs that are specific to their group. These shared customs represent a subculture within the larger culture. Now, can anyone think of an example of a subculture in the United States?

> Now get ready to answer the questions

Audio

26. What is the topic of this lecture?

Answer

(B) "In anthropology, however, culture is defined in a very different way. To an anthropologist, culture refers to. . . . " Choices (A), (C), and (D) are secondary themes used to support the main theme of the lecture, culture in anthropology.

Audio

27. According to the speaker, what do most people mean when they use the word *culture* in ordinary conversation?

Answer

(D) "In informal conversation, the word *culture* refers to a desirable personal attribute . . . And that's what most people think of when they hear the word culture." Choices (A), (B), and (C) refer to the definition of culture in anthropology, not in informal conversation.

Audio

28. According to the speaker, what do anthropologists mean when they say a thought or activity is to be included as part of culture?

Answer

(C) "For a thought or activity to be included as part of a culture, it must be commonly shared by or considered appropriate for the group." Choice (A) refers to a subculture, not a culture. Choice (B) refers to the word culture as it is understood in informal conversation. Choice (D) refers to the United States and societies like it.

Audio

29. How does the professor explain American culture?

Answer

(A) ". . . in . . . the United States, which comprises many diverse ethnic groups, there are practices common to all Americans, and these practices constitute American culture." Choice (B) refers to a subculture, not to the culture of the United States. Choice (C) is not correct because the practices are common to all Americans. Choice (D) is not correct because the practices are common to all, not just the majority, of Americans.

Audio

30. According to the speaker, what is a subculture?

Answer

(C) ". . . the smaller groups within the larger society have shared customs that are specific to their group . . . a subculture." Choices (A) and (B) refer to an informal definition of culture, not to subcultures. Choice (D) refers to a definition of culture by an anthropologist, not to a definition of a subculture.

Audio Talk

Narrator: A medical doctor has been invited to talk about AIDS to a biology class. Listen to the beginning of the talk.

In 1992, the World Health Organization (WHO) reported that ten to twelve million adults and one million children worldwide had contracted HIV, the virus that causes AIDS, and they estimated that by the twenty-first century, forty million people would be infected. If the current trends continue, however, that estimate will fall far short of actual numbers, which may reach one hundred ten million.

In addition, there appears to be a change in the characteristics of AIDS victims. In the 1980s, homosexual men in large urban areas accounted for approximately two thirds of all AIDS cases. Women and children seemed to be on the periphery of the AIDS epidemic. But today almost ninety percent of new adult infections result from heterosexual contact. Consequently, the rates of exposure and infection are rising for women, with an accompanying rise in the number of children born to them with HIV. In the twenty-first century, it is expected that the majority of AIDS victims will be heterosexual women and their young children.

Furthermore, research by WHO reveals that women around the world are more susceptible to the AIDS virus for a number of reasons. First, women are biologically more susceptible to all sexually transmitted diseases; second, women tend to have sexual relationships with older men who are more likely to have had multiple partners; and last, the traditional role of the man as the partner in control of the sexual activity inhibits women in many cultures from using protection.

> Now get ready to answer the questions

Audio

31. How does the World Health Organization estimate compare with actual trends?

Answer

(B) "If the current trends continue, however, that estimate will fall far short of actual numbers. . . . " Choices (A) and (C) are not correct because the estimate is lower than the actual numbers, not the same or higher. The fraction in Choice (D) refers to the AIDS cases accounted for by homosexual men in the 1980s, not to the actual numbers compared with the estimate.

Audio

32. The guest speaker briefly discusses a trend. Summarize the trend by putting the events in order.

Answer

(D) (A) (C) (B) "In the 1980s, homosexual men…accounted for . . . two thirds of all AIDS cases . . . today almost ninety percent of new adult infections result from heterosexual contact . . . the rates of exposure and infection are rising for women, with an accompanying rise in the number of children . . . with HIV. . . . "

Audio

33. Why are women so susceptible to the AIDS virus?

Answer

(C) (D) ". . . women are biologically more susceptible to all sexually transmitted diseases . . . and the traditional role of the man as the partner in control of the sexual activity inhibits women in many cultures. . . . " The multiple partners in Choice (A) refer to those of older men, not women. The cultures in Choice (B) refer to restrictions for women using protection, not to restrictions on the use of protection.

Audio

34. Which segments of the population will probably constitute the majority of AIDS cases in the twenty-first century?

Answer

(A) (C) "In the twenty-first century, it is expected that the majority of AIDS victims will be heterosexual women and their young children." Choices (B) and (D) are not mentioned in the estimate and may not be concluded from information in the talk.

Audio Discussion

Narrator:	Listen to part of a class discussion in a psychology class.
Professor:	How many of you have experienced jet lag? Almost everyone? Do you know what causes it? Jennifer?
Jennifer:	The difference in time that occurs when we cross time zones.
Professor:	Yes. That's right. You see we all have an internal clock that determines when we should sleep, wake up, eat, or perform other bodily functions during a twenty-four-hour period. So most travelers are not able to adjust to the shorter or longer day.
David:	Excuse me, Professor Roberts.
Professor:	Yes, David.
David:	Is it true that jet lag is worse after a flight east than it is after a flight west?
Professor:	Very good question. Yes, most people can adjust a little better to a longer day than they can to a shorter day. It's also true that people over thirty who tend to have a more established routine are likely to suffer the most from jet lag.
Jennifer:	Excuse me, Professor. But is there any research on how we can deal with jet lag?
Professor:	Yes, Jennifer, there is. Probably the most interesting research studies on how to minimize the effects of jet lag are those that show the value of scheduling an early evening arrival. Can you imagine why that might be helpful?
Jennifer:	Because you would probably just go to bed?
Professor:	True enough. But there is also some evidence that light plays a role in accommodating a new sleep cycle. In addition, it seems that a full stomach increases the symptoms of restlessness and fatigue. In fact, eating a small meal on the plane should help as long as you don't find the nearest restaurant when you land. Finally, alcohol tends to dehydrate the body, which appears to make jet lag worse. So that's why it's better to drink lots of water and avoid drinking alcohol on the plane. Yes, Jennifer?
Jennifer:	Does the research tell us how long it takes to adjust to a new time zone? When I visit my sister, I am waking up at three in the morning for most of my visit.
Professor:	And then it's time to go home.
Jennifer:	Exactly.
Professor:	Well, Jennifer, some studies show that we require half a day for each time zone crossed. So if you can't include a stopover on a long flight, it is better not to schedule an important meeting for the day after your arrival.

> Now get ready to answer the questions

Audio

35. What causes jet lag?

Answer

(A) ". . . most travelers are not able to adjust to the shorter or longer day." Choice (B) refers to a situation that affects the severity of jet lag, not to the cause. Choices (C) and (D) are not mentioned and may not be concluded from information in the discussion.

Audio

36. Who would suffer most from jet lag?

Answer

(C) ". . . people over thirty who tend to have a more established routine are likely to suffer the most from jet lag." Choice (A) is not correct because people over thirty, not younger people, suffer the most. Choice (B) is not correct because an adjustment from air travel east to west is a little easier. Choice (D) is not mentioned and may not be concluded from information in the discussion.

Audio

37. How can jet lag be minimized?

Answer

(B) (C) ". . . to minimize the effects of jet lag . . . [try] scheduling an early evening arrival . . . drink lots of water." Choice (A) is not correct because a full stomach increases the symptoms of jet lag. Choice (D) is not mentioned and may not be concluded from information in the discussion.

Audio

38. How long does it take to adjust to a new time zone?

Answer

(A) ". . . studies show that we require half a day for each time zone crossed." Choices (B), (C), and (D) contradict the research results.

Audio Talk

Narrator: A guest speaker has been invited to talk to an education class about adult education. Listen to the beginning of the talk.

One of the most successful educational programs for adults is the Elderhostel, designed for students over the age of sixty. Initiated in 1975 by five colleges in New Hampshire, Elderhostel was originally a one-week summer program for senior citizens combining travel and college residence with enrichment courses. The concept has been so popular that it has grown rapidly to include a network of more than three hundred colleges and universities in all fifty states. Host institutions have expanded to include museums, parks, and other outdoor centers as well as traditional college campuses, and one, two, or three-week programs are now available year round. Although courses are not offered for credit, and no exams are required, the classes are taught by highly qualified faculty at the host college.

Let me write Elderhostel on the board for you. Elderhostel.

To date, hundreds of thousands of students from sixty to one hundred years old have participated in Elderhostel. Students usually live in dormitories, eat in cafeterias, and attend social, recreational, and cultural functions. All services available to students during the academic year are offered to Elderhostel students. Registration fees vary from as little as twenty dollars to as much as three hundred dollars, excluding books and transportation to the campus or community site. For many senior citizens, Elderhostel offers the opportunity for lifelong learning, companionship, and fun.

If you know someone sixty years old or older and you think they might enjoy learning, call your local college. There is probably an Elderhostel program right in your community.

> Now get ready to answer the questions

Audio
39. What is Elderhostel?

Answer
(C) "One of the most successful educational programs for adults is the Elderhostel. . . . " Choice (A) is not correct because the classes are taught by highly qualified faculty at the host college, not by retired professors. Although Elderhostel was originally a summer program, Choice (B) is not correct because it is now offered year round. Choice (D) is not correct because Elderhostel is an educational program with travel included, not a travel program.

Audio
40. Which of the statements is true of Elderhostel?

Answer
(B) (D) "Although courses are not offered for credit, and no exams are required, the classes are taught by highly qualified faculty at the host college." Choice (A) is not correct because the courses are not offered for credit. Choice (C) is not correct because Elderhostel is for people over the age of sixty.

Audio
41. Which of the people in the picture would most probably be enrolled in an Elderhostel program?

Answer
(C) "Elderhostel [is] designed for students over the age of sixty." Choice (C) is a person sixty years or older. The other people in the pictures, Choices (A), (B), and (D), are too young to enroll in Elderhostel.

Audio
42. What should you do if you are interested in finding out more about Elderhostel?

Answer
(B) ". . . call your local college." Choices (A), (C), and (D) are not mentioned and may not be concluded from information in the talk.

Audio Lecture

Narrator: Listen to part of a lecture in an earth science class. The professor will talk about pyrite.

I will be putting another specimen in the mineral lab for you after today's lecture. It is pyrite, also known as iron disulfide, but more commonly called fool's gold.

This is a very fine example of pyrite because this particular specimen shows the well-defined cubic or isometric crystal formations quite well. There are a lot of flat facets on the face of this pyrite. As you can see, the mineral is a brassy yellow with some green and brown streaks running through it, and it has a metallic luster. It does, in fact, look a little bit like gold, doesn't it?

But really, pyrite and gold have very different scientific properties. Pyrite is much harder than gold—about 6 on the Mohs scale. As you will recall, gold is quite soft—only about 3 on the Mohs scale. And pyrite is much more brittle than gold, too.

But what if you are on a dig, and you want to tell the difference? Well, all you have to do is heat your sample. Gold will not react at all, but pyrite will smoke and produce an unpleasant odor, a little like sulfuric acid, which is, in fact, made from pyrite. And when pyrite is struck with a hammer, it will create sparks. Actually, the term *pyrite* is derived from the Greek word for fire, and there is speculation that mankind may have used pyrite to make the first fires for cooking and heating.

Large deposits of pyrite are found throughout the world, in igneous rocks in all kinds of geological environments. It is a very common mineral. And, yes, the resemblance of pyrite to gold causes prospectors worldwide to mistake fool's gold for real gold.

Now get ready to answer the questions

Audio
43. What problem does the lecturer point out?

Answer
(A) ". . . the resemblance of pyrite to gold causes prospectors worldwide to mistake fool's gold [pyrite] for real gold." Choice (C) is not correct because it is a very common mineral. Choice (D) is not correct because the specimen [of pyrite] shows well-defined crystal formations. Choice (B) is true, but it is referred to as an advantageous characteristic, not a problem.

Audio

44. What will the professor do with the specimen he has brought to class?

Answer

(D) "I will be putting another specimen in the mineral lab for you after today's lecture." Choices (A), (B), and (C) are not mentioned and may not be concluded from information in the lecture.

Audio

45. Select the specimen that is most similar to the one that the professor showed in class.

Answer

(C) Choice (C) is the most similar to the specimen that the professor showed in class. Choices (A) and (B) are not minerals.

Audio

46. Identify the properties of pyrite.

Answer

(B) (C) ". . . pyrite is much more brittle than gold . . . and when pyrite is struck with a hammer, it will create sparks." Choice (A) refers to a property of gold, not to that of pyrite. Choice (D) is not correct because pyrite is found in all kinds of geological environments and is considered a very common mineral.

Audio

47. What is an easy way to identify pyrite?

Answer

(A) ". . . all you have to do [to tell the difference between pyrite and gold] is heat your sample." Choices (B) and (D) refer to the smell of sulfuric acid that pyrite produces when heated, but using acid or smelling the sample are not mentioned as tests for pyrite. Choice (C) refers to the description of the pyrite specimen that the professor has brought to class. However, the fact that so many prospectors worldwide mistake pyrite for gold implies that pyrite cannot be identified by looking at it.

Audio Conversation

Narrator:	Listen to part of a conversation on campus between two students.
Man:	Excuse me. Has anyone turned in a calculus book?
Woman:	I don't think so. Where did you leave it?
Man:	I'm not sure. I was sitting over there by the window, and I think I left it under the table. But it isn't there now.
Woman:	When did you lose it? Today?
Man:	Yes, just about an hour ago when I was in here for lunch. I didn't notice until I got to the library to study for my test.
Woman:	That's too bad. Well, listen, sometimes people don't turn in lost items to us. There's a lost-and-found in the Student Union by the entrance to the auditorium. Maybe someone found your book and took it there.
Man:	Maybe.
Woman:	Do you know where the Student Union is?
Man:	Yes, I do. Thanks a lot for your help.
Woman:	You're welcome. Oh, wait. Another thing. If you don't find it there today, you should probably check again tomorrow. Sometimes people get busy, and don't get over there right away to turn something in.

Man: Good idea. Thanks again.
Woman: Good luck. I hope it's there.

> Now get ready to answer the questions

Audio

48. What prompted this conversation?

Answer

(C) Since the man begins the conversation by asking whether anyone has turned in a lost book, it must be concluded that the lost book is the reason for the conversation. Choice (A) is true, but it is not the reason for the conversation. Choice (B) is not correct because the man knows where the Student Union is. Choice (D) is not mentioned and may not be concluded from information in the conversation.

Audio

49. Where does the man think he left his book?

Answer

(C) ". . . I think I left it [my book] under the table . . . when I was in here [the cafeteria]." Choice (B) refers to the location of the lost-and-found, not to where the man left his book. Choice (D) refers to where the man noticed that his book was missing. Choice (A) is not mentioned and may not be concluded from information in the conversation.

Audio

50. What does the woman suggest that the man do?

Answer

(A) (D) "There's a lost-and-found in the Student Union. . . . If you don't find it there today, you should probably check again tomorrow." Choices (B) and (C) are not mentioned and may not be concluded from information in the conversation.

Section 2: Structure

1. **(C)** *Similar* is used after the two nouns *protoplasm* and *glue* to compare them. Choice (A) is redundant because the pronoun *they* is used consecutively after the nouns to which it refers. Choice (B) has the same meaning as the correct answer, but *similar to* is used before, not after, the second noun compared. Choice (D) does not have a verb.

2. **(D)** *Oil* is a noncount noun because it is a liquid that can change shape, depending on the shape of the container.

3. **(C)** Every sentence must have a main verb. Choices (A), (B), and (D) are not main verbs.

4. **(D)** In order to refer to a gallon of water being *moved to a higher place, raise* not *rise* should be used. To *raise* means to move to a higher place. To *rise* means to go up without assistance; to increase.

5. **(D)** *Unless* introduces a subject and verb that express a change in conditions. Choices (A), (B), and (C) do not have a subject and verb.

6. **(A)** The word order for a passive sentence is BE followed by a participle. Choice (B) is a participle, but the form of BE is missing. Choice (C) is redundant because the pronoun *it* is used consecutively after the subject *path*. Choice (D) is an *-ing* form, not a passive.

7. (**B**) *From* introduces cause. Choices (A), (C), and (D) are not idiomatic.

8. (**A**) *Wholly* should be *As a whole. As a whole* means *generally. Wholly* means *completely.*

9. (**A**) *More than* is used before a specific number to express an estimate. "As many as two hundred" would also be correct.

10. (**A**) *There* introduces inverted order, but there must still be agreement between subject and verb. *Is* should be *are* to agree with the plural subject, *so many variables.*

11. (**D**) No article before a noncount noun or a plural count noun means *all.* Choice (A) would be an incomplete sentence because it is missing a main verb. Choices (B) and (C) contain articles and would change the meaning of the sentence.

12. (**D**) Either an *-ing* form or an infinitive may be used as the subject of a sentence. Choice (A) is an infinitive that means *to establish,* not *to identify.* Choice (B) is a verb word. Choice (C) is a noun. "To find" would also be correct.

13. (**D**) *By* expresses means before an *-ing* form. *Provide* should be *providing.*

14. (**D**) *Had* and a participle in the condition requires *would have* and a participle in the result. *Will* should be *would.*

15. (**D**) *Besides* is used before a noun or an adjective. It means *in addition to.* Choices (A) and (C) include the word *beside,* which means *near,* not *besides.* In Choice (B), the word *besides* is used after, not before, the noun.

16. (**D**) *No* is used before a noun phrase like *definite shape. Not* in Choice (A) should be used before a verb. *None* in Choice (B) and *nothing* in Choice (C) are pronouns that are used instead of the noun phrase.

17. (**D**) To *differ from* is a verb that expresses difference. Because Choices (A) and (C) are not verbs, the sentence would not have a main verb in it. Choice (B) is a verb, but the preposition *from* is missing. "A dolphin is different from a porpoise" would also be correct.

18. (**C**) *Do* is usually used before complements that describe work and chores. *Make* should be *do* before the complement *research.*

19. (**B**) *That most natural time units are not simple multiples of each other* functions as the noun phrase subject of the main verb *is.* Choice (A) is redundant because the pronoun *it* is used consecutively after the noun phrase subject. In Choice (C), the usual subject-verb-object order of English sentences is reversed. Choice (D) does not include a main verb.

20. (**C**) *Believe* should be *belief. Believe* is a verb. *Belief* is a noun.

21. (**C**) A negative phrase introduces inverted order. *Only after* requires an auxiliary verb, subject, and main verb. In Choices (A) and (D) the subject precedes the auxiliary. In Choice (B) there is no subject.

22. (**D**) A present tense verb is used after *when* to express future. *Will limit* should be *limit.*

23. (**C**) Because the verb *to fail* requires an infinitive in the complement, *recognizing* should be *to recognize.*

24. (**A**) An introductory phrase should immediately precede the subject noun that it modifies. It does not have a main verb. Choices (B) and (C) contain both subjects and verbs. Choice (D) does not modify the subject noun, *Carl Sandburg.*

25. (**C**) Ideas in a series should be expressed by parallel structures. *Writing* should be *to write* to provide for parallelism with the infinitives *to understand* and *to read.*

Section 3: Reading

1. (**D**) The other choices are secondary ideas that are used to develop the main idea, "Seismography." Choices (A), (B), and (C) are important to the discussion as they relate to the Richter scale.

2. (**B**) The Richter scale was developed "to measure the amplitude of the largest trace…." Choices (A) and (D) refer to the placement of the seismograph in order to record the amplitude. Choice (C) refers to the numerical reference that estimates the degree of damage.

3. (**C**) In the context of this passage, standard could best be replaced by conventional. Choices (A), (B), and (D) are not accepted definitions of the word.

4. (**A**) The "tables have been formulated to demonstrate the magnitude of any earthquake…." Choice (D) refers to the release of

energy, one of the factors that is considered in formulating the magnitude. Choices (B) and (C) are not mentioned in reference to the value of the tables.

5. **(B)** "…each number on the Richter scale represents an earthquake ten times as strong as one of the next lower magnitude." Choices (A), (C), and (D) are not correct because each magnitude is ten times stronger than the previous one.

6. "An earthquake that reads 4 to 5.5 would be expected to cause localized damage, and those [earthquakes] of magnitude 2 on the Richter scale may be felt." Other choices would change the meaning of the sentence.

7. **(A)** Choice (A) is a restatement of the sentence referred to in the passage. *Site* means location. Choices (B), (C), and (D) would change the meaning of the original sentence.

8. In the context of this passage, the word basically is closest in meaning to roughly. No other words or phrases in the **bold** text are close to the meaning of the word roughly.

9. **(B)** In the context of this passage, undetected is closest in meaning to with no notice. Choices (A), (C), and (D) are not accepted definitions of the word.

10. **(D)** Because the author states that "Earthquakes of Mercalli 2 or 3 are basically the same as those of Richter 3 or 4" and "measurements of 11 or 12 on the Mercalli scale can be roughly correlated with magnitudes of 8 or 9 on the Richter scale," it must be concluded that the two scales are different but can be compared. Choice (A) is not correct because two scales of measurement describe earthquakes in quantitative terms. Choice (B) is not correct because the Richter scale measures the amplitude of the largest trace, and the Mercalli scale measures the intensity of the shaking. Choice (C) is not correct because most earthquakes are so minor that they pass undetected.

11. **(C)** "…the Richter scale,…developed and introduced by American seismologist Charles R. Richter in 1935." Choices (A) and (B) are both mentioned in the reference to the Richter scale. Choice (D) refers to the purpose of the scale, which is "to measure the amplitude of the largest trace…." Choice (C) refers to the Mercalli scale, not to the Richter scale.

12. **(B)** The passage mainly discusses Charles Ives' life, including references to the details referred to in Choices (A), (C), and (D).

13. **(B)** "…the use of dissonance and special effects was just too different for the musical mainstream." Choice (A) is true but is not a reason that the public did not appreciate his music. Choice (D) is not correct because he wrote music. In Choice (C), although the performers felt his music was unplayable, there is no reference to the fact that they did not play it well.

14. In the context of this passage, the phrase clash of keys with conflicting rhythms is closest in meaning to the word dissonance. No other words or phrases in the **bold** text are close to the meaning of the word dissonance.

15. **(D)** "Even the few conductors and performers he tried to interest in his compositions felt that they [the compositions] were unplayable." Choices (A), (B), and (C) would change the meaning of the sentence.

16. **(C)** "…he became a successful insurance executive…." Choice (A) refers to his father's profession. Choice (B) refers to Horatio Parker's profession. Although it is true that Ives published his own music as in Choice (D), he did not make a living from it.

17. **(A)** In the context of this passage, became reconciled to is closest in meaning to accepted. Choices (B), (C), and (D) are not accepted definitions of the word.

18. **(A)** "…he published his work privately and distributed it free." Choice (C) refers to the fact that he occasionally hired musicians to play his works, but they were private, not public performances. Choices (B) and (D) are not mentioned and may not be concluded from information in the passage.

19. **(D)** Choice (A) refers to the fact that Ives "…quoted, combined, insinuated, and distorted familiar hymns, marches, and battle songs…." Choice (B) refers to the fact that Ives was "…experimenting with polytonality…and dissonance…." Choice (C) refers to the fact that "the few conductors and performers he tried to interest in his composi-

tions felt that they were unplayable." Choice (D) is not correct because Ives became "famous" near the end of his life and "received the Pulitzer Prize."

20. **(D)** "...the greatest music composed by an American." Choice (A) is not correct because the reviews were laudatory. Choices (B) and (C) refer to Ives' music prior to the *Concord Sonata* performance.

21. "John Kirkpatrick played *Concord Sonata* in Town Hall.... One reviewer proclaimed it [*Concord Sonata*] 'the greatest music composed by an American.' " Other choices would change the meaning of the sentence.

22. "Instead, he became a successful insurance executive, building his company into the largest agency in the country in only two decades. Even during such a busy time in his career, he still dedicated himself to composing music in the evenings, on weekends, and during vacations." The connection between the two sentences is the reference to "building his company into the largest agency" and "such a busy time in his career." Chronological order requires the second sentence to follow the first.

23. **(C)** Because the author states that bats are "not...dirty...groom themselves carefully...and help reforest barren land," it must be concluded that the author views bats as clean, helpful members of the animal world. Choice (A) is not correct because bats are not dirty and only rarely carry rabies. Choice (B) is not correct because bats are not the monsters that they are portrayed in vampire films. Choice (D) is not correct because bats consume pests, pollinate plants, and reforest land, all of which are important contributions to the animal world.

24. **(B)** "...the majority [of bats] eat fruit, insects, spiders or other small animals." Choice (A) is not correct because of the fact that only three species rely on blood meals. Choice (D) is not correct because bats eat small, not large, animals. Choice (C) is not mentioned and may not be concluded from information in the passage.

25. In the context of this passage, the word huge is closest in meaning to enormous. No other words or phrases in the **bold** text are close to the meaning of the word enormous.

26. **(C)** "They...help reforest...barren land by excreting millions of undigested seeds." Choices (A), (B), and (D) all refer to the activities of bats, but not to how they reforest the land.

27. **(D)** "Of the hundreds of species of bats, only three rely on blood meals." Choice (A) is not correct because bats pollinate many varieties of plant life. Choice (B) is not correct because bats assume specialized roles within their social system. Choice (C) is not correct because almost all bats use echolocation.

28. **(A)** In the context of this passage, emit is closest in meaning to send. Choices (B), (C), and (D) are not accepted definitions of the word.

29. **(A)** "As these signals bounce off objects in their path, an echo is detected by the bats' sensitive ears...[and] they...undertake corrective or evasive action." Choice (B) refers to one of the roles of bats within their social system, not to their navigational skills. Choice (C) is not correct because the number fifty refers to the number of high-pitched squeaks per minute, not to the number of times bats beat their wings. Choice (D) is true, but the specific noises they hear are the echoes referred to in Choice (A).

30. **(C)** "As these signals bounce off objects in their path, an echo is detected by the bats' sensitive ears that informs them [the bats] of the direction, distance, and nature of obstacles..." Other choices would change the meaning of the sentence.

31. "In fact, all species of bats can see, probably about as well as human beings." Quotation from sentence 6, paragraph 2.

32. "Within their social systems, bats assume specialized roles. Some [bats] may guard the entrance to their caves, others may scout for food, and still others may warn the colony of approaching danger." Other choices would change the meaning of the sentence.

33. "It is a little known fact that bats are highly social creatures. Aggregation during the day may vary from small groups consisting of a single male and a dozen or more females to huge colonies of many thousands or even millions of individuals, hanging upside down in caves or in hollow trees, buildings, and other protected shelters." The connec-

tion between the two sentences is the social nature of bats. The first sentence is a general statement followed by examples in the second sentence.

34. **(B)** The passage includes descriptions of various kinds of population centers. Choices (A) and (D) are two kinds of population centers described in the passage. Choice (C) refers to the source of the information about population centers, not to the topic of the passage.

35. **(B)** "…more Americans live in the suburbs of large metropolitan areas than in the cities themselves." Choice (A) is not correct because more Americans live in the suburbs. Choices (C) and (D) are not mentioned and may not be concluded from information in the passage.

36. In the context of this passage, the word live is closest in meaning to reside. No other words or phrases in the **bold** text are close to the meaning of the word reside.

37. **(A)** "The Bureau of the Census regards any area with more than 2500 people as an urban area…." Choice (B) refers to an MSA, not to an urban area. The number in Choice (C) refers to megapolises, not to urban areas. Choice (D) refers to the definition of a megapolis.

38. **(A)** "…the political boundaries are less significant than the social and economic relationships and the transportation and communication systems…." Because the political boundaries are less significant, it must be concluded that the factors in Choices (B), (C), and (D) are more significant.

39. **(C)** In the context of this passage, integrate is closest in meaning to unite. Choices (A), (B), and (D) are not accepted definitions of the word.

40. In the context of this passage, the word area is closest in meaning to locale. No other words or phrases in the **bold** text are close to the meaning of the word locale.

41. **(C)** "…an MSA is any area that contains a city and its [the city's] surrounding suburbs and has a total population of 50,000…." Other choices would change the meaning of the sentence.

42. "…the Bureau reports more than 280 MSAs, which together account for 75 percent of the US population." Quotation from sentence 1, paragraph 3. Paragraph 2 defines an MSA by the number of people living in it but does not contain any references to the total population living in all MSAs.

43. **(A)** In the context of this passage, the phrase beside each other is closest in meaning to the word adjacent. Choices (B), (C), and (D) describe megapolises, but they are not close in meaning to the word adjacent.

44. **(D)** "…the Bureau recognizes eighteen megapolises, that is, continuous adjacent metropolitan areas." Choices (A), (B), and (C) are not correct because a megapolis includes more than one adjacent city.

45. **(A)** "One of the most obvious megapolises [is]…the Eastern Corridor…. Another megapolis that is growing rapidly is the California coast…." Choice (B) refers to the population of all the MSAs, not to the population of the Eastern Corridor and the California coast. Choice (C) is true, but it is not the reason that the Eastern Corridor and the California coast are mentioned. Choice (D) is not mentioned and may not be concluded from information in the passage.

Writing Section

Question:

Read and think about the following statement: The college years are the best time in a person's life. Do you agree or disagree with the statement? Give reasons to support your opinion.

Outline
College years not best
• Stress
     Decisions—career, job, marriage
     Competition
• Dependence
     Family
     Debts
The best is yet to be

Map

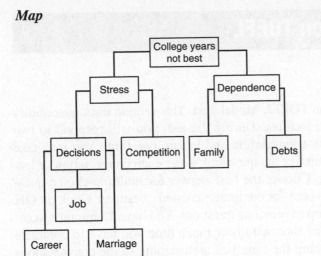

The best is yet to be

Example Essay

I disagree that the college years are the best time in a person's life. Admittedly, college often corresponds with a time when people are young, healthy, and physically strong, and those attributes are highly regarded in Western cultures; however, the college years must also be viewed as a period of high stress and a certain uncomfortable dependence.

Stress converges on college students from many directions. First, there is the pressure to choose a major field of study and, ultimately, to select a career, choices that will affect the rest of their lives. These choices often coincide with another life choice—the selection of a marriage partner. In combination, the stress associated with such important decisions can be very high. Second, there is the daily stress from competition in the classroom, exacerbated by staying up too late studying for tests, preparing papers, and reading assignments. It is well documented that college students tend to gain weight and suffer from many stress-related illnesses.

In addition to the stressful environment, most college students are not financially independent. Many rely on their families for funding, a circumstance that is often uncomfortable for young adults. Asking for money usually requires an explanation of why it is needed. In other words, financial dependence for college results in dependence in other areas of life at a time when young people are beginning to think for themselves and are old enough to be independent. Besides the embarrassment involved in negotiating for necessities, there is often a strict budget. For some students, there is also a debt to repay.

As a college student myself, I view this time of life as an opportunity to prepare for the next, and more important, stage of life, when I am independent and productive. I am eager to begin working and earning my own way. I look forward to the years after college with the hope that the best is yet to be.

Model Test 9—Next Generation TOEFL

Listening Section

This is the Listening Section of the Next Generation TOEFL Model Test. This section tests your ability to understand campus conversations and academic lectures. During the test, you will respond to two conversations and four lectures. You will hear each conversation and lecture one time. You may take notes while you listen. You may use your notes to answer the questions. After each conversation or lecture, you will have five or six questions to answer. Choose the best answer for multiple-choice questions. Follow the directions on the page or on the screen for computer-assisted questions. Click on **OK** and **Next** to go to the next question. You cannot return to previous questions. You have 25 minutes to answer all of the questions. A clock on the screen will show you how much time you have to complete your answers for the section. The clock does not count the time you are listening to the conversations and lectures.

Independent Listening 1: "Career Counseling"

Audio Conversation

Narrator: Now get ready to listen to a conversation and take notes about it.

Listen to a conversation on campus between two students. They are both in their last year of college.

Man: I wish I were as sure about my future as you seem to be. I . . . I really don't know what I want to do after I graduate.

Woman: Well, have you talked with a counselor over at the Office of Career Development?

Man: No. . . . I talked to my academic advisor, though.

Woman: That's good, but it's really better to see someone who specializes in helping people make career decisions. You see, an academic advisor is there to help you work out your academic program. You know, figure out what your major is going to be and which courses to take and all that. But a career counselor has a lot of experience and resources to help you decide what you want to do in the work world.

Man: Did you see a career counselor?

Woman: I sure did. Last semester. I was . . . well, I didn't even know what I would be good at, for a career, I mean. So I made an appointment at the Office of Career Development, and I talked with a counselor.

Man: Do you remember who it was?

Woman: Sure. It was Ruth Jackson.

Man: Oh, but since I'm interested in careers for math majors, probably I should see someone else.

Woman: Not really. Any of the counselors can help you. Look, first I took some aptitude tests and something called a . . . uh . . . I think it was called a *career inventory*. Anyway, I took several tests, and then the counselor gave me some ideas about different careers. I even went to some group sessions with some other students for a few weeks. Mrs. Jackson was the group leader, so um that's how I met her, and then I just sort of naturally started making my appointments with her when I needed some advice.

Man: It sounds like it took a lot of time. I'm so busy already.

Woman: Well, it did take time. Probably three hours for the tests, and I think I went to maybe four group sessions, and then I saw Ruth a couple of times. I guess about nine or ten hours probably. But it was worth it.

Man:	So, is that why you decided to go into library science? Because of the tests and every-thing?
Woman:	In part. But, mostly it was because of the internship. You see, I also got my internship through the Office of Career Development. And when I was working as an intern in the public library, it all sort of came together for me. I really liked what I was doing, and I realized that I didn't want the internship to end.
Man:	And you get paid for working there in the library too, don't you?
Woman:	I get paid, and I get credit toward my degree. But even better, I have a job offer from the library where I'm doing my internship.
Man:	Wow! Are you going to take it?
Woman:	I think so. I have to let them know next week. If I do take the job, I'll have to go to graduate school to get a degree in library science, but I can do that part-time while I'm working, and I had thought about graduate school anyway. So, I'm leaning toward taking the job.
Man:	That's great, Anne. I'm glad for you. So uh I guess I'd better make an appointment with Ruth Jackson. Maybe she can find me an internship.
Woman:	Maybe.

> Now get ready to answer the questions. You may use your notes.

Audio

1. What are the students mainly discussing?

Answer

(B) Because the woman shares her positive experience at the Office of Career Development and recommends career counseling to the man, it may be concluded that the main topic is the advantages of career counseling for the man. Choices (A) and (C) are mentioned in reference to the main topic, "the advantages of career counseling for the man." Choice (D) is not mentioned and may not be concluded from information in the conversation.

Audio

2. What is the man's problem?

Answer

(C) "I wish I were as sure about my future as you seem to be. I . . . I really don't know what I want to do after I graduate." Choice (A) is not correct because it is a concern that the man expresses when the woman suggests career counseling, but it is not the main problem that the man brings up at the beginning of the conversation. Choice (B) is not correct because the internship is an idea that occurs to him after he hears about the woman's internship. Choice (D) is not mentioned and may not be concluded from information in the conversation.

Audio

3. Why does the woman tell the man about her experience?

Answer

(A) Because the woman's experience at the Office of Career Development was positive, it may be concluded that she told the man about it in order to demonstrate the benefits. Choice (B) is not correct because the woman encourages the man to talk to a counselor about a career choice, not an internship. Choice (C) is not correct because the woman does not suggest that the man change his major to library science, the major field that she is pursuing. Choice (D) is not correct because the man has not made a career decision.

Audio

4. What is the woman's attitude toward her internship?

Answer

(C) "I really liked what I was doing, and I realized that I didn't want the internship to end." Because the woman doesn't want the internship to end, it must be a very positive experience. Choice (A) is not correct because she is thinking about going to graduate school part-time, but she does mention that she would rather go to graduate school than continue her internship. Choice (B) is not correct because the woman is already interning. Choice (D) is not correct because she does not want the internship to end.

Audio

5. What will the man probably do?

Answer

(B) "So uh I guess I'd better make an appointment with Ruth Jackson." Choice (A) is not correct because Ruth Jackson is a career counselor at the Office of Career Development, not an academic advisor. Choices (C) and (D) are not mentioned and may not be concluded from information in the conversation.

Independent Listening 2: "Admission"

Audio Conversation

Narrator: Now get ready to listen to a conversation and take notes about it.

Listen to a conversation on campus between a student and an admissions officer.

Student: Excuse me, but the secretary referred me to your office.

Assistant: Yes?

Student: I'm a new student . . . well, actually, I'm not enrolled yet, but I'm trying to get all my admissions applications turned in today.

Assistant: What's your name?

Student: Robert Franklin.

Assistant: Middle initial?

Student: T.

Assistant: Oh, I see. Wait a minute and we'll see what you have to do. . . . Well, according to the records here, you have your admissions form, a financial aid application, three letters of recommendation, transcripts from Regional College . . . so that's everything you need except a transcript from County Community College.

Student: That's what I thought. You see, I took a couple of courses there during the summer because it's close to my parent's house. Anyway, almost all of my first two years is from Regional College, and uh that's where I'm transferring from. In fact, the credit for the community college courses appears on the transcript from Regional College as transfer credit, but uh it doesn't show my final grades in the courses.

Assistant: Oh, and you haven't been able to register for your courses here at State University because the computer shows that you are missing some of your application materials. Is that it?

Student: Exactly. What I was wondering is whether you have like a policy for this kind of situation so I could go ahead and register for this first semester while we wait for the transcript to get here. It should be here now. I requested it the same time that I requested a transcript from Regional College, but they're just slow at County Community.

Assistant: That happens sometimes. . . . Do you have a copy of your transcript from County Community College?

Student: Yes, I do. It's right here. Of course, it isn't an official copy. It's stamped "unofficial copy."

Assistant: But I can use this one until the official copy gets here. Here's the best way to handle this. We can give you a provisional admission. That means that you're admitted contingent upon the receipt of your official transcript. That will allow you to register for your courses this semester. When County Community College sends us your official transcript, then I can change your status from provisional admission to regular admission.

Student: Oh, that's great!

Assistant: Is this the only copy you have of your transcript?

Student: No. I have another one.

Assistant: Good. Then I'll just keep this in your file.

Student: Okay.

Assistant: Now the only problem is you can't register for next semester without regular admission status, and you need the official transcript for me to do that, so you still need to keep after them to get everything sent to us as soon as possible.

Student: Right. Well, I'll do that. But at least I have some time to get it done. . . . Um . . . what do I need to do now . . . to get registered, I mean.

Assistant: Just wait here while I enter everything into the computer, and then you can take a copy of your provisional admission along with you to the Office for Transfer Students. They'll assign you an advisor and help you get registered later today.

> Now get ready to answer the questions. You may use your notes.

Audio

6. Why does the student go to the admissions office?

Answer

(D) ". . . I'm not enrolled yet, but I'm trying to get all my admissions applications turned in today." Choice (A) is not correct because his financial aid form is already on file. Choice (B) is not correct because he has requested an official transcript from another college to include in his admissions applications. Choice (C) is not correct because he is transferring from another college, not to another college.

Audio

7. What is missing from the student's file?

Answer

(B) ". . so that's everything you need except a transcript from County Community College." Choice (A) is not correct because the woman confirms that the financial aid application is already on file. Choice (C) is not correct because the grades from Regional College would be on the transcript that is in the man's file. Choice (D) is not correct because the admissions form is the official copy of the application.

Audio

8. Listen again to part of the conversation. Then answer the question.

"Oh, and you haven't been able to register for your courses here at State University because the computer shows that you are missing some of your application materials. Is that it?"

Why does the woman say, "Is that it?"

Answer

(B) The woman paraphrases the problem and then asks for confirmation that she has understood. *Is that it* means "Is that your problem?" Choice (A) is not correct because the woman has already paraphrased the situation. Choice (C) is not correct because the woman's tone is helpful, not impatient. Choice (D) is not correct because the man has explained a problem but he has not asked a question yet.

Audio

9. What does the woman suggest that the man do?

Answer

(D) ". . . you still need to keep after them to get everything [the official transcript from County Community College] sent to us as soon as possible." Choice (A) is not correct because he already has an unofficial copy of his transcripts. Choice (B) is not correct because, according to their records, the admission form is already on file. Choice (C) is not correct because he must have his official transcript before he can change his provisional status to regular status next semester and because he will register this semester with provisional status.

Audio

10. What will the student most probably do now?

Answer

(B) "...you can take a copy of your provisional admission along with you to the Office for Transfer Students. They'll assign you an advisor and help you get registered. . . . " Choice (A) is not correct because the man will see an advisor, not the woman, later today. Choice (C) is not correct because it refers to what the woman, not the man, will do. Choice (D) is not correct because the woman is assigning the provisional status to the man without her superior's approval.

Independent Listening 3: "Groups"

Audio Lecture

Narrator: Now get ready to listen to a lecture and take notes about it.
              Listen to part of a lecture in a sociology class.

Professor:

Social influence involves the changes in behavior influenced by the actions of other people. Social influence can come about for a variety of reasons, on a continuum from mere suggestion to, in the more severe form, well, to torture. How does social influence work? Well, first we must become aware of a difference between ourselves and the values or behaviors of other people. There are a great many studies of social influence that demonstrate how the presence of others can cause us to change our attitudes or actions. Studies show that people eat more when dining with others than, and I'm talking about dining out here, so they eat more in the company of others than they do when they're alone. They also run faster when others are running with them. There's even some interesting research on social influence among animals with similar results to . . . to those of human studies.

Probably one of the most interesting aspects of social influence is the pressure for conformity. Conformity is a process by which an individual's opinion or behavior moves toward the norms of the group. In a classic study by Solomon Asch, seven people were shown cards with three lines drawn on them. Here's an example:

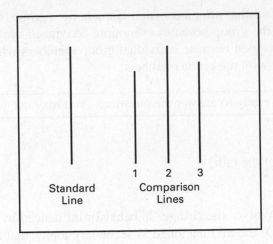

So, they were shown the lines, and then they were asked to select the line among the three that matched the uh . . . the uh . . . standard line. Here's the standard. So there's no question as to the comparison. This has to be easy, right? Wrong. You see, Asch enlisted the cooperation of six of the seven participants in the experiment. On the first card, the six respond correctly—they . . . they identify the lines of the same length—so the seventh person, who is the only real subject in the experiment, well, the seventh person answers correctly, in agreement with the others. But on the next card, four of the cooperating participants choose an incorrect answer, but they're in agreement, so the problem for the subject is whether to conform to the opinion of the peer group, even though the answer um . . . is in conflict with the answer that the subject knows to be correct.

So what do you think happened? Well, subjects who were tested alone made errors in answers fewer than 1 percent of the time. This was the control group. But of those tested in groups of seven, let's see um, 75 percent yielded at least once to conform to a group answer that was clearly incorrect, and on average, subjects conformed to the group in about 37 percent of the critical trials. This means that they were bringing their behavior into agreement with group norms in . . . in spite of what they were seeing.

Later Asch manipulated the size of the control group . . . I'm sorry, the experimental group . . . to see whether group size would affect pressure, and it did, but probably less than you might expect. Um . . . groups of four demonstrated about the same results as groups of eight. Interestingly enough, a unanimous agreement by the group was more important than the number. In other words, a unanimous opinion by three exerted more pressure to conform than a majority of seven with a dissenting opinion in a group of eight.

Similar experiments have been performed in various countries, among diverse cultural groups, with um comparable results. Of course, people in cultures that emphasize group cooperation tended to be more willing to conform, but remember that many of the original studies were done in the United States where there's a high value placed on individualism. In an interesting variation on the study, Abrams found that conformity is especially strong when the group is selected from among those people that the subject clearly identifies with, either because, um…they have characteristics in common or . . . or they know each other and interact in a peer group outside of the experimental situation.

So what does all of this mean in the real world? Well, since group members can influence one another to conform to the opinion of the group, the group . . . decisions of a group uh may be called into question. What about decisions by political committees or parliaments? What about juries who are charged with convicting or acquitting an accused defendant? Clearly, social influence will play a part in these critical group decisions.

Also interesting is the fact that after a decision is made by a group, there's a tendency to solidify, and by that I mean that the group becomes even more convinced of the validity of the group opinion. Um . . . this may happen because individual group members who strongly support the group tend to be more popular with the group members.

Now get ready to answer the questions. You may use your notes.

Audio

11. What is the main topic of the talk?

Answer

(C) "Social influence involves the changes in behavior influenced by the actions of other people." Choices (A), (B), and (D) are all mentioned as secondary topics that are used to develop the main topic of the lecture, "the influence of groups on individual behavior."

Audio

12. According to the professor, what two results were reported in the Asch and Abrams studies?

Answer

(B) (C) ". . . subjects conformed to the group in about 37 percent of the critical trials. . . . Abrams found that conformity is especially strong when the group is selected from among those people . . . [who] interact in a peer group outside of the experimental situation." Choice (A) is not correct because a larger group of eight demonstrated about the same results as a smaller group of four. Choice (D) is not correct because a unanimous opinion by three exerted more pressure to conform than a majority of seven with a dissenting opinion in a group of eight.

Audio

13. Listen again to part of the lecture. Then answer the question.

"Later Asch manipulated the size of the control group . . . I'm sorry . . . the experimental group . . . to see whether group size would affect pressure, and it did, but probably less than you might expect."

Why does the professor say this: "I'm sorry . . . the experimental group . . ."

Answer

(C) Professors occasionally misspeak and must correct themselves. The professor is talking about the experimental group, and incorrectly refers to the control group. Choice (D) is not correct because she is providing the facts in logical sequence. She is not returning to a previous point in the lecture to add important facts. Choices (A) and (B) are not mentioned and may not be concluded from information in the lecture.

Audio

14. What generally happens after a group makes a decision?

Answer

(C) ". . . after a decision is made by a group, there's a tendency to solidify . . . the group becomes even more convinced of the validity of the group opinion." Choice (D) refers to the fact that those who support the group most strongly tend to be more popular with the group, but competition for leadership is not mentioned and may not be concluded from information in the lecture. Choices (A) and (B) are not mentioned and may not be concluded from information in the lecture.

Audio

15. Based on information in the lecture, indicate whether the statements describe the Asch study. For each sentence, click in the YES or NO column.

Answer

(A) is YES. ". . . the seventh person . . . is the only real subject in the experiment. . . . " **(B)** is NO. ". . . there's no question as to the comparison." **(C)** is YES. " . . . Asch enlisted the cooperation of six of the seven participants in the experiment."

Independent Listening 4: "Photography"

Audio Lecture

Narrator: Now get ready to listen to a lecture and take notes about it.
            Listen to part of a lecture in an art history class.

Professor:

We know that the Chinese had been aware of basic photographic principles as early as the fifth century B.C., and Leonardo da Vinci had experimented with a dark room in the 1500s, but it was a number of discoveries in chemistry during the eighteenth century that uh . . . accelerated the development of modern photography. The discovery that silver salts were light sensitive led to . . . experimentation with images of light on a . . . a surface that had been coated with silver. Often glass was used in the early images. But the problem was that these images were ephemeral—fading after only a short time. Some of the chemists who worked with them called them fairy pictures, and considered them uh . . . that they were only momentary creations uh . . . that they would disappear.

Okay. How to fix the image permanently was one of the most important uh . . . challenges . . . of the early photographer chemists. In France, in about 1820, Nicephore Niepce discovered a method for fixing the image after a long exposure time, oh, probably eight hours. So, although his work was considered interesting, it was uh . . . uh . . . largely dismissed for . . . as impractical. Nevertheless, one of his associates, Louis Daguerre, managed to find a way to uh . . . reduce . . . the exposure time to less than twenty minutes. So the story goes, in 1835, Daguerre was experimenting with some exposed plates, and he put a couple of them into his chemical cupboard, so a few days later, he opened the cupboard, and uh . . . to his surprise, the latent images on the plates had developed. At first, he couldn't figure out why, but eventually, he concluded that this must have occurred as a result of mercury vapor . . . from a broken thermometer that was also in the . . . uh . . . enclosed in the cupboard. Supposedly, from this fortunate accident, he was able to invent a process for developing latent images on . . . on exposed plates.

The process itself was somewhat complicated. First, he exposed copper plates to iodine which released fumes of uh . . . of light-sensitive silver iodide. These copper plates were used to capture the image, and by the way, they had to be used almost immediately after their exposure to the iodine. So, the image on the plate was then exposed to light for ten to twenty minutes. The plate was developed over mercury heated to about 75 degrees centigrade, which . . . that caused the mercury to amalgamate with the silver. Now here's the ingenious part—he then fixed the image in a warm solution of common salt, but later he began using sodium sulphite. Anyway, after he rinsed the plate in hot distilled water, a white image was left permanently on the plate. And the quality was really quite amazing.

But, um . . . the process had its limitations. First, the images couldn't be reproduced, so each one was a unique piece, and that uh greatly increased the cost of photography. Second, the image was reversed, so the subjects would actually see themselves as though they were looking in a mirror, although, uh . . . in the case of portraits, the fact that people were accustomed to seeing themselves in a mirror made this less . . . this problem less urgent than some of the others. Nevertheless, some photographers did point their cameras at a mirrored reflection of the image that they wanted to capture so that the reflection would be reversed, and a true image could be produced. Okay. Third, the chemicals and the fumes that they released were highly toxic, so photography was a very dangerous occupation. Fourth, the surface of the image was extremely fragile and…had to be protected, often under glass, so they didn't disintegrate from being . . . from handling. The beautiful cases that were made to hold the early images became popular not only for aesthetic purposes but uh . . . but also for very practical reasons. And finally, although the exposure time had been radically reduced, it was still . . . inconveniently long . . . at twenty minutes, especially for portraits, since people would have to sit still in the sun for that length of time. Elaborate headrests were constructed to keep the subjects from moving so that the image wouldn't be ruined, and uh . . . many people simply didn't want to endure the discomfort.

But, by the mid 1800s, improvements in chemistry and optics had resolved most of these issues. Bromide as well as iodine sensitized the plates, and some photographers were even using chlorine in an effort to decrease exposure time. The . . . the portrait lens was also improved by reducing the size of the opening, and limiting the amount of light that could enter, so the exposure time was about twenty seconds instead of twenty minutes. And negative film had been introduced in France, sorry, in England, and negatives permitted the production of multiple copies from a single image. So, photography was on its way to becoming a popular profession and pastime.

> Now get ready to answer the questions. You may use your notes.

Audio

16. What is the main topic of this lecture?

Answer

(D) The lecture begins with historical background information and then focuses on the history of early photography in the 1800s when it was evolving into modern photography. Choices (A), (B), and (C) are all mentioned as secondary topics that are used to develop the main topic of the lecture, "the history of early photography."

Audio

17. According to the professor, what two limitations were noted in Daguerre's process for developing and fixing latent images?

Answer

(B) (C) "But . . . the process had its limitations. First, the images couldn't be reproduced, so each one was a unique piece. . . . Fourth, the surfaces of the image were extremely fragile and . . . had to be protected . . . so they didn't disintegrate . . . from handling." Choice (A) is not correct because Daguerre had resolved the problem of fixing the image in his process. Choice (D) is not correct because Daguerre's process had reduced the exposure time to twenty minutes.

Audio

18. Listen again to part of the lecture. Then answer the question.

"At first, he couldn't figure out why, . . . but eventually, he concluded that this must have occurred as a result of mercury vapor from a broken thermometer that was also in the uh . . . enclosed in the cupboard. Supposedly, from this fortunate accident, he was able to invent a process for developing latent images on . . . on exposed plates."

Why does the professor say this:
"Supposedly, from this fortunate accident, he was able to invent a process for developing latent images on . . . on exposed plates."

Answer

(C) The word *supposedly* implies that the speaker is not sure about the information. Choice (A) is not correct because she would not use such a neutral tone if she were trying to draw students into the story. Choice (D) is not correct because she does not invite them to use their imaginations while she is recounting the story. Choice (B) is not correct because the origin of the story is not mentioned.

Audio

19. What substance was first used to fix the images?

Answer

(B) "Now here's the ingenious part—he then fixed the image in a warm solution of common salt. . . . " Choice (A) is not correct because copper was the substance used for sensitizing the plates, not for fixing the images. Choice (C) is not correct because mercury vapor was the substance used to develop the plates, not to fix the images. Choice (D) is not correct because hot water was the substance used to rinse the plates after the images were fixed.

Audio

20. What can we assume about photographers in the 1800s?

Answer

(D) Because "the chemicals and the fumes that they released were highly toxic" and photography was "a very dangerous occupation," it may be concluded that some photographers must have experienced health problems as a result of their laboratory work. Choice (B) is not correct because many people didn't want to endure the discomfort associated with sitting still for a long time in order to have a portrait done. Choices (A) and (C) are not mentioned and may not be concluded from information in the lecture.

Independent Listening 5: "Authority"

Audio Lecture

Narrator: Now get ready to listen to a lecture and take notes about it.
             Listen to part of a lecture in an anthropology class.

Professor:
The concepts of power and authority are related, but they're not the same. Power is the ability to exercise influence . . . and control over others. And this can be observed on every level of society, from, well . . . the relationships within a family to the relationships among nations. Power is usually structured by customs and . . . and social institutions or laws and tends to be exerted by persuasive arguments or coercion or . . . or even brute force. In general, groups with the greatest uh . . . resources tend to have the advantage in power struggles. So, is power always legitimate? Is it viewed by members of society as justified? Well, no. Power can be realized by individuals or groups . . . even when it involves the resistance of others if . . . as long as . . . as long as they're in a position to impose their will. But what about power that is accepted by members of society as right and just, that is, legitimate power? Now we're talking about authority. And that is what I want to focus on today.

Okay. When individuals or institutions possess authority, they have um . . . a recognized and established right . . . to determine policies, with the acceptance of those over . . . over . . . whom they exercise control. Max Weber, the German classical sociologist, proposed three types of authority in society: traditional, charismatic, and rational or legal authority. In all three types, he uh . . . he acknowledged the right of those in positions of power to lead . . . with the consent of the governed. So, how did Weber differentiate among the three types of authority? Well, he divided them according to how the right to lead and the duty to follow are uh interpreted. In traditional authority, power resides in customs and conventions that provide certain people or groups with legitimate power in their societies. Often their origin is found in sacred traditions. The example that most often comes to mind is a monarchy in which kings or queens rule . . . uh . . . by birthright, not because of any particular . . . quality of leadership or political election, just because they have a claim to authority, based on traditional acceptance of their position, and in some cases, their uh their uh . . . unique relationship with and uh responsibility in religious practices. The royal families in Europe or the emperors in Asia are . . . come to mind as examples of traditional authority.

Okay. This contrasts sharply with charismatic authority, which is . . . uh . . . derived . . . because of personal attributes that inspire admiration, loyalty, and . . . and even devotion. Leaders who exercise this type of authority may be the founders of religious movements or political parties, but it's not their traditional right to lead. What's important here is that their followers are mobilized more by . . . by the force of the leader's personality than by the tradition or the law. So when we think of "charismatic" leaders in the United States, perhaps John Kennedy would be an example because he was able to project a youthful and energetic image that people were proud to identify with, or, if you prefer Republicans, you may argue that Ronald Reagan was able to exercise authority by virtue of his charismatic appeal. In any case, going back to Weber, to qualify for charismatic authority, a leader must be able to enlist others in the service of a . . . a cause that transforms the social structure in some way.

Which leaves us with legal rational authority, or power that is legitimized by rules, uh laws, and procedures. In such a system, leaders gain authority not by traditional birthrights or by charismatic appeal but . . . but rather because they're elected or appointed in accordance with the law, and power is delegated to layers of officials who owe their allegiance to the uh . . . principles that are agreed upon rationally, and because they accept the ideal that the law is supreme. In a legal rational society, people accept the legitimacy of authority as a government of laws, not of leaders. So, an example of this type of authority might be a president, like Richard Nixon, who was threatened with uh impeachment because he was perceived as not governing within the law.

Some sociologists have postulated that the three types of authority represent stages of evolution in society. That preindustrial societies tend to respect traditional authority, but um . . . as societies move into an industrial age, the importance of tradition . . . wanes . . . in favor of charismatic authority, with a natural rise of charismatic leaders. Then, as . . . as the modern era evolves, the rational legal authority, embodied by rules and regulations, replaces the loyalty to leaders in favor of . . . a respect for law. Of course, other sociologists argue that in practice, authority may be represented by a combination of several of these ideal types at any one time.

> Now get ready to answer the questions. You may use your notes.

Audio

21. What is the main purpose of this lecture?

Answer

(A) "Max Weber, the German classical sociologist, proposed three types of authority in society: traditional, charismatic, and rational or legal authority." Choice (B) refers to the introduction, not to the main purpose of the lecture. Choices (C) and (D) are not mentioned and may not be concluded from information in the lecture.

Audio

22. According to the professor, what two factors are associated with charismatic authority?

Answer

(B) (C) ". . . charismatic authority, which is . . . derived . . . because of personal attributes that inspire admiration . . . . [A] leader must be able to enlist others in the service of a . . . cause that transforms the social structure in some way." Choice (A) refers to traditional authority, not to charismatic authority. Choice (D) refers to rational or legal authority, not to charismatic authority.

Audio

23. Listen again to part of the lecture. Then answer the question.

"But what about power that is accepted by members of society as right and just, that is, legitimate power? Now we're talking about authority. And that is what I want to focus on today."

Why does the professor say this:
"But what about power that is accepted by members of society as right and just, that is, legitimate power?"

Answer

(B) Professors often ask questions to introduce a topic. After the question, he continues, "Now we're talking about authority. And that is what I want to focus on today." Choice (A) is not correct because the professor doesn't pause long enough to invite answers. Choice (C) is not correct because he doesn't express an opinion after the question. Choice (D) is not correct because the previous point is about power, not authority.

Audio

24. In an evolutionary model, how is rational legal authority viewed?

Answer

(A) "Then, as . . . the modern era evolves, the rational legal authority, embodied by rules and regulations, replaces the loyalty to leaders in favor of . . . a respect for the law." Choice (B) refers to charismatic authority, not to rational legal authority. Choice (C) refers to the preindustrial age. Choice (D) is not correct because rational legal authority is one of the three ideal types, not a replacement for the three.

Audio

25. What does the professor imply about the three types of authority?

Answer

(B) Because the professor presents both an evolutionary model and an argument for an inclusive model that combines several types of authority, it must be concluded that sociologists do not agree. Choice (A) is not correct because the professor defines authority as "legitimate power." Choice (C) is not correct because at least some sociologists believe that societies evolve from one type of authority structure to another. Choice (D) is not mentioned and may not be concluded from information in the lecture.

Independent Listening 6: "Mineral Exploitation"

Audio Lecture

Narrator: Now get ready to listen to a lecture and take notes about it.
              Listen to part of a discussion in an environmental science class.

Professor: The exploitation of minerals involves five steps. First, you have to explore and locate the mineral deposits, then you set up a mining operation, next, you must refine the raw minerals and transport the refined minerals to the manufacturer.

Student 1:   Excuse me. Sorry. I only have four steps. Could you . . . ?

Professor: Sure. That's exploration, mining, refining, transportation, and manufacturing.

Student 1:   Thanks.

Professor: So, each of these activities involves costs, there are costs associated with them, and the costs can be economic, but not necessarily so. Mineral exploitation also has environmental costs associated with it. For example, the exploration stage will clearly have a high economic cost because of . . . of personnel and technology, but the environmental cost will probably be quite low. Why would that be, do you think?

Student 2:   Because you aren't actually disturbing the environment. You're just looking, I mean, after you find a mineral deposit, you don't do anything about it at that stage.

Professor: Right. So the environmental costs would be low. But what happens when you use up all the resources that are easy to find? Then what?

Student 2:   Then the costs go up for exploration.

Professor: Which costs?

Student 2:   Well, probably both of them, but I can see where the economic costs would increase.

Professor: Okay. Let's say, for example, that some areas such as national parks or historic reserves have been . . . off-limits to exploration. What will happen when we use up the minerals outside of these areas? Remember now that these are uh . . . nonrenewable resources that we're looking for.

Student 1:   Then there will be a lot of pressure . . . you know . . . to open up these areas to exploration and exploitation.

Professor: Probably so. And that means that there could be a high environmental cost. Any other options?

Student 1:   Find an alternative.

Professor: Yes. You're on the right track.

Student 1:   Okay. Find an alternative, I mean a substitute, something that will substitute for the mineral. Maybe something man-made?

Professor: Good. That will involve a different kind of exploration, again with economic costs. I'm talking about basic research here to find synthetics. But uh...let's go on to the other steps, and we'll see if we can pull this all together. How about mining? Now, we're looking at high environmental costs because of the destruction of the landscape and . . .

and the accumulation . . . of waste products that have to be dealt with. Air and water pollution is almost always a problem. . . . Any ideas on refining?

Student 2: Wouldn't it be the same as mining? I mean, you would have high costs because of labor and equipment, and there would be problems of waste and pollution, like you said.

Professor: True. True. And in refining, well that often involves the separation of a small amount of a valuable mineral from a large amount of surrounding rock. So that means that . . . that uh . . . refining also carries the additional cost of cleanup. And don't forget that it's often difficult to get vegetation to grow on piles of waste. In fact, some of it, the waste piles I mean, they can even be dangerous to living creatures, including people. Not to mention the appearance of the area. So the environmental costs can be extremely high. Isn't it sad and ironic that so much of the mining and refining must take place in areas of great natural beauty?

Student 1: So you're saying that both mining and refining have heavy costs . . . heavy economic and environmental costs.

Professor: Right. And in both mining and refining, you would need transportation to support the movement of supplies, equipment, and personnel. But, after the minerals are mined and refined, then transportation becomes even more essential.

Student 2: And I was just thinking that in addition to the economic costs of the transportation for trucks and fuel and labor and everything, there could be, there might be some construction too, if there aren't any roads in and out of the area.

Professor: And that would mean . . .

Student 2: That would mean that the landscape and even the ecosystem for the plants and animal life could be altered, so . . . so that's an environmental cost.

Professor: It is indeed. Good point. That leaves us with manufacturing. After we find it, mine it, refine it, and transport it, we still have to manufacture it. What are the costs associated with that? Well, construction again, for factories, then there would be energy costs, technology, and labor.

Student 1: So all that's economic. No environmental costs in manufacturing then.

Professor: Well, yes there are actually. Pollution is often a costly problem for uh . . . manufacturing plants.

Student 1: Oh right. I was thinking of the natural landscape, and the manufacturing is often positioned near cities to take advantage of the labor pool. But, um . . . cities have the environmental problems associated with pollution. So, every step has both economic and environmental costs then.

Professor: Right.

Now get ready to answer the questions. You may use your notes.

Audio

26. What is the main topic of this lecture?

Answer

(D) "So, each of these activities involves costs . . . [that] can be economic, but . . . also environmental. . . ." Choices (A), (B), and (C) are all mentioned as secondary topics that are used to develop the main topic of the lecture, "the economic and environmental costs of mineral exploitation."

Audio

27. According to the professor, what are two problems that can be anticipated when roads are cut into an area for mining?

Answer

(B) (D) ". . . the landscape and even the ecosystem for the plants and animal life could be altered, . . . so that's an environmental cost." Choice (C) refers to the waste piles that are created in mining, but they are not mentioned in reference to the roadbeds. Choice (A) is not mentioned and may not be concluded from information in the lecture.

Audio

28. Listen again to part of the lecture. Then answer the question.

"And I was just thinking that in addition to the economic costs of the transportation for trucks and fuel and labor and everything, there could be, there might be some construction too, if there aren't any roads in and out of the area." "And that would mean. . . ."

Why does the professor say this, "And that would mean…"

Answer

(A) Professors often begin a sentence and then wait for the student to complete it. In this case, the professor is encouraging the student to continue by adding information to the answer that she gave initially. Choice (B) is not correct because the professor does not tell the student that he doesn't understand and does not ask the student to explain the answer that she gave initially. Choice (C) is not correct because the professor continues to direct his comments to the same student who has been speaking, not to another student. Choice (D) is not correct because the professor does not offer praise.

Audio

29. What option is proposed as an alternative when all of the mineral resources in easily accessible locations have been depleted?

Answer

(C) "Find an alternative. . . . Maybe something man-made . . . . I'm talking about basic research here to find synthetics." Choice (A) is not correct because minerals are *nonrenewable* resources, but converting to nonrenewable resources would imply that minerals are renewable. Choices (B) and (D) are not mentioned and may not be concluded from information in the lecture.

Audio

30. What does the professor imply about the environmental costs of mineral exploitation?

Answer

(B) Because the professor comments that it is "sad and ironic that so much of the mining and refining must take place in areas of great natural beauty," it may be concluded that he regrets that the environment is damaged during mineral exploitation. Choice (A) is not correct because the professor does not compare the costs. Choice (C) is not correct because the professor agrees with a student's view regarding the problems of pollution in cities, but the professor does not say that he opposes mineral exploitation near urban areas. Choice (D) is not correct because the professor poses the question but does not give his opinion about exploiting minerals in national parks and historic reserves.

Speaking Section

This is the Speaking Section of the Next Generation TOEFL Model Test. This section tests your ability to communicate in English in an academic context. During the test, you will respond to six speaking questions. You may take notes as you listen. You may use your notes to answer the questions. The reading passages and the questions are printed in the book, but most of the directions will be spoken. Your speaking will be evaluated on both the fluency of the language and the accuracy of the content. A clock on the screen will show you how much time you have to prepare your answer and how much time you have to record it.

Independent Speaking Question 1: "A Book"

Narrator 2: Number 1. Listen for a question about a familiar topic. After you hear the question, you have 15 seconds to prepare and 45 seconds to record your answer.

Narrator 1: Think about a book that you have enjoyed reading. Why did you like it? What was especially interesting about the book? Use specific details and examples to support your response.

Narrator 2: Please prepare your answer after the beep.

Beep

[Preparation time: 15 seconds]

Narrator 2: Please begin speaking after the beep.

Beep

[Recording time: 45 seconds]

Beep

Narrator 1: Now listen to an example answer.

Example Answer
The Power of Positive Thinking by Dr. Norman Vincent Peale is one of my favorite books. Um . . . according to Dr. Peale, a positive outlook is essential to a happy, successful life. But what is especially interesting about the book are the practical strategies that help maintain an optimistic approach to living, even when uh things don't happen to be going well. He recommends reflection on all the aspects of life that are positive, and cultivating an "attitude of gratitude." He also recommends positive statements and mental pictures to encourage and motivate and . . . and to replace negative thoughts that come to mind.

Beep

Independent Speaking Question 2: "Foreign Travel"

Narrator 2: Number 2. Listen for a question that asks your opinion about a familiar topic. After you hear the question, you have 15 seconds to prepare and 45 seconds to record your answer.

Narrator 1: Some people think that it is better to travel as part of a tour group when they are visiting a foreign country. Other people prefer to make their own travel plans so that they can travel independently. Which approach do you think is better and why? Use specific reasons and examples to support your opinion.

Narrator 2: Please prepare your answer after the beep.

Beep

[Preparation time: 15 seconds]

Narrator 2: Please begin speaking after the beep.

Beep

[Recording time: 45 seconds]

Beep

Narrator 1: Now listen to an example answer.

Example Answer
I've taken several tours, but I prefer to make my own travel plans because . . . I don't want to spend a lot of time at tourist hotels. In my experience, large hotels insulate travelers from the foreign culture. Instead of eating typical food, they prepare special meals for the tourists. And when I'm with groups of tourists, it's less likely that local people will approach me to talk. On my own, I've had some wonderful conversations with locals. Another reason that I like to travel independently is because I'm kind of a . . . a spontaneous person, so I like to take advantage of opportunities that present themselves on the trip.

Beep

Integrated Speaking Question 3: "Old Main"

Narrator 2: Number 3. Read a short passage and listen to a talk on the same topic. Then listen for a question about them. After you hear the question, you have 30 seconds to prepare and 60 seconds to record your answer.

Narrator 1: A public meeting is planned to discuss alternatives for renovating the original building on campus. Read the notice from the college newspaper printed on page 458. You have 45 seconds to complete it. Please begin reading now.

[Reading time: 45 seconds]

Narrator 1: Now listen to a faculty member who is speaking at the meeting. She is expressing her opinion about the proposals.

Woman professor: Although there may be some practical reasons for tearing down the structure surrounding the clock tower, I urge the committee to consider the historical importance of Old Main and opt for renovation of the original structure. I think we all agree that the brick structure is quite beautiful and basically sound. Only a few minor repairs would be necessary to preserve it. The cost of new electrical and plumbing systems for the old structure would be less than the cost of a new building with the same systems. And if a new building were to be erected, the clock tower would seem out of place somehow.

Narrator 1: The professor expresses her opinion of the plan for the renovation of Old Main. Report her opinion and explain the reasons that she gives for having that opinion.

Narrator 2: Please prepare your answer after the beep.

Beep

[Preparation time: 30 seconds]

Narrator 2: Please begin speaking after the beep.

Beep

[Recording time: 60 seconds]

Beep

Narrator 1: Now listen to an example answer.

Example Answer

The professor doesn't support the plan to demolish the main structure of Old Main and build a new structure around the original clock tower. She presents three arguments. Um . . . first, she says that the brick structure now standing is strong and it would require only minor repairs. And second, she points out that the electrical and plumbing problems in the old building could be repaired for less than the . . . the expenditure for a new building. Finally, she opposes the construction of a new building around the original clock tower because she thinks that the tower would be . . . would look odd in the new setting. She would probably support the alternative plan, which is um . . . to repair the original building.

Beep

Integrated Speaking Question 4: "Communication with Primates"

Narrator 2: Number 4. Read a short passage and then listen to a lecture on the same topic. Then listen for a question about them. After you hear the question, you have 30 seconds to prepare and 60 seconds to record your answer.

Narrator 1: Now read the passage about communication with primates printed on page 458. You have 45 seconds to complete it. Please begin reading now.

[Reading time: 45 seconds]

Narrator 1: Now listen to part of a lecture in a zoology class. The professor is talking about a primate experiment.

Professor: Let me tell you about an experiment that didn't turn out quite like the researcher had expected. Dr. Sue Savage-Rumbaugh had been trying to train a chimpanzee to use a keyboard adapted with symbols. But no luck. What is interesting about the experiment is that the chimpanzee's adopted son Kanzi, also a bonobo Chimpanzee, well, Kanzi had been observing the lessons and had acquired a rather impressive vocabulary. After that, Kanzi was not given structured training, but he was taught language while walking through the forest or in other informal settings with his trainers. By six years of age, Kanzi had acquired a vocabulary of more than 200 words and was able to form sentences by combining words with gestures or with other words. So, the question is this: should we proceed by trying to teach language to primates in a classroom environment, or should we simply live with them and interact informally like we do with beginning learners of language in our own species? I tend to side with those who elect to support language acquisition in natural settings.

Narrator 1: Explain the importance of the Kanzi experiment in the context of research on primate communication.

Narrator 2: Please prepare your answer after the beep.

Beep

[Preparation time: 30 seconds]

Narrator 2: Please begin speaking after the beep.

Beep

[Recording time: 60 seconds]

Beep

Narrator 1: Now listen to an example answer.

Example Answer

The experiment with Kanzi is important because it supports the theory that language should be acquired in natural settings instead of in a formal classroom. Previous research to teach primates to communicate included direct instruction in American Sign Language and uh also plastic shapes that could be arranged on a magnetic board. Earlier research . . . I think it was with Kanzi's mother . . . it replicated this formal approach. But when Kanzi learned vocabulary by observing the lessons, the direction of the experiment changed. In informal settings with trainers, Kanzi acquired a vocabulary of about 200 words, and began to create sentences with words and gestures to . . . to communicate with human uh companions. Children of our own species learn by informal interaction with adults. The Kanzi experiment suggests that this may be a better way to teach language to primates.

Beep

Integrated Speaking Question 5: "Headaches"

Narrator 2: Number 5. Listen to a short conversation. Then listen for a question about it. After you hear the question, you have 20 seconds to prepare and 60 seconds to record your answer.

Narrator 1: Now listen to a conversation between a student and her friend.

Friend: Are you still having headaches?

Student: Yeah. I'm taking Tylenol every day.

Friend: That doesn't sound good. Why don't you go over to the Health Center?

Student: I keep thinking it'll go away. Probably just a tension headache. I feel really stressed out this semester.

Friend: Well, you're probably right, but it still wouldn't hurt to get a checkup. Maybe the doctor will refer you for an eye exam. I used to get headaches from eyestrain, especially when I was using my computer a lot. And guess what? I needed to get my glasses changed.

Student: No kidding? I hadn't thought about that, but I do notice that it gets worse after I've been using my computer.

Friend: Well, then. That's important to mention when you see the doctor at the Health Center.

Student: You think I should still go to the Health Center? I mean, if it's my eyes, I . . . I could just make an appointment with the eye doctor.

Friend: You could, but you really aren't sure what it is. I'd go to the doctor at the Health Center, and I'd ask for a referral to the eye doctor. Besides, if you get referred, I think your student health insurance will pay most of the cost of new glasses.

Narrator 1: Describe the woman's problem, and the two suggestions that her friend makes about how to handle it. What do you think the woman should do, and why?

Narrator 2: Please prepare your answer after the beep.

Beep

[Preparation time: 20 seconds]

Narrator 2: Please begin speaking after the beep.

Beep

[Recording time: 60 seconds]

Beep

Narrator 1: Now listen to an example answer.

Example Answer

The woman's suffering from daily headaches, and she's controlling the pain by taking Tylenol. The man suggests that she make an appointment with a doctor at the Health Center because the problem should be diagnosed by a professional, but he also mentions the possibility that the doctor might refer her for an eye exam. Apparently, the problem's worse when she's been staring at the computer for long periods of time. Um . . . he reminds her that if the doctor at the Health Center refers her for the eye exam, the student health insurance may pay a large percentage of the cost for glasses. So . . . I think the woman should take the man's advice because eyestrain's a common problem for college students, and she probably does need an eye appointment, but by going to the doctor at the Health Center first, she can be certain that there isn't something more serious going on, and if she needs glasses, the referral will probably allow her to use her insurance benefit.

Beep

Integrated Speaking Question 6: "Fax Machines"

Narrator 2: Number 6. Listen to part of a lecture. Then listen for a question about it. After you hear the question, you have 20 seconds to prepare, and 60 seconds to record your answer.

Narrator 1: Now listen to part of a lecture in an engineering class. The professor is discussing the way that a fax machine transmits and receives data.

Professor: Okay, to illustrate my point that many new machines are simply combinations of machines that are already available, let's talk about the fax machine. To understand how a fax machine works, I'd like you to think of it as three machines—a copier, a modem, and a printer. First, the data is copied. How does that happen? Well, when you load paper into the fax machine, a light shines on it and optical sensors read whether a specific point on the paper is black or white. These sensors communicate the digital information into a microprocessor, where a copy of the page is made of black or white dots. Thus, you see that in the first step, the fax machine functions like a copier. Next, the fax machine works like a modem. Remember, a modem takes a black-and-white image and converts this digital data into an analog signal, that is, electronic impulses that can be sent over a phone line. The fax machine calls another fax machine to transmit, using two different types of tones to represent the black and white dots in the document. For example, it might send an 800-Hertz tone for white and a 1,300-Hertz tone for black. The last part of a fax machine is the printer. After the receiving fax machine answers the sending fax machine, it begins to accept the electronic impulses, and then it converts them back to the black-and-white dots in a digital image. Finally, it prints the image out on paper just like any other printer.

Narrator 1: Using the main points and examples from the lecture, describe the three parts of a fax machine and then explain how the fax process works.

Narrator 2: Please prepare your answer after the beep.

Beep

[Preparation time: 20 seconds]

Narrator 2: Please begin speaking after the beep.

Beep

[Recording time: 60 seconds]

Beep

Narrator 1: Now listen to an example answer.

Example Answer

A fax machine has three parts. The fax that's sending text and images has sensors to read black-and-white points on paper and communicate the patterns digitally to a microprocessor, and the microprocessor . . . it recreates the images in black-and-white dots. So this part of the process is like a copy machine. So then the digital information . . . I mean the image in black-and-white dots . . . is converted into an analog signal that's made up of electronic impulses. The impulses are sent over a phone line, like a modem. Then the fax machine that's sending the information connects with another fax machine that's receiving the information. They communicate with two tones, one that signals a black dot and another that signals a white dot. And the fax machine that receives the tones begins to print the dots on paper in the same way that any printer produces an image. So a fax is really a combination copier, modem, and printer.

Beep

Reading Section

This is the Reading Section of the Next Generation TOEFL Model Test. This section tests your ability to understand reading passages like those in college textbooks. There are three passages. After each passage, you will answer twelve or thirteen questions about it. Most questions are worth one point, but one question in each passage is worth more than one point. You will have 25 minutes to read each passage and answer the comprehension questions. You may take notes while you read. You may use your notes to answer the questions. Choose the best answer for multiple-choice questions. Follow the directions on the page or on the screen for computer-assisted questions. Click on **Next** to go to the next question. Click on **Back** to return to the previous question. You may return to previous questions in the same reading passage, but after you go to the next passage, you may not return to a previous passage. A clock on the screen will show you how much time you have to complete each passage.

Independent Reading 1: *"Symbiotic Relationships"*

1. **(C)** In the context of this passage, *derives* means "obtains." Choices (A), (B), and (D) are not accepted meanings of the word *derives*.

2. **(C)** "Parasitism is a relationship in which one organism, known as the parasite, lives in or on another organism, known as the host, from which it [the parasite] derives nourishment." The pronoun *it* does not refer to Choices (A), (B), or (D).

3. **(A)** In the context of this passage, *relatively* means "comparatively." Choices (B), (C), and (D) are not accepted meanings of the word *relatively*.

4. **(A)** Choice (A) is a paraphrase of the statement. Choices (B), (C), and (D) change the meaning of the statement.

5. **(A)** In the context of this passage, *tolerate* means "permit." Choices (B), (C), and (D) are not accepted meanings of the word *tolerate*.

6. **(D)** "Parasites that live on the surface of their hosts are known as **ectoparasites**." Choice (A) is not correct because mold and mildew are examples of ectoparasites, not a description of the way they survive. Choice (B) is not correct because it refers to endoparasites, not ectoparasites. Choice (C) is not correct because bacteria are an example of endoparasites.

7. **(A)** "There are many examples of commensal relationships. Many orchids use trees as a surface upon which to grow." Choice (B) refers to a parasite, not a member of a commensal relationship. Choice (C) refers to a member of a mutualistic relationship. Choice (D) refers to a parasite.

8. **(C)** In the context of this passage, *actually* means "really." Choices (A), (B), and (D) are not accepted meanings of the word *actually*.

9. **(B)** ". . . the species can exist separately but are more successful when they are involved in a mutualistic relationship. Some species of *Acacia*. . . . " Choice (A) is not correct because the ants could exist separately but they are more successful living in the *Acacia* trees. Choice (C) is not correct because the example refers to a specific plant [*Acacia*] and animal [ant], not to all plants and animals. Choice (D) is not correct because mutualism is a solution, not a problem.

10. **(C)** ". . . have bacteria that live in their roots. . . . The bacteria do not cause disease but provide the plants with nitrogen-containing molecules that the plants can use for growth." Choice (B) is not correct because the plants use the nitrogen supplied by bacteria for growth. Choice (D) is not correct because the nodules are helpful, not harmful. Choice (A) is not mentioned and may not be concluded from information in the passage.

11. **(B)** Pronoun reference is a transitional device that connects the insert sentence with the previous sentence. The two sentences are related by the reference to "molds" and "mildews" in the previous sentence and the pronoun "they" in the insert sentence.

12. **(A)** Because the passage is about the relationship between organisms, it may be concluded

that the passage would most probably appear in the chapter, "Environment and Organisms." Choices (B), (C), and (D) would probably not include a passage on symbiosis.

13. **(A) (C) (E)** summarize the lecture. Choice (B) is true, but it is a minor point mentioned as an example of a parasitic relationship. Choice (D) is true, but it is a minor point mentioned as an example of a mutalistic relationship. Choice (F) is true, but it is a minor point mentioned as an example of a commensal relationship.

Independent Reading 2: "Civilization"

1. **(B)** "...Neolithic settlements were hardly more than villages. But as their inhabitants mastered the art of farming, they gradually began to give birth to more complex human societies [civilizations]." Choice (A) is not correct because the Neolithic settlements preceded civilizations. Choice (C) is not correct because agriculture is mentioned as a cause of the rise in complex cultures, not as a definition of civilization. Choice (D) is not correct because the population centers increased in size as civilizations grew, but other basic characteristics had to be present as well.

2. **(B)** "Although copper was the first metal to be utilized in producing tools, after 4000 B.C., craftspeople in western Asia discovered that a combination of copper and tin produced bronze, a much harder and more durable metal than copper. Its [bronze's] widespread use has led historians to speak of a Bronze Age. . . ." The pronoun *its* does not refer to Choices (A), (C), or (D).

3. **(B)** "As wealth increased, such societies began to develop armies and to build walled cities." Choices (A), (C), and (D) may be logical, but they are not mentioned and may not be concluded from information in the passage.

4. **(C)** In the context of this passage, *hardly* means "barely." Choices (A), (B), and (D) are not accepted meanings of the word *hardly*.

5. **(D)** Because the author states that Neolithic towns were transformed, it may be concluded that they are mentioned to contrast them with the civilizations that evolved. Choice (A) is not correct because a Neolithic town does not qualify as a civilization. Choice (B) is not correct because writing systems were not part of Neolithic settlements. Choice (C) is not correct because Neolithic settlements were referred to as villages, and no argument was made for the classification.

6. **(B)** ". . . . a new social structure . . . [included] kings and an upper class . . . free people . . . and a class of slaves. . . ." Choice (A) is not correct because it does not include free people. Choice (C) is not correct because it does not include free people. Choice (D) is not mentioned and may not be concluded from information in the passage. The new structure described is based on economics, not education.

7. **(A)** Choice (A) is a paraphrase of the statement. Choices (B), (C), and (D) change the meaning of the statement.

8. **(A)** In the context of this passage, *crucial* means "fundamental." Choices (B), (C), and (D) are not accepted meanings of the word *crucial*.

9. **(B)** In the context of this passage, *prominent* means "important." Choices (A), (C), and (D) are not accepted meanings of the word *prominent*.

10. **(B)** "A number of possible explanations of the beginning of civilization have been suggested." Choice (A) is not correct because scholars do not agree on one explanation. Choice (C) is not correct because trade routes are not mentioned in paragraph 4. Choice (D) is not correct because coincidence is not mentioned as one of the possible explanations.

11. **(C)** Choice (A) is mentioned in paragraph 4, sentence 9. Choice (B) is mentioned in paragraph 4, sentence 8. Choice (D) is mentioned in paragraph 4, sentence 6.

12. **(B)** A rhetorical question is a question that is asked and answered by the same speaker. Response is a transitional device that connects the insert sentence with the previous rhetorical question. Choices (A), (C), and (D) do not include transitional devices that connect the insert sentence with the sentences marked in the passage.

13. **(B) (E) (F)** summarize the passage. Choice (A) is true, but it is a minor point that is mentioned as an example in the characteristic of a class structure. Choice (C) is not mentioned in the passage. Choice (D) is not mentioned in the passage.

Independent Reading 3: "The Scientific Method"

1. **(B)** In the context of this passage, *obvious* means "clear." Choices (A), (C), and (D) are not accepted meanings of the word *obvious*.

2. **(B)** " . . . our interpretations of facts often are based on beliefs about the world that others might not share. For example . . . that the Sun rises . . . [is] an idea that might not have been accepted by ancient Egyptians. . . . " Choice (A) is not correct because the rotation might not have been accepted by ancient Egyptians. Choices (C) and (D) are not mentioned and may not be concluded from information in the passage.

3. **(C)** In the context of this passage, *essentially* means "basically." Choices (A), (B), and (D) are not accepted meanings of the word *essentially*.

4. **(A)** In the context of this passage, *flawed* means "not perfect." Choices (B), (C), and (D) are not accepted meanings of the word *flawed*.

5. **(B)** Choice (B) is a paraphrase of the statement. Choices (A), (C), and (D) change the meaning of the statement.

6. **(B)** " . . . its [the Ptolemaic model's] predictions didn't quite match actual observations—a key reason why the Earth-centered model of the universe finally was discarded." The pronoun *its* does not refer to Choices (A), (C), or (D).

7. **(A)** "Therefore, even well-established theories must be subject to continuing challenges through further observations and experiments." Choice (C) is not correct because a theory that is generally accepted by the scientific community would have to be subject to scientific observation and experimentation. Choices (B) and (D) are not mentioned and may not be concluded from information in the passage.

8. **(C)** " . . . Kepler . . . tested his model against observations that had been made previously, rather than verifying new predictions. . . . " Choice (A) is not correct because the predictions do not verify a model. Predictions must be verified by the model. Choices (B) and (D) are not mentioned and may not be concluded from information in the passage.

9. **(D)** In the context of this passage, *plenty* means "numerous." Choices (A), (B), and (C) are not accepted meanings of the word *plenty*.

10. **(D)** Choice (A) is mentioned in paragraph 2, sentence 2. Choice (B) is mentioned in paragraph 2, sentence 8. Choice (C) is mentioned in paragraph 2, sentence 5.

11. **(A)** Because the Ptolemaic model "didn't quite match actual observations. . . . " it may be concluded that a model does not always reflect observations. Choice (B) is not correct because theories are more firmly established than models. Choice (C) is not correct because a theory can never be "true beyond all doubt." Choice (D) is not correct because "a model must be continually challenged with new observations or experiments."

12. **(C)** Paraphrase is a transitional device that connects the insert sentence with a previous sentence. " . . . our [cultural] interpretations of facts" in a previous sentence is a paraphrase of "cultural orientation" in the insert sentence. Choices (A), (B), and (D) do not include transitional devices that connect the insert sentence with the sentences marked in the passage.

13. **(A) (C) (E)** summarize the lecture. Choice (B) is true, but it is a minor point mentioned in reference to the fourth and final step of the method. Choice (D) is true, but it is mentioned after the discussion of the steps in the scientific method. Choice (F) is not mentioned in the passage.

Writing Section

This is the Writing Section of the Next Generation TOEFL Model Test. This section tests your ability to write essays in English. During the test, you will write two essays. The independent essay usually asks for your opinion about a familiar topic. The integrated essay asks for your response to an academic reading passage, a lecture, or both. You may take notes as you read and listen. You may use your notes to write the essays. If a lecture is included, it will be spoken, but the directions and the questions will be written. A clock on the screen will show you how much time you have to complete each essay.

Independent Writing: "Study in the United States"

Question:
You are planning to study in the United States. What do you think you will like and dislike about this experience? Why? Use specific reasons and details to support your answer.

Outline
Like
- Improve language proficiency
- Participate in culture
- College courses

Dislike
- Miss family
- Rely on fast food
- Compete with Americans

Map

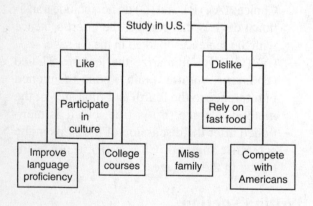

Example Essay
Living abroad provides many opportunities and challenges. When I study in the United States, I look forward to making friends with Americans. By getting to know people, I will be able to improve my English language proficien-

cy. There are idioms and words that are best learned within the context of real conversations with native speakers. I also look forward to being a participant in a new culture. At the end of my stay in the United States, I hope that I will understand American culture in a different and deeper way than is possible when the information is derived from only movies and books. In addition, I am excited about studying on an American campus. I expect the college courses to be challenging, and I am eager to learn about the latest technological advances in my field of study.

I am realistic about the disadvantages of foreign study, however. I know that I will miss my family very much. It will be too expensive to return to my country to spend holidays with them, and I will be very lonely during the times when I know that they are gathered for special celebrations. Another aspect of the experience that I do not look forward to is the reliance on fast food that is so typical of American college students. Pizza, hamburgers, and other junk foods are easier to find and prepare than the meals that I enjoy in my country, but they aren't as good, and they probably aren't as healthy. Finally, I imagine that my life will be very stressful because I will be competing with students who know the language of the classroom and are accustomed to the expectations that American professors have for their students. I am a competitive person by nature, and I am apprehensive about my ability to compete with my classmates.

Once I am in the United States, I will no doubt find many other opportunities to take advantage of and many challenges that I must confront. Nevertheless, I expect my experience to be overwhelmingly positive, and I intend to see the lessons in both adventures and adversity.

Integrated Writing: "Problem Solving"

Audio
Narrator: Now listen to a lecture on the same topic as the reading passage on page 477.

Professor:
Now that you've read the article on problem solving, let's talk about the role of breaks. We all know that taking a break is a good strategy for

solving a problem, but how does a break really influence the solution? Well, some researchers feel that rest allows the brain to analyze the problem more clearly. We're advised to "sleep on it" when a problem is difficult to solve. Okay, but what if there's some type of *incubation effect* during sleep that allows the brain to continue working on a solution? Here's what I mean. F. A. Kekule was puzzled by the structure of benzene. One night, he dreamed about a snake biting its tail while whirling around in a circle. And when he awoke, it occurred to him that the carbon atoms of benzene might be arranged in a ring. He attributed the solution of the problem directly to the dream. But Kekule's experience and others like it present researchers with a dilemma because there's disagreement about whether unconscious mental activity exists. Were the dreamers really asleep or were they relaxed but awake when they solved the problem?

Two explanations have been proposed to explain why a break supports problem solving while we're awake. One possibility is that during the break, information may appear that provides a solution. For example, Buckminster Fuller was looking at a triangle when he saw the structure of multiple triangles as the solution for constructing a geodesic dome. Of course, another possibility is much more simplistic. It could be that the value of taking a break is as basic as interfering with an ineffective pattern of thinking. By focusing on something else, we may return to the problem in a different frame of mind and think about it in a different, and more productive, way.

Question:
Summarize the main points in the lecture, referring to the way that they relate to the reading passage on page 477.

Outline
Sleeping
• Rest to function at higher capacity
• "Incubation effect"—Kekule structure benzene
• "Functional fixedness" released

Waking
• Input during break—Fuller geodesic dome
• Interruption unsuccessful process
• Different "mental set"

Map

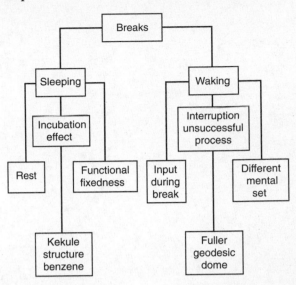

Example Essay

Although researchers do not agree about the way that a break contributes to problem solving, it is clear that breaks during sleeping hours and those that we take during waking hours are both helpful. The value of sleep may be related to the brain's requirement for rest in order to function at a higher capacity. On the other hand, it is possible that there is an "incubation effect," that is, that the brain continues to problem solve at a different level of consciousness during a sleep break. For example, Kekule had insight into the structure of benzene during a dream. Although researchers are not in agreement as to the level of unconscious activity of dreamers, and some argue that dreamers who solve problems are not really asleep, it remains that the sleep break was helpful. It may even be that "functional fixedness" described in the text is somehow released in sleep so that preconceived notions are less limiting.

In contrast, breaks during waking hours appear to be more straightforward. Sometimes input during the break period will contribute to the solution. For example, Fuller's inspiration for the geodesic dome occurred while he was looking at a triangle during a break. However, merely interrupting an unsuccessful problem-solving process could be helpful. By taking a break, we may be more willing to abandon a strategy that is not working, or, as the text states, we return to the problem with a different "mental set."

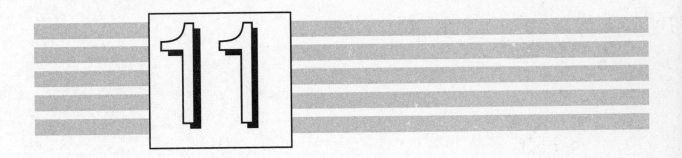

SCORE
ESTIMATES

Important Background Information

It is not possible for you to determine the exact score that you will receive on the TOEFL. There are three reasons why this is true. First, the testing conditions on the day of your official TOEFL will affect your score. If you are in an uncomfortable room, if there are noisy distractions, if you are upset because you almost arrived late for the test, or if you are very nervous, then these factors can affect your score. The administration of a Model Test is more controlled. You will probably not be as stressed when you take one of the tests in this book. Second, the Model Tests in the book are designed to help you practice the most frequently tested item types on the official TOEFL. Because they are constructed to teach as well as to test, there is more repetition in Model Tests than there is on official TOEFL tests. Tests that are not constructed for exactly the same purposes are not exactly comparable. Third, the TOEFL scores received by the same student will vary from one official Computer-Based TOEFL examination to another official Computer-Based TOEFL examination by as many as 20 points, even when the examinations are taken on the same day. In testing and assessment, this is called a standard error of measurement. Therefore, a TOEFL score cannot be predicted precisely even when two official tests are used.

But, of course, you would like to know how close you are to your goal. To do that, you can use the following procedure to estimate your TOEFL score. An estimate is an approximation. In this case, it is a range of scores.

Score Correspondence Procedure

1. Use the charts on the following pages to determine your percentage scores for each section of the TOEFL.

2. Determine the total percentage score for the TOEFL.
   Listening Section = one-third the total
   Structure Section = one-sixth the total
   Reading Section = one-third the total
   Writing Section = one-sixth the total

3. Use the Score Correspondence Table to estimate an official TOEFL score.

Listening Section

Number Correct	Percentage Score
50	100
49	98
48	96
47	94
46	92
45	90
44	88
43	86
42	84
41	82
40	80
39	78
38	76
37	74
36	72
35	70
34	68
33	66
32	64
31	62
30	60
29	58
28	56
27	54
26	52
25	50
24	48
23	46
22	44
21	42
20	40
19	38
18	36
17	34
16	32
15	30
14	28
13	26
12	24
11	22
10	20
9	18
8	16
7	14
6	12
5	10
4	8
3	6
2	4
1	2
0	0

Structure Section

Number Correct	Percentage Score
25	100
24	96
23	94
22	88
21	84
20	80
19	76
18	72
17	68
16	64
15	60
14	56
13	52
12	48
11	44
10	40
9	36
8	32
7	28
6	24
5	20
4	16
3	12
2	8
1	4
0	0

Reading Section

Number Correct	Percentage Score
45	100
44	98
43	96
42	93
41	91
40	89
39	87
38	84
37	82
36	80
35	78
34	76
33	73
32	71
31	69
30	67
29	64
28	62
27	60
26	58
25	56
24	53
23	51
22	49
21	47
20	44
19	42
18	40
17	38
16	36
15	33
14	31
13	29
12	27
11	24
10	22
9	20
8	18
7	16
6	13
5	11
4	9
3	7
2	4
1	2
0	0

Writing Section

Scaled Score	Percentage Score
6.0	100
5.5	92
5.0	84
4.5	76
4.0	68
3.5	60
3.0	52
2.5	44
2.0	36
1.5	28
1.0	20
0	0

Score Correspondence Table

Model Test Percentage Scores	Computer-Based TOEFL Score Ranges	Paper-Based TOEFL Score Ranges
100	287–300	660–677
95	273–283	640–657
90	260–270	620–637
85	250–260	600–617
80	237–247	580–597
75	220–233	560–577
70	207–220	540–557
65	190–203	520–537
60	173–187	500–517
55	157–170	480–497
50	140–153	460–477
45	123–137	440–457
40	110–123	420–437
35	97–107	400–417
30	83–93	380–397
25	70–80	360–377
20	60–70	340–357
15	47–57	320–337
10	40–47	310–317
5		
0		

Progress Chart

Percentage Scores

	Listening ⅓	Structure ⅙	Reading ⅓	Writing ⅙	=	Total	=	Score Ranges
One								
Two								
Three								
Four								
Five								
Six								
Seven								
Eight								

Scores for the Next Generation TOEFL

The Next Generation TOEFL will have section scores for each of the four sections. The range for the section scores will be 0–25. Then the scores for the four sections will be added together. Although final scoring has not been determined, the total score range for the Next Generation TOEFL will probably be 0–100. To estimate your score on Model Test 9, the Next Generation TOEFL Model Test, determine your percentage of correct answers on each section and divide by four. This is a very rough estimate, but until a more refined scoring scale is published, it will give you a general idea of how you would score. Continue to watch the TOEFL web site at *www.toefl.org* for the latest information about the official scoring scale.

RESOURCES

Featured Colleges and Universities

Many students have written to me to ask my advice about language programs and degree programs in American colleges and universities. Which college or university to attend is a very personal decision, and only you can know where you will be happy. In order to decide, you should get as much information about the school or program as you can. Use reference books like *Barron's Profiles of American Colleges* and visit web sites of language programs and schools.

The language programs featured here collaborated with me on field tests or revisions of items for the Computer-Based TOEFL Model Tests in this book and on the CD-ROM that supplements this book. All of the programs are members of the American Association of Intensive English Programs, are eligible to issue the form I-20 for you to obtain a student visa to enter the United States, and offer special TOEFL preparation courses as part of their curricula. These programs also advertise that they will provide professional ESL instructors on the faculty; multiple levels of instruction; small classes (ten to twenty students); and a safe campus area. In addition, each program has some unique features that may be important to you as you consider your options.

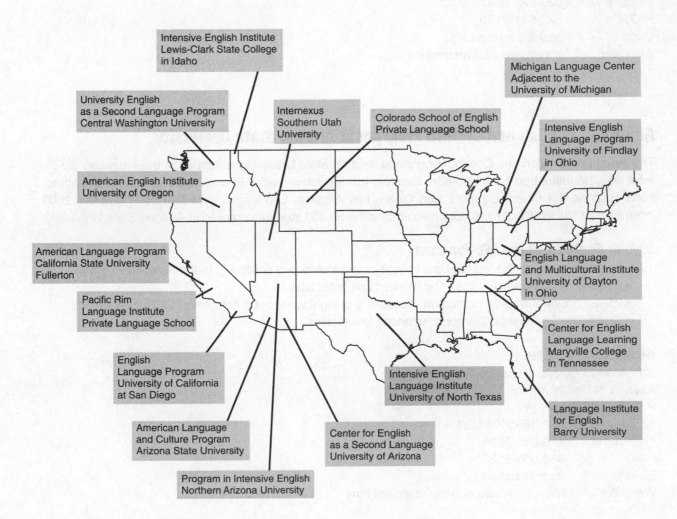

Center for English as a Second Language at the University of Arizona

The Center for English as a Second Language (CESL) at the University of Arizona in Tucson is located in the Arizona-Sonora Desert of the American Southwest, sixty miles from Mexico. There are 2150 international students among the 35,000 students enrolled in the University of Arizona.

Unique Features of the ESL Program
- Located at one of the top twenty research universities in the nation
- An international campus with students from over 115 countries
- Access to extensive facilities and services on campus
- Exceptional qualifications for faculty
- Auditing and credit courses available for qualified students

Admissions Contact
Center for English as a Second Language
The University of Arizona
P.O. Box 210024
Tucson, Arizona 85721-0024 USA
Telephone: 520-621-3637
FAX: 520-621-9180
E-mail: cesl@u.arizona.edu
Web site: http://www.cesl.arizona.edu

American English and Culture Program at Arizona State University

The American English and Culture Program at Arizona State University is located in the American Southwest on a beautiful tree-lined 800-acre campus, just ten miles east of Phoenix, and close to many attractions such as the Grand Canyon, San Diego, Los Angeles, Las Vegas, and Mexico. There are 2000 international students from 140 countries among the 50,000 students enrolled in Arizona State University.

Unique Features of the ESL Program
- Located in one of the top ten best college towns in America according to the *New York Times*
- Full use of university facilities and modern computer labs
- 21–24 hours of weekly instruction in sessions of eight weeks and complete TOEFL preparation
- Considered a "best buy" among American universities

Admissions Contact
American English and Culture Program
Arizona State University
P.O. Box 873504
Tempe, Arizona 85287-3504 USA
Telephone: 480-965-2376
FAX: 480-965-8529
E-mail: aecp@asu.edu
Web site: http://www.asu.edu/xed/aecp/esl.html

The Program in Intensive English at Northern Arizona University

The Program in Intensive English (PIE) is located in Flagstaff, Arizona, with a wonderful four-season climate. The program offers complete preparation for university course work. Northern Arizona University is a comprehensive university with degrees in many areas of study.

Unique Features of the ESL Program
- Near the Grand Canyon and many other scenic attractions
- Many extra-curricular activities available
- Curriculum designed to prepare students for success
- Automatic admission upon meeting TOEFL requirements
- English-only option available

Admissions Contact
Program in Intensive English
Box 6032
Northern Arizona University
Flagstaff, Arizona 86011-6032 USA
Telephone: 520-523-7503
FAX: 520-523-7074
E-mail: pie.nau@nau.edu
Web site: www.nau.edu/~english/tesl/pie.html

English Language Program at the University of California at San Diego

The English Language Program at the University of California at San Diego is located less than a mile from the Pacific Ocean on a 1200-acre campus in La Jolla, one of the most prestigious seaside neighborhoods on the California coast. There are 4500 international students and scholars among the 18,000 students enrolled in the University of California at San Diego.

Unique Features of the ESL Program
- Customized scheduling from a list of electives that account for 50 percent of the student's schedule
- Professional certificate programs including business management; U.S. legal systems; travel, tourism, and hospitality management
- Exceptional computer facilities and the latest computer-based instruction
- Location in an area that enjoys one of the finest climates in the United States
- Affiliation with one of the premier research universities in the United States

Admissions Contact
English Language Programs
University of California at San Diego
9500 Gilman Drive
La Jolla, California 92093-0176 USA
Telephone: 619-534-6784
FAX: 619-534-5703
E-mail: elp@ucsd.edu
Web site: http://www-esps.ucsd.edu/elp

American Language Program at California State University, Fullerton

The American Language Program is located in safe suburban Orange County 30 miles south of Los Angeles and close to beaches, cultural attractions, and entertainment. The program offers small classes with TOEFL instruction at every level and conditional admission to Cal State Fullerton, which has the second largest undergraduate business program in the United States.

Unique Features of the ESL Program
- TOEFL preparation and TOEFL examinations in all levels
- High-quality instruction and service by experienced, well-educated professionals
- Social, recreational, and cultural activities and trips included
- University courses available for advanced-level students
- Homestay and conversation partner programs

Admissions Contact
American Language Program
California State University
800 N. State College Boulevard
Fullerton, CA 92831 USA
Telephone: 714-278-2909
FAX: 714-278-7114
E-mail: alp@fullerton.edu
Web site: http://alp.fullerton.edu

Pacific Rim Language Institute

The Pacific Rim Language Institute is a private adult language school located in a quiet residential suburb, twenty minutes east of downtown Los Angeles. The school is approved by the Bureau for Private Post-secondary and Vocational Education and is a member of the American Association of Intensive English Programs (AAIEP).

Unique Features of the ESL Program
- Focus on conversation skills and spoken English
- Two levels of TOEFL preparation—450–500 range and 550–600 range
- Located in Asian-American community, with many stores and restaurants
- Excellent relationships with local community colleges
- Assistance with transfer to degree programs

Admissions Contact
Pacific Rim Language Institute
1719 Fullerton Road
Rowland Heights, California 91748 USA
Telephone: 626-964-0888
FAX: 626-913-9658
E-mail: admissions@prli.com
Web site: http://www.prli.com

American English Institute at the University of Oregon

The American English Institute at the University of Oregon is located in the beautiful Willamette Valley of the Pacific Northwest on a 250-acre campus in a suburban area. There are 1650 international students among the 17,000 students enrolled in the University of Oregon.

Unique Features of the ESL Program

- Affiliation with a highly ranked university in the Oregon system of higher education
- Orientation program before the beginning of the term
- Two hours of tutoring per week included in the tuition
- Graduation credit for ESL courses for matriculated students
- University credit courses for advanced language students

Admissions Contact

American English Institute
107 Pacific Hall
5212 University of Oregon
Eugene, Oregon 97403-5121 USA
Telephone: 541-346-3945
FAX: 541-346-3917
E-mail: aeiadmit@oregon.uoregon.edu
Web site: http://babel.uoregon.edu/aei/aei.html

University English as a Second Language Program at Central Washington University

The University English as a Second Language (UESL) Program at Central Washington University is located in Ellensburg, Washington, one hundred miles east of Seattle on a 380-acre campus. There are 400 international students among the 7000 students enrolled in Central Washington University.

Unique Features of the ESL Program

- Active conversation partners program
- Workshops to provide help with college applications
- Supervised visitations to regular university classes
- Conditional admission to Central Washington University through the UESL program with program recommendation accepted in place of TOEFL score
- Partnerships with other colleges and universities in the Washington state university system

Admissions Contact

University English as a Second Language Program
Central Washington University
400 East 8th Avenue
Ellensburg, Washington 98926-7562 USA
Telephone: 509-963-1375
FAX: 509-963-1380
E-mail: horowitz@CWU.edu
Web site: http://www.cwu.edu/~intlprog/uesl.html

Michigan Language Center, adjacent to the University of Michigan

The Michigan Language Center (MLC) is a private language school located in the Midwestern United States in Ann Arbor, Michigan, adjacent to the University of Michigan. There are 3050 international students among the 22,000 students enrolled in the neighboring academic community at the University of Michigan.

Unique Features of the ESL Program
- New sessions every six weeks
- Special seminars offered each term at no extra charge
- Conversation partner program
- Location in a small, safe, but exciting city near the University of Michigan, one of the best academic institutions in the United States
- Assistance by the MLC academic counselor in applying to American colleges and universities, as well as arrangements with some institutions for conditional admission

Admissions Contact
Michigan Language Center
309 South State Street
P.O. Box 8231
Ann Arbor, Michigan 48107 USA
Telephone: 734-663-9415
FAX: 734-663-9623
E-mail: mlc-usa@att.net
Web site: www.englishclasses.com

Intensive English Language Program at the University of Findlay

The Intensive English Language Program (IELP) at the University of Findlay is located in Findlay, Ohio, a small city in the Midwestern United States. Nearly 300 international students among the 4000 students enrolled in the University of Findlay attend classes on the 160-acre campus.

Unique Features of the ESL Program
- Long-standing tradition of educating international students from thirty countries
- Computer skills course offered as part of the advanced curriculum
- University credit awarded for intensive English students majoring in English as an International Language
- Location in an area named the best micropolitan (small city) in Ohio and one of the top places to live in the United States—near Detroit, Chicago, Cleveland, Columbus, Cincinnati
- Affiliation with a small liberal arts university that offers a large number of degree programs

Admissions Contact
Intensive English Language Institute
The University of Findlay
1000 N. Main Street
Findlay, Ohio 45840-3695 USA
Telephone: 419-424-4558
FAX: 419-424-5507
E-mail: international@findlay.edu
Web site: http://www.findlay.edu

English Language and Multicultural Institute at the University of Dayton

The English Language and Multicultural Institute (ELMI) at the University of Dayton, Ohio, is located in the heart of the Midwestern United States in a safe, suburban setting. There are 190 international students among the 9900 students enrolled in the University of Dayton, as well as 250 international students in the ESL program, preparing for study at the university of their choice.

Unique Features of the ESL Program
- Personal academic counseling by caring faculty advisors
- Highly individualized approach to language learning
- Special programs for business professionals and family members
- Supervised activities and field trips; strong host family and conversation partner programs
- Affiliation with a university recognized as a national leader in Catholic higher education and one of the top five regional universities in the Midwest

Admissions Contact
English Language and Multicultural Institute
300 College Park
Dayton, Ohio 45469-0319 USA
Telephone: 937-229-3729
FAX: 937-229-3700
E-mail: elmi@udayton.edu
Web site: http://www.udayton.edu/~elmi/

Center for English Language Learning at Maryville College

The Center for English Language Learning at Maryville College in Maryville, Tennessee, is located sixteen miles from Knoxville, near the Great Smoky Mountains National Park on a 350-acre park-like campus. There are sixty-five international students among the 900 students enrolled in Maryville College.

Unique Features of the ESL Program
- Very small classes, usually six to twelve students
- Low costs in comparison with similar colleges
- New sessions every five weeks
- Undergraduate college credit for twelve hours of ESL courses
- Affiliation with a college recognized among *U.S. News and World Report*'s top regional four-year liberal arts institutions

Admissions Contact
Center for English Language Learning
Maryville College
Maryville, Tennessee 37804-5907 USA
Telephone: 865-981-8186
FAX: 865-983-0581
E-mail: Internat@MaryvilleCollege.edu
Web site: http://www.MaryvilleCollege.edu

Language Institute for English at Barry University

The Language Institute for English at Barry University in Miami Shores, Florida, is located twelve miles north of Miami on a ninety-acre campus. There are 450 international students among the 2,000 students enrolled in Barry University.

Unique Features of the ESL Program
- Twelve levels of instruction which allow for very accurate placement
- New sessions every four weeks
- Many elective courses for advanced students
- Arrangements for conditional admission to more than 100 universities, preparatory high schools, and vocational schools
- Exceptional social, cultural, and sports activities

Admissions Contact
Language Institute for English
Barry University
11300 Northeast Second Avenue
Miami Shores, Florida 33161 USA
Telephone: 305-899-3128
FAX: 305-892-2229
E-mail: admissions@mail.barry.edu
Web site: http://www.barry.edu

Intensive English Language Institute at the University of North Texas

The Intensive English Language Institute (IELI) at the University of North Texas is located in a small university city in the Southern United States, thirty minutes from Dallas, Texas. There are 1500 international students among the 26,000 students enrolled in the University of North Texas.

Unique Features of the ESL Program
- Accredited by the Commission on English Language Program Accreditation (CELPA)
- Full-time, professional teachers and student counselors with a 12:1 student/teacher ratio, year-round classes at levels 0–6
- Graduate Preparation Course (GPC) offered by IELI, waives the GRE verbal score for admission to many UNT graduate programs
- Conditional admission for level 5 IELI/UNT students with TOEFL waiver
- Affiliation with the fourth largest university in Texas, University of North Texas (UNT), listed in "America's 100 Best College Buys," and "One of America's 100 Most Wired Colleges" according to Yahoo

Admissions Contact
Intensive English Language Institute
P.O. Box 310739
Denton, Texas 76203-0739 USA
Telephone: 940-565-2003
FAX: 940-565-4822
E-mail: intl@isp.admin.unt.edu
Web site: http://www.unt.edu/isp/

Internexus at Southern Utah University

Internexus at Southern Utah University is located in Cedar City on a 120-acre campus, within a short drive of Las Vegas as well as several national parks. There are 175 international students among the 6,000 students enrolled in Southern Utah University.

Unique Features of the ESL Program
- English Plus Program which includes activities for youth and summer travel in the national parks
- Admission for students as young as 14 years of age for short-term group programs
- Half-Half Program for students who are eligible to enroll in a part-time program of university courses
- Living language laboratory
- Affiliation with other private language schools hosted by colleges and universities in the United States and the United Kingdom

Admissions Contact
Internexus
Southern Utah University
351 West Center Street
Cedar City, Utah 84720 USA
Telephone: 435-865-8033
FAX: 435-865-8013
E-mail: sutah@internexus
Web site: http://www.suu.edu/webpages/contedu/elsc

Colorado School of English

Colorado School of English is a private language school with a campus in downtown Denver.

Unique Features of the ESL Program
- Custom programs designed for groups
- Private classes designed for the special language needs of one student
- Partnering programs for executives in the same field of work
- Sight-seeing tours combined with language study
- New courses beginning every Monday

Admissions Contact
Colorado School of English
1325 S. Colorado Boulevard, Suite 101
Denver, Colorado 80222 USA
Telephone: 303-758-3123
FAX: 303-758-3002
E-mail: cse@englishamerica.com
Web site: http://www.englishamerica.com

The Intensive English Institute at Lewis-Clark State College

The Intensive English Institute (IEI) at Lewis-Clark State College is located in a typical American town settled in a scenic river valley. There are 120 international students among the 3100 students enrolled in Lewis-Clark State College.

Unique Features of the ESL Program
- Location in an area with a mild climate
- Exceptional commitment to student services
- More home-stay opportunities than the average college program
- Courses for computer and keyboarding skills in English
- Cross-registration with three Idaho universities for students enrolled in degree programs

Admissions Contact
Intensive English Institute
Lewis-Clark State College
Lewiston, Idaho 83501 USA
Telephone: 208-799-2321
FAX: 208-799-2824
E-mail: ieiprog@lcsc.edu
Web site: http://www.iei-USA.com

Glossary of Campus Vocabulary

ace   v.   to receive a grade of A
    Example: I *aced* that exam.
    Suggestion: Find someone who *aced* the course to help you.
    Assumption: Kathy *aced* her computer science class?
    Problem: If I don't *ace* the final, I'll get a B in the class.

admissions office   n.   the administrative office where students apply for admission to a college or university
    Example: I have an appointment at the *admissions office* to review my application.
    Suggestion: Why don't you go over to the *admissions office*?
    Assumption: You mean you couldn't find the *admissions office*?
    Problem: I need to get to the *admissions office* before five o'clock.

advisor   n.   a person who helps students make decisions about their academic programs
    Example: Dr. Jones is the *academic advisor* for the engineering students.
    Suggestion: You should see your *academic advisor* before you decide.
    Assumption: Dr. Jones is your *academic advisor*?
    Problem: I can't see my *academic advisor* until Friday.

all-nighter   n.   a study session that lasts all night
    Example: We had to pull an *all-nighter* to get ready for the final exam.
    Suggestion: If I were you, I wouldn't pull another *all-nighter*.
    Assumption: So you did pull another *all-nighter*.
    Problem: I have to pull an *all-nighter* in order to be ready for the final exam.

article   n.   a publication about an academic subject
    Example: We read six *articles* in addition to the reading in the textbook.
    Suggestion: You had better read the *articles* that were assigned.
    Assumption: You read the *articles* already?
    Problem: I need to read the *articles* again.

assignment   n.   work that must be done as part of the requirements for a class
    Example: The *assignment* was to read two chapters in the text book.
    Suggestion: You had better read the *assignment* before class.
    Assumption: So you did read the *assignment* after all.
    Problem: I can't finish the *assignment* before class.

assistant professor   n.   a college or university teacher who ranks above a lecturer and below an associate professor
    Example: Dr. Green is an *assistant professor*.
    Suggestion: Why don't you find out whether he is a lecturer or an *assistant professor*?
    Assumption: You mean Dr. Green isn't an *assistant professor*?
    Problem: I need to find out whether Dr. Green is an *assistant professor*.

assistantship   n.   an opportunity for a graduate student to teach or do research in exchange for a stipend
    Example: Terry got an *assistantship* from State University.
    Suggestion: If I were you, I would apply for an *assistantship*.
    Assumption: So you did get an *assistantship* from State University.
    Problem: The *assistantship* doesn't pay as much as I thought it would.

associate professor   n.   a college or university teacher who ranks above an assistant professor
and below a professor

Example: Dr. Peterson is an *associate professor* now, but she will be promoted to a full
professor at the end of the year.

Suggestion: You could ask the secretary if Dr. Peterson is an *associate professor*.

Assumption: Dr. Peterson isn't an *associate professor*, is she?

Problem: If Dr. Peterson is an *associate professor*, I used the wrong title in my letter to her.

audit   v.   to attend a course without credit

Example: It usually costs as much to *audit* a course as to take it for credit.

Suggestion: You could *audit* the course if you don't need the credit.

Assumption: You mean you are *auditing* the course?

Problem: If I *audit* the course, I won't get credit for it.

bear   n.   a difficult class

Example: That computer science course was a *bear*.

Suggestion: I heard that Dr. Young's class is a real *bear*, so I would advise against it this
semester.

Assumption: Your roommate thought this class was a *bear*?

Problem: Two of the classes I am in are real *bears*.

be behind   v.   to be late; to have a lot of work to do

Example: I *am behind* in my physics class.

Suggestion: You *are behind* in your psychology class so you should study.

Assumption: Bill *is behind*?

Problem: I can't go to the party because I *am behind* in my classes.

bike   n.   an abbreviation of the word *bicycle*

Example: Many students ride their *bikes* on campus.

Suggestion: You could park your *bike* outside the student union building.

Assumption: Your *bike* was locked?

Problem: I can't ride my *bike* to the pizza parlor because there isn't any parking for it.

bike rack   n.   the metal supports where bicycles are parked

Example: That *bike rack* is full, but there is another one by the library.

Suggestion: If I were you, I would use the *bike rack* closest to the door.

Assumption: The *bike rack* was moved from in front of the library?

Problem: The *bike racks* at my dormitory will not hold all of the students' bikes.

blackboard   n.   the writing surface in the front of the classroom

Example: Dr. Mitchell always writes the important words on the *blackboard*.

Suggestion: You had better copy everything the instructor writes on the *blackboard*.

Assumption: You mean you copied all of the material that was on the *blackboard*?

Problem: I can't see what is written on the *blackboard*.

book   n.   a written work

Example: The *books* for this class cost eighty dollars.

Suggestion: You shouldn't wait too long to buy your *books*.

Assumption: You didn't buy all of your *books*?

Problem: I can't buy all of my *books* with only fifty dollars.

book bag   n.   a bag in which to carry books and school supplies
Example: This *book bag* is very heavy.
Suggestion: Why don't you buy a sturdy *book bag* so it will last longer?
Assumption: Your brand new *book bag* fell apart?
Problem: I can't carry all of my books at one time because my *book bag* is too small.

bookstore   n.   the store on campus where students buy their text books
Example: The *bookstore* opens at seven in the morning.
Suggestion: You should be at the *bookstore* before it opens so that you can get a used book.
Assumption: You mean that you were at the *bookstore* early and there were still no used books?
Problem: The *bookstore* is too far from my apartment for me to walk.

break   n.   a pause in work or study
Example: Let's take a *break* after we finish our homework.
Suggestion: If I were you, I would take a *break* before I began a new project.
Assumption: You mean you're taking a *break* right now?
Problem: I can't take a *break* until I complete this section of the problem.

bring up   v.   to improve
Example: If Jack doesn't *bring up* his grades, he won't get into graduate school.
Suggestion: If you want to *bring up* your grades, you will have to study more.
Assumption: You *brought up* your grades without studying?
Problem: If I don't study more, I won't be able to *bring up* my grades.

cafeteria   n.   a restaurant where students can select food from several choices and carry their
                meals on trays to their tables
Example: Let's order a pizza instead of going to the *cafeteria.*
Suggestion: Why don't we meet in the *cafeteria* before going to see our advisor?
Assumption: You mean you like the food in the *cafeteria*?
Problem: I can't meet you in the *cafeteria* because I have to speak with my professor after
                class.

call on   v.   to acknowledge in class; to invite to speak
Example: The professor *calls on* students who sit in the front more often than those who sit
                in back.
Suggestion: If you want the professor to *call on* you frequently, then sit in the front of the room.
Assumption: You sat in the front of the room and weren't *called on*?
Problem: I didn't know the answer when the professor *called on* me.

call the roll   v.   to read the names on a class roster in order to take attendance
Example: Some professors don't *call the roll*, but Dr. Peterson always does.
Suggestion: You should always find out whether or not the professor *calls the roll.*
Assumption: You mean you weren't there when Dr. Peterson *called the roll*?
Problem: I need to get to class earlier so that I will be there when Dr. Peterson *calls the roll.*

campus   n.   the buildings and grounds of a college or university
Example: State University has a beautiful *campus.*
Suggestion: You should see the *campus* before you decide to apply to school here.
Assumption: You mean you walked the entire *campus* by yourself?
Problem: I can't go with you to see the *campus* if you go this afternoon.

campus security   n.   the police on campus
    Example: In an emergency, call *campus security*.
    Suggestion: You had better call *campus security* to report that your bicycle is missing.
    Assumption: The *campus security* is understaffed, isn't it?
    Problem: Carol had to call *campus security* to help her get her car started.

carrel   n.   a private study space in the stacks of the library
    Example: There are never enough *carrels* for all of the graduate students.
    Suggestion: You should go to the library early in the evening if you want a *carrel*.
    Assumption: You mean the *carrels* are free?
    Problem: There aren't enough *carrels* in the library.

chapter   n.   a division in a book
    Example: The professor assigned three *chapters* in the textbook.
    Suggestion: If I were you, I would set aside several hours to read all of the *chapters* assigned today.
    Assumption: So you did allow enough time to finish the *chapters*.
    Problem: I have to go to the lab and I am in the middle of a *chapter*.

cheat   v.   to act dishonestly
    Example: Students who *cheat* may be expelled from the university.
    Suggestion: You should not *cheat* because the penalty is serious.
    Assumption: Gary was expelled because he *cheated*?
    Problem: I know that some of my friends *cheated*, but I don't know what to do about it.

cheating   n.   a dishonest act
    Example: Sharing answers on an exam is *cheating*.
    Suggestion: You could sit alone during the exam so that the professor knows you are not *cheating*.
    Assumption: You consider copying a few sentences from a book *cheating*?
    Problem: Should I report it to the professor if I see someone *cheating*?

check out   v.   to borrow
    Example: You must have a library card to *check out* books.
    Suggestion: If you want to *check out* books for your research paper, you had better go to the library soon.
    Assumption: So you didn't go to the library to *check out* the books you needed?
    Problem: I need a new library card to be able to *check out* books.

class   n.   the meeting place and the content of a course
    Example: We have three *classes* together this term.
    Suggestion: You could arrange your schedule so that you have three *classes* on the same day.
    Assumption: So you wanted your *classes* to be on Friday.
    Problem: I have to work on Tuesdays and Thursdays, so I can't have *classes* on those days.

class discussion   n.   an exchange of ideas during a class
    Example: Dr. Green often has *class discussions* instead of lectures.
    Suggestion: If I were you I would prepare for a *class discussion* in tomorrow's class.
    Assumption: You prepared for the *class discussion*, didn't you?
    Problem: I am not ready for the *class discussion* today.

closed out adj. to be denied access to a class
    Example: Register early so that you aren't *closed out* of the classes you want.
    Suggestion: Why don't you plan to register tomorrow before you are *closed out* of the classes you need to graduate?
    Assumption: Sue registered early to avoid being *closed out* of her classes?
    Problem: I was *closed out* of the English class I needed.

coed adj. an abbreviation for *coeducational,* which is a system of education in which both men and women attend the same school or classes
    Example: Most of the schools in the United States are *coed*.
    Suggestion: If I were you, I would live in a *coed* dormitory.
    Assumption: You mean you don't attend a *coed* school?
    Problem: My parents don't want me to live in a *coed* dormitory.

college n. a school that grants a bachelor's degree; an undergraduate division or a school within a university
    Example: Steve applied to the *college* of business at State University.
    Suggestion: You need to apply to the *college* of nursing early.
    Assumption: So you did apply to several *colleges* after all.
    Problem: The *college* of education requires three letters of recommendation.

commencement n. a graduation ceremony
    Example: Larger colleges and universities usually have *commencement* more than once each year.
    Suggestion: You had better be early for *commencement* because it starts on time.
    Assumption: So you did attend last year's *commencement* exercises.
    Problem: I don't have a cap and gown for *commencement*.

committee n. a group of professors who guide a graduate student's program and approve the thesis or dissertation
    Example: Bill's *committee* signed his dissertation today.
    Suggestion: You should be prepared before you meet with your *committee*.
    Assumption: Your *committee* didn't approve your dissertation topic?
    Problem: I need to do more research before I meet with my *committee*.

computer n. a programmable electronic machine that calculates, processes, and stores information
    Example: At some universities, students must bring their own *computers* with them to school.
    Suggestion: If I were you, I would purchase a *computer* before going to college.
    Assumption: You mean you don't know how to use a *computer*?
    Problem: I need to have my *computer* repaired.

computer disk n. a magnetic disk on which computer data is stored
    Example: It's a good idea to save a copy of your papers and projects on a *computer disk*.
    Suggestion: You should always have extra *computer disks*.
    Assumption: You mean you didn't save your work on a *computer disk*?
    Problem: I can't print my paper until I find my *computer disk*.

counselor n. a person who gives advice, often of a personal nature
    Example: See your advisor for academic advice and a *counselor* for personal advice.
    Suggestion: Why don't you speak with your *counselor* about the problems with your roommate?
    Assumption: You mean you have to make an appointment before seeing your *counselor*?
    Problem: I can't see my *counselor* until tomorrow.

course   n.   a class
> Example: How many *courses* are you taking this semester?
> Suggestion: If I were you, I would take fewer *courses* this semester.
> Assumption: You registered for your *courses* already?
> Problem: I need to take *courses* that apply to my major.

course request (form)   n.   a form used to register for a class
> Example: A student's academic advisor usually signs a *course request* form.
> Suggestion: You should pick up a *course request* form from the registrar's office today.
> Assumption: So you did pick up your *course request* form.
> Problem: I need to speak with my advisor about my *course request* form.

cram   v.   to study at the last minute
> Example: Nancy always *crams* for the quizzes in her math class.
> Suggestion: Why don't you study each night instead of *cramming* the night before the test?
> Assumption: You mean you *crammed* for the biology final?
> Problem: I need to be more organized so I won't have to *cram* for my tests.

credit   n.   a unit of study
> Example: I have thirty *credits* toward my master's degree.
> Suggestion: Why don't you check your *credits* with your advisor?
> Assumption: You mean you have enough *credits* to graduate?
> Problem: I have to take thirty more *credits* in my major area.

credit hour   n.   the number that represents one hour of class per week for one term
> Example: This course is three *credit hours*.
> Suggestion: You could take eighteen *credit hours* this semester.
> Assumption: So you did complete fifteen *credit hours* last summer.
> Problem: I can't take enough *credit hours* to graduate this semester.

curve   n.   a grading system that relies on the normal curve of distribution, resulting in a few
>   A grades, the majority C grades, and a few failing grades
> Example: Grading on the *curve* encourages competition.
> Suggestion: Forget about the *curve*, and just do your best.
> Assumption: Dr. Graham grades his tests on the *curve*?
> Problem: Since the exams were graded on the *curve*, a 95 was a B.

cut class   v.   to be absent from class, usually without a good excuse
> Example: My roommate *cut class* on Monday because he didn't come back to campus until
>   late Sunday night.
> Suggestion: You had better not *cut class* on Thursday.
> Assumption: You *cut class* to sleep in?
> Problem: I can't *cut class* because I have too many absences.

dean   n.   an administrator who ranks above a department chair and below a vice president
> Example: The *dean* called a meeting with the department chair.
> Suggestion: You should meet with the *dean* about your problem.
> Assumption: So you did speak with the *dean*.
> Problem: Vicki has to prepare a presentation for the *dean*.

dean's list   n.   the honor roll at a college or university
   Example: You must maintain a 3.5 grade point average to be on the *dean's list*.
   Suggestion: You had better improve your grades if your want to make the *dean's list*.
   Assumption: Jack made the *dean's list* last semester?
   Problem: I can't make the *dean's list* this semester.

declare   v.   to make an official decision about a major field of study
   Example: Most students *declare* their major in their third year at the university.
   Suggestion: If I were you, I would *declare* my major before I take any more classes.
   Assumption: You mean you *declared* your major last year?
   Problem: Joe needs to *declare* his major soon.

degree   n.   an academic title awarded to a student who completes a course of study
   Example: The three most common *degrees* are a bachelor's, a master's, and a doctorate.
   Suggestion: You should get your *degree* before you get married.
   Assumption: So you did graduate with a *degree* in music theory.
   Problem: I can't get a good job without a *degree*.

department   n.   a division of a college or university organized by subject
   Example: The English *department* offers classes for international students.
   Suggestion: Why don't you check the *department's* phone number again?
   Assumption: So you worked in the English *department* office.
   Problem: I can't find the list of the *department* offices.

department chair   n.   a university administrator for a division of a college or university
   Example: The professors in a department report to the *department chair*.
   Suggestion: You could speak to the *department chair* about auditing the class.
   Assumption: You mean Dr. Carlson is the new *department chair*?
   Problem: I can't meet with the *department chair* until after registration.

diploma   n.   the certificate of completion for a degree
   Example: Students receive their *diplomas* at the graduation ceremony.
   Suggestion: You should get your *diploma* framed.
   Assumption: So you did show your family your *diploma*.
   Problem: I need to mail this form and pay my fees before I can get my *diploma*.

dissertation   n.   a thesis that is written in partial fulfillment of the requirements for a doctorate.
   Example: Dr. Green wrote his *dissertation* on global warming.
   Suggestion: If I were you, I would consider several ideas before selecting a *dissertation* topic.
   Assumption: You mean you already started your *dissertation*?
   Problem: I can't find enough research on my *dissertation* topic.

distance learning   n.   courses organized so that students can complete the requirements by computer, or other media, often without going to campus
   Example: There are several *distance learning* opportunities for working adults.
   Suggestion: Why don't you sign up for that course through *distance learning*?
   Assumption: So you did take that *distance learning* class.
   Problem: I can only take three *distance learning* classes.

division   n.   a group of departments in a college or university
Example: The *division* of modern languages includes both the Spanish department and the French department as well as the German department.
Suggestion: Why don't you go to the *division* of math and sciences to find more information about biology instructors?
Assumption: You mean you've already spoken to Dr. Conrad about the entrance exam for the *division* of social sciences?
Problem: I need to find out what opportunities the *division* of modern languages offers for foreign study.

doctorate   n.   the degree after a master's degree awarded to an academic doctor
Example: Karen will receive her *doctorate* in the spring.
Suggestion: You should meet with your academic advisor to discuss a *doctorate*.
Assumption: So you did receive your *doctorate* from State University.
Problem: I must complete my dissertation before I get my *doctorate*.

dorm   n.   an abbreviation for *dormitory*
Example: Living on campus in a *dorm* is often cheaper than living off campus.
Suggestion: You should live in a *dorm* for at least one year.
Assumption: You lived in a *dorm* for four years?
Problem: Sue needs to apply now for a room in the *dorm*.

draft   n.   a preliminary copy of a paper or other written document
Example: A good student does not turn in a first *draft* of a paper.
Suggestion: You should edit each *draft* on the computer.
Assumption: You wrote the first *draft* in one night?
Problem: I can't turn in my essay because I have only the first *draft* written.

drop   v.   to withdraw from a course
Example: If you *drop* a course early in the term, you may get a partial refund.
Suggestion: If I were you, I would *drop* the class immediately.
Assumption: You mean you *dropped* the class because it was too hard?
Problem: Bill needs to *drop* one of his classes because he is taking too many credit hours.

drop out   v.   to withdraw from a college or university
Example: Mark *dropped out* because he needed to work full-time.
Suggestion: You could *drop out* and then reenter next semester.
Assumption: Diane *dropped out* after her junior year?
Problem: I have to *drop out* because I don't have enough money for tuition.

due   adj.   expected on a certain date
Example: The assignment is *due* on Friday.
Suggestion: Why don't you turn in the paper before it's *due*?
Assumption: You mean the project is *due* this week?
Problem: I can't complete the assignment by the *due* date.

elective (course)   n., adj.   an optional academic course
Example: In the junior year, most students are taking *elective* courses as well as requirements.
Suggestion: Take some *elective* classes in your areas of outside interest.
Assumption: So you did take an *elective* in art appreciation.
Problem: I can't take any *elective* classes this semester.

enrolled   adj.   registered for a course or a university program
    Example: Only a few students are *enrolled* in seminars.
    Suggestion: Why don't you *enroll* early before the class fills up?
    Assumption: You mean you didn't *enroll* in the computer class?
    Problem: I can't *enroll* in that class without taking the introductory class first.

essay   n.   a short composition on a single subject, usually presenting the personal opinion of the author
    Example: An *essay* is often five paragraphs long.
    Suggestion: If I were you, I would make an outline before writing the *essay*.
    Assumption: So you did pass the *essay* class.
    Problem: I have to write an *essay* for my class on Friday.

exam   n.   an abbreviation for *examination*
    Example: The professor scheduled several quizzes and one *exam*.
    Suggestion: You had better prepare for the *exam* in chemistry.
    Assumption: You studied for the physics *exam*?
    Problem: I have to meet with my study group before the *exam*.

excused absence   n.   absence with the permission of the professor
    Example: Dr. Mitchell allows every student one *excused absence* each semester.
    Suggestion: You could take an *excused absence* in your Friday class so we could leave early.
    Assumption: You mean you have two *excused absences* in biology?
    Problem: I already have one *excused absence* in Dr. Mitchell's class.

expel   v.   to dismiss from school
    Example: Gary was *expelled* because he cheated on an exam.
    Suggestion: You should avoid getting *expelled* at all costs.
    Assumption: Gary was *expelled* from the university?
    Problem: I would be *expelled* if I helped you.

extension   n.   additional time
    Example: We asked Dr. Peterson for an *extension* in order to complete the group project.
    Suggestion: You should organize your time so that you will not have to ask for an *extension*.
    Assumption: You mean your request for an *extension* was denied?
    Problem: I need to meet with my professor to discuss an *extension*.

faculty member   n.   a teacher in a college or university
    Example: Dr. Baker is a *faculty member* at State University.
    Suggestion: Why don't you ask a *faculty member* for directions?
    Assumption: You didn't meet any of the new *faculty members* when you visited the campus?
    Problem: I don't know the other *faculty members* in my department very well.

fail   v.   to receive an unacceptable grade
    Example: If Mary gets another low grade, she will *fail* the course.
    Suggestion: You had better complete the project or you will *fail* the class.
    Assumption: You mean you *failed* the exam?
    Problem: I have to study tonight or I will *fail* the test tomorrow.

fee   n.   a charge for services
    Example: You must pay a *fee* to park your car on campus.
    Suggestion: If I were you, I would pay my *fees* before the late penalty applies.
    Assumption: You mean there are *fees* for using the recreational facilities?
    Problem: I need to go to the business office to pay my *fees*.

field trip   n.   a trip for observation and education
    Example: The geology class usually takes several *field trips* to the museum.
    Suggestion: You should wear sturdy shoes on the *field trip*.
    Assumption: You didn't sign up for the *field trip* to the art gallery?
    Problem: I have to go on a *field trip* Saturday morning, but my boss won't let me off work.

fill-in-the-blank (test)   n., adj.   an objective test in which the student completes sentences by writing in the missing words
    Example: Dr. Stephens always gives *fill-in-the-blank* tests during the semester, but he gives short-essay finals.
    Suggestion: You had better study the definitions for the *fill-in-the-blank* portion of the test.
    Assumption: You mean the test was all *fill-in-the-blank*?
    Problem: Kathy needs to do better on the *fill-in-the-blank* questions.

final (exam)   n.   the last examination of an academic course
    Example: The *final* will include questions from the notes as well as from the textbook.
    Suggestion: You should use both your notes and the text to review for the *final* exam.
    Assumption: You finished your *final* in an hour?
    Problem: I have to prepare for two *final* exams on the same day.

fine   n.   a sum of money paid for violation of a rule
    Example: The *fine* for keeping a library book after the due date is one dollar per day.
    Suggestion: You should move your car to avoid a *fine*.
    Assumption: You mean you were charged a *fine* for parking there?
    Problem: I need to pay my *fines* before the end of the semester.

fraternity   n.   a social organization for male college students
    Example: Bill is going to join a *fraternity*.
    Suggestion: You could join a professional *fraternity*.
    Assumption: You were invited to join three *fraternities*?
    Problem: I can't afford to join a *fraternity*.

fraternity row   n.   a street where many fraternity houses are located
    Example: I live on Fifth Street, near *fraternity row*.
    Suggestion: Why don't you walk down *fraternity row* to look at the homecoming decorations?
    Assumption: Isn't Ken going to live on *fraternity row* next year?
    Problem: I can't find a place to park on *fraternity row*.

freshman   n.   a first-year college student
    Example: Most of the students in Manchester Hall are *freshmen*.
    Suggestion: You should establish good study habits while you are a *freshman*.
    Assumption: Didn't you live in a dorm when you were a *freshman*?
    Problem: The *freshmen* have to take requirements.

full-time adj. the number of hours for standard tuition at a college or university, usually 9 hours for a graduate student and 12–15 hours for an undergraduate student

Example: Tom is a *full-time* student this semester.
Suggestion: If I were you, I would register as a *full-time* student this semester.
Assumption: You mean the scholarship is only available to *full-time* students?
Problem: I need to register as a *full-time* student to be eligible for a loan.

get behind v. to be late or off schedule

Example: I am *getting behind* in my math class.
Suggestion: You had better study this weekend or you will *get behind* in English.
Assumption: Ken *got behind* in his classes?
Problem: I *got behind* in French, and now my class is really confusing.

get caught up v. to bring up to date

Example: We are going to *get caught up* in our classes this weekend.
Suggestion: Why don't you *get caught up* in English before you start your next project?
Assumption: Sue *got caught up* over vacation?
Problem: I need to *get caught up* before final exams.

G.P.A. n. abbreviation for grade point average

Example: Kathy's *G.P.A.* as an undergraduate was 4.0, but she isn't doing as well in graduate school.
Suggestion: You should be concerned about your *G.P.A.*
Assumption: Laura's *G.P.A.* dropped last semester?
Problem: I can't raise my *G.P.A.* if I take calculus.

grade point average n. a scale, usually 0–4, on which grades are calculated

Example: If students' *grade point averages* fall below 2.0, they will be placed on probation.
Suggestion: If I were you, I would speak to my academic advisor about your *grade point average*.
Assumption: You mean your *grade point average* is more important than work experience?
Problem: I need to improve my *grade point average*.

grades n. a standard number or letter indicating a student's level of performance

Example: We will get our *grades* in the mail a week after the semester is over.
Suggestion: You should check the *grades* that the professor posted.
Assumption: Our *grades* are already in the mail?
Problem: I have to have better *grades* to get into the college of business.

graduate school n. a division of a college or university to serve students who are pursuing masters or doctoral degrees

Example: I would like to apply to *graduate school* after I complete my bachelor's degree.
Suggestion: Why don't you work a year before applying to *graduate school*?
Assumption: So Tracy did get accepted to *graduate school*?
Problem: I have to get letters of recommendation to apply to *graduate school*.

graduate student n. a student who is pursuing a master's or doctorate

Example: *Graduate students* must maintain higher grades than undergraduate students.
Suggestion: You had better work with the other *graduate students* on this project.
Assumption: You mean only *graduate students* are allowed to take this class?
Problem: All of the students in the class are *graduate students* except me.

grant   n.   funds for research or study
    Example: Carol received a *grant* for her research in psychology.
    Suggestion: You should apply for a summer *grant*.
    Assumption: You mean there are *grants* available for undergraduate students?
    Problem: Bill needs to write a proposal before Tuesday if he wants to be considered for a *grant*.

group project   n.   an assignment to be completed by three or more students
    Example: I prefer to work on *group projects* instead of on assignments by myself.
    Suggestion: You should select your *group project* before midterm.
    Assumption: You've chosen your *group project* already?
    Problem: The *group project* will take more time than I thought.

hand back   v.   return an assignment
    Example: Dr. Graham always *hands back* our assignments the next day.
    Suggestion: You had better be there when Dr. Mitchell *hands back* your exam.
    Assumption: Dr. Mitchell hasn't *handed back* your exam yet?
    Problem: I can't find the exam that he *handed back*.

handout   n.   prepared notes that a teacher provides to the class
    Example: Dr. Stephen's *handouts* are always very helpful.
    Suggestion: You had better save all of your *handouts*.
    Assumption: You lost the *handouts*?
    Problem: I need to organize all of my *handouts* before I start to study for the final.

head resident   n.   the advisor for a dormitory
    Example: The *head resident* can help you resolve problems with your roommate.
    Suggestion: If I were you, I would introduce myself to the *head resident*.
    Assumption: So you did speak with the *head resident*.
    Problem: I can't find the *head resident*.

health center   n.   the clinic on campus to provide basic health care for students
    Example: We are going to the *health center* for a free eye examination.
    Suggestion: You had better go to the *health center* for that cough.
    Assumption: You mean the *health center* is closed?
    Problem: I am too sick to go to the *health center*.

health insurance   n.   protection for students who may need medical attention
    Example: *Health insurance* is required on most campuses.
    Suggestion: You need to purchase *health insurance* through the university.
    Assumption: You don't have a *health insurance* policy?
    Problem: I have to earn some more money to pay for my *health insurance*.

hit the books   v.   to study very hard
    Example: I have to *hit the books* tonight and tomorrow to get ready for the midterm.
    Suggestion: You had better *hit the books* for Dr. Sheridan's exam.
    Assumption: You mean you didn't *hit the books* for the psychology exam?
    Problem: My friends have to *hit the books* this weekend so they can't go to the party with me.

homework n.   schoolwork done at home
    Example: If I do my *homework* every day, I understand the lectures better.
    Suggestion: Why don't you do your *homework* before dinner?
    Assumption: There wasn't any *homework* last night, was there?
    Problem: I have to do my *homework* in order to be prepared for the class discussion.

honors n.   a program of study or a special recognition for exceptional students
    Example: Jane is graduating with *honors*.
    Suggestion: You could live in an *honors* dorm.
    Assumption: So you did enroll in the *honors* program.
    Problem: The courses in the *honors* program are much harder than the regular courses.

housing office n.   an administrative office for residence halls and off-campus rentals
    Example: Let's go over to the *housing office* to ask about apartments near the campus.
    Suggestion: If I were you, I would check at the *housing office* for a dorm application.
    Assumption: You mean the *housing office* closed early?
    Problem: I need to speak with someone in the *housing office* about my application.

incomplete n.   a grade in a course that allows students to complete requirements the following term
    Example: I asked Dr. Young for an *incomplete* in his class.
    Suggestion: You should request an *incomplete* at least two weeks before the end of the term.
    Assumption: Bill took an *incomplete* in sociology last semester?
    Problem: I can't ask Dr. Young for another *incomplete*.

instructor n.   a college or university teacher who ranks below an assistant professor
    Example: My *instructor* for math is from Hawaii.
    Suggestion: You should check with the *instructor* to see if there is room in the class.
    Assumption: The *instructor* was absent?
    Problem: I can't seem to get along with my *instructor*.

interactive television (course) n.   a distance learning course that is taught on two-way television connections
    Example: The instructor for our *interactive television* course is on a campus about fifty miles away.
    Suggestion: You could take that class on the *interactive television*.
    Assumption: Dr. Stephen's class is offered on *interactive television*?
    Problem: *Interactive television* classes make me uncomfortable.

interlibrary loan n.   a system that allows students on one campus to borrow books from other libraries on other campuses
    Example: It takes at least a week to receive a book by *interlibrary loan*.
    Suggestion: You could see if the book is available through *interlibrary loan*.
    Assumption: Your *interlibrary loan* books arrived in time?
    Problem: I can't seem to find the desk for *interlibrary loans*.

internship n.   a training opportunity for an advanced student or a recent graduate
    Example: Bill got an *internship* at the University Hospital.
    Suggestion: You should apply for an *internship* very early.
    Assumption: You are getting paid for your *internship*?
    Problem: I need to serve a two-year *internship*.

junior   n.   a third-year college student
Example:	When I am a *junior*, I plan to study abroad for a semester.
Suggestion:	You could concentrate on your major your *junior* year.
Assumption:	A *junior* can study abroad?
Problem:	I need to carry eighteen credit hours both semesters of my *junior* year.

keep grades up   v.   to maintain a good grade point average
Example:	If Joanne doesn't *keep her grades up*, she will lose her scholarship.
Suggestion:	You need to study harder if you want to *keep your grades up*.
Assumption:	Kathy didn't *keep her grades up* this semester?
Problem:	I can't *keep my grades up* and work full-time.

lab   n.   abbreviation for laboratory
Example:	The course includes a five-hour *lab*.
Suggestion:	You had better allow sufficient time for your biology *lab*.
Assumption:	You missed the last *lab* session?
Problem:	I need to find a partner for my psychology *lab*.

lab assistant   n.   a graduate student who helps in the lab
Example:	Bill is Dr. Peterson's *lab assistant*.
Suggestion:	You could ask the *lab assistant* for help.
Assumption:	You are the *lab assistant*, aren't you?
Problem:	I need to speak with the *lab assistant* before class.

laboratory   n.   a classroom equipped for experiments and research
Example:	The physics *laboratory* at State University is very old.
Suggestion:	You could meet your biology study group in the *laboratory*.
Assumption:	The *laboratory* isn't closed Saturday, is it?
Problem:	I have to get directions to the *laboratory*.

lab report   n.   a written description of the laboratory activities
Example:	Our *lab reports* are due every Friday.
Suggestion:	If I were you, I wouldn't wait to start my *lab report*.
Assumption:	You mean the *lab reports* have to be typed?
Problem:	I have to turn in my *lab report* tomorrow.

learning assistance center   n.   an area used for tutoring and special programs to help students with their classes
Example:	I have to meet my tutor at the *learning assistance center* at four o'clock.
Suggestion:	You should go to the *learning assistance center* for help in the morning.
Assumption:	So Nancy did go to the *learning assistance center* for tutoring.
Problem:	The tutors at the *learning assistance center* are all juniors and seniors, so I don't qualify.

lecture   n.   a presentation for a class, delivered by the professor
Example:	The *lectures* are really interesting, but I don't enjoy the labs as much.
Suggestion:	You should take more notes during Dr. Mitchell's *lectures*.
Assumption:	The *lecture* is canceled for today?
Problem:	I can't keep up with the *lectures*.

lecturer   n.   a college or university teacher, usually without rank
  Example: Mr. Lewis is only a *lecturer*, but his classes are very good.
  Suggestion: If I were you, I would speak with the *lecturer* about your questions.
  Assumption: The *lecturer* isn't here?
  Problem: I can't take notes because the *lecturer* speaks too fast.

library   n.   the building on campus where books and other research materials are kept
  Example: Vicki has a job in the *library*.
  Suggestion: Your study group could reserve a study room in the *library*.
  Assumption: You mean the *library* is within walking distance?
  Problem: I need to return my books to the *library*.

library card   n.   an identification card that permits the holder to borrow books and materials from the library
  Example: Without a *library card*, you can't borrow books here.
  Suggestion: You should get a *library card* right away.
  Assumption: So you did bring your *library card* with you.
  Problem: I can't use my *library card* because I owe a fine.

library fine   n.   a payment for returning books and materials after the due date
  Example: You can't get your grade report unless you pay your *library fines*.
  Suggestion: You should pay your *library fines* immediately.
  Assumption: You owe ten dollars in *library fines*?
  Problem: Nancy needs to pay her *library fines* before she checks out any more books.

lost and found   n.   an area on campus where items are kept for their owners to reclaim
  Example: Maybe someone picked up your book and took it to the *lost and found*.
  Suggestion: Why don't you check at the *lost and found* for your backpack?
  Assumption: You mean Sue's wallet wasn't at the *lost and found*?
  Problem: Sue needs to fill out a report at the *lost and found*.

lower-division (course)   adj.   introductory-level courses for first- and second-year students
  Example: Seniors don't usually take *lower-division* courses.
  Suggestion: You should take *lower-division* classes your first year.
  Assumption: You mean all of the *lower-division* classes are full?
  Problem: I have to take a *lower-division* class before I can take the advanced course.

major   n.   a field of study chosen as an academic specialty
  Example: My *major* is environmental studies.
  Suggestion: You should declare your *major* by your junior year.
  Assumption: You mean you have to declare a *major* to graduate?
  Problem: I have to tell my advisor my *major* tomorrow.

makeup test   n.   a test taken after the date of the original administration
  Example: Dr. Stephens usually allows her students to take a *makeup test* if there is a good reason for being absent.
  Suggestion: You could speak with Dr. Stephens about taking a *makeup test*.
  Assumption: Dr. Peterson let you take a *makeup test*?
  Problem: Dana needs to take a *makeup test* before spring break.

married student housing   n.   apartments on or near campus for married students
    Example: There is usually a waiting list to be assigned to *married student housing*.
    Suggestion: If I were you, I would get an application for *married student housing* today.
    Assumption: You mean there are no vacancies in *married student housing*?
    Problem: We need to pick up an application for *married student housing*.

Mickey Mouse course   n.   a very easy course
    Example: This is a *Mickey Mouse course,* but it is on my program of study.
    Suggestion: Why don't you take one *Mickey Mouse course* this semester just for fun?
    Assumption: You thought physics was a *Mickey Mouse course*?
    Problem: I have to take this *Mickey Mouse course* to fulfill my physical education requirement.

midterm   n.   an exam that is given in the middle of the term
    Example: I got an A on my *midterm* in accounting.
    Suggestion: Why don't you study with your study group for the music theory *midterm*?
    Assumption: You mean Sue failed her economics *midterm*?
    Problem: I have three *midterms* in one day.

minor   n.   a secondary area of study
    Example: With a major in international business, I decided to do my *minor* in English.
    Suggestion: You should *minor* in economics since you're studying prelaw.
    Assumption: You mean you've completed all of your *minor* classes?
    Problem: I need one more class to complete my *minor*.

miss (class)   v.   to be absent
    Example: My roommate is *missing* a lot of classes lately.
    Suggestion: If I were you I wouldn't *miss* Dr. Mitchell's class today.
    Assumption: So you did *miss* class last Friday.
    Problem: I can't *miss* any more of Dr. Mitchell's classes or my grade will be lowered by one
                 letter.

multiple-choice test   n.   an objective test with questions that provide several possible answer choices
    Example: We usually have *multiple-choice tests* in Dr. Graham's classes.
    Suggestion: You had better study very carefully for Dr. Graham's *multiple-choice test*.
    Assumption: It was a *multiple-choice test*?
    Problem: I don't usually do well on *multiple-choice tests*.

notebook   n.   a bound book with blank pages in it for notes
    Example: I lost the *notebook* with my biology notes in it.
    Suggestion: You should make sure that your *notebook* is well organized.
    Assumption: You lost your *notebook*?
    Problem: I need to organize my *notebook* this weekend.

notebook computer   n.   a computer the size of a notebook
    Example: Joe has a *notebook computer* that he uses in class.
    Suggestion: Why don't you use my *notebook computer* to see whether you like it?
    Assumption: So you did purchase a *notebook computer*.
    Problem: I can't possibly afford a *notebook computer* right now.

notes   n.   a brief record of a lecture to help students recall the important points
  Example: We didn't take *notes* in class today because most of the lecture was from the book.
  Suggestion: You should copy Tracy's *notes* before the next test.
  Assumption: You mean you lent your *notes* to someone?
  Problem: I need to recopy my *notes* this evening.

objective test   n.   a test with questions that have one possible answer, usually presented in a multiple-choice, matching, or true-false format
  Example: The final exam will be an *objective test*, not an essay test.
  Suggestion: You should probably prepare for an *objective test* in math.
  Assumption: The final exam was an *objective test*?
  Problem: I have to study harder for *objective tests*.

off campus   adj.   not on university property
  Example: There are some very nice apartments just *off campus* on State Street.
  Suggestion: You should come to campus early unless you want to park *off campus*.
  Assumption: You mean Carol doesn't want to live *off campus*?
  Problem: I need to live *off campus* to save money.

office   n.   a place for university faculty and staff to meet with students and do their work
  Example: Mr. Lewis has an *office* in Madison Hall.
  Suggestion: Most of the advisors' *offices* are in Sycamore Hall.
  Assumption: So you did find Mr. Lewis's *office* before he left for the day.
  Problem: I have to go to the business *office* tomorrow to ask about my bill.

office hours   n.   a schedule when faculty are in their offices to meet with students
  Example: *Office hours* are usually posted on the door of the professor's office.
  Suggestion: You should write down the instructor's *office hours* in your notebook.
  Assumption: You don't know Dr. Miller's *office hours*?
  Problem: I can't find my copy of Dr. Miller's *office hours*.

online course   n.   a course taught on the Internet
  Example: There is a separate list of *online courses* this semester.
  Suggestion: Why don't you consider an *online course* in economics?
  Assumption: Joe took an *online course* last year?
  Problem: I need a computer to take an *online course*.

on probation   prep.   experiencing a trial period to improve grades before disciplinary action
  Example: Kathy is *on probation,* so she will probably be studying this weekend.
  Suggestion: You had better keep up your grades or you will end up *on probation*.
  Assumption: Sue couldn't be *on probation* again.
  Problem: I can't let my parents find out that I am *on probation*.

on reserve   prep.   retained in a special place in the library, usually for use only in the library.
  Example: Dr. Young always puts a lot of books *on reserve* for his classes.
  Suggestion: You could check to see if the book is *on reserve*.
  Assumption: You mean the articles are *on reserve*?
  Problem: I have to find out which books are *on reserve*.

open-book test   n.   a test during which students may consult their books and notes
Example: *Open-book tests* are often longer than other tests.
Suggestion: You should still prepare even though it is an *open-book test*.
Assumption: You mean you didn't know it was an *open-book test*?
Problem: I can't find my notes for the *open-book test*.

orientation   n.   a program for new students at a college or university during which they receive
                          information about the school
Example: I missed the first day of *orientation*, so I didn't get a map.
Suggestion: You should sit near the front during *orientation*.
Assumption: So you did go to freshman *orientation*.
Problem: I have to go to *orientation* tomorrow evening.

override   n.   permission to enter a class for which the student does not qualify
Example: Dr. Stephens will usually give you an *override* if you need the class.
Suggestion: You should speak to the professor about getting an *override* for that class.
Assumption: You mean your request for an *override* was denied?
Problem: I need to get an *override* so that I can take that class.

paper   n.   a research report
Example: The *papers* for this class should be at least ten pages long.
Suggestion: You had better follow Dr. Carlyle's guidelines for this *paper*.
Assumption: Laura turned in her *paper* late?
Problem: I can't print my *paper* because I need an ink cartridge for my printer.

parking garage   n.   a structure for parking, usually requiring payment
Example: The *parking garages* are too far away from the classrooms.
Suggestion: You had better get a parking permit for the *parking garage*.
Assumption: You mean you don't know which *parking garage* you used?
Problem: I have to find a *parking garage* with a vacancy.

parking lot   n.   an area for parking
Example: This *parking lot* is for students only.
Suggestion: You should avoid leaving your car in the *parking lot* overnight.
Assumption: You mean your car was towed from the *parking lot*?
Problem: I have to leave early to get a spot in the *parking lot* beside the dorm.

parking permit   n.   permission to park in certain parking lots or garages
Example: Your *parking permit* expires at the end of the month.
Suggestion: If I were you, I would get a *parking permit* when you register.
Assumption: My *parking permit* has expired?
Problem: I need to pay my fines before they will issue me another *parking permit*.

parking space   n.   a designated area for one car
Example: There is a car in my *parking space*.
Suggestion: You should not use a reserved *parking space*.
Assumption: So you did park in someone else's *parking space*.
Problem: I can't find a *parking space*.

parking ticket n.   notice of a fine due for parking in a restricted area
    Example: If you don't take care of your *parking tickets*, you won't be able to register for classes next semester.
    Suggestion: You could avoid getting *parking tickets* by using the student parking lots.
    Assumption: You mean Carol got a *parking ticket* because she didn't have a permit?
    Problem: I have to save money to pay my *parking ticket*s.

part-time adj.   less than the full work day or school day
    Example: Laura has a *part-time* job after school.
    Suggestion: Why don't you get a *part-time* job to pay for your books?
    Assumption: You applied for a *part-time* job on campus?
    Problem: I need to find a *part-time* job this summer.

pass back v.   to return tests and assignments to the owner
    Example: Dr. Young is going to *pass back* our quizzes today.
    Suggestion: You should ask Dr. Young for an appointment after he *passes back* the tests.
    Assumption: Dr. Young didn't *pass back* the papers?
    Problem: I have to get my paper from Dr. Young because I wasn't there when he *passed them back*.

placement office n.   the office where students receive assistance in locating employment
    Example: Several companies are interviewing students at the *placement office* this week.
    Suggestion: Why don't you check the interview listing in the *placement office* on Monday?
    Assumption: Joe got his job through the *placement office*?
    Problem: I need to schedule an interview in the *placement office*.

plagiarize v.   to use someone else's written work without giving that person credit
    Example: To avoid *plagiarizing*, always cite the source.
    Suggestion: If you change this sentence, it will keep you from *plagiarizing*.
    Assumption: You mean you know someone who *plagiarized*?
    Problem: The professor thought that I had *plagiarized* a report.

pop quiz n.   a quiz that is given without notice
    Example: We had a *pop quiz* in our sociology class today.
    Suggestion: You should always be prepared for a *pop quiz*.
    Assumption: You passed all of the *pop quizzes*?
    Problem: I have to be on time to class in case there is a *pop quiz* at the beginning of class.

post (grade) v.   to publish a list and display it in a public place
    Example: The grades for the exams are *posted* on Dr. Graham's door.
    Suggestion: You should see if the grades have been *posted* yet.
    Assumption: The assignments aren't *posted* yet, are they?
    Problem: I can't get to campus to see if the grades are *posted*.

prerequisite n.   a course required before a student is eligible to take a higher-level course
    Example: This English class has two *prerequisites*.
    Suggestion: You should check the *prerequisites* before seeing your advisor.
    Assumption: You took the *prerequisites* last year?
    Problem: I have to pass the *prerequisites* before I can register for the next class.

presentation   n.   a lecture, speech, or demonstration in front of the class
    Example: Your *presentation* in our anthropology class was very interesting.
    Suggestion: You could use more pictures in your *presentation*.
    Assumption: You mean your *presentation* is fifty minutes long?
    Problem: I need to get over my fear of public speaking before I give my *presentation*.

professor   n.   a college or university teacher who ranks above an associate professor
    Example: Dr. Baker is a *professor* of English.
    Suggestion: Why don't you speak with your *professor* about the project?
    Assumption: The *professor's* office hours are posted, aren't they?
    Problem: I need to speak to my *professor* before class on Friday.

program of study   n.   a list of the courses that a student must take to fulfill the requirements for
                                    graduation
    Example: If you want to change your *program of study*, you must see your advisor.
    Suggestion: Why don't you review your *program of study* in your catalog?
    Assumption: The *program of study* is a four-year plan, isn't it?
    Problem: I need to become familiar with my *program of study*

project   n.   an assignment that often involves the application of knowledge
    Example: We can do the *project* by ourselves or in a group.
    Suggestion: Why don't you and your study group do the *project* together?
    Assumption: You did the *project* that everyone is talking about?
    Problem: I have to present my *project* to the class.

quarter   n.   a school term that is usually ten to twelve weeks in length
    Example: This *quarter* has gone by very quickly.
    Suggestion: You could take fewer classes next *quarter*.
    Assumption: You mean you have to finish your thesis this *quarter*?
    Problem: I need to study harder next *quarter*.

quiz   n.   an evaluation that is usually shorter and worth fewer points than a test
    Example: We have a *quiz* in our algebra class every week.
    Suggestion: You should always be prepared for a *quiz*.
    Assumption: The *quiz* doesn't include last night's reading, does it?
    Problem: We have a *quiz* in chemistry this week.

registrar   n.   a university official in charge of keeping records
    Example: You need to see the *registrar* about your grade change.
    Suggestion: If I were you, I would check with the *registrar* about your transcript.
    Assumption: So you did file a change of address with the *registrar*.
    Problem: The *registrar* is unavailable until next week.

registration   n.   the process for enrolling in courses at a college or university
    Example: *Registration* always takes longer than I think it will.
    Suggestion: You should meet with your advisor before *registration*.
    Assumption: You mean that early *registration* is available for graduate students?
    Problem: I can't get to *registration* before noon.

report   n.   a written or oral presentation of results, either of research or experimentation
Example:	Ken gave an excellent *report* in our management class today.
Suggestion:	If I were you, I would allow more time for my next *report*.
Assumption:	So you did listen to Ken's *report*.
Problem:	I have to do five oral *reports* for speech class.

research   n.   investigation or study
Example:	Dr. Peterson is going to give a lecture about her *research* on cross-cultural interaction.
Suggestion:	You could use my class for your *research*.
Assumption:	Your *research* is complete, isn't it?
Problem:	I need more sources for my *research*.

research assistant   n.   a research position under the supervision of a faculty member
Example:	The *research assistants* get to know the faculty better than the other graduate students do.
Suggestion:	You could apply to be a *research assistant* next year.
Assumption:	You mean Ken's a *research assistant*?
Problem:	I need to speak to the *research assistant* who works in the psychology lab.

research paper   n.   a written report based on research
Example:	Use at least ten references for your *research papers*.
Suggestion:	You had better go to the library soon if you want that book for your *research paper*.
Assumption:	You mean we have to present our *research paper* to the class?
Problem:	I can't get started on my *research paper*.

resident advisor   n.   an advisor who lives in a dormitory in order to provide supervision and counseling for the students
Example:	We call our *resident advisor* the "head resident."
Suggestion:	Why don't you speak to the *resident advisor* about your problem?
Assumption:	You live next door to the *resident advisor*?
Problem:	I need to speak with the *resident advisor* regarding the desk in my room.

review session   n.   a study meeting to review material before a test, often led by the professor
Example:	I'm on my way to a *review session* for my art appreciation class.
Suggestion:	You could schedule a *review session* with your study group.
Assumption:	The *review session* was productive?
Problem:	I can't meet Thursday afternoon for the *review session*.

room and board   n.   fees for room rent and meals
Example:	The fees for *room and board* go up every year.
Suggestion:	You should plan to include the price of *room and board* in your budget.
Assumption:	You mean your scholarship covers *room and board*?
Problem:	I need to find a part-time job to pay for *room and board*.

roommate   n.   a person who shares a room or rooms
Example:	I think Diane is looking for a *roommate*.
Suggestion:	Why don't you and Diane get another *roommate*?
Assumption:	You mean you're looking for another *roommate*?
Problem:	I need a *roommate* to share my rent.

schedule   n.   a list of courses with days, times, and locations
  Example: My *schedule* this semester allows me to work in the afternoons.
  Suggestion: With your *schedule*, you could get a job at school.
  Assumption: Your *schedule* doesn't include evening classes?
  Problem: I can't fit that class into my *schedule*.

scholarship   n.   a grant awarded to a student
  Example: Tracy got a *scholarship* to attend a special summer course abroad.
  Suggestion: Why don't you apply for a *scholarship*?
  Assumption: There aren't any *scholarships* available for international students, are there?
  Problem: I have to turn the application in tomorrow to be eligible for the *scholarship*.

section   n.   one of several options for the same course
  Example: Everyone wants to take the *section* that Mrs. McNiel teaches.
  Suggestion: You could ask Mrs. McNiel to let you into her *section*.
  Assumption: You mean there are no *sections* open in the morning?
  Problem: I can't get into that *section* because it is closed.

semester   n.   a school term that is usually fifteen to eighteen weeks in length
  Example: When the *semester* is over, I am going to visit my family.
  Suggestion: You could sign up for more classes this *semester*.
  Assumption: This *semester* ends before winter break, doesn't it?
  Problem: I need to take eighteen credit hours next *semester*.

senior   n.   a fourth-year student
  Example: Laura will be a *senior* next semester.
  Suggestion: If I were you, I would take that class as a *senior*.
  Assumption: You mean Dana is a *senior*?
  Problem: I have to take five classes when I'm a *senior*.

short-essay test   n.   a test with questions that require a written response of one sentence to one
                            paragraph in length
  Example: I would rather take a *short-essay test* than an objective test.
  Suggestion: You had better study your notes for Dr. Mitchell's *short-essay test*.
  Assumption: You think a *short-essay test* is easier than an objective test?
  Problem: I have three *short-essay tests* in that class.

shuttle   n.   a bus that has a short route around the campus area
  Example: Carol has a car, but she still uses the campus *shuttle* most of the time.
  Suggestion: If I were you, I would take the *shuttle* at night.
  Assumption: You mean there's no *shuttle* on Sundays?
  Problem: I need to leave early to catch the *shuttle*.

sign up (for a class)   v.   to enroll (in a class)
  Example: Let's *sign up* for the same geology class.
  Suggestion: You should *sign up* for Dr. Brown's music theory class.
  Assumption: So you did *sign up* for the field trip.
  Problem: I can't *sign up* for that class because it conflicts with my schedule.

skip class v. to be absent

Example:	Nancy has been *skipping* class again.
Suggestion:	If I were you, I wouldn't *skip class* this week.
Assumption:	Ken *skipped class* yesterday?
Problem:	Bill *skipped class* on the day of the test.

snack bar n. a small restaurant area where a limited menu is available

Example:	We usually meet at the *snack bar* for a quick lunch.
Suggestion:	You could meet me at the *snack bar*.
Assumption:	So you did go to the *snack bar* after class.
Problem:	I need to go to the *snack bar* between classes because I don't have a break for lunch.

social security number n. a nine-digit number that is often used for student identification as well as for employment purposes

Example:	What is your *social security number*?
Suggestion:	You should memorize your *social security number*.
Assumption:	Your *social security number* is on your license, isn't it?
Problem:	Anna doesn't have a *social security number*.

sophomore n. a second-year college student

Example:	A full-time student is usually a *sophomore* by the third semester.
Suggestion:	You had better complete your general education classes by the end of your *sophomore* year.
Assumption:	You mean Bill is only a *sophomore*?
Problem:	I can't take advanced psychology because I am only a *sophomore*.

sorority n. a social organization for female college students

Example:	About a dozen *sororities* are on campus.
Suggestion:	You should consider joining a *sorority*.
Assumption:	So you did join a *sorority*.
Problem:	*Sororities* require a lot of time.

spring break n. a short vacation in the middle of the spring semester

Example:	Some of my friends are going to Florida for *spring break*.
Suggestion:	Why don't you visit your family over *spring break*?
Assumption:	You got your research paper done over *spring break*?
Problem:	I have to work during *spring break*.

stacks n. the area of the library where most of the books are shelved

Example:	At a small college, the *stacks* are usually open to all of the students.
Suggestion:	You should look in the *stacks* for that book.
Assumption:	The librarian let you go up in the *stacks* to look for your own book?
Problem:	I need to find a carrel in the *stacks*.

student n. one who attends a school

Example:	State University has more than fifty-thousand *students* enrolled on the main campus.
Suggestion:	If you tell them that you are a *student*, maybe you will get a discount.
Assumption:	You mean you aren't a *student*?
Problem:	I need to find five *students* to complete my study.

student I.D. number   n.   a number used for identification at a college or university, often a social security number

Example: Your social security number is your *student I.D. number*.
Suggestion: You should write your *student I.D. number* on all of your papers.
Assumption: Pat has a *student I.D. number*?
Problem: I can't seem to remember my *student I.D. number*.

student services   n.   an administrative branch of a college or university that provides noninstructional support services for students

Example: I have to go over to *student services* to meet with a financial aid advisor.
Suggestion: You had better go to *student services* to check on your dorm application.
Assumption: The *student services* office is open during registration, isn't it?
Problem: I have to go to the *student services* office before the end of the day.

student union   n.   a building on campus where students can relax

Example: There is a movie at the *student union* tonight.
Suggestion: You could meet Ken in the *student union* before the concert.
Assumption: You mean the *student union* is closed over the holidays?
Problem: The *student union* closes at 10:00 P.M.

studies   n.   research investigations

Example: Many *studies* have been conducted here at State University.
Suggestion: Why don't you speak with Dr. Mason about her *studies*?
Assumption: So you did begin your *studies*.
Problem: I have to complete my *studies* by the end of the semester.

study   v.   to acquire knowledge or understanding of a subject

Example: I have to *study* if I want to get a good grade in this class.
Suggestion: Why don't you plan to *study* at my house this weekend?
Assumption: You mean you *studied* for that test?
Problem: I need to allow more time to *study*.

study date   n.   a date in which the activity is studying

Example: Joe and Diane have *study dates* most of the time.
Suggestion: You could arrange a *study date* with Jack before the test.
Assumption: You mean you don't have a *study date* tonight?
Problem: I have to meet Jack at the library for our *study date*.

study lounge   n.   a quiet area of a dormitory where students can go to study

Example: Even the *study lounge* is noisy in this dorm.
Suggestion: Why don't you meet me in the *study lounge* this evening?
Assumption: Did you say that the *study lounge* is quiet?
Problem: I can't concentrate in the *study lounge*.

subject   n.   an area of study

Example: Math is my favorite *subject*.
Suggestion: Why don't you ask Tracy for help with the *subjects* she tutors?
Assumption: You can get tutoring in all of the *subjects* taught at the university?
Problem: I have to take a lot of classes in *subjects* that I don't really like.

summer school   n.   the summer sessions, which are usually June through August
Example:	*Summer school* starts the second week of June this year.
Suggestion:	Why don't you take the art appreciation course in *summer school*?
Assumption:	You mean you've gone to *summer school* every summer?
Problem:	I can't go to *summer school* this year.

T.A.   n.   an abbreviation for teaching assistant
Example:	Laura has applied to be Dr. Graham's *T.A.*
Suggestion:	You should see the *T.A.* if you have questions about the lecture.
Assumption:	So Bill did apply to be a *T.A.*
Problem:	I have to find Dr. Graham's *T.A.* before class tomorrow.

teaching assistant   n.   a graduate student whose teaching duties are supervised by a faculty member
Example:	We have a *teaching assistant* for the discussion session of this class.
Suggestion:	You had better speak with the *teaching assistant* before the next lab session.
Assumption:	You mean you haven't spoken with the *teaching assistant*?
Problem:	The *teaching assistant* is really difficult to understand.

tenure   n.   an academic rank that guarantees permanent status
Example:	Professor Peterson has *tenure*, but Mr. Lewis doesn't.
Suggestion:	Why don't you request the requirements for *tenure*?
Assumption:	You mean Dr. Peterson has *tenure*?
Problem:	Mr. Lewis will have to get his Ph.D. to qualify for *tenure*.

term   n.   a time period when school is in session, usually a quarter or a semester
Example:	Dana needs two more *terms* to graduate.
Suggestion:	Dana had better take statistics next *term*.
Assumption:	Nancy passed all of her classes last *term*?
Problem:	I have to complete my dissertation in three *terms*.

test   n.   an evaluation that is usually longer and worth more points than a quiz but shorter and worth fewer points than an exam
Example:	You will have a *test* every week in this class.
Suggestion:	If I were you, I would work with my study group before the *test*.
Assumption:	You mean you forgot about the *test*?
Problem:	I have to study for two *tests* next week.

textbook   n.   a book that is used for a course
Example:	The *textbooks* can be purchased at the bookstore or ordered over the Internet.
Suggestion:	You could purchase used *textbooks* for some of your classes.
Assumption:	You mean you had to buy new *textbooks*?
Problem:	I can't find good used *textbooks* anywhere.

thesis   n.   a written research report in partial fulfillment of a graduate degree
Example:	Tracy isn't taking any courses this semester because she is writing her *thesis*.
Suggestion:	You should get the handbook at the graduate school before starting your *thesis*.
Assumption:	Tracy isn't writing her *thesis* this semester, is she?
Problem:	I need to allow at least one semester to write my *thesis*.

transcript   n.   a printed copy of a student's grades
Example: The admissions office requires two *transcripts* with every application.
Suggestion: Why don't you request an extra copy of your *transcript*?
Assumption: You mean you still haven't received your *transcripts*?
Problem: I have to have those *transcripts* by next Monday.

transfer   v.   to change schools
Example: It is better to *transfer* at the beginning of the third year.
Suggestion: If I were you, I would *transfer* as soon as possible.
Assumption: Dana *transferred* to State University?
Problem: I can't *transfer* colleges because I would lose credits.

tuition   n.   fees for instruction at a school
Example: The *tuition* is different from school to school.
Suggestion: You should check the *tuition* before deciding on a college.
Assumption: *Tuition* at private colleges is more?
Problem: I need a scholarship to pay my *tuition*.

tuition hike   n.   an increase in the fees for instruction
Example: There is a *tuition hike* every year at State University.
uggestion: You should sign the petition protesting the *tuition hike*.
Assumption: You mean you graduated before the *tuition hike*?
Problem: I can't afford another *tuition hike*.

turn in   v.   to submit an assignment
Example: Please *turn in* your homework before you leave.
Suggestion: You had better *turn in* your paper before the end of the day.
Assumption: You mean I could have *turned in* my paper tomorrow?
Problem: I have to *turn in* the paper by Friday or I will get an F.

tutor   n.   a private instructor, often another student
Example: I have to meet my *tutor* at the library.
Suggestion: Why don't you get a *tutor* for your accounting class?
Assumption: You mean Jack is your *tutor*?
Problem: I can't afford to hire a *tutor*.

tutoring   n.   private instruction
Example: Nancy needs some *tutoring* in this class.
Suggestion: You could earn extra money *tutoring* for math.
Assumption: So you did get the *tutoring* job.
Problem: *Tutoring* takes a lot of time.

undergrad   n., adj.   abbreviation for undergraduate
Example: I think that Dana is an *undergrad*.
Suggestion: You could still enroll for *undergrad* classes while you are waiting to hear from the
                  graduate school admissions office.
Assumption: You mean you're an *undergrad*?
Problem: I need to apply for an *undergrad* scholarship.

undergraduate (student)   n., adj.   a student pursuing a bachelor's degree
Example: Some *undergraduates* require five years to complete a four-year program.
Suggestion: You should look at more than one *undergraduate* program.
Assumption: You mean you completed your *undergraduate* courses in three years?
Problem: I can't complete my *undergraduate* degree before we move.

upper-division (course)   adj.   advanced courses for third- and fourth-year students.
Example: Most of the *upper-division* courses are numbered 400 or above.
Suggestion: Why don't you take an *upper-division* music class?
Assumption: You mean grammar is an *upper-division* course?
Problem: Dana needs to take an *upper-division* math class.

withdraw   v.   to leave school
Example: My roommate *withdrew* from school.
Suggestion: You should *withdraw* so that you won't have failing grades on your transcript.
Assumption: You mean your parents want you to *withdraw* from school?
Problem: I have to *withdraw* from school at the end of the semester.

work-study (student)   n.   a student who works on campus in a special program that allows study
                                time when there is nothing to do on the job
Example: There are several *work-study* positions open in the finance office.
Suggestion: Dana should apply for the *work-study* program next semester.
Assumption: You mean Vicki's library job is a *work-study* position?
Problem: The *work-study* students couldn't answer my questions.

Xerox (machine)   n.   a copy machine
Example: There is a long line at the *Xerox* machine.
Suggestion: You could use the *Xerox* machine in the library.
Assumption: You mean there are only three *Xerox* machines on campus?
Problem: I need to find a *Xerox* machine.

Index

Barron's TOEFL Audio Compact Disk

The four compact disks available can be used in your compact disk player to provide the audio for the TOEFL Model Tests. You should hear audio only. If you want to simulate the Computer-Based TOEFL, with both audio and visuals, you need a CD-ROM, not a compact disk. The CD-ROM is available from Barron's Educational Series, Inc.

Telephone: 800-645-3476   E-mail: customer.service@barronseduc.com
FAX: 631-434-3723   Web site: http://www.barronseduc.com

TOEFL CD-ROM Minimum Requirements

The following documentation applies if you purchased *How to Prepare for the TOEFL, 11th Edition* book with CD-ROM. Please disregard this information if your version does not contain the CD-ROM.

Documentation

MINIMUM HARDWARE REQUIREMENTS

The program will run on a PC with	The program will run on a Macintosh® with
1. 166 MHz Intel Pentium processor or greater	1. Macintosh PowerPC processor (G3 or higher recommended)
2. Windows 98/ME/NT/2000/ XP	2. Mac OS 8.6 to OS X
3. 32 MB or more of installed RAM (64 MB RAM Recommended)	3. 32 MB or more of installed RAM
4. SVGA (256 Colors) Monitor	4. SVGA (256 Colors) Monitor
5. Sound card with speakers or SoundBlaster	5. Sound card with speakers or SoundBlaster
6. 16X CD-ROM drive	6. 16X CD-ROM drive
7. Keyboard, Mouse	7. Keyboard, Mouse

LAUNCHING THE APPLICATION

Barron's TOEFL CD-ROM includes an "autorun" feature that automatically launches the application when the CD is inserted into the CD drive. In the unlikely event that the autorun features are disabled, alternate launching instructions are provided below.

Launching instructions for the PC	Launching instructions for the MAC
Windows® 95/98/NT/2000: 1. Put the Barron's TOEFL CD-ROM into the CD-ROM drive. 2. Click on the Start button and choose Run. 3. Type *D:\TOEFL.EXE* (assuming the CD is in the drive D), then click OK.	1. Put the Barron's TOEFL CD-ROM into the CD-ROM drive. 2. Double-click the TOEFL Installer icon. 3. Follow the onscreen instructions.